SOLUTIONS MANUAL

Chapters 1-15 + Combination Journal Module

College Accounting

20th EDITION

James A. Heintz, DBA, CPA

Professor of Accounting
School of Business
University of Kansas

Robert W. Parry, Jr., Ph.D.

Professor of Accounting
Kelley School of Business
Indiana University

SOUTH-WESTERN
CENGAGE Learning

Australia • Brazil • Japan • Korea • Mexico • Singapore • Spain • United Kingdom • United States

SOUTH-WESTERN
CENGAGE Learning

ISBN-13: 978-0-538-75088-2
ISBN-10: 0-538-75088-X

South-Western Cengage Learning
5191 Natorp Boulevard
Mason, OH 45040
USA

Cengage Learning is a leading provider of customized learning solutions with office locations around the globe, including Singapore, the United Kingdom, Australia, Mexico, Brazil, and Japan. Locate your local office at: **international.cengage.com/region**.

Cengage Learning products are represented in Canada by Nelson Education, Ltd.

For your course and learning solutions, visit **www.cengage.com**.

Purchase any of our products at your local college store or at our preferred online store **www.ichapters.com**.

READ IMPORTANT LICENSE INFORMATION

Printed in the United States of America
1 2 3 4 5 6 7   14 13 12 11 10

Table of Contents

CHAPTER 1

INTRODUCTION TO ACCOUNTING

REVIEW QUESTIONS

1. The purpose of accounting is to provide financial information about a business to individuals and organizations.

2. Four user groups normally interested in financial information about a business are owners, managers, creditors, and government agencies.

3. The six major steps of the accounting process are listed below.
   a. Analyzing is looking at events that have taken place and thinking about how these affect the business.
   b. Recording is entering financial information into the accounting system.
   c. Classifying is sorting and grouping like items together.
   d. Summarizing is the aggregation of many similar events to provide information that is easy to understand.
   e. Reporting is telling the results.
   f. Interpreting is deciding the importance of information in the various reports.

4. Generally accepted accounting principles (GAAP) are the rules that businesses must follow when preparing financial statements.

5. FASB takes the following steps to develop an accounting standard:

   1. The issue is placed on the Board's agenda.
   2. After researching the issue, a discussion memorandum is issued.
   3. Public hearings are held.
   4. An exposure draft is issued.
   5. The statement of financial accounting standards (SFAS) is issued.

6. The International Accounting Standards Board.

7. The three types of ownership structures are listed below.
   a. A sole proprietorship is owned by one person. The owner assumes all risks for the business. The advantage is that the owner can make all of the business decisions.
   b. A partnership is owned by more than one person. Partners assume the risks for the business, and their assets may be taken to pay creditors. An advantage of a partnership is that owners share risks and decision making. A disadvantage is that partners may disagree about the best way to run the business.
   c. A corporation is owned by stockholders. The owners' risk is usually limited to their initial investment, but they typically have very little influence on business decisions.

8. Three types of businesses classified by activities are service businesses, merchandising businesses, and manufacturing businesses.

9. An accounting clerk performs accounting tasks such as recording, sorting, and filing accounting information.

10. Three areas of specialization for a public accountant are auditing, taxation, and management advisory services.

    Auditing—Auditing involves the application of standard review and testing procedures to be certain that proper accounting policies and practices have been followed. The purpose of the audit is to provide an independent opinion that the financial information about a business is fairly presented.

    Taxation—The work of tax specialists includes offering advice on tax planning, preparing tax returns, and representing clients before governmental agencies such as the Internal Revenue Service.

    Management Advisory Services—Given the financial training and business experience of public accountants, many businesses seek their advice on a wide variety of managerial issues.

11. The Sarbanes-Oxley Act (SOX) was passed by Congress to help improve reporting practices of public companies. One important provision prohibits accounting firms from providing audit and management advisory services to the same company.

12. Six areas of specialization for a managerial accountant are accounting information systems, financial accounting, cost accounting, budgeting, tax accounting, and internal auditing.

    Accounting Information Systems—Accountants in this area design and implement manual and computerized accounting systems.

    Financial Accounting—Based on the accounting data prepared by the bookkeepers and accounting clerks, the accountant prepares various reports and financial statements.

    Cost Accounting—The cost of producing specific products or providing services must be measured. Further analysis is also done to determine whether the products and services are produced in the most cost-effective manner.

    Budgeting—In the budgeting process, accountants help management develop a financial plan for the future.

    Tax Accounting—A firm may have its own accountants to focus on tax planning, preparation of tax returns, and dealing with the Internal Revenue Service and other governmental agencies.

    Internal Auditing—The main functions of an internal auditor are to review the operating and accounting control procedures adopted by management and to see that accurate and timely information is provided.

Exercise 1-1A

1. _____*d*_____ Owners   a. Whether the firm can pay its bills on time

2. _____*b*_____ Managers   b. Detailed, up-to-date information to measure business performance (and plan for future operations)

3. _____*a*_____ Creditors   c. To determine taxes to be paid and whether other regulations are met

4. _____*c*_____ Government agencies   d. The firm's current financial condition

Exercise 1-2A

Order	Accounting Process	Definition
2	Recording	*entering financial information into the accounting system*
4	Summarizing	*aggregating many similar events to provide information that is easy to understand*
5	Reporting	*telling the results*
1	Analyzing	*looking to see what events have taken place and thinking about how these affect the business*
6	Interpreting	*deciding the importance of information on the various reports*
3	Classifying	*sorting and grouping like items together*

Exercise 1-1B

Users	Information
Owners (present and future):	*firm's profitability and current financial condition*
Managers:	*detailed, up-to-date information about the business to measure performance*
Creditors (present and future):	*firm's profitability, debt outstanding, and assets that could be used to secure debt*
Government agencies:	*firm's profitability, cash flows, and overall financial condition*

Exercise 1-2B

Letter	Accounting Process		Definition
b	Analyzing	a.	Telling the results
f	Recording	b.	Looking at events that have taken place and thinking about how they affect the business
e	Classifying	c.	Deciding the importance of the various reports
d	Summarizing	d.	Aggregating many similar events to provide information that is easy to understand
a	Reporting	e.	Sorting and grouping like items together
c	Interpreting	f.	Entering financial information into the accounting system

MANAGING YOUR WRITING

The purpose of this writing assignment is to give the students an opportunity to dream about the type of business they might enjoy. In the current economy, most opportunities are with smaller, start-up companies. The student should demonstrate an understanding of the different forms of ownership and describe the advantages and disadvantages of each form. Further, they should demonstrate an understanding of the different types of businesses: service, merchandising, and manufacturing.

CHAPTER 2

ANALYZING TRANSACTIONS: THE ACCOUNTING EQUATION

REVIEW QUESTIONS

1. It is necessary to distinguish between business assets and liabilities and nonbusiness assets and liabilities of a single proprietor because, according to the business entity concept, nonbusiness assets and liabilities are not included in the business entity's accounting records. These distinctions allow the owner to make decisions based on the financial condition and results of the business apart from nonbusiness activities.

2. The six major elements of the accounting equation are listed below.
    a. Assets are items owned by a business that will provide future benefits.
    b. Liabilities are items owed to another business.
    c. Owner's equity is the amount by which the business assets exceed the business liabilities. Other terms used for owner's equity include net worth and capital.
    d. Revenues represent the amount a business charges customers for products sold or services performed.
    e. Expenses represent the decrease in assets (or increase in liabilities) as a result of efforts made to produce revenues.
    f. Withdrawals, or drawing, reduce owner's equity as a result of the owner taking cash or other assets out of the business for personal use.

3. The three basic questions that must be answered when analyzing the effects of a business transaction on the accounting equation are as follows:
    a. What happened?
    b. Which accounts are affected?
    c. How is the accounting equation affected?

4. The function of an income statement is to report the profitability of business operations for a specific period of time.

5. The function of a statement of owner's equity is to report the investments and withdrawals by the owner and the profits and losses generated through operating activities for a specific period of time.

6. The function of a balance sheet is to report the assets, liabilities, and owner's equity on a specific date. It is called a balance sheet because it confirms that the accounting equation is in balance.

7. The three basic phases of the accounting process are listed below.
    Input—Business transactions are used as input to the accounting process.
    Processing—The transactions are processed by recognizing their effects on assets, liabilities, owner's equity, revenues, and expenses.
    Output—Output from the accounting process is provided in the form of financial statements.

Exercise 2-1A

Item	Account	Classification
Money in bank	Cash	A
Office supplies	Supplies	A
Money owed	Accounts Payable	L
Office chairs	Office Furniture	A
Net worth of owner	John Smith, Capital	OE
Money withdrawn by owner	John Smith, Drawing	OE
Money owed by customers	Accounts Receivable	A

Exercise 2-2A

Assets	=	Liabilities	+	Owner's Equity
$34,000	=	$24,000	+	$10,000
$25,000	=	$18,000	+	$ 7,000
$40,000	=	$25,000	+	$15,000

Exercise 2-3A

	Assets	=	Liabilities	+	Owner's Equity
(a)	20,000				20,000
Bal.	20,000				20,000
(b)	3,500		3,500		
Bal.	23,500		3,500		20,000
(c)	(1,200)				
	1,200				
Bal.	23,500		3,500		20,000
(d)	(1,500)		(1,500)		
Bal.	22,000		2,000		20,000

Exercise 2-4A

	Assets	=	Liabilities	+	Capital	−	Drawing	+	Revenues	−	Expenses	Description
								Owner's Equity				
Bal. from E 2-3A	22,000		2,000		20,000							
(d)	2,500								2,500			Service fees
(e)	(900)										900	Rent expense
(f)	(73)										73	Telephone exp.
(g)	(500)						500					
(h)	1,000								1,000			Service fees
(i)	(600)										600	Wages expense
(j)	600											
(k)	(600)											
Bal.	23,427		2,000		20,000		500		3,500		1,573	

Total Assets $23,427

Total Liabilities	$ 2,000
Capital	20,000
Drawing	(500)
Revenues	3,500
Expenses	(1,573)
Total Liabilities and Owner's Equity	$23,427

Exercise 2-5A

Account	Classification	Financial Statement
Cash	A	BS
Rent Expense	E	IS
Accounts Payable	L	BS
Service Fees	R	IS
Supplies	A	BS
Wages Expense	E	IS
Ramon Martinez, Drawing	OE	SOE
Ramon Martinez, Capital	OE	SOE, BS
Prepaid Insurance	A	BS
Accounts Receivable	A	BS

Exercise 2-6A

Betsy Ray's Accounting Service

Statement of Owner's Equity

For Month Ended June 30, 20--

Betsy Ray, capital, June 1, 20--		$ - - -
Investment during June		20 0 0 0 00
Total investment		$20 0 0 0 00
Net income for June	$10 0 0 0 00	
Less withdrawals for June	8 0 0 0 00	
Increase in capital		2 0 0 0 00
Betsy Ray, capital, June 30, 20--		$22 0 0 0 00

Exercise 2-7A

Betsy Ray's Accounting Service

Statement of Owner's Equity

For Month Ended June 30, 20--

Betsy Ray, capital, June 1, 20--		$	- - -
Investment during June		20 0 0 0	00
Total investment		$20 0 0 0	00
Less: Net loss for June	$3 0 0 0 00		
Withdrawals for June	8 0 0 0 00		
Decrease in capital		11 0 0 0	00
Betsy Ray, capital, June 30, 20--		$ 9 0 0 0	00

Problem 2-8A

	Assets	=	Liabilities	+	Owner's Equity
1.	$30,550		$ 6,160		$24,390
2.	$37,840		$10,370		$27,470
3.	$34,920		$12,570		$22,350

Problem 2-9A: See page 10

Problem 2-10A

Jay Pembroke

Income Statement

For Month Ended April 30, 20--

Revenues:		
Service fees		$3 3 0 0 00
Expenses:		
Rent expense		7 5 0 00
Net income		$2 5 5 0 00

Problem 2-9A

	Assets (Items Owned)				=	Liabilities (Amts. Owed)	+	Owner's Equity						
								(Owner's Investment)			(Earnings)			
	Cash	+ Accounts Receivable	+ Office Supplies	+ Prepaid Insurance	=	Accounts Payable	+	J. Pembroke, Capital	− J. Pembroke, Drawing	+	Revenues	−	Expenses	Description
(a)	18,000							18,000						
(b)	(2,000)		4,600			2,600								
(c)	(1,200)			1,200										
(d)	1,300	2,000									3,300			Service fees
(e)	(2,300)					(2,300)								
(f)	(750)												750	Rent exp.
(g)	(100)								100					
Bal.	12,950	2,000	4,600	1,200		300		18,000	100		3,300		750	

Cash	$12,950
Accounts Receivable	2,000
Office Supplies	4,600
Prepaid Insurance	1,200
Total Assets	$20,750

Accounts Payable	$ 300
Jay Pembroke, Capital	18,000
Jay Pembroke, Drawing	(100)
Service Fees	3,300
Rent Expense	(750)
Total Liabilities and Owner's Equity	$20,750

Problem 2-11A

Jay Pembroke										
Statement of Owner's Equity										
For Month Ended April 30, 20--										
Jay Pembroke, capital, April 1, 20--							$	-	-	-
Investment during April							18	0	00	00
Total investment							$18	0	00	00
Net income for April	$2	5	5	0	00					
Less withdrawals for April		1	0	0	00					
Increase in capital							2	4	50	00
Jay Pembroke, capital, April 30, 20--							$20	4	50	00

Problem 2-12A

Jay Pembroke										
Balance Sheet										
April 30, 20--										
Assets						**Liabilities**				
Cash	$12	9	5	0	00	Accounts payable	$	3	00	00
Accounts receivable	2	0	0	0	00					
Office supplies	4	6	0	0	00	**Owner's Equity**				
Prepaid insurance	1	2	0	0	00	Jay Pembroke, capital	20	4	50	00
Total assets	$20	7	5	0	00	Total liab. & owner's equity	$20	7	50	00

Exercise 2-1B

Account	Classification
Cash	A
Accounts Payable	L
Supplies	A
Bill Jones, Drawing	OE
Prepaid Insurance	A
Accounts Receivable	A
Bill Jones, Capital	OE

Exercise 2-2B

Assets	=	Liabilities	+	Owner's Equity
$25,000	=	$20,000	+	$5,000
$30,000	=	$15,000	+	*$15,000*
$20,000	=	*$10,000*	+	$10,000

Exercise 2-3B

	Assets	=	Liabilities	+	Owner's Equity
(a)	*30,000*				*30,000*
Bal.	*30,000*				*30,000*
(b)	*4,500*		*4,500*		
Bal.	*34,500*		*4,500*		*30,000*
(c)	*1,600*				
	(1,600)				
Bal.	*34,500*		*4,500*		*30,000*
(d)	*(2,000)*		*(2,000)*		
Bal.	*32,500*		*2,500*		*30,000*

Exercise 2-4B

	Assets	=	Liabilities	+	Capital	−	Drawing	+	Revenues	−	Expenses	Description
									Owner's Equity			
Bal. from E 2-3B	32,500		2,500		30,000							
(d)	3,000								3,000			Service fees
(e)	(1,000)										1,000	Rent expense
(f)	(68)										68	Telephone exp.
(g)	(800)						800					
(h)	900								900			Service fees
(i)	(500)										500	Wages expense
(j)	500											
(k)	(500)											
Bal.	34,032		2,500		30,000		800		3,900		1,568	

Total Assets $34,032

Total Liabilities	$ 2,500
Capital	30,000
Drawing	(800)
Revenues	3,900
Expenses	(1,568)
Total Liabilities and Owner's Equity	$34,032

Exercise 2-5B

Account	Classification	Financial Statement
Cash	A	BS
Rent Expense	E	IS
Accounts Payable	L	BS
Service Fees	R	IS
Supplies	A	BS
Wages Expense	E	IS
Amanda Wong, Drawing	OE	SOE
Amanda Wong, Capital	OE	SOE, BS
Prepaid Insurance	A	BS
Accounts Receivable	A	BS

Exercise 2-6B

Lopez Financial Consulting

Statement of Owner's Equity

For Month Ended June 30, 20--

Efran Lopez, capital, June 1, 20--		$ - - -
Investment during June		15 0 0 0 00
Total investment		$15 0 0 0 00
Net income for June	$6 0 0 0 00	
Less withdrawals for June	7 0 0 0 00	
Decrease in capital		1 0 0 0 00
Efran Lopez, capital, June 30, 20--		$14 0 0 0 00

Exercise 2-7B

Lopez Financial Consulting

Statement of Owner's Equity

For Month Ended June 30, 20--

Efran Lopez, capital, June 1, 20--		$ - - -
Investment during June		15 000 00
Total investment		$15 000 00
Less: Net loss for June	$2 000 00	
Withdrawals for June	7 000 00	
Decrease in capital		9 000 00
Efran Lopez, capital, June 30, 20--		$ 6 000 00

Problem 2-8B

	Assets	=	Liabilities	+	Owner's Equity
1.	$22,860		$ 4,605		$18,255
2.	$27,425		$ 8,515		$18,910
3.	$25,235		$10,165		$15,070

Problem 2-9B: See page 16

Problem 2-10B

David Segal

Income Statement

For Month Ended October 31, 20--

Revenues:	
Service fees	$2 700 00
Expenses:	
Rent expense	650 00
Net income	$2 050 00

Problem 2-9B

| | Assets | | | | = | Liabilities | + | Owner's Equity | | | | |
| | (Items Owned) | | | | | (Amts' Owed) | | (Owner's Investment) | | (Earnings) | | |
	Cash	+ Accounts Receivable	+ Office Supplies	+ Prepaid Insurance	=	Accounts Payable	+	D. Segal, Capital	− D. Segal, Drawing	+ Revenues	− Expenses	Description
(a)	15,000							15,000				
(b)	(1,800)		3,800			2,000						
(c)	(1,000)			1,000								
(d)	1,700	1,000								2,700		Service fees
(e)	(1,800)					(1,800)						
(f)	(650)										650	Rent expense
(g)	(150)								150			
Bal.	11,300	1,000	3,800	1,000		200		15,000	150	2,700	650	

Cash	$11,300
Accounts Receivable	1,000
Office Supplies	3,800
Prepaid Insurance	1,000
Total Assets	$17,100

Accounts Payable	$ 200
David Segal, Capital	15,000
David Segal, Drawing	(150)
Service Fees	2,700
Rent Expense	(650)
Total Liabilities and Owner's Equity	$17,100

Problem 2-11B

David Segal

Statement of Owner's Equity

For Month Ended October 31, 20--

David Segal, capital, October 1, 20--		$ - - -
Investment during October		15 0 0 0 00
Total investment		$15 0 0 0 00
Net income for October	$2 0 5 0 00	
Less withdrawals for October	1 5 0 00	
Increase in capital		1 9 0 0 00
David Segal, capital, October 31, 20--		$16 9 0 0 00

Problem 2-12B

David Segal

Balance Sheet

October 31, 20--

Assets		Liabilities	
Cash	$11 3 0 0 00	Accounts payable	$ 2 0 0 00
Accounts receivable	1 0 0 0 00		
Office supplies	3 8 0 0 00	Owner's Equity	
Prepaid insurance	1 0 0 0 00	David Segal, capital	16 9 0 0 00
Total assets	$17 1 0 0 00	Total liab. & owner's equity	$17 1 0 0 00

MANAGING YOUR WRITING

The students should focus on the following differences:

1. An expense is an outflow of assets or increase in liabilities as a result of the efforts made to earn revenues. A withdrawal is an outflow of assets for the owner's personal use. The withdrawal is not related to the earning process.
2. A withdrawal that increases a liability would be unusual. Expenses often increase liabilities.

The student should focus on the following similarity:

1. Expenses and withdrawals reduce owner's equity.

Mastery Problem

CHAPTER 2 — 19

1.

| | Assets (Items Owned) | | | | | = | Liabilities (Amts. Owed) | + | Owner's Equity | | | | |
	Cash +	Accts. Rec. +	Sup-plies +	Prepaid Ins. +	Tools +	Van	=	Accts. Payable	+	(Owner's Investment) L. Vozniak, Capital −	L. Vozniak, Drawing +	(Earnings) Rev. −	Exp.	Description
(a)	8,000									8,000				
(b)	(150)												150	Rent exp.
(c)	(5,000)					5,000								
(d)					600			600						
(e)	(200)		300					100						
(f)	(100)												100	Wages exp.
(g)	(75)												75	Adver. exp.
(h)	(480)			480										
(i)	800											800		Cleaning fees
(j)		500										500		Cleaning fees
(k)	(40)												40	Telephone exp.
(l)	200	(200)												
(m)	(150)												150	Wages exp.
(n)	(200)							(200)						
(o)	600	200										800		Cleaning fees
(p)	(100)										100			
2. Bal.	3,105	500	300	480	600	5,000		500		8,000	100	2,100	515	

Mastery Problem (Continued)

3.

We Do Windows

Income Statement

For Month Ended July 31, 20--

Revenues:														
Cleaning fees									$2	1	0	0	00	
Expenses:														
Wages expense		$2	5	0	00									
Rent expense		1	5	0	00									
Advertising expense			7	5	00									
Telephone expense			4	0	00									
Total expenses										5	1	5	00	
Net income									$1	5	8	5	00	

4.

We Do Windows

Statement of Owner's Equity

For Month Ended July 31, 20--

Lisa Vozniak, capital, July 1, 20--									$	-	-	-		
Investment in July									8	0	0	0	00	
Total investment									$8	0	0	0	00	
Net income for July		$1	5	8	5	00								
Less withdrawals for July		1	0	0	00									
Increase in capital									1	4	8	5	00	
Lisa Vozniak, capital, July 31, 20--									$9	4	8	5	00	

Mastery Problem (Concluded)

5.

We Do Windows						
Balance Sheet						
July 31, 20--						

Assets			Liabilities		
Cash	$3 1 0 5 00		Accounts payable	$ 5 0 0 00	
Accounts receivable	5 0 0 00				
Supplies	3 0 0 00				
Prepaid insurance	4 8 0 00				
Tools	6 0 0 00		Owner's Equity		
Van	5 0 0 0 00		Lisa Vozniak, capital	9 4 8 5 00	
Total assets	$9 9 8 5 00		Total liab. & owner's equity	$9 9 8 5 00	

Challenge Problem

Cash from customers							$3	7	0 0	00
Cash paid for wages	$4	5	0	00						
Cash paid for rent	3	0	0	00						
Cash paid for utilities		5	0	00						
Cash paid for insurance	6	0	0	00						
Cash paid for supplies	1	0	0	00						
Cash paid for telephone		3	5	00						
Total cash paid for operating items							1	5	3 5	00
Difference between cash received from customers and										
cash paid for goods and services							$2	1	6 5	00

Yes, there is a difference of $2,000. Net income does a better job of measuring profits because it offers a better matching of revenues and expenses. However, cash flows are important. If you don't have enough cash to pay your bills, you will go out of business.

CHAPTER 3

THE DOUBLE-ENTRY FRAMEWORK

REVIEW QUESTIONS

1. The three major parts of the T account are:
   a. the title.
   b. the debit or left side.
   c. the credit or right side.

2. The left side of the T account is called the debit side. The right side of the T account is called the credit side.

3. The totals on the debit side and the credit side of the T account are called footings.

4. The relationship between revenues and expenses and owner's equity is:
   a. revenues increase owner's equity. Revenues could be recorded directly on the credit side of the owner's capital account; however, specific revenue accounts are maintained because readers of financial statements want to see the specific types of revenues.
   b. expenses decrease owner's equity. Expenses could be recorded directly on the debit side of the owner's capital account; however, specific expense accounts are maintained because readers of financial statements want to see the specific types of expenses.

5. The function of the trial balance is to list all account titles and balances and show that the debits and credits are equal.

Exercise 3-1A

	Cash		
500		100	
400		<u>200</u>	
<u>600</u>		*300*	
1,500			
Bal.	*1,200*		

Exercise 3-2A

a.	The cash account is increased with a	*debit*
b.	The owner's capital account is increased with a	*credit*
c.	The delivery equipment account is increased with a..	*debit*
d.	The cash account is decreased with a	*credit*
e.	The liability account Accounts Payable is increased with a	*credit*
f.	The revenue account Delivery Fees is increased with a..	*credit*
g.	The asset account Accounts Receivable is increased with a..	*debit*
h.	The rent expense account is increased with a	*debit*
i.	The owner's drawing account is increased with a..	*debit*

Exercise 3-3A

1. and 2.

	Cash					Jim Arnold, Capital	
(a)	*5,000*	*(b)*	*800*			*(a)*	*5,000*
		(c)	*1,500*				
			2,300				
Bal.	*2,700*						

	Supplies				Utilities Expense	
(b)	*800*			*(c)*	*1,500*	

Exercise 3-4A

Account	Debit or Credit
1. Cash	debit
2. Wages Expense	debit
3. Accounts Payable	credit
4. Owner's Drawing	debit
5. Supplies	debit
6. Owner's Capital	credit
7. Equipment	debit

Exercises 3-5A and 3-6A: See page 26.

Exercises 3-5A and 3-6A

Assets		=	Liabilities		+	Owner's Equity	
Dr. +	Cr. −		Dr. −	Cr. +		Dr. −	Cr. +

Cash

Dr.		Cr.
(a) 4,000	(b)	500
	(d)	300
	(e)	700
		1,500
Bal. 2,500		

Equipment

(b) 500	
(c) 800	
Bal. 1,300	

Accounts Payable

Dr. −	Cr. +
(d) 300	(c) 800
	Bal. 500

Sheryl Hansen, Capital

Dr. −	Cr. +
	(a) 4,000

Drawing

Dr. +	Cr. −

Sheryl Hansen, Drawing

(e) 700	

Expenses

Dr. +	Cr. −

Revenues

Dr. −	Cr. +

Exercise 3-7A

Assets = Liabilities + Owner's Equity

Assets

Dr. +		Cr. –

Cash

(a)	30,000	(b)	300
(e)	3,000	(c)	5,000
(j)	6,000	(f)	4,000
	39,000	(h)	1,500
		(i)	800
		(k)	3,000
			14,600
Bal.	24,400		

Accounts Receivable

(g)	9,000	(j)	6,000
Bal.	3,000		

Office Supplies

(b)	300	

Computer Equipment

(d)	8,000	

Office Furniture

(c)	5,000	

Liabilities

Dr. –		Cr. +

Accounts Payable

(f)	4,000	(d)	8,000
		Bal.	4,000

Owner's Equity

Dr. –		Cr. +

Charles Chadwick, Capital

		(a)	30,000

Drawing

Dr. +		Cr. –

C. Chadwick, Drawing

(k)	3,000	

Revenues

Dr. –		Cr. +

Professional Fees

		(e)	3,000
		(g)	9,000
		Bal.	12,000

Expenses

Dr. +		Cr. –

Rent Expense

(h)	1,500	

Utilities Expense

(i)	800	

Exercise 3-8A

Charlie's Detective Service

Trial Balance

January 31, 20--

ACCOUNT	DEBIT BALANCE	CREDIT BALANCE
Cash	24 4 0 0 00	
Accounts Receivable	3 0 0 0 00	
Office Supplies	3 0 0 00	
Computer Equipment	8 0 0 0 00	
Office Furniture	5 0 0 0 00	
Accounts Payable		4 0 0 0 00
Charles Chadwick, Capital		30 0 0 0 00
Charles Chadwick, Drawing	3 0 0 0 00	
Professional Fees		12 0 0 0 00
Rent Expense	1 5 0 0 00	
Utilities Expense	8 0 0 00	
	46 0 0 0 00	46 0 0 0 00

Exercise 3-9A

Damon's Lawn Service

Trial Balance

September 30, 20--

ACCOUNT	DEBIT BALANCE	CREDIT BALANCE
Cash	10 000 00	
Accounts Receivable	6 000 00	
Supplies	1 600 00	
Prepaid Insurance	1 200 00	
Delivery Equipment	16 000 00	
Accounts Payable		4 000 00
Damon Young, Capital		20 000 00
Damon Young, Drawing	2 000 00	
Delivery Fees		18 800 00
Wages Expense	4 200 00	
Rent Expense	1 800 00	
	42 800 00	42 800 00

Exercise 3-10A

Juanita's Delivery Service

Income Statement

For Month Ended September 30, 20--

Revenue:		
Delivery fees		$9 400 00
Expenses:		
Wages expense	$2 100 00	
Rent expense	900 00	
Total expenses		3 000 00
Net income		$6 400 00

Exercise 3-11A

Juanita's Delivery Service

Statement of Owner's Equity

For Month Ended September 30, 20--

Juanita Raye, capital, September 1, 20--		$10 0 0 0 00
Net income for September	$6 4 0 0 00	
Less withdrawals for September	1 0 0 0 00	
Increase in capital		5 4 0 0 00
Juanita Raye, capital, September 30, 20--		$15 4 0 0 00

Exercise 3-12A

Juanita's Delivery Service

Balance Sheet

September 30, 20--

Assets		Liabilities	
Cash	$ 5 0 0 0 00	Accounts payable	$ 2 0 0 0 00
Accounts receivable	3 0 0 0 00		
Supplies	8 0 0 00	**Owner's Equity**	
Prepaid insurance	6 0 0 00	Juanita Raye, capital	15 4 0 0 00
Delivery equipment	8 0 0 00		
Total assets	$17 4 0 0 00	Total liab. & owner's equity	$17 4 0 0 00

Problem 3-13A
1. and 2.

Assets = **Liabilities** + **Owner's Equity**

Assets

Cash

Dr. +		Cr. –	
(a)	20,000	(b)	7,000
(d)	6,000	(e)	2,000
(l)	3,000	(f)	900
(o)	1,800	(g)	200
	30,800	(i)	120
		(j)	600
		(k)	1,200
		(m)	160
		(n)	1,000
		(p)	2,800
			15,980
Bal.	14,820		

Accts. Receivable

Dr. +		Cr. –	
(h)	4,000	(l)	3,000
(o)	1,400		
	5,400		
Bal.	2,400		

Office Supplies

Dr. +		Cr. –
(i)	120	

Prepaid Insurance

Dr. +		Cr. –
(k)	1,200	

Equipment

Dr. +		Cr. –
(c)	5,000	
(n)	3,000	
Bal.	8,000	

Van

Dr. +		Cr. –
(b)	7,000	

Liabilities

Accounts Payable

Dr. –		Cr. +	
(e)	2,000	(c)	5,000
		(n)	2,000
			7,000
		Bal.	5,000

Owner's Equity

Dr. –	Cr. +

Harold Long, Capital

Dr. –	Cr. +	
	(a)	20,000

Revenues

Dr. –	Cr. +

Service Fees

Dr. –	Cr. +	
	(d)	6,000
	(h)	4,000
	(o)	3,200
	Bal.	13,200

Drawing

Dr. +	Cr. –

H. Long, Drawing

Dr. +		Cr. –
(p)	2,800	

Expenses

Dr. +	Cr. –

Rent Expense

Dr. +		Cr. –
(f)	900	

Wages Expense

Dr. +		Cr. –
(j)	600	

Telephone Expense

Dr. +		Cr. –
(g)	200	

Gas & Oil Expense

Dr. +		Cr. –
(m)	160	

Problem 3-13A (Concluded)

3.

Harold's Home Repair

Trial Balance

May 31, 20--

ACCOUNT	DEBIT BALANCE	CREDIT BALANCE
Cash	14 8 2 0 00	
Accounts Receivable	2 4 0 0 00	
Office Supplies	1 2 0 00	
Prepaid Insurance	1 2 0 0 00	
Equipment	8 0 0 0 00	
Van	7 0 0 0 00	
Accounts Payable		5 0 0 0 00
Harold Long, Capital		20 0 0 0 00
Harold Long, Drawing	2 8 0 0 00	
Service Fees		13 2 0 0 00
Rent Expense	9 0 0 00	
Wages Expense	6 0 0 00	
Telephone Expense	2 0 0 00	
Gas and Oil Expense	1 6 0 00	
	38 2 0 0 00	38 2 0 0 00

Problem 3-14A

1.

a. Total revenue for the month $13,200

b. Total expenses for the month... $ 1,860

c. Net income for the month $11,340

2.

a. Harold Long's original investment in the business $20,000

   + Net income for the month....................................... $11,340

   – Owner's drawing... $ 2,800

   Increase in capital .... $ 8,540

   = Ending owner's equity $28,540

b. End-of-month accounting equation:

Assets	=	Liabilities	+	Owner's Equity
$33,540		$5,000		$28,540

Problem 3-15A

1.

Harold's Home Repair

Income Statement

For Month Ended May 31, 20--

Revenue:			
Service fees			$13 2 0 0 00
Expenses:			
Rent expense	$9 0 0 00		
Wages expense	6 0 0 00		
Telephone expense	2 0 0 00		
Gas and oil expense	1 6 0 00		
Total expenses		1 8 6 0 00	
Net income			$11 3 4 0 00

Problem 3-15A (Concluded)

2.

Harold's Home Repair
Statement of Owner's Equity
For Month Ended May 31, 20--

Harold Long, capital, May 1, 20--		$	—
Investments during May		20 0 0 0 00	
Total investment		$20 0 0 0 00	
Net income for May	$11 3 4 0 00		
Less withdrawals for May	2 8 0 0 00		
Increase in capital		8 5 4 0 00	
Harold Long, capital, May 31, 20--		$28 5 4 0 00	

3.

Harold's Home Repair
Balance Sheet
May 31, 20--

Assets		Liabilities	
Cash	$14 8 2 0 00	Accounts payable	$ 5 0 0 0 00
Accounts receivable	2 4 0 0 00		
Office supplies	1 2 0 00	Owner's Equity	
Prepaid insurance	1 2 0 0 00	Harold Long, capital	28 5 4 0 00
Equipment	8 0 0 0 00		
Van	7 0 0 0 00		
Total assets	$33 5 4 0 00	Total liab. & owner's equity	$33 5 4 0 00

Exercise 3-1B

Accounts Payable	
300	450
250	350
550	150
	950
Bal.	**400**

Exercise 3-2B

a. The asset account Prepaid Insurance is increased with a .... *debit*

b. The owner's drawing account is increased with a .... *debit*

c. The asset account Accounts Receivable is decreased with a .... *credit*

d. The liability account Accounts Payable is decreased with a .... *debit*

e. The owner's capital account is increased with a .... *credit*

f. The revenue account Professional Fees is increased with a .... *credit*

g. The expense account Repair Expense is increased with a .... *debit*

h. The asset account Cash is decreased with a .... *credit*

i. The asset account Delivery Equipment is decreased with a .... *credit*

Exercise 3-3B

1. and 2.

Cash						Roberto Alvarez, Capital			
(a)	6,000	(b)	1,200					(a)	6,000
		(c)	900						
			2,100						
Bal.	3,900								

Supplies				Utilities Expense		
(b)	1,200			(c)	900	

Exercise 3-4B

	Account	Debit or Credit
1.	Cash	debit
2.	Rent Expense	debit
3.	Notes Payable	credit
4.	Owner's Drawing	debit
5.	Accounts Receivable	debit
6.	Owner's Capital	credit
7.	Tools	debit

Exercises 3-5B and 3-6B: See page 37.

Exercises 3-5B and 3-6B

Assets		=	Liabilities		+	Owner's Equity	
Dr. +	Cr. –		Dr. –	Cr. +		Dr. –	Cr. +

Cash

(a) 7,000	(b) 900	
	(d) 800	
	(e) 1,100	
	2,800	
Bal. 4,200		

Equipment

(b) 900	
(c) 1,500	
Bal. 2,400	

Accounts Payable

(d) 800	(c) 1,500
	Bal. 700

George Atlas, Capital

Dr. –	Cr. +
	(a) 7,000

Drawing

Dr. +	Cr. –

Expenses

Dr. +	Cr. –

Revenues

Dr. –	Cr. +

G. Atlas, Drawing

(e) 1,100	

Exercise 3-7B

Assets = Liabilities + Owner's Equity

Assets

Dr. +	Cr. −

Cash

Dr.	Cr.
(a) 18,000	(b) 500
(e) 4,000	(c) 8,000
(j) 3,000	(f) 2,000
25,000	(h) 900
	(i) 600
	(k) 4,000
	16,000
Bal. 9,000	

Accts. Receivable

Dr.	Cr.
(g) 7,000	(j) 3,000
Bal. 4,000	

Office Supplies

Dr.	Cr.
(b) 500	

Computer Equip.

Dr.	Cr.
(d) 5,000	

Office Furniture

Dr.	Cr.
(c) 8,000	

Liabilities

Dr. −	Cr. +

Accounts Payable

Dr.	Cr.
(f) 2,000	(d) 5,000
	Bal. 3,000

Owner's Equity

Dr. −	Cr. +

Nicole Lawrence, Capital

Dr.	Cr.
	(a) 18,000

Drawing

Dr. +	Cr. −

N. Lawrence, Drawing

Dr.	Cr.
(k) 4,000	

Revenues

Dr. −	Cr. +

Professional Fees

Dr.	Cr.
	(e) 4,000
	(g) 7,000
	Bal. 11,000

Expenses

Dr. +	Cr. −

Rent Expense

Dr.	Cr.
(h) 900	

Utilities Expense

Dr.	Cr.
(i) 600	

Exercise 3-8B

Nickie's Neat Ideas

Trial Balance

January 31, 20--

ACCOUNT	DEBIT BALANCE	CREDIT BALANCE
Cash	9 0 0 0 00	
Accounts Receivable	4 0 0 0 00	
Office Supplies	5 0 0 00	
Computer Equipment	5 0 0 0 00	
Office Furniture	8 0 0 0 00	
Accounts Payable		3 0 0 0 00
Nicole Lawrence, Capital		18 0 0 0 00
Nicole Lawrence, Drawing	4 0 0 0 00	
Professional Fees		11 0 0 0 00
Rent Expense	9 0 0 00	
Utilities Expense	6 0 0 00	
	32 0 0 0 00	32 0 0 0 00

Exercise 3-9B

Betty's Cleaning Service

Trial Balance

September 30, 20--

ACCOUNT	DEBIT BALANCE	CREDIT BALANCE
Cash	14 0 0 0 00	
Accounts Receivable	8 0 0 0 00	
Supplies	1 2 0 0 00	
Prepaid Insurance	1 8 0 0 00	
Delivery Equipment	18 0 0 0 00	
Accounts Payable		6 0 0 0 00
Betty Par, Capital		24 0 0 0 00
Betty Par, Drawing	4 0 0 0 00	
Delivery Fees		25 0 0 0 00
Wages Expense	6 0 0 0 00	
Rent Expense	2 0 0 0 00	
	55 0 0 0 00	55 0 0 0 00

Exercise 3-10B

Bill's Delivery Service

Income Statement

For Month Ended September 30, 20--

Revenue:		
Delivery fees		$12 5 0 0 00
Expenses:		
Wages expense	$3 0 0 0 00	
Rent expense	1 0 0 0 00	
Total expenses		4 0 0 0 00
Net income		$ 8 5 0 0 00

Exercise 3-11B

Bill's Delivery Service
Statement of Owner's Equity
For Month Ended September 30, 20--

Bill Swift, capital, September 1, 20--			$12 000 00
Net income for September	$8 500 00		
Less withdrawals for September	2 000 00		
Increase in capital			6 500 00
Bill Swift, capital, September 30, 20--			$18 500 00

Exercise 3-12B

Bill's Delivery Service
Balance Sheet
September 30, 20--

Assets		Liabilities	
Cash	$ 7 000 00	Accounts payable	$ 3 000 00
Accounts receivable	4 000 00		
Supplies	600 00	Owner's Equity	
Prepaid insurance	900 00	Bill Swift, capital	18 500 00
Delivery equipment	9 000 00		
Total assets	$21 500 00	Total liab. & owner's equity	$21 500 00

Problem 3-13B

1. and 2.

Assets = **Liabilities** + **Owner's Equity**

Assets (Dr. + / Cr. –)

Cash

Dr. +		Cr. –	
(a) 30,000		(b) 8,000	
(d) 3,000		(e) 1,000	
(l) 3,000		(f) 700	
(o) 1,100		(g) 100	
37,100		(i) 300	
		(j) 500	
		(k) 800	
		(m) 2,000	
		(n) 500	
		(p) 3,000	
		16,900	
Bal. 20,200			

Accts. Receivable

Dr. +	Cr. –
(h) 4,000	(l) 3,000
(o) 1,700	
5,700	
Bal. 2,700	

Office Supplies

Dr. +	Cr. –
(i) 300	

Prepaid Insurance

Dr. +	Cr. –
(k) 800	

Plumbing Equip.

Dr. +	Cr. –
(c) 4,000	
(n) 2,000	
Bal. 6,000	

Van

Dr. +	Cr. –
(b) 8,000	

Liabilities (Dr. – / Cr. +)

Accounts Payable

Dr. –	Cr. +
(e) 1,000	(c) 4,000
	(n) 1,500
	5,500
	Bal. 4,500

Owner's Equity

Sue Jantz, Capital (Dr. – / Cr. +)

Dr. –	Cr. +
	(a) 30,000

Drawing

Sue Jantz, Drawing (Dr. + / Cr. –)

Dr. +	Cr. –
(p) 3,000	

Revenues (Dr. – / Cr. +)

Service Fees

Dr. –	Cr. +
	(d) 3,000
	(h) 4,000
	(o) 2,800
	Bal. 9,800

Expenses (Dr. + / Cr. –)

Rent Expense

Dr. +	Cr. –
(f) 700	

Wages Expense

(j) 500	

Telephone Expense

(g) 100	

Advertising Expense

(m) 2,000	

Problem 3-13B (Concluded)

3.

Jantz Plumbing Service

Trial Balance

August 31, 20--

ACCOUNT	DEBIT BALANCE	CREDIT BALANCE
Cash	20 2 0 0 00	
Accounts Receivable	2 7 0 0 00	
Office Supplies	3 0 0 00	
Prepaid Insurance	8 0 0 00	
Plumbing Equipment	6 0 0 0 00	
Van	8 0 0 0 00	
Accounts Payable		4 5 0 0 00
Sue Jantz, Capital		30 0 0 0 00
Sue Jantz, Drawing	3 0 0 0 00	
Service Fees		9 8 0 0 00
Rent Expense	7 0 0 00	
Wages Expense	5 0 0 00	
Telephone Expense	1 0 0 00	
Advertising Expense	2 0 0 00	
	44 3 0 0 00	44 3 0 0 00

Problem 3-14B

1.

 a. Total revenue for the month .... $ 9,800

 b. Total expenses for the month .... $ 3,300

 c. Net income for the month .... $ 6,500

2.

 a. Sue Jantz's original investment in the business $30,000

     + Net income for the month $6,500

     – Owner's drawing $3,000

     Increase in capital .... $ 3,500

     = Ending owner's equity $33,500

 b. End-of-month accounting equation:

Assets	=	Liabilities	+	Owner's Equity
$38,000		$4,500		$33,500

Problem 3-15B

1.

Jantz Plumbing Service

Income Statement

For Month Ended August 31, 20--

Revenue:			
Service fees			$9 8 0 0 00
Expenses:			
Advertising expense	$2 0 0 0 00		
Rent expense	7 0 0 00		
Wages expense	5 0 0 00		
Telephone expense	1 0 0 00		
Total expenses		3 3 0 0 00	
Net income		$6 5 0 0 00	

Problem 3-15B (Concluded)

2.

Jantz Plumbing Service
Statement of Owner's Equity
For Month Ended August 31, 20--

Sue Jantz, capital, August 1, 20--		$
Investments during August		30 0 0 0 00
Total investment		$30 0 0 0 00
Net income for August	$ 6 5 0 0 00	
Less withdrawals for August	3 0 0 0 00	
Increase in capital		3 5 0 0 00
Sue Jantz, capital, August 31, 20--		$33 5 0 0 00

3.

Jantz Plumbing Service
Balance Sheet
August 31, 20--

Assets		Liabilities	
Cash	$20 2 0 0 00	Accounts payable	$ 4 5 0 0 00
Accounts receivable	2 7 0 0 00		
Office supplies	3 0 0 00	Owner's Equity	
Prepaid insurance	8 0 0 00	Sue Jantz, capital	33 5 0 0 00
Plumbing equipment	6 0 0 0 00		
Van	8 0 0 0 00		
Total assets	$38 0 0 0 00	Total liab. & owner's equity	$38 0 0 0 00

MANAGING YOUR WRITING

This writing assignment will give students a chance to think about how they might apply the accounting techniques learned in the first three chapters to their personal lives. They will have various types of assets: cash, clothing, automobiles, books, stereos, etc. They may wonder whether cash on hand, in the checking account, and in the savings account should be one account, or three. Some students may have liabilities: car loans, student loans, and amounts owed on credit cards. Wages from part-time or full-time jobs represent revenue. Cash received from family members may be viewed as revenue or a liability, depending on whether the student is expected to repay the family member. Expenses include all types of spending on food, rent, tuition, and entertainment.

Mastery Problem

1. and 2.

Assets = Liabilities + Owner's Equity

Assets

Cash

Dr. +		Cr. −	
(a)	3,000	(b)	200
(f)	500	(c)	50
(h)	400	(e)	30
(l)	600	(g)	480
	4,500	(i)	350
		(j)	60
		(k)	200
		(m)	700
		(n)	150
		(o)	100
		(p)	200
			2,520

Bal. 1,980

Accts. Receivable

Dr. +		Cr. −	
(d)	520	(h)	400
(l)	720		
	1,240		

Bal. 840

Mowing Equipment

Dr. +		Cr. −	
(b)	1,000		

Lawn Tools

Dr. +		Cr. −	
(g)	480		

Liabilities

Accounts Payable

Dr. −		Cr. +	
(k)	200	(b)	800
		Bal.	600

Notes Payable

Dr. −		Cr. +	
(o)	100	(f)	500
		Bal.	400

Owner's Equity

Craig Fisher, Capital

Dr. −		Cr. +	
		(a)	3,000

Drawing

C. Fisher, Drawing

Dr. +		Cr. −	
(p)	200		

Revenues

Lawn Fees

Dr. −		Cr. +	
		(d)	520
		(l)	1,320
		Bal.	1,840

Expenses

Rent Expense

Dr. +		Cr. −	
(c)	50		

Wages Expense

Dr. +		Cr. −	
(i)	350		
(m)	700		
Bal.	1,050		

Telephone Expense

Dr. +		Cr. −	
(e)	30		

Gas & Oil Expense

Dr. +		Cr. −	
(j)	60		

Trans. Expense

Dr. +		Cr. −	
(n)	150		

Mastery Problem (Continued)

3.

Craig's Quick Cut

Trial Balance

June 30, 20--

ACCOUNT	DEBIT BALANCE	CREDIT BALANCE
Cash	1 9 8 0 00	
Accounts Receivable	8 4 0 00	
Mowing Equipment	1 0 0 0 00	
Lawn Tools	4 8 0 00	
Accounts Payable		6 0 0 00
Notes Payable		4 0 0 00
Craig Fisher, Capital		3 0 0 0 00
Craig Fisher, Drawing	2 0 0 00	
Lawn Fees		1 8 4 0 00
Rent Expense	5 0 00	
Wages Expense	1 0 5 0 00	
Telephone Expense	3 0 00	
Gas and Oil Expense	6 0 00	
Transportation Expense	1 5 0 00	
	5 8 4 0 00	5 8 4 0 00

4.

Craig's Quick Cut

Income Statement

For Month Ended June 30, 20--

Revenue:		
Lawn fees		$1 8 4 0 00
Expenses:		
Wages expense	$1 0 5 0 00	
Transportation expense	1 5 0 00	
Gas and oil expense	6 0 00	
Rent expense	5 0 00	
Telephone expense	3 0 00	
Total expenses		1 3 4 0 00
Net income		$ 5 0 0 00

Mastery Problem (Concluded)

5.

Craig's Quick Cut
Statement of Owner's Equity
For Month Ended June 30, 20--

Craig Fisher, capital, June 1, 20--			$	
Investments during June			3 0 0 0 00	
Total investment			$3 0 0 0 00	
Net income for June	$ 5 0 0 00			
Less withdrawals for June	2 0 0 00			
Increase in capital			3 0 0 00	
Craig Fisher, capital, June 30, 20--			$3 3 0 0 00	

6.

Craig's Quick Cut
Balance Sheet
June 30, 20--

Assets		Liabilities	
Cash	$1 9 8 0 00	Accounts payable	$ 6 0 0 00
Accounts receivable	8 4 0 00	Notes payable	4 0 0 00
Mowing equipment	1 0 0 0 00	Total liabilities	$1 0 0 0 00
Lawn tools	4 8 0 00		
		Owner's Equity	
		Craig Fisher, capital	3 3 0 0 00
Total assets	$4 3 0 0 00	Total liab. & owner's equity	$4 3 0 0 00

Challenge Problem

1.

Chris Stevick's Business									
Statement of Owner's Equity									
For Month Ended August 31, 20--									
Chris Stevick, capital, August 1, 20--						$ 4 0 0	00		
Net income for August	$ 3 0 0	00							
Less withdrawals for August	1 0 0	00							
Increase in capital						2 0 0	00		
Chris Stevick, capital, August 31, 20--						$ 6 0 0	00		

2.

Improvements that students might suggest for the income statement:

1. *Categorize the types of revenues that Chris generates if she provides more than*

    one type of service.

2. *Categorize the types of expenses that Chris incurred.*

CHAPTER 4

JOURNALIZING AND POSTING TRANSACTIONS

REVIEW QUESTIONS

1. The flow of accounting information from source documents to trial balance includes the following steps:
    a. Analyze what has happened by using the chart of accounts and information from the source documents.
    b. Enter the business transactions in the general journal.
    c. Post entries to the accounts in the general ledger.
    d. Prepare a trial balance.

2. The purpose of a chart of accounts is to list and classify all the accounts used by a business.

3. The five types of financial statement items for which it is ordinarily desirable to keep separate accounts are assets, liabilities, owner's equity, revenues, and expenses.

4. Examples of source documents are as follows (students are required to list only one):
    a. Cash payment—check stub or carbon copies of checks.
    b. Cash receipt—receipt stubs, carbon copies of receipts, cash register tapes, or memos of cash register totals.
    c. Sale of goods or services—copies of sales tickets or sales invoices issued to customers or clients.
    d. Purchase of goods or services—purchase invoices received from suppliers.

5. The first formal accounting record of a business transaction is usually made in the journal, which is called a book of original entry.

6. The four steps required to journalize a business transaction in a general journal are as follows:
    Step 1: Enter the date.
    Step 2: Enter the debit.
    Step 3: Enter the credit.
    Step 4: Enter the explanation.

7. The accounts are placed in the ledger in the same order as in the chart of accounts, in numeric order grouped by classification.

8. The primary advantage of a general ledger account is that it maintains a running balance.

9. The five steps required when posting the journal to the ledger are as follows:
    In the ledger account:
    Step 1: Enter the date of each transaction in the Date column.
    Step 2: Enter the amount of each transaction in the Debit or Credit column.
    Step 3: Enter the new balance in the Balance columns under Debit or Credit. If the balance of the account is zero, draw a line through the Debit and Credit columns.
    Step 4: Enter the page number of the journal from which each transaction is posted in the Posting Reference column.
    In the journal:
    Step 5: Enter the account number in the Posting Reference column of the journal for each transaction that is posted.

10. As an amount is posted to the proper account in the ledger, the appropriate account number is entered in the Posting Reference column of the journal.

11. If a journal entry was debited or credited to the wrong account(s), or if an item was posted to the wrong account, the ledger will still be in balance.

12. A slide occurs when debit or credit amounts "slide" a digit or two to the left or right when entered. An example of a slide is if $250 was entered as $25.

13. A transposition error occurs when two digits are reversed (for example, if $520 was entered as $250).

14. The ruling method of correcting an error is to draw a line through the incorrect account title or amount and write the correct information directly above the line. The correction is then initialed so the source and reason for the correction can be traced.

15. If an incorrect entry has been journalized and posted to the wrong account, a correcting entry must be made. This is called the correcting entry method.

Exercise 4-1A

1.	*c*	Check stubs or check register	a.	A good or service has been sold.
2.	*d*	Purchase invoice from suppliers (vendors)	b.	Cash has been received by the business.
3.	*a*	Sales tickets or invoices to customers	c.	Cash has been paid by the business.
4.	*b*	Receipts or cash register tapes	d.	Goods or services have been purchased by the business.

Exercise 4-2A

Transaction	Debit	Credit
1. Invested cash in the business, $5,000.	*Cash*	*Owner's Capital*
2. Paid office rent, $500.	*Rent Expense*	*Cash*
3. Purchased office supplies on account, $300.	*Office Supplies*	*Accounts Payable*
4. Received cash for services rendered (fees), $400.	*Cash*	*Fees*
5. Paid cash on account, $50.	*Accounts Payable*	*Cash*
6. Rendered services on account, $300.	*Accounts Receivable*	*Fees*
7. Received cash for an amount owed by a customer, $100.	*Cash*	*Accounts Receivable*

Exercise 4-3A

	Cash					Accounts Receivable			
1.	5,000	2.	500		6.	300	7.		100
4.	400	5.	50		Bal.	200			
7.	100		550						
	5,500								
Bal.	4,950								

	Office Supplies				Accounts Payable			
3.	300			5.	50	3.		300
						Bal.		250

Exercise 4-3A (Concluded)

Owner's Capital				Fees		
	1.	5,000		4.		400
				6.		300
				Bal.		700

Rent Expense			Total Debits:		Total Credits:	
2.	500		Cash	4,950	Accts. Pay.	250
			Accts. Rec.	200	Owner's Cap.	5,000
			Off. Sup.	300	Fees	700
			Rent Exp.	500		5,950
				5,950		

Exercise 4-4A

GENERAL JOURNAL   PAGE 1

	DATE		DESCRIPTION	POST. REF.	DEBIT	CREDIT	
1	20-- Jan.	1	Cash	101	10 000 00		1
2			Jean Jones, Capital	311		10 000 00	2
3			Owner's original investment				3
4							4
5		2	Rent Expense	521	5 00 00		5
6			Cash	101		5 00 00	6
7			Paid office rent for January				7
8							8
9		3	Office Equipment	181	1 5 00 00		9
10			Accounts Payable	202		1 5 00 00	10
11			Purchased office equipment on account				11
12							12
13		5	Cash	101	7 50 00		13
14			Consulting Fees	401		7 50 00	14
15			Received cash for consulting services				15
16							16
17		8	Telephone Expense	525	6 5 00		17
18			Cash	101		6 5 00	18
19			Paid telephone bill				19
20							20
21		10	Miscellaneous Expense	549	1 5 00		21
22			Cash	101		1 5 00	22
23			Purchased magazine subscription				23
24							24

CHAPTER 4

55

Exercise 4-4A (Concluded)

GENERAL JOURNAL

PAGE 2

	DATE		DESCRIPTION	POST. REF.	DEBIT	CREDIT	
1	20-- Jan.	11	Office Supplies	142	3 0 0 00		1
2			Accounts Payable	202		3 0 0 00	2
3			Purchased office supplies on account				3
4							4
5		15	Accounts Payable	202	1 5 0 00		5
6			Cash	101		1 5 0 00	6
7			Made partial payment on office equipment				7
8							8
9		18	Wages Expense	511	5 0 0 00		9
10			Cash	101		5 0 0 00	10
11			Paid employee				11
12							12
13		21	Cash	101	3 5 0 00		13
14			Consulting Fees	401		3 5 0 00	14
15			Received cash for consulting services				15
16							16
17		25	Utilities Expense	533	8 5 00		17
18			Cash	101		8 5 00	18
19			Paid utilities bill				19
20							20
21		27	Jean Jones, Drawing	312	1 0 0 00		21
22			Cash	101		1 0 0 00	22
23			Owner's withdrawal				23
24							24
25		29	Wages Expense	511	5 0 0 00		25
26			Cash	101		5 0 0 00	26
27			Paid employee				27

© 2011 Cengage Learning. All Rights Reserved. May not be scanned, copied or duplicated, or posted to a publicly accessible website, in whole or in part.

Exercise 4-5A

GENERAL LEDGER

ACCOUNT **Cash**   ACCOUNT NO. **101**

DATE		ITEM	POST. REF.	DEBIT	CREDIT	BALANCE DEBIT	BALANCE CREDIT
20-- Jan.	1		J1	10 0 0 0 00		10 0 0 0 00	
	2		J1		5 0 0 00	9 5 0 0 00	
	5		J1	7 5 0 00		10 2 5 0 00	
	8		J1		6 5 00	10 1 8 5 00	
	10		J1		1 5 00	10 1 7 0 00	
	15		J2		1 5 0 00	10 0 2 0 00	
	18		J2		5 0 0 00	9 5 2 0 00	
	21		J2	3 5 0 00		9 8 7 0 00	
	25		J2		8 5 00	9 7 8 5 00	
	27		J2		1 0 0 00	9 6 8 5 00	
	29		J2		5 0 0 00	9 1 8 5 00	

ACCOUNT **Office Supplies**   ACCOUNT NO. **142**

DATE		ITEM	POST. REF.	DEBIT	CREDIT	BALANCE DEBIT	BALANCE CREDIT
20-- Jan.	11		J2	3 0 0 00		3 0 0 00	

ACCOUNT **Office Equipment**   ACCOUNT NO. **181**

DATE		ITEM	POST. REF.	DEBIT	CREDIT	BALANCE DEBIT	BALANCE CREDIT
20-- Jan.	3		J1	1 5 0 0 00		1 5 0 0 00	

Exercise 4-5A (Continued)

ACCOUNT **Accounts Payable**   ACCOUNT NO. **202**

DATE		ITEM	POST. REF.	DEBIT	CREDIT	BALANCE DEBIT	BALANCE CREDIT
20-- Jan.	3		J1		1 5 0 0 00		1 5 0 0 00
	11		J2		3 0 0 00		1 8 0 0 00
	15		J2	1 5 0 00			1 6 5 0 00

ACCOUNT **Jean Jones, Capital**   ACCOUNT NO. **311**

DATE		ITEM	POST. REF.	DEBIT	CREDIT	BALANCE DEBIT	BALANCE CREDIT
20-- Jan.	1		J1		10 0 0 0 00		10 0 0 0 00

ACCOUNT **Jean Jones, Drawing**   ACCOUNT NO. **312**

DATE		ITEM	POST. REF.	DEBIT	CREDIT	BALANCE DEBIT	BALANCE CREDIT
20-- Jan.	27		J2	1 0 0 00		1 0 0 00	

ACCOUNT **Consulting Fees**   ACCOUNT NO. **401**

DATE		ITEM	POST. REF.	DEBIT	CREDIT	BALANCE DEBIT	BALANCE CREDIT
20-- Jan.	5		J1		7 5 0 00		7 5 0 00
	21		J2		3 5 0 00		1 1 0 0 00

Exercise 4-5A (Continued)

ACCOUNT **Wages Expense**   ACCOUNT NO. **511**

DATE		ITEM	POST. REF.	DEBIT	CREDIT	BALANCE DEBIT	BALANCE CREDIT
20-- Jan.	18		J2	5 0 0 00		5 0 0 00	
	29		J2	5 0 0 00		1 0 0 0 00	

ACCOUNT **Rent Expense**   ACCOUNT NO. **521**

DATE		ITEM	POST. REF.	DEBIT	CREDIT	BALANCE DEBIT	BALANCE CREDIT
20-- Jan.	2		J1	5 0 0 00		5 0 0 00	

ACCOUNT **Telephone Expense**   ACCOUNT NO. **525**

DATE		ITEM	POST. REF.	DEBIT	CREDIT	BALANCE DEBIT	BALANCE CREDIT
20-- Jan.	8		J1	6 5 00		6 5 00	

ACCOUNT **Utilities Expense**   ACCOUNT NO. **533**

DATE		ITEM	POST. REF.	DEBIT	CREDIT	BALANCE DEBIT	BALANCE CREDIT
20-- Jan.	25		J2	8 5 00		8 5 00	

ACCOUNT **Miscellaneous Expense**   ACCOUNT NO. **549**

DATE		ITEM	POST. REF.	DEBIT	CREDIT	BALANCE DEBIT	BALANCE CREDIT
20-- Jan.	10		J1	1 5 00		1 5 00	

Exercise 4-5A (Concluded)

Jones Consulting

Trial Balance

January 31, 20--

ACCOUNT TITLE	ACCT. NO.	DEBIT BALANCE	CREDIT BALANCE
Cash	101	9 1 8 5 00	
Office Supplies	142	3 0 0 00	
Office Equipment	181	1 5 0 0 00	
Accounts Payable	202		1 6 5 0 00
Jean Jones, Capital	311		10 0 0 0 00
Jean Jones, Drawing	312	1 0 0 00	
Consulting Fees	401		1 1 0 0 00
Wages Expense	511	1 0 0 0 00	
Rent Expense	521	5 0 0 00	
Telephone Expense	525	6 5 00	
Utilities Expense	533	8 5 00	
Miscellaneous Expense	549	1 5 00	
		12 7 5 0 00	12 7 5 0 00

Exercise 4-6A

Jones Consulting

Income Statement

For Month Ended January 31, 20--

Revenue:		
Consulting fees		$1 1 0 0 00
Expenses:		
Wages expense	$1 0 0 0 00	
Rent expense	5 0 0 00	
Telephone expense	6 5 00	
Utilities expense	8 5 00	
Miscellaneous expense	1 5 00	
Total expenses		1 6 6 5 00
Net loss		$ 5 6 5 00

Exercise 4-6A (Concluded)

Jones Consulting
Statement of Owner's Equity
For Month Ended January 31, 20--

Jean Jones, capital, January 1, 20--			$
Investments during January			10 000 00
Total investment			$10 000 00
Less: Net loss for January	$ 5 65 00		
Withdrawals for January	1 00 00		
Decrease in capital			6 65 00
Jean Jones, capital, January 31, 20--			$ 9 335 00

Jones Consulting
Balance Sheet
January 31, 20--

Assets		Liabilities	
Cash	$ 9 185 00	Accounts payable	$ 1 650 00
Office supplies	3 00 00		
Office equipment	1 500 00	Owner's Equity	
		Jean Jones, capital	9 335 00
Total assets	$10 985 00	Total liab. & owner's equity	$10 985 00

Exercise 4-7A

TJ's Paint Service

Income Statement

For Month Ended July 31, 20--

Revenue:			
Painting fees			$3 6 0 0 00
Expenses:			
Wages expense	$9 0 0 00		
Rent expense	2 5 0 00		
Telephone expense	5 0 00		
Transportation expense	6 0 00		
Utilities expense	7 0 00		
Miscellaneous expense	2 5 00		
Total expenses			1 3 5 5 00
Net income			$2 2 4 5 00

TJ's Paint Service

Statement of Owner's Equity

For Month Ended July 31, 20--

TJ Ulza, capital, July 1, 20--			$
Investments during July			3 2 0 5 00
Total investment			$3 2 0 5 00
Net income for July	$2 2 4 5 00		
Less withdrawals for July	5 0 0 00		
Increase in capital			1 7 4 5 00
TJ Ulza, capital, July 31, 20--			$4 9 5 0 00

Exercise 4-7A (Concluded)

TJ's Paint Service			
Balance Sheet			
July 31, 20--			

Assets		Liabilities	
Cash	$4 3 0 0 00	Accounts payable	$2 1 5 0 00
Accounts receivable	1 1 0 0 00		
Supplies	8 0 0 00	Owner's Equity	
Paint equipment	9 0 0 00	TJ Ulza, capital	4 9 5 0 00
Total assets	$7 1 0 0 00	Total liab. & owner's equity	$7 1 0 0 00

Exercise 4-8A

GENERAL JOURNAL   PAGE

	DATE		DESCRIPTION	POST. REF.	DEBIT	CREDIT	
15	May	17	Office ~~Equipment~~ *Supplies* ← Student Initials		5 0 0 00 / 4 0 0 00		15
16			*Accounts Payable* ← / ~~Cash~~			5 0 0 00 / 4 0 0 00	16
17			Purchased copy paper *on account*				17
18							18
23		23	Cash	101	10 0 0 00		23
24			Service Fees	401		10 0 0 00	24
25			Received cash for services previously earned				25
26							26
27		25	Service Fees		1 0 0 0 00		27
28			Accounts Receivable			1 0 0 0 00	28
29			To correct entry of May 23				29
30							30
31							31
32							32
33							33

Problem 4-9A
2. (For 1. and 3., see page 66.)

GENERAL JOURNAL   PAGE 1

	DATE		DESCRIPTION	POST. REF.	DEBIT	CREDIT	
1	20-- Jan.	1	Cash	101	10 0 0 0 00		1
2			Annette Creighton, Capital	311		10 0 0 0 00	2
3			Original investment in the business				3
4							4
5		1	Rent Expense	521	5 0 0 00		5
6			Cash	101		5 0 0 00	6
7			Paid rent				7
8							8
9		2	Office Supplies	142	3 0 0 00		9
10			Accounts Payable	202		3 0 0 00	10
11			Purchased office supplies				11
12							12
13		4	Office Equipment	181	1 5 0 0 00		13
14			Accounts Payable	202		1 5 0 0 00	14
15			Purchased office equipment				15
16							16
17		6	Cash	101	5 8 0 00		17
18			Consulting Fees	401		5 8 0 00	18
19			Earned consulting fees				19
20							20
21		7	Telephone Expense	525	4 2 00		21
22			Cash	101		4 2 00	22
23			Paid telephone bill				23
24							24
25		8	Utilities Expense	533	3 8 00		25
26			Cash	101		3 8 00	26
27			Paid utilities bill				27
28							28
29		10	Cash	101	3 6 0 00		29
30			Consulting Fees	401		3 6 0 00	30
31			Earned consulting fees				31
32							32
33							33
34							34

Problem 4-9A (Continued)

GENERAL JOURNAL

PAGE 2

	DATE		DESCRIPTION	POST. REF.	DEBIT	CREDIT	
1	20-- Jan.	12	Accounts Payable	202	5 0 00		1
2			Cash	101		5 0 00	2
3			Paid cash on account				3
4							4
5		13	Transportation Expense	526	1 5 0 00		5
6			Cash	101		1 5 0 00	6
7			Paid for car rental				7
8							8
9		15	Wages Expense	511	3 6 0 00		9
10			Cash	101		3 6 0 00	10
11			Paid employee				11
12							12
13		17	Cash	101	4 2 0 00		13
14			Consulting Fees	401		4 2 0 00	14
15			Earned consulting fees				15
16							16
17		18	Annette Creighton, Drawing	312	1 0 0 00		17
18			Cash	101		1 0 0 00	18
19			Owner's withdrawal				19
20							20
21		20	Advertising Expense	512	2 6 00		21
22			Cash	101		2 6 00	22
23			Paid for newspaper ad				23
24							24
25		22	Transportation Expense	526	3 5 00		25
26			Cash	101		3 5 00	26
27			Paid cab fare				27
28							28
29		24	Miscellaneous Expense	549	2 8 00		29
30			Cash	101		2 8 00	30
31			Purchased books				31
32							32
33							33
34							34

Problem 4-9A (Continued)

GENERAL JOURNAL

PAGE 3

	DATE		DESCRIPTION	POST. REF.	DEBIT	CREDIT	
1	20-- Jan.	25	*Cash*	*101*	3 2 0 00		1
2			*Consulting Fees*	*401*		3 2 0 00	2
3			*Earned consulting fees*				3
4							4
5		27	**Accounts Payable**	*202*	1 5 0 00		5
6			*Cash*	*101*		1 5 0 00	6
7			**Paid cash on account**				7
8							8
9		29	*Wages Expense*	*511*	3 6 0 00		9
10			*Cash*	*101*		3 6 0 00	10
11			**Paid employee**				11
12							12
13		30	*Cash*	*101*	1 8 0 00		13
14			*Consulting Fees*	*401*		1 8 0 00	14
15			*Earned consulting fees*				15
16							16
17							17
18							18
19							19
20							20
21							21
22							22
23							23
24							24
25							25
26							26
27							27
28							28
29							29
30							30
31							31
32							32
33							33
34							34

Problem 4-9A (Continued)

1. and 3.

GENERAL LEDGER

ACCOUNT Cash   ACCOUNT NO. 101

DATE		ITEM	POST. REF.	DEBIT	CREDIT	BALANCE DEBIT	BALANCE CREDIT
20-- Jan.	1		J1	10 0 0 0 00		10 0 0 0 00	
	1		J1		5 0 0 00	9 5 0 0 00	
	6		J1	5 8 0 00		10 0 8 0 00	
	7		J1		4 2 00	10 0 3 8 00	
	8		J1		3 8 00	10 0 0 0 00	
	10		J1	3 6 0 00		10 3 6 0 00	
	12		J2		5 0 00	10 3 1 0 00	
	13		J2		1 5 0 00	10 1 6 0 00	
	15		J2		3 6 0 00	9 8 0 0 00	
	17		J2	4 2 0 00		10 2 2 0 00	
	18		J2		1 0 0 00	10 1 2 0 00	
	20		J2		2 6 00	10 0 9 4 00	
	22		J2		3 5 00	10 0 5 9 00	
	24		J2		2 8 00	10 0 3 1 00	
	25		J3	3 2 0 00		10 3 5 1 00	
	27		J3		1 5 0 00	10 2 0 1 00	
	29		J3		3 6 0 00	9 8 4 1 00	
	30		J3	1 8 0 00		10 0 2 1 00	

ACCOUNT Office Supplies   ACCOUNT NO. 142

DATE		ITEM	POST. REF.	DEBIT	CREDIT	BALANCE DEBIT	BALANCE CREDIT
20-- Jan.	2		J1	3 0 0 00		3 0 0 00	

Problem 4-9A (Continued)

ACCOUNT Office Equipment ACCOUNT NO. 181

DATE		ITEM	POST. REF.	DEBIT	CREDIT	BALANCE DEBIT	BALANCE CREDIT
20-- Jan.	4		J1	1 5 0 0 00		1 5 0 0 00	

ACCOUNT Accounts Payable ACCOUNT NO. 202

DATE		ITEM	POST. REF.	DEBIT	CREDIT	BALANCE DEBIT	BALANCE CREDIT
20-- Jan.	2		J1		3 0 0 00		3 0 0 00
	4		J1		1 5 0 0 00		1 8 0 0 00
	12		J2	5 0 00			1 7 5 0 00
	27		J3	1 5 0 00			1 6 0 0 00

ACCOUNT Annette Creighton, Capital ACCOUNT NO. 311

DATE		ITEM	POST. REF.	DEBIT	CREDIT	BALANCE DEBIT	BALANCE CREDIT
20-- Jan.	1		J1		10 0 0 0 00		10 0 0 0 00

ACCOUNT Annette Creighton, Drawing ACCOUNT NO. 312

DATE		ITEM	POST. REF.	DEBIT	CREDIT	BALANCE DEBIT	BALANCE CREDIT
20-- Jan.	18		J2	1 0 0 00		1 0 0 00	

Problem 4-9A (Continued)

ACCOUNT Consulting Fees

ACCOUNT NO. 401

DATE		ITEM	POST. REF.	DEBIT	CREDIT	BALANCE	
						DEBIT	CREDIT
20-- Jan.	6		J1		5 8 0 00		5 8 0 00
	10		J1		3 6 0 00		9 4 0 00
	17		J2		4 2 0 00		1 3 6 0 00
	25		J3		3 2 0 00		1 6 8 0 00
	30		J3		1 8 0 00		1 8 6 0 00

ACCOUNT Wages Expense

ACCOUNT NO. 511

DATE		ITEM	POST. REF.	DEBIT	CREDIT	BALANCE	
						DEBIT	CREDIT
20-- Jan.	15		J2	3 6 0 00		3 6 0 00	
	29		J3	3 6 0 00		7 2 0 00	

ACCOUNT Advertising Expense

ACCOUNT NO. 512

DATE		ITEM	POST. REF.	DEBIT	CREDIT	BALANCE	
						DEBIT	CREDIT
20-- Jan.	20		J2	2 6 00		2 6 00	

ACCOUNT Rent Expense

ACCOUNT NO. 521

DATE		ITEM	POST. REF.	DEBIT	CREDIT	BALANCE	
						DEBIT	CREDIT
20-- Jan.	1		J1	5 0 0 00		5 0 0 00	

Problem 4-9A (Continued)

ACCOUNT Telephone Expense   ACCOUNT NO. 525

DATE		ITEM	POST. REF.	DEBIT	CREDIT	BALANCE DEBIT	BALANCE CREDIT
20-- Jan.	7		J1	4 2 00		4 2 00	

ACCOUNT   Transportation Expense   ACCOUNT NO 526

DATE		ITEM	POST. REF.	DEBIT	CREDIT	BALANCE DEBIT	BALANCE CREDIT
20-- Jan.	13		J2	1 5 0 00		1 5 0 00	
	22		J2	3 5 00		1 8 5 00	

ACCOUNT Utilities Expense   ACCOUNT NO. 533

DATE		ITEM	POST. REF.	DEBIT	CREDIT	BALANCE DEBIT	BALANCE CREDIT
20-- Jan.	8		J1	3 8 00		3 8 00	

ACCOUNT Miscellaneous Expense   ACCOUNT NO. 549

DATE		ITEM	POST. REF.	DEBIT	CREDIT	BALANCE DEBIT	BALANCE CREDIT
20-- Jan.	24		J2	2 8 00		2 8 00	

Problem 4-9A (Continued)

4.

Creighton Consulting
Trial Balance
January 31, 20--

ACCOUNT TITLE	ACCT. NO.	DEBIT BALANCE	CREDIT BALANCE
Cash	101	10 0 2 1 00	
Office Supplies	142	3 0 0 00	
Office Equipment	181	1 5 0 0 00	
Accounts Payable	202		1 6 0 0 00
Annette Creighton, Capital	311		10 0 0 0 00
Annette Creighton, Drawing	312	1 0 0 00	
Consulting Fees	401		1 8 6 0 00
Wages Expense	511	7 2 0 00	
Advertising Expense	512	2 6 00	
Rent Expense	521	5 0 0 00	
Telephone Expense	525	4 2 00	
Transportation Expense	526	1 8 5 00	
Utilities Expense	533	3 8 00	
Miscellaneous Expense	549	2 8 00	
		13 4 6 0 00	13 4 6 0 00

Problem 4-9A (Continued)

5.

Creighton Consulting

Income Statement

For Month Ended January 31, 20--

Revenue:									
Consulting fees						$1	8	6 0	00
Expenses:									
Wages expense	$7	2	0	00					
Advertising expense		2	6	00					
Rent expense	5	0	0	00					
Telephone expense		4	2	00					
Transportation expense	1	8	5	00					
Utilities expense		3	8	00					
Miscellaneous expense		2	8	00					
Total expenses						1	5 3	9	00
Net income						$	3 2	1	00

Problem 4-9A (Concluded)

Creighton Consulting
Statement of Owner's Equity
For Month Ended January 31, 20--

Annette Creighton, capital, January 1, 20--						$					
Investments during January							10	0	0	0	00
Total investment						$10	0	0	0	00
Net income for January	$	3	2	1	00						
Less withdrawals for January		1	0	0	00						
Increase in capital								2	2	1	00
Annette Creighton, capital, January 31, 20--						$10	2	2	1	00

Creighton Consulting
Balance Sheet
January 31, 20--

Assets						Liabilities					
Cash	$10	0	2	1	00	Accounts payable	$	1	6	0	0	00
Office supplies		3	0	0	00						
Office equipment	1	5	0	0	00	Owner's Equity					
						Annette Creighton, capital	10	2	2	1	00
Total assets	$11	8	2	1	00	Total liab. & owner's equity	$11	8	2	1	00

Problem 4-10A

2. (For 1. and 3., see page 76.)

GENERAL JOURNAL

PAGE 7

	DATE		DESCRIPTION	POST. REF.	DEBIT	CREDIT	
1	20-- June	1	Rent Expense	521	3 0 0 00		1
2			Cash	101		3 0 0 00	2
3			Paid rent for June				3
4							4
5		2	Cash	101	1 0 0 00		5
6			Accounts Receivable	122	2 0 0 00		6
7			Delivery Fees	401		3 0 0 00	7
8			Deliveries made for cash and on account				8
9							9
10		4	Advertising Expense	512	1 5 00		10
11			Cash	101		1 5 00	11
12			Paid advertising expense				12
13							13
14		6	Office Supplies	142	1 8 0 00		14
15			Accounts Payable	202		1 8 0 00	15
16			Purchased office supplies				16
17							17
18		7	Cash	101	2 6 0 00		18
19			Delivery Fees	401		2 6 0 00	19
20			Received cash for delivery services				20
21							21
22		9	Accounts Payable	202	2 0 0 00		22
23			Cash	101		2 0 0 00	23
24			Made partial payment on truck				24
25							25
26		10	Office Equipment	181	7 0 0 00		26
27			Cash	101		1 0 0 00	27
28			Accounts Payable	202		6 0 0 00	28
29			Purchased copier				29
30							30
31							31
32							32
33							33
34							34

Problem 4-10A (Continued)

GENERAL JOURNAL

PAGE 8

	DATE		DESCRIPTION	POST. REF.	DEBIT		CREDIT		
1	20-- June	11	*Charitable Contributions Expense*	534	2 0 00				1
2			*Cash*	101			2 0 00		2
3			*Made contribution to Red Cross*						3
4									4
5		12	Cash	101	3 8 0 00				5
6			*Delivery Fees*	401			3 8 0 00		6
7			*Received cash for delivery services*						7
8									8
9		13	Cash	101	1 0 0 00				9
10			*Accounts Receivable*	122			1 0 0 00		10
11			*Received cash on account*						11
12									12
13		15	Wages Expense	511	2 0 0 00				13
14			*Cash*	101			2 0 0 00		14
15			*Paid employee*						15
16									16
17		16	Electricity Expense	533	3 6 00				17
18			*Cash*	101			3 6 00		18
19			*Paid electric bill*						19
20									20
21		18	Telephone Expense	525	4 6 00				21
22			*Cash*	101			4 6 00		22
23			*Paid telephone bill*						23
24									24
25		19	Cash	101	1 0 0 00				25
26			*Accounts Receivable*	122			1 0 0 00		26
27			*Received cash on account*						27
28									28
29		20	*Jim Andrews, Drawing*	312	2 0 0 00				29
30			*Cash*	101			2 0 0 00		30
31			*Owner's withdrawal*						31
32									32
33									33
34									34

Problem 4-10A (Continued)

	DATE		DESCRIPTION	POST. REF.	DEBIT	CREDIT	
1	20-- June	21	Gas and Oil Expense	538	3 2 00		1
2			Cash	101		3 2 00	2
3			Purchased gas and oil				3
4							4
5		22	Accounts Payable	202	4 0 00		5
6			Cash	101		4 0 00	6
7			Paid cash on account				7
8							8
9		24	Cash	101	3 4 0 00		9
10			Delivery Fees	401		3 4 0 00	10
11			Received cash for delivery services				11
12							12
13		26	Miscellaneous Expense	549	1 5 00		13
14			Cash	101		1 5 00	14
15			Paid for magazine subscription				15
16							16
17		27	Cash	101	1 8 0 00		17
18			Delivery Fees	401		1 8 0 00	18
19			Received cash for delivery services				19
20							20
21		27	Cash	101	1 0 0 00		21
22			Accounts Receivable	122		1 0 0 00	22
23			Received cash on account				23
24							24
25		29	Gas and Oil Expense	538	2 4 00		25
26			Cash	101		2 4 00	26
27			Purchased gasoline				27
28							28
29		30	Wages Expense	511	2 0 0 00		29
30			Cash	101		2 0 0 00	30
31			Paid employee				31
32							32
33							33
34							34

Problem 4-10A (Continued)

1. and 3.

ACCOUNT Cash   **GENERAL LEDGER**   ACCOUNT NO. 101

DATE		ITEM	POST. REF.	DEBIT	CREDIT	BALANCE DEBIT	BALANCE CREDIT
20-- June	1	Balance	✓			3 8 2 6 00	
	1		J7		3 0 0 00	3 5 2 6 00	
	2		J7	1 0 0 00		3 6 2 6 00	
	4		J7		1 5 00	3 6 1 1 00	
	7		J7	2 6 0 00		3 8 7 1 00	
	9		J7		2 0 0 00	3 6 7 1 00	
	10		J7		1 0 0 00	3 5 7 1 00	
	11		J8		2 0 00	3 5 5 1 00	
	12		J8	3 8 0 00		3 9 3 1 00	
	13		J8	1 0 0 00		4 0 3 1 00	
	15		J8		2 0 0 00	3 8 3 1 00	
	16		J8		3 6 00	3 7 9 5 00	
	18		J8		4 6 00	3 7 4 9 00	
	19		J8	1 0 0 00		3 8 4 9 00	
	20		J8		2 0 0 00	3 6 4 9 00	
	21		J9		3 2 00	3 6 1 7 00	
	22		J9		4 0 00	3 5 7 7 00	
	24		J9	3 4 0 00		3 9 1 7 00	
	26		J9		1 5 00	3 9 0 2 00	
	27		J9	1 8 0 00		4 0 8 2 00	
	27		J9	1 0 0 00		4 1 8 2 00	
	29		J9		2 4 00	4 1 5 8 00	
	30		J9		2 0 0 00	3 9 5 8 00	

Problem 4-10A (Continued)

ACCOUNT Accounts Receivable   ACCOUNT NO. 122

DATE		ITEM	POST. REF.	DEBIT	CREDIT	BALANCE DEBIT	BALANCE CREDIT
20-- June	1	Balance	✓			1 2 1 2 00	
	2		J7	2 0 0 00		1 4 1 2 00	
	13		J8		1 0 0 00	1 3 1 2 00	
	19		J8		1 0 0 00	1 2 1 2 00	
	27		J9		1 0 0 00	1 1 1 2 00	

ACCOUNT Office Supplies   ACCOUNT NO. 142

DATE		ITEM	POST. REF.	DEBIT	CREDIT	BALANCE DEBIT	BALANCE CREDIT
20-- June	1	Balance	✓			6 4 8 00	
	6		J7	1 8 0 00		8 2 8 00	

ACCOUNT Office Equipment   ACCOUNT NO. 181

DATE		ITEM	POST. REF.	DEBIT	CREDIT	BALANCE DEBIT	BALANCE CREDIT
20-- June	1	Balance	✓			2 1 0 0 00	
	10		J7	7 0 0 00		2 8 0 0 00	

ACCOUNT Delivery Truck   ACCOUNT NO. 185

DATE		ITEM	POST. REF.	DEBIT	CREDIT	BALANCE DEBIT	BALANCE CREDIT
20-- June	1	Balance	✓			8 0 0 0 00	

Problem 4-10A (Continued)

ACCOUNT Accounts Payable   ACCOUNT NO. 202

DATE		ITEM	POST. REF.	DEBIT	CREDIT	BALANCE DEBIT	BALANCE CREDIT
20-- June	1	Balance	✓				6 0 0 0 00
	6		J7		1 8 0 00		6 1 8 0 00
	9		J7	2 0 0 00			5 9 8 0 00
	10		J7		6 0 0 00		6 5 8 0 00
	22		J9	4 0 00			6 5 4 0 00

ACCOUNT Jim Andrews, Capital   ACCOUNT NO. 311

DATE		ITEM	POST. REF.	DEBIT	CREDIT	BALANCE DEBIT	BALANCE CREDIT
20-- June	1	Balance	✓				4 4 7 8 00

ACCOUNT Jim Andrews, Drawing   ACCOUNT NO. 312

DATE		ITEM	POST. REF.	DEBIT	CREDIT	BALANCE DEBIT	BALANCE CREDIT
20-- June	1	Balance	✓			1 8 0 0 00	
	20		J8	2 0 0 00		2 0 0 0 00	

ACCOUNT Delivery Fees   ACCOUNT NO. 401

DATE		ITEM	POST. REF.	DEBIT	CREDIT	BALANCE DEBIT	BALANCE CREDIT
20-- June	1	Balance	✓				9 8 8 0 00
	2		J7		3 0 0 00		10 1 8 0 00
	7		J7		2 6 0 00		10 4 4 0 00
	12		J8		3 8 0 00		10 8 2 0 00
	24		J9		3 4 0 00		11 1 6 0 00
	27		J9		1 8 0 00		11 3 4 0 00

Problem 4-10A (Continued)

ACCOUNT Wages Expense   ACCOUNT NO. 511

DATE		ITEM	POST. REF.	DEBIT	CREDIT	BALANCE DEBIT	BALANCE CREDIT
20-- June	1	Balance	✔			1 2 0 0 00	
	15		J8	2 0 0 00		1 4 0 0 00	
	30		J9	2 0 0 00		1 6 0 0 00	

ACCOUNT Advertising Expense   ACCOUNT NO. 512

DATE		ITEM	POST. REF.	DEBIT	CREDIT	BALANCE DEBIT	BALANCE CREDIT
20-- June	1	Balance	✔			9 0 00	
	4		J7	1 5 00		1 0 5 00	

ACCOUNT Rent Expense   ACCOUNT NO. 521

DATE		ITEM	POST. REF.	DEBIT	CREDIT	BALANCE DEBIT	BALANCE CREDIT
20-- June	1	Balance	✔			9 0 0 00	
	1		J7	3 0 0 00		1 2 0 0 00	

ACCOUNT Telephone Expense   ACCOUNT NO. 525

DATE		ITEM	POST. REF.	DEBIT	CREDIT	BALANCE DEBIT	BALANCE CREDIT
20-- June	1	Balance	✔			1 2 6 00	
	18		J8	4 6 00		1 7 2 00	

Problem 4-10A (Continued)

ACCOUNT   Electricity Expense   ACCOUNT NO. 533

DATE		ITEM	POST. REF.	DEBIT	CREDIT	BALANCE	
						DEBIT	CREDIT
20-- June	1	Balance	✔			9 8 00	
	16		J8	3 6 00		1 3 4 00	

ACCOUNT   Charitable Contributions Expense   ACCOUNT NO. 534

DATE		ITEM	POST. REF.	DEBIT	CREDIT	BALANCE	
						DEBIT	CREDIT
20-- June	1	Balance	✔			6 0 00	
	11		J8	2 0 00		8 0 00	

ACCOUNT   Gas and Oil Expense   ACCOUNT NO. 538

DATE		ITEM	POST. REF.	DEBIT	CREDIT	BALANCE	
						DEBIT	CREDIT
20-- June	1	Balance	✔			1 8 6 00	
	21		J9	3 2 00		2 1 8 00	
	29		J9	2 4 00		2 4 2 00	

ACCOUNT   Miscellaneous Expense   ACCOUNT NO. 549

DATE		ITEM	POST. REF.	DEBIT	CREDIT	BALANCE	
						DEBIT	CREDIT
20-- June	1	Balance	✔			1 1 2 00	
	26		J9	1 5 00		1 2 7 00	

Problem 4-10A (Concluded)
4.

Jim's Quick Delivery

Trial Balance

June 30, 20--

ACCOUNT TITLE	ACCT. NO.	DEBIT BALANCE	CREDIT BALANCE
Cash	101	3 9 5 8 00	
Accounts Receivable	122	1 1 1 2 00	
Office Supplies	142	8 2 8 00	
Office Equipment	181	2 8 0 0 00	
Delivery Truck	185	8 0 0 0 00	
Accounts Payable	202		6 5 4 0 00
Jim Andrews, Capital	311		4 4 7 8 00
Jim Andrews, Drawing	312	2 0 0 0 00	
Delivery Fees	401		11 3 4 0 00
Wages Expense	511	1 6 0 0 00	
Advertising Expense	512	1 0 5 00	
Rent Expense	521	1 2 0 0 00	
Telephone Expense	525	1 7 2 00	
Electricity Expense	533	1 3 4 00	
Charitable Contributions Expense	534	8 0 00	
Gas and Oil Expense	538	2 4 2 00	
Miscellaneous Expense	549	1 2 7 00	
		22 3 5 8 00	22 3 5 8 00

Problem 4-11A

GENERAL JOURNAL

	DATE		DESCRIPTION	POST. REF.	DEBIT	CREDIT	
1		(1)	Cash		5 0 0 00		1
2			Accounts Payable			5 0 0 00	2
3			To correct error in which purchase of				3
4			supplies on account was credited to Cash				4
5							5
6		(2)	Wages Expense		3 0 0 00		6
7			Rent Expense			3 0 0 00	7
8			To correct error in which a payment of				8
9			wages was debited to Rent Expense				9
10							10
11		(3)	Accounts Payable		2 0 0 00		11
12			Supplies			1 0 0 00	12
13			Cash			1 0 0 00	13
14			To correct error in which a $200 payment				14
15			on account was recorded as a $100 cash				15
16			purchase of supplies				16
17							17
18							18
19							19
20							20

Exercise 4-1B

1. Cash register tape   *The cash register tape is evidence of cash receipts.*

2. Sales ticket (issued to customer)   *The sales ticket is evidence of sales of goods or services (for cash or on account).*

3. Purchase invoice (received from supplier or vendor)   *The purchase invoice is evidence of purchases (accounts payable) of goods or services.*

4. Check stub   *A check stub is evidence of a cash payment.*

Exercise 4-2B

Transaction	Debit	Credit
1. Invested cash in the business, $1,000.	Cash	Owner's Capital
2. Performed services on account, $200.	Accounts Receivable	Fees
3. Purchased office equipment on account, $500.	Office Equipment	Accounts Payable
4. Received cash on account for services previously rendered, $200.	Cash	Accounts Receivable
5. Made a payment on account, $100.	Accounts Payable	Cash

Exercise 4-3B

	Cash		
1.	1,000	5.	100
4.	200		
	1,200		
Bal.	1,100		

	Accounts Receivable		
2.	200	4.	200
Bal.	—		

	Office Equipment		
3.	500		

	Accounts Payable		
5.	100	3.	500
		Bal.	400

	Owner's Capital		
		1.	1,000

	Fees		
		2.	200

Total Debits:		Total Credits:	
Cash	1,100	Accts. Pay.	400
Off. Equip.	500	Owner's Cap.	1,000
	1,600	Fees	200
			1,600

Exercise 4-4B

GENERAL JOURNAL

PAGE 1

	DATE		DESCRIPTION	POST. REF.	DEBIT	CREDIT	
1	20-- Oct.	1	Cash	101	15 0 0 0 00		1
2			Sengel Moon, Capital	311		15 0 0 0 00	2
3			Investment by owner				3
4							4
5		2	Rent Expense	521	3 0 0 00		5
6			Cash	101		3 0 0 00	6
7			Paid rent for October				7
8							8
9		3	Bicycle Parts	141	2 0 0 0 00		9
10			Accounts Payable	202		2 0 0 0 00	10
11			Purchased bicycle parts on account				11
12							12
13		5	Office Supplies	142	2 5 0 00		13
14			Accounts Payable	202		2 5 0 00	14
15			Purchased office supplies on account				15
16							16
17		8	Telephone Expense	525	3 8 00		17
18			Cash	101		3 8 00	18
19			Paid telephone bill				19
20							20
21		9	Cash	101	1 4 0 00		21
22			Repair Fees	401		1 4 0 00	22
23			Received cash for repair services				23
24							24
25		11	Miscellaneous Expense	549	1 5 00		25
26			Cash	101		1 5 00	26
27			Paid for magazine subscription				27
28							28
29		12	Accounts Payable	202	1 0 0 00		29
30			Cash	101		1 0 0 00	30
31			Made payment on account				31
32							32
33							33
34							34

Exercise 4-4B (Concluded)

GENERAL JOURNAL

	DATE		DESCRIPTION	POST. REF.	DEBIT	CREDIT	
1	20-- Oct.	14	Wages Expense	511	3 0 0 00		1
2			Cash	101		3 0 0 00	2
3			Paid employee				3
4							4
5		15	Cash	101	3 5 0 00		5
6			Repair Fees	401		3 5 0 00	6
7			Received cash for repair services				7
8							8
9		16	Utilities Expense	533	4 8 00		9
10			Cash	101		4 8 00	10
11			Paid utilities bill				11
12							12
13		19	Cash	101	2 5 0 00		13
14			Repair Fees	401		2 5 0 00	14
15			Received cash for repair services				15
16							16
17		23	Sengel Moon, Drawing	312	5 0 00		17
18			Cash	101		5 0 00	18
19			Owner's withdrawal				19
20							20
21		25	Accounts Payable	202	5 0 00		21
22			Cash	101		5 0 00	22
23			Made payment on account				23
24							24
25		29	Wages Expense	511	3 0 0 00		25
26			Cash	101		3 0 0 00	26
27			Paid employee				27
28							28

Exercise 4-5B

GENERAL LEDGER

ACCOUNT *Cash*　　　　　　　　　　　　　　　　　　　　　　　ACCOUNT NO.　**101**

DATE		ITEM	POST. REF.	DEBIT	CREDIT	BALANCE DEBIT	BALANCE CREDIT
20-- Oct.	1		J1	15 0 0 0 00		15 0 0 0 00	
	2		J1		3 0 0 00	14 7 0 0 00	
	8		J1		3 8 00	14 6 6 2 00	
	9		J1	1 4 0 00		14 8 0 2 00	
	11		J1		1 5 00	14 7 8 7 00	
	12		J1		1 0 0 00	14 6 8 7 00	
	14		J2		3 0 0 00	14 3 8 7 00	
	15		J2	3 5 0 00		14 7 3 7 00	
	16		J2		4 8 00	14 6 8 9 00	
	19		J2	2 5 0 00		14 9 3 9 00	
	23		J2		5 0 00	14 8 8 9 00	
	25		J2		5 0 00	14 8 3 9 00	
	29		J2		3 0 0 00	14 5 3 9 00	

ACCOUNT *Bicycle Parts*　　　　　　　　　　　　　　　　　　　ACCOUNT NO.　**141**

DATE		ITEM	POST. REF.	DEBIT	CREDIT	BALANCE DEBIT	BALANCE CREDIT
20-- Oct.	3		J1	2 0 0 0 00		2 0 0 0 00	

ACCOUNT *Office Supplies*　　　　　　　　　　　　　　　　　　ACCOUNT NO.　**142**

DATE		ITEM	POST. REF.	DEBIT	CREDIT	BALANCE DEBIT	BALANCE CREDIT
20-- Oct.	5		J1	2 5 0 00		2 5 0 00	

Exercise 4-5B (Continued)

ACCOUNT   **Accounts Payable**   ACCOUNT NO.   **202**

DATE		ITEM	POST. REF.	DEBIT	CREDIT	BALANCE DEBIT	BALANCE CREDIT
20-- Oct.	3		J1		2 0 0 0 00		2 0 0 0 00
	5		J1		2 5 0 00		2 2 5 0 00
	12		J1	1 0 0 00			2 1 5 0 00
	25		J2	5 0 00			2 1 0 0 00

ACCOUNT   **Sengel Moon, Capital**   ACCOUNT NO.   **311**

DATE		ITEM	POST. REF.	DEBIT	CREDIT	BALANCE DEBIT	BALANCE CREDIT
20-- Oct.	1		J1		15 0 0 0 00		15 0 0 0 00

ACCOUNT   **Sengel Moon, Drawing**   ACCOUNT NO.   **312**

DATE		ITEM	POST. REF.	DEBIT	CREDIT	BALANCE DEBIT	BALANCE CREDIT
20-- Oct.	23		J2	5 0 00		5 0 00	

ACCOUNT   **Repair Fees**   ACCOUNT NO.   **401**

DATE		ITEM	POST. REF.	DEBIT	CREDIT	BALANCE DEBIT	BALANCE CREDIT
20-- Oct.	9		J1		1 4 0 00		1 4 0 00
	15		J2		3 5 0 00		4 9 0 00
	19		J2		2 5 0 00		7 4 0 00

Exercise 4-5B (Continued)

ACCOUNT **Wages Expense** ACCOUNT NO. **511**

DATE		ITEM	POST. REF.	DEBIT	CREDIT	BALANCE DEBIT	BALANCE CREDIT
20-- Oct.	14		J2	3 0 0 00		3 0 0 00	
	29		J2	3 0 0 00		6 0 0 00	

ACCOUNT **Rent Expense** ACCOUNT NO. **521**

DATE		ITEM	POST. REF.	DEBIT	CREDIT	BALANCE DEBIT	BALANCE CREDIT
20-- Oct.	2		J1	3 0 0 00		3 0 0 00	

ACCOUNT **Telephone Expense** ACCOUNT NO. **525**

DATE		ITEM	POST. REF.	DEBIT	CREDIT	BALANCE DEBIT	BALANCE CREDIT
20-- Oct.	8		J1	3 8 00		3 8 00	

ACCOUNT **Utilities Expense** ACCOUNT NO. **533**

DATE		ITEM	POST. REF.	DEBIT	CREDIT	BALANCE DEBIT	BALANCE CREDIT
20-- Oct.	16		J2	4 8 00		4 8 00	

ACCOUNT **Miscellaneous Expense** ACCOUNT NO. **549**

DATE		ITEM	POST. REF.	DEBIT	CREDIT	BALANCE DEBIT	BALANCE CREDIT
20-- Oct.	11		J1	1 5 00		1 5 00	

Exercise 4-5B (Concluded)

The Bike Doctor

Trial Balance

October 31, 20--

ACCOUNT TITLE	ACCT. NO.	DEBIT BALANCE	CREDIT BALANCE
Cash	*101*	14 5 3 9 00	
Bicycle Parts	*141*	2 0 0 0 00	
Office Supplies	*142*	2 5 0 00	
Accounts Payable	*202*		2 1 0 0 00
Sengel Moon, Capital	*311*		15 0 0 0 00
Sengel Moon, Drawing	*312*	5 0 00	
Repair Fees	*401*		7 4 0 00
Wages Expense	*511*	6 0 0 00	
Rent Expense	*521*	3 0 0 00	
Telephone Expense	*525*	3 8 00	
Utilities Expense	*533*	4 8 00	
Miscellaneous Expense	*549*	1 5 00	
		17 8 4 0 00	17 8 4 0 00

Exercise 4-6B

The Bike Doctor

Income Statement

For Month Ended October 31, 20--

Revenue:			
Repair fees			$ 7 4 0 00
Expenses:			
Wages expense	$ 6 0 0 00		
Rent expense	3 0 0 00		
Telephone expense	3 8 00		
Utilities expense	4 8 00		
Miscellaneous expense	1 5 00		
Total expenses			1 0 0 1 00
Net loss			$ 2 6 1 00

Exercise 4-6B (Concluded)

The Bike Doctor

Statement of Owner's Equity

For Month Ended October 31, 20--

Sengel Moon, capital, October 1, 20--			$
Investments during October			15 000 00
Total investment			$15 000 00
Less: Net loss for October	$ 261 00		
Withdrawals for October	50 00		
Decrease in capital			311 00
Sengel Moon, capital, October 31, 20--			$14 689 00

The Bike Doctor

Balance Sheet

October 31, 20--

Assets		Liabilities	
Cash	$14 539 00	Accounts payable	$ 2 100 00
Bicycle parts	2 000 00		
Office supplies	250 00	**Owner's Equity**	
		Sengel Moon, capital	14 689 00
Total assets	$16 789 00	Total liab. & owner's equity	$16 789 00

Exercise 4-7B

AT Speaker's Bureau
Income Statement
For Month Ended March 31, 20--

Revenue:										
Speaking fees							$4 8 0 0 00			
Expenses:										
Wages expense	$4 0 0 00									
Rent expense	2 0 0 00									
Telephone expense	3 5 00									
Travel expense	4 5 0 00									
Utilities expense	8 8 00									
Miscellaneous expense	2 5 00									
Total expenses							1 1 9 8 00			
Net income							$3 6 0 2 00			

AT Speaker's Bureau
Statement of Owner's Equity
For Month Ended March 31, 20--

AT Speaker, capital, March 1, 20--							$			
Investments during March							6 0 9 8 00			
Total investment							$6 0 9 8 00			
Net income for March	$3 6 0 2 00									
Less withdrawals for March	8 0 0 00									
Increase in capital							2 8 0 2 00			
AT Speaker, capital, March 31, 20--							$8 9 0 0 00			

Exercise 4-7B (Concluded)

AT Speaker's Bureau

Balance Sheet

March 31, 20--

Assets		Liabilities	
Cash	$ 6 600 00	Accounts payable	$ 3 000 00
Accounts receivable	2 800 00		
Office supplies	1 000 00	**Owner's Equity**	
Office equipment	1 500 00	AT Speaker, capital	8 900 00
Total assets	$11 900 00	Total liab. & owner's equity	$11 900 00

Exercise 4-8B

GENERAL JOURNAL

PAGE

	DATE		DESCRIPTION	POST. REF.	DEBIT	CREDIT	
15	Apr.	6	Office ~~Supplies~~ *Equipment* ← Student Initials		3 5 0 00 ~~5 3 0 00~~		15
16			~~Cash~~ *Accounts Payable*			3 5 0 00 ~~5 3 0 00~~	16
17			Purchased office equipment *on account*				17
18							18
23		21	Cash	101	3 0 0 00		23
24			Service Fees	401		3 0 0 00	24
25			Revenue earned from services				25
26			previously rendered				26
27							27
28		25	**Accounts Receivable**		3 0 0 00		28
29			**Cash**			3 0 0 00	29
30			**To correct entry of April 21**				30
31							31
32							32
33							33

Problem 4-9B
2. (For 1. and 3., see page 96.)

GENERAL JOURNAL

PAGE 1

	DATE		DESCRIPTION	POST. REF.	DEBIT	CREDIT	
1	20-- May	1	Cash	101	5 0 0 0 00		1
2			Benito Mendez, Capital	311		5 0 0 0 00	2
3			Original investment				3
4							4
5		2	Rent Expense	521	5 0 0 00		5
6			Cash	101		5 0 0 00	6
7			Paid rent for May				7
8							8
9		3	Office Supplies	142	1 0 0 00		9
10			Cash	101		1 0 0 00	10
11			Purchased office supplies				11
12							12
13		4	Office Equipment	181	2 0 0 0 00		13
14			Accounts Payable	202		2 0 0 0 00	14
15			Purchased office equipment on account				15
16							16
17		5	Cash	101	2 8 0 00		17
18			Appraisal Fees	401		2 8 0 00	18
19			Earned appraisal fees				19
20							20
21		8	Telephone Expense	525	3 8 00		21
22			Cash	101		3 8 00	22
23			Paid telephone bill				23
24							24
25		9	Electricity Expense	533	4 2 00		25
26			Cash	101		4 2 00	26
27			Paid electric bill				27
28							28
29		10	Cash	101	3 1 0 00		29
30			Appraisal Fees	401		3 1 0 00	30
31			Earned appraisal fees				31
32							32
33							33
34							34

Problem 4-9B (Continued)

GENERAL JOURNAL

PAGE 2

	DATE		DESCRIPTION	POST. REF.	DEBIT	CREDIT	
1	20-- May	13	Wages Expense	511	500 00		1
2			Cash	101		500 00	2
3			Paid employee				3
4							4
5		14	Transportation Expense	526	200 00		5
6			Cash	101		200 00	6
7			Paid for car rental				7
8							8
9		15	Advertising Expense	512	30 00		9
10			Cash	101		30 00	10
11			Paid for newspaper ad				11
12							12
13		18	Cash	101	620 00		13
14			Appraisal Fees	401		620 00	14
15			Earned appraisal fees				15
16							16
17		19	Transportation Expense	526	22 00		17
18			Cash	101		22 00	18
19			Paid mileage reimbursement				19
20							20
21		21	Benito Mendez, Drawing	312	50 00		21
22			Cash	101		50 00	22
23			Owner's withdrawal				23
24							24
25		23	Accounts Payable	202	200 00		25
26			Cash	101		200 00	26
27			Paid cash on account				27
28							28
29		24	Accounts Receivable	122	500 00		29
30			Appraisal Fees	401		500 00	30
31			Earned appraisal fees				31
32							32
33							33
34							34

Problem 4-9B (Continued)

GENERAL JOURNAL

PAGE 3

	DATE		DESCRIPTION	POST. REF.	DEBIT				CREDIT				
1	20-- May	26	Advertising Expense	512		3	0	00					1
2			Cash	101						3	0	00	2
3			Paid for newspaper ad										3
4													4
5		27	Miscellaneous Expense	549		1	5	00					5
6			Cash	101						1	5	00	6
7			Paid softball team sponsorship										7
8													8
9		28	Wages Expense	511	5	0	0	00					9
10			Cash	101					5	0	0	00	10
11			Paid employee										11
12													12
13		29	Cash	101	2	5	0	00					13
14			Accounts Receivable	122					2	5	0	00	14
15			Received cash on account										15
16													16
17		30	Cash	101	2	8	0	00					17
18			Appraisal Fees	401					2	8	0	00	18
19			Earned appraisal fees										19
20													20
21		31	Transportation Expense	526		1	3	00					21
22			Cash	101						1	3	00	22
23			Paid cab fare										23
24													24
25													25
26													26
27													27
28													28
29													29
30													30
31													31
32													32
33													33
34													34

Problem 4-9B (Continued)

1. and 3.

GENERAL LEDGER

ACCOUNT Cash   ACCOUNT NO. 101

DATE		ITEM	POST. REF.	DEBIT	CREDIT	BALANCE DEBIT	BALANCE CREDIT
20-- May	1		J1	5 0 0 0 00		5 0 0 0 00	
	2		J1		5 0 0 00	4 5 0 0 00	
	3		J1		1 0 0 00	4 4 0 0 00	
	5		J1	2 8 0 00		4 6 8 0 00	
	8		J1		3 8 00	4 6 4 2 00	
	9		J1		4 2 00	4 6 0 0 00	
	10		J1	3 1 0 00		4 9 1 0 00	
	13		J2		5 0 0 00	4 4 1 0 00	
	14		J2		2 0 0 00	4 2 1 0 00	
	15		J2		3 0 00	4 1 8 0 00	
	18		J2	6 2 0 00		4 8 0 0 00	
	19		J2		2 2 00	4 7 7 8 00	
	21		J2		5 0 00	4 7 2 8 00	
	23		J2		2 0 0 00	4 5 2 8 00	
	26		J3		3 0 00	4 4 9 8 00	
	27		J3		1 5 00	4 4 8 3 00	
	28		J3		5 0 0 00	3 9 8 3 00	
	29		J3	2 5 0 00		4 2 3 3 00	
	30		J3	2 8 0 00		4 5 1 3 00	
	31		J3		1 3 00	4 5 0 0 00	

ACCOUNT Accounts Receivable   ACCOUNT NO. 122

DATE		ITEM	POST. REF.	DEBIT	CREDIT	BALANCE DEBIT	BALANCE CREDIT
20-- May	24		J2	5 0 0 00		5 0 0 00	
	29		J3		2 5 0 00	2 5 0 00	

Problem 4-9B (Continued)

ACCOUNT Office Supplies   ACCOUNT NO. 142

DATE		ITEM	POST. REF.	DEBIT	CREDIT	BALANCE DEBIT	BALANCE CREDIT
20-- May	3		J1	1 0 0 00		1 0 0 00	

ACCOUNT Office Equipment   ACCOUNT NO. 181

DATE		ITEM	POST. REF.	DEBIT	CREDIT	BALANCE DEBIT	BALANCE CREDIT
20-- May	4		J1	2 0 0 0 00		2 0 0 0 00	

ACCOUNT Accounts Payable   ACCOUNT NO. 202

DATE		ITEM	POST. REF.	DEBIT	CREDIT	BALANCE DEBIT	BALANCE CREDIT
20-- May	4		J1		2 0 0 0 00		2 0 0 0 00
	23		J2	2 0 0 00			1 8 0 0 00

ACCOUNT Benito Mendez, Capital   ACCOUNT NO. 311

DATE		ITEM	POST. REF.	DEBIT	CREDIT	BALANCE DEBIT	BALANCE CREDIT
20-- May	1		J1		5 0 0 0 00		5 0 0 0 00

Problem 4-9B (Continued)

ACCOUNT Benito Mendez, Drawing   ACCOUNT NO. 312

DATE		ITEM	POST. REF.	DEBIT	CREDIT	BALANCE DEBIT	BALANCE CREDIT
20-- May	21		J2	5 0 00		5 0 00	

ACCOUNT Appraisal Fees   ACCOUNT NO. 401

DATE		ITEM	POST. REF.	DEBIT	CREDIT	BALANCE DEBIT	BALANCE CREDIT
20-- May	5		J1		2 8 0 00		2 8 0 00
	10		J1		3 1 0 00		5 9 0 00
	18		J2		6 2 0 00		1 2 1 0 00
	24		J2		5 0 0 00		1 7 1 0 00
	30		J3		2 8 0 00		1 9 9 0 00

ACCOUNT Wages Expense   ACCOUNT NO. 511

DATE		ITEM	POST. REF.	DEBIT	CREDIT	BALANCE DEBIT	BALANCE CREDIT
20-- May	13		J2	5 0 0 00		5 0 0 00	
	28		J3	5 0 0 00		1 0 0 0 00	

ACCOUNT Advertising Expense   ACCOUNT NO. 512

DATE		ITEM	POST. REF.	DEBIT	CREDIT	BALANCE DEBIT	BALANCE CREDIT
20-- May	15		J2	3 0 00		3 0 00	
	26		J3	3 0 00		6 0 00	

Problem 4-9B (Continued)

ACCOUNT Rent Expense   ACCOUNT NO. 521

DATE		ITEM	POST. REF.	DEBIT	CREDIT	BALANCE DEBIT	BALANCE CREDIT
20-- May	2		J1	5 0 0 00		5 0 0 00	

ACCOUNT Telephone Expense   ACCOUNT NO. 525

DATE		ITEM	POST. REF.	DEBIT	CREDIT	BALANCE DEBIT	BALANCE CREDIT
20-- May	8		J1	3 8 00		3 8 00	

ACCOUNT Transportation Expense   ACCOUNT NO 526

DATE		ITEM	POST. REF.	DEBIT	CREDIT	BALANCE DEBIT	BALANCE CREDIT
20-- May	14		J2	2 0 0 00		2 0 0 00	
	19		J2	2 2 00		2 2 2 00	
	31		J3	1 3 00		2 3 5 00	

ACCOUNT Electricity Expense   ACCOUNT NO. 533

DATE		ITEM	POST. REF.	DEBIT	CREDIT	BALANCE DEBIT	BALANCE CREDIT
20-- May	9		J1	4 2 00		4 2 00	

ACCOUNT Miscellaneous Expense   ACCOUNT NO. 549

DATE		ITEM	POST. REF.	DEBIT	CREDIT	BALANCE DEBIT	BALANCE CREDIT
20-- May	27		J3	1 5 00		1 5 00	

Problem 4-9B (Continued)

4.

Mendez Appraisals

Trial Balance

May 31, 20--

ACCOUNT TITLE	ACCT. NO.	DEBIT BALANCE	CREDIT BALANCE
Cash	101	4 5 0 0 00	
Accounts Receivable	122	2 5 0 00	
Office Supplies	142	1 0 0 00	
Office Equipment	181	2 0 0 0 00	
Accounts Payable	202		1 8 0 0 00
Benito Mendez, Capital	311		5 0 0 0 00
Benito Mendez, Drawing	312	5 0 00	
Appraisal Fees	401		1 9 9 0 00
Wages Expense	511	1 0 0 0 00	
Advertising Expense	512	6 0 00	
Rent Expense	521	5 0 0 00	
Telephone Expense	525	3 8 00	
Transportation Expense	526	2 3 5 00	
Electricity Expense	533	4 2 00	
Miscellaneous Expense	549	1 5 00	
		8 7 9 0 00	8 7 9 0 00

Problem 4-9B (Continued)

5.

Mendez Appraisals
Income Statement
For Month Ended May 31, 20--

Revenue:			
Appraisal fees			$1 9 9 0 00
Expenses:			
Wages expense	$1 0 0 0 00		
Advertising expense	6 0 00		
Rent expense	5 0 0 00		
Telephone expense	3 8 00		
Transportation expense	2 3 5 00		
Electricity expense	4 2 00		
Miscellaneous expense	1 5 00		
Total expenses			1 8 9 0 00
Net income			$ 1 0 0 00

Mendez Appraisals
Statement of Owner's Equity
For Month Ended May 31, 20--

Benito Mendez, capital, May 1, 20--			$
Investments during May			5 0 0 0 00
Total investment			$5 0 0 0 00
Net income for May	$ 1 0 0 00		
Less withdrawals for May	5 0 00		
Increase in capital			5 0 00
Benito Mendez, capital, May 31, 20--			$5 0 5 0 00

Problem 4-9B (Concluded)

Mendez Appraisals
Balance Sheet
May 31, 20--

Assets						Liabilities					
Cash	$4	5	0	0	00	Accounts payable	$1	8	0	0	00
Accounts receivable		2	5	0	00						
Office supplies		1	0	0	00	Owner's Equity					
Office equipment		2	0	0	00	Benito Mendez, capital		5	0	5	0	00
Total assets	$6	8	5	0	00	Total liab. & owner's equity	$6	8	5	0	00

Problem 4-10B
2. (For 1. and 3., see page 106.)

GENERAL JOURNAL   PAGE 7

	DATE		DESCRIPTION	POST. REF.	DEBIT	CREDIT	
1	20-- Nov.	1	Rent Expense	521	3 0 0 00		1
2			Cash	101		3 0 0 00	2
3			Paid rent				3
4							4
5		2	Tailoring Supplies	141	1 5 0 00		5
6			Accounts Payable	202		1 5 0 00	6
7			Purchased tailoring supplies on account				7
8							8
9		3	Tailoring Equipment	183	3 0 0 00		9
10			Accounts Payable	202		3 0 0 00	10
11			Purchased machine on account				11
12							12
13		5	Cash	101	1 0 0 00		13
14			Accounts Receivable	122	3 0 0 00		14
15			Tailoring Fees	401		4 0 0 00	15
16			Earned tailoring fees				16
17							17
18		8	Advertising Expense	512	1 3 00		18
19			Cash	101		1 3 00	19
20			Paid for newspaper ad				20
21							21
22		9	Telephone Expense	525	2 8 00		22
23			Cash	101		2 8 00	23
24			Paid telephone bill				24
25							25
26		10	Electricity Expense	533	2 1 00		26
27			Cash	101		2 1 00	27
28			Paid electric bill				28
29							29
30		11	Cash	101	2 0 0 00		30
31			Accounts Receivable	122		2 0 0 00	31
32			Received cash on account				32
33							33
34							34

Problem 4-10B (Continued)

GENERAL JOURNAL

	DATE		DESCRIPTION	POST. REF.	DEBIT	CREDIT	
1	20-- Nov.	12	Cash	101	2 0 0 00		1
2			Accounts Receivable	122	2 5 0 00		2
3			Tailoring Fees	401		4 5 0 00	3
4			Earned tailoring fees				4
5							5
6		15	Wages Expense	511	4 0 0 00		6
7			Cash	101		4 0 0 00	7
8			Paid employee				8
9							9
10		16	Accounts Payable	202	1 0 0 00		10
11			Cash	101		1 0 0 00	11
12			Paid cash on account				12
13							13
14		17	Miscellaneous Expense	549	1 2 00		14
15			Cash	101		1 2 00	15
16			Paid for magazine subscription				16
17							17
18		19	Cash	101	3 0 0 00		18
19			Accounts Receivable	122	1 5 0 00		19
20			Tailoring Fees	401		4 5 0 00	20
21			Earned tailoring fees				21
22							22
23		23	Cash	101	3 0 0 00		23
24			Accounts Receivable	122		3 0 0 00	24
25			Received cash on account				25
26							26
27		24	Advertising Expense	512	1 3 00		27
28			Cash	101		1 3 00	28
29			Paid for newspaper ad				29
30							30
31							31
32							32
33							33
34							34

Problem 4-10B (Continued)

	DATE		DESCRIPTION	POST. REF.	DEBIT		CREDIT	
1	20-- Nov.	26	*Miscellaneous Expense*	549	1 2 00			1
2			*Cash*	101			1 2 00	2
3			*Paid for postage*					3
4								4
5		27	*Cash*	101	2 0 0 00			5
6			*Accounts Receivable*	122	4 0 0 00			6
7			*Tailoring Fees*	401			6 0 0 00	7
8			*Earned tailoring fees*					8
9								9
10		30	*Cash*	101	4 0 0 00			10
11			*Accounts Receivable*	122			4 0 0 00	11
12			*Received cash on account*					12
13								13
14								14
15								15
16								16
17								17
18								0
19								19
20								20
21								21
22								22
23								23
24								24
25								25
26								26
27								27
28								28
29								29
30								30
31								31
32								32
33								33
34								34

Problem 4-10B (Continued)

1. and 3.

GENERAL LEDGER

ACCOUNT Cash   ACCOUNT NO. 101

DATE		ITEM	POST. REF.	DEBIT	CREDIT	BALANCE DEBIT	BALANCE CREDIT
20-- Nov.	1	Balance	✓			6 2 1 1 00	
	1		J7		3 0 0 00	5 9 1 1 00	
	5		J7	1 0 0 00		6 0 1 1 00	
	8		J7		1 3 00	5 9 9 8 00	
	9		J7		2 8 00	5 9 7 0 00	
	10		J7		2 1 00	5 9 4 9 00	
	11		J7	2 0 0 00		6 1 4 9 00	
	12		J8	2 0 0 00		6 3 4 9 00	
	15		J8		4 0 0 00	5 9 4 9 00	
	16		J8		1 0 0 00	5 8 4 9 00	
	17		J8		1 2 00	5 8 3 7 00	
	19		J8	3 0 0 00		6 1 3 7 00	
	23		J8	3 0 0 00		6 4 3 7 00	
	24		J8		1 3 00	6 4 2 4 00	
	26		J9		1 2 00	6 4 1 2 00	
	27		J9	2 0 0 00		6 6 1 2 00	
	30		J9	4 0 0 00		7 0 1 2 00	

ACCOUNT Accounts Receivable   ACCOUNT NO. 122

DATE		ITEM	POST. REF.	DEBIT	CREDIT	BALANCE DEBIT	BALANCE CREDIT
20-- Nov.	1	Balance	✓			4 8 4 00	
	5		J7	3 0 0 00		7 8 4 00	
	11		J7		2 0 0 00	5 8 4 00	
	12		J8	2 5 0 00		8 3 4 00	
	19		J8	1 5 0 00		9 8 4 00	
	23		J8		3 0 0 00	6 8 4 00	
	27		J9	4 0 0 00		1 0 8 4 00	
	30		J9		4 0 0 00	6 8 4 00	

Problem 4-10B (Continued)

ACCOUNT Tailoring Supplies   ACCOUNT NO. 141

DATE		ITEM	POST. REF.	DEBIT	CREDIT	BALANCE DEBIT	BALANCE CREDIT
20-- Nov.	1	Balance	✓			1 0 0 0 00	
	2		J7	1 5 0 00		1 1 5 0 00	

ACCOUNT Tailoring Equipment   ACCOUNT NO. 183

DATE		ITEM	POST. REF.	DEBIT	CREDIT	BALANCE DEBIT	BALANCE CREDIT
20-- Nov.	1	Balance	✓			3 8 0 0 00	
	3		J7	3 0 0 00		4 1 0 0 00	

ACCOUNT Accounts Payable   ACCOUNT NO. 202

DATE		ITEM	POST. REF.	DEBIT	CREDIT	BALANCE DEBIT	BALANCE CREDIT
20-- Nov.	1	Balance	✓				4 1 2 5 00
	2		J7		1 5 0 00		4 2 7 5 00
	3		J7		3 0 0 00		4 5 7 5 00
	16		J8	1 0 0 00			4 4 7 5 00

ACCOUNT Ann Taylor, Capital   ACCOUNT NO. 311

DATE		ITEM	POST. REF.	DEBIT	CREDIT	BALANCE DEBIT	BALANCE CREDIT
20-- Nov.	1	Balance	✓				6 1 3 0 00

Problem 4-10B (Continued)

ACCOUNT Ann Taylor, Drawing   ACCOUNT NO. 312

DATE		ITEM	POST. REF.	DEBIT	CREDIT	BALANCE DEBIT	BALANCE CREDIT
20-- Nov.	1	Balance	✓			8 0 0 00	

ACCOUNT Tailoring Fees   ACCOUNT NO. 401

DATE		ITEM	POST. REF.	DEBIT	CREDIT	BALANCE DEBIT	BALANCE CREDIT
20-- Nov.	1	Balance	✓				3 6 0 0 00
	5		J7		4 0 0 00		4 0 0 0 00
	12		J8		4 5 0 00		4 4 5 0 00
	19		J8		4 5 0 00		4 9 0 0 00
	27		J9		6 0 0 00		5 5 0 0 00

ACCOUNT Wages Expense   ACCOUNT NO. 511

DATE		ITEM	POST. REF.	DEBIT	CREDIT	BALANCE DEBIT	BALANCE CREDIT
20-- Nov.	1	Balance	✓			8 0 0 00	
	15		J8	4 0 0 00		1 2 0 0 00	

ACCOUNT Advertising Expense   ACCOUNT NO. 512

DATE		ITEM	POST. REF.	DEBIT	CREDIT	BALANCE DEBIT	BALANCE CREDIT
20-- Nov.	1	Balance	✓			3 4 00	
	8		J7	1 3 00		4 7 00	
	24		J8	1 3 00		6 0 00	

Problem 4-10B (Continued)

ACCOUNT Rent Expense   ACCOUNT NO. 521

DATE		ITEM	POST. REF.	DEBIT	CREDIT	BALANCE DEBIT	BALANCE CREDIT
20-- Nov.	1	Balance	✓			6 0 0 00	
	1		J7	3 0 0 00		9 0 0 00	

ACCOUNT Telephone Expense   ACCOUNT NO. 525

DATE		ITEM	POST. REF.	DEBIT	CREDIT	BALANCE DEBIT	BALANCE CREDIT
20-- Nov.	1	Balance	✓			6 0 00	
	9		J7	2 8 00		8 8 00	

ACCOUNT Electricity Expense   ACCOUNT NO. 533

DATE		ITEM	POST. REF.	DEBIT	CREDIT	BALANCE DEBIT	BALANCE CREDIT
20-- Nov.	1	Balance	✓			4 4 00	
	10		J7	2 1 00		6 5 00	

ACCOUNT Miscellaneous Expense   ACCOUNT NO. 549

DATE		ITEM	POST. REF.	DEBIT	CREDIT	BALANCE DEBIT	BALANCE CREDIT
20-- Nov.	1	Balance	✓			2 2 00	
	17		J8	1 2 00		3 4 00	
	26		J9	1 2 00		4 6 00	

Problem 4-10B (Concluded)

4.

Taylor Tailoring

Trial Balance

November 30, 20--

ACCOUNT TITLE	ACCT. NO.	DEBIT BALANCE	CREDIT BALANCE
Cash	101	7 0 1 2 00	
Accounts Receivable	122	6 8 4 00	
Tailoring Supplies	141	1 1 5 0 00	
Tailoring Equipment	183	4 1 0 0 00	
Accounts Payable	202		4 4 7 5 00
Ann Taylor, Capital	311		6 1 3 0 00
Ann Taylor, Drawing	312	8 0 0 00	
Tailoring Fees	401		5 5 0 0 00
Wages Expense	511	1 2 0 0 00	
Advertising Expense	512	6 0 00	
Rent Expense	521	9 0 0 00	
Telephone Expense	525	8 8 00	
Electricity Expense	533	6 5 00	
Miscellaneous Expense	549	4 6 00	
		16 1 0 5 00	16 1 0 5 00

Problem 4-11B

GENERAL JOURNAL

PAGE

	DATE	DESCRIPTION	POST. REF.	DEBIT	CREDIT	
1	(1)	Equipment		4 0 0 00		1
2		Supplies			4 0 0 00	2
3		Correction in which purchase of				3
4		equipment was debited to Supplies				4
5						5
6		Cash		4 0 0 00		6
7		Accounts Payable			4 0 0 00	7
8		Correction in which purchase on account				8
9		was credited to Cash				9
10						10
11	(2)	Advertising Expense		2 0 0 00		11
12		Repair Expense			2 0 0 00	12
13		Correction in which a payment for				13
14		advertising was debited to Repair Expense				14
15						15
16	(3)	Accounts Payable		6 0 0 00		16
17		Prepaid Insurance			4 0 0 00	17
18		Cash			2 0 0 00	18
19		Correction in which a $600 payment				19
20		on account was recorded as a $400				20
21		insurance premium payment				21
22						22
23						23

MANAGING YOUR WRITING

The student should make the following points:

1.   The method of entering information into the accounting system is based on a double-entry framework. This means that every transaction will affect at least two accounts. Some accounts will be debited and others will be credited. The sum of the debits must equal the sum of the credits for every transaction.

     The double-entry framework helps ensure that complete information on each transaction is entered. If only the increase in the asset is recorded, valuable information on why an asset increased is lost. Cash could have increased because the business borrowed the money, sold another asset, earned the money by providing a service, or received an additional investment by the owner. Thus, the debit to Cash must be offset, or explained, by a credit to some other account.

2.   The accounting system is based on a simple accounting equation (Assets = Liabilities + Owner's Equity) that must remain in balance as each transaction is recorded. This means, for example, that an increase in an asset must be offset by a decrease in another asset, an increase in liabilities, or an increase in owner's equity.

3.   The trial balance provides a check of whether the sum of the debits equals the sum of the credits. If the columns of the trial balance are not equal, an error has been made. The following errors are possibilities:
     a.   Making a math error in the trial balance, or in the ledger accounts.
     b.   Failing to post all debits and credits to the ledger accounts.
     c.   Failing to enter all debits and credits in the journal.
     d.   Posting a debit as a credit, or a credit as a debit.
     e.   Entering different amounts for the debits and credits.
          (This list is not intended to be all inclusive. It should be interesting to read about other errors that the students suggest.)

4.   Tips for finding errors are specifically addressed in the text. They include the following:
     a.   Double check your addition.
     b.   Find the difference between the debits and the credits.
          (1)   If the difference is equal to the amount of a specific transaction, perhaps you forgot to post the debit or credit portion of this transaction.
          (2)   Divide the difference by 2. If a debit were posted as a credit, it would mean that one transaction had two credits and no debits. The difference between the total debits and credits would be twice the amount of the debit that was posted as a credit.
          (3)   Divide the difference by 9. If the difference is evenly divisible by 9, you may have committed a slide error or a transposition error.

Mastery Problem

1.

GENERAL JOURNAL

PAGE 1

	DATE		DESCRIPTION	POST. REF.	DEBIT	CREDIT	
1	20-- June	1	Cash	101	10 0 0 0 00		1
2			Barry Bird, Capital	311		10 0 0 0 00	2
3			Owner's original investment				3
4							4
5		1	Athletic Equipment	183	3 0 0 0 00		5
6			Cash	101		3 0 0 0 00	6
7			Purchased athletic equipment				7
8							8
9		2	Advertising Expense	512	5 0 0 00		9
10			Cash	101		5 0 0 00	10
11			Paid for advertising				11
12							12
13		2	Cash	101	15 0 0 0 00		13
14			Registration Fees	401		15 0 0 0 00	14
15			Collected registration fees				15
16							16
17		2	Basketball Facilities	184	12 0 0 0 00		17
18			Accounts Payable	202		12 0 0 0 00	18
19			Completed construction of basketball court				19
20							20
21		5	Office Supplies	142	3 0 0 00		21
22			Accounts Payable	202		3 0 0 00	22
23			Purchased office supplies on account				23
24			from Gordon Office Supplies				24
25							25
26		6	Food Expense	524	5 8 0 0 00		26
27			Accounts Payable	202		5 8 0 0 00	27
28			Campers' meals charged at Magic's				28
29			Restaurant				29
30							30
31							31
32							32
33							33
34							34
35							35

Mastery Problem (Continued)

GENERAL JOURNAL   PAGE 2

	DATE		DESCRIPTION	POST. REF.	DEBIT	CREDIT	
1	20-- June	7	Cash	101	16 2 0 0 00		1
2			Registration Fees	401		16 2 0 0 00	2
3			Collected registration fees				3
4							4
5		10	Wages Expense	511	5 0 0 00		5
6			Cash	101		5 0 0 00	6
7			Paid wages to camp counselors				7
8							8
9		14	Cash	101	13 5 0 0 00		9
10			Registration Fees	401		13 5 0 0 00	10
11			Collected registration fees				11
12							12
13		14	Food Expense	524	6 2 0 0 00		13
14			Accounts Payable	202		6 2 0 0 00	14
15			Campers' meals charged at Magic's				15
16			Restaurant				16
17							17
18		17	Wages Expense	511	5 0 0 00		18
19			Cash	101		5 0 0 00	19
20			Paid wages to camp counselors				20
21							21
22		18	Postage Expense	536	8 5 00		22
23			Cash	101		8 5 00	23
24			Paid postage				24
25							25
26		21	Cash	101	15 2 0 0 00		26
27			Registration Fees	401		15 2 0 0 00	27
28			Collected registration fees				28
29							29
30		22	Food Expense	524	6 5 0 0 00		30
31			Accounts Payable	202		6 5 0 0 00	31
32			Campers' meals charged at Magic's				32
33			Restaurant				33
34							34
35							35

Mastery Problem (Continued)

GENERAL JOURNAL

	DATE		DESCRIPTION	POST. REF.	DEBIT	CREDIT	
1	20-- June	24	Wages Expense	511	5 0 0 00		1
2			Cash	101		5 0 0 00	2
3			Paid wages to camp counselors				3
4							4
5		28	Cash	101	14 0 0 0 00		5
6			Registration Fees	401		14 0 0 0 00	6
7			Collected registration fees				7
8							8
9		30	Food Expense	524	7 2 0 0 00		9
10			Accounts Payable	202		7 2 0 0 00	10
11			Campers' meals charged at Magic's				11
12			Restaurant				12
13							13
14		30	Wages Expense	511	5 0 0 00		14
15			Cash	101		5 0 0 00	15
16			Paid wages to camp counselors				16
17							17
18		30	Accounts Payable	202	25 7 0 0 00		18
19			Cash	101		25 7 0 0 00	19
20			Made payment on account to Magic's				20
21			Restaurant				21
22							22
23		30	Utilities Expense	533	5 0 0 00		23
24			Cash	101		5 0 0 00	24
25			Paid utility bill				25
26							26
27		30	Telephone Expense	525	1 2 0 00		27
28			Cash	101		1 2 0 00	28
29			Paid phone bill				29
30							30
31		30	Barry Bird, Drawing	312	2 0 0 0 00		31
32			Cash	101		2 0 0 0 00	32
33			Withdrawal by Bird				33
34							34
35							35

Mastery Problem (Continued)

2.

ACCOUNT Cash   **GENERAL LEDGER**   ACCOUNT NO. 101

DATE		ITEM	POST. REF.	DEBIT	CREDIT	BALANCE DEBIT	BALANCE CREDIT
20-- June	1		J1	10 0 0 0 00		10 0 0 0 00	
	1		J1		3 0 0 0 00	7 0 0 0 00	
	2		J1		5 0 0 0 00	2 0 0 0 00	
	2		J1	15 0 0 0 00		17 0 0 0 00	
	7		J2	16 2 0 0 00		33 2 0 0 00	
	10		J2		5 0 0 00	32 7 0 0 00	
	14		J2	13 5 0 0 00		46 2 0 0 00	
	17		J2		5 0 0 00	45 7 0 0 00	
	18		J2		8 5 00	45 6 1 5 00	
	21		J2	15 2 0 0 00		60 8 1 5 00	
	24		J3		5 0 0 00	60 3 1 5 00	
	28		J3	14 0 0 0 00		74 3 1 5 00	
	30		J3		5 0 0 00	73 8 1 5 00	
	30		J3		25 7 0 0 00	48 1 1 5 00	
	30		J3		5 0 0 00	47 6 1 5 00	
	30		J3		1 2 0 00	47 4 9 5 00	
	30		J3		2 0 0 0 00	45 4 9 5 00	

ACCOUNT Office Supplies   ACCOUNT NO. 142

DATE		ITEM	POST. REF.	DEBIT	CREDIT	BALANCE DEBIT	BALANCE CREDIT
20-- June	5		J1	3 0 0 00		3 0 0 00	

ACCOUNT Athletic Equipment   ACCOUNT NO. 183

DATE		ITEM	POST. REF.	DEBIT	CREDIT	BALANCE DEBIT	BALANCE CREDIT
20-- June	1		J1	3 0 0 0 00		3 0 0 0 00	

Mastery Problem (Continued)

ACCOUNT Basketball Facilities   ACCOUNT NO. 184

DATE		ITEM	POST. REF.	DEBIT	CREDIT	BALANCE DEBIT	BALANCE CREDIT
20-- June	2		J1	12 0 0 0 00		12 0 0 0 00	

ACCOUNT Accounts Payable   ACCOUNT NO. 202

DATE		ITEM	POST. REF.	DEBIT	CREDIT	BALANCE DEBIT	BALANCE CREDIT
20-- June	2		J1		12 0 0 0 00		12 0 0 0 00
	5		J1		3 0 0 00		12 3 0 0 00
	6		J1		5 8 0 0 00		18 1 0 0 00
	14		J2		6 2 0 0 00		24 3 0 0 00
	22		J2		6 5 0 0 00		30 8 0 0 00
	30		J3		7 2 0 0 00		38 0 0 0 00
	30		J3	25 7 0 0 00			12 3 0 0 00

ACCOUNT Barry Bird, Capital   ACCOUNT NO. 311

DATE		ITEM	POST. REF.	DEBIT	CREDIT	BALANCE DEBIT	BALANCE CREDIT
20-- June	1		J1		10 0 0 0 00		10 0 0 0 00

ACCOUNT Barry Bird, Drawing   ACCOUNT NO. 312

DATE		ITEM	POST. REF.	DEBIT	CREDIT	BALANCE DEBIT	BALANCE CREDIT
20-- June	30		J3	2 0 0 0 00		2 0 0 0 00	

Mastery Problem (Continued)

ACCOUNT Registration Fees

ACCOUNT NO. 401

DATE		ITEM	POST. REF.	DEBIT	CREDIT	BALANCE DEBIT	BALANCE CREDIT
20-- June	2		J1		15 0 0 0 00		15 0 0 0 00
	7		J2		16 2 0 0 00		31 2 0 0 00
	14		J2		13 5 0 0 00		44 7 0 0 00
	21		J2		15 2 0 0 00		59 9 0 0 00
	28		J3		14 0 0 0 00		73 9 0 0 00

ACCOUNT Wages Expense

ACCOUNT NO. 511

DATE		ITEM	POST. REF.	DEBIT	CREDIT	BALANCE DEBIT	BALANCE CREDIT
20-- June	10		J2	5 0 0 00		5 0 0 00	
	17		J2	5 0 0 00		1 0 0 0 00	
	24		J3	5 0 0 00		1 5 0 0 00	
	30		J3	5 0 0 00		2 0 0 0 00	

ACCOUNT Advertising Expense

ACCOUNT NO. 512

DATE		ITEM	POST. REF.	DEBIT	CREDIT	BALANCE DEBIT	BALANCE CREDIT
20-- June	2		J1	5 0 0 0 00		5 0 0 0 00	

Mastery Problem (Continued)

ACCOUNT Food Expense

ACCOUNT NO. 524

DATE		ITEM	POST. REF.	DEBIT	CREDIT	BALANCE	
						DEBIT	CREDIT
20-- June	6		J1	5 8 0 0 00		5 8 0 0 00	
	14		J2	6 2 0 0 00		12 0 0 0 00	
	22		J2	6 5 0 0 00		18 5 0 0 00	
	30		J3	7 2 0 0 00		25 7 0 0 00	

ACCOUNT Telephone Expense

ACCOUNT NO. 525

DATE		ITEM	POST. REF.	DEBIT	CREDIT	BALANCE	
						DEBIT	CREDIT
20-- June	30		J3	1 2 0 00		1 2 0 00	

ACCOUNT Utilities Expense

ACCOUNT NO. 533

DATE		ITEM	POST. REF.	DEBIT	CREDIT	BALANCE	
						DEBIT	CREDIT
20-- June	30		J3	5 0 0 00		5 0 0 00	

ACCOUNT Postage Expense

ACCOUNT NO. 536

DATE		ITEM	POST. REF.	DEBIT	CREDIT	BALANCE	
						DEBIT	CREDIT
20-- June	18		J2	8 5 00		8 5 00	

Mastery Problem (Concluded)

3.

ACCOUNT TITLE	ACCT. NO.	DEBIT BALANCE	CREDIT BALANCE
Barry Bird Basketball Camp			
Trial Balance			
June 30, 20--			
Cash	101	45 4 9 5 00	
Office Supplies	142	3 0 0 00	
Athletic Equipment	183	3 0 0 0 00	
Basketball Facilities	184	12 0 0 0 00	
Accounts Payable	202		12 3 0 0 00
Barry Bird, Capital	311		10 0 0 0 00
Barry Bird, Drawing	312	2 0 0 0 00	
Registration Fees	401		73 9 0 0 00
Wages Expense	511	2 0 0 0 00	
Advertising Expense	512	5 0 0 0 00	
Food Expense	524	25 7 0 0 00	
Telephone Expense	525	1 2 0 00	
Utilities Expense	533	5 0 0 00	
Postage Expense	536	8 5 00	
		96 2 0 0 00	96 2 0 0 00

Challenge Problem

1. and 2.

The errors in the trial balance were caused by the following:

1. June 12—The debit to Automobile Expense was made for $50,000 instead of $50. This is called a "slide."
2. June 14—A credit was made to Cash instead of Accounts Payable.
3. June 21—The debit to Drawing was made for $2,100 instead of $1,200. This is called a transposition error.
4. In the trial balance, Cash was listed as a credit balance instead of a debit balance.

3.

Fred Phaler Consulting

Trial Balance

June 30, 20--

ACCOUNT TITLE	ACCT. NO.	DEBIT BALANCE	CREDIT BALANCE
Cash	101	14 1 5 0 00	
Accounts Receivable	122	2 0 0 00	
Office Supplies	142	2 5 0 00	
Accounts Payable	202		1 5 0 00
Fred Phaler, Capital	311		10 0 0 0 00
Fred Phaler, Drawing	312	1 2 0 0 00	
Professional Fees	401		9 0 0 0 00
Wages Expense	511	8 0 0 00	
Rent Expense	521	5 0 0 00	
Telephone Expense	525	1 0 0 00	
Automobile Expense	526	5 0 00	
Utilities Expense	533	1 0 0 00	
		19 1 5 0 00	19 1 5 0 00

CHAPTER 5

ADJUSTING ENTRIES AND THE WORK SHEET

REVIEW QUESTIONS

1. The matching principle requires the matching of revenues earned during an accounting period with the expenses incurred to produce the revenues.

2. Under the historical cost principle, assets are recorded at their actual cost.

3. A plant asset is expected to provide benefits over more than one year.

4. A contra-asset has a credit balance and is deducted from the related asset account on the balance sheet.

5. The useful life of an asset is the period of time that an asset is expected to help produce revenues.

6. The purpose of depreciation is to provide a method of matching the cost of the assets against the revenues the assets will help to produce over their useful lives.

7. An asset's depreciable cost is the cost of the asset that is subject to depreciation.

8. The book value of an asset is the difference between the asset's cost and the related accumulated depreciation.

9. The purpose of a work sheet is to help in preparing end-of-period adjustments and financial statements. The work sheet pulls together all of the information needed to enter adjusting entries and prepare the financial statements.

10. The five major column headings on a work sheet are Trial Balance, Adjustments, Adjusted Trial Balance, Income Statement, and Balance Sheet.

11. The five steps when preparing a work sheet are as follows:
    Step 1: Prepare the trial balance.
    Step 2: Prepare the adjustments.
    Step 3: Prepare the adjusted trial balance.
    Step 4: Extend adjusted balances to the Income Statement and Balance Sheet columns.
    Step 5: Complete the work sheet by summing the Income Statement and Balance Sheet columns and computing net income or net loss.

12. Four tips for finding errors on the work sheet are as follows:
    a. Check the addition of all columns.
    b. Check the addition and subtraction required when extending to the Adjusted Trial Balance columns.
    c. Make sure the adjusted account balances have been extended to the appropriate columns.
    d. Make sure that the net income or net loss has been added to the appropriate columns.

13. Under the accrual basis of accounting, revenues are recorded when earned. Revenues are considered earned when a service is provided or a product sold, regardless of whether cash has been received. Under the cash and modified cash bases of accounting, revenues are recorded when cash is received.

14. Under the accrual basis of accounting, expenses are recorded when incurred. Expenses are considered incurred when a service is received or an asset consumed, regardless of when cash is paid. Under the cash basis, expenses are recorded when cash is paid. Under the modified cash basis, a firm uses the cash basis for recording most expenses. However, under the modified cash basis when cash is paid for assets with useful lives greater than one accounting period, the cash payment is recorded as an asset and adjustments are made each period as under the accrual basis of accounting.

Exercise 5-1A

(Balance Sheet) Supplies					(Income Statement) Supplies Expense		
TB	320	Adj.	230		Adj.	230	
Bal.	90						

GENERAL JOURNAL   PAGE

	DATE		DESCRIPTION	POST. REF.	DEBIT	CREDIT	
1			*Adjusting Entries*				1
2	20-- Dec.	31	**Supplies Expense**		2 3 0 00		2
3			**Supplies**			2 3 0 00	3
4							4
5							5
6							6

Exercise 5-2A

(Balance Sheet) Prepaid Insurance					(Income Statement) Insurance Expense		
TB	900	Adj.	150		Adj.	150	
Bal.	750						

GENERAL JOURNAL   PAGE

	DATE		DESCRIPTION	POST. REF.	DEBIT	CREDIT	
1			*Adjusting Entries*				1
2	20-- Dec.	31	*Insurance Expense*		1 5 0 00		2
3			*Prepaid Insurance*			1 5 0 00	3
4							4
5							5
6							6

Exercise 5-3A

	(Income Statement) Wages Expense			(Balance Sheet) Wages Payable	
TB	600		Adj.		200
Adj.	200				
Bal.	800				

GENERAL JOURNAL   PAGE

	DATE		DESCRIPTION	POST. REF.	DEBIT	CREDIT	
1			*Adjusting Entries*				1
2	20-- Dec.	31	Wages Expense		2 0 0 00		2
3			Wages Payable			2 0 0 00	3
4							4

Exercise 5-4A

$$\frac{\$7,200}{48} = \$150$$

	(Income Statement) Depr. Expense—Delivery Equipment		(Balance Sheet) Accum. Depr.—Delivery Equipment	
Adj.	150	Adj.	150

GENERAL JOURNAL   PAGE

	DATE		DESCRIPTION	POST. REF.	DEBIT	CREDIT	
1			*Adjusting Entries*				1
2	20-- Dec.	31	Depr. Expense—Delivery Equipment		1 5 0 00		2
3			Accum. Depr.—Delivery Equipment			1 5 0 00	3
4							4

Exercise 5-5A

Original cost	= $5,400
Less: Accumulated depreciation	= 630 (5,400/60 × 7 mos.)
Book value, December 31, 20--	= $4,770

Exercise 5-6A

1.

(Balance Sheet) Supplies			(Income Statement) Supplies Expense	
TB	460			
		Adj.	*330*	Adj.	*330*
Bal.	*130*			

2.

(Balance Sheet) Supplies			(Income Statement) Supplies Expense	
TB	545			
		Adj.	*320*	Adj.	*320*
Bal.	*225*			

Exercise 5-7A

1.

(Balance Sheet) Prepaid Insurance			(Income Statement) Insurance Expense	
TB	1,300			
		Adj.	*900*	Adj.	*900*
Bal.	*400*			

2.

(Balance Sheet) Prepaid Insurance			(Income Statement) Insurance Expense	
TB	860			
		Adj.	*675*	Adj.	*675*
Bal.	*185*			

Exercise 5-8A

GENERAL JOURNAL

	DATE		DESCRIPTION	POST. REF.	DEBIT	CREDIT	
1			Adjusting Entries				1
2	20-- Dec.	31	Supplies Expense	523	8 5 00		2
3			Supplies	141		8 5 00	3
4							4
5		31	Wages Expense	511	2 2 0 00		5
6			Wages Payable	219		2 2 0 00	6
7							7
8							8
9							9
10							10
11							11
12							12
13							13
14							14
15							15
16							16
17							17
18							18

Exercise 5-8A (Concluded)

GENERAL LEDGER

ACCOUNT   Supplies   ACCOUNT NO.   141

DATE		ITEM	POST. REF.	DEBIT	CREDIT	BALANCE	
						DEBIT	CREDIT
20-- Dec.	1	Balance	✓			1 5 0 00	
	15		J8	5 0 00		2 0 0 00	
	31	*Adjusting*	*J9*		8 5 00	*1 1 5 00*	

ACCOUNT   Wages Payable   ACCOUNT NO.   219

DATE		ITEM	POST. REF.	DEBIT	CREDIT	BALANCE	
						DEBIT	CREDIT
20-- Dec.	31	*Adjusting*	*J9*		2 2 0 00		2 2 0 00

ACCOUNT   Wages Expense   ACCOUNT NO.   511

DATE		ITEM	POST. REF.	DEBIT	CREDIT	BALANCE	
						DEBIT	CREDIT
20-- Dec.	1	Balance	✓			9 0 0 00	
	15		J8	3 0 0 00		1 2 0 0 00	
	31	*Adjusting*	*J9*	*2 2 0 00*		*1 4 2 0 00*	

ACCOUNT   Supplies Expense   ACCOUNT NO.   523

DATE		ITEM	POST. REF.	DEBIT	CREDIT	BALANCE	
						DEBIT	CREDIT
20-- Dec.	31	*Adjusting*	*J9*	8 5 00		8 5 00	

Exercise 5-9A

Jim Jacobs' Furniture Repair
Work Sheet (Partial)
For Year Ended December 31, 20--

ACCOUNT TITLE	TRIAL BALANCE Debit	TRIAL BALANCE Credit	ADJUSTMENTS Debit	ADJUSTMENTS Credit	ADJUSTED TRIAL BALANCE Debit	ADJUSTED TRIAL BALANCE Credit
1 Cash	1 0 0 00				1 0 0 00	
2 Supplies	8 5 0 00			(a) 6 5 0 00	2 0 0 00	
3 Prepaid Insurance	9 0 0 00			(b) 6 0 0 00	3 0 0 00	
4 Delivery Equipment	3 6 0 0 00				3 6 0 0 00	
5 Accum. Depr.—Delivery Equip.		6 0 0 00		(c) 2 0 0 00		8 0 0 00
6 Wages Payable				(d) 1 0 0 00		1 0 0 00
7 Jim Jacobs, Capital		4 0 0 0 00				4 0 0 0 00
8 Repair Fees		1 6 5 0 00				1 6 5 0 00
9 Wages Expense	6 0 0 00		(d) 1 0 0 00		7 0 0 00	
10 Advertising Expense	2 0 0 00				2 0 0 00	
11 Supplies Expense			(a) 6 5 0 00		6 5 0 00	
12 Insurance Expense			(b) 6 0 0 00		6 0 0 00	
13 Depr. Exp.—Delivery Equip.			(c) 2 0 0 00		2 0 0 00	
14	6 2 5 0 00	6 2 5 0 00	1 5 5 0 00	1 5 5 0 00	6 5 5 0 00	6 5 5 0 00

Exercise 5-10A

GENERAL JOURNAL   PAGE

	DATE		DESCRIPTION	POST. REF.	DEBIT	CREDIT	
1			*Adjusting Entries*				1
2	20-- Dec.	31	**Supplies Expense**		6 5 0 00		2
3			**Supplies**			6 5 0 00	3
4							4
5		31	**Insurance Expense**		6 0 0 00		5
6			**Prepaid Insurance**			6 0 0 00	6
7							7
8		31	**Depreciation Expense—Delivery Equipment**		2 0 0 00		8
9			**Accum. Depreciation—Delivery Equipment**			2 0 0 00	9
10							10
11		31	**Wages Expense**		1 0 0 00		11
12			**Wages Payable**			1 0 0 00	12
13							13
14							14
15							15

Exercise 5-11A

	Income Statement		Balance Sheet	
	Debit	**Credit**	**Debit**	**Credit**
Cash			X	
Accounts Receivable			X	
Supplies			X	
Prepaid Insurance			X	
Delivery Equipment			X	
Accum. Depr.—Delivery Equip.				X
Accounts Payable				X
Wages Payable				X
Owner, Capital				X
Owner, Drawing			X	
Delivery Fees		X		
Wages Expense	X			
Rent Expense	X			

Exercise 5-11A (Concluded)

	Income Statement		Balance Sheet	
	Debit	**Credit**	**Debit**	**Credit**
Supplies Expense	X			
Insurance Expense	X			
Depr. Exp.—Delivery Equip.	X			

Exercise 5-12A

	Income Statement		Balance Sheet	
	Debit	**Credit**	**Debit**	**Credit**
Net Income	X			X
Net Loss		X	X	

Exercise 5-13A

	Cash Basis	Modified Cash Basis	Accrual Basis

1. Purchase supplies on account.	*No entry*	*Supplies*
		  Accts. Payable
			Supplies
			  Accts. Payable

2. Make payment on asset previously purchased.	*Expense*
	  Cash
		Accts. Payable
		  Cash
			Accts. Payable
			  Cash

3. Purchase supplies for cash.	*Supplies Expense*
	  Cash
		Supplies
		  Cash
			Supplies
			  Cash

4. Purchase insurance for cash.	*Insurance Exp.*
	  Cash
		Prepaid Insurance
		  Cash
			Prepaid Insurance
			  Cash

5. Pay cash for wages.	*Wages Expense*
	  Cash
		Wages Expense
		  Cash
			Wages Expense
			  Cash

6. Pay cash for telephone expense.	*Telephone Exp.*
	  Cash
		Telephone Exp.
		  Cash
			Telephone Exp.
			  Cash

7. Pay cash for new equipment.	*Equipment Exp.*
	  Cash
		Equipment
		  Cash
			Equipment
			  Cash

8. Wages earned but not paid.	*No entry*	*No entry*	*Wages Expense* *Wages Payable*

9. Prepaid item purchased, partly used.	*No entry*	*Expense*
		  Prepaid Asset
			Expense
			  Prepaid Asset

10. Depreciation on long-term assets.	*No entry*	*Depr. Exp.*
		  Accum. Depr.
			Depr. Exp.
			  Accum. Depr.

Problem 5-14A

Mason's Delivery

Work

For Month Ended

	ACCOUNT TITLE	BALANCE DEBIT					BALANCE CREDIT					ADJUSTMENTS DEBIT					ADJUSTMENTS CREDIT				
1	Cash	1	6	0	0	00															
2	Accounts Receivable		9	4	0	00															
3	Supplies		6	3	5	00											(a)	4	7	0	00
4	Prepaid Insurance	1	2	0	0	00											(b)	8	0	0	00
5	Delivery Equipment	6	4	0	0	00															
6	Accum. Depr.—Delivery Equip.																(c)	4	0	0	00
7	Accounts Payable						1	2	2	0	00										
8	Wages Payable																(d)	2	2	5	00
9	Jill Mason, Capital						8	0	0	0	00										
10	Jill Mason, Drawing	1	4	0	0	00															
11	Delivery Fees						6	2	0	0	00										
12	Wages Expense	1	5	0	0	00						(d)	2	2	5	00					
13	Advertising Expense		4	6	0	00															
14	Rent Expense		8	0	0	00															
15	Supplies Expense											(a)	4	7	0	00					
16	Telephone Expense		1	6	5	00															
17	Insurance Expense											(b)	8	0	0	00					
18	Repair Expense		2	3	0	00															
19	Oil and Gas Expense			9	0	00															
20	Depr. Exp.—Delivery Equip.											(c)	4	0	0	00					
21		15	4	2	0	00	15	4	2	0	00	1	8	9	5	00	1	8	9	5	00
22	*Net Income*																				
23																					
24																					
25																					
26																					
27																					
28																					
29																					
30																					
31																					
32																					
33																					

Problem 5-14A (Concluded)

Service

Sheet

September 30, 20--

ADJUSTED TRIAL BALANCE		INCOME STATEMENT		BALANCE SHEET		
DEBIT	CREDIT	DEBIT	CREDIT	DEBIT	CREDIT	
1 6 0 0 00				1 6 0 0 00		1
9 4 0 00				9 4 0 00		2
1 6 5 00				1 6 5 00		3
4 0 0 00				4 0 0 00		4
6 4 0 0 00				6 4 0 0 00		5
	4 0 0 00				4 0 0 00	6
	1 2 2 0 00				1 2 2 0 00	7
	2 2 5 00				2 2 5 00	8
	8 0 0 0 00				8 0 0 0 00	9
1 4 0 0 00				1 4 0 0 00		10
	6 2 0 0 00		6 2 0 0 00			11
1 7 2 5 00		1 7 2 5 00				12
4 6 0 00		4 6 0 00				13
8 0 0 00		8 0 0 00				14
4 7 0 00		4 7 0 00				15
1 6 5 00		1 6 5 00				16
8 0 0 00		8 0 0 00				17
2 3 0 00		2 3 0 00				18
9 0 00		9 0 00				19
4 0 0 00		4 0 0 00				20
16 0 4 5 00	16 0 4 5 00	5 1 4 0 00	6 2 0 0 00	10 9 0 5 00	9 8 4 5 00	21
		1 0 6 0 00			1 0 6 0 00	22
		6 2 0 0 00	6 2 0 0 00	10 9 0 5 00	10 9 0 5 00	23

Problem 5-15A

Campus Delivery

Work

For Month Ended

ACCOUNT TITLE	TRIAL BALANCE DEBIT	TRIAL BALANCE CREDIT	ADJUSTMENTS DEBIT	ADJUSTMENTS CREDIT
1 Cash	9 8 0 00			
2 Accounts Receivable	5 9 0 00			
3 Supplies	5 7 5 00			(a) 3 9 0 00
4 Prepaid Insurance	1 3 0 0 00			(b) 5 0 0 00
5 Van	5 8 0 0 00			
6 Accumulated Depreciation—Van				(c) 3 0 0 00
7 Accounts Payable		9 6 0 00		
8 Wages Payable				(d) 1 9 0 00
9 Jason Armstrong, Capital		10 0 0 0 00		
10 Jason Armstrong, Drawing	6 0 0 00			
11 Delivery Fees		2 6 0 0 00		
12 Wages Expense	1 8 0 0 00		(d) 1 9 0 00	
13 Advertising Expense	3 8 0 00			
14 Rent Expense	9 0 0 00			
15 Supplies Expense			(a) 3 9 0 00	
16 Telephone Expense	2 2 0 00			
17 Insurance Expense			(b) 5 0 0 00	
18 Repair Expense	3 1 5 00			
19 Oil and Gas Expense	1 0 0 00			
20 Depreciation Expense—Van			(c) 3 0 0 00	
21	13 5 6 0 00	13 5 6 0 00	1 3 8 0 00	1 3 8 0 00
22 **Net Loss**				
23				
24				
25				
26				
27				
28				
29				
30				
31				
32				
33				

Problem 5-15A (Concluded)

Service

Sheet

November 30, 20--

ADJUSTED TRIAL BALANCE								INCOME STATEMENT								BALANCE SHEET								
DEBIT				CREDIT				DEBIT				CREDIT				DEBIT				CREDIT				
	9	8	0	00														9	8	0	00					1
	5	9	0	00														5	9	0	00					2
	1	8	5	00														1	8	5	00					3
	8	0	0	00														8	0	0	00					4
5	8	0	0	00												5	8	0	0	00					5
					3	0	0	00														3	0	0	00	6
					9	6	0	00														9	6	0	00	7
					1	9	0	00														1	9	0	00	8
				10	0	0	0	00													10	0	0	0	00	9
	6	0	0	00														6	0	0	00					10
					2	6	0	0	00						2	6	0	0	00							11
1	9	9	0	00					1	9	9	0	00													12
	3	8	0	00						3	8	0	00													13
	9	0	0	00						9	0	0	00													14
	3	9	0	00						3	9	0	00													15
	2	2	0	00						2	2	0	00													16
	5	0	0	00						5	0	0	00													17
	3	1	5	00						3	1	5	00													18
	1	0	0	00						1	0	0	00													19
	3	0	0	00						3	0	0	00													20
14	0	5	0	00	14	0	5	0	00	5	0	9	5	00	2	6	0	0	00	8	9	5	5	00	11	4	5	0	00	21
														2	4	9	5	00	2	4	9	5	00						22
									5	0	9	5	00	5	0	9	5	00	11	4	5	0	00	11	4	5	0	00	23

Problem 5-16A

1.   **GENERAL JOURNAL**   PAGE 5

	DATE		DESCRIPTION	POST. REF.	DEBIT	CREDIT	
1			*Adjusting Entries*				1
2	20-- Nov.	30	Supplies Expense	523	3 9 0 00		2
3			Supplies	141		3 9 0 00	3
4							4
5		30	Insurance Expense	535	5 0 0 00		5
6			Prepaid Insurance	145		5 0 0 00	6
7							7
8		30	Depreciation Expense—Van	541	3 0 0 00		8
9			Accumulated Depreciation—Van	185.1		3 0 0 00	9
10							10
11		30	Wages Expense	511	1 9 0 00		11
12			Wages Payable	219		1 9 0 00	12
13							13
14							14
15							15
16							16
17							17
18							18
19							19
20							20
21							21
22							22
23							23
24							24
25							25
26							26
27							27
28							28
29							29
30							30
31							31
32							32
33							33
34							34
35							35
36							36

Problem 5-16A (Continued)

2.   **GENERAL LEDGER**

ACCOUNT   Supplies   ACCOUNT NO.   141

DATE		ITEM	POST. REF.	DEBIT	CREDIT	BALANCE	
						DEBIT	CREDIT
20-- Nov.	1		J1	4 7 5 00		4 7 5 00	
	15		J4	1 0 0 00		5 7 5 00	
	30	*Adjusting*	*J5*		3 9 0 00	1 8 5 00	

ACCOUNT   Prepaid Insurance   ACCOUNT NO.   145

DATE		ITEM	POST. REF.	DEBIT	CREDIT	BALANCE	
						DEBIT	CREDIT
20-- Nov.	1		J1	1 3 0 0 00		1 3 0 0 00	
	30	*Adjusting*	*J5*		5 0 0 00	8 0 0 00	

ACCOUNT   Accumulated Depreciation—Van   ACCOUNT NO.   185.1

DATE		ITEM	POST. REF.	DEBIT	CREDIT	BALANCE	
						DEBIT	CREDIT
20-- Nov.	30	*Adjusting*	*J5*		3 0 0 00		3 0 0 00

ACCOUNT   Wages Payable   ACCOUNT NO.   219

DATE		ITEM	POST. REF.	DEBIT	CREDIT	BALANCE	
						DEBIT	CREDIT
20-- Nov.	30	*Adjusting*	*J5*		1 9 0 00		1 9 0 00

Problem 5-16A (Concluded)

ACCOUNT Wages Expense   ACCOUNT NO. 511

DATE		ITEM	POST. REF.	DEBIT	CREDIT	BALANCE DEBIT	BALANCE CREDIT
20-- Nov.	15		J3	9 0 0 00		9 0 0 00	
	26		J4	9 0 0 00		1 8 0 0 00	
	30	*Adjusting*	J5	1 9 0 00		1 9 9 0 00	

ACCOUNT Supplies Expense   ACCOUNT NO. 523

DATE		ITEM	POST. REF.	DEBIT	CREDIT	BALANCE DEBIT	BALANCE CREDIT
20-- Nov.	30	*Adjusting*	J5	3 9 0 00		3 9 0 00	

ACCOUNT Insurance Expense   ACCOUNT NO. 535

DATE		ITEM	POST. REF.	DEBIT	CREDIT	BALANCE DEBIT	BALANCE CREDIT
20-- Nov.	30	*Adjusting*	J5	5 0 0 00		5 0 0 00	

ACCOUNT Depreciation Expense—Van   ACCOUNT NO. 541

DATE		ITEM	POST. REF.	DEBIT	CREDIT	BALANCE DEBIT	BALANCE CREDIT
20-- Nov.	30	*Adjusting*	J5	3 0 0 00		3 0 0 00	

Problem 5-17A: See pages 142 and 143

Exercise 5-1B

(Balance Sheet) Supplies				(Income Statement) Supplies Expense	
TB	430	Adj.	310	Adj.	310
Bal.	120				

GENERAL JOURNAL

PAGE

	DATE		DESCRIPTION	POST. REF.	DEBIT	CREDIT	
1			*Adjusting Entries*				1
2	20-- July	31	**Supplies Expense**		3 1 0 00		2
3			**Supplies**			3 1 0 00	3
4							4
5							5
6							6

Exercise 5-2B

(Balance Sheet) Prepaid Insurance				(Income Statement) Insurance Expense	
TB	750	Adj.	125	Adj.	125
Bal.	625				

GENERAL JOURNAL

PAGE

	DATE		DESCRIPTION	POST. REF.	DEBIT	CREDIT	
1			*Adjusting Entries*				1
2	20-- July	31	**Insurance Expense**		1 2 5 00		2
3			**Prepaid Insurance**			1 2 5 00	3
4							4
5							5
6							6

Problem 5-17A

	ACCOUNT TITLE	TRIAL BALANCE						ADJUSTMENTS						
		DEBIT				CREDIT		DEBIT				CREDIT		
1	Cash	1	7	2	5	00								
2	Accounts Receivable		9	6	0	00								
3	Supplies		5	2	5	00						(a) 3	6	5	00
4	Prepaid Insurance		9	3	0	00						(b) 4	1	0	00
5	Office Equipment	5	4	5	0	00								
6	Accum. Depr.—Office Equipment											(c) 2	7	5	00
7	Accounts Payable						4	8	0	00					
8	Wages Payable											(d) 1	1	0	00
9	Joyce Lee, Capital						7	5	0	0	00				
10	Joyce Lee, Drawing	1	1	2	5	00								
11	Professional Fees						5	7	0	0	00				
12	Wages Expense	1	4	2	0	00				(d) 1	1	0	00		
13	Advertising Expense		3	5	0	00								
14	Rent Expense		7	0	0	00								
15	Supplies Expense									(a) 3	6	5	00		
16	Telephone Expense		1	3	0	00								
17	Utilities Expense		1	9	0	00								
18	Insurance Expense									(b) 4	1	0	00		
19	Depr. Expense—Office Equipment									(c) 2	7	5	00		
20	Miscellaneous Expense		1	7	5	00								
21		13	6	8	0	00	13	6	8	0	00	1 1	6	0	00	1 1	6	0	00
22	**Net Income**													
23														
24														
25														
26														
27														
28														
29														
30														
31														

Note: Shaded areas indicate where corrections were made.

Problem 5-17A (Concluded)

Tax Service

Sheet

March 31, 20--

ADJUSTED TRIAL BALANCE		INCOME STATEMENT		BALANCE SHEET		
DEBIT	CREDIT	DEBIT	CREDIT	DEBIT	CREDIT	
1 7 2 5 00				1 7 2 5 00		1
9 6 0 00				9 6 0 00		2
1 6 0 00				1 6 0 00		3
5 2 0 00				5 2 0 00		4
5 4 5 0 00				5 4 5 0 00		5
	2 7 5 00				2 7 5 00	6
	4 8 0 00				4 8 0 00	7
	1 1 0 00				1 1 0 00	8
	7 5 0 0 00				7 5 0 0 00	9
1 1 2 5 00				1 1 2 5 00		10
	5 7 0 0 00		5 7 0 0 00			11
1 5 3 0 00		1 5 3 0 00				12
3 5 0 00		3 5 0 00				13
7 0 0 00		7 0 0 00				14
3 6 5 00		3 6 5 00				15
1 3 0 00		1 3 0 00				16
1 9 0 00		1 9 0 00				17
4 1 0 00		4 1 0 00				18
2 7 5 00		2 7 5 00				19
1 7 5 00		1 7 5 00				20
14 0 6 5 00	14 0 6 5 00	4 1 2 5 00	5 7 0 0 00	9 9 4 0 00	8 3 6 5 00	21
		1 5 7 5 00			1 5 7 5 00	22
		5 7 0 0 00	5 7 0 0 00	9 9 4 0 00	9 9 4 0 00	23

Exercise 5-3B

	(Income Statement) Wages Expense		(Balance Sheet) Wages Payable	
TB	800		Adj.	150
Adj.	150			
Bal.	950			

GENERAL JOURNAL   PAGE

	DATE		DESCRIPTION	POST. REF.	DEBIT	CREDIT	
1			**Adjusting Entries**				1
2	20-- July	31	**Wages Expense**		1 5 0 00		2
3			**Wages Payable**			1 5 0 00	3
4							4

Exercise 5-4B

$$\frac{\$4,320}{36} = \$120$$

	(Income Statement) Depr. Expense—Delivery Equipment		(Balance Sheet) Accum. Depr.—Delivery Equipment	
Adj.	120		Adj.	120

GENERAL JOURNAL   PAGE

	DATE		DESCRIPTION	POST. REF.	DEBIT	CREDIT	
1			**Adjusting Entries**				1
2	20-- July	31	**Depr. Expense—Delivery Equipment**		1 2 0 00		2
3			**Accumulated Depr.—Delivery Equipment**			1 2 0 00	3
4							4

Exercise 5-5B

Original cost	= $5,760	
Less: Accumulated depreciation	= 720	(5,760/48 × 6 mos.)
Book value, July 1, 20--	= $5,040	

Exercise 5-6B

1.

(Balance Sheet) Supplies				(Income Statement) Supplies Expense	
TB	540				
		Adj.	*445*	Adj.	*445*
Bal.	*95*				

2.

(Balance Sheet) Supplies				(Income Statement) Supplies Expense	
TB	330				
		Adj.	*280*	Adj.	*280*
Bal.	*50*				

Exercise 5-7B

1.

(Balance Sheet) Prepaid Insurance				(Income Statement) Insurance Expense	
TB	960				
		Adj.	*830*	Adj.	*830*
Bal.	*130*				

2.

(Balance Sheet) Prepaid Insurance				(Income Statement) Insurance Expense	
TB	1,135				
		Adj.	*795*	Adj.	*795*
Bal.	*340*				

Exercise 5-8B

GENERAL JOURNAL

PAGE 7

	DATE		DESCRIPTION	POST. REF.	DEBIT	CREDIT	
1			Adjusting Entries				1
2	20-- July	31	Insurance Expense	535	3 2 0 00		2
3			Prepaid Insurance	145		3 2 0 00	3
4							4
5		31	Depreciation Expense—Cleaning Equipment	541	1 4 5 00		5
6			Accumulated Depreciation—Cleaning Equipment	183.1		1 4 5 00	6
7							7
8							8
9							9
10							10
11							11
12							12
13							13
14							14
15							15
16							16

Exercise 5-8B (Concluded)

GENERAL LEDGER

ACCOUNT   Prepaid Insurance   ACCOUNT NO.   145

DATE		ITEM	POST. REF.	DEBIT	CREDIT	BALANCE	
						DEBIT	CREDIT
20-- July	1	Balance	✓			3 2 0 00	
	15		J6	6 4 0 00		9 6 0 00	
	31	*Adjusting*	*J7*		3 2 0 00	6 4 0 00	

ACCOUNT   Accumulated Depreciation—Cleaning Equipment   ACCOUNT NO.   183.1

DATE		ITEM	POST. REF.	DEBIT	CREDIT	BALANCE	
						DEBIT	CREDIT
20-- July	1	Balance	✓				8 7 0 00
	31	*Adjusting*	*J7*		1 4 5 00		1 0 1 5 00

ACCOUNT   Insurance Expense   ACCOUNT NO.   535

DATE		ITEM	POST. REF.	DEBIT	CREDIT	BALANCE	
						DEBIT	CREDIT
20-- July	31	*Adjusting*	*J7*	3 2 0 00		3 2 0 00	

ACCOUNT   Depreciation Expense—Cleaning Equipment   ACCOUNT NO.   541

DATE		ITEM	POST. REF.	DEBIT	CREDIT	BALANCE	
						DEBIT	CREDIT
20-- July	31	*Adjusting*	*J7*	1 4 5 00		1 4 5 00	

Exercise 5-9B

Jasmine Kah's Auto Detailing
Work Sheet (Partial)
For Month Ended June 30, 20--

	ACCOUNT TITLE	TRIAL BALANCE Debit	TRIAL BALANCE Credit	ADJUSTMENTS Debit	ADJUSTMENTS Credit	ADJUSTED TRIAL BALANCE Debit	ADJUSTED TRIAL BALANCE Credit
1	Cash	1 5 0 00				1 5 0 00	
2	Supplies	5 2 0 00			(a) 4 3 0 00	9 0 00	
3	Prepaid Insurance	7 5 0 00			(b) 5 5 0 00	2 0 0 00	
4	Cleaning Equipment	5 4 0 0 00				5 4 0 0 00	
5	Accum. Depr.—Cleaning Equip.		8 5 0 00		(c) 3 0 0 00		1 1 5 0 00
6	Wages Payable				(d) 2 5 0 00		2 5 0 00
7	Jasmine Kah, Capital		4 6 0 0 00				4 6 0 0 00
8	Detailing Fees		2 2 2 0 00				2 2 2 0 00
9	Wages Expense	7 0 0 00		(d) 2 5 0 00		9 5 0 00	
10	Advertising Expense	1 5 0 00				1 5 0 00	
11	Supplies Expense			(a) 4 3 0 00		4 3 0 00	
12	Insurance Expense			(b) 5 5 0 00		5 5 0 00	
13	Depr. Exp.—Cleaning Equip.			(c) 3 0 0 00		3 0 0 00	
14		7 6 7 0 00	7 6 7 0 00	1 5 3 0 00	1 5 3 0 00	8 2 2 0 00	8 2 2 0 00

Exercise 5-10B

GENERAL JOURNAL   PAGE

	DATE		DESCRIPTION	POST. REF.	DEBIT	CREDIT	
1			*Adjusting Entries*				1
2	20-- June	30	Supplies Expense		4 3 0 00		2
3			Supplies			4 3 0 00	3
4							4
5		30	Insurance Expense		5 5 0 00		5
6			Prepaid Insurance			5 5 0 00	6
7							7
8		30	Depreciation Expense—Cleaning Equipment		3 0 0 00		8
9			Accum. Depreciation—Cleaning Equipment			3 0 0 00	9
10							10
11		30	Wages Expense		2 5 0 00		11
12			Wages Payable			2 5 0 00	12
13							13
14							14
15							15

Exercise 5-11B

	Income Statement Debit	Credit	Balance Sheet Debit	Credit
Cash			X	
Accounts Receivable			X	
Supplies			X	
Prepaid Insurance			X	
Automobile			X	
Accum. Depr.—Automobile				X
Accounts Payable				X
Wages Payable				X
Owner, Capital				X
Owner, Drawing			X	
Service Fees		X		
Wages Expense	X			
Supplies Expense	X			

Exercise 5-11B (Concluded)

	Income Statement		Balance Sheet	
	Debit	**Credit**	**Debit**	**Credit**
Utilities Expense	X			
Insurance Expense	X			
Depr. Exp.—Automobile	X			

Exercise 5-12B

	Income Statement		Balance Sheet	
	Debit	**Credit**	**Debit**	**Credit**
Net Income	2,500			2,500
Net Loss		1,900	1,900	

Exercise 5-13B

	Cash Basis	Modified Cash Basis	Accrual Basis

1. Office Equipment
    Cash
        Purchased equipment for cash
	Debit Expense	✔	✔

2. Office Equipment
    Accounts Payable
        Purchased equipment on account
	No entry	✔	✔

3. Cash
    Revenue
        Cash receipts for week
	✔	✔	✔

4. Accounts Receivable
    Revenue
        Services performed on account
	No entry	*No entry*	✔

5. Prepaid Insurance
    Cash
        Purchased prepaid asset
	Debit Expense	✔	✔

6. Supplies
    Accounts Payable
        Purchased prepaid asset
	No entry	✔	✔

7. Telephone Expense
    Cash
        Paid telephone bill
	✔	✔	✔

8. Wages Expense
    Cash
        Paid wages for month
	✔	✔	✔

9. Accounts Payable
    Cash
        Made payment on account
	Accounts Payable not used. Debit Expense	✔	✔

10. Supplies Expense Supplies	*No entry*	✔	✔

Exercise 5-13B (Concluded)

	Cash Basis	Modified Cash Basis	Accrual Basis
11. Wages Expense Wages Payable	*No entry*	*No entry*	✔
12. Depreciation Expense—Office Equipment Accum. Depr.—Office Equipment	*No entry*	✔	✔

✔ Indicates accounting method for which the entry would be appropriate.

This page left intentionally blank.

Problem 5-14B

Louie's Lawn

Work

For Month Ended

	ACCOUNT TITLE	TRIAL BALANCE			ADJUSTMENTS		
		DEBIT	CREDIT		DEBIT		CREDIT
1	Cash	1 3 7 5 00					
2	Accounts Receivable	8 8 0 00					
3	Supplies	4 9 0 00					(a) 3 2 5 00
4	Prepaid Insurance	8 0 0 00					(b) 1 0 0 00
5	Lawn Equipment	5 7 0 0 00					
6	Accum. Depr.—Lawn Equipment						(c) 2 0 0 00
7	Accounts Payable		7 8 0 00				
8	Wages Payable						(d) 1 8 0 00
9	Louie Long, Capital		6 5 0 0 00				
10	Louie Long, Drawing	1 2 5 0 00					
11	Lawn Service Fees		6 1 0 0 00				
12	Wages Expense	1 1 4 5 00			(d) 1 8 0 00		
13	Advertising Expense	5 4 0 00					
14	Rent Expense	7 2 5 00					
15	Supplies Expense				(a) 3 2 5 00		
16	Telephone Expense	1 6 0 00					
17	Insurance Expense				(b) 1 0 0 00		
18	Repair Expense	2 5 0 00					
19	Depr. Expense—Lawn Equipment				(c) 2 0 0 00		
20	Miscellaneous Expense	6 5 00					
21		13 3 8 0 00	13 3 8 0 00		8 0 5 00		8 0 5 00
22	*Net Income*						
23							
24							
25							
26							
27							
28							
29							
30							
31							
32							
33							

Problem 5-14B (Concluded)

Service

Sheet

March 31, 20--

ADJUSTED TRIAL BALANCE DEBIT	ADJUSTED TRIAL BALANCE CREDIT	INCOME STATEMENT DEBIT	INCOME STATEMENT CREDIT	BALANCE SHEET DEBIT	BALANCE SHEET CREDIT	
1 3 7 5 00				1 3 7 5 00		1
8 8 0 00				8 8 0 00		2
1 6 5 00				1 6 5 00		3
7 0 0 00				7 0 0 00		4
5 7 0 0 00				5 7 0 0 00		5
	2 0 0 00				2 0 0 00	6
	7 8 0 00				7 8 0 00	7
	1 8 0 00				1 8 0 00	8
	6 5 0 0 00				6 5 0 0 00	9
1 2 5 0 00				1 2 5 0 00		10
	6 1 0 0 00		6 1 0 0 00			11
1 3 2 5 00		1 3 2 5 00				12
5 4 0 00		5 4 0 00				13
7 2 5 00		7 2 5 00				14
3 2 5 00		3 2 5 00				15
1 6 0 00		1 6 0 00				16
1 0 0 00		1 0 0 00				17
2 5 0 00		2 5 0 00				18
2 0 0 00		2 0 0 00				19
6 5 00		6 5 00				20
13 7 6 0 00	13 7 6 0 00	3 6 9 0 00	6 1 0 0 00	10 0 7 0 00	7 6 6 0 00	21
		2 4 1 0 00			2 4 1 0 00	22
		6 1 0 0 00	6 1 0 0 00	10 0 7 0 00	10 0 7 0 00	23
						24
						25
						26
						27
						28
						29
						30
						31
						32
						33

Problem 5-15B

Nolan's Home

Work

For Month Ended

	ACCOUNT TITLE	TRIAL BALANCE DEBIT	TRIAL BALANCE CREDIT	ADJUSTMENTS DEBIT	ADJUSTMENTS CREDIT
1	Cash	830 00			
2	Accounts Receivable	760 00			
3	Supplies	625 00			(a) 415 00
4	Prepaid Insurance	950 00			(b) 150 00
5	Automobile	6500 00			
6	Accum. Depr.—Automobile				(c) 250 00
7	Accounts Payable		1500 00		
8	Wages Payable				(d) 175 00
9	Val Nolan, Capital		9900 00		
10	Val Nolan, Drawing	1100 00			
11	Appraisal Fees		3000 00		
12	Wages Expense	1560 00		(d) 175 00	
13	Advertising Expense	420 00			
14	Rent Expense	1050 00			
15	Supplies Expense			(a) 415 00	
16	Telephone Expense	255 00			
17	Insurance Expense			(b) 150 00	
18	Repair Expense	270 00			
19	Oil and Gas Expense	80 00			
20	Depr. Expense—Automobile			(c) 250 00	
21		14400 00	14400 00	990 00	990 00
22	*Net Loss*				
23					
24					
25					
26					
27					
28					
29					
30					
31					
32					
33					

Problem 5-15B (Concluded)

Appraisals

Sheet

October 31, 20--

ADJUSTED TRIAL BALANCE		INCOME STATEMENT		BALANCE SHEET		
DEBIT	CREDIT	DEBIT	CREDIT	DEBIT	CREDIT	
8 3 0 00				8 3 0 00		1
7 6 0 00				7 6 0 00		2
2 1 0 00				2 1 0 00		3
8 0 0 00				8 0 0 00		4
6 5 0 0 00				6 5 0 0 00		5
	2 5 0 00				2 5 0 00	6
	1 5 0 0 00				1 5 0 0 00	7
	1 7 5 00				1 7 5 00	8
	9 9 0 0 00				9 9 0 0 00	9
1 1 0 0 00				1 1 0 0 00		10
	3 0 0 0 00		3 0 0 0 00			11
1 7 3 5 00		1 7 3 5 00				12
4 2 0 00		4 2 0 00				13
1 0 5 0 00		1 0 5 0 00				14
4 1 5 00		4 1 5 00				15
2 5 5 00		2 5 5 00				16
1 5 0 00		1 5 0 00				17
2 7 0 00		2 7 0 00				18
8 0 00		8 0 00				19
2 5 0 00		2 5 0 00				20
14 8 2 5 00	14 8 2 5 00	4 6 2 5 00	3 0 0 0 00	10 2 0 0 00	11 8 2 5 00	21
			1 6 2 5 00	1 6 2 5 00		22
		4 6 2 5 00	4 6 2 5 00	11 8 2 5 00	11 8 2 5 00	23
						24
						25
						26
						27
						28
						29
						30
						31
						32
						33

Problem 5-16B

1.

GENERAL JOURNAL

PAGE 3

	DATE		DESCRIPTION	POST. REF.	DEBIT	CREDIT	
1			*Adjusting Entries*				1
2	20-- Oct.	31	**Supplies Expense**	523	4 1 5 00		2
3			**Supplies**	141		4 1 5 00	3
4							4
5		31	**Insurance Expense**	535	1 5 0 00		5
6			**Prepaid Insurance**	145		1 5 0 00	6
7							7
8		31	**Depreciation Expense—Automobile**	541	2 5 0 00		8
9			**Accumulated Depreciation—Automobile**	185.1		2 5 0 00	9
10							10
11		31	**Wages Expense**	511	1 7 5 00		11
12			**Wages Payable**	219		1 7 5 00	12
13							13
14							14
15							15
16							16
17							17
18							18
19							19
20							20
21							21
22							22
23							23
24							24
25							25
26							26
27							27
28							28
29							29
30							30
31							31
32							32
33							33
34							34
35							35
36							36

Problem 5-16B (Continued)

2.   **GENERAL LEDGER**

ACCOUNT Supplies   ACCOUNT NO. 141

DATE		ITEM	POST. REF.	DEBIT	CREDIT	BALANCE	
						DEBIT	CREDIT
20-- Oct.	2		J1	6 2 5 00		6 2 5 00	
	31	Adjusting	J3		4 1 5 00	2 1 0 00	

ACCOUNT Prepaid Insurance   ACCOUNT NO. 145

DATE		ITEM	POST. REF.	DEBIT	CREDIT	BALANCE	
						DEBIT	CREDIT
20-- Oct.	3		J1	9 5 0 00		9 5 0 00	
	31	Adjusting	J3		1 5 0 00	8 0 0 00	

ACCOUNT Accumulated Depreciation—Automobile   ACCOUNT NO. 185.1

DATE		ITEM	POST. REF.	DEBIT	CREDIT	BALANCE	
						DEBIT	CREDIT
20-- Oct.	31	Adjusting	J3		2 5 0 00		2 5 0 00

Problem 5-16B (Continued)

ACCOUNT   Wages Payable   ACCOUNT NO.   219

DATE		ITEM	POST. REF.	DEBIT	CREDIT	BALANCE	
						DEBIT	CREDIT
20-- Oct.	31	Adjusting	J3		1 7 5 00		1 7 5 00

ACCOUNT   Wages Expense   ACCOUNT NO.   511

DATE		ITEM	POST. REF.	DEBIT	CREDIT	BALANCE	
						DEBIT	CREDIT
20-- Oct.	15		J2	7 0 0 00		7 0 0 00	
	26		J2	8 6 0 00		1 5 6 0 00	
	31	Adjusting	J3	1 7 5 00		1 7 3 5 00	

ACCOUNT   Supplies Expense   ACCOUNT NO.   523

DATE		ITEM	POST. REF.	DEBIT	CREDIT	BALANCE	
						DEBIT	CREDIT
20-- Oct.	31	Adjusting	J3	4 1 5 00		4 1 5 00	

Problem 5-16B (Concluded)

ACCOUNT   Insurance Expense   ACCOUNT NO.   535

DATE		ITEM	POST. REF.	DEBIT	CREDIT	BALANCE DEBIT	BALANCE CREDIT
20-- Oct.	31	Adjusting	J3	1 5 0 00		1 5 0 00	

ACCOUNT   Depreciation Expense—Automobile   ACCOUNT NO.   541

DATE		ITEM	POST. REF.	DEBIT	CREDIT	BALANCE DEBIT	BALANCE CREDIT
20-- Oct.	31	Adjusting	J3	2 5 0 00		2 5 0 00	

Problem 5-17B

	ACCOUNT TITLE	TRIAL BALANCE		ADJUSTMENTS	
		DEBIT	CREDIT	DEBIT	CREDIT
1	Cash	1 3 6 5 00			
2	Accounts Receivable	8 4 5 00			
3	Supplies	6 2 0 00			(a) 4 9 0 00
4	Prepaid Insurance	1 1 5 0 00			(b) 7 3 0 00
5	Office Equipment	6 4 0 0 00			
6	Accum. Depr.—Office Equipment				(c) 3 2 5 00
7	Accounts Payable		7 3 5 00		
8	Wages Payable				(d) 9 5 00
9	Dick Ady, Capital		7 8 0 0 00		
10	Dick Ady, Drawing	1 2 0 0 00			
11	Professional Fees		6 3 5 0 00		
12	Wages Expense	1 4 9 5 00		(d) 9 5 00	
13	Advertising Expense	3 8 0 00			
14	Rent Expense	8 5 0 00			
15	Supplies Expense			(a) 4 9 0 00	
16	Telephone Expense	2 0 5 00			
17	Utilities Expense	2 8 5 00			
18	Insurance Expense			(b) 7 3 0 00	
19	Depr. Expense—Office Equipment			(c) 3 2 5 00	
20	Miscellaneous Expense	9 0 00			
21		14 8 8 5 00	14 8 8 5 00	1 6 4 0 00	1 6 4 0 00
22	**Net Income**				

Note: Shaded areas indicate where corrections were made.

Problem 5-17B (Concluded)

Bookkeeping Service

Sheet

July 31, 20--

ADJUSTED TRIAL BALANCE		INCOME STATEMENT		BALANCE SHEET		
DEBIT	CREDIT	DEBIT	CREDIT	DEBIT	CREDIT	
1 3 6 5 00				1 3 6 5 00		1
8 4 5 00				8 4 5 00		2
1 3 0 00				1 3 0 00		3
4 2 0 00				4 2 0 00		4
6 4 0 0 00				6 4 0 0 00		5
	3 2 5 00				3 2 5 00	6
	7 3 5 00				7 3 5 00	7
	9 5 00				9 5 00	8
	7 8 0 0 00				7 8 0 0 00	9
1 2 0 0 00				1 2 0 0 00		10
	6 3 5 0 00		6 3 5 0 00			11
1 5 9 0 00		1 5 9 0 00				12
3 8 0 00		3 8 0 00				13
8 5 0 00		8 5 0 00				14
4 9 0 00		4 9 0 00				15
2 0 5 00		2 0 5 00				16
2 8 5 00		2 8 5 00				17
7 3 0 00		7 3 0 00				18
3 2 5 00		3 2 5 00				19
9 0 00		9 0 00				20
15 3 0 5 00	15 3 0 5 00	4 9 4 5 00	6 3 5 0 00	10 3 6 0 00	8 9 5 5 00	21
		1 4 0 5 00			1 4 0 5 00	22
		6 3 5 0 00	6 3 5 0 00	10 3 6 0 00	10 3 6 0 00	23
						24
						25
						26
						27
						28
						29
						30
						31
						32

MANAGING YOUR WRITING

Adjusting entries are important because the bank will want a proper matching of expenses and revenues for the year and proper measures of assets and liabilities as of December 31, 20--. Failure to make these adjustments not only leads to incorrect financial statements, but also conveys the impression that Ms. Alvarez is not knowledgeable about business matters.

Students should request additional information on the following accounts:

Supplies: What was the cost of supplies remaining on 12/31? This amount should be reported as an asset. The supplies used during the period should be recognized as an expense.

Prepaid Insurance: How much of the amount applies to insurance for next year? That amount should be reported as an asset. The remainder is an expense.

Lawn Equipment: How long has the equipment been owned? What is its expected life and salvage value? This information would be used to recognize depreciation expense and to reduce the book value of the asset by establishing a contra-asset account for accumulated depreciation.

Rent Expense: Was this amount paid only for 20--? Or, was part of it paid for next year? If so, prepaid rent should be recognized and the expense should be reduced.

Wages Expense: Did the employees earn wages in 20-- that were not paid by 12/31/--? If so, additional wages expense and wages payable should be recognized.

Gas and Oil Expense: How much gas and oil still remains on 12/31? If it is just the amounts in the tanks and engines of the equipment, an adjustment is not worthwhile. However, if several cases of oil were stored on 12/31, an adjustment should be made to recognize this asset and reduce the expense.

Later in the text, we will cover the need to adjust Accounts Receivable for estimated bad debts. Some students may also request this information.

Note: The potential adjustments for rent, gas, and oil were not discussed in the text. The assignment provides an excellent opportunity to gauge student understanding of the concept of adjusting entries and their ability to apply this concept to new situations.

This page left intentionally blank.

Mastery Problem

1.

Kristi Williams Family

Work

For Year Ended

	ACCOUNT TITLE	TRIAL BALANCE		ADJUSTMENTS	
		DEBIT	CREDIT	DEBIT	CREDIT
1	Cash	8 7 3 0 00			
2	Office Supplies	7 0 0 00			(a) 6 0 0 00
3	Prepaid Insurance	6 0 0 00			(d) 1 0 0 00
4	Office Equipment	18 0 0 0 00			
5	*Accum. Depr.—Office Equip.*				(b) 1 8 0 0 00
6	Computer Equipment	6 0 0 0 00			
7	*Accum. Depr.—Computer Equip.*				(c) 1 0 0 0 00
8	Notes Payable		8 0 0 0 00		
9	Accounts Payable		5 0 0 00		
10	Kristi Williams, Capital		11 4 0 0 00		
11	Kristi Williams, Drawing	3 0 0 0 00			
12	Client Fees		35 8 0 0 00		
13	Wages Expense	9 5 0 0 00			
14	Rent Expense	6 0 0 0 00			
15	*Office Supplies Expense*			(a) 6 0 0 00	
16	Utilities Expense	2 1 7 0 00			
17	*Insurance Expense*			(d) 1 0 0 00	
18	*Depr. Expense—Office Equip.*			(b) 1 8 0 0 00	
19	*Depr. Exp.—Computer Equip.*			(c) 1 0 0 0 00	
20	Miscellaneous Expense	1 0 0 0 00			
21		55 7 0 0 00	55 7 0 0 00	3 5 0 0 00	3 5 0 0 00
22	*Net Income*				
23					
24					
25					
26					
27					
28					
29					
30					
31					
32					

Mastery Problem (Continued)

Counseling Services

Sheet

December 31, 20--

ADJUSTED TRIAL BALANCE		INCOME STATEMENT		BALANCE SHEET		
DEBIT	CREDIT	DEBIT	CREDIT	DEBIT	CREDIT	
8 7 3 0 00				8 7 3 0 00		1
1 0 0 00				1 0 0 00		2
5 0 0 00				5 0 0 00		3
18 0 0 0 00				18 0 0 0 00		4
	1 8 0 0 00				1 8 0 0 00	5
6 0 0 0 00				6 0 0 0 00		6
	1 0 0 0 00				1 0 0 0 00	7
	8 0 0 0 00				8 0 0 0 00	8
	5 0 0 00				5 0 0 00	9
	11 4 0 0 00				11 4 0 0 00	10
3 0 0 0 00				3 0 0 0 00		11
	35 8 0 0 00		35 8 0 0 00			12
9 5 0 0 00		9 5 0 0 00				13
6 0 0 0 00		6 0 0 0 00				14
6 0 0 00		6 0 0 00				15
2 1 7 0 00		2 1 7 0 00				16
1 0 0 00		1 0 0 00				17
1 8 0 0 00		1 8 0 0 00				18
1 0 0 0 00		1 0 0 0 00				19
1 0 0 0 00		1 0 0 0 00				20
58 5 0 0 00	58 5 0 0 00	22 1 7 0 00	35 8 0 0 00	36 3 3 0 00	22 7 0 0 00	21
		13 6 3 0 00			13 6 3 0 00	22
		35 8 0 0 00	35 8 0 0 00	36 3 3 0 00	36 3 3 0 00	23

Mastery Problem (Concluded)

2.

GENERAL JOURNAL

PAGE

	DATE		DESCRIPTION	POST. REF.	DEBIT	CREDIT	
1			*Adjusting Entries*				1
2	20-- Dec.	31	Office Supplies Expense		6 0 0 00		2
3			Office Supplies			6 0 0 00	3
4							4
5		31	Depreciation Expense—Office Equipment		1 8 0 0 00		5
6			Accumulated Depreciation—Office Equipment			1 8 0 0 00	6
7							7
8		31	Depreciation Expense—Computer Equipment		1 0 0 0 00		8
9			Accum. Depreciation—Computer Equipment			1 0 0 0 00	9
10							10
11		31	Insurance Expense		1 0 0 00		11
12			Prepaid Insurance			1 0 0 00	12
13							13
14							14
15							15
16							16
17							17
18							18
19							19
20							20
21							21
22							22
23							23
24							24
25							25
26							26
27							27
28							28
29							29
30							30
31							31
32							32
33							33
34							34
35							35

Challenge Problem

See pages 170–171 for work sheet for Challenge Problem.

Challenge Problem

1.

Diane Kiefner's Wilderness

Work

For Summer

	ACCOUNT TITLE	TRIAL BALANCE DEBIT	TRIAL BALANCE CREDIT	ADJUSTMENTS DEBIT	ADJUSTMENTS CREDIT
1	Cash	11 5 0 0 00			
2	*Prepaid Advertising Supplies*			7 5 0 00	
3	*Kayak & Paddles*			3 5 0 0 00	
4	*Accum. Depr.—Kayak & Paddles*				7 0 0 00
5	Diane Kiefner, Capital		15 0 0 0 00		
6	Tour Revenue		10 0 0 0 00		
7	Advertising Supplies Expense	1 0 0 0 00			7 5 0 00
8	Food Expense	2 0 0 0 00			
9	Equipment Rental Expense	3 0 0 0 00			
10	Travel Expense	4 0 0 0 00			
11	Kayak Expense	3 5 0 0 00			3 5 0 0 00
12	*Depr. Exp.—Kayak & Paddles*			7 0 0 00	
13		25 0 0 0 00	25 0 0 0 00	4 9 5 0 00	4 9 5 0 00
14	*Net Income*				
15					
16					
17					
18					
19					

Challenge Problem (Concluded)

Kayaking Tours

Sheet

Ended 20--

ADJUSTED TRIAL BALANCE		INCOME STATEMENT		BALANCE SHEET		
DEBIT	CREDIT	DEBIT	CREDIT	DEBIT	CREDIT	
11 5 0 0 00				11 5 0 0 00		1
7 5 0 00				7 5 0 00		2
3 5 0 0 00				3 5 0 0 00		3
	7 0 0 00				7 0 0 00	4
	15 0 0 0 00				15 0 0 0 00	5
	10 0 0 0 00		10 0 0 0 00			6
2 5 0 00		2 5 0 00				7
2 0 0 0 00		2 0 0 0 00				8
3 0 0 0 00		3 0 0 0 00				9
4 0 0 0 00		4 0 0 0 00				10
						11
7 0 0 00		7 0 0 00				12
25 7 0 0 00	25 7 0 0 00	9 9 5 0 00	10 0 0 0 00	15 7 5 0 00	15 7 0 0 00	13
		5 0 00			5 0 00	14
		10 0 0 0 00	10 0 0 0 00	15 7 5 0 00	15 7 5 0 00	15
						16
						17
						18
						19

2. *Diane thought she lost $3,500. She actually made net income of $50. Although she did not actually lose money this summer, buying her own kayak did significantly reduce her profitability. Note the depreciation expense of $700.*

APPENDIX: DEPRECIATION METHODS

REVIEW QUESTIONS

1. straight-line
   double-declining-balance
   sum-of-the-years'-digits

2. Modified Accelerated Cost Recovery System

Exercise 5Apx-1A

Straight-Line Depreciation

Year	Depreciable Cost	×	Rate	=	Depreciation Expense	Accumulated Depreciation End of Year	Book Value End of Year
1	$20,000		25%		$5,000	$ 5,000	$20,000
2	20,000		25%		5,000	10,000	15,000
3	20,000		25%		5,000	15,000	10,000
4	20,000		25%		5,000	20,000	5,000

Exercise 5Apx-2A

Sum-of-the-Years'-Digits

Year	Depreciable Cost	×	Rate	=	Depreciation Expense	Accumulated Depreciation End of Year	Book Value End of Year
1	$20,000		4/10		$8,000	$ 8,000	$17,000
2	20,000		3/10		6,000	14,000	11,000
3	20,000		2/10		4,000	18,000	7,000
4	20,000		1/10		2,000	20,000	5,000

Exercise 5Apx-3A

Double-Declining-Balance Method

Year	Book Value Beginning of Year	×	Rate	=	Depreciation Expense	Accumulated Depreciation End of Year	Book Value End of Year
1	$25,000		50%		$12,500	$12,500	$12,500
2	12,500		50%		6,250	18,750	6,250
3	6,250				1,250	20,000	5,000
4	5,000				0	20,000	5,000

Exercise 5Apx-4A

Modified Accelerated Cost Recovery System

Year	Cost	×	Rate	=	Depreciation Expense	Accumulated Depreciation End of Year	Book Value End of Year
1	$25,000		20.00%		$5,000	$ 5,000	$20,000
2	25,000		32.00%		8,000	13,000	12,000
3	25,000		19.20%		4,800	17,800	7,200
4	25,000		11.52%		2,880	20,680	4,320
5	25,000		11.52%		2,880	23,560	1,440
6	25,000		5.76%		1,440	25,000	0

Exercise 5Apx-1B

Straight-Line Depreciation

Year	Depreciable Cost	×	Rate	=	Depreciation Expense	Accumulated Depreciation End of Year	Book Value End of Year
1	$4,500		20%		$900	$ 900	$4,100
2	4,500		20%		900	1,800	3,200
3	4,500		20%		900	2,700	2,300
4	4,500		20%		900	3,600	1,400
5	4,500		20%		900	4,500	500

Exercise 5Apx-2B

Sum-of-the-Years'-Digits

Year	Depreciable Cost	×	Rate	=	Depreciation Expense	Accumulated Depreciation End of Year	Book Value End of Year
1	$4,500		5/15		$1,500	$1,500	$3,500
2	4,500		4/15		1,200	2,700	2,300
3	4,500		3/15		900	3,600	1,400
4	4,500		2/15		600	4,200	800
5	4,500		1/15		300	4,500	500

Exercise 5Apx-3B

Double-Declining-Balance Method

Year	Book Value Beginning of Year	×	Rate	=	Depreciation Expense	Accumulated Depreciation End of Year	Book Value End of Year
1	$5,000		40%		$2,000	$2,000	$3,000
2	3,000		40%		1,200	3,200	1,800
3	1,800		40%		720	3,920	1,080
4	1,080		40%		432	4,352	648
5	648				148	4,500	500

Exercise 5Apx-4B

Modified Accelerated Cost Recovery System

Year	Cost	×	Rate	=	Depreciation Expense	Accumulated Depreciation End of Year	Book Value End of Year
1	$5,000		20.00%		$1,000	$1,000	$4,000
2	5,000		32.00%		1,600	2,600	2,400
3	5,000		19.20%		960	3,560	1,440
4	5,000		11.52%		576	4,136	864
5	5,000		11.52%		576	4,712	288
6	5,000		5.76%		288	5,000	0

CHAPTER 6

FINANCIAL STATEMENTS AND THE CLOSING PROCESS

REVIEW QUESTIONS

1. The information needed to prepare the income statement is found in the Income Statement columns of the work sheet. Revenue is shown first, followed by an itemized and totaled list of expenses. Net income may be calculated or copied from the Income Statement columns of the work sheet.

2. Two approaches to listing the expenses in the income statement are:
    a. the expenses could be listed in the same order that they appear in the chart of accounts.
    b. the expenses could be listed in descending order, by dollar amount.

3. The Balance Sheet columns of the work sheet provide most of the information needed to prepare a statement of owner's equity. The capital account balance and the drawing account balance are in the Balance Sheet columns of the work sheet. The net income for the year can be found either on the work sheet at the bottom of the Balance Sheet columns or on the income statement. Additional investments must be identified in the owner's capital account.

4. If additional investments are made during the year, the owner's capital account in the general ledger must be reviewed. The owner's capital account in the general ledger contains the beginning balance. The additional investments will also be shown in the owner's capital account in the general ledger.

5. The work sheet and the statement of owner's equity are used to prepare the balance sheet. The asset and liability amounts can be found in the Balance Sheet columns of the work sheet. The ending balance for the owner's capital has been computed on the statement of owner's equity. This amount should be copied from the statement of owner's equity to the balance sheet.

6. A permanent account is an account in which the balance is brought forward for each new period. Assets, liabilities, and the owner's capital account accumulate information across accounting periods. Their balances are brought forward for each new period. All accounts reported on the balance sheet are permanent accounts.

7. Three types of temporary accounts are revenue, expense, and drawing accounts. These accounts accumulate information for a specific accounting period.

8. The four steps in the closing process are:
    Step 1: Close revenue accounts to Income Summary.
    Step 2: Close expense accounts to Income Summary.
    Step 3: Close Income Summary to the owner's capital account.
    Step 4: Close Drawing to the owner's capital account.

9. The net effect of the four closing entries on the balance of the owner's capital account is that the balance from Income Summary is transferred to the owner's capital account and the drawing account is closed to the owner's capital account. Upon completion of the four steps, all temporary accounts have zero balances and the earnings and withdrawals for the period have been transferred to the owner's capital account. This same amount, the increase or decrease in capital, is calculated on the statement of owner's equity.

10. The purpose of the post-closing trial balance is to prove the equality of the debit and credit balances in the general ledger accounts, after posting the closing entries.

11. The 10 steps in the accounting cycle are:

During the Accounting Period
1. Analyze source documents.
2. Journalize the transactions.
3. Post to the ledger accounts.

End of Accounting Period
4. Prepare a trial balance.
5. Determine and prepare the needed adjustments on the work sheet.
6. Complete an end-of-period work sheet.
7. Journalize and post the adjusting entries.
8. Prepare an income statement, a statement of owner's equity, and a balance sheet.
9. Journalize and post the closing entries.
10. Prepare a post-closing trial balance.

Exercise 6-1A

Case Advising
Income Statement
For Month Ended January 31, 20--

Revenue:							
Advising fees					$3 7 9 3 00		
Expenses:							
Wages expense	$8 0 0 00						
Advertising expense	8 0 00						
Rent expense	5 0 0 00						
Supplies expense	1 2 0 00						
Telephone expense	5 8 00						
Electricity expense	4 4 00						
Insurance expense	3 0 00						
Gas and oil expense	3 8 00						
Depreciation expense—office equipment	1 0 0 00						
Miscellaneous expense	3 3 00						
Total expenses					1 8 0 3 00		
Net income					$1 9 9 0 00		

Exercise 6-2A

Case Advising
Statement of Owner's Equity
For Month Ended January 31, 20--

Bill Case, capital, January 1, 20--					$4 0 0 0 00		
Net income for January	$1 9 9 0 00						
Less withdrawals for January	8 0 0 00						
Increase in capital					1 1 9 0 00		
Bill Case, capital, January 31, 20--					$5 1 9 0 00		

Exercise 6-3A

Case Advising

Balance Sheet

January 31, 20--

Assets								
Current assets:								
Cash	$1	2	1	2	00			
Accounts receivable		8	9	6	00			
Supplies		4	8	2	00			
Prepaid insurance		9	0	0	00			
Total current assets						$3	4 9 0	00
Property, plant, and equipment:								
Office equipment	$3	0	0	0	00			
Less accumulated depreciation		1	0	0	00	2	9 0 0	00
Total assets						$6	3 9 0	00
Liabilities								
Current liabilities:								
Accounts payable	$1	0	0	0	00			
Wages payable		2	0	0	00			
Total current liabilities						$1	2 0 0	00
Owner's Equity								
Bill Case, capital						5	1 9 0	00
Total liabilities and owner's equity						$6	3 9 0	00

Exercise 6-4A

GENERAL JOURNAL   PAGE 1

	DATE		DESCRIPTION	POST. REF.	DEBIT	CREDIT	
1			*Closing Entries*				1
2	20-- Jan.	31	Advising Fees	401	3 7 9 3 00		2
3			Income Summary	313		3 7 9 3 00	3
4							4
5		31	Income Summary	313	1 8 0 3 00		5
6			Wages Expense	511		8 0 0 00	6
7			Advertising Expense	512		8 0 00	7
8			Rent Expense	521		5 0 0 00	8
9			Supplies Expense	524		1 2 0 00	9
10			Telephone Expense	525		5 8 00	10
11			Electricity Expense	533		4 4 00	11
12			Insurance Expense	535		3 0 00	12
13			Gas and Oil Expense	538		3 8 00	13
14			Depreciation Expense—Office Equipment	541		1 0 0 00	14
15			Miscellaneous Expense	549		3 3 00	15
16							16
17		31	Income Summary	313	1 9 9 0 00		17
18			Bill Case, Capital	311		1 9 9 0 00	18
19							19
20		31	Bill Case, Capital	311	8 0 0 00		20
21			Bill Case, Drawing	312		8 0 0 00	21
22							22
23							23

Cash 101 — Bal. 1,212

Accounts Receivable 122 — Bal. 896

Supplies 141 — Bal. 482

Prepaid Insurance 145 — Bal. 900

Office Equipment 181 — Bal. 3,000

Accum. Depr.—Office Equip. 181.1 — Bal. 100

Exercise 6-4A (Concluded)

	Accounts Payable	202				*Wages Payable*	219
	Bal.	1,000				Bal.	200

	Bill Case, Capital	311				*Bill Case, Drawing*	312
Closing	800	Bal.	4,000	Bal.	800	Closing	800
		Closing	1,990	—		—	
			5,990				
		Bal.	5,190				

	Income Summary	313				*Advising Fees*	401
Closing	1,803	Closing	3,793	Closing	3,793	Bal.	3,793
Closing	1,990	—		—		—	
	3,793						
	—						

	Wages Expense	511				*Advertising Expense*	512
Bal.	800	Closing	800	Bal.	80	Closing	80
—		—		—		—	

	Rent Expense	521				*Supplies Expense*	524
Bal.	500	Closing	500	Bal.	120	Closing	120
—		—		—		—	

	Telephone Expense	525				*Electricity Expense*	533
Bal.	58	Closing	58	Bal.	44	Closing	44
—		—		—		—	

	Insurance Expense	535				*Gas and Oil Expense*	538
Bal.	30	Closing	30	Bal.	38	Closing	38
—		—		—		—	

	Depr. Exp.—Office Equip.	541				*Miscellaneous Expense*	549
Bal.	100	Closing	100	Bal.	33	Closing	33
—		—		—		—	

Exercise 6-5A

GENERAL JOURNAL

PAGE

	DATE		DESCRIPTION	POST. REF.	DEBIT	CREDIT	
1			*Closing Entries*				1
2	20— Apr.	30	**Golf Instruction Fees**	401	4 0 0 0 00		2
3			**Income Summary**	313		4 0 0 0 00	3
4							4
5		30	**Income Summary**	313	2 4 8 0 00		5
6			**Wages Expense**	511		8 0 0 00	6
7			**Advertising Expense**	512		2 0 0 00	7
8			**Travel Expense**	515		6 0 0 00	8
9			**Supplies Expense**	524		5 0 0 00	9
10			**Insurance Expense**	535		1 0 0 00	10
11			**Postage Expense**	536		5 0 00	11
12			**Gas and Oil Expense**	538		1 5 0 00	12
13			**Miscellaneous Expense**	549		8 0 00	13
14							14
15		30	**Income Summary**	313	1 5 2 0 00		15
16			**Chris Williams, Capital**	311		1 5 2 0 00	16
17							17
18		30	**Chris Williams, Capital**	311	1 0 0 0 00		18
19			**Chris Williams, Drawing**	312		1 0 0 0 00	19
20							20
21							21
22							22
23							23
24							24
25							25
26							26
27							27
28							28
29							29
30							30
31							31

Exercise 6-5A (Concluded)

Cash		101
Bal.	500	

Accounts Receivable		122
Bal.	1,500	

Wages Payable		219
	Bal.	400

Chris Williams, Capital		311
	Bal.	9,000
Closing	1,000	Closing	1,520
		10,520
	Bal.	9,520

Chris Williams, Drawing		312
Bal.	1,000	Closing	1,000
—		—

Income Summary		313
Closing	2,480	Closing	4,000
Closing	1,520	
	4,000	
—		—

Golf Instruction Fees		401
Closing	4,000	Bal.	4,000
—		—

Wages Expense		511
Bal.	800	Closing	800
—		—

Advertising Expense		512
Bal.	200	Closing	200
—		—

Travel Expense		515
Bal.	600	Closing	600

Supplies Expense		524
Bal.	500	Closing	500
—		—

Insurance Expense		535
Bal.	100	Closing	100
—		—

Postage Expense		536
Bal.	50	Closing	50
—		—

Gas and Oil Expense		538
Bal.	150	Closing	150
—		—

Miscellaneous Expense		549
Bal.	80	Closing	80
—		—

Exercise 6-6A

| | GENERAL JOURNAL | | | | PAGE | |

	DATE		DESCRIPTION	POST. REF.	DEBIT	CREDIT	
1			***Closing Entries***				1
2	20-- Jan.	31	**Delivery Fees**	401	2 2 0 0 00		2
3			**Income Summary**	313		2 2 0 0 00	3
4							4
5		31	**Income Summary**	313	2 8 0 3 00		5
6			**Wages Expense**	511		1 8 0 0 00	6
7			**Advertising Expense**	512		8 0 00	7
8			**Rent Expense**	521		5 0 0 00	8
9			**Supplies Expense**	523		1 2 0 00	9
10			**Telephone Expense**	525		5 8 00	10
11			**Electricity Expense**	533		4 4 00	11
12			**Insurance Expense**	535		3 0 00	12
13			**Gas and Oil Expense**	538		3 8 00	13
14			**Depreciation Expense—Delivery Equipment**	541		1 0 0 00	14
15			**Miscellaneous Expense**	549		3 3 00	15
16							16
17		31	**Saburo Goto, Capital**	311	6 0 3 00		17
18			**Income Summary**	313		6 0 3 00	18
19							19
20		31	**Saburo Goto, Capital**	311	8 0 0 00		20
21			**Saburo Goto, Drawing**	312		8 0 0 00	21
22							22
23							23
24							24
25							25
26							26

Exercise 6-6A (Concluded)

Accum. Depr.—Delivery Equip.		185.1
	Bal.	100

Wages Payable		219
	Bal.	200

Saburo Goto, Capital			311
Closing	*603*	Bal.	4,000
Closing	*800*		
	1,403		
		Bal.	*2,597*

Saburo Goto, Drawing			312
Bal.	800	*Closing*	*800*
	—		—

Income Summary			313
Closing	*2,803*	*Closing*	*2,200*
		Closing	*603*
			2,803
	—		—

Delivery Fees			401
Closing	*2,200*	Bal.	2,200
	—		—

Wages Expense			511
Bal.	1,800	*Closing*	*1,800*
	—		—

Advertising Expense			512
Bal.	80	*Closing*	*80*
	—		—

Rent Expense			521
Bal.	500	*Closing*	*500*
	—		—

Supplies Expense			523
Bal.	120	*Closing*	*120*
	—		—

Telephone Expense			525
Bal.	58	*Closing*	*58*
	—		—

Electricity Expense			533
Bal.	44	*Closing*	*44*
	—		—

Insurance Expense			535
Bal.	30	*Closing*	*30*
	—		—

Gas and Oil Expense			538
Bal.	38	*Closing*	*38*
	—		—

Depr. Exp.—Delivery Equip.			541
Bal.	100	*Closing*	*100*
	—		—

Miscellaneous Expense			549
Bal.	33	*Closing*	*33*
	—		—

Problem 6-7A

1.

Monte's Repairs
Income Statement
For Month Ended January 31, 20--

Revenue:		
Repair fees		$4 2 3 0 00
Expenses:		
Wages expense	$1 8 0 0 00	
Advertising expense	1 7 0 00	
Rent expense	4 2 0 00	
Supplies expense	2 0 0 00	
Telephone expense	4 9 00	
Insurance expense	1 0 0 00	
Gas and oil expense	3 3 00	
Depreciation expense—delivery equipment	3 0 00	
Miscellaneous expense	2 8 00	
Total expenses		2 8 3 0 00
Net income		$1 4 0 0 00

2.

Monte's Repairs
Statement of Owner's Equity
For Month Ended January 31, 20--

Monte Eli, capital, January 1, 20--		$7 0 0 0 00
Net income for January	$1 4 0 0 00	
Less withdrawals for January	1 0 0 0 00	
Increase in capital		4 0 0 00
Monte Eli, capital, January 31, 20--		$7 4 0 0 00

Problem 6-7A (Concluded)

3.

Monte's Repairs

Balance Sheet

January 31, 20--

Assets												
Current assets:												
Cash	$3	0	8	0	00							
Accounts receivable	1	2	0	0	00							
Supplies		6	0	0	00							
Prepaid insurance		8	0	0	00							
Total current assets						$5	6	8	0	00		
Property, plant, and equipment:												
Delivery equipment	$3	0	0	0	00							
Less accumulated depreciation			3	0	00		2	9	7	0	00	
Total assets						$8	6	5	0	00		
Liabilities												
Current liabilities:												
Accounts payable	$1	1	0	0	00							
Wages payable		1	5	0	00							
Total current liabilities						$1	2	5	0	00		
Owner's Equity												
Monte Eli, capital							7	4	0	0	00	
Total liabilities and owner's equity						$8	6	5	0	00		

Problem 6-8A

			Autumn's Home Designs								

Autumn's Home Designs
Statement of Owner's Equity
For Month Ended January 31, 20--

Autumn Chou, capital, January 1, 20--							$4	8	0	0	00
Investments during January							1	2	0	0	00
Total investment							$6	0	0	0	00
Net income for January	$1	8	2	0	00						
Less withdrawals for January	1	0	0	0	00						
Increase in capital								8	2	0	00
Autumn Chou, capital, January 31, 20--							$6	8	2	0	00

Problem 6-9A

1.

GENERAL JOURNAL

DATE		DESCRIPTION	POST. REF.	DEBIT	CREDIT	
1		*Adjusting Entries*				1
2	20-- Jan. 31	**Supplies Expense**	523	2 0 0 00		2
3		**Supplies**	141		2 0 0 00	3
4						4
5	31	**Insurance Expense**	535	1 0 0 00		5
6		**Prepaid Insurance**	145		1 0 0 00	6
7						7
8	31	*Wages Expense*	511	1 5 0 00		8
9		**Wages Payable**	219		1 5 0 00	9
10						10
11	31	**Depreciation Expense—Delivery Equipment**	541	3 0 00		11
12		*Accumulated Depreciation—Delivery Equip.*	185.1		3 0 00	12
13						13
14						14
15						15
16						16
17						17
18						18

Problem 6-9A (Continued)

2.

GENERAL JOURNAL   PAGE 11

	DATE		DESCRIPTION	POST. REF.	DEBIT	CREDIT	
1			*Closing Entries*				1
2	20-- Jan.	31	*Repair Fees*	401	4 2 3 0 00		2
3			*Income Summary*	313		4 2 3 0 00	3
4							4
5		31	*Income Summary*	313	2 8 3 0 00		5
6			*Wages Expense*	511		1 8 0 0 00	6
7			*Advertising Expense*	512		1 7 0 00	7
8			*Rent Expense*	521		4 2 0 00	8
9			*Supplies Expense*	523		2 0 0 00	9
10			*Telephone Expense*	525		4 9 00	10
11			*Insurance Expense*	535		1 0 0 00	11
12			*Gas and Oil Expense*	538		3 3 00	12
13			*Depreciation Expense—Delivery Equipment*	541		3 0 00	13
14			*Miscellaneous Expense*	549		2 8 00	14
15							15
16		31	*Income Summary*	313	1 4 0 0 00		16
17			*Monte Eli, Capital*	311		1 4 0 0 00	17
18							18
19		31	*Monte Eli, Capital*	311	1 0 0 0 00		19
20			*Monte Eli, Drawing*	312		1 0 0 0 00	20
21							21
22							22
23							23

GENERAL LEDGER

1. and 2.

ACCOUNT Cash   ACCOUNT NO. 101

DATE		ITEM	POST. REF.	DEBIT	CREDIT	BALANCE DEBIT	BALANCE CREDIT
20-- Jan.	31	Balance	✓			3 0 8 0 00	

Problem 6-9A (Continued)

ACCOUNT Accounts Receivable   ACCOUNT NO. 122

DATE		ITEM	POST. REF.	DEBIT	CREDIT	BALANCE	
						DEBIT	CREDIT
20-- Jan.	31	Balance	✓			1 2 0 0 00	

ACCOUNT Supplies   ACCOUNT NO. 141

DATE		ITEM	POST. REF.	DEBIT	CREDIT	BALANCE	
						DEBIT	CREDIT
20-- Jan.	31	Balance	✓			8 0 0 00	
	31	Adjusting	J10		2 0 0 00	6 0 0 00	

ACCOUNT Prepaid Insurance   ACCOUNT NO. 145

DATE		ITEM	POST. REF.	DEBIT	CREDIT	BALANCE	
						DEBIT	CREDIT
20-- Jan.	31	Balance	✓			9 0 0 00	
	31	Adjusting	J10		1 0 0 00	8 0 0 00	

ACCOUNT Delivery Equipment   ACCOUNT NO. 185

DATE		ITEM	POST. REF.	DEBIT	CREDIT	BALANCE	
						DEBIT	CREDIT
20-- Jan.	31	Balance	✓			3 0 0 0 00	

ACCOUNT Accumulated Depreciation—Delivery Equipment   ACCOUNT NO. 185.1

DATE		ITEM	POST. REF.	DEBIT	CREDIT	BALANCE	
						DEBIT	CREDIT
20-- Jan.	31	Adjusting	J10		3 0 00		3 0 00

Problem 6-9A (Continued)

ACCOUNT   Accounts Payable   ACCOUNT NO. 202

DATE		ITEM	POST. REF.	DEBIT	CREDIT	BALANCE DEBIT	BALANCE CREDIT
20-- Jan.	31	Balance	✓				1 1 0 0 00

ACCOUNT   Wages Payable   ACCOUNT NO. 219

DATE		ITEM	POST. REF.	DEBIT	CREDIT	BALANCE DEBIT	BALANCE CREDIT
20-- Jan.	31	Adjusting	J10		1 5 0 00		1 5 0 00

ACCOUNT   Monte Eli, Capital   ACCOUNT NO. 311

DATE		ITEM	POST. REF.	DEBIT	CREDIT	BALANCE DEBIT	BALANCE CREDIT
20-- Jan.	31	Balance	✓				7 0 0 0 00
	31	Closing	J11		1 4 0 0 00		8 4 0 0 00
	31	Closing	J11	1 0 0 0 00			7 4 0 0 00

ACCOUNT   Monte Eli, Drawing   ACCOUNT NO. 312

DATE		ITEM	POST. REF.	DEBIT	CREDIT	BALANCE DEBIT	BALANCE CREDIT
20-- Jan.	31	Balance	✓			1 0 0 0 00	
	31	Closing	J11		1 0 0 0 00	—	—

ACCOUNT   Income Summary   ACCOUNT NO. 313

DATE		ITEM	POST. REF.	DEBIT	CREDIT	BALANCE DEBIT	BALANCE CREDIT
20-- Jan.	31	Closing	J11		4 2 3 0 00		4 2 3 0 00
	31	Closing	J11	2 8 3 0 00			1 4 0 0 00
	31	Closing	J11	1 4 0 0 00		—	—

Problem 6-9A (Continued)

ACCOUNT   Repair Fees

ACCOUNT NO.   401

DATE		ITEM	POST. REF.	DEBIT	CREDIT	BALANCE DEBIT	BALANCE CREDIT
20-- Jan.	31	Balance	✓				4 2 3 0 00
	31	Closing	J11	4 2 3 0 00			

ACCOUNT   Wages Expense

ACCOUNT NO.   511

DATE		ITEM	POST. REF.	DEBIT	CREDIT	BALANCE DEBIT	BALANCE CREDIT
20-- Jan.	31	Balance	✓			1 6 5 0 00	
	31	Adjusting	J10	1 5 0 00		1 8 0 0 00	
	31	Closing	J11		1 8 0 0 00		

ACCOUNT   Advertising Expense

ACCOUNT NO.   512

DATE		ITEM	POST. REF.	DEBIT	CREDIT	BALANCE DEBIT	BALANCE CREDIT
20-- Jan.	31	Balance	✓			1 7 0 00	
	31	Closing	J11		1 7 0 00		

ACCOUNT   Rent Expense

ACCOUNT NO.   521

DATE		ITEM	POST. REF.	DEBIT	CREDIT	BALANCE DEBIT	BALANCE CREDIT
20-- Jan.	31	Balance	✓			4 2 0 00	
	31	Closing	J11		4 2 0 00		

ACCOUNT   Supplies Expense

ACCOUNT NO.   523

DATE		ITEM	POST. REF.	DEBIT	CREDIT	BALANCE DEBIT	BALANCE CREDIT
20-- Jan.	31	Adjusting	J10	2 0 0 00		2 0 0 00	
	31	Closing	J11		2 0 0 00		

Problem 6-9A (Continued)

ACCOUNT   Telephone Expense   ACCOUNT NO.   525

DATE		ITEM	POST. REF.	DEBIT	CREDIT	BALANCE DEBIT	BALANCE CREDIT
20-- Jan.	31	Balance	✓			4 9 00	
	31	Closing	J11		4 9 00	——	——

ACCOUNT   Insurance Expense   ACCOUNT NO.   535

DATE		ITEM	POST. REF.	DEBIT	CREDIT	BALANCE DEBIT	BALANCE CREDIT
20-- Jan.	31	Adjusting	J10	1 0 0 00		1 0 0 00	
	31	Closing	J11		1 0 0 00	——	——

ACCOUNT   Gas and Oil Expense   ACCOUNT NO.   538

DATE		ITEM	POST. REF.	DEBIT	CREDIT	BALANCE DEBIT	BALANCE CREDIT
20-- Jan.	31	Balance	✓			3 3 00	
	31	Closing	J11		3 3 00	——	——

ACCOUNT   Depreciation Expense—Delivery Equipment   ACCOUNT NO.   541

DATE		ITEM	POST. REF.	DEBIT	CREDIT	BALANCE DEBIT	BALANCE CREDIT
20-- Jan.	31	Adjusting	J10	3 0 00		3 0 00	
	31	Closing	J11		3 0 00	——	——

ACCOUNT   Miscellaneous Expense   ACCOUNT NO.   549

DATE		ITEM	POST. REF.	DEBIT	CREDIT	BALANCE DEBIT	BALANCE CREDIT
20-- Jan.	31	Balance	✓			2 8 00	
	31	Closing	J11		2 8 00	——	——

Problem 6-9A (Concluded)

3.

Monte's Repairs

Post-Closing Trial Balance

January 31, 20--

ACCOUNT	ACCT. NO.	DEBIT BALANCE	CREDIT BALANCE
Cash	*101*	3 0 8 0 00	
Accounts Receivable	*122*	1 2 0 0 00	
Supplies	*141*	6 0 0 00	
Prepaid Insurance	*145*	8 0 0 00	
Delivery Equipment	*185*	3 0 0 0 00	
Accumulated Depreciation—Delivery Equipment	*185.1*		3 0 00
Accounts Payable	*202*		1 1 0 0 00
Wages Payable	*219*		1 5 0 00
Monte Eli, Capital	*311*		7 4 0 0 00
		8 6 8 0 00	8 6 8 0 00

Exercise 6-1B

Adams' Shoe Shine

Income Statement

For Month Ended June 30, 20--

Revenue:				
Service fees			$4 8 1 3 00	
Expenses:				
Wages expense	$1 0 8 0 00			
Advertising expense	3 4 00			
Rent expense	9 0 0 00			
Supplies expense	3 2 2 00			
Telephone expense	1 3 3 00			
Utilities expense	1 0 2 00			
Insurance expense	1 2 0 00			
Gas and oil expense	8 8 00			
Depreciation expense—office equipment	1 1 0 00			
Miscellaneous expense	9 8 00			
Total expenses			2 9 8 7 00	
Net income			$1 8 2 6 00	

Exercise 6-2B

Adams' Shoe Shine

Statement of Owner's Equity

For Month Ended June 30, 20--

Mary Adams, capital, June 1, 20--		$6 0 0 0 00	
Net income for June	$1 8 2 6 00		
Less withdrawals for June	2 0 0 0 00		
Decrease in capital		(1 7 4 00)	
Mary Adams, capital, June 30, 20--		$5 8 2 6 00	

Exercise 6-3B

Adams' Shoe Shine

Balance Sheet

June 30, 20--

Assets			
Current assets:			
Cash	$3 2 6 2 00		
Accounts receivable	1 2 4 4 00		
Supplies	8 0 0 00		
Prepaid insurance	6 4 0 00		
Total current assets		$5 9 4 6 00	
Property, plant, and equipment:			
Office equipment	$2 1 0 0 00		
Less accumulated depreciation—office equipment	1 1 0 00	1 9 9 0 00	
Total assets		$7 9 3 6 00	
Liabilities			
Current liabilities:			
Accounts payable	$1 8 5 0 00		
Wages payable	2 6 0 00		
Total current liabilities		$2 1 1 0 00	
Owner's Equity			
Mary Adams, capital		5 8 2 6 00	
Total liabilities and owner's equity		$7 9 3 6 00	

Exercise 6-4B

GENERAL JOURNAL   PAGE 1

	DATE		DESCRIPTION	POST. REF.	DEBIT	CREDIT	
1			**Closing Entries**				1
2	20-- June	30	Service Fees	401	4 8 1 3 00		2
3			Income Summary	313		4 8 1 3 00	3
4							4
5		30	Income Summary	313	2 9 8 7 00		5
6			Wages Expense	511		1 0 8 0 00	6
7			Advertising Expense	512		3 4 00	7
8			Rent Expense	521		9 0 0 00	8
9			Supplies Expense	523		3 2 2 00	9
10			Telephone Expense	525		1 3 3 00	10
11			Utilities Expense	533		1 0 2 00	11
12			Insurance Expense	535		1 2 0 00	12
13			Gas and Oil Expense	538		8 8 00	13
14			Depreciation Expense—Office Equipment	542		1 1 0 00	14
15			Miscellaneous Expense	549		9 8 00	15
16							16
17		30	Income Summary	313	1 8 2 6 00		17
18			Mary Adams, Capital	311		1 8 2 6 00	18
19							19
20		30	Mary Adams, Capital	311	2 0 0 0 00		20
21			Mary Adams, Drawing	312		2 0 0 0 00	21
22							22
23							23

Cash 101	Accounts Receivable 122
Bal. 3,262	Bal. 1,244

Supplies 141	Prepaid Insurance 145
Bal. 800	Bal. 640

Office Equipment 181	Accum. Depr.—Office Equip. 181.1
Bal. 2,100	Bal. 110

Exercise 6-4B (Concluded)

Accounts Payable			202
		Bal.	1,850

Wages Payable			219
		Bal.	260

Mary Adams, Capital			311
Closing	2,000	Bal.	6,000
		Closing	1,826
			7,826
		Bal.	5,826

Mary Adams, Drawing			312
Bal.	2,000	Closing	2,000
	—		—

Income Summary			313
Closing	2,987	Closing	4,813
Closing	1,826		
	4,813		
	—		—

Service Fees			401
Closing	4,813	Bal.	4,813
	—		—

Wages Expense			511
Bal.	1,080	Closing	1,080
	—		

Advertising Expense			512
Bal.	34	Closing	34
	—		

Rent Expense			521
Bal.	900	Closing	900
	—		—

Supplies Expense			523
Bal.	322	Closing	322
	—		—

Telephone Expense			525
Bal.	133	Closing	133
	—		—

Utilities Expense			533
Bal.	102	Closing	102
	—		—

Insurance Expense			535
Bal.	120	Closing	120
	—		—

Gas and Oil Expense			538
Bal.	88	Closing	88
	—		—

Depr. Exp.—Office Equip.			542
Bal.	110	Closing	110
	—		—

Miscellaneous Expense			549
Bal.	98	Closing	98
	—		—

Exercise 6-5B

GENERAL JOURNAL

PAGE

	DATE		DESCRIPTION	POST. REF.	DEBIT	CREDIT	
1			*Closing Entries*				1
2	20-- May	31	**Lawn Service Fees**	401	5 0 0 0 00		2
3			**Income Summary**	313		5 0 0 0 00	3
4							4
5		31	**Income Summary**	313	3 2 4 0 00		5
6			**Wages Expense**	511		4 0 0 00	6
7			**Advertising Expense**	512		6 0 0 00	7
8			**Travel Expense**	515		1 0 0 00	8
9			**Supplies Expense**	524		9 0 0 00	9
10			**Insurance Expense**	535		3 0 0 00	10
11			**Postage Expense**	536		4 0 00	11
12			**Gas and Oil Expense**	538		7 0 0 00	12
13			**Miscellaneous Expense**	549		2 0 0 00	13
14							14
15		31	**Income Summary**	313	1 7 6 0 00		15
16			**Mark Thrasher, Capital**	311		1 7 6 0 00	16
17							17
18		31	**Mark Thrasher, Capital**	311	8 0 0 00		18
19			**Mark Thrasher, Drawing**	312		8 0 0 00	19
20							20
21							21
22							22
23							23
24							24
25							25
26							26
27							27
28							28
29							29
30							30
31							31
32							32
33							33
34							34

Exercise 6-5B (Concluded)

Cash		101			Advertising Expense		512
Bal.	600			Bal.	600	*Closing*	*600*
					—		—

Accounts Receivable		122			Travel Expense		515
Bal.	1,800			Bal.	100	*Closing*	*100*
					—		—

Wages Payable		219			Supplies Expense		524
	Bal.	500		Bal.	900	*Closing*	*900*
					—		—

Mark Thrasher, Capital		311			Insurance Expense		535
	Bal.	8,000		Bal.	300	*Closing*	*300*
Closing	*800*	*Closing*	*1,760*		—		—
		9,760					
	Bal.	**8,960**					

Mark Thrasher, Drawing		312			Postage Expense		536
Bal.	800	*Closing*	*800*	Bal.	40	*Closing*	*40*
—		—			—		—

Income Summary		313			Gas and Oil Expense		538
Closing	*3,240*	*Closing*	*5,000*	Bal.	700	*Closing*	*700*
Closing	*1,760*				—		—
	5,000						
—		—					

Lawn Service Fees		401			Miscellaneous Expense		549
Closing	*5,000*	Bal.	5,000	Bal.	200	*Closing*	*200*
		—			—		—

Wages Expense		511
Bal.	400	*Closing*	*400*
—		—

Exercise 6-6B

GENERAL JOURNAL   PAGE

	DATE		DESCRIPTION	POST. REF.	DEBIT	CREDIT	
1			*Closing Entries*				1
2	20-- June	30	**Referral Fees**	401	2 8 1 3 00		2
3			**Income Summary**	313		2 8 1 3 00	3
4							4
5		30	**Income Summary**	313	2 9 8 7 00		5
6			**Wages Expense**	511		1 0 8 0 00	6
7			**Advertising Expense**	512		3 4 00	7
8			**Rent Expense**	521		9 0 0 00	8
9			**Supplies Expense**	523		3 2 2 00	9
10			**Telephone Expense**	525		1 3 3 00	10
11			**Utilities Expense**	533		1 0 2 00	11
12			**Insurance Expense**	535		1 2 0 00	12
13			**Gas and Oil Expense**	538		8 8 00	13
14			**Depreciation Expense—Office Equipment**	541		1 1 0 00	14
15			**Miscellaneous Expense**	549		9 8 00	15
16							16
17		30	**Raquel Zapata, Capital**	311	1 7 4 00		17
18			**Income Summary**	313		1 7 4 00	18
19							19
20		30	**Raquel Zapata, Capital**	311	2 0 0 0 00		20
21			**Raquel Zapata, Drawing**	312		2 0 0 0 00	21
22							22
23							23
24							24
25							25
26							26
27							27
28							28
29							29
30							30
31							31
32							32
33							33
34							34
35							35
36							36

Exercise 6-6B (Concluded)

Accum. Depr.—Office Equip.		181.1
	Bal.	110

Wages Payable		219
	Bal.	260

Raquel Zapata, Capital		311
Closing 174	Bal.	6,000
Closing 2,000		
2,174		
	Bal.	*3,826*

Raquel Zapata, Drawing		312
Bal. 2,000	*Closing*	*2,000*
—		—

Income Summary		313
Closing 2,987	*Closing*	2,813
	Closing	174
		2,987
—		

Referral Fees		401
Closing 2,813	Bal.	2,813
—		

Wages Expense		511
Bal. 1,080	*Closing*	*1,080*
—		—

Advertising Expense		512
Bal. 34	*Closing*	*34*
—		—

Rent Expense		521
Bal. 900	*Closing*	*900*
—		—

Supplies Expense		523
Bal. 322	*Closing*	*322*
—		—

Telephone Expense		525
Bal. 133	*Closing*	*133*
—		—

Utilities Expense		533
Bal. 102	*Closing*	*102*
—		—

Insurance Expense		535
Bal. 120	*Closing*	*120*
—		—

Gas and Oil Expense		538
Bal. 88	*Closing*	*88*
—		—

Depr. Exp.—Office Equip.		541
Bal. 110	*Closing*	*110*
—		—

Miscellaneous Expense		549
Bal. 98	*Closing*	*98*
—		—

Problem 6-7B

1.

Juanita's Consulting										
Income Statement										
For Month Ended June 30, 20--										

Revenue:										
Consulting fees						$4	2	0	4	00
Expenses:										
Wages expense	$1	6	0	0	00					
Advertising expense		6	0	00						
Rent expense		5	0	0	00					
Supplies expense		2	5	0	00					
Telephone expense			4	6	00					
Electricity expense			3	9	00					
Insurance expense		1	0	0	00					
Gas and oil expense			2	8	00					
Depreciation expense—office equipment		1	1	0	00					
Miscellaneous expense			2	1	00					
Total expenses							2	7	5	4	00
Net income						$1	4	5	0	00

2.

Juanita's Consulting										
Statement of Owner's Equity										
For Month Ended June 30, 20--										

Juanita Alvarez, capital, June 1, 20--						$7	0	0	0	00
Net income for June	$1	4	5	0	00					
Less withdrawals for June		8	0	0	00					
Increase in capital							6	5	0	00
Juanita Alvarez, capital, June 30, 20--						$7	6	5	0	00

Problem 6-7B (Concluded)

3.

Juanita's Consulting

Balance Sheet

June 30, 20--

Assets			
Current assets:			
Cash	$5 2 8 5 00		
Accounts receivable	1 0 7 5 00		
Supplies	5 0 0 00		
Prepaid insurance	4 0 0 00		
Total current assets			$7 2 6 0 00
Property, plant, and equipment:			
Office equipment	$2 2 0 0 00		
Less accumulated depreciation	1 1 0 00		2 0 9 0 00
Total assets			$9 3 5 0 00
Liabilities			
Current liabilities:			
Accounts payable	$1 5 0 0 00		
Wages payable	2 0 0 00		
Total current liabilities			$1 7 0 0 00
Owner's Equity			
Juanita Alvarez, capital			7 6 5 0 00
Total liabilities and owner's equity			$9 3 5 0 00

Problem 6-8B

Minta's Editorial Services

Statement of Owner's Equity

For Month Ended January 31, 20--

Minta Berry, capital, January 1, 20--		$3 6 0 0 00
Investments during January		2 9 0 0 00
Total investment		$6 5 0 0 00
Net income for January	$5 1 7 5 00	
Less withdrawals for January	1 7 0 0 00	
Increase in capital		3 4 7 5 00
Minta Berry, capital, January 31, 20--		$9 9 7 5 00

Problem 6-9B

1.

GENERAL JOURNAL

PAGE 10

	DATE		DESCRIPTION	POST. REF.	DEBIT	CREDIT	
1			**Adjusting Entries**				1
2	20-- June	30	Supplies Expense	523	2 5 0 00		2
3			Supplies	141		2 5 0 00	3
4							4
5		30	Insurance Expense	535	1 0 0 00		5
6			Prepaid Insurance	145		1 0 0 00	6
7							7
8		30	Wages Expense	511	2 0 0 00		8
9			Wages Payable	219		2 0 0 00	9
10							10
11		30	Depreciation Expense—Office Equipment	541	1 1 0 00		11
12			Accumulated Depreciation—Office Equipment	181.1		1 1 0 00	12
13							13
14							14
15							15
16							16
17							17
18							18

Problem 6-9B (Continued)

2.

	GENERAL JOURNAL				PAGE 11

	DATE		DESCRIPTION	POST. REF.	DEBIT	CREDIT	
1			*Closing Entries*				1
2	20-- June	30	Consulting Fees	401	4 2 0 4 00		2
3			Income Summary	313		4 2 0 4 00	3
4							4
5		30	Income Summary	313	2 7 5 4 00		5
6			Wages Expense	511		1 6 0 0 00	6
7			Advertising Expense	512		6 0 00	7
8			Rent Expense	521		5 0 0 00	8
9			Supplies Expense	523		2 5 0 00	9
10			Telephone Expense	525		4 6 00	10
11			Electricity Expense	533		3 9 00	11
12			Insurance Expense	535		1 0 0 00	12
13			Gas and Oil Expense	538		2 8 00	13
14			Depreciation Expense—Office Equipment	541		1 1 0 00	14
15			Miscellaneous Expense	549		2 1 00	15
16							16
17		30	Income Summary	313	1 4 5 0 00		17
18			Juanita Alvarez, Capital	311		1 4 5 0 00	18
19							19
20		30	Juanita Alvarez, Capital	311	8 0 0 00		20
21			Juanita Alvarez, Drawing	312		8 0 0 00	21
22							22
23							23

GENERAL LEDGER

1. and 2.

ACCOUNT   Cash   ACCOUNT NO.   101

DATE		ITEM	POST. REF.	DEBIT	CREDIT	BALANCE DEBIT	BALANCE CREDIT
20-- June	30	Balance	✓			5 2 8 5 00	

Problem 6-9B (Continued)

ACCOUNT Accounts Receivable ACCOUNT NO. 122

DATE		ITEM	POST. REF.	DEBIT	CREDIT	BALANCE DEBIT	BALANCE CREDIT
20-- June	30	Balance	✓			1 0 7 5 00	

ACCOUNT Supplies ACCOUNT NO. 141

DATE		ITEM	POST. REF.	DEBIT	CREDIT	BALANCE DEBIT	BALANCE CREDIT
20-- June	30	Balance	✓			7 5 0 00	
	30	Adjusting	J10		2 5 0 00	5 0 0 00	

ACCOUNT Prepaid Insurance ACCOUNT NO. 145

DATE		ITEM	POST. REF.	DEBIT	CREDIT	BALANCE DEBIT	BALANCE CREDIT
20-- June	30	Balance	✓			5 0 0 00	
	30	Adjusting	J10		1 0 0 00	4 0 0 00	

ACCOUNT Office Equipment ACCOUNT NO. 181

DATE		ITEM	POST. REF.	DEBIT	CREDIT	BALANCE DEBIT	BALANCE CREDIT
20-- June	30	Balance	✓			2 2 0 0 00	

ACCOUNT Accumulated Depreciation—Office Equipment ACCOUNT NO. 181.1

DATE		ITEM	POST. REF.	DEBIT	CREDIT	BALANCE DEBIT	BALANCE CREDIT
20-- June	30	Adjusting	J10		1 1 0 00		1 1 0 00

Problem 6-9B (Continued)

ACCOUNT Accounts Payable   ACCOUNT NO. 202

DATE		ITEM	POST. REF.	DEBIT	CREDIT	BALANCE DEBIT	BALANCE CREDIT
20-- June	30	Balance	✓				1 5 0 0 00

ACCOUNT Wages Payable   ACCOUNT NO. 219

DATE		ITEM	POST. REF.	DEBIT	CREDIT	BALANCE DEBIT	BALANCE CREDIT
20-- June	30	Adjusting	J10		2 0 0 00		2 0 0 00

ACCOUNT Juanita Alvarez, Capital   ACCOUNT NO. 311

DATE		ITEM	POST. REF.	DEBIT	CREDIT	BALANCE DEBIT	BALANCE CREDIT
20-- June	30	Balance	✓				7 0 0 0 00
	30	Closing	J11		1 4 5 0 00		8 4 5 0 00
	30	Closing	J11	8 0 0 00			7 6 5 0 00

ACCOUNT Juanita Alvarez, Drawing   ACCOUNT NO. 312

DATE		ITEM	POST. REF.	DEBIT	CREDIT	BALANCE DEBIT	BALANCE CREDIT
20-- June	30	Balance	✓			8 0 0 00	
	30	Closing	J11		8 0 0 00	—	—

ACCOUNT Income Summary   ACCOUNT NO. 313

DATE		ITEM	POST. REF.	DEBIT	CREDIT	BALANCE DEBIT	BALANCE CREDIT
20-- June	30	Closing	J11		4 2 0 4 00		4 2 0 4 00
	30	Closing	J11	2 7 5 4 00			1 4 5 0 00
	30	Closing	J11	1 4 5 0 00		—	—

Problem 6-9B (Continued)

ACCOUNT   Consulting Fees   ACCOUNT NO.   401

DATE		ITEM	POST. REF.	DEBIT	CREDIT	BALANCE DEBIT	BALANCE CREDIT
20-- June	30	Balance	✓				4 2 0 4 00
	30	*Closing*	*J11*	4 2 0 4 00			

ACCOUNT   Wages Expense   ACCOUNT NO.   511

DATE		ITEM	POST. REF.	DEBIT	CREDIT	BALANCE DEBIT	BALANCE CREDIT
20-- June	30	Balance	✓			1 4 0 0 00	
	30	*Adjusting*	*J10*	2 0 0 00		1 6 0 0 00	
	30	*Closing*	*J11*		1 6 0 0 00		

ACCOUNT   Advertising Expense   ACCOUNT NO.   512

DATE		ITEM	POST. REF.	DEBIT	CREDIT	BALANCE DEBIT	BALANCE CREDIT
20-- June	30	Balance	✓			6 0 00	
	30	*Closing*	*J11*		6 0 00		

ACCOUNT   Rent Expense   ACCOUNT NO.   521

DATE		ITEM	POST. REF.	DEBIT	CREDIT	BALANCE DEBIT	BALANCE CREDIT
20-- June	30	Balance	✓			5 0 0 00	
	30	*Closing*	*J11*		5 0 0 00		

ACCOUNT   Supplies Expense   ACCOUNT NO.   523

DATE		ITEM	POST. REF.	DEBIT	CREDIT	BALANCE DEBIT	BALANCE CREDIT
20-- June	30	*Adjusting*	*J10*	2 5 0 00		2 5 0 00	
	30	*Closing*	*J11*		2 5 0 00		

Problem 6-9B (Continued)

ACCOUNT   Telephone Expense   ACCOUNT NO.   525

DATE		ITEM	POST. REF.	DEBIT	CREDIT	BALANCE	
						DEBIT	CREDIT
20-- June	30	Balance	✓			4 6 00	
	30	Closing	J11		4 6 00		

ACCOUNT   Electricity Expense   ACCOUNT NO.   533

DATE		ITEM	POST. REF.	DEBIT	CREDIT	BALANCE	
						DEBIT	CREDIT
20-- June	30	Balance	✓			3 9 00	
	30	Closing	J11		3 9 00		

ACCOUNT   Insurance Expense   ACCOUNT NO.   535

DATE		ITEM	POST. REF.	DEBIT	CREDIT	BALANCE	
						DEBIT	CREDIT
20-- June	30	Adjusting	J10	1 0 0 00		1 0 0 00	
	30	Closing	J11		1 0 0 00		

ACCOUNT   Gas and Oil Expense   ACCOUNT NO.   538

DATE		ITEM	POST. REF.	DEBIT	CREDIT	BALANCE	
						DEBIT	CREDIT
20-- June	30	Balance	✓			2 8 00	
	30	Closing	J11		2 8 00		

ACCOUNT   Depreciation Expense—Office Equipment   ACCOUNT NO.   541

DATE		ITEM	POST. REF.	DEBIT	CREDIT	BALANCE	
						DEBIT	CREDIT
20-- June	30	Adjusting	J10	1 1 0 00		1 1 0 00	
	30	Closing	J11		1 1 0 00		

Problem 6-9B (Concluded)

ACCOUNT Miscellaneous Expense   ACCOUNT NO. 549

DATE		ITEM	POST. REF.	DEBIT	CREDIT	BALANCE DEBIT	BALANCE CREDIT
20-- June	30	Balance	✓			2 1 00	
	30	Closing	J11		2 1 00		

3.

Juanita's Consulting

Post-Closing Trial Balance

June 30, 20--

ACCOUNT	ACCT. NO.	DEBIT BALANCE	CREDIT BALANCE
Cash	101	5 2 8 5 00	
Accounts Receivable	122	1 0 7 5 00	
Supplies	141	5 0 0 00	
Prepaid Insurance	145	4 0 0 00	
Office Equipment	181	2 2 0 0 00	
Accumulated Depreciation—Office Equipment	181.1		1 1 0 00
Accounts Payable	202		1 5 0 0 00
Wages Payable	219		2 0 0 00
Juanita Alvarez, Capital	311		7 6 5 0 00
		9 4 6 0 00	9 4 6 0 00

MANAGING YOUR WRITING

The purposes of closing entries are listed below.

1. To prepare temporary accounts (revenue, expense, and drawing) for the next accounting period by giving them zero balances.

2. To transfer the balances of revenue and expense accounts to Income Summary, and then to the owner's capital account.

3. To transfer the balance of the drawing account to the owner's capital account.

Students are often concerned about when closing entries should be made. Some argue that they should be made before preparing the financial statements. Others argue that "closing the books" is the last thing done in the accounting cycle. If the financial statements are prepared from the work sheet, it does not really matter when the closing entries are made. The amounts reported in the Income Statement and Balance Sheet columns are the amounts that should be used when preparing the financial statements, *except for the owner's capital account*. The ending balance of the capital account reported on the statement of owner's equity and balance sheet should reflect the net income and withdrawals for the accounting period. Of course, revenues, expenses, and drawing will not be reflected in the capital account until the closing entries are made. Thus, when using the work sheet, the ending balance of the capital account must be computed on the statement of owner's equity and transferred to the balance sheet.

If accounting software is used, the closing entries should be made in a manner consistent with the design of the software. Generally, closing entries are made following preparation of the financial statements. This implies that accounting software follows the same approach described above. The ending balance of the owner's capital account must be computed (by the software) on the statement of owner's equity and transferred to the balance sheet.

Mastery Problem

GENERAL JOURNAL

PAGE 4

	DATE		DESCRIPTION	POST. REF.	DEBIT	CREDIT	
1			*Adjusting Entries*				1
2	20-- Dec.	31	Styling Supplies Expense		1 4 5 0 00		2
3			Styling Supplies			1 4 5 0 00	3
4							4
5		31	Insurance Expense		6 5 0 00		5
6			Prepaid Insurance			6 5 0 00	6
7							7
8		31	Wages Expense		4 0 00		8
9			Wages Payable			4 0 00	9
10							10
11		31	Depreciation Expense—Salon Equipment		9 0 0 00		11
12			Accumulated Depreciation—Salon Equipment			9 0 0 00	12
13							13
14							14
15			*Closing Entries*				15
16		31	Styling Fees		32 0 0 0 00		16
17			Income Summary			32 0 0 0 00	17
18							18
19		31	Income Summary		18 2 9 0 00		19
20			Wages Expense			8 0 4 0 00	20
21			Rent Expense			6 0 0 00	21
22			Styling Supplies Expense			1 4 5 0 00	22
23			Telephone Expense			4 5 0 00	23
24			Utilities Expense			8 0 0 00	24
25			Insurance Expense			6 5 0 00	25
26			Depreciation Expense—Salon Equipment			9 0 0 00	26
27							27
28		31	Income Summary		13 7 1 0 00		28
29			Elizabeth Soltis, Capital			13 7 1 0 00	29
30							30
31		31	Elizabeth Soltis, Capital		12 0 0 0 00		31
32			Elizabeth Soltis, Drawing			12 0 0 0 00	32
33							33
34							34
35							35
36							36

Mastery Problem (Continued)

Aunt Ibby's Styling Salon

Income Statement

For Year Ended December 31, 20--

Revenue:			
Styling fees			$32 0 0 0 00
Expenses:			
Wages expense	$8 0 4 0 00		
Rent expense	6 0 0 0 00		
Styling supplies expense	1 4 5 0 00		
Telephone expense	4 5 0 00		
Utilities expense	8 0 0 00		
Insurance expense	6 5 0 00		
Depreciation expense—salon equipment	9 0 0 00		
Total expenses			18 2 9 0 00
Net income			$13 7 1 0 00

Aunt Ibby's Styling Salon

Statement of Owner's Equity

For Year Ended December 31, 20--

Elizabeth Soltis, capital, January 1, 20--		$2 7 6 5 00
Net income for 20--	$13 7 1 0 00	
Less withdrawals for 20--	12 0 0 0 00	
Increase in capital		1 7 1 0 00
Elizabeth Soltis, capital, December 31, 20--		$4 4 7 5 00

Mastery Problem (Concluded)

Aunt Ibby's Styling Salon
Balance Sheet
December 31, 20--

Assets									
Current assets:									
Cash	$	9 4 0	00						
Styling supplies		5 0	00						
Prepaid insurance		1 5 0	00						
Total current assets				$1 1 4 0	00				
Property, plant, and equipment:									
Salon equipment	$4 5 0 0	00							
Less accumulated depreciation		9 0 0	00		3 6 0 0	00			
Total assets				$4 7 4 0	00				
Liabilities									
Current liabilities:									
Accounts payable	$	2 2 5	00						
Wages payable		4 0	00						
Total current liabilities				$	2 6 5	00			
Owner's Equity									
Elizabeth Soltis, capital					4 4 7 5	00			
Total liabilities and owner's equity				$4 7 4 0	00				

Challenge Problem

Ardery Advising
Income Statement
For Month Ended January 31, 20--

Revenue:				
Advising fees			$ 3 8 0 2 00	
Expenses:				
Wages expense	$1 8 0 0 00			
Advertising expense	4 0 0 00			
Rent expense	1 5 0 0 00			
Supplies expense	1 2 0 00			
Telephone expense	3 0 0 00			
Electricity expense	4 4 00			
Insurance expense	2 0 0 00			
Gas and oil expense	3 8 00			
Depreciation expense—office equipment	1 0 0 0 00			
Miscellaneous expense	5 0 0 00			
Total expenses			5 9 0 2 00	
Net loss			$(2 1 0 0 00)	

Ardery Advising
Statement of Owner's Equity
For Month Ended January 31, 20--

Sam Ardery, capital, January 1, 20--		$ 1 0 0 0 00	
Investments during January		1 2 0 0 00	
Total investment		$ 2 2 0 0 00	
Net loss for January	$2 1 0 0 00		
Plus withdrawals for January	8 0 0 00		
Net decrease in capital		(2 9 0 0 00)	
Sam Ardery, capital, January 31, 20--		$ (7 0 0 00)	

Challenge Problem (Concluded)

Ardery Advising

Balance Sheet

January 31, 20--

Assets				
Current assets:				
Cash	$2 4 1 2 00			
Accounts receivable	8 9 6 00			
Supplies	4 8 2 00			
Prepaid insurance	9 0 0 00			
Total current assets			$4 6 9 0 00	
Property, plant, and equipment:				
Office equipment	$3 0 0 0 00			
Less accumulated depreciation	2 0 0 0 00		1 0 0 0 00	
Total assets			$5 6 9 0 00	
Liabilities				
Current liabilities:				
Accounts payable	$2 1 9 0 00			
Wages payable	1 2 0 0 00			
Notes payable	3 0 0 0 00			
Total current liabilities			$6 3 9 0 00	
Owner's Equity				
Sam Ardery, capital			(7 0 0 00)	
Total liabilities and owner's equity			$5 6 9 0 00	

APPENDIX: STATEMENT OF CASH FLOWS

REVIEW QUESTIONS

1. The purpose of the statement of cash flows is to explain what the business did to generate cash and how the cash was used. This is done by categorizing all cash transactions into three types of activities: operating, investing, and financing.

2. **Operating activities** are related to the revenues and expenses reported on the income statement. Examples include cash received for services performed and the payment of cash for expenses.

   Investing activities are those transactions involving the purchase and sale of long-term assets, lending money, and collecting the principal on related loans. Examples include buying trucks and equipment.

   Financing activities are those transactions dealing with the exchange of cash between the business and its owners and creditors. Examples include cash received from the owner to finance the operations and cash paid to the owner as withdrawals. Financing activities also include the receipt of cash from loans and the repayment of the loans.

Exercise 6Apx-1A

a.	*Financing*	g.	*Operating*
b.	*Operating*	h.	*Operating*
c.	*Investing*	i.	*Operating*
d.	*Operating*	j.	*Financing*
e.	*Operating*	k.	*Operating*
f.	*Financing*		

Problem 6Apx-2A

Dolores Lopez, Consulting

Statement of Cash Flows

For Month Ended January 31, 20--

Cash flows from operating activities:			
Cash received from clients			$ 1 7 0 0 00
Cash paid for rent	$ (5 0 0 00)		
Cash paid for telephone	(6 5 00)		
Cash paid for wages	(1 0 0 0 00)		
Cash paid for electricity	(8 5 00)		
Total cash paid for operations		(1 6 5 0 00)	
Net cash provided by operating activities		$ 5 0 00	
Cash flows from investing activities:			
Cash paid for office equipment	$ (1 5 0 0 00)		
Net cash used for investing activities		(1 5 0 0 00)	
Cash flows from financing activities:			
Cash investment by owner	$10 0 0 0 00		
Cash withdrawal by owner	(1 0 0 00)		
Payment made on loan	(5 0 0 00)		
Net cash provided by financing activities		9 4 0 0 00	
Net increase in cash		$ 7 9 5 0 00	

Exercise 6Apx-1B

a. _Financing_   g. _Financing_

b. _Investing_   h. _Operating_

c. _Operating_   i. _Operating_

d. _Operating_   j. _Financing_

e. _Operating_   k. _Operating_

f. _Operating_

Problem 6Apx-2B

Bob Jacobs Advertising Agency
Statement of Cash Flows
For Month Ended January 31, 20--

Cash flows from operating activities:		
Cash received from clients		$ 1 3 0 0 00
Cash paid for rent	$ (4 0 0 00)	
Cash paid for telephone	(9 5 00)	
Cash paid for wages	(1 4 0 0 00)	
Cash paid for electricity	(1 0 0 00)	
Total cash paid for operations		(1 9 9 5 00)
Net cash used for operating activities		$ (6 9 5 00)
Cash flows from investing activities:		
Cash paid for office equipment	$(2 5 0 0 00)	
Net cash used for investing activities		(2 5 0 0 00)
Cash flows from financing activities:		
Cash investment by owner	$ 5 0 0 0 00	
Cash withdrawal by owner	(5 0 0 00)	
Payment made on loan	(5 0 0 00)	
Net cash provided by financing activities		4 0 0 0 00
Net increase in cash		$ 8 0 5 00

Comprehensive Problem 1: The Accounting Cycle

1.

GENERAL JOURNAL

PAGE 1

	DATE		DESCRIPTION	POST. REF.	DEBIT	CREDIT	
1	20-- Apr.	1	Cash	101	90 000 00		1
2			Bob Night, Capital	311		90 000 00	2
3			Owner's original investment				3
4							4
5		1	Prepaid Insurance	145	9 000 00		5
6			Cash	101		9 000 00	6
7			Paid insurance premium for camping				7
8			season				8
9							9
10		2	Rent Expense	521	40 000 00		10
11			Cash	101		40 000 00	11
12			Paid rent for April				12
13							13
14		2	Cash	101	35 000 00		14
15			Registration Fees	401		35 000 00	15
16			Collected registration fees				16
17							17
18		2	Fishing Boats	181	60 000 00		18
19			Accounts Payable	202		60 000 00	19
20			Purchased fishing boats on account				20
21							21
22		3	Food Supplies	144	7 000 00		22
23			Accounts Payable	202		7 000 00	23
24			Purchased food supplies on account				24
25			from Acme Super Market				25
26							26
27		5	Office Supplies	142	5 00 00		27
28			Accounts Payable	202		5 00 00	28
29			Purchased office supplies on account				29
30			from Gordon Office Supplies				30
31							31
32							32
33							33
34							34

Comprehensive Problem 1 (Continued)

GENERAL JOURNAL   PAGE 2

	DATE		DESCRIPTION	POST. REF.	DEBIT	CREDIT	
1	20-- Apr.	7	Cash	101	38 6 0 0 00		1
2			Registration Fees	401		38 6 0 0 00	2
3			Collected registration fees				3
4							4
5		10	Food Supplies	144	8 2 0 0 00		5
6			Accounts Payable	202		8 2 0 0 00	6
7			Purchased food supplies on account				7
8			from Acme Super Market				8
9							9
10		10	Wages Expense	511	10 0 0 0 00		10
11			Cash	101		10 0 0 0 00	11
12			Paid wages to guides				12
13							13
14		14	Cash	101	30 5 0 0 00		14
15			Registration Fees	401		30 5 0 0 00	15
16			Collected registration fees				16
17							17
18		16	Food Supplies	144	9 0 0 0 00		18
19			Accounts Payable	202		9 0 0 0 00	19
20			Purchased food supplies on account				20
21			from Acme Super Market				21
22							22
23		17	Wages Expense	511	10 0 0 0 00		23
24			Cash	101		10 0 0 0 00	24
25			Paid wages to guides				25
26							26
27		18	Postage Expense	536	1 5 0 00		27
28			Cash	101		1 5 0 00	28
29			Paid postage				29
30							30
31							31
32							32
33							33
34							34
35							35

Comprehensive Problem 1 (Continued)

GENERAL JOURNAL

PAGE 3

	DATE		DESCRIPTION	POST. REF.	DEBIT	CREDIT	
1	20-- Apr.	21	Cash	101	35 6 0 0 00		1
2			Registration Fees	401		35 6 0 0 00	2
3			Collected registration fees				3
4							4
5		24	Food Supplies	144	8 5 0 0 00		5
6			Accounts Payable	202		8 5 0 0 00	6
7			Purchased food supplies on account				7
8			from Acme Super Market				8
9							9
10		24	Wages Expense	511	10 0 0 0 00		10
11			Cash	101		10 0 0 0 00	11
12			Paid wages to guides				12
13							13
14		28	Cash	101	32 0 0 0 00		14
15			Registration Fees	401		32 0 0 0 00	15
16			Collected registration fees				16
17							17
18		29	Wages Expense	511	10 0 0 0 00		18
19			Cash	101		10 0 0 0 00	19
20			Paid wages to guides				20
21							21
22		30	Food Supplies	144	6 0 0 0 00		22
23			Accounts Payable	202		6 0 0 0 00	23
24			Purchased food supplies on account				24
25			from Acme Super Market				25
26							26
27		30	Accounts Payable	202	32 7 0 0 00		27
28			Cash	101		32 7 0 0 00	28
29			Made payment on account to				29
30			Acme Super Market				30
31							31
32							32
33							33
34							34
35							35

Comprehensive Problem 1 (Continued)

GENERAL JOURNAL

PAGE 4

	DATE		DESCRIPTION	POST. REF.	DEBIT	CREDIT	
1	20-- Apr.	30	Utilities Expense	533	2 0 0 0 00		1
2			Cash	101		2 0 0 0 00	2
3			Paid utility bill				3
4							4
5		30	Telephone Expense	525	1 2 0 0 00		5
6			Cash	101		1 2 0 0 00	6
7			Paid phone bill				7
8							8
9		30	Bob Night, Drawing	312	6 0 0 0 00		9
10			Cash	101		6 0 0 0 00	10
11			Owner's withdrawal				11

2., 6., and 11.

GENERAL LEDGER

ACCOUNT   Cash   ACCOUNT NO.   101

DATE		ITEM	POST. REF.	DEBIT	CREDIT	BALANCE DEBIT	BALANCE CREDIT
20-- Apr.	1		J1	90 0 0 0 00		90 0 0 0 00	
	1		J1		9 0 0 0 00	81 0 0 0 00	
	2		J1		40 0 0 0 00	41 0 0 0 00	
	2		J1	35 0 0 0 00		76 0 0 0 00	
	7		J2	38 6 0 0 00		114 6 0 0 00	
	10		J2		10 0 0 0 00	104 6 0 0 00	
	14		J2	30 5 0 0 00		135 1 0 0 00	
	17		J2		10 0 0 0 00	125 1 0 0 00	
	18		J2		1 5 0 00	124 9 5 0 00	
	21		J3	35 6 0 0 00		160 5 5 0 00	
	24		J3		10 0 0 0 00	150 5 5 0 00	
	28		J3	32 0 0 0 00		182 5 5 0 00	
	29		J3		10 0 0 0 00	172 5 5 0 00	
	30		J3		32 7 0 0 00	139 8 5 0 00	
	30		J4		2 0 0 0 00	137 8 5 0 00	
	30		J4		1 2 0 0 00	136 6 5 0 00	
	30		J4		6 0 0 0 00	130 6 5 0 00	

Comprehensive Problem 1 (Continued)

ACCOUNT   Office Supplies   ACCOUNT NO.   142

DATE		ITEM	POST. REF.	DEBIT	CREDIT	BALANCE DEBIT	BALANCE CREDIT
20-- Apr.	5		J1	5 0 0 00		5 0 0 00	
	30	Adjusting	J5		4 0 0 00	1 0 0 00	

ACCOUNT   Food Supplies   ACCOUNT NO.   144

DATE		ITEM	POST. REF.	DEBIT	CREDIT	BALANCE DEBIT	BALANCE CREDIT
20-- Apr.	3		J1	7 0 0 0 00		7 0 0 0 00	
	10		J2	8 2 0 0 00		15 2 0 0 00	
	16		J2	9 0 0 0 00		24 2 0 0 00	
	24		J3	8 5 0 0 00		32 7 0 0 00	
	30		J3	6 0 0 0 00		38 7 0 0 00	
	30	Adjusting	J5		30 7 0 0 00	8 0 0 0 00	

ACCOUNT   Prepaid Insurance   ACCOUNT NO.   145

DATE		ITEM	POST. REF.	DEBIT	CREDIT	BALANCE DEBIT	BALANCE CREDIT
20-- Apr.	1		J1	9 0 0 0 00		9 0 0 0 00	
	30	Adjusting	J5		1 5 0 0 00	7 5 0 0 00	

ACCOUNT   Fishing Boats   ACCOUNT NO.   181

DATE		ITEM	POST. REF.	DEBIT	CREDIT	BALANCE DEBIT	BALANCE CREDIT
20-- Apr.	2		J1	60 0 0 0 00		60 0 0 0 00	

Comprehensive Problem 1 (Continued)

ACCOUNT Accumulated Depreciation—Fishing Boats   ACCOUNT NO. 181.1

DATE	ITEM	POST. REF.	DEBIT	CREDIT	BALANCE DEBIT	BALANCE CREDIT
20-- Apr. 30	Adjusting	J5		1 0 0 0 00		1 0 0 0 00

ACCOUNT Accounts Payable   ACCOUNT NO. 202

DATE	ITEM	POST. REF.	DEBIT	CREDIT	BALANCE DEBIT	BALANCE CREDIT
20-- Apr. 2		J1		60 0 0 0 00		60 0 0 0 00
3		J1		7 0 0 0 00		67 0 0 0 00
5		J1		5 0 0 00		67 5 0 0 00
10		J2		8 2 0 0 00		75 7 0 0 00
16		J2		9 0 0 0 00		84 7 0 0 00
24		J3		8 5 0 0 00		93 2 0 0 00
30		J3		6 0 0 0 00		99 2 0 0 00
30		J3	32 7 0 0 00			66 5 0 0 00

ACCOUNT Wages Payable   ACCOUNT NO. 219

DATE	ITEM	POST. REF.	DEBIT	CREDIT	BALANCE DEBIT	BALANCE CREDIT
20-- Apr. 30	Adjusting	J5		5 0 0 00		5 0 0 00

ACCOUNT Bob Night, Capital   ACCOUNT NO. 311

DATE	ITEM	POST. REF.	DEBIT	CREDIT	BALANCE DEBIT	BALANCE CREDIT
20-- Apr. 1		J1		90 0 0 0 00		90 0 0 0 00
30	Closing	J6		54 2 5 0 00		144 2 5 0 00
30	Closing	J6	6 0 0 0 00			138 2 5 0 00

Comprehensive Problem 1 (Continued)

ACCOUNT Bob Night, Drawing   ACCOUNT NO. 312

DATE		ITEM	POST. REF.	DEBIT	CREDIT	BALANCE DEBIT	BALANCE CREDIT
20--Apr.	30		J4	6 0 0 0 00		6 0 0 0 00	
	30	Closing	J6		6 0 0 0 00	——	——

ACCOUNT Income Summary   ACCOUNT NO. 313

DATE		ITEM	POST. REF.	DEBIT	CREDIT	BALANCE DEBIT	BALANCE CREDIT
20--Apr.	30	Closing	J5		171 7 0 0 00		171 7 0 0 00
	30	Closing	J5	117 4 5 0 00			54 2 5 0 00
	30	Closing	J6	54 2 5 0 00		——	——

ACCOUNT Registration Fees   ACCOUNT NO. 401

DATE		ITEM	POST. REF.	DEBIT	CREDIT	BALANCE DEBIT	BALANCE CREDIT
20--Apr.	2		J1		35 0 0 0 00		35 0 0 0 00
	7		J2		38 6 0 0 00		73 6 0 0 00
	14		J2		30 5 0 0 00		104 1 0 0 00
	21		J3		35 6 0 0 00		139 7 0 0 00
	28		J3		32 0 0 0 00		171 7 0 0 00
	30	Closing	J5	171 7 0 0 00		——	——

Comprehensive Problem 1 (Continued)

ACCOUNT   Wages Expense   ACCOUNT NO.   511

DATE		ITEM	POST. REF.	DEBIT	CREDIT	BALANCE DEBIT	BALANCE CREDIT
20-- Apr.	10		J2	10 0 0 0 00		10 0 0 0 00	
	17		J2	10 0 0 0 00		20 0 0 0 00	
	24		J3	10 0 0 0 00		30 0 0 0 00	
	29		J3	10 0 0 0 00		40 0 0 0 00	
	30	Adjusting	J5	5 0 0 00		40 5 0 0 00	
	30	Closing	J5		40 5 0 0 00	——	——

ACCOUNT   Rent Expense   ACCOUNT NO.   521

DATE		ITEM	POST. REF.	DEBIT	CREDIT	BALANCE DEBIT	BALANCE CREDIT
20-- Apr.	2		J1	40 0 0 0 00		40 0 0 0 00	
	30	Closing	J5		40 0 0 0 00	——	——

ACCOUNT   Office Supplies Expense   ACCOUNT NO.   523

DATE		ITEM	POST. REF.	DEBIT	CREDIT	BALANCE DEBIT	BALANCE CREDIT
20-- Apr.	30	Adjusting	J5	4 0 0 00		4 0 0 00	
	30	Closing	J5		4 0 0 00	——	——

ACCOUNT   Food Supplies Expense   ACCOUNT NO.   524

DATE		ITEM	POST. REF.	DEBIT	CREDIT	BALANCE DEBIT	BALANCE CREDIT
20-- Apr.	30	Adjusting	J5	30 7 0 0 00		30 7 0 0 00	
	30	Closing	J5		30 7 0 0 00	——	——

Comprehensive Problem 1 (Continued)

ACCOUNT   Telephone Expense   ACCOUNT NO.   525

DATE		ITEM	POST. REF.	DEBIT	CREDIT	BALANCE DEBIT	BALANCE CREDIT
20-- Apr.	30		J4	1 2 0 0 00		1 2 0 0 00	
	30	Closing	J5		1 2 0 0 00	—	—

ACCOUNT   Utilities Expense   ACCOUNT NO.   533

DATE		ITEM	POST. REF.	DEBIT	CREDIT	BALANCE DEBIT	BALANCE CREDIT
20-- Apr.	30		J4	2 0 0 0 00		2 0 0 0 00	
	30	Closing	J5		2 0 0 0 00	—	—

ACCOUNT   Insurance Expense   ACCOUNT NO.   535

DATE		ITEM	POST. REF.	DEBIT	CREDIT	BALANCE DEBIT	BALANCE CREDIT
20-- Apr.	30	Adjusting	J5	1 5 0 0 00		1 5 0 0 00	
	30	Closing	J5		1 5 0 0 00	—	—

ACCOUNT   Postage Expense   ACCOUNT NO.   536

DATE		ITEM	POST. REF.	DEBIT	CREDIT	BALANCE DEBIT	BALANCE CREDIT
20-- Apr.	18		J2	1 5 0 00		1 5 0 00	
	30	Closing	J5		1 5 0 00	—	—

ACCOUNT   Depreciation Expense—Fishing Boats   ACCOUNT NO.   542

DATE		ITEM	POST. REF.	DEBIT	CREDIT	BALANCE DEBIT	BALANCE CREDIT
20-- Apr.	30	Adjusting	J5	1 0 0 0 00		1 0 0 0 00	
	30	Closing	J5		1 0 0 0 00	—	—

Comprehensive Problem 1 (Continued)
3. and 4.

The General's Favorite

Work

For the Month Ended

	ACCOUNT TITLE	TRIAL BALANCE DEBIT	TRIAL BALANCE CREDIT	ADJUSTMENTS DEBIT	ADJUSTMENTS CREDIT
1	Cash	130 6 5 0 00			
2	Office Supplies	5 0 0 00			(a) 4 0 0 00
3	Food Supplies	38 7 0 0 00			(b)30 7 0 0 00
4	Prepaid Insurance	9 0 0 0 00			(c) 1 5 0 0 00
5	Fishing Boats	60 0 0 0 00			
6	Accum. Depr.—Fishing Boats				(d) 1 0 0 0 00
7	Accounts Payable		66 5 0 0 00		
8	Wages Payable				(e) 5 0 0 00
9	Bob Night, Capital		90 0 0 0 00		
10	Bob Night, Drawing	6 0 0 0 00			
11	Registration Fees		171 7 0 0 00		
12	Wages Expense	40 0 0 0 00		(e) 5 0 0 00	
13	Rent Expense	40 0 0 0 00			
14	Office Supplies Expense			(a) 4 0 0 00	
15	Food Supplies Expense			(b)30 7 0 0 00	
16	Telephone Expense	1 2 0 0 00			
17	Utilities Expense	2 0 0 0 00			
18	Insurance Expense			(c) 1 5 0 0 00	
19	Postage Expense	1 5 0 00			
20	Depr. Exp.—Fishing Boats			(d) 1 0 0 0 00	
21		328 2 0 0 00	328 2 0 0 00	34 1 0 0 00	34 1 0 0 00
22	Net Income				
23					
24					
25					
26					
27					
28					
29					
30					
31					

Comprehensive Problem 1 (Continued)

Fishing Hole

Sheet

April 30, 20--

ADJUSTED TRIAL BALANCE		INCOME STATEMENT		BALANCE SHEET		
DEBIT	CREDIT	DEBIT	CREDIT	DEBIT	CREDIT	
130 6 5 0 00				130 6 5 0 00		1
1 0 0 00				1 0 0 00		2
8 0 0 0 00				8 0 0 0 00		3
7 5 0 0 00				7 5 0 0 00		4
60 0 0 0 00				60 0 0 0 00		5
	1 0 0 0 00				1 0 0 0 00	6
	66 5 0 0 00				66 5 0 0 00	7
	5 0 0 00				5 0 0 00	8
	90 0 0 0 00				90 0 0 0 00	9
6 0 0 0 00				6 0 0 0 00		10
	171 7 0 0 00		171 7 0 0 00			11
40 5 0 0 00		40 5 0 0 00				12
40 0 0 0 00		40 0 0 0 00				13
4 0 0 00		4 0 0 00				14
30 7 0 0 00		30 7 0 0 00				15
1 2 0 0 00		1 2 0 0 00				16
2 0 0 0 00		2 0 0 0 00				17
1 5 0 0 00		1 5 0 0 00				18
1 5 0 00		1 5 0 00				19
1 0 0 0 00		1 0 0 0 00				20
329 7 0 0 00	329 7 0 0 00	117 4 5 0 00	171 7 0 0 00	212 2 5 0 00	158 0 0 0 00	21
		54 2 5 0 00			54 2 5 0 00	22
		171 7 0 0 00	171 7 0 0 00	212 2 5 0 00	212 2 5 0 00	23
						24
						25
						26
						27
						28
						29
						30
						31

Comprehensive Problem 1 (Continued)

7.

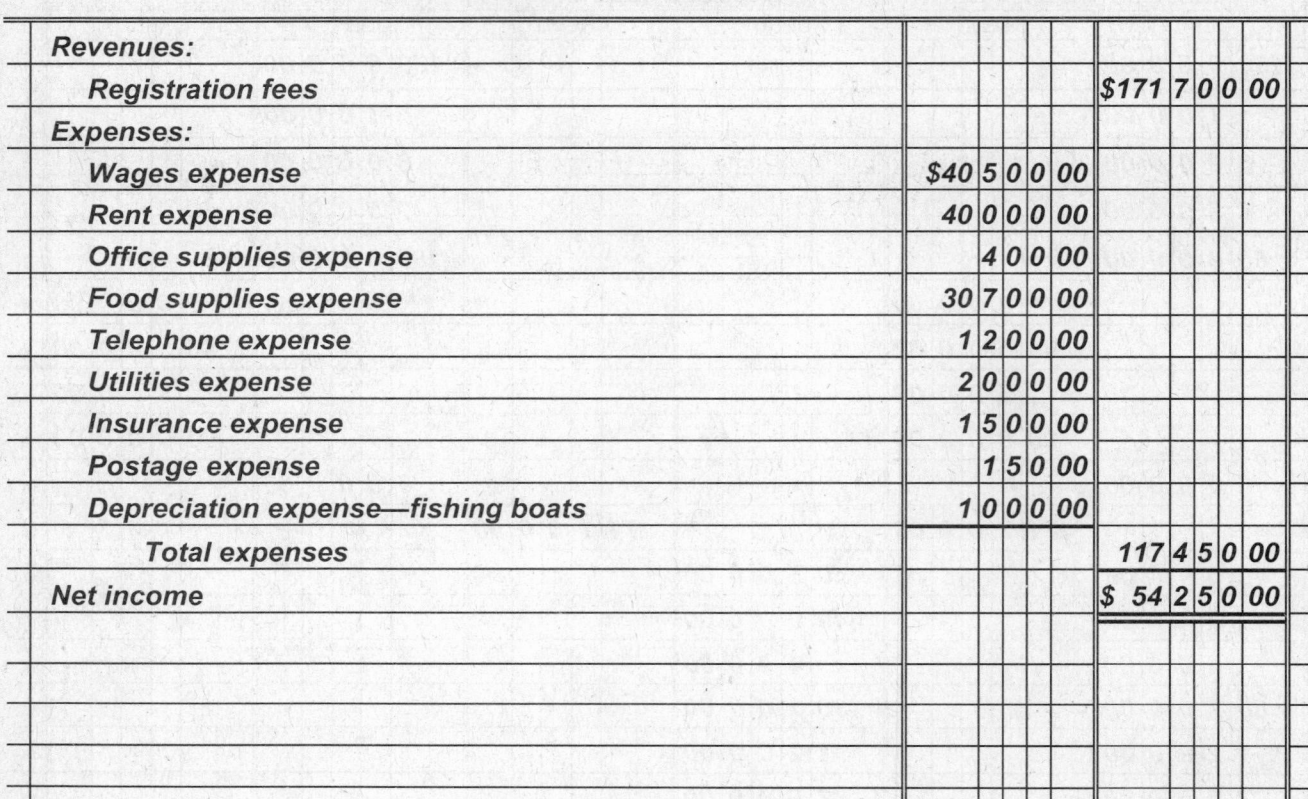

The General's Favorite Fishing Hole
Income Statement
For Month Ended April 30, 20--

Revenues:			
Registration fees			$171 700 00
Expenses:			
Wages expense	$40 500 00		
Rent expense	40 000 00		
Office supplies expense	400 00		
Food supplies expense	30 700 00		
Telephone expense	1 200 00		
Utilities expense	2 000 00		
Insurance expense	1 500 00		
Postage expense	150 00		
Depreciation expense—fishing boats	1 000 00		
Total expenses			117 450 00
Net income			$ 54 250 00

8.

The General's Favorite Fishing Hole
Statement of Owner's Equity
For Month Ended April 30, 20--

Bob Night, capital, April 1, 20--			$
Investments during April			90 000 00
Total investment			$ 90 000 00
Net income for April	$54 250 00		
Less withdrawals for April	6 000 00		
Increase in capital			48 250 00
Bob Night, capital, April 30, 20--			$138 250 00

Comprehensive Problem 1 (Continued)

9.

The General's Favorite Fishing Hole															
Balance Sheet															
April 30, 20--															
Assets															
Current assets:															
Cash	$130	6	5	0	00										
Office supplies			1	0	0	00									
Food supplies		8	0	0	00										
Prepaid insurance		7	5	0	00										
Total current assets						$146	2	5	0	00					
Property, plant, and equipment:															
Fishing boats	$ 60	0	0	0	00										
Less accumulated depreciation		1	0	0	0	00	59	0	0	0	00				
Total assets						$205	2	5	0	00					
Liabilities															
Current liabilities:															
Accounts payable	$ 66	5	0	0	00										
Wages payable		5	0	0	00										
Total current liabilities						$ 67	0	0	0	00					
Owner's Equity															
Bob Night, capital						138	2	5	0	00					
Total liabilities and owner's equity						$205	2	5	0	00					

Comprehensive Problem 1 (Continued)

5. and 10.

GENERAL JOURNAL   PAGE 5

	DATE		DESCRIPTION	POST. REF.	DEBIT	CREDIT	
1	20-- Apr.		*Adjusting Entries*				1
2		30	**Office Supplies Expense**	523	4 0 0 00		2
3			**Office Supplies**	142		4 0 0 00	3
4							4
5		30	**Food Supplies Expense**	524	30 7 0 0 00		5
6			**Food Supplies**	144		30 7 0 0 00	6
7							7
8		30	**Insurance Expense**	535	1 5 0 0 00		8
9			**Prepaid Insurance**	145		1 5 0 0 00	9
10							10
11		30	**Depreciation Expense—Fishing Boats**	542	1 0 0 0 00		11
12			**Accum. Depreciation—Fishing Boats**	181.1		1 0 0 0 00	12
13							13
14		30	**Wages Expense**	511	5 0 0 00		14
15			**Wages Payable**	219		5 0 0 00	15
16							16
17			*Closing Entries*				17
18		30	**Registration Fees**	401	171 7 0 0 00		18
19			**Income Summary**	313		171 7 0 0 00	19
20							20
21		30	**Income Summary**	313	117 4 5 0 00		21
22			**Wages Expense**	511		40 5 0 0 00	22
23			**Rent Expense**	521		40 0 0 0 00	23
24			**Office Supplies Expense**	523		4 0 0 00	24
25			**Food Supplies Expense**	524		30 7 0 0 00	25
26			**Telephone Expense**	525		1 2 0 0 00	26
27			**Utilities Expense**	533		2 0 0 0 00	27
28			**Insurance Expense**	535		1 5 0 0 00	28
29			**Postage Expense**	536		1 5 0 00	29
30			**Depreciation Expense—Fishing Boats**	542		1 0 0 0 00	30
31							31
32							32
33							33
34							34
35							35

Comprehensive Problem 1 (Concluded)

GENERAL JOURNAL   PAGE 6

	DATE		DESCRIPTION	POST. REF.	DEBIT	CREDIT	
1	20-- Apr.	30	Income Summary	313	54 2 5 0 00		1
2			Bob Night, Capital	311		54 2 5 0 00	2
3							3
4		30	Bob Night, Capital	311	6 0 0 0 00		4
5			Bob Night, Drawing	312		6 0 0 0 00	5
6							6
7							7
8							8
9							9

12.

The General's Favorite Fishing Hole
Post-Closing Trial Balance
April 30, 20--

ACCOUNT	ACCT. NO.	DEBIT BALANCE	CREDIT BALANCE
Cash	101	130 6 5 0 00	
Office Supplies	142	1 0 0 00	
Food Supplies	144	8 0 0 0 00	
Prepaid Insurance	145	7 5 0 0 00	
Fishing Boats	181	60 0 0 0 00	
Accumulated Depreciation—Fishing Boats	181.1		1 0 0 0 00
Accounts Payable	202		66 5 0 0 00
Wages Payable	219		5 0 0 00
Bob Night, Capital	311		138 2 5 0 00
		206 2 5 0 00	206 2 5 0 00

Comprehensive Problem 1, Period 2: The Accounting Cycle

1.

GENERAL JOURNAL

PAGE 5

	DATE		DESCRIPTION	POST. REF.	DEBIT	CREDIT	
1	20-- May	1	Cash	101	2 0 0 00		1
2			Vending Commission Revenue	404		2 0 0 00	2
3							3
4		2	Surround Sound System	182	3 6 0 0 00		4
5			Cash	101		3 6 0 0 00	5
6							6
7		2	Big Screen TV	183	8 0 0 00		7
8			Cash	101		8 0 0 00	8
9							9
10		2	Satellite Programming Expense	546	1 2 5 00		10
11			Cash	101		1 2 5 00	11
12							12
13		3	Accounts Payable	202	1 0 0 00		13
14			Office Supplies	142		1 0 0 00	14
15							15
16		3	Cash	101	52 7 0 0 00		16
17			Registration Fees	401		52 7 0 0 00	17
18							18
19		3	Rent Expense	521	40 0 0 00		19
20			Cash	101		40 0 0 00	20
21							21
22		3	Cash	101	600 0 0 00		22
23			Bob Night, Capital	311		600 0 0 00	23
24							24
25		4	Accounts Payable	202	4 0 0 00		25
26			Cash	101		4 0 0 00	26
27							27
28		4	Land	161	100 0 0 00		28
29			Buildings	171	530 0 0 00		29
30			Fishing Boats	181	9 0 0 00		30
31			Cash	101		639 0 0 00	31
32							32
33							33
34							34
35							35

Comprehensive Problem 1, Period 2 (Continued)

GENERAL JOURNAL   PAGE 6

	DATE		DESCRIPTION	POST. REF.	DEBIT	CREDIT	
1	20-- May	5	Insurance Expense	535	1 0 0 0 00		1
2			Cash	101		1 0 0 0 00	2
3							3
4		5	Food Supplies	144	22 9 5 0 00		4
5			Accounts Payable	202		22 9 5 0 00	5
6							6
7		5	Office Supplies	142	1 2 0 0 00		7
8			Accounts Payable	202		1 2 0 0 00	8
9							9
10		7	Prepaid Subscriptions	146	1 2 0 00		10
11			Cash	101		1 2 0 00	11
12							12
13		10	Cash	101	62 7 5 0 00		13
14			Registration Fees	401		62 7 5 0 00	14
15							15
16		13	Wages Expense	511	29 5 0 0 00		16
17			Wages Payable	219	5 0 0 00		17
18			Cash	101		30 0 0 0 00	18
19							19
20		14	Registration Fees	401	1 0 0 0 00		20
21			Cash	101		1 0 0 0 00	21
22							22
23		17	Cash	101	63 0 0 0 00		23
24			Registration Fees	401		63 0 0 0 00	24
25							25
26		19	Food Supplies	144	18 4 0 0 00		26
27			Accounts Payable	202		18 4 0 0 00	27
28							28
29		21	Cash	101	63 4 0 0 00		29
30			Registration Fees	401		63 4 0 0 00	30
31							31
32		23	Advertising Expense	512	2 5 0 0 00		32
33			Cash	101		2 5 0 0 00	33
34							34
35		25	Repair Expense	537	8 5 0 00		35
36			Cash	101		8 5 0 00	36
37							37
38		27	Wages Expense	511	30 0 0 0 00		38
39			Cash	101		30 0 0 0 00	39
40							40
41		28	Advertising Expense	512	1 8 0 0 00		41
42			Cash	101		1 8 0 0 00	42

Comprehensive Problem 1, Period 2 (Continued)

GENERAL JOURNAL

	DATE		DESCRIPTION	POST. REF.	DEBIT	CREDIT	
1	20-- May	29	Food Supplies	144	14 3 2 5 00		1
2			Accounts Payable	202		14 3 2 5 00	2
3							3
4		30	Utilities Expense	533	3 3 0 0 00		4
5			Cash	101		3 3 0 0 00	5
6							6
7		30	Telephone Expense	525	1 8 0 0 00		7
8			Cash	101		1 8 0 0 00	8
9							9
10		30	Accounts Payable	202	47 3 5 0 00		10
11			Cash	101		47 3 5 0 00	11
12							12
13		31	Bob Night, Drawing	312	7 5 0 0 00		13
14			Cash	101		7 5 0 0 00	14
15							15
16							16
17							17
18							18
19							19
20							20
21							21
22							22
23							23
24							24
25							25
26							26
27							27
28							28
29							29
30							30
31							31
32							32
33							33
34							34

Comprehensive Problem 1, Period 2 (Continued)

2., 6., and 11.

GENERAL LEDGER

ACCOUNT Cash   ACCOUNT NO. 101

DATE		ITEM	POST. REF.	DEBIT	CREDIT	BALANCE DEBIT	BALANCE CREDIT
20-- Apr.	30	Balance	✓			130 6 5 0 00	
May	1		J5	2 0 0 00		130 8 5 0 00	
	2		J5		3 6 0 0 00	127 2 5 0 00	
	2		J5		8 0 0 0 00	119 2 5 0 00	
	2		J5		1 2 5 00	119 1 2 5 00	
	3		J5	52 7 0 0 00		171 8 2 5 00	
	3		J5		40 0 0 0 00	131 8 2 5 00	
	3		J5	600 0 0 0 00		731 8 2 5 00	
	4		J5		4 0 0 00	731 4 2 5 00	
	4		J5		639 0 0 0 00	92 4 2 5 00	
	5		J6		1 0 0 0 00	91 4 2 5 00	
	7		J6		1 2 0 00	91 3 0 5 00	
	10		J6	62 7 5 0 00		154 0 5 5 00	
	13		J6		30 0 0 0 00	124 0 5 5 00	
	14		J6		1 0 0 0 00	123 0 5 5 00	
	17		J6	63 0 0 0 00		186 0 5 5 00	
	21		J6	63 4 0 0 00		249 4 5 5 00	
	23		J6		2 5 0 0 00	246 9 5 5 00	
	25		J6		8 5 0 00	246 1 0 5 00	
	27		J6		30 0 0 0 00	216 1 0 5 00	
	28		J6		1 8 0 0 00	214 3 0 5 00	
	30		J7		3 3 0 0 00	211 0 0 5 00	
	30		J7		1 8 0 0 00	209 2 0 5 00	
	30		J7		47 3 5 0 00	161 8 5 5 00	
	31		J7		7 5 0 0 00	154 3 5 5 00	

ACCOUNT Accounts Receivable   ACCOUNT NO. 122

DATE		ITEM	POST. REF.	DEBIT	CREDIT	BALANCE DEBIT	BALANCE CREDIT
20-- May	31	Adjusting	J8	3 0 00		3 0 00	

Comprehensive Problem 1, Period 2 (Continued)

ACCOUNT **Office Supplies** ACCOUNT NO. **142**

DATE		ITEM	POST. REF.	DEBIT	CREDIT	BALANCE DEBIT	BALANCE CREDIT
20-- Apr.	30	Balance	✓			1 0 0 00	
May	3		J5		1 0 0 00	—	
	5		J6	1 2 0 0 00		1 2 0 0 00	
	31	Adjusting	J8		1 0 5 0 00	1 5 0 00	

ACCOUNT **Food Supplies** ACCOUNT NO. **144**

DATE		ITEM	POST. REF.	DEBIT	CREDIT	BALANCE DEBIT	BALANCE CREDIT
20-- Apr.	30	Balance	✓			8 0 0 0 00	
May	5		J6	22 9 5 0 00		30 9 5 0 00	
	19		J6	18 4 0 0 00		49 3 5 0 00	
	29		J7	14 3 2 5 00		63 6 7 5 00	
	31	Adjusting	J8		57 7 5 0 00	5 9 2 5 00	

ACCOUNT **Prepaid Insurance** ACCOUNT NO. **145**

DATE		ITEM	POST. REF.	DEBIT	CREDIT	BALANCE DEBIT	BALANCE CREDIT
20-- Apr.	30	Balance	✓			7 5 0 0 00	
May	31	Adjusting	J8		1 5 0 0 00	6 0 0 0 00	

ACCOUNT **Prepaid Subscriptions** ACCOUNT NO. **146**

DATE		ITEM	POST. REF.	DEBIT	CREDIT	BALANCE DEBIT	BALANCE CREDIT
20-- May	7		J6	1 2 0 00		1 2 0 00	
	31	Adjusting	J8		1 0 00	1 1 0 00	

Comprehensive Problem 1, Period 2 (Continued)

ACCOUNT Land   ACCOUNT NO. 161

DATE		ITEM	POST. REF.	DEBIT	CREDIT	BALANCE DEBIT	BALANCE CREDIT
20-- May	4		J5	100 0 0 0 00		100 0 0 0 00	

ACCOUNT Buildings   ACCOUNT NO. 171

DATE		ITEM	POST. REF.	DEBIT	CREDIT	BALANCE DEBIT	BALANCE CREDIT
20-- May	4		J5	530 0 0 0 00		530 0 0 0 00	

ACCOUNT Accumulated Depreciation—Buildings   ACCOUNT NO. 171.1

DATE		ITEM	POST. REF.	DEBIT	CREDIT	BALANCE DEBIT	BALANCE CREDIT
20-- May	31	Adjusting	J8		8 0 0 00		8 0 0 00

ACCOUNT Fishing Boats   ACCOUNT NO. 181

DATE		ITEM	POST. REF.	DEBIT	CREDIT	BALANCE DEBIT	BALANCE CREDIT
20-- Apr.	30	Balance	✓			60 0 0 0 00	
May	4		J5	9 0 0 0 00		69 0 0 0 00	

Comprehensive Problem 1, Period 2 (Continued)

ACCOUNT Accumulated Depreciation—Fishing Boats   ACCOUNT NO. 181.1

DATE		ITEM	POST. REF.	DEBIT	CREDIT	BALANCE DEBIT	BALANCE CREDIT
20-- Apr.	30	Balance	✓				1 0 0 0 00
May	31	Adjusting	J8		1 1 5 0 00		2 1 5 0 00

ACCOUNT Surround Sound System   ACCOUNT NO. 182

DATE		ITEM	POST. REF.	DEBIT	CREDIT	BALANCE DEBIT	BALANCE CREDIT
20-- May	2		J5	3 6 0 0 00		3 6 0 0 00	

ACCOUNT Accumulated Depreciation—Surround Sound System   ACCOUNT NO. 182.1

DATE		ITEM	POST. REF.	DEBIT	CREDIT	BALANCE DEBIT	BALANCE CREDIT
20-- May	31	Adjusting	J8		6 0 00		6 0 00

ACCOUNT Big Screen TV   ACCOUNT NO. 183

DATE		ITEM	POST. REF.	DEBIT	CREDIT	BALANCE DEBIT	BALANCE CREDIT
20-- May	2		J5	8 0 0 0 00		8 0 0 0 00	

ACCOUNT Accumulated Depreciation—Big Screen TV   ACCOUNT NO. 183.1

DATE		ITEM	POST. REF.	DEBIT	CREDIT	BALANCE DEBIT	BALANCE CREDIT
20-- May	31	Adjusting	J8		7 5 00		7 5 00

Comprehensive Problem 1, Period 2 (Continued)

ACCOUNT Accounts Payable   ACCOUNT NO. 202

DATE		ITEM	POST. REF.	DEBIT	CREDIT	BALANCE DEBIT	BALANCE CREDIT
20-- Apr.	30	Balance	✓				66 5 0 0 00
May	3		J5	1 0 0 00			66 4 0 0 00
	4		J5	4 0 0 00			66 0 0 0 00
	5		J6		22 9 5 0 00		88 9 5 0 00
	5		J6		1 2 0 0 00		90 1 5 0 00
	19		J6		18 4 0 0 00		108 5 5 0 00
	29		J7		14 3 2 5 00		122 8 7 5 00
	30		J7	47 3 5 0 00			75 5 2 5 00

ACCOUNT Wages Payable   ACCOUNT NO. 219

DATE		ITEM	POST. REF.	DEBIT	CREDIT	BALANCE DEBIT	BALANCE CREDIT
20-- Apr.	30	Balance	✓				5 0 0 00
May	13		J6	5 0 0 00		—	—
	31	Adjusting	J8		6 0 0 00		6 0 0 00

ACCOUNT Bob Night, Capital   ACCOUNT NO. 311

DATE		ITEM	POST. REF.	DEBIT	CREDIT	BALANCE DEBIT	BALANCE CREDIT
20-- Apr.	30	Balance	✓				138 2 5 0 00
May	3		J5		600 0 0 0 00		738 2 5 0 00
	31	Closing	J9		61 8 1 0 00		800 0 6 0 00
	31	Closing	J9	7 5 0 0 00			792 5 6 0 00

ACCOUNT Bob Night, Drawing   ACCOUNT NO. 312

DATE		ITEM	POST. REF.	DEBIT	CREDIT	BALANCE DEBIT	BALANCE CREDIT
20-- May	31		J7	7 5 0 0 00		7 5 0 0 00	
	31	Closing	J9		7 5 0 0 00	—	—

Comprehensive Problem 1, Period 2 (Continued)

ACCOUNT   Income Summary   ACCOUNT NO.   313

DATE		ITEM	POST. REF.	DEBIT	CREDIT	BALANCE DEBIT	BALANCE CREDIT
20-- May	31	Closing	J9		241 0 8 0 00		241 0 8 0 00
	31	Closing	J9	179 2 7 0 00			61 8 1 0 00
	31	Closing	J9	61 8 1 0 00		—	—

ACCOUNT   Registration Fees   ACCOUNT NO.   401

DATE		ITEM	POST. REF.	DEBIT	CREDIT	BALANCE DEBIT	BALANCE CREDIT
20-- May	3		J5		52 7 0 0 00		52 7 0 0 00
	10		J6		62 7 5 0 00		115 4 5 0 00
	14		J6	1 0 0 0 00			114 4 5 0 00
	17		J6		63 0 0 0 00		177 4 5 0 00
	21		J6		63 4 0 0 00		240 8 5 0 00
	31	Closing	J9	240 8 5 0 00		—	—

ACCOUNT   Vending Commission Revenue   ACCOUNT NO.   404

DATE		ITEM	POST. REF.	DEBIT	CREDIT	BALANCE DEBIT	BALANCE CREDIT
20-- May	1		J5		2 0 0 00		2 0 0 00
	31	Adjusting	J8		3 0 00		2 3 0 00
	31	Closing	J9	2 3 0 00		—	—

ACCOUNT   Wages Expense   ACCOUNT NO.   511

DATE		ITEM	POST. REF.	DEBIT	CREDIT	BALANCE DEBIT	BALANCE CREDIT
20-- May	13		J6	29 5 0 0 00		29 5 0 0 00	
	27		J6	30 0 0 0 00		59 5 0 0 00	
	31	Adjusting	J8	6 0 0 0 00		65 5 0 0 00	
	31	Closing	J9		65 5 0 0 00	—	—

Comprehensive Problem 1, Period 2 (Continued)

ACCOUNT   Advertising Expense   ACCOUNT NO.   512

DATE		ITEM	POST. REF.	DEBIT	CREDIT	BALANCE DEBIT	BALANCE CREDIT
20-- May	23		J6	2 5 0 0 00		2 5 0 0 00	
	28		J6	1 8 0 0 00		4 3 0 0 00	
	31	Closing	J9		4 3 0 0 00		

ACCOUNT   Rent Expense   ACCOUNT NO.   521

DATE		ITEM	POST. REF.	DEBIT	CREDIT	BALANCE DEBIT	BALANCE CREDIT
20-- May	3		J5	40 0 0 0 00		40 0 0 0 00	
	31	Closing	J9		40 0 0 0 00		

ACCOUNT   Office Supplies Expense   ACCOUNT NO.   523

DATE		ITEM	POST. REF.	DEBIT	CREDIT	BALANCE DEBIT	BALANCE CREDIT
20-- May	31	Adjusting	J8	1 0 5 0 00		1 0 5 0 00	
	31	Closing	J9		1 0 5 0 00		

ACCOUNT   Food Supplies Expense   ACCOUNT NO.   524

DATE		ITEM	POST. REF.	DEBIT	CREDIT	BALANCE DEBIT	BALANCE CREDIT
20-- May	31	Adjusting	J8	57 7 5 0 00		57 7 5 0 00	
	31	Closing	J9		57 7 5 0 00		

Comprehensive Problem 1, Period 2 (Continued)

ACCOUNT   Telephone Expense   ACCOUNT NO.   525

DATE		ITEM	POST. REF.	DEBIT	CREDIT	BALANCE DEBIT	BALANCE CREDIT
20-- May	30		J7	1 8 0 0 00		1 8 0 0 00	
	31	Closing	J9		1 8 0 0 00	—	—

ACCOUNT   Utilities Expense   ACCOUNT NO.   533

DATE		ITEM	POST. REF.	DEBIT	CREDIT	BALANCE DEBIT	BALANCE CREDIT
20-- May	30		J7	3 3 0 0 00		3 3 0 0 00	
	31	Closing	J9		3 3 0 0 00	—	—

ACCOUNT   Insurance Expense   ACCOUNT NO.   535

DATE		ITEM	POST. REF.	DEBIT	CREDIT	BALANCE DEBIT	BALANCE CREDIT
20-- May	5		J6	1 0 0 0 00		1 0 0 0 00	
	31	Adjusting	J8	1 5 0 0 00		2 5 0 0 00	
	31	Closing	J9		2 5 0 0 00	—	—

ACCOUNT   Postage Expense   ACCOUNT NO.   536

DATE	ITEM	POST. REF.	DEBIT	CREDIT	BALANCE DEBIT	BALANCE CREDIT

Comprehensive Problem 1, Period 2 (Continued)

ACCOUNT Repair Expense   ACCOUNT NO. 537

DATE		ITEM	POST. REF.	DEBIT	CREDIT	BALANCE DEBIT	BALANCE CREDIT
20-- May	25		J6	8 5 0 00		8 5 0 00	
	31	Closing	J9		8 5 0 00	———	———

ACCOUNT Depreciation Expense—Buildings   ACCOUNT NO. 540

DATE		ITEM	POST. REF.	DEBIT	CREDIT	BALANCE DEBIT	BALANCE CREDIT
20-- May	31	Adjusting	J8	8 0 0 00		8 0 0 00	
	31	Closing	J9		8 0 0 00	———	———

ACCOUNT Depreciation Expense—Surround Sound System   ACCOUNT NO. 541

DATE		ITEM	POST. REF.	DEBIT	CREDIT	BALANCE DEBIT	BALANCE CREDIT
20-- May	31	Adjusting	J8	6 0 00		6 0 00	
	31	Closing	J9		6 0 00	———	———

ACCOUNT Depreciation Expense—Fishing Boats   ACCOUNT NO. 542

DATE		ITEM	POST. REF.	DEBIT	CREDIT	BALANCE DEBIT	BALANCE CREDIT
20-- May	31	Adjusting	J8	1 1 5 0 00		1 1 5 0 00	
	31	Closing	J9		1 1 5 0 00	———	———

Comprehensive Problem 1, Period 2 (Continued)

ACCOUNT   Depreciation Expense—Big Screen TV   ACCOUNT NO.   543

	DATE	ITEM	POST. REF.	DEBIT	CREDIT	BALANCE DEBIT	BALANCE CREDIT
20-- May	31	Adjusting	J8	7 5 00		7 5 00	
	31	Closing	J9		7 5 00	—	—

ACCOUNT   Satellite Programming Expense   ACCOUNT NO.   546

	DATE	ITEM	POST. REF.	DEBIT	CREDIT	BALANCE DEBIT	BALANCE CREDIT
20-- May	2		J5	1 2 5 00		1 2 5 00	
	31	Closing	J9		1 2 5 00	—	—

ACCOUNT   Subscriptions Expense   ACCOUNT NO.   548

	DATE	ITEM	POST. REF.	DEBIT	CREDIT	BALANCE DEBIT	BALANCE CREDIT
20-- May	31	Adjusting	J8	1 0 00		1 0 00	
	31	Closing	J9		1 0 00	—	—

Comprehensive Problem 1, Period 2 (Continued)
3. and 4.

The General's Favorite

Work

For Month Ended

	ACCOUNT TITLE	TRIAL BALANCE DEBIT	TRIAL BALANCE CREDIT	ADJUSTMENTS DEBIT	ADJUSTMENTS CREDIT
1	Cash	154 3 5 5 00			
2	Accounts Receivable			(a) 3 0 00	
3	Office Supplies	1 2 0 0 00			(h) 1 0 5 0 00
4	Food Supplies	63 6 7 5 00			(i) 57 7 5 0 00
5	Prepaid Insurance	7 5 0 0 00			(f) 1 5 0 0 00
6	Prepaid Subscriptions	1 2 0 00			(g) 1 0 00
7	Land	100 0 0 0 00			
8	Buildings	530 0 0 0 00			
9	Accum. Depr.—Buildings				(e) 8 0 0 00
10	Fishing Boats	69 0 0 0 00			
11	Accum. Depr.—Fishing Boats		1 0 0 0 00		(b) 1 1 5 0 00
12	Surround Sound System	3 6 0 0 00			
13	Accum. Depr.—Surround Sound				(c) 6 0 00
14	Big Screen TV	8 0 0 0 00			
15	Accum. Depr.—Big Screen TV				(d) 7 5 00
16	Accounts Payable		75 5 2 5 00		
17	Wages Payable				(j) 6 0 0 00
18	Bob Night, Capital		738 2 5 0 00		
19	Bob Night, Drawing	7 5 0 0 00			
20	Registration Fees		240 8 5 0 00		
21	Vending Commission Revenue		2 0 0 00		(a) 3 0 00
22	Wages Expense	59 5 0 0 00		(j) 6 0 0 0 00	
23	Advertising Expense	4 3 0 0 00			
24	Rent Expense	40 0 0 0 00			
25	Office Supplies Expense			(h) 1 0 5 0 00	
26	Food Supplies Expense			(i) 57 7 5 0 00	
27	Telephone Expense	1 8 0 0 00			
28	Utilities Expense	3 3 0 0 00			
29	Insurance Expense	1 0 0 0 00		(f) 1 5 0 0 00	
30	Repair Expense	8 5 0 00			
31	Depr. Exp.—Buildings			(e) 8 0 0 00	
32	Depr. Exp.—Surround Sound			(c) 6 0 00	
33	Depr. Exp.—Fishing Boats			(b) 1 1 5 0 00	
34	Depr. Exp.—Big Screen TV			(d) 7 5 00	
35	Satellite Programming Expense	1 2 5 00			
36	Subscriptions Expense			(g) 1 0 00	
37		1,055 8 2 5 00	1,055 8 2 5 00	68 4 2 5 00	68 4 2 5 00
38	Net Income				
39					
40					

Comprehensive Problem 1, Period 2 (Continued)

Fishing Hole

Sheet

May 31, 20--

ADJUSTED TRIAL BALANCE		INCOME STATEMENT		BALANCE SHEET		
DEBIT	CREDIT	DEBIT	CREDIT	DEBIT	CREDIT	
154 3 5 5 00				154 3 5 5 00		1
3 0 00				3 0 00		2
1 5 0 00				1 5 0 00		3
5 9 2 5 00				5 9 2 5 00		4
6 0 0 0 00				6 0 0 0 00		5
1 1 0 00				1 1 0 00		6
100 0 0 0 00				100 0 0 0 00		7
530 0 0 0 00				530 0 0 0 00		8
	8 0 0 00				8 0 0 00	9
69 0 0 0 00				69 0 0 0 00		10
	2 1 5 0 00				2 1 5 0 00	11
3 6 0 0 00				3 6 0 0 00		12
	6 0 00				6 0 00	13
8 0 0 0 00				8 0 0 0 00		14
	7 5 00				7 5 00	15
	75 5 2 5 00				75 5 2 5 00	16
	6 0 0 0 00				6 0 0 0 00	17
	738 2 5 0 00				738 2 5 0 00	18
7 5 0 0 00				7 5 0 0 00		19
	240 8 5 0 00		240 8 5 0 00			20
	2 3 0 00		2 3 0 00			21
65 5 0 0 00		65 5 0 0 00				22
4 3 0 0 00		4 3 0 0 00				23
40 0 0 0 00		40 0 0 0 00				24
1 0 5 0 00		1 0 5 0 00				25
57 7 5 0 00		57 7 5 0 00				26
1 8 0 0 00		1 8 0 0 00				27
3 3 0 0 00		3 3 0 0 00				28
2 5 0 0 00		2 5 0 0 00				29
8 5 0 00		8 5 0 00				30
8 0 0 00		8 0 0 00				31
6 0 00		6 0 00				32
1 1 5 0 00		1 1 5 0 00				33
7 5 00		7 5 00				34
1 2 5 00		1 2 5 00				35
1 0 00		1 0 00				36
1,063 9 4 0 00	1,063 9 4 0 00	179 2 7 0 00	241 0 8 0 00	884 6 7 0 00	822 8 6 0 00	37
		61 8 1 0 00			61 8 1 0 00	38
		241 0 8 0 00	241 0 8 0 00	884 6 7 0 00	884 6 7 0 00	39
						40

Comprehensive Problem 1, Period 2 (Continued)

5.

GENERAL JOURNAL

PAGE 8

	DATE		DESCRIPTION	POST. REF.	DEBIT	CREDIT	
1			*Adjusting Entries*				1
2	20-- May	31	Accounts Receivable	122	3 0 00		2
3			Vending Commission Revenue	404		3 0 00	3
4							4
5		31	Depreciation Expense—Fishing Boats	542	1 1 5 0 00		5
6			Accumulated Depreciation—Fishing Boats	181.1		1 1 5 0 00	6
7							7
8		31	Depreciation Expense—Surround Sound System	541	6 0 00		8
9			Accum. Depr.—Surround Sound System	182.1		6 0 00	9
10							10
11		31	Depreciation Expense—Big Screen TV	543	7 5 00		11
12			Accumulated Depreciation—Big Screen TV	183.1		7 5 00	12
13							13
14		31	Depreciation Expense—Buildings	540	8 0 0 00		14
15			Accumulated Depreciation—Buildings	171.1		8 0 0 00	15
16							16
17		31	Insurance Expense	535	1 5 0 0 00		17
18			Prepaid Insurance	145		1 5 0 0 00	18
19							19
20		31	Subscriptions Expense	548	1 0 00		20
21			Prepaid Subscriptions	146		1 0 00	21
22							22
23		31	Office Supplies Expense	523	1 0 5 0 00		23
24			Office Supplies	142		1 0 5 0 00	24
25							25
26		31	Food Supplies Expense	524	57 7 5 0 00		26
27			Food Supplies	144		57 7 5 0 00	27
28							28
29		31	Wages Expense	511	6 0 0 0 00		29
30			Wages Payable	219		6 0 0 0 00	30

Comprehensive Problem 1, Period 2 (Continued)

7.

The General's Favorite Fishing Hole
Income Statement
For Month Ended May 31, 20--

Revenues:														
Registration fees	$240	8	5	0	00									
Vending commission revenue		2	3	0	00									
Total revenues						$241	0	8	0	00					
Expenses:														
Wages expense	$ 65	5	0	0	00									
Advertising expense	4	3	0	0	00									
Rent expense	40	0	0	0	00									
Office supplies expense	1	0	5	0	00									
Food supplies expense	57	7	5	0	00									
Telephone expense	1	8	0	0	00									
Utilities expense	3	3	0	0	00									
Insurance expense	2	5	0	0	00									
Repair expense		8	5	0	00									
Depreciation expense—buildings		8	0	0	00									
Depreciation expense—surround sound system			6	0	00									
Depreciation expense—fishing boats	1	1	5	0	00									
Depreciation expense—big screen TV			7	5	00									
Satellite programming expense		1	2	5	00									
Subscriptions expense			1	0	00									
Total expenses						179	2	7	0	00					
Net income						$ 61	8	1	0	00					

8.

The General's Favorite Fishing Hole
Statement of Owner's Equity
For Month Ended May 31, 20--

Bob Night, capital, May 1, 20--						$138	2	5	0	00
Investments during May						600	0	0	0	00
Total investment						$738	2	5	0	00
Net income for May	$ 61	8	1	0	00					
Less withdrawals for May	7	5	0	0	00					
Increase in capital						54	3	1	0	00
Bob Night, capital, May 31, 20--						$792	5	6	0	00

Comprehensive Problem 1, Period 2 (Continued)

9.

The General's Favorite Fishing Hole

Balance Sheet

May 31, 20--

Assets			
Current assets:			
Cash		$154 355 00	
Accounts receivable		30 00	
Office supplies		150 00	
Food supplies		5 925 00	
Prepaid insurance		6 000 00	
Prepaid subscriptions		110 00	
Total current assets			$166 570 00
Property, plant, and equipment:			
Land		$100 000 00	
Buildings	$530 000 00		
Less accum. depr.—buildings	800 00	529 200 00	
Fishing boats	$ 69 000 00		
Less accum. depr.—fishing boats	2 150 00	66 850 00	
Surround sound system	$ 3 600 00		
Less accum. depr.—surround sound sys.	60 00	3 540 00	
Big screen TV	$ 8 000 00		
Less accum. depr.—big screen TV	75 00	7 925 00	
Total property, plant, and equipment			707 515 00
Total assets			$874 085 00
Liabilities			
Current liabilities:			
Accounts payable		$ 75 525 00	
Wages payable		6 000 00	
Total current liabilities			$ 81 525 00
Owner's Equity			
Bob Night, capital			792 560 00
Total liabilities and owner's equity			$874 085 00

Comprehensive Problem 1, Period 2 (Continued)
10.

GENERAL JOURNAL

PAGE 9

	DATE		DESCRIPTION	POST. REF.	DEBIT	CREDIT	
1			*Closing Entries*				1
2	20-- May	31	*Registration Fees*	401	240 8 5 0 00		2
3			*Vending Commission Revenue*	404	2 3 0 00		3
4			*Income Summary*	313		241 0 8 0 00	4
5							5
6		31	*Income Summary*	313	179 2 7 0 00		6
7			*Wages Expense*	511		65 5 0 0 00	7
8			*Advertising Expense*	512		4 3 0 0 00	8
9			*Rent Expense*	521		40 0 0 0 00	9
10			*Office Supplies Expense*	523		1 0 5 0 00	10
11			*Food Supplies Expense*	524		57 7 5 0 00	11
12			*Telephone Expense*	525		1 8 0 0 00	12
13			*Utilities Expense*	533		3 3 0 0 00	13
14			*Insurance Expense*	535		2 5 0 0 00	14
15			*Repair Expense*	537		8 5 0 00	15
16			*Depreciation Expense—Buildings*	540		8 0 0 00	16
17			*Depreciation Exp.—Surround Sound System*	541		6 0 00	17
18			*Depreciation Expense—Fishing Boats*	542		1 1 5 0 00	18
19			*Depreciation Expense—Big Screen TV*	543		7 5 00	19
20			*Satellite Programming Expense*	546		1 2 5 00	20
21			*Subscriptions Expense*	548		1 0 00	21
22							22
23		31	*Income Summary*	313	61 8 1 0 00		23
24			*Bob Night, Capital*	311		61 8 1 0 00	24
25							25
26		31	*Bob Night, Capital*	311	7 5 0 0 00		26
27			*Bob Night, Drawing*	312		7 5 0 0 00	27
28							28
29							29
30							30
31							31
32							32
33							33
34							34
35							35

Comprehensive Problem 1, Period 2 (Concluded)
12.

The General's Favorite Fishing Hole
Post-Closing Trial Balance
May 31, 20--

ACCOUNT TITLE	ACCT. NO.	DEBIT BALANCE	CREDIT BALANCE
Cash	101	154 355 00	
Accounts Receivable	122	30 00	
Office Supplies	142	150 00	
Food Supplies	144	5 925 00	
Prepaid Insurance	145	6 000 00	
Prepaid Subscriptions	146	110 00	
Land	161	100 000 00	
Buildings	171	530 000 00	
Accumulated Depreciation—Buildings	171.1		800 00
Fishing Boats	181	69 000 00	
Accumulated Depreciation—Fishing Boats	181.1		2 150 00
Surround Sound System	182	3 600 00	
Accumulated Depreciation—Surround Sound System	182.1		60 00
Big Screen TV	183	8 000 00	
Accumulated Depreciation—Big Screen TV	183.1		75 00
Accounts Payable	202		75 525 00
Wages Payable	219		600 00
Bob Night, Capital	311		792 560 00
		877 170 00	877 170 00

CHAPTER 7

ACCOUNTING FOR CASH

REVIEW QUESTIONS

1. A signature card must be filled out and signed to open a checking account because the bank uses this card to verify the depositor's signature on any banking transactions.

2. With a blank endorsement, the depositor simply signs on the back of the check. This makes the check payable to any bearer. With a restrictive endorsement, the depositor adds words, such as "For deposit," "Pay to any bank," or "Pay to Daryl Beck only," to restrict the payment of the check.

3. The three parties to every check are the drawer, the drawee, and the payee.

4. The three steps to follow in preparing a check are as follows:
   a. Complete the check stub or register.
   b. Enter the date, payee name, and amount on the check.
   c. Sign the check.

5. The most common reasons for differences between the book and bank cash balances are deposits in transit, outstanding checks, service charges, collections, not sufficient funds checks, and errors.

6. The three steps to follow in preparing a bank reconciliation are as follows:
   a. Identify deposits in transit and any related errors.
   b. Identify outstanding checks and any related errors.
   c. Identify additional reconciling items.

7. The two kinds of items on a bank reconciliation that require journal entries are errors in the books and bank additions and deductions that do not already appear in the books.

8. Five applications of electronic funds transfer in current use are payrolls, social security payments, retail purchases, mortgage payments, and ATM transactions.

9. The purpose of a petty cash fund is to pay for small items with cash rather than spending the time and cost of writing checks for small items.

10. Every time a petty cash payment is made, a petty cash voucher should be prepared.

11. The petty cash fund should be replenished whenever the fund runs low and at the end of each accounting period so that the accounts are brought up to date.

12. The information for issuing a check to replenish the petty cash fund is obtained from the petty cash payments record.

13. An entry is made affecting the change fund when the fund is established and when the amount of the fund is being changed.

14. A debit balance in the cash short and over account represents a net shortage and is treated as an expense. A credit balance in the account represents a net overage and is treated as revenue.

Exercise 7-1A

1. _____c_____   5. _____f_____
2. _____e_____   6. _____g_____
3. _____a_____   7. _____b_____
4. _____d_____

Exercise 7-2A

63-1209
631

DEPOSIT TICKET

WIZARD BANK
3711 Buena Vista Dr.
Orlando, FL 32811-1314

Date _January 15_ 20 __

CHECKS AND OTHER ITEMS ARE RECEIVED FOR DEPOSIT SUBJECT TO THE TERMS AND CONDITIONS OF THIS FINANCIAL INSTITUTION'S ACCOUNT AGREEMENT.

_____
SIGN HERE ONLY IF CASH RECEIVED FROM DEPOSIT

⑆063112094⑆ 0001632475⑈

CURRENCY		334	00
COIN		26	00
CHECKS	4-11	311	00
	80-322	108	00
	3-9	38	00
TOTAL FROM OTHER SIDE			
SUBTOTAL		817	00
LESS CASH RECEIVED			
NET DEPOSIT		817	00

Exercise 7-3A

No. 1

DATE _Jan 15_ 20 __
TO _J.M. Suppliers_
FOR _office sup._

ACCT. _Office Sup._

	DOLLARS	CENTS
BAL BRO'T FOR'D	2,841	50
AMT. DEPOSITED	817	00
TOTAL	3,658	50
AMT. THIS CHECK	150	00
BAL CAR'D FOR'D	3,508	50

No. 1   63-1209 / 631

January 15 20 __

PAY TO THE ORDER OF _J.M. Suppliers_ $ _150.00_

One hundred fifty and ⁰⁰/100 _____ Dollars

FOR CLASSROOM USE ONLY

WIZARD BANK
3711 Buena Vista Dr.
Orlando, FL 32811-1314

MEMO _____

BY _Student's Signature_

⑆063112094⑆ 0001632475⑈

Exercise 7-4A

	Ending Bank Balance	Ending Check-book Balance
1.	+	
2.		+
3.		−
4.	−	
5.		−
6.		−
7.		+

Exercise 7-5A

GENERAL JOURNAL   PAGE

	DATE		DESCRIPTION	POST. REF.	DEBIT	CREDIT	
1	20-- July	31	Cash		2 3 00		1
2			Accounts Payable			2 3 00	2
3			Error on Check No. 394				3
4							4
5		31	Accounts Receivable		3 9 0 00		5
6			Cash			3 9 0 00	6
7			NSF check				7
8							8
9		31	Miscellaneous Expense		1 0 00		9
10			Cash			1 0 00	10
11			Bank service charge				11
12							12
13							13
14							14
15							15
16							16
17							17
18							18
19							19
20							20
21							21

Exercise 7-6A

GENERAL JOURNAL

PAGE

	DATE		DESCRIPTION	POST. REF.	DEBIT	CREDIT	
1	20-- Jan.	1	Petty Cash		2 0 0 00		1
2			Cash			2 0 0 00	2
3			Establish petty cash fund				3
4							4
5		31	Telephone Expense		1 7 50		5
6			Automobile Expense		3 3 00		6
7			Joseph Levine, Drawing		7 0 00		7
8			Postage Expense		1 2 50		8
9			Charitable Contributions Expense		1 5 00		9
10			Miscellaneous Expense		4 9 00		10
11			Cash			1 9 7 00	11
12			Replenish petty cash fund				12
13							13
14							14
15							15
16							16
17							17
18							18
19							19
20							20
21							21
22							22
23							23
24							24
25							25
26							26
27							27
28							28
29							29
30							30
31							31
32							32
33							33
34							34
35							35
36							36

Exercise 7-7A

GENERAL JOURNAL   PAGE

	DATE		DESCRIPTION	POST. REF.	DEBIT	CREDIT	
1	20-- Apr.	2	Cash		266 50		1
2			Cash Short and Over		2 00		2
3			Service Fees			268 50	3
4			Record service fees and cash shortage				4
5							5
6		9	Cash		233 50		6
7			Cash Short and Over		4 25		7
8			Service Fees			237 75	8
9			Record service fees and cash shortage				9
10							10
11		16	Cash		311 00		11
12			Cash Short and Over			1 75	12
13			Service Fees			309 25	13
14			Record service fees and cash overage				14
15							15
16		23	Cash		224 00		16
17			Cash Short and Over		2 50		17
18			Service Fees			226 50	18
19			Record service fees and cash shortage				19
20							20
21		30	Cash		322 00		21
22			Cash Short and Over			4 00	22
23			Service Fees			318 00	23
24			Record service fees and cash overage				24
25							25
26							26
27							27
28							28
29							29
30							30
31							31
32							32
33							33
34							34
35							35
36							36

Problem 7-8A

1.

Volman Enterprises					
Bank Reconciliation					
October 31, 20--					
Bank statement balance, October 31				$4 3 4 8 00	
Add deposits in transit:					
October 29	$1 7 5 00				
October 30	3 3 4 00		5 0 9 00		
			$4 8 5 7 00		
Deduct outstanding checks:					
No. 1764	$ 4 7 00				
No. 1767	1 4 6 00				
No. 1772	1 1 3 00				
No. 1781	3 6 9 00		6 7 5 00		
Adjusted bank balance				$4 1 8 2 00	
Book balance, October 31				$4 7 6 5 00	
Add error on Check No. 1754				1 0 00	
				$4 7 7 5 00	
Deduct: Unrecorded ATM withdrawal	$1 8 0 00				
Bank service charge	4 3 00				
NSF check	3 7 0 00		5 9 3 00		
Adjusted book balance				$4 1 8 2 00	

Problem 7-8A (Concluded)
2.

GENERAL JOURNAL PAGE

	DATE		DESCRIPTION	POST. REF.	DEBIT	CREDIT	
1	20-- Oct.	31	Gary Volman, Drawing		1 8 0 00		1
2			Cash			1 8 0 00	2
3			Unrecorded ATM withdrawal				3
4							4
5		31	Cash		1 0 00		5
6			Accounts Payable			1 0 00	6
7			Error on Check No. 1754				7
8							8
9		31	Miscellaneous Expense		4 3 00		9
10			Cash			4 3 00	10
11			Bank service charge				11
12							12
13		31	Accounts Receivable		3 7 0 00		13
14			Cash			3 7 0 00	14
15			NSF check				15

Problem 7-9A

1.

Lyle's Salon

Bank Reconciliation

November 30, 20--

Bank statement balance, November 30		$2 127 00
Add deposit in transit		1 177 00
		$3 304 00
Deduct outstanding checks:		
No. 471	$ 18 65	
No. 549	1 85 00	
No. 561	21 00	
No. 562	9 40	234 05
Adjusted bank balance		$3 069 95
Book balance, November 30		$3 282 95
Add interest earned		19 00
		$3 301 95
Deduct: Unrecorded ATM withdrawal	$1 50 00	
NSF check	19 50	
Bank service charge	17 50	
Error in recording Check No. 523	45 00	232 00
Adjusted book balance		$3 069 95

Problem 7-9A (Concluded)

2.

GENERAL JOURNAL PAGE

	DATE		DESCRIPTION	POST. REF.	DEBIT	CREDIT	
1	20-- Nov.	30	Cash		1 9 00		1
2			Interest Earned			1 9 00	2
3			Interest earned for November				3
4							4
5		30	Lyle, Drawing		1 5 0 00		5
6			Cash			1 5 0 00	6
7			Unrecorded ATM withdrawal				7
8							8
9		30	Accounts Receivable		1 9 50		9
10			Cash			1 9 50	10
11			NSF check				11
12							12
13		30	Miscellaneous Expense		1 7 50		13
14			Cash			1 7 50	14
15			Bank service charge				15
16							16
17		30	Accounts Payable		4 5 00		17
18			Cash			4 5 00	18
19			Error in recording Check No. 523				19

Problem 7-10A

1. and 3.

GENERAL JOURNAL

PAGE

	DATE		DESCRIPTION	POST. REF.	DEBIT	CREDIT	
1	20-- May	1	Petty Cash		1 5 0 00		1
2			Cash			1 5 0 00	2
3			Establish petty cash fund				3
4							4
5		31	Office Supplies		1 1 00		5
6			Postage Expense		7 00		6
7			Charitable Contributions Expense		3 0 00		7
8			Telephone Expense		5 00		8
9			Travel and Entertainment Expense		2 8 00		9
10			Miscellaneous Expense		4 3 00		10
11			J. Adams, Drawing		2 5 00		11
12			Cash			1 4 9 00	12
13			Replenish petty cash fund				13

Problem 7-10A (Concluded)
2. and 3.

PETTY CASH PAYMENTS FOR MONTH OF   May   20--   PAGE

DAY	DESCRIPTION	VOU. NO.	TOTAL AMOUNT	OFFICE SUPPLIES	POSTAGE EXPENSE	CHARIT. CONTRIB. EXPENSE	TELEPHONE EXPENSE	TRAVEL & ENTER. EXPENSE	MISC. EXPENSE	ACCOUNT	AMOUNT	
1	Received in fund, $150											1
1	Postage	1	3 50		3 50							2
3	Supplies	2	11 00	11 00								3
5	Auto repair	3	43 00						43 00			4
7	J. Adams, drawing	4	25 00							J. Adams, Drawing	25 00	5
11	Donation	5	10 00			10 00						6
15	Travel expenses	6	28 00					28 00				7
22	Postage	7	3 50		3 50							8
26	Telephone call	8	5 00				5 00					9
30	Donation	9	20 00			20 00						10
			149 00	11 00	7 00	30 00	5 00	28 00	43 00		25 00	11
31	Balance		$ 1.00									12
31	Replenished fund		149.00									13
	Total		$150.00									14

DISTRIBUTION OF PAYMENTS

Problem 7-11A

1.

GENERAL JOURNAL PAGE 8

	DATE		DESCRIPTION	POST. REF.	DEBIT	CREDIT	
1	20-- July	2	Cash		287 00		1
2			Cash Short and Over	516	2 50		2
3			Service Fees			289 50	3
4			Record service fees and cash shortage				4
5							5
6		9	Cash		311 50		6
7			Service Fees			311 50	7
8			Record service fees				8
9							9
10		16	Cash		308 50		10
11			Cash Short and Over	516		2 50	11
12			Service Fees			306 00	12
13			Record service fees and cash overage				13
14							14
15		23	Cash		315 00		15
16			Cash Short and Over	516	2 50		16
17			Service Fees			317 50	17
18			Record service fees and cash shortage				18
19							19
20		30	Cash		299 50		20
21			Cash Short and Over	516		3 50	21
22			Service Fees			296 00	22
23			Record service fees and cash overage				23

2.

ACCOUNT *Cash Short and Over*   ACCOUNT NO. 516

DATE		ITEM	POST. REF.	DEBIT	CREDIT	BALANCE DEBIT	BALANCE CREDIT
20-- July	2		J8	2 50		2 50	
	16		J8		2 50		
	23		J8	2 50		2 50	
	30		J8		3 50		1 00

3. The balance represents:
Revenue

Exercise 7-1B

1. _____g_____   5. _____d_____
2. _____c_____   6. _____a_____
3. _____f_____   7. _____b_____
4. _____e_____

Exercise 7-2B

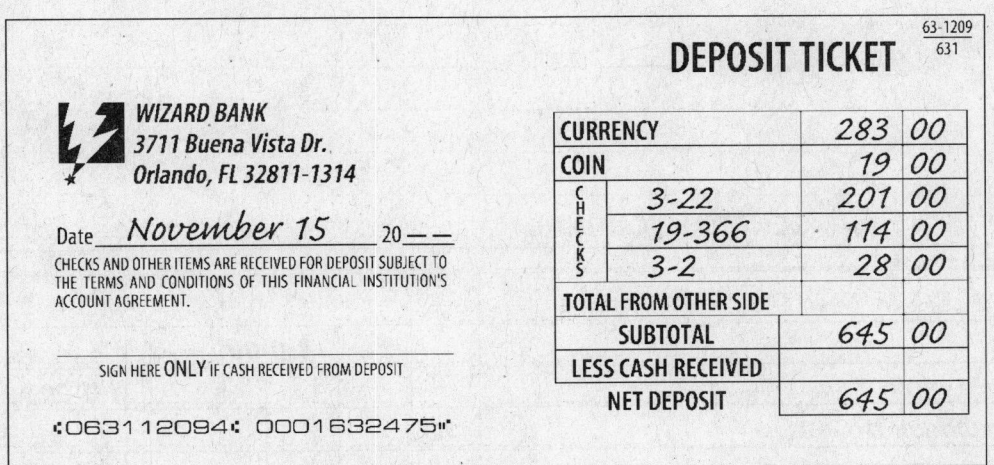

Exercise 7-3B

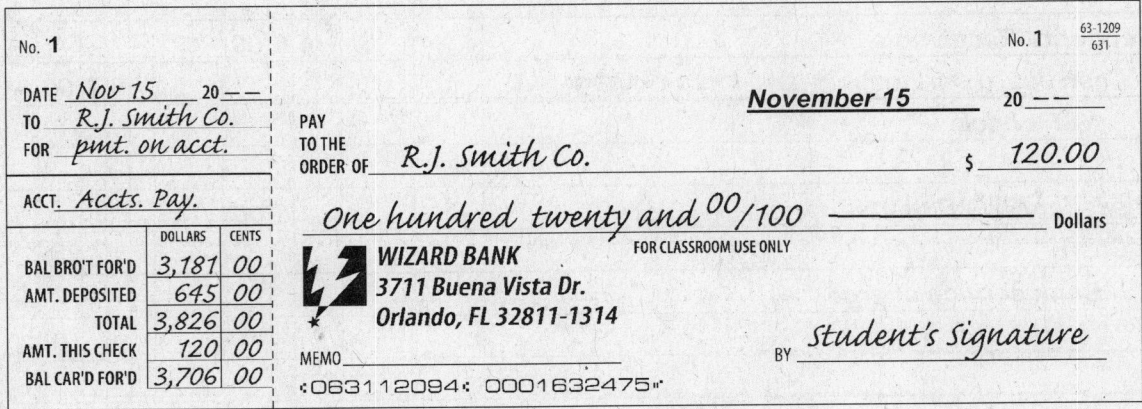

Exercise 7-4B

	Ending Bank Balance	Ending Check-book Balance
1.	_____	–
2.	–	_____
3.	_____	+
4.	_____	–
5.	_____	+
6.	+	_____
7.	_____	–

Exercise 7-5B

GENERAL JOURNAL   PAGE

	DATE		DESCRIPTION	POST. REF.	DEBIT	CREDIT	
1	20-- July	31	Cash		10 00		1
2			Accounts Payable			10 00	2
3			Error on Check No. 191				3
4							4
5		31	Cash		2 00		5
6			Interest Earned			2 00	6
7			Interest earned for July				7
8							8
9		31	Accounts Receivable		66 00		9
10			Cash			66 00	10
11			NSF check				11
12							12
13		31	Miscellaneous Expense		15 00		13
14			Cash			15 00	14
15			Bank service charge				15
16							16
17							17
18							18
19							19
20							20
21							21

Exercise 7-6B

GENERAL JOURNAL

	DATE		DESCRIPTION	POST. REF.	DEBIT	CREDIT	
1	20-- Oct.	1	Petty Cash		2 0 0 00		1
2			Cash			2 0 0 00	2
3			Establish petty cash fund				3
4							4
5		31	Postage Expense		1 3 00		5
6			Miscellaneous Expense		1 7 00		6
7			John Flanagan, Drawing		4 5 00		7
8			Telephone Expense		3 6 00		8
9			Charitable Contributions Expense		5 0 00		9
10			Automobile Expense		2 9 00		10
11			Cash			1 9 0 00	11
12			Replenish petty cash fund				12
13							13
14							14
15							15
16							16
17							17
18							18
19							19
20							20
21							21
22							22
23							23
24							24
25							25
26							26
27							27
28							28
29							29
30							30
31							31
32							32
33							33
34							34
35							35
36							36

Exercise 7-7B

GENERAL JOURNAL

PAGE

	DATE		DESCRIPTION	POST. REF.	DEBIT	CREDIT	
1	20-- June	1	Cash		3 3 3 00		1
2			Cash Short and Over			3 00	2
3			Service Fees			3 3 0 00	3
4			Record service fees and cash overage				4
5							5
6		8	Cash		3 0 0 00		6
7			Cash Short and Over			3 00	7
8			Service Fees			2 9 7 00	8
9			Record service fees and cash overage				9
10							10
11		15	Cash		2 3 1 00		11
12			Cash Short and Over		2 00		12
13			Service Fees			2 3 3 00	13
14			Record service fees and cash shortage				14
15							15
16		22	Cash		2 9 6 50		16
17			Cash Short and Over		5 50		17
18			Service Fees			3 0 2 00	18
19			Record service fees and cash shortage				19
20							20
21		29	Cash		3 1 2 00		21
22			Cash Short and Over		4 00		22
23			Service Fees			3 1 6 00	23
24			Record service fees and cash shortage				24
25							25
26							26
27							27
28							28
29							29
30							30
31							31
32							32
33							33
34							34
35							35
36							36

Problem 7-8B

1.

Kyri Enterprises

Bank Reconciliation

November 30, 20--

Bank statement balance, November 30								$2	5	2	5	00
Add deposits in transit:												
November 29	$1	2	5	00								
November 30	2	0	0	00			3	2	5	00		
							$2	8	5	0	00	
Deduct outstanding checks:												
No. 322	$	1	7	00								
No. 324	1	0	5	00								
No. 327		5	4	00			1	7	6	00		
Adjusted bank balance							$2	6	7	4	00	
Book balance, November 30							$2	9	6	4	00	
Add error on Check No. 321									2	0	00	
							$2	9	8	4	00	
Deduct: Unrecorded ATM withdrawal	$1	0	0	00								
Bank service charge		2	5	00								
NSF check	1	8	5	00			3	1	0	00		
Adjusted book balance							$2	6	7	4	00	

Problem 7-8B (Concluded)

2.

GENERAL JOURNAL

PAGE

	DATE		DESCRIPTION	POST. REF.	DEBIT	CREDIT	
1	20-- Nov.	30	Susan Kyri, Drawing		1 0 0 00		1
2			Cash			1 0 0 00	2
3			Unrecorded ATM withdrawal				3
4							4
5		30	Miscellaneous Expense		2 5 00		5
6			Cash			2 5 00	6
7			Bank service charge				7
8							8
9		30	Accounts Receivable		1 8 5 00		9
10			Cash			1 8 5 00	10
11			NSF check				11
12							12
13		30	Cash		2 0 00		13
14			Accounts Payable			2 0 00	14
15			Error on Check No. 321				15

Problem 7-9B

1.

Tori's Health Center

Bank Reconciliation

April 30, 20--

Bank statement balance, April 30				$3 2 7 5 60
Add deposit in transit				1 5 9 2 00
				$4 8 6 7 60
Deduct outstanding checks:				
No. 397	$	3 8 60		
No. 481		2 1 5 00		
No. 493		7 1 00		
No. 494		2 4 30		3 4 8 90
Adjusted bank balance				$4 5 1 8 70
Book balance, April 30				$4 6 9 0 30
Add: Interest earned	$	2 8 00		
Error in recording Check No. 422		5 4 00		8 2 00
				$4 7 7 2 30
Deduct: Unrecorded ATM withdrawal	$	2 0 0 00		
NSF check		2 9 10		
Bank service charge		2 4 50		2 5 3 60
Adjusted book balance				$4 5 1 8 70

Problem 7-9B (Concluded)
2.

GENERAL JOURNAL

PAGE

	DATE		DESCRIPTION	POST. REF.	DEBIT	CREDIT	
1	20-- Apr.	30	Cash		2 8 00		1
2			Interest Earned			2 8 00	2
3			Interest earned for April				3
4							4
5		30	Cash		5 4 00		5
6			Accounts Payable			5 4 00	6
7			Error in recording Check No. 422				7
8							8
9		30	Tori, Drawing		2 0 0 00		9
10			Cash			2 0 0 00	10
11			Unrecorded ATM withdrawal				11
12							12
13		30	Accounts Receivable		2 9 10		13
14			Cash			2 9 10	14
15			NSF check				15
16							16
17		30	Miscellaneous Expense		2 4 50		17
18			Cash			2 4 50	18
19			Bank service charge				19

Problem 7-10B

1. and 3.

GENERAL JOURNAL

	DATE		DESCRIPTION	POST. REF.	DEBIT	CREDIT	
1	20-- July	1	Petty Cash		1 0 0 00		1
2			Cash			1 0 0 00	2
3			Establish petty cash fund				3
4							4
5		31	Office Supplies		7 00		5
6			Postage Expense		5 50		6
7			Charitable Contributions Expense		1 5 00		7
8			Telephone Expense		5 00		8
9			Travel and Entertainment Expense		1 6 00		9
10			Miscellaneous Expense		1 8 50		10
11			L. Ortiz, Drawing		2 0 00		11
12			Cash			8 7 00	12
13			Replenish petty cash fund				13

Problem 7-10B (Concluded)
2. and 3.

PETTY CASH PAYMENTS FOR MONTH OF July 20--   PAGE

DAY	DESCRIPTION	VOU. NO.	TOTAL AMOUNT	OFFICE SUPPLIES	POSTAGE EXPENSE	CHARIT. CONTRIB. EXPENSE	TELEPHONE EXPENSE	TRAVEL & ENTER. EXPENSE	MISC. EXPENSE	ACCOUNT	AMOUNT
							DISTRIBUTION OF PAYMENTS				
1	Received in fund, $100										
1	Office supplies	1	3 00	3 00							
3	Donation	2	15 00			15 00					
5	Travel expenses	3	5 00					5 00			
7	Postage due	4	2 00		2 00						
8	Office supplies	5	4 00	4 00							
11	Postage due	6	3 50		3 50						
15	Telephone call	7	5 00				5 00				
21	Travel expenses	8	11 00					11 00			
25	Withdrawal	9	20 00							L. Ortiz, Drawing	20 00
26	Copier repair	10	18 50						18 50		
			87 00	7 00	5 50	15 00	5 00	16 00	18 50		20 00
31	Balance		$ 13.00								
31	Replenished fund		87.00								
	Total		$100.00								

Problem 7-11B

1.

GENERAL JOURNAL

	DATE		DESCRIPTION	POST. REF.	DEBIT	CREDIT	
1	20-- Aug.	1	Cash		2 9 5 00		1
2			Cash Short and Over	516		2 50	2
3			Service Fees			2 9 2 50	3
4			Record service fees and cash overage				4
5							5
6		8	Cash		3 0 1 50		6
7			Cash Short and Over	516	3 50		7
8			Service Fees			3 0 5 00	8
9			Record service fees and cash shortage				9
10							10
11		15	Cash		2 8 6 00		11
12			Service Fees			2 8 6 00	12
13			Record service fees				13
14							14
15		22	Cash		3 3 2 75		15
16			Cash Short and Over	516		2 50	16
17			Service Fees			3 3 0 25	17
18			Record service fees and cash overage				18
19							19
20		29	Cash		2 9 5 00		20
21			Cash Short and Over	516	4 20		21
22			Service Fees			2 9 9 20	22
23			Record service fees and cash shortage				23

2.

ACCOUNT **Cash Short and Over**   ACCOUNT NO. **516**

DATE		ITEM	POST. REF.	DEBIT	CREDIT	BALANCE DEBIT	BALANCE CREDIT
20-- Aug.	1		J8		2 50		2 50
	8		J8	3 50		1 00	
	22		J8		2 50		1 50
	29		J8	4 20		2 70	

3. The balance represents:
Expense

MANAGING YOUR WRITING

This situation presents an ethical dilemma similar to receiving too much change from a store clerk. The only difference is the amount is larger in this case. There would be no legal obligation to notify the bank (or the store clerk). But the ethical obligation is clear. A mistake has been made and the money is not yours. You should make a reasonable effort to notify the bank of the error. A reasonable effort in this case could be simply a phone call or a note to the bank.

ETHICS CASE: SUGGESTED SOLUTIONS

1. Ben did something that was dishonest, and dishonest actions are unethical. The fact that he intended to repay the "loan" is not relevant to the act. It is Naomi's responsibility to take corrective action in this situation because she is responsible for supervising Ben. She has been entrusted with that responsibility by the bank, her employer.

2. Naomi could ignore Ben's actions since he repaid the money and keep it a secret from the branch manager. Naomi could report the incident to the branch manager and let him decide what action to take. Naomi could report the incident to the branch manager and the internal auditor.

3. Answers will vary. Students should include an accurate description of the incident and possibly a recommendation of corrective action.

4. Answers will vary. Some possible suggestions are dual control of all cash funds, separation of duties involving reconciliation of cash, minimizing the amount of cash kept on hand, and strict disciplinary action when cash is mismanaged.

Mastery Problem
1.

PETTY CASH PAYMENTS FOR MONTH OF July 20-- PAGE

DAY	VOU. NO.	DESCRIPTION	TOTAL AMOUNT	TRUCK EXPENSE	POSTAGE EXPENSE	CHARIT. CONTRIB. EXPENSE	TELEPHONE EXPENSE	ADVERT. EXPENSE	MISC. EXPENSE	ACCOUNT	AMOUNT
2		Received in fund, $100									
5	1	Postage	25 00		25 00						
7	2	Flowers	30 00						30 00		
8	3	Truck repair	20 00	20 00							
12	4	Newspaper advertisement	22 00					22 00			
			97 00	20 00	25 00			22 00	30 00		
13		Balance $ 3.00									
13		Replenished fund 97.00									
		Total $100.00									
20	5	Truck repair	26 00	26 00							
24	6	Telephone	12 50				12 50				
28	7	YMCA contribution	25 00			25 00					
			63 50	26 00		25 00	12 50				
31		Balance $ 36.50									
31		Replenished fund 63.50									
		Total $100.00									

Mastery Problem (Continued)

2. and 3.

GENERAL JOURNAL

	DATE		DESCRIPTION	POST. REF.	DEBIT	CREDIT	
1	20-- July	2	Petty Cash		1 0 0 00		1
2			Cash			1 0 0 00	2
3			Established petty cash fund				3
4							4
5		5	Rent Expense		6 5 0 00		5
6			Cash			6 5 0 00	6
7			Paid office rent				7
8							8
9		13	Truck Expense		2 0 00		9
10			Postage Expense		2 5 00		10
11			Advertising Expense		2 2 00		11
12			Miscellaneous Expense		3 0 00		12
13			Cash			9 7 00	13
14			Replenishment of petty cash fund				14
15							15
16		15	Office Equipment		5 2 5 00		16
17			Cash			5 2 5 00	17
18			Purchased office equipment				18
19							19
20		17	Supplies		1 3 3 00		20
21			Cash			1 3 3 00	21
22			Purchased supplies				22
23							23
24		18	Legal Expense		1 0 0 0 00		24
25			Cash			1 0 0 0 00	25
26			Paid attorney fees				26
27							27
28		30	Advertising Expense		2 0 0 20		28
29			Cash			2 0 0 20	29
30			Paid for newspaper ads				30
31							31
32							32
33							33
34							34
35							35

Mastery Problem (Concluded)

GENERAL JOURNAL

PAGE 2

	DATE		DESCRIPTION	POST. REF.	DEBIT	CREDIT	
1	July 20--	31	Truck Expense		2 6 00		1
2			Charitable Contributions Expense		2 5 00		2
3			Telephone Expense		1 2 50		3
4			Cash			6 3 50	4
5			Replenishment of petty cash fund				5
6							6
7		31	Miscellaneous Expense		2 50		7
8			Cash			2 50	8
9			Bank service charge				9
10							10
11		31	Rent Expense		5 00		11
12			Cash			5 00	12
13			Error in recording Check No. 302				13
14							14

3.

Turner Excavation
Bank Reconciliation
July 31, 20--

Bank statement balance, July 31		$3 2 3 7 75
Add deposit in transit		2 3 5 0 00
		$5 5 8 7 75
Deduct outstanding checks:		
No. 306	$1 0 0 0 00	
No. 307	2 0 0 20	
No. 308	6 3 50	1 2 6 3 70
Adjusted bank balance		$4 3 2 4 05
Book balance, July 31		$4 3 3 1 55
Deduct: Bank service charge	$ 2 50	
Error on Check No. 302	5 00	7 50
Adjusted book balance		$4 3 2 4 05

Challenge Problem

1. Panera Bakery

GENERAL JOURNAL

PAGE

	DATE		DESCRIPTION	POST. REF.	DEBIT	CREDIT	
1	20-- June	30	Susan Panera, Drawing		2 0 0 00		1
2			Cash			2 0 0 00	2
3			Unrecorded ATM withdrawal				3
4							4
5		30	Deposit in transit—no entry required				5
6							6
7		30	Cash		9 0 00		7
8			Accounts Payable			9 0 00	8
9			Error in recording check				9
10							10
11		30	Bank error—no entry required				11
12							12
13		30	Accounts Payable		2 6 0 00		13
14			Cash			2 6 0 00	14
15			Unrecorded EFT payment				15
16							16
17		30	Outstanding checks—no entry required				17
18							18
19							19
20							20
21							21
22							22
23							23
24							24
25							25
26							26
27							27
28							28
29							29

Challenge Problem (Concluded)

2. Lawrence Bank

GENERAL JOURNAL

	DATE		DESCRIPTION	POST. REF.	DEBIT	CREDIT	
1	20-- June	30	*Depositor error—no entry required*				1
2							2
3		30	*Deposit in transit—no entry required*				3
4							4
5		30	*Cash*		1 9 0 00		5
6			*Depositor Accounts (or similar liability acct.)*			1 9 0 00	6
7			*Error in recording depositor check*				7
8							8
9		30	*Depositor Accounts*		3 5 0 00		9
10			*Cash*			3 5 0 00	10
11			*Duplicate recording of ATM deposit*				11
12							12
13		30	*Depositor error—no entry required*				13
14							14
15		30	*Outstanding checks—no entry required*				15
16							16
17							17
18							18
19							19
20							20
21							21
22							22
23							23
24							24
25							25
26							26
27							27
28							28
29							29

APPENDIX: Internal Controls

REVIEW QUESTIONS

1. Section 404 of the Sarbanes-Oxley Act requires publicly held companies to report annually on the effectiveness of internal control over financial reporting.

2. Internal control is a system developed by a company to provide reasonable assurance of achieving (1) effective and efficient operations, (2) reliable financial reporting, and (3) compliance with laws and regulations.

3. Control environment
   Risk assessment
   Control activities
   Information and communication system
   Monitoring processes

4. Segregation of duties
   Authorization procedures and related responsibilities
   Adequate documents and records
   Protection of assets and records

5. The main purposes of internal controls over cash receipts are to make sure that (1) all cash received by the business is recorded in the accounts, and (2) the cash is promptly deposited in the business bank account.

6. The main purpose of internal controls over cash payments is to make sure cash is paid only for goods and services received by the business, consistent with its best interests.

7. A voucher system is a control technique that requires every acquisition and subsequent payment to be supported by an approved voucher.

8. Voucher
   Purchase invoice
   Receiving report
   Purchase order
   Purchase requisition

9. This prevents a voucher from being processed again to create a duplicate payment.

Exercise 7Apx-1A

1. The control environment is the policies, procedures, and attitudes of the top management and owners of the business.

2. Risk assessment is management's process for identifying, analyzing, and responding to its business risks.

3. Control activities are the policies and procedures established to help management meet its control objectives.

4. The information and communication system is the set of procedures, processes, and records established to initiate, process, record, and report the business's transactions.

5. Monitoring processes are the methods used by management to determine that controls are operating properly, and that the controls are modified in response to changes in assessed risks.

Exercise 7Apx-2A

1. a

2. d

3. e

4. c

5. b

Exercise 7Apx-3A

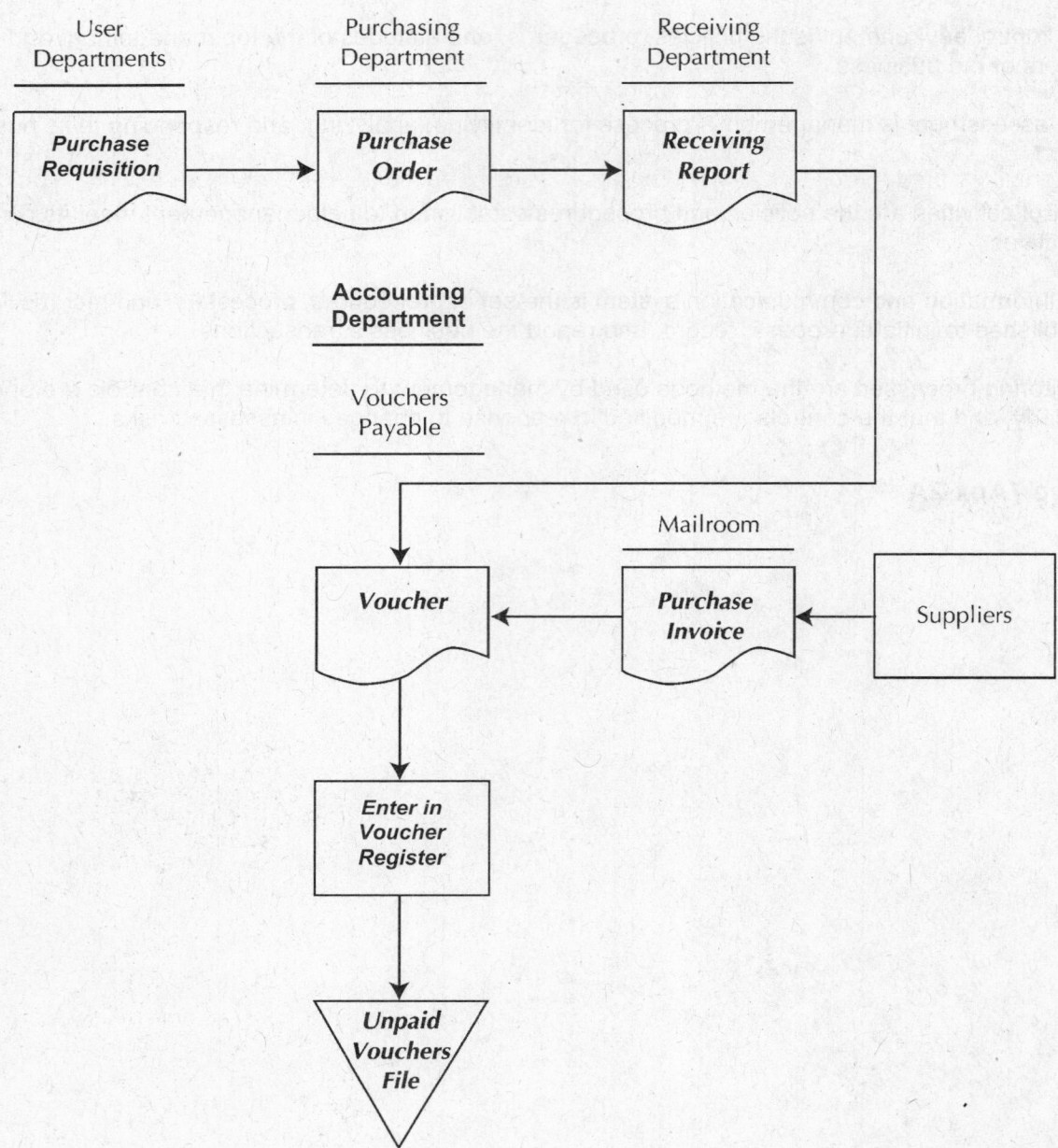

Problem 7Apx-4A

1. Require a voucher and supporting documents (including receiving report) for all payments.

2. Require cancelation of vouchers and supporting documents when payment is made.

3. Require password protection of all computer files and programs.

4. Require the bank reconciliation to be prepared by someone with no other cash handling responsibilities.

Exercise 7Apx-1B

1. Segregation of duties means that:

   a. Different employees should be responsible for different parts of a transaction; and
   b. Employees who account for transactions should not also have custody of the assets.

2. Authorization procedures and related responsibilities means that every business activity should be properly authorized. In addition, it should be possible to identify who is responsible for every activity that has occurred.

3. Adequate documents and records means that accounting documents and records should be used so that all business transactions are recorded.

4. Protection of assets and records means that assets and records should be physically and logically protected.

Exercise 7Apx-2B

1. d

2. b

3. c

4. a

Exercise 7Apx-3B

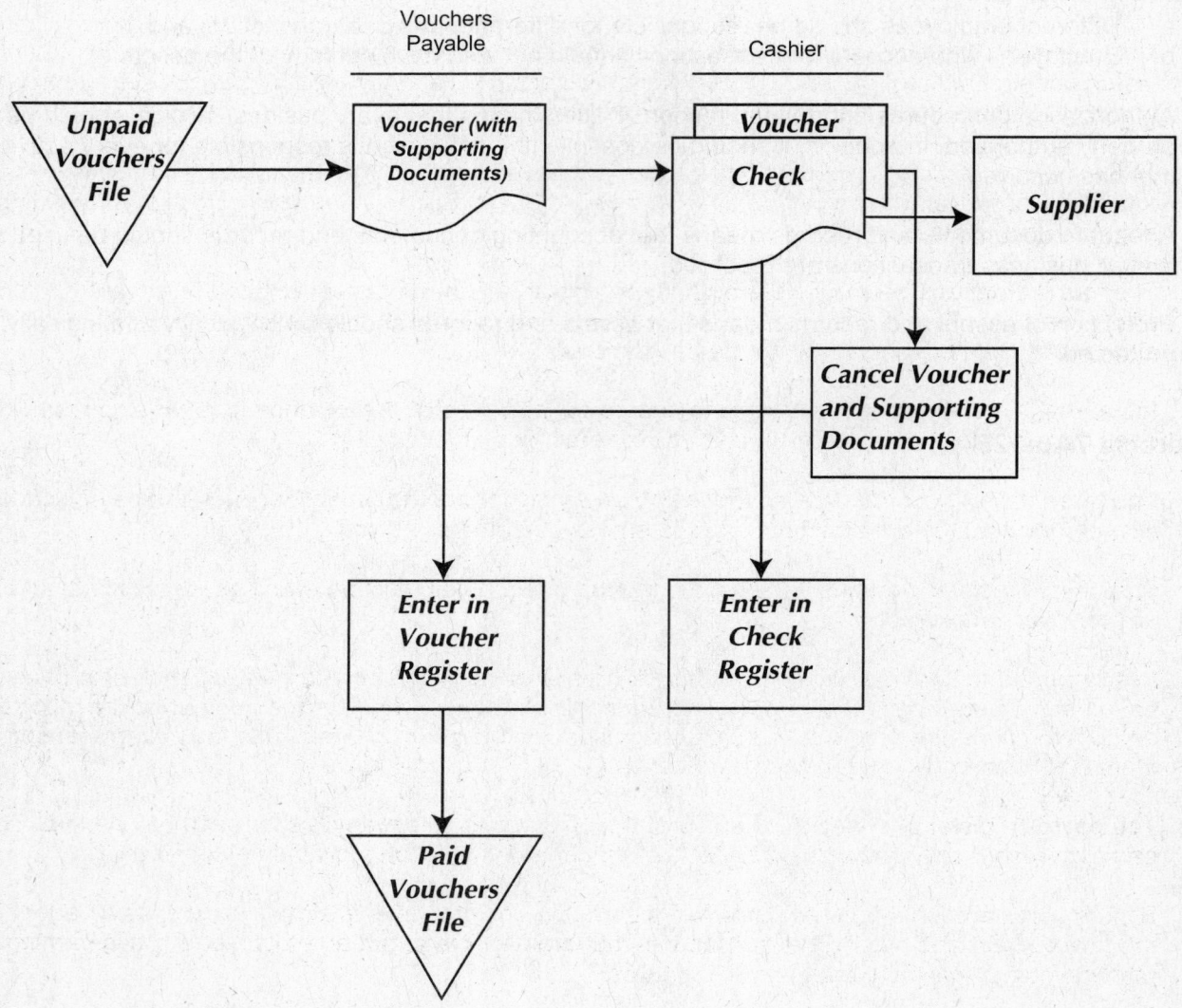

Problem 7Apx-4B

1. Require a voucher and supporting documents (including purchase order) for all payments.

2. Require a voucher and supporting documents (compare sales invoice with receiving report and purchase order) for all payments.

3. Physically protect valuable inventory by storing it in a secure location.

4. Require prenumbering and accounting for all key documents.

CHAPTER 8

PAYROLL ACCOUNTING: EMPLOYEE EARNINGS AND DEDUCTIONS

REVIEW QUESTIONS

1. It is important for payroll accounting purposes to distinguish between an employee and an independent contractor because government laws and regulations regarding payroll are much more complex for employees than for independent contractors.

2. Three major categories of deductions from an employee's gross pay are federal (and possibly state and city) income tax withholding, employee's FICA (Social Security and Medicare) tax withholding, and voluntary deductions.

3. The four factors that determine the amount of federal income tax that is withheld from an employee's pay each pay period are total earnings, marital status, number of withholding allowances claimed, and length of the pay period.

4. In general, each employee is entitled to one personal withholding allowance, one for a spouse who does not also claim an allowance, and one for each dependent.

5. The three payroll records usually needed by an employer are the payroll register, the payroll check with earnings statement attached, and the employee earnings record.

6. The payroll register contains detailed information on earnings, taxable earnings, deductions, and net pay for each employee.

7. It is important to total and verify the totals of the payroll register after the data for each employee have been entered because an error in the payroll register could cause the payment of an incorrect amount to an employee. It also could result in sending an incorrect amount to the government or other agencies for whom funds are withheld.

8. The payroll register provides a summary of the earnings of all employees for each pay period. The earnings record provides a summary of the annual earnings of an individual employee.

9. By deducting amounts from an employee's earnings, the employer is simply serving as an agent for the government and other groups. Amounts that are deducted from an employee's gross earnings must be paid by the employer to these groups.

10. Payroll processing centers and electronic systems are commonly used in payroll accounting because they make payroll accounting more efficient and accurate.

Exercise 8-1A

a.	__40__ regular hours × $10.00 per hour	$400.00
b.	__6__ overtime hours × $15.00 per hour	90.00
c.	Total gross wages	$490.00
d.	Federal income tax withholding (from tax tables in Figure 8-4)	$ 6.00
e.	Social Security withholding at 6.2%	30.38
f.	Medicare withholding at 1.45%	7.11
g.	Total withholding	43.49
h.	Net pay	$446.51

Exercise 8-2A

Regular hours	40 hours × $15	=	$600
Time-and-a-half overtime	2 hours × $22.50	=	45
Double-time overtime	5 hours × $30	=	150
Gross pay			$795

Exercise 8-3A

a. $2,600 × 12 = $31,200 annual pay

$31,200/52 = $600 pay per week

$600/40 = $15 regular pay per hour

$15 × 1.5 = $22.50 overtime pay per hour

b.	Regular pay	40 hours × $15 = $600.00
	Overtime pay	5 hours × $22.50 = 112.50
	Gross pay	$712.50

Exercise 8-4A

	Marital Status	Total Weekly Earnings	Number of Allowances	Amount of Withholding
a.	S	$327.90	2	$13
b.	S	410.00	1	37
c.	M	438.16	3	7
d.	S	518.25	0	62
e.	M	603.98	5	10

Exercise 8-5A

Cumul. Pay Before Current Weekly Payroll	Current Gross Pay	Year-to-Date Earnings	Soc. Sec. Maximum	Amount Over Max. Soc. Sec.	Amount Subject to Soc. Sec.	Soc. Sec. Tax Withheld	Medicare Tax Withheld
$ 22,000	$1,200	**$ 23,200**	$106,800	*none*	**$1,200**	**$ 74.40**	**$17.40**
54,000	4,200	**58,200**	106,800	*none*	**4,200**	**260.40**	**60.90**
104,200	3,925	**108,125**	106,800	**$1,325**	**2,600**	**161.20**	**56.91**
106,200	4,600	**110,800**	106,800	**4,000**	**600**	**37.20**	**66.70**

Exercise 8-6A

Social Security tax:
 $8,000 × 0.062 = $496

Medicare tax:
 $8,700 × 0.0145 = $126.15

GENERAL JOURNAL   PAGE

	DATE		DESCRIPTION	POST. REF.	DEBIT	CREDIT	
1	20-- Dec.	31	*Wages and Salaries Expense*		8 7 0 0 00		1
2			*Employee Income Tax Payable*			9 2 0 00	2
3			*Social Security Tax Payable*			4 9 6 00	3
4			*Medicare Tax Payable*			1 2 6 15	4
5			*United Way Contributions Payable*			2 0 0 00	5
6			*Cash*			6 9 5 7 85	6
7			*Payroll for week ended December 31*				7
8							8
9							9

Exercise 8-7A

GENERAL JOURNAL   PAGE

	DATE		DESCRIPTION	POST. REF.	DEBIT	CREDIT	
1	20-- Apr.	15	*Wages and Salaries Expense*		6 2 4 2 00		1
2			*Employee Income Tax Payable*			5 9 3 00	2
3			*Social Security Tax Payable*			3 8 7 00	3
4			*Medicare Tax Payable*			9 0 51	4
5			*Pension Plan Payable*			9 0 00	5
6			*Health Insurance Premiums Payable*			2 2 5 00	6
7			*United Way Contributions Payable*			1 0 0 00	7
8			*Cash*			4 7 5 6 49	8
9			*Payroll for week ended April 15*				9

Problem 8-8A

1.

Regular pay (40 × $8.50)	$340.00
Overtime pay (8 × $12.75)	102.00
Gross pay	$442.00
Deductions:	
Employee income tax	$ 8.00
Social Security tax ($442 × 0.062)	27.40
Medicare tax ($442 × 0.0145)	6.41
Health insurance premium	85.00
Credit union	125.00
United Way contribution	10.00
Total deductions	261.81
Net pay	$180.19

2.

GENERAL JOURNAL

PAGE

	DATE		DESCRIPTION	POST. REF.	DEBIT	CREDIT	
1	20-- Jan.	31	Wages and Salaries Expense		442 00		1
2			Employee Income Tax Payable			8 00	2
3			Social Security Tax Payable			27 40	3
4			Medicare Tax Payable			6 41	4
5			Health Insurance Premiums Payable			85 00	5
6			Credit Union Payable			125 00	6
7			United Way Contributions Payable			10 00	7
8			Cash			180 19	8
9			Payroll for week ended January 31				9
10							10
11							11
12							12
13							13
14							14
15							15

Problem 8-9A

1. The Payroll Register can be found on pages 296-297.

2.

GENERAL JOURNAL   PAGE

	DATE		DESCRIPTION	POST. REF.	DEBIT	CREDIT	
1	20-- Mar.	24	Wages and Salaries Expense		2 2 7 4 25		1
2			Employee Income Tax Payable			1 1 3 00	2
3			Social Security Tax Payable			1 4 1 00	3
4			Medicare Tax Payable			3 2 98	4
5			City Tax Payable			2 2 74	5
6			Health Insurance Premiums Payable			4 0 00	6
7			Credit Union Payable			4 0 00	7
8			U.S. Savings Bonds Payable			5 7 50	8
9			Cash			1 8 2 7 03	9
10			Payroll for week ended March 22				10
11							11
12							12
13							13
14							14

Problem 8-9A (Continued)

1.

PAYROLL REGISTER

	NAME	NO. ALLOW.	MARIT. STATUS	EARNINGS						TAXABLE EARNINGS			
				REGULAR		OVERTIME		TOTAL		CUMULATIVE TOTAL		UNEMPLOY. COMP.		SOCIAL SECURITY
1	Ali, Loren	4	M	440	00	82	50	522	50	5,802	50	522	50	522	50
2	Carson, Judy	1	S	480	00			480	00	6,240	00	480	00	480	00
3	Hernandez, Maria	3	M	380	00	42	75	422	75	4,982	75	422	75	422	75
4	Knox, Wayne	1	S	429	00			429	00	5,554	50	429	00	429	00
5	Paglione, Jim	2	M	420	00			420	00	5,140	50	420	00	420	00
6				2,149	00	125	25	2,274	25	27,720	25	2,274	25	2,274	25
7															
8															
9															
10															
11															
12															
13															
14															

Problem 8-9A (Concluded)

FOR PERIOD ENDED   *March 22*   20--

				DEDUCTIONS												
FEDERAL INCOME TAX		SOCIAL SECURITY TAX		MEDICARE TAX		CITY TAX		HEALTH INSUR.		OTHER				TOTAL		NET PAY		CK. NO.	
9	00	32	40	7	58	5	22	15	00	Credit Union	20	00	89	20	433	30	423	1
47	00	29	76	6	96	4	80	5	00	Bonds	38	75	132	27	347	73	424	2
6	00	26	20	6	13	4	23	5	00	Bonds	18	75	66	31	356	44	425	3
38	00	26	60	6	22	4	29	15	00	Credit Union	20	00	110	11	318	89	426	4
13	00	26	04	6	09	4	20						49	33	370	67	427	5
113	00	141	00	32	98	22	74	40	00		97	50	447	22	1,827	03		6
																		7
																		8
																		9
																		10
																		11
																		12
																		13
																		14

Problem 8-10A

EMPLOYEE EARNINGS RECORD

20 -- PERIOD ENDED	EARNINGS				TAXABLE EARNINGS		DEDUCTIONS	
	REGULAR	OVERTIME	TOTAL	CUMULATIVE TOTAL	UNEMPLOY. COMP.	SOCIAL SECURITY	FEDERAL INCOME TAX	SOCIAL SECURITY TAX
3/8								
3/15								
3/22	480 00		480 00	6,240 00	480 00	480 00	47 00	29 76
3/29								

GENDER	DEPARTMENT	OCCUPATION	SOCIAL SECURITY NO.	MARITAL STATUS	ALLOW- ANCES
M (F)	Ticket Sales	Manager	544-67-1283	S	1

Problem 8-10A (Concluded)

FOR PERIOD ENDED   *March 22*   20--

			DEDUCTIONS								
MEDICARE TAX		CITY TAX		HEALTH INSURANCE		OTHER				TOTAL		CK. NO.	AMOUNT	
6	96	4	80	5	00	Savings Bond		38	75	132	27	424	347	73

PAY RATE		DATE OF BIRTH		DATE HIRED		NAME/ADDRESS	EMP. NO.
$12.00		5/8/59		6/1/--		*Judy Carson*	62
						28 Quarry Drive	
						Vernon, CT 06066	

Exercise 8-1B

a.	_____40_____	regular hours × $12.00 per hour	$480.00
b.	_____5 ½_____	overtime hours × $18.00 per hour	99.00
c.	Total gross wages		$579.00
d.	Federal income tax withholding (from tax tables in Figure 8-4)		$ 7.00
e.	Social Security withholding at 6.2%		35.90
f.	Medicare withholding at 1.45%		8.40
g.	Total withholding		51.30
h.	Net pay		$527.70

Exercise 8-2B

Regular hours	**40 hours × $12 = $480**
Time-and-a-half overtime	**3 hours × $18 = 54**
Double-time overtime	**6 hours × $24 = 144**
Gross pay	**$678**

Exercise 8-3B

a. **$3,250 × 12 = $39,000 annual pay**

$39,000/52 = $750.00 pay per week

$750.00/40 = $18.75 regular pay per hour

$18.75 × 1.5 = $28.125 overtime pay per hour

b.	**Regular pay**	**40 hours × $18.75 = $750.00**
	Overtime pay	**6 hours × $28.125 = 168.75**
	Gross pay	**$918.75**

Exercise 8-4B

	Marital Status	Total Weekly Earnings	Number of Allowances	Amount of Withholding
a.	M	$546.00	4	$11
b.	M	390.00	3	3
c.	S	461.39	2	34
d.	M	522.88	2	23
e.	S	612.00	0	77

Exercise 8-5B

Cumul. Pay Before Current Weekly Payroll	Current Gross Pay	Year-to-Date Earnings	Soc. Sec. Maximum	Amount Over Max. Soc. Sec.	Amount Subject to Soc. Sec.	Soc. Sec. Tax Withheld	Medicare Tax Withheld
$ 31,000	$1,500	$ 32,500	$106,800	none	$1,500	$ 93.00	$21.75
53,000	2,860	55,860	106,800	none	2,860	177.32	41.47
103,900	3,140	107,040	106,800	$ 240	2,900	179.80	45.53
106,200	2,920	109,120	106,800	2,320	600	37.20	42.34

Exercise 8-6B

Social Security tax:
$9,400 × 0.062 = $582.80

Medicare tax:
$9,400 × 0.0145 = $136.30

GENERAL JOURNAL   PAGE

	DATE		DESCRIPTION	POST. REF.	DEBIT	CREDIT	
1	20-- Nov.	30	*Wages and Salaries Expense*		9 4 0 0 00		1
2			*Employee Income Tax Payable*			9 8 5 00	2
3			*Social Security Tax Payable*			5 8 2 80	3
4			*Medicare Tax Payable*			1 3 6 30	4
5			*United Way Contributions Payable*			2 0 0 00	5
6			*Cash*			7 4 9 5 90	6
7			*Payroll for week ended November 30*				7
8							8
9							9
10							10
11							11
12							12
13							13
14							14
15							15
16							16
17							17
18							18
19							19
20							20
21							21
22							22

Exercise 8-7B

GENERAL JOURNAL   PAGE

	DATE		DESCRIPTION	POST. REF.	DEBIT	CREDIT	
1	20-- June	12	Wages and Salaries Expense		7 4 7 0 00		1
2			Employee Income Tax Payable			7 8 2 00	2
3			Social Security Tax Payable			4 6 3 14	3
4			Medicare Tax Payable			1 0 8 32	4
5			Pension Plan Payable			8 0 00	5
6			Health Insurance Premiums Payable			1 9 0 00	6
7			United Way Contributions Payable			1 5 0 00	7
8			Cash			5 6 9 6 54	8
9			Payroll for week ended June 12				9
10							10
11							11
12							12
13							13

Problem 8-8B

1.

Regular pay (40 × $9.00)	$360.00
Overtime pay (6 × $13.50)	81.00
Gross pay	$441.00
Deductions:	
Employee income tax	$ 15.00
Social Security tax ($441 × 0.062)	27.34
Medicare tax ($441 × 0.0145)	6.39
Health insurance premium	92.00
Credit union	110.00
United Way contributions	5.00
Total deductions	255.73
Net pay	$185.27

Problem 8-8B (Concluded)

2.

GENERAL JOURNAL

	DATE		DESCRIPTION	POST. REF.	DEBIT	CREDIT	
1	20-- Jan.	31	*Wages and Salaries Expense*		4 4 1 00		1
2			*Employee Income Tax Payable*			1 5 00	2
3			*Social Security Tax Payable*			2 7 34	3
4			*Medicare Tax Payable*			6 39	4
5			*Health Insurance Premiums Payable*			9 2 00	5
6			*Credit Union Payable*			1 1 0 00	6
7			*United Way Contributions Payable*			5 00	7
8			*Cash*			1 8 5 27	8
9			*Payroll for week ended January 31*				9
10							10
11							11
12							12
13							13
14							14
15							15
16							16
17							17
18							18
19							19
20							20
21							21
22							22
23							23
24							24
25							25
26							26
27							27
28							28
29							29
30							30
31							31
32							32
33							33
34							34
35							35

Problem 8-9B

1.

PAYROLL REGISTER

	NAME	NO. ALLOW.	MARIT. STATUS	EARNINGS						TAXABLE EARNINGS			
				REGULAR		OVERTIME		TOTAL		CUMULATIVE TOTAL		UNEMPLOY. COMP.		SOCIAL SECURITY
1	Barone, W.	1	S	400	00			400	00	2,800	00	400	00	400	00
2	Hastings, G.	4	M	480	00	90	00	570	00	3,930	00	570	00	570	00
3	Nitobe, I.	3	M	350	00	78	75	428	75	3,363	75	428	75	428	75
4	Smith, J.	4	M	440	00	33	00	473	00	3,218	00	473	00	473	00
5	Tarshis, D.	1	S	409	50			409	50	3,060	25	409	50	409	50
6				2,079	50	201	75	2,281	25	16,372	00	2,281	25	2,281	25
7															
8															
9															
10															
11															
12															
13															
14															

Problem 8-9B (Concluded)

FOR PERIOD ENDED *February 15* 20--

				DEDUCTIONS										
FEDERAL INCOME TAX		SOCIAL SECURITY TAX		MEDICARE TAX		CITY TAX		HEALTH INSUR.		OTHER		TOTAL		NET PAY	CK. NO.	
35	00	24	80	5	80	4	00					69	60	330	40	365	1
14	00	35	34	8	27	5	70	35	00	Bonds	18	75	117	06	452	94	366	2
6	00	26	58	6	22	4	29	15	00	Credit Union	25	00	83	09	345	66	367	3
4	00	29	33	6	86	4	73	35	00	Bonds	43	75	123	67	349	33	368	4
35	00	25	39	5	94	4	10	15	00	Credit Union	25	00	110	43	299	07	369	5
94	00	141	44	33	09	22	82	100	00		112	50	503	85	1,777	40		6

2.

GENERAL JOURNAL

PAGE

	DATE		DESCRIPTION	POST. REF.	DEBIT	CREDIT	
1	20-- Feb.	17	Wages and Salaries Expense		2 2 8 1 25		1
2			Employee Income Tax Payable			9 4 00	2
3			Social Security Tax Payable			1 4 1 44	3
4			Medicare Tax Payable			3 3 09	4
5			City Tax Payable			2 2 82	5
6			Health Insurance Premiums Payable			1 0 0 00	6
7			Credit Union Payable			5 0 00	7
8			U.S. Savings Bonds Payable			6 2 50	8
9			Cash			1 7 7 7 40	9
10			Payroll for week ended February 15				10
11							11
12							12
13							13
14							14

Problem 8-10B

EMPLOYEE EARNINGS RECORD

20 -- PERIOD ENDED	EARNINGS				TAXABLE EARNINGS		DEDUCTIONS	
	REGULAR	OVERTIME	TOTAL	CUMULATIVE TOTAL	UNEMPLOY. COMP.	SOCIAL SECURITY	FEDERAL INCOME TAX	SOCIAL SECURITY TAX
2/8								
2/15	400 00		400 00	2,800 00	400 00	400 00	35 00	24 80
2/22								

GENDER	DEPARTMENT	OCCUPATION	SOCIAL SECURITY NO.	MARITAL STATUS	ALLOW-ANCES
(M) F	Desserts	Baker	342-73-4681	S	1

Problem 8-10B (Concluded)

FOR PERIOD ENDED   *February 15*   20--

DEDUCTIONS								
MEDICARE TAX	CITY TAX	HEALTH INSURANCE	OTHER		TOTAL	CK. NO.	AMOUNT	
5 80	4 00				69 60	365	330	40

PAY RATE	DATE OF BIRTH	DATE HIRED	NAME/ADDRESS	EMP. NO.
$10.00	8/26/59	10/1/--	*William Barone*	19
			30 Timber Lane	
			Willington, CT 06279	

MANAGING YOUR WRITING

For: Respect for human dignity demands that the minimum wage be raised. The current minimum wage hardly enables a worker to live above the poverty level. In addition, as the cost of living increases, the minimum wage must be increased just to help workers stay at their current inadequate level.

Against: If the minimum wage is increased too much, jobs will be lost because businesses will be able to afford fewer employees, or will move to areas with lower labor costs. The net effect of this will be to help those who still have jobs but worsen the situation for the workers overall. In addition, higher labor costs will cause businesses to increase prices. This will make it more costly to live, so that the net benefit of the increased minimum wage is unclear.

ETHICS CASE: SUGGESTED SOLUTIONS

1. No. Simon agreed to have these amounts withheld from his pay by accepting employment at N & L and completing the payroll paperwork. Also, Simon might be trying to take advantage of a new employee.
2. Current liabilities would be understated.
3. Answers will vary. Students not aware of the employer's payroll tax, which is introduced in the next chapter, might recognize that cash will be lower than it should be and current liabilities will not reflect proper withholding amounts.
4. Answers will vary. Students should recognize that Simon was wrong to ask Maura not to withhold taxes and Maura would be wrong to honor his request. Also, they might suggest that Maura report the incident to her supervisor for direction.

Mastery Problem

1.

PAYROLL REGISTER

	NAME	NO. ALLOW.	MARIT. STATUS	EARNINGS REGULAR		OVERTIME		TOTAL		CUMULATIVE TOTAL		TAXABLE EARNINGS UNEMPLOY. COMP.		SOCIAL SECURITY	
1	Berling, J.	3	M	480	00	168	00	648	00	25,173	00			648	00
2	Merz, L.	4	M	400	00	185	00	585	00	21,065	00			585	00
3	Goetz, K.	2	M	440	00			440	00	21,940	00			440	00
4	Menick, J.	2	S	275	00	352	00	627	00	23,252	00			627	00
5	Morales, E.	3	M	494	00			494	00	25,224	00			494	00
6	Heimbrock, J.	5	M	1,360	00			1,360	00	107,200	00			960	00
7	Townsley, S.	2	M	252	00	72	00	324	00	21,749	00			324	00
8	Salzman, B.	4	M	374	00	176	00	550	00	7,185	00	365	00	550	00
9	Layton, E.	3	M	440	00			440	00	6,075	00	440	00	440	00
10	Thompson, D.	5	M	440	00	93	50	533	50	22,168	50			533	50
11	Vadillo, C.	2	S	481	00	208	00	689	00	24,804	00			689	00
12				5,436	00	1,254	50	6,690	50	305,835	50	805	00	6,290	50
13															
14															

3.

EMPLOYEE EARNINGS RECORD

20 -- PERIOD ENDED	EARNINGS REGULAR		OVERTIME		TOTAL		CUMULATIVE TOTAL		TAXABLE EARNINGS UNEMPLOY. COMP.		SOCIAL SECURITY		FEDERAL INCOME TAX	
11/4	330	00	33	00	363	00	6,145	50	363	00	363	00	0	00
11/11	440	00	49	50	489	50	6,635	00	489	50	489	50	5	00
11/18	374	00	176	00	550	00	7,185	00	365	00	550	00	12	00
11/25														

GENDER	DEPARTMENT	OCCUPATION	SOCIAL SECURITY NO.	MARITAL STATUS
(M) F	Administration	Office Manager	446-46-6321	M

Mastery Problem (Continued)

FOR PERIOD ENDED *November 18* 20--

FEDERAL INCOME TAX		SOCIAL SECURITY TAX		MEDICARE TAX		STATE INCOME TAX		HEALTH INSURANCE		CREDIT UNION		TOTAL		NET PAY		CK. NO.	
28	00	40	17	9	40	22	68	5	00	149	60	254	85	393	15	331	1
15	00	36	27	8	48	20	48	5	00	117	00	202	23	382	77	332	2
15	00	27	28	6	38	15	40	5	00	91	30	160	36	279	64	333	3
58	00	38	88	9	09	21	95	5	00	126	50	259	42	367	58	334	4
13	00	30	63	7	16	17	29	5	00	117	05	190	13	303	87	335	5
114	00	59	52	19	72	47	60	5	00	154	25	400	09	959	91	336	6
3	00	20	09	4	70	11	34	5	00	83	05	127	18	196	82	337	7
12	00	34	09	7	98	19	25	5	00	130	00	208	32	341	68	338	8
8	00	27	28	6	38	15	40	5	00	88	00	150	06	289	94	339	9
3	00	33	08	7	73	18	67	5	00	128	90	196	38	337	12	340	10
67	00	42	72	9	99	24	12	5	00	139	11	287	94	401	06	341	11
336	00	390	01	97	01	234	18	55	00	1,324	76	2,436	96	4,253	54		12
																	13
																	14

FOR PERIOD ENDED 20--

SOCIAL SECURITY TAX		MEDICARE TAX		STATE INCOME TAX		HEALTH INSURANCE		CREDIT UNION		TOTAL		CK. NO.		AMOUNT	
22	51	5	26	12	71			72	60	113	08	121		249	92
30	35	7	10	17	13			97	90	157	48	229		332	02
34	09	7	98	19	25	5	00	130	00	208	32	338		341	68

ALLOWANCES	PAY RATE	DATE OF BIRTH	DATE HIRED	NAME/ADDRESS	EMP. NO.
4	$11.00	4/5/64	7/22/--	*Ben F. Salzman*	8
				12 Windmill Lane	
				Trumbull, CT 06611	

Mastery Problem (Concluded)

2.

GENERAL JOURNAL

PAGE

	DATE		DESCRIPTION	POST. REF.	DEBIT	CREDIT	
1	20-- Nov.	21	Wages and Salaries Expense		6 6 9 0 50		1
2			Employee Income Tax Payable			3 3 6 00	2
3			Social Security Tax Payable			3 9 0 01	3
4			Medicare Tax Payable			9 7 01	4
5			State Income Tax Payable			2 3 4 18	5
6			Health Insurance Premiums Payable			5 5 00	6
7			Credit Union Payable			1 3 2 4 76	7
8			Cash			4 2 5 3 54	8
9			Payroll for week ended November 18				9
10							10
11							11
12							12
13							13
14							14
15							15
16							16
17							17
18							18
19							19
20							20
21							21
22							22
23							23
24							24
25							25
26							26
27							27
28							28
29							29
30							30
31							31
32							32
33							33
34							34
35							35

Challenge Problem

1.

GENERAL JOURNAL

PAGE

	DATE		DESCRIPTION	POST. REF.	DEBIT	CREDIT	
1	20-2 Jan.	4	Wages and Salaries Payable		1 7 5 4 00		1
2			Wages and Salaries Expense		1 5 9 6 00		2
3			Employee Income Tax Payable			3 4 2 00	3
4			Social Security Tax Payable			2 0 7 70	4
5			Medicare Tax Payable			4 8 58	5
6			Health Insurance Premiums Payable			5 0 00	6
7			United Way Contributions Payable			8 0 00	7
8			Cash			2 6 2 1 72	8
9			To record Jan. 4 payroll				9
10							10

2.

Wages and Salaries Expense		Wages and Salaries Payable		
20-2 Jan. 4 1,596.00		20-2 Jan. 4 1,754.00	Jan. 1 Bal.	1,754.00

CHAPTER 9

PAYROLL ACCOUNTING: EMPLOYER TAXES AND REPORTS

REVIEW QUESTIONS

1. The various employee payroll taxes are levied on the employee, not the employer.

2. The text assumes the rate is 6.2% on an earnings base of $106,800.

3. The purpose of the FUTA tax is to raise funds to administer the federal/state unemployment compensation program. The employer must pay this tax.

4. The purpose of the state unemployment tax is to raise funds to pay unemployment benefits. In most states, the employer must pay this tax.

5. When employer payroll taxes are properly recorded, the following accounts are affected: Payroll Taxes Expense, Social Security Tax Payable, Medicare Tax Payable, FUTA Tax Payable, and SUTA Tax Payable.

6. Social Security taxes withheld from employees' earnings and imposed on the employer are credited to Social Security Tax Payable. The payment of Social Security tax is debited to Social Security Tax Payable. Similarly, Medicare taxes withheld from employees' earnings and imposed on the employer are credited to Medicare Tax Payable. The payment of Medicare tax is debited to Medicare Tax Payable.

7. The total cost of an employee to the employer includes Social Security, Medicare, SUTA, and FUTA taxes in addition to the employee's gross wages.

8. The purpose of Form 8109 is for deposits made at an authorized commercial bank of federal income tax withheld and Social Security and Medicare taxes.

9. Form 941 is a report of employee federal income tax and employee and employer Social Security and Medicare taxes for the quarter.

10. Employers file an annual report of federal unemployment tax on Form 940.

11. Form W-2 shows the total amount of wages paid to the employee and the amounts of taxes withheld during the preceding tax year.

12. The purpose of Form I-9 is to document that each employee is authorized to work in the United States.

13. Workers' compensation insurance provides insurance for employees who suffer a job-related illness or injury. The entire cost of workers' compensation insurance usually is paid by the employer.

Exercise 9-1A

Social Security tax	= $12,200 × 0.062	= $ 756.40
Medicare tax	= $12,200 × 0.0145	= 176.90
FUTA tax	= $10,500 × 0.008	= 84.00
SUTA tax	= $10,500 × 0.054	= 567.00
Total employer payroll taxes		$1,584.30

GENERAL JOURNAL   PAGE

	DATE		DESCRIPTION	POST. REF.	DEBIT	CREDIT	
1	20-- July	15	Payroll Taxes Expense		1 5 8 4 30		1
2			Social Security Tax Payable			7 5 6 40	2
3			Medicare Tax Payable			1 7 6 90	3
4			FUTA Tax Payable			8 4 00	4
5			SUTA Tax Payable			5 6 7 00	5
6			To record employer payroll taxes expense				6
7							7

Exercise 9-2A

Total unemployment taxable		= $ 710.00
Total Social Security taxable		= $4,000.00
Total earnings		= $4,000.00

Social Security tax	= $4,000 × 0.062	= $248.00
Medicare tax	= $4,000 × 0.0145	= 58.00
FUTA tax	= $710 × 0.008	= 5.68
SUTA tax	= $710 × 0.054	= 38.34
Total employer payroll taxes		$350.02

GENERAL JOURNAL   PAGE

	DATE		DESCRIPTION	POST. REF.	DEBIT	CREDIT	
1	20-- Mar.	12	Payroll Taxes Expense		3 5 0 02		1
2			Social Security Tax Payable			2 4 8 00	2
3			Medicare Tax Payable			5 8 00	3
4			FUTA Tax Payable			5 68	4
5			SUTA Tax Payable			3 8 34	5
6			To record employer payroll taxes expense				6
7							7

Exercise 9-3A

		Taxable Earnings	
Name	Current Earnings	Unemploy. Comp.	Social Security
Burgos	$ 1,250	$200	$ 1,250
Ellis	1,100	700	1,100
Lewis	2,320	—	2,320
Mason	2,270	—	2,270
Yates	1,900	—	1,900
Zielke	2,680	—	1,870
Total	$11,520	$900	$10,710

Social Security tax	= $10,710 × 0.062	= $664.02
Medicare tax	= $11,520 × 0.0145	= $167.04
FUTA tax	= $900 × 0.008	= $ 7.20
SUTA tax	= $900 × 0.054	= $ 48.60

GENERAL JOURNAL   PAGE

	DATE		DESCRIPTION	POST. REF.	DEBIT	CREDIT	
1	20-- Sept.	14	Payroll Taxes Expense		8 8 6 86		1
2			Social Security Tax Payable			6 6 4 02	2
3			Medicare Tax Payable			1 6 7 04	3
4			FUTA Tax Payable			7 20	4
5			SUTA Tax Payable			4 8 60	5
6			To record employer payroll taxes expense				6
7							7

Exercise 9-4A

Salary of Knox	$32,000
Social Security tax ($32,000 × 0.062)	1,984
Medicare tax ($32,000 × 0.0145)	464
FUTA tax ($7,000 × 0.008)	56
SUTA tax ($7,000 × 0.054)	378
Total cost of employee	$34,882

Exercise 9-5A

GENERAL JOURNAL

PAGE

	DATE		DESCRIPTION	POST. REF.	DEBIT	CREDIT	
1	20-- Apr.	15	Employee Income Tax Payable		6 8 2 5 00		1
2			Social Security Tax Payable		11 2 5 0 00		2
3			Medicare Tax Payable		2 6 2 5 00		3
4			Cash			20 7 0 0 00	4
5			Deposit of employee federal income tax and				5
6			Social Security and Medicare taxes				6
7		30	FUTA Tax Payable		6 0 0 00		7
8			Cash			6 0 0 00	8
9			Paid FUTA tax				9
10		30	SUTA Tax Payable		4 0 5 0 00		10
11			Cash			4 0 5 0 00	11
12			Paid SUTA tax				12

Exercise 9-6A

1. Workers' compensation insurance premium = $425,000 × 0.002 = $850.00

GENERAL JOURNAL

PAGE

	DATE		DESCRIPTION	POST. REF.	DEBIT	CREDIT	
1	20-- Jan.	2	Workers' Compensation Insurance Expense		8 5 0 00		1
2			Cash			8 5 0 00	2
3			Paid estimated workers'				3
4			compensation insurance premium				4
5							5

2.

Actual payroll = $432,000 × 0.002 = $864.00

Actual amount owed	= $864.00
Less estimated premium paid	= 850.00
Additional premium due	= $ 14.00

GENERAL JOURNAL

PAGE

	DATE		DESCRIPTION	POST. REF.	DEBIT	CREDIT	
1	20-- Dec.	31	Workers' Compensation Insurance Expense		1 4 00		1
2			Workers' Compensation Insurance Payable			1 4 00	2
3			Adjustment for insurance premium				3
4							4

Problem 9-7A

1.

		Taxable Earnings	
Name	Current Earnings	Unemploy. Comp.	Social Security
Barnum, Alex	$ 820	$250	$ 820
Duel, Richard	725	660	725
Hunt, J. B.	1,235	—	1,235
Larson, Susan	910	50	910
Mercado, Denise	3,520	—	1,350
Swan, Judy	1,125	—	1,125
Yates, Keith	1,300	—	1,300
Total	$9,635	$960	$7,465

Social Security tax	*= $7,465 × 0.062*	*= $462.83*
Medicare tax	*= $9,635 × 0.0145*	*= 139.71*
FUTA tax	*= $960 × 0.008*	*= 7.68*
SUTA tax	*= $960 × 0.054*	*= 51.84*
Total employer payroll taxes		*$662.06*

2.

GENERAL JOURNAL   PAGE

	DATE		DESCRIPTION	POST. REF.	DEBIT	CREDIT	
1	20-- July	7	*Payroll Taxes Expense*		6 6 2 06		1
2			*Social Security Tax Payable*			4 6 2 83	2
3			*Medicare Tax Payable*			1 3 9 71	3
4			*FUTA Tax Payable*			7 68	4
5			*SUTA Tax Payable*			5 1 84	5
6			*To record employer's payroll taxes expense*				6
7							7
8							8
9							9
10							10

Problem 9-8A

1.

GENERAL JOURNAL

PAGE

	DATE		DESCRIPTION	POST. REF.	DEBIT	CREDIT	
1	20-- June	15	Employee Income Tax Payable	211	3 5 5 3 00		1
2			Social Security Tax Payable	212	5 1 0 3 00		2
3			Medicare Tax Payable	213	1 1 9 7 00		3
4			Cash	101		9 8 5 3 00	4
5			Deposit of employee federal income tax and				5
6			Social Security and Medicare taxes				6
7							7
8		30	Wages and Salaries Expense	511	42 0 0 0 00		8
9			Employee Income Tax Payable	211		3 5 7 0 00	9
10			Social Security Tax Payable	212		2 6 0 4 00	10
11			Medicare Tax Payable	213		6 0 9 00	11
12			Savings Bond Deductions Payable	218		1 2 2 5 00	12
13			Cash	101		33 9 9 2 00	13
14			To record June payroll				14
15							15
16		30	Savings Bond Deductions Payable	218	2 4 5 0 00		16
17			Cash	101		2 4 5 0 00	17
18			Purchased U.S. savings bonds				18
19			for employees				19
20							20
21		30	Payroll Taxes Expense	530	3 8 6 4 00		21
22			Social Security Tax Payable	212		2 6 0 4 00	22
23			Medicare Tax Payable	213		6 0 9 00	23
24			FUTA Tax Payable	221		8 4 00	24
25			SUTA Tax Payable	222		5 6 7 00	25
26			To record employer payroll taxes expense				26
27							27
28	July	15	Employee Income Tax Payable	211	3 5 7 0 00		28
29			Social Security Tax Payable	212	5 2 0 8 00		29
30			Medicare Tax Payable	213	1 2 1 8 00		30
31			Cash	101		9 9 9 6 00	31
32			Deposit of employee federal income tax and				32
33			Social Security and Medicare taxes				33
34							34
35							35
36							36

Problem 9-8A (Continued)

GENERAL JOURNAL

PAGE

	DATE		DESCRIPTION	POST. REF.	DEBIT	CREDIT	
1	20-- July	31	SUTA Tax Payable	222	3 4 0 2 00		1
2			Cash	101		3 4 0 2 00	2
3			Paid SUTA tax				3
4							4
5		31	FUTA Tax Payable	221	6 5 8 00		5
6			Cash	101		6 5 8 00	6
7			Paid FUTA tax				7
8							8
9							9
10							10
11							11
12							12
13							13
14							14
15							15
16							16
17							17
18							18
19							19
20							20
21							21
22							22
23							23
24							24
25							25
26							26
27							27
28							28
29							29
30							30
31							31
32							32
33							33
34							34
35							35

Problem 9-8A (Concluded)

2.

	Cash		101		Employee Income Tax Payable		211
Bal.	**70,200**	6/15	9,853	6/15	3,553	**Bal.**	**3,553**
		6/30	33,992	7/15	3,570	6/30	3,570
		6/30	2,450				
		7/15	9,996				
		7/31	3,402				
		7/31	658				

	Social Security Tax Payable		212		Medicare Tax Payable		213
6/15	5,103	**Bal.**	**5,103**	6/15	1,197	**Bal.**	**1,197**
7/15	5,208	6/30	2,604	7/15	1,218	6/30	609
		6/30	2,604			6/30	609

	Savings Bond Deductions Payable		218		FUTA Tax Payable		221
6/30	2,450	**Bal.**	**1,225**	7/31	658	**Bal.**	**574**
		6/30	1,225			6/30	84

	SUTA Tax Payable		222		Wages and Salaries Expense		511
7/31	3,402	**Bal.**	**2,835**	6/30	42,000		
		6/30	567				

	Payroll Taxes Expense		530
6/30	3,864		

Problem 9-9A

1.

$650,000 × 0.003 = $1,950.00

GENERAL JOURNAL   PAGE

	DATE		DESCRIPTION	POST. REF.	DEBIT	CREDIT	
1	20-- Jan.	2	Workers' Compensation Insurance Expense		1 9 5 0 00		1
2			Cash			1 9 5 0 00	2
3			Paid estimated workers' compensation				3
4			insurance premium				4
5							5
6							6

2.

$672,000 × 0.003	$2,016.00
Less estimated premium paid	1,950.00
Additional premium due	$ 66.00

GENERAL JOURNAL   PAGE

	DATE		DESCRIPTION	POST. REF.	DEBIT	CREDIT	
1	20-- Dec.	31	Workers' Compensation Insurance Expense		6 6 00		1
2			Workers' Compensation Insurance Payable			6 6 00	2
3			Adjustment for insurance premium				3
4							4
5							5
6							6

Problem 9-9A (Concluded)

3.

$634,000 × 0.003	$1,902.00
Less estimated premium paid	1,950.00
Refund due	$ (48.00)

GENERAL JOURNAL   PAGE

	DATE		DESCRIPTION	POST. REF.	DEBIT	CREDIT	
1	20-- Dec.	31	Insurance Refund Receivable		4 8 00		1
2			Workers' Compensation Insurance Expense			4 8 00	2
3			Adjustment for insurance premium				3
4							4
5							5

Exercise 9-1B

Social Security tax	= $15,680 × 0.062	= $ 972.16	
Medicare tax	= $15,680 × 0.0145	= 227.36	
FUTA tax	= $12,310 × 0.008	= 98.48	
SUTA tax	= $12,310 × 0.054	= 664.74	
Total employer payroll taxes		$1,962.74	

GENERAL JOURNAL   PAGE

	DATE		DESCRIPTION	POST. REF.	DEBIT	CREDIT	
1	20-- June	21	Payroll Taxes Expense		1 9 6 2 74		1
2			Social Security Tax Payable			9 7 2 16	2
3			Medicare Tax Payable			2 2 7 36	3
4			FUTA Tax Payable			9 8 48	4
5			SUTA Tax Payable			6 6 4 74	5
6			To record employer payroll taxes expense				6
7							7
8							8
9							9

Exercise 9-2B

Total unemployment taxable	*= $1,380.00*
Total Social Security taxable	*= $5,465.00*
Total earnings	*= $5,465.00*

Social Security tax	*= $5,465 × 0.062*	*= $338.83*
Medicare tax	*= $5,465 × 0.0145*	*= 79.24*
FUTA tax	*= $1,380 × 0.008*	*= 11.04*
SUTA tax	*= $1,380 × 0.054*	*= 74.52*
Total employer payroll taxes		*$503.63*

GENERAL JOURNAL

PAGE

	DATE		DESCRIPTION	POST. REF.	DEBIT	CREDIT	
1	20-- Apr.	7	Payroll Taxes Expense		503 63		1
2			Social Security Tax Payable			338 83	2
3			Medicare Tax Payable			79 24	3
4			FUTA Tax Payable			11 04	4
5			SUTA Tax Payable			74 52	5
6			To record employer payroll taxes expense				6
7							7
8							8

Exercise 9-3B

		Taxable Earnings	
Name	**Current Earnings**	**Unemploy. Comp.**	**Social Security**
Carlson	$ 950	$ 365	$ 950
Delgado	1,215	850	1,215
Lewis	2,415	—	2,415
Nixon	1,750	—	1,750
Shippe	1,450	—	1,450
Watts	2,120	—	1,400
Total	$9,900	$1,215	$9,180

Exercise 9-3B (Concluded)

Social Security tax	= $9,180 × 0.062	= $569.16
Medicare tax	= $9,900 × 0.0145	= $143.55
FUTA tax	= $1,215 × 0.008	= $ 9.72
SUTA tax	= $1,215 × 0.054	= $ 65.61

GENERAL JOURNAL   PAGE

	DATE		DESCRIPTION	POST. REF.	DEBIT	CREDIT	
1	20-- Oct.	7	Payroll Taxes Expense		788 04		1
2			Social Security Tax Payable			569 16	2
3			Medicare Tax Payable			143 55	3
4			FUTA Tax Payable			9 72	4
5			SUTA Tax Payable			65 61	5
6			To record employer payroll taxes expense				6
7							7

Exercise 9-4B: See page 325.

Exercise 9-5B

GENERAL JOURNAL   PAGE

	DATE		DESCRIPTION	POST. REF.	DEBIT	CREDIT	
1	20-- July	15	Employee Income Tax Payable		7245 00		1
2			Social Security Tax Payable		9563 00		2
3			Medicare Tax Payable		2250 00		3
4			Cash			19058 00	4
5			Deposit of employee federal income tax and				5
6			Social Security and Medicare taxes				6
7							7
8		31	FUTA Tax Payable		504 00		8
9			Cash			504 00	9
10			Paid FUTA tax				10
11							11
12		31	SUTA Tax Payable		3402 00		12
13			Cash			3402 00	13
14			Paid SUTA tax				14

Exercise 9-4B

Salary of Gonzales	*$46,000*
Social Security tax ($46,000 × 0.062)	*2,852*
Medicare tax ($46,000 × 0.0145)	*667*
FUTA tax ($7,000 × 0.008)	*56*
SUTA tax ($7,000 × 0.054)	*378*
Total cost of employee	*$49,953*

Exercise 9-6B

1.

Workers' compensation insurance premium = $385,000 × 0.002 = $770.00

GENERAL JOURNAL   PAGE

	DATE		DESCRIPTION	POST. REF.	DEBIT	CREDIT	
1	20-- Jan.	2	*Workers' Compensation Insurance Expense*		7 7 0 00		1
2			*Cash*			7 7 0 00	2
3			*Paid estimated workers'*				3
4			*compensation insurance premium*				4
5							5

2.

Actual payroll = $396,000 × 0.002 = $792.00

Actual amount owed	*= $792.00*
Less estimated premium paid	*= 770.00*
Additional premium due	*= $ 22.00*

GENERAL JOURNAL   PAGE

	DATE		DESCRIPTION	POST. REF.	DEBIT	CREDIT	
1	20-- Dec.	31	*Workers' Compensation Insurance Expense*		2 2 00		1
2			*Workers' Compensation Insurance Payable*			2 2 00	2
3			*Adjustment for insurance premium*				3
4							4
5							5

Problem 9-7B

1.

Name	Current Earnings	Taxable Earnings Unemploy. Comp.	Social Security
Ackers, Alice	$ 645	$540	$ 645
Conley, Dorothy	1,025	—	1,025
Davis, James	565	150	565
Lawrence, Kevin	2,875	—	2,875
Rawlings, Judy	985	—	985
Tanaka, Sumio	835	—	835
Vadillo, Raynette	3,540	—	1,840
Total	$10,470	$690	$8,770

Social Security tax	= $8,770 × 0.062	= $543.74
Medicare tax	= $10,470 × 0.0145	= 151.82
FUTA tax	= $690 × 0.008	= 5.52
SUTA tax	= $690 × 0.054	= 37.26
Total employer payroll taxes		$738.34

2.

GENERAL JOURNAL

PAGE

	DATE		DESCRIPTION	POST. REF.	DEBIT	CREDIT	
1	20-- July	14	Payroll Taxes Expense		7 3 8 34		1
2			Social Security Tax Payable			5 4 3 74	2
3			Medicare Tax Payable			1 5 1 82	3
4			FUTA Tax Payable			5 52	4
5			SUTA Tax Payable			3 7 26	5
6			To record employer payroll taxes expense				6
7							7
8							8
9							9
10							10
11							11
12							12

Problem 9-8B

1.

GENERAL JOURNAL   PAGE

	DATE		DESCRIPTION	POST. REF.	DEBIT	CREDIT	
1	20-- June	15	Employee Income Tax Payable	211	2 0 1 8 00		1
2			Social Security Tax Payable	212	2 7 3 5 00		2
3			Medicare Tax Payable	213	6 4 1 00		3
4			Cash	101		5 3 9 4 00	4
5			Deposit of employee federal income tax and				5
6			Social Security and Medicare taxes				6
7							7
8		30	Wages and Salaries Expense	511	22 0 5 0 00		8
9			Employee Income Tax Payable	211		1 9 2 0 00	9
10			Social Security Tax Payable	212		1 3 6 7 10	10
11			Medicare Tax Payable	213		3 1 9 73	11
12			Savings Bond Deductions Payable	218		7 8 7 50	12
13			Cash	101		17 6 5 5 67	13
14			To record June payroll				14
15							15
16		30	Savings Bond Deductions Payable	218	1 5 7 5 00		16
17			Cash	101		1 5 7 5 00	17
18			Purchased U.S. savings bonds				18
19			for employees				19
20							20
21		30	Payroll Taxes Expense	530	2 1 0 5 33		21
22			Social Security Tax Payable	212		1 3 6 7 10	22
23			Medicare Tax Payable	213		3 1 9 73	23
24			FUTA Tax Payable	221		5 4 00	24
25			SUTA Tax Payable	222		3 6 4 50	25
26			To record employer payroll taxes expense				26
27							27
28	July	15	Employee Income Tax Payable	211	1 9 2 0 00		28
29			Social Security Tax Payable	212	2 7 3 4 20		29
30			Medicare Tax Payable	213	6 3 9 46		30
31			Cash	101		5 2 9 3 66	31
32			Deposit of employee federal income tax and				32
33			Social Security and Medicare taxes				33
34							34
35							35
36							36

Problem 9-8B (Continued)

GENERAL JOURNAL

PAGE ____

	DATE		DESCRIPTION	POST. REF.	DEBIT	CREDIT	
1	20-- July	31	SUTA Tax Payable	222	1 7 4 4 50		1
2			Cash	101		1 7 4 4 50	2
3			Paid SUTA tax				3
4							4
5		31	FUTA Tax Payable	221	5 9 4 00		5
6			Cash	101		5 9 4 00	6
7			Paid FUTA tax				7
8							8
9							9
10							10
11							11
12							12
13							13
14							14
15							15
16							16
17							17
18							18
19							19
20							20
21							21
22							22
23							23
24							24
25							25
26							26
27							27
28							28
29							29
30							30
31							31
32							32
33							33
34							34
35							35

Problem 9-8B (Concluded)

2.

	Cash		101
Bal.	69,500.00	6/15	5,394.00
		6/30	17,655.67
		6/30	1,575.00
		7/15	5,293.66
		7/31	1,744.50
		7/31	594.00

	Employee Income Tax Payable		211
6/15	2,018.00	Bal.	2,018.00
7/15	1,920.00	6/30	1,920.00

	Social Security Tax Payable		212
6/15	2,735.00	Bal.	2,735.00
7/15	2,734.20	6/30	1,367.10
		6/30	1,367.10

	Medicare Tax Payable		213
6/15	641.00	Bal.	641.00
7/15	639.46	6/30	319.73
		6/30	319.73

	Savings Bond Deductions Payable		218
6/30	1,575.00	Bal.	787.50
		6/30	787.50

	FUTA Tax Payable		221
7/31	594.00	Bal.	540.00
		6/30	54.00

	SUTA Tax Payable		222
7/31	1,744.50	Bal.	1,380.00
		6/30	364.50

	Wages and Salaries Expense		511
6/30	22,050.00		

	Payroll Taxes Expense		530
6/30	2,105.33		

Problem 9-9B

1.

$540,000 × 0.002 = $1,080.00

GENERAL JOURNAL   PAGE

	DATE		DESCRIPTION	POST. REF.	DEBIT	CREDIT	
1	20-- Jan.	2	Workers' Compensation Insurance Expense		1 0 8 0 00		1
2			Cash			1 0 8 0 00	2
3			Paid insurance premium				3
4							4
5							5
6							6

2.

$562,000 × 0.002	$1,124.00
Less estimated premium paid	1,080.00
Additional premium due	$ 44.00

GENERAL JOURNAL   PAGE

	DATE		DESCRIPTION	POST. REF.	DEBIT	CREDIT	
1	20-- Dec.	31	Workers' Compensation Insurance Expense		4 4 00		1
2			Workers' Compensation Insurance Payable			4 4 00	2
3			Adjustment for insurance premium				3
4							4
5							5
6							6

Problem 9-9B (Concluded)

3.

$532,000 × 0.002	$1,064.00
Less estimated premium paid	1,080.00
Refund due	$ (16.00)

GENERAL JOURNAL   PAGE

	DATE		DESCRIPTION	POST. REF.	DEBIT	CREDIT	
1	20-- Dec.	31	Insurance Refund Receivable		1 6 00		1
2			Workers' Compensation Insurance Expense			1 6 00	2
3			Adjustment for insurance premium				3
4							4

MANAGING YOUR WRITING

Every employer is required to pay a percentage of wages for various government programs for employees. Costs that are part of this element of these fringe benefits are as follows:

Social Security	6.20%
Medicare	1.45
FUTA	0.80
SUTA	5.40
Total	13.85%

In addition to this approximately 14% required by the government, various other programs could easily make up the rest of the 30% of fringe benefits. Some common examples include the following:

Health insurance	10–15%
Retirement program	5–10%
Vacation support program	2–5%
Family leave program	5–10%

All things considered, the art director is probably fortunate to be held responsible for only 30% in fringes.

ETHICS CASE: SUGGESTED SOLUTIONS

1. No. Bob injured his back at home. Workers' compensation is for injuries and illnesses incurred while on the job.
2. Bob's claim could potentially increase Cliffrock Company's premium because premiums are based, in part, on the number of work-related accidents and illnesses that have occurred at the company.
3. Answers will vary. Students should include the purpose of workers' compensation and the procedures to follow when a workers' compensation claim is filed.
4. Answers will vary. Possible risks might include repeated stress injuries to wrists; back, neck, and shoulder strains; headaches; and eyestrain. Employers could minimize these risks by encouraging input operators to sit properly and take stretching breaks. Employers could also invest in ergonomic chairs and keyboards as well as high resolution monitors to prevent eyestrain.

Mastery Problem

1., 2., and 3.

GENERAL JOURNAL

PAGE

	DATE		DESCRIPTION	POST. REF.	DEBIT	CREDIT	
1	20-- Mar.	31	Wages and Salaries Expense		5 5 0 0 00		1
2			Employee Income Tax Payable			5 0 0 00	2
3			Social Security Tax Payable			3 4 1 00	3
4			Medicare Tax Payable			7 9 75	4
5			Health Insurance Premiums Payable			1 6 5 00	5
6			Life Insurance Premiums Payable			2 0 0 00	6
7			Cash			4 2 1 4 25	7
8			To record Mar. 31 payroll				8
9							9
10		31	Payroll Taxes Expense		7 3 0 75		10
11			Social Security Tax Payable			3 4 1 00	11
12			Medicare Tax Payable			7 9 75	12
13			FUTA Tax Payable			4 0 00	13
14			SUTA Tax Payable			2 7 0 00	14
15			To record employer payroll taxes expense				15
16							16
17	Apr.	15	Employee Income Tax Payable		3 0 0 0 00		17
18			Social Security Tax Payable		2 6 9 0 00		18
19			Medicare Tax Payable		6 2 9 50		19
20			Cash			6 3 1 9 50	20
21			Deposit of employee federal income tax and				21
22			Social Security and Medicare taxes				22
23							23
24		30	FUTA Tax Payable		5 6 0 00		24
25			Cash			5 6 0 00	25
26			Paid FUTA tax				26
27							27
28		30	SUTA Tax Payable		3 7 8 0 00		28
29			Cash			3 7 8 0 00	29
30			Paid SUTA tax				30
31							31
32							32
33							33
34							34
35							35

Mastery Problem (Concluded)

GENERAL JOURNAL

	DATE		DESCRIPTION	POST. REF.	DEBIT	CREDIT	
1	20-- Dec.	31	Insurance Refund Receivable		2 0 00		1
2			Workers' Compensation Insurance Expense			2 0 00	2
3			Adjustment for insurance premium				3
4							4
5							5
6							6
7							7
8							8
9							9
10							10
11							11
12							12
13							13
14							14
15							15
16							16
17							17
18							18
19							19
20							20
21							21
22							22
23							23
24							24
25							25
26							26
27							27
28							28
29							29
30							30
31							31
32							32
33							33
34							34
35							35

Challenge Problem

1.

Social Security tax	= $12,500 × 0.062	= $775.00
Medicare tax	= $12,500 × 0.0145	= $181.25
FUTA tax	= $12,500 × 0.008	= $100.00
SUTA tax	= $12,500 × 0.020	= $250.00

2.

GENERAL JOURNAL

PAGE

	DATE		DESCRIPTION	POST. REF.	DEBIT	CREDIT	
1	20-- Jan.	7	Payroll Taxes Expense		1 3 0 6 25		1
2			Social Security Tax Payable			7 7 5 00	2
3			Medicare Tax Payable			1 8 1 25	3
4			FUTA Tax Payable			1 0 0 00	4
5			SUTA Tax Payable			2 5 0 00	5
6			Employer payroll taxes for week				6
7			ended Jan. 7				7

3.

$12,500 × 0.054	= $675.00
$12,500 × 0.020	= 250.00
Savings	$425.00

CHAPTER 10

ACCOUNTING FOR SALES AND CASH RECEIPTS

REVIEW QUESTIONS

1. In retail businesses, a cash register tape summary and a sales ticket are commonly used. In wholesale businesses, a sales invoice is commonly used. When merchandise is returned, a credit memo would be used by both retailers and wholesalers.

2. A credit memo is issued by the seller for the amount involved when credit is given for merchandise returned or for an allowance.

3. The sales account is a revenue account used to record sales of merchandise. Sales Tax Payable is a liability account that is credited for the amount of tax imposed on sales. Sales Returns and Allowances is a contra-revenue account to which sales returns and sales allowances are debited. Sales Discounts is a contra-revenue account to which cash discounts allowed are debited.

4. To post sales from the general journal to the general ledger:

    In the general ledger account:
    Step 1: Enter the date of the transaction in the Date column.
    Step 2: Enter the amount of the debit or credit in the Debit or Credit column.
    Step 3: Enter the new balance in the Balance columns under Debit or Credit.
    Step 4: Enter the journal page number from which each transaction is posted in the Posting Reference column.

    In the journal:
    Step 5: Enter the ledger account number in the Posting Reference column of the journal for each transaction that is posted.

5. To post sales from the general journal to the accounts receivable ledger:

    In the accounts receivable ledger account:
    Step 1: Enter the date of the transaction in the Date column.
    Step 2: Enter the amount of the debit or credit in the Debit or Credit column.
    Step 3: Enter the new balance in the Balance column.
    Step 4: Enter the journal page number from which each transaction is posted in the Posting Reference column.

    In the journal:
    Step 5: Enter a slash (/) followed by a check mark (✓) in the Posting Reference column of the journal for each transaction that is posted.

6. To post sales returns and allowances from the general journal to the general ledger and accounts receivable ledger:

    The general ledger is posted using the same five steps as are illustrated for sales transactions in Figure 10-13. The accounts receivable ledger is posted using the following five steps:

    In the accounts receivable ledger account:
    Step 1: Enter the date of the transaction in the Date column.
    Step 2: Enter the amount of the debit or credit in the Debit or Credit column.
    Step 3: Enter the new balance in the Balance column.
    Step 4: Enter the journal page number from which each transaction is posted in the Posting Reference column.

In the journal:
Step 5: Enter a slash (/) followed by a check mark (✓) in the Posting Reference column of the journal for each transaction that is posted.

7. To post cash receipts from the general journal to the general ledger:

Cash receipts transactions are posted to the general ledger in the same manner as is illustrated for sales transactions in Figure 10-13.

8. To post cash receipts from the general journal to the accounts receivable ledger:

In the accounts receivable ledger account:
Step 1: Enter the date of the transaction in the Date column.
Step 2: Enter the amount of the debit or credit in the Debit or Credit column.
Step 3: Enter the new balance in the Balance column.
Step 4: Enter the journal page number from which each transaction is posted in the Posting Reference column.

In the journal:
Step 5: Enter a slash (/) followed by a check mark (✓) in the Posting Reference column of the journal for each transaction that is posted.

9. To find the error, use the following steps:
Step 1: Verify the total of the schedule.
Step 2: Verify the postings to the accounts receivable ledger.
Step 3: Verify the postings to Accounts Receivable in the general ledger.

Exercise 10-1A

1. *Retail*   4. *Retail*
2. *Wholesale*   5. *Wholesale and retail*
3. *Wholesale*   6. *Wholesale*

Exercise 10-2A

1.

Cash				Accounts Receivable			
(a)	300.00			*(b)*	285.00	*(c)*	285.00
(c)	285.00						

Sales Tax Payable				Sales			
						(a)	300.00
						(b)	285.00

Sales Returns and Allowances		Sales Discounts	

2.

Cash				Accounts Receivable			
(a)	315.00			*(b)*	299.25	*(c)*	299.25
(c)	299.25						

Sales Tax Payable				Sales			
		(a)	15.00			*(a)*	300.00
		(b)	14.25			*(b)*	285.00

Sales Returns and Allowances		Sales Discounts	

Exercise 10-2A (Concluded)

3.

Cash					Accounts Receivable				
(a)	325.00	(b)	25.00		(c)	350.00	(d)	35.00
(e)	315.00						(e)	315.00

Sales Tax Payable					Sales				
							(a)	325.00
							(c)	350.00

Sales Returns and Allowances					Sales Discounts				
(b)	25.00							
(d)	35.00							

4.

Cash					Accounts Receivable				
(c)	378.00	(e)	21.00		(a)	420.00	(b)	42.00
(d)	294.00						(c)	378.00

Sales Tax Payable					Sales				
(b)	2.00	(a)	20.00				(a)	400.00
(e)	1.00	(d)	14.00				(d)	280.00

Sales Returns and Allowances					Sales Discounts				
(b)	40.00							
(e)	20.00							

5.

Cash					Accounts Receivable				
(b)	343.00				(a)	350.00	(b)	350.00
(d)	290.00				(c)	290.00	(d)	290.00

Sales Tax Payable					Sales				
							(a)	350.00
							(c)	290.00

Sales Returns and Allowances					Sales Discounts				
					(b)	7.00		

Exercise 10-3A

Sales		$3,580	
Less: Sales returns and allowances	$428		
Sales discounts	73	501	
Net sales		$3,079	

Exercise 10-4A

GENERAL JOURNAL   PAGE

	DATE		DESCRIPTION	POST. REF.	DEBIT	CREDIT	
1	20-- Aug.	4	Accounts Receivable/F. Graves		3 5 3 60		1
2			Sales			3 4 0 00	2
3			Sales Tax Payable			1 3 60	3
4			Made credit sale				4
5							5
6		6	Accounts Receivable/B. Feikert		1 8 7 20		6
7			Sales			1 8 0 00	7
8			Sales Tax Payable			7 20	8
9			Made credit sale				9
10							10
11		10	Sales Returns and Allowances		3 0 00		11
12			Sales Tax Payable		1 20		12
13			Accounts Receivable/F. Graves			3 1 20	13
14			Returned merchandise				14
15							15
16		13	Cash		3 1 6 20		16
17			Sales Discounts		6 20		17
18			Accounts Receivable/F. Graves			3 2 2 40	18
19			Received cash on account				19
20							20

Exercise 10-4A (Concluded)

GENERAL JOURNAL

PAGE

	DATE		DESCRIPTION	POST. REF.	DEBIT	CREDIT	
21	20-- Aug.	15	**Sales Returns and Allowances**		5 0 00		21
22			**Sales Tax Payable**		2 00		22
23			**Accounts Receivable/B. Feikert**			5 2 00	23
24			**Returned merchandise**				24
25							25
26		20	**Cash**		1 3 5 20		26
27			**Accounts Receivable/B. Feikert**			1 3 5 20	27
28			**Received cash on account**				28

Exercise 10-5A

GENERAL JOURNAL

PAGE

	DATE		DESCRIPTION	POST. REF.	DEBIT	CREDIT	
1	20-- May	1	**Accounts Receivable/J. Adams**		2 1 2 0 00		1
2			**Sales**			2 0 0 0 00	2
3			**Sales Tax Payable**			1 2 0 00	3
4			**Sale No. 488**				4
5							5
6		4	**Accounts Receivable/B. Clark**		1 9 0 8 00		6
7			**Sales**			1 8 0 0 00	7
8			**Sales Tax Payable**			1 0 8 00	8
9			**Sale No. 489**				9
10							10
11		8	**Accounts Receivable/A. Duck**		1 5 9 0 00		11
12			**Sales**			1 5 0 0 00	12
13			**Sales Tax Payable**			9 0 00	13
14			**Sale No. 490**				14
15							15
16		11	**Accounts Receivable/E. Hill**		2 0 6 7 00		16
17			**Sales**			1 9 5 0 00	17
18			**Sales Tax Payable**			1 1 7 00	18
19			**Sale No. 491**				19
20							20
21							21
22							22

Exercise 10-6A

GENERAL JOURNAL

	DATE		DESCRIPTION	POST. REF.	DEBIT	CREDIT	
1	20-- June	1	Sales Returns and Allowances	401.1	7 3 00		1
2			Accounts Receivable/J. Abramowitz	122/✓		7 3 00	2
3			Returned merchandise				3
4							4
5		6	Sales Returns and Allowances	401.1	4 4 00		5
6			Accounts Receivable/M. Perez	122/✓		4 4 00	6
7			Returned merchandise				7
8							8
9		8	Sales Returns and Allowances	401.1	2 4 00		9
10			Accounts Receivable/L. B. Gruder	122/✓		2 4 00	10
11			Returned merchandise				11
12							12
13							13
14							14
15							15

GENERAL LEDGER

ACCOUNT Accounts Receivable   ACCOUNT NO. 122

DATE		ITEM	POST. REF.	DEBIT	CREDIT	BALANCE DEBIT	BALANCE CREDIT
20-- June	1	Balance	✓			4 2 0 0 00	
	1		J60		7 3 00	4 1 2 7 00	
	6		J60		4 4 00	4 0 8 3 00	
	8		J60		2 4 00	4 0 5 9 00	

ACCOUNT Sales Returns and Allowances   ACCOUNT NO. 401.1

DATE		ITEM	POST. REF.	DEBIT	CREDIT	BALANCE DEBIT	BALANCE CREDIT
20-- June	1		J60	7 3 00		7 3 00	
	6		J60	4 4 00		1 1 7 00	
	8		J60	2 4 00		1 4 1 00	

Exercise 10-6A (Concluded)

ACCOUNTS RECEIVABLE LEDGER

NAME John B. Abramowitz

ADDRESS 3201 West Judkins Road, Seattle, WA 98201-1079

DATE		ITEM	POST. REF.	DEBIT	CREDIT	BALANCE
20-- June	1	Balance	✓			8 5 0 00
	1		J60		7 3 00	7 7 7 00

NAME L. B. Gruder

ADDRESS 44 Western Blvd., Spokane, WA 98601-4092

DATE		ITEM	POST. REF.	DEBIT	CREDIT	BALANCE
20-- June	1	Balance	✓			4 2 8 00
	8		J60		2 4 00	4 0 4 00

NAME Marie L. Perez

ADDRESS 158 West Adams Point, Bellevue, WA 98401-0663

DATE		ITEM	POST. REF.	DEBIT	CREDIT	BALANCE
20-- June	1	Balance	✓			1 0 1 8 00
	6		J60		4 4 00	9 7 4 00

Exercise 10-7A

GENERAL JOURNAL

PAGE

	DATE		DESCRIPTION	POST. REF.	DEBIT	CREDIT	
1	20-- July	6	Cash		6 4 3 00		1
2			Accounts Receivable/J. Adler			6 4 3 00	2
3			Received cash on account				3
4							4
5		10	Cash		2 3 2 0 00		5
6			Sales			2 3 2 0 00	6
7			Made cash sales				7
8							8
9		14	Cash		4 3 0 00		9
10			Accounts Receivable/B. Havel			4 3 0 00	10
11			Received cash on account				11
12							12
13		15	Cash		1 1 7 00		13
14			Accounts Receivable/J. L. Borg			1 1 7 00	14
15			Received cash on account				15
16							16
17		17	Cash		2 2 3 7 00		17
18			Sales			2 2 3 7 00	18
19			Made cash sales				19
20							20
21							21
22							22

Exercise 10-8A

Pheng Co.

Schedule of Accounts Receivable

August 31, 20--

B & G Distributors	$1 2 4 0 00
B. J. Hinschliff & Co.	1 4 9 0 00
Sally M. Pitts	8 3 8 00
Trendsetters, Inc.	1 0 1 8 00
Total	$4 5 8 6 00

Problem 10-9A

1.

GENERAL JOURNAL

PAGE 15

	DATE		DESCRIPTION	POST. REF.	DEBIT	CREDIT	
1	20-- Aug.	1	Accounts Receivable/Jung Manufacturing Co.	122/✓	1 2 7 2 00		1
2			Sales	401		1 2 0 0 00	2
3			Sales Tax Payable	231		7 2 00	3
4			Sale No. 213				4
5							5
6		3	Accounts Receivable/Hassad Co.	122/✓	3 8 1 6 00		6
7			Sales	401		3 6 0 0 00	7
8			Sales Tax Payable	231		2 1 6 00	8
9			Sale No. 214				9
10							10
11		7	Accounts Receivable/Helsinki, Inc.	122/✓	1 4 8 4 00		11
12			Sales	401		1 4 0 0 00	12
13			Sales Tax Payable	231		8 4 00	13
14			Sale No. 215				14
15							15
16		11	Accounts Receivable/Ardis Myler	122/✓	1 3 5 6 80		16
17			Sales	401		1 2 8 0 00	17
18			Sales Tax Payable	231		7 6 80	18
19			Sale No. 216				19
20							20
21		18	Accounts Receivable/Hassad Co.	122/✓	4 5 8 9 80		21
22			Sales	401		4 3 3 0 00	22
23			Sales Tax Payable	231		2 5 9 80	23
24			Sale No. 217				24
25							25
26		22	Accounts Receivable/Jung Manufacturing Co.	122/✓	2 1 2 0 00		26
27			Sales	401		2 0 0 0 00	27
28			Sales Tax Payable	231		1 2 0 00	28
29			Sale No. 218				29
30							30
31		30	Accounts Receivable/Ardis Myler	122/✓	1 7 0 6 60		31
32			Sales	401		1 6 1 0 00	32
33			Sales Tax Payable	231		9 6 60	33
34			Sale No. 219				34

Problem 10-9A (Continued)

2.

GENERAL LEDGER

ACCOUNT Accounts Receivable   ACCOUNT NO. 122

DATE	ITEM	POST. REF.	DEBIT	CREDIT	BALANCE DEBIT	BALANCE CREDIT
20-- Aug. 1		J15	1 2 7 2 00		1 2 7 2 00	
3		J15	3 8 1 6 00		5 0 8 8 00	
7		J15	1 4 8 4 00		6 5 7 2 00	
11		J15	1 3 5 6 80		7 9 2 8 80	
18		J15	4 5 8 9 80		12 5 1 8 60	
22		J15	2 1 2 0 00		14 6 3 8 60	
30		J15	1 7 0 6 60		16 3 4 5 20	

ACCOUNT Sales Tax Payable   ACCOUNT NO. 231

DATE	ITEM	POST. REF.	DEBIT	CREDIT	BALANCE DEBIT	BALANCE CREDIT
20-- Aug. 1		J15		7 2 00		7 2 00
3		J15		2 1 6 00		2 8 8 00
7		J15		8 4 00		3 7 2 00
11		J15		7 6 80		4 4 8 80
18		J15		2 5 9 80		7 0 8 60
22		J15		1 2 0 00		8 2 8 60
30		J15		9 6 60		9 2 5 20

ACCOUNT Sales   ACCOUNT NO. 401

DATE	ITEM	POST. REF.	DEBIT	CREDIT	BALANCE DEBIT	BALANCE CREDIT
20-- Aug. 1		J15		1 2 0 0 00		1 2 0 0 00
3		J15		3 6 0 0 00		4 8 0 0 00
7		J15		1 4 0 0 00		6 2 0 0 00
11		J15		1 2 8 0 00		7 4 8 0 00
18		J15		4 3 3 0 00		11 8 1 0 00
22		J15		2 0 0 0 00		13 8 1 0 00
30		J15		1 6 1 0 00		15 4 2 0 00

Problem 10-9A (Concluded)

ACCOUNTS RECEIVABLE LEDGER

NAME Hassad Co.

ADDRESS 1225 W. Temperance Street, Elletsville, IN 47429-9976

DATE		ITEM	POST. REF.	DEBIT	CREDIT	BALANCE
20-- Aug.	3		J15	3 8 1 6 00		3 8 1 6 00
	18		J15	4 5 8 9 80		8 4 0 5 80

NAME Helsinki, Inc.

ADDRESS 125 Fishers Drive, Noblesville, IN 47870-8867

DATE		ITEM	POST. REF.	DEBIT	CREDIT	BALANCE
20-- Aug.	7		J15	1 4 8 4 00		1 4 8 4 00

NAME Jung Manufacturing Co.

ADDRESS 8825 Old State Road, Bloomington, IN 47401-8823

DATE		ITEM	POST. REF.	DEBIT	CREDIT	BALANCE
20-- Aug.	1		J15	1 2 7 2 00		1 2 7 2 00
	22		J15	2 1 2 0 00		3 3 9 2 00

NAME Ardis Myler

ADDRESS 2100 Greer Lane, Bedford, IN 47421-8876

DATE		ITEM	POST. REF.	DEBIT	CREDIT	BALANCE
20-- Aug.	11		J15	1 3 5 6 80		1 3 5 6 80
	30		J15	1 7 0 6 60		3 0 6 3 40

Problem 10-10A

1.

GENERAL JOURNAL

	DATE		DESCRIPTION	POST. REF.	DEBIT	CREDIT	
1	20-- Dec.	1	Cash	101	1 3 6 0 00		1
2			Accounts Receivable/M. Anderson	122/✓		1 3 6 0 00	2
3			Received cash on account				3
4							4
5		2	Cash	101	3 8 2 00		5
6			Accounts Receivable/Ansel Manufacturing	122/✓		3 8 2 00	6
7			Received cash on account				7
8							8
9		7	Cash	101	3 3 4 9 60		9
10			Sales	401		3 1 6 0 00	10
11			Sales Tax Payable	231		1 8 9 60	11
12			Made cash sales				12
13							13
14		7	Cash	101	1 0 2 8 20		14
15			Bank Credit Card Expense	513	3 1 80		15
16			Sales	401		1 0 0 0 00	16
17			Sales Tax Payable	231		6 0 00	17
18			Made credit card sales				18
19							19
20		8	Cash	101	8 8 0 00		20
21			Accounts Receivable/J. Gorbea	122/✓		8 8 0 00	21
22			Received cash on account				22
23							23
24		11	Sales Returns and Allowances	401.1	6 0 00		24
25			Sales Tax Payable	231	3 60		25
26			Accounts Receivable/M. Anderson	122/✓		6 3 60	26
27			Returned merchandise				27
28							28
29		14	Cash	101	2 9 6 8 00		29
30			Sales	401		2 8 0 0 00	30
31			Sales Tax Payable	231		1 6 8 00	31
32			Made cash sales				32
33							33
34							34

Problem 10-10A (Continued)

GENERAL JOURNAL

	DATE		DESCRIPTION	POST. REF.	DEBIT	CREDIT	
1	20-- Dec.	14	Cash	101	8 2 2 56		1
2			Bank Credit Card Expense	513	2 5 44		2
3			Sales	401		8 0 0 00	3
4			Sales Tax Payable	231		4 8 00	4
5			Made credit card sales				5
6							6
7		20	Cash	101	1 1 1 0 00		7
8			Accounts Receivable/T. Wilson	122/✓		1 1 1 0 00	8
9			Received cash on account				9
10							10
11		21	Sales Returns and Allowances	401.1	2 2 00		11
12			Sales Tax Payable	231	1 32		12
13			Accounts Receivable/Ansel Manufacturing	122/✓		2 3 32	13
14			Returned merchandise				14
15							15
16		21	Cash	101	3 3 9 2 00		16
17			Sales	401		3 2 0 0 00	17
18			Sales Tax Payable	231		1 9 2 00	18
19			Made cash sales				19
20							20
21		24	Cash	101	2 0 0 0 00		21
22			Accounts Receivable/R. Carson	122/✓		2 0 0 0 00	22
23			Received cash on account				23
24							24
25							25
26							26
27							27
28							28
29							29
30							30
31							31
32							32
33							33
34							34

Problem 10-10A (Continued)

2.

GENERAL LEDGER

ACCOUNT   Cash   ACCOUNT NO.   101

DATE		ITEM	POST. REF.	DEBIT	CREDIT	BALANCE DEBIT	BALANCE CREDIT
20-- Dec.	1	Balance	✓			9 8 6 2 00	
	1		J20	1 3 6 0 00		11 2 2 2 00	
	2		J20	3 8 2 00		11 6 0 4 00	
	7		J20	3 3 4 9 60		14 9 5 3 60	
	7		J20	1 0 2 8 20		15 9 8 1 80	
	8		J20	8 8 0 00		16 8 6 1 80	
	14		J20	2 9 6 8 00		19 8 2 9 80	
	14		J21	8 2 2 56		20 6 5 2 36	
	20		J21	1 1 1 0 00		21 7 6 2 36	
	21		J21	3 3 9 2 00		25 1 5 4 36	
	24		J21	2 0 0 0 00		27 1 5 4 36	

ACCOUNT   Accounts Receivable   ACCOUNT NO.   122

DATE		ITEM	POST. REF.	DEBIT	CREDIT	BALANCE DEBIT	BALANCE CREDIT
20-- Dec.	1	Balance	✓			9 3 5 2 00	
	1		J20		1 3 6 0 00	7 9 9 2 00	
	2		J20		3 8 2 00	7 6 1 0 00	
	8		J20		8 8 0 00	6 7 3 0 00	
	11		J20		6 3 60	6 6 6 6 40	
	20		J21		1 1 1 0 00	5 5 5 6 40	
	21		J21		2 3 32	5 5 3 3 08	
	24		J21		2 0 0 0 00	3 5 3 3 08	

Problem 10-10A (Continued)

ACCOUNT   Sales Tax Payable   ACCOUNT NO.   231

DATE		ITEM	POST. REF.	DEBIT	CREDIT	BALANCE DEBIT	BALANCE CREDIT
20-- Dec.	7		J20		1 8 9 60		1 8 9 60
	7		J20		6 0 00		2 4 9 60
	11		J20	3 60			2 4 6 00
	14		J20		1 6 8 00		4 1 4 00
	14		J21		4 8 00		4 6 2 00
	21		J21	1 32			4 6 0 68
	21		J21		1 9 2 00		6 5 2 68

ACCOUNT   Sales   ACCOUNT NO.   401

DATE		ITEM	POST. REF.	DEBIT	CREDIT	BALANCE DEBIT	BALANCE CREDIT
20-- Dec.	7		J20		3 1 6 0 00		3 1 6 0 00
	7		J20		1 0 0 0 00		4 1 6 0 00
	14		J20		2 8 0 0 00		6 9 6 0 00
	14		J21		8 0 0 00		7 7 6 0 00
	21		J21		3 2 0 0 00		10 9 6 0 00

ACCOUNT   Sales Returns and Allowances   ACCOUNT NO.   401.1

DATE		ITEM	POST. REF.	DEBIT	CREDIT	BALANCE DEBIT	BALANCE CREDIT
20-- Dec.	11		J20	6 0 00		6 0 00	
	21		J21	2 2 00		8 2 00	

ACCOUNT   Bank Credit Card Expense   ACCOUNT NO.   513

DATE		ITEM	POST. REF.	DEBIT	CREDIT	BALANCE DEBIT	BALANCE CREDIT
20-- Dec.	7		J20	3 1 80		3 1 80	
	14		J21	2 5 44		5 7 24	

Problem 10-10A (Continued)

ACCOUNTS RECEIVABLE LEDGER

NAME Michael Anderson

ADDRESS 233 West 11th Avenue, Detroit, MI 59500-1154

DATE		ITEM	POST. REF.	DEBIT	CREDIT	BALANCE
20-- Dec.	1	Balance	✓			2 4 8 0 00
	1		J20		1 3 6 0 00	1 1 2 0 00
	11		J20		6 3 60	1 0 5 6 40

NAME Ansel Manufacturing

ADDRESS 284 West 88 Street, Detroit, MI 59522-1168

DATE		ITEM	POST. REF.	DEBIT	CREDIT	BALANCE
20-- Dec.	1	Balance	✓			9 8 2 00
	2		J20		3 8 2 00	6 0 0 00
	21		J21		2 3 32	5 7 6 68

NAME J. Gorbea

ADDRESS P.O. Box 864, Detroit, MI 59552-0864

DATE		ITEM	POST. REF.	DEBIT	CREDIT	BALANCE
20-- Dec.	1	Balance	✓			8 8 0 00
	8		J20		8 8 0 00	—

Problem 10-10A (Concluded)

NAME Rachel Carson

ADDRESS 11312 Fourteenth Avenue South, Detroit, MI 59221-1142

DATE		ITEM	POST. REF.	DEBIT	CREDIT	BALANCE
20-- Dec.	1	Balance	✓			3 2 0 0 00
	24		J21		2 0 0 0 00	1 2 0 0 00

NAME Tom Wilson

ADDRESS 100 NW Seward St., Detroit, MI 59210-1337

DATE		ITEM	POST. REF.	DEBIT	CREDIT	BALANCE
20-- Dec.	1	Balance	✓			1 8 1 0 00
	20		J21		1 1 1 0 00	7 0 0 00

Problem 10-11A

1.

GENERAL JOURNAL

PAGE 7

	DATE		DESCRIPTION	POST. REF.	DEBIT	CREDIT	
1	20-- Mar.	1	Accounts Receivable/Able & Co.	122/✓	1 9 4 4 00		1
2			Sales	401		1 8 0 0 00	2
3			Sales Tax Payable	231		1 4 4 00	3
4			Sale No. 33C				4
5							5
6		3	Accounts Receivable/R. J. Kalas, Inc.	122/✓	2 4 1 9 20		6
7			Sales	401		2 2 4 0 00	7
8			Sales Tax Payable	231		1 7 9 20	8
9			Sale No. 33D				9
10							10
11		5	Sales Returns and Allowances	401.1	3 0 00		11
12			Sales Tax Payable	231	2 40		12
13			Accounts Receivable/Able & Co.	122/✓		3 2 40	13
14			Returned merchandise—Credit Memo #66				14
15							15
16		7	Cash	101	3 4 1 2 80		16
17			Sales	401		3 1 6 0 00	17
18			Sales Tax Payable	231		2 5 2 80	18
19			Made cash sales				19
20							20
21		10	Cash	101	1 9 1 1 60		21
22			Accounts Receivable/Able & Co.	122/✓		1 9 1 1 60	22
23			Received cash on account				23
24							24
25		11	Accounts Receivable/Blevins Bakery	122/✓	1 3 0 6 80		25
26			Sales	401		1 2 1 0 00	26
27			Sales Tax Payable	231		9 6 80	27
28			Sale No. 33E				28
29							29
30		13	Cash	101	2 4 1 9 20		30
31			Accounts Receivable/R. J. Kalas, Inc.	122/✓		2 4 1 9 20	31
32			Received cash on account				32
33							33
34							34

Problem 10-11A (Continued)

GENERAL JOURNAL

	DATE		DESCRIPTION	POST. REF.	DEBIT	CREDIT	
1	20-- Mar.	14	Cash	101	4 5 3 6 00		1
2			Sales	401		4 2 0 0 00	2
3			Sales Tax Payable	231		3 3 6 00	3
4			Made cash sales				4
5							5
6		16	Sales Returns and Allowances	401.1	4 4 00		6
7			Sales Tax Payable	231	3 52		7
8			Accounts Receivable/Blevins Bakery	122/✓		4 7 52	8
9			Returned merchandise—Credit Memo #67				9
10							10
11		18	Accounts Receivable/R. J. Kalas, Inc.	122/✓	2 8 2 9 60		11
12			Sales	401		2 6 2 0 00	12
13			Sales Tax Payable	231		2 0 9 60	13
14			Sale No. 33F				14
15							15
16		20	Cash	101	1 2 5 9 28		16
17			Accounts Receivable/Blevins Bakery	122/✓		1 2 5 9 28	17
18			Received cash on account				18
19							19
20		21	Cash	101	2 5 9 2 00		20
21			Sales	401		2 4 0 0 00	21
22			Sales Tax Payable	231		1 9 2 00	22
23			Made cash sales				23
24							24
25		25	Accounts Receivable/Blevins Bakery	122/✓	2 0 6 8 20		25
26			Sales	401		1 9 1 5 00	26
27			Sales Tax Payable	231		1 5 3 20	27
28			Sale No. 33G				28
29							29
30		27	Accounts Receivable/Thompson Group	122/✓	2 1 7 7 28		30
31			Sales	401		2 0 1 6 00	31
32			Sales Tax Payable	231		1 6 1 28	32
33			Sale No. 33H				33
34							34

Problem 10-11A (Continued)

GENERAL JOURNAL

	DATE		DESCRIPTION	POST. REF.	DEBIT	CREDIT	
1	20-- Mar.	28	Cash	101	3 7 8 0 00		1
2			Sales	401		3 5 0 0 00	2
3			Sales Tax Payable	231		2 8 0 00	3
4			Made cash sales				4
5							5
6							6
7							7
8							8
9							9
10							10

2.

GENERAL LEDGER

ACCOUNT Cash

ACCOUNT NO. 101

DATE		ITEM	POST. REF.	DEBIT	CREDIT	BALANCE DEBIT	BALANCE CREDIT
20-- Mar.	1	Balance	✓			9 7 4 1 00	
	7		J7	3 4 1 2 80		13 1 5 3 80	
	10		J7	1 9 1 1 60		15 0 6 5 40	
	13		J7	2 4 1 9 20		17 4 8 4 60	
	14		J8	4 5 3 6 00		22 0 2 0 60	
	20		J8	1 2 5 9 28		23 2 7 9 88	
	21		J8	2 5 9 2 00		25 8 7 1 88	
	28		J9	3 7 8 0 00		29 6 5 1 88	

Problem 10-11A (Continued)

ACCOUNT   Accounts Receivable

ACCOUNT NO.   122

DATE		ITEM	POST. REF.	DEBIT	CREDIT	BALANCE DEBIT	BALANCE CREDIT
20-- Mar.	1	Balance	✓			1 0 5 8 25	
	1		J7	1 9 4 4 00		3 0 0 2 25	
	3		J7	2 4 1 9 20		5 4 2 1 45	
	5		J7		3 2 40	5 3 8 9 05	
	10		J7		1 9 1 1 60	3 4 7 7 45	
	11		J7	1 3 0 6 80		4 7 8 4 25	
	13		J7		2 4 1 9 20	2 3 6 5 05	
	16		J8		4 7 52	2 3 1 7 53	
	18		J8	2 8 2 9 60		5 1 4 7 13	
	20		J8		1 2 5 9 28	3 8 8 7 85	
	25		J8	2 0 6 8 20		5 9 5 6 05	
	27		J8	2 1 7 7 28		8 1 3 3 33	

ACCOUNT   Sales Tax Payable

ACCOUNT NO.   231

DATE		ITEM	POST. REF.	DEBIT	CREDIT	BALANCE DEBIT	BALANCE CREDIT
20-- Mar.	1		J7		1 4 4 00		1 4 4 00
	3		J7		1 7 9 20		3 2 3 20
	5		J7	2 40			3 2 0 80
	7		J7		2 5 2 80		5 7 3 60
	11		J7		9 6 80		6 7 0 40
	14		J8		3 3 6 00		1 0 0 6 40
	16		J8	3 52			1 0 0 2 88
	18		J8		2 0 9 60		1 2 1 2 48
	21		J8		1 9 2 00		1 4 0 4 48
	25		J8		1 5 3 20		1 5 5 7 68
	27		J8		1 6 1 28		1 7 1 8 96
	28		J9		2 8 0 00		1 9 9 8 96

Problem 10-11A (Continued)

ACCOUNT Sales   ACCOUNT NO. 401

DATE		ITEM	POST. REF.	DEBIT	CREDIT	BALANCE DEBIT	BALANCE CREDIT
20-- Mar.	1		J7		1 8 0 0 00		1 8 0 0 00
	3		J7		2 2 4 0 00		4 0 4 0 00
	7		J7		3 1 6 0 00		7 2 0 0 00
	11		J7		1 2 1 0 00		8 4 1 0 00
	14		J8		4 2 0 0 00		12 6 1 0 00
	18		J8		2 6 2 0 00		15 2 3 0 00
	21		J8		2 4 0 0 00		17 6 3 0 00
	25		J8		1 9 1 5 00		19 5 4 5 00
	27		J8		2 0 1 6 00		21 5 6 1 00
	28		J9		3 5 0 0 00		25 0 6 1 00

ACCOUNT Sales Returns and Allowances   ACCOUNT NO. 401.1

DATE		ITEM	POST. REF.	DEBIT	CREDIT	BALANCE DEBIT	BALANCE CREDIT
20-- Mar.	5		J7	3 0 00		3 0 00	
	16		J8	4 4 00		7 4 00	

ACCOUNTS RECEIVABLE LEDGER

NAME Able & Co.

ADDRESS 1424 Jackson Creek Road, Nashville, IN 47448-2245

DATE		ITEM	POST. REF.	DEBIT	CREDIT	BALANCE
20-- Mar.	1		J7	1 9 4 4 00		1 9 4 4 00
	5		J7		3 2 40	1 9 1 1 60
	10		J7		1 9 1 1 60	———

Problem 10-11A (Concluded)

NAME Blevins Bakery

ADDRESS 6422 E. Bender Road, Bloomington, IN 47401-7756

DATE		ITEM	POST. REF.	DEBIT	CREDIT	BALANCE
20-- Mar.	11		J7	1 3 0 6 80		1 3 0 6 80
	16		J8		4 7 52	1 2 5 9 28
	20		J8		1 2 5 9 28	———
	25		J8	2 0 6 8 20		2 0 6 8 20

NAME R. J. Kalas, Inc.

ADDRESS 3315 Longview Avenue, Bloomington, IN 47401-7223

DATE		ITEM	POST. REF.	DEBIT	CREDIT	BALANCE
20-- Mar.	3		J7	2 4 1 9 20		2 4 1 9 20
	13		J7		2 4 1 9 20	———
	18		J8	2 8 2 9 60		2 8 2 9 60

NAME Thompson Group

ADDRESS 2300 E. National Road, Cumberland, IN 46229-4824

DATE		ITEM	POST. REF.	DEBIT	CREDIT	BALANCE
20-- Mar.	1	Balance	✓			1 0 5 8 25
	27		J8	2 1 7 7 28		3 2 3 5 53

Problem 10-12A

Owens Distributors

Schedule of Accounts Receivable

March 31, 20--

Blevins Bakery	$2 0 6 8 20
R. J. Kalas, Inc.	2 8 2 9 60
Thompson Group	3 2 3 5 53
Total	$8 1 3 3 33

Exercise 10-1B

1. *Retail*   4. *Retail*

2. *Wholesale*   5. *Wholesale*

3. *Wholesale*   6. *Wholesale*

Exercise 10-2B

1.

Cash				Accounts Receivable			
(a)	250.00			*(b)*	225.00	*(c)*	225.00
(c)	225.00						

Sales Tax Payable				Sales			
						(a)	250.00
						(b)	225.00

Sales Returns and Allowances		Sales Discounts	

2.

Cash				Accounts Receivable			
(a)	265.00			*(b)*	238.50	*(c)*	238.50
(c)	238.50						

Sales Tax Payable				Sales			
		(a)	15.00			*(a)*	250.00
		(b)	13.50			*(b)*	225.00

Sales Returns and Allowances		Sales Discounts	

Exercise 10-2B (Concluded)

3.

Cash			
(a)	481.00	(b)	18.00
(e)	364.00		

Accounts Receivable			
(c)	388.00	(d)	24.00
		(e)	364.00

Sales Tax Payable	

Sales			
		(a)	481.00
		(c)	388.00

Sales Returns and Allowances	
(b)	18.00
(d)	24.00

Sales Discounts	

4.

Cash			
(c)	477.00	(e)	31.80
(d)	318.00		

Accounts Receivable			
(a)	508.80	(b)	31.80
		(c)	477.00

Sales Tax Payable			
(b)	1.80	(a)	28.80
(e)	1.80	(d)	18.00

Sales			
		(a)	480.00
		(d)	300.00

Sales Returns and Allowances	
(b)	30.00
(e)	30.00

Sales Discounts	

5.

Cash			
(b)	274.40		
(d)	203.00		

Accounts Receivable			
(a)	280.00	(b)	280.00
(c)	203.00	(d)	203.00

Sales Tax Payable	

Sales			
		(a)	280.00
		(c)	203.00

Sales Returns and Allowances	

Sales Discounts	
(b)	5.60

Exercise 10-3B

Sales			$2,880
Less: Sales returns and allowances	$322		
Sales discounts	56	378	
Net sales			$2,502

Exercise 10-4B

GENERAL JOURNAL

PAGE

	DATE		DESCRIPTION	POST. REF.	DEBIT		CREDIT		
1	20-- Oct.	5	Accounts Receivable/B. Farsnby		291 20				1
2			Sales				280 00		2
3			Sales Tax Payable				11 20		3
4			Made credit sale						4
5									5
6		8	Accounts Receivable/F. Preetee		249 60				6
7			Sales				240 00		7
8			Sales Tax Payable				9 60		8
9			Made credit sale						9
10									10
11		11	Sales Returns and Allowances		50 00				11
12			Sales Tax Payable		2 00				12
13			Accounts Receivable/F. Preetee				52 00		13
14			Returned merchandise						14
15									15
16		17	Cash		193 80				16
17			Sales Discounts		3 80				17
18			Accounts Receivable/F. Preetee				197 60		18
19			Received cash on account						19
20									20

Exercise 10-4B (Concluded)

GENERAL JOURNAL   PAGE

	DATE		DESCRIPTION	POST. REF.	DEBIT	CREDIT	
21	20-- Oct.	18	Sales Returns and Allowances		6 0 00		21
22			Sales Tax Payable		2 40		22
23			Accounts Receivable/B. Farnsby			6 2 40	23
24			Returned merchandise				24
25							25
26		20	Cash		2 2 8 80		26
27			Accounts Receivable/B. Farsnby			2 2 8 80	27
28			Received cash on account				28

Exercise 10-5B

GENERAL JOURNAL   PAGE

	DATE		DESCRIPTION	POST. REF.	DEBIT	CREDIT	
1	20-- Sept.	1	Accounts Receivable/K. Smith		1 8 9 0 00		1
2			Sales			1 8 0 0 00	2
3			Sales Tax Payable			9 0 00	3
4			Sale No. 228				4
5							5
6		3	Accounts Receivable/J. Arnes		3 2 5 5 00		6
7			Sales			3 1 0 0 00	7
8			Sales Tax Payable			1 5 5 00	8
9			Sale No. 229				9
10							10
11		5	Accounts Receivable/M. Denison		2 9 4 0 00		11
12			Sales			2 8 0 0 00	12
13			Sales Tax Payable			1 4 0 00	13
14			Sale No. 230				14
15							15
16		7	Accounts Receivable/B. Marshall		1 9 9 5 00		16
17			Sales			1 9 0 0 00	17
18			Sales Tax Payable			9 5 00	18
19			Sale No. 231				19
20							20
21							21
22							22

Exercise 10-6B

	DATE		DESCRIPTION	POST. REF.	DEBIT	CREDIT	
1	20-- June	1	Sales Returns and Allowances	401.1	4 3 00		1
2			Accounts Receivable/M. Phillips	122/✓		4 3 00	2
3			Returned merchandise				3
4							4
5		11	Sales Returns and Allowances	401.1	5 9 00		5
6			Accounts Receivable/J. Adams	122/✓		5 9 00	6
7			Returned merchandise				7
8							8
9		15	Sales Returns and Allowances	401.1	2 1 00		9
10			Accounts Receivable/L. B. Greene	122/✓		2 1 00	10
11			Returned merchandise				11
12							12
13							13
14							14

GENERAL LEDGER

ACCOUNT Accounts Receivable   ACCOUNT NO. 122

DATE		ITEM	POST. REF.	DEBIT	CREDIT	BALANCE DEBIT	BALANCE CREDIT
20-- June	1	Balance	✓			3 9 0 0 00	
	1		J60		4 3 00	3 8 5 7 00	
	11		J60		5 9 00	3 7 9 8 00	
	15		J60		2 1 00	3 7 7 7 00	

ACCOUNT Sales Returns and Allowances   ACCOUNT NO. 401.1

DATE		ITEM	POST. REF.	DEBIT	CREDIT	BALANCE DEBIT	BALANCE CREDIT
20-- June	1		J60	4 3 00		4 3 00	
	11		J60	5 9 00		1 0 2 00	
	15		J60	2 1 00		1 2 3 00	

Exercise 10-6B (Concluded)

ACCOUNTS RECEIVABLE LEDGER

NAME John B. Adams

ADDRESS 127 Strawberry Lane, Manchester, CT 06040-0865

DATE		ITEM	POST. REF.	DEBIT	CREDIT	BALANCE
20-- June	1	Balance	✓			8 5 0 00
	11		J60		5 9 00	7 9 1 00

NAME L. B. Greene

ADDRESS 2254 Blackrock, Bronx, NY 10472-1974

DATE		ITEM	POST. REF.	DEBIT	CREDIT	BALANCE
20-- June	1	Balance	✓			4 2 8 00
	15		J60		2 1 00	4 0 7 00

NAME Marie L. Phillips

ADDRESS 334 Fern St., W. Hartford, CT 06119-2314

DATE		ITEM	POST. REF.	DEBIT	CREDIT	BALANCE
20-- June	1	Balance	✓			1 0 1 8 00
	1		J60		4 3 00	9 7 5 00

Exercise 10-7B

GENERAL JOURNAL   PAGE 1

	DATE		DESCRIPTION	POST. REF.	DEBIT	CREDIT	
1	20-- Nov.	1	Cash		7 5 0 00		1
2			Accounts Receivable/J. Haghighat			7 5 0 00	2
3			Received cash on account				3
4							4
5		12	Cash		4 6 4 00		5
6			Accounts Receivable/M. Antonoff			4 6 4 00	6
7			Received cash on account				7
8							8
9		15	Cash		3 7 6 3 00		9
10			Sales			3 7 6 3 00	10
11			Made cash sales				11
12							12
13		18	Cash		2 4 1 00		13
14			Accounts Receivable/W. Mossein			2 4 1 00	14
15			Received cash on account				15
16							16
17		25	Cash		2 6 4 8 00		17
18			Sales			2 6 4 8 00	18
19			Made cash sales				19
20							20
21							21
22							22
23							23

Exercise 10-8B

Gelph Co.

Schedule of Accounts Receivable

November 30, 20--

James L. Adams Co.	$3 2 0 0 00
Trish Berens	1 3 6 0 00
R & J Travis	1 8 4 2 00
Total	$6 4 0 2 00

Problem 10-9B

1.

GENERAL JOURNAL

	DATE		DESCRIPTION	POST. REF.	DEBIT	CREDIT	
1	20-- July	1	Accounts Receivable/Saga, Inc.	122/✓	1260 00		1
2			Sales	401		1200 00	2
3			Sales Tax Payable	231		60 00	3
4			Sale No. 101				4
5							5
6		8	Accounts Receivable/V. Ward	122/✓	2205 00		6
7			Sales	401		2100 00	7
8			Sales Tax Payable	231		105 00	8
9			Sale No. 102				9
10							10
11		15	Accounts Receivable/Dvorak Manufacturing	122/✓	4515 00		11
12			Sales	401		4300 00	12
13			Sales Tax Payable	231		215 00	13
14			Sales No. 103				14
15							15
16		21	Accounts Receivable/V. Ward	122/✓	1890 00		16
17			Sales	401		1800 00	17
18			Sales Tax Payable	231		90 00	18
19			Sale No. 104				19
20							20
21		24	Accounts Receivable/Zapata Co.	122/✓	1680 00		21
22			Sales	401		1600 00	22
23			Sales Tax Payable	231		80 00	23
24			Sale No. 105				24
25							25
26		29	Accounts Receivable/Saga, Inc.	122/✓	1522 50		26
27			Sales	401		1450 00	27
28			Sales Tax Payable	231		72 50	28
29			Sale No. 106				29
30							30
31							31
32							32
33							33
34							34

Problem 10-9B (Continued)

2.

GENERAL LEDGER

ACCOUNT   Accounts Receivable   ACCOUNT NO.   122

DATE		ITEM	POST. REF.	DEBIT	CREDIT	BALANCE	
						DEBIT	CREDIT
20-- July	1		J15	1 2 6 0 00		1 2 6 0 00	
	8		J15	2 2 0 5 00		3 4 6 5 00	
	15		J15	4 5 1 5 00		7 9 8 0 00	
	21		J15	1 8 9 0 00		9 8 7 0 00	
	24		J15	1 6 8 0 00		11 5 5 0 00	
	29		J15	1 5 2 2 50		13 0 7 2 50	

ACCOUNT   Sales Tax Payable   ACCOUNT NO.   231

DATE		ITEM	POST. REF.	DEBIT	CREDIT	BALANCE	
						DEBIT	CREDIT
20-- July	1		J15		6 0 00		6 0 00
	8		J15		1 0 5 00		1 6 5 00
	15		J15		2 1 5 00		3 8 0 00
	21		J15		9 0 00		4 7 0 00
	24		J15		8 0 00		5 5 0 00
	29		J15		7 2 50		6 2 2 50

ACCOUNT   Sales   ACCOUNT NO.   401

DATE		ITEM	POST. REF.	DEBIT	CREDIT	BALANCE	
						DEBIT	CREDIT
20-- July	1		J15		1 2 0 0 00		1 2 0 0 00
	8		J15		2 1 0 0 00		3 3 0 0 00
	15		J15		4 3 0 0 00		7 6 0 0 00
	21		J15		1 8 0 0 00		9 4 0 0 00
	24		J15		1 6 0 0 00		11 0 0 0 00
	29		J15		1 4 5 0 00		12 4 5 0 00

Problem 10-9B (Concluded)

ACCOUNTS RECEIVABLE LEDGER

NAME Dvorak Manufacturing

ADDRESS 2105 Williams Drive, Muncie, IN 47304-2437

DATE		ITEM	POST. REF.	DEBIT	CREDIT	BALANCE
20-- July	15		J15	4 5 1 5 00		4 5 1 5 00

NAME Saga, Inc.

ADDRESS 1453 Parnell Avenue, Indianapolis, IN 46201-6870

DATE		ITEM	POST. REF.	DEBIT	CREDIT	BALANCE
20-- July	1		J15	1 2 6 0 00		1 2 6 0 00
	29		J15	1 5 2 2 50		2 7 8 2 50

NAME Vinnie Ward

ADDRESS 308 So. Muirhead Drive, Okemos, MI 48864-5356

DATE		ITEM	POST. REF.	DEBIT	CREDIT	BALANCE
20-- July	8		J15	2 2 0 5 00		2 2 0 5 00
	21		J15	1 8 9 0 00		4 0 9 5 00

NAME Zapata Co.

ADDRESS 789 N. Stafford Dr., Bloomington, IN 47401-6201

DATE		ITEM	POST. REF.	DEBIT	CREDIT	BALANCE
20-- July	24		J15	1 6 8 0 00		1 6 8 0 00

Problem 10-10B

1.

GENERAL JOURNAL

	DATE		DESCRIPTION	POST. REF.	DEBIT	CREDIT	
1	20-- Jan.	1	Cash	101	8 80 00		1
2			Accounts Receivable/R. Boyd	122/✓		8 80 00	2
3			Received cash on account				3
4							4
5		3	Cash	101	2 71 00		5
6			Accounts Receivable/C. Hassell	122/✓		2 71 00	6
7			Received cash on account				7
8							8
9		5	Cash	101	2 9 40 00		9
10			Sales	401		2 8 00 00	10
11			Sales Tax Payable	231		1 40 00	11
12			Made cash sales				12
13							13
14		5	Cash	101	1 2 22 20		14
15			Bank Credit Card Expense	513	3 7 80		15
16			Sales	401		1 2 00 00	16
17			Sales Tax Payable	231		6 00 00	17
18			Made credit card sales				18
19							19
20		8	Cash	101	9 12 00		20
21			Accounts Receivable/J. Sowada	122/✓		9 12 00	21
22			Received cash on account				22
23							23
24		11	Sales Returns and Allowances	401.1	4 0 00		24
25			Sales Tax Payable	231	2 00		25
26			Accounts Receivable/R. Boyd	122/✓		4 2 00	26
27			Returned merchandise				27
28							28
29		12	Cash	101	3 2 55 00		29
30			Sales	401		3 1 00 00	30
31			Sales Tax Payable	231		1 55 00	31
32			Made cash sales				32
33							33
34							34

Problem 10-10B (Continued)

GENERAL JOURNAL

	DATE		DESCRIPTION	POST. REF.	DEBIT	CREDIT	
1	20-- Jan.	12	Cash	101	1 9 3 5 15		1
2			Bank Credit Card Expense	513	5 9 85		2
3			Sales	401		1 9 0 0 00	3
4			Sales Tax Payable	231		9 5 00	4
5			Made credit card sales				5
6							6
7		15	Cash	101	1 1 0 0 00		7
8			Accounts Receivable/R. Zehnle	122/✓		1 1 0 0 00	8
9			Received cash on account				9
10							10
11		18	Sales Returns and Allowances	401.1	3 1 00		11
12			Sales Tax Payable	231	1 55		12
13			Accounts Receivable/R. Zehnle	122/✓		3 2 55	13
14			Returned merchandise				14
15							15
16		19	Cash	101	2 3 4 1 50		16
17			Sales	401		2 2 3 0 00	17
18			Sales Tax Payable	231		1 1 1 50	18
19			Made cash sales				19
20							20
21		25	Cash	101	3 1 8 00		21
22			Accounts Receivable/Dazai Manufacturing	122/✓		3 1 8 00	22
23			Received cash on account				23
24							24
25							25
26							26
27							27
28							28
29							29
30							30
31							31
32							32
33							33
34							34

Problem 10-10B (Continued)

2.

GENERAL LEDGER

ACCOUNT   Cash   ACCOUNT NO.   101

DATE		ITEM	POST. REF.	DEBIT	CREDIT	BALANCE DEBIT	BALANCE CREDIT
20-- Jan.	1	Balance	✓			2 8 9 0 75	
	1		J20	8 8 0 00		3 7 7 0 75	
	3		J20	2 7 1 00		4 0 4 1 75	
	5		J20	2 9 4 0 00		6 9 8 1 75	
	5		J20	1 2 2 2 20		8 2 0 3 95	
	8		J20	9 1 2 00		9 1 1 5 95	
	12		J20	3 2 5 5 00		12 3 7 0 95	
	12		J21	1 9 3 5 15		14 3 0 6 10	
	15		J21	1 1 0 0 00		15 4 0 6 10	
	19		J21	2 3 4 1 50		17 7 4 7 60	
	25		J21	3 1 8 00		18 0 6 5 60	

ACCOUNT   Accounts Receivable   ACCOUNT NO.   122

DATE		ITEM	POST. REF.	DEBIT	CREDIT	BALANCE DEBIT	BALANCE CREDIT
20-- Jan.	1	Balance	✓			6 3 0 0 00	
	1		J20		8 8 0 00	5 4 2 0 00	
	3		J20		2 7 1 00	5 1 4 9 00	
	8		J20		9 1 2 00	4 2 3 7 00	
	11		J20		4 2 00	4 1 9 5 00	
	15		J21		1 1 0 0 00	3 0 9 5 00	
	18		J21		3 2 55	3 0 6 2 45	
	25		J21		3 1 8 00	2 7 4 4 45	

Problem 10-10B (Continued)

ACCOUNT Sales Tax Payable ACCOUNT NO. 231

DATE		ITEM	POST. REF.	DEBIT	CREDIT	BALANCE	
						DEBIT	CREDIT
20-- Jan.	5		J20		1 4 0 00		1 4 0 00
	5		J20		6 0 00		2 0 0 00
	11		J20	2 00			1 9 8 00
	12		J20		1 5 5 00		3 5 3 00
	12		J21		9 5 00		4 4 8 00
	18		J21	1 55			4 4 6 45
	19		J21		1 1 1 50		5 5 7 95

ACCOUNT Sales ACCOUNT NO. 401

DATE		ITEM	POST. REF.	DEBIT	CREDIT	BALANCE	
						DEBIT	CREDIT
20-- Jan.	5		J20		2 8 0 0 00		2 8 0 0 00
	5		J20		1 2 0 0 00		4 0 0 0 00
	12		J20		3 1 0 0 00		7 1 0 0 00
	12		J21		1 9 0 0 00		9 0 0 0 00
	19		J21		2 2 3 0 00		11 2 3 0 00

ACCOUNT Sales Returns and Allowances ACCOUNT NO. 401.1

DATE		ITEM	POST. REF.	DEBIT	CREDIT	BALANCE	
						DEBIT	CREDIT
20-- Jan.	11		J20	4 0 00		4 0 00	
	18		J21	3 1 00		7 1 00	

ACCOUNT Bank Credit Card Expense ACCOUNT NO. 513

DATE		ITEM	POST. REF.	DEBIT	CREDIT	BALANCE	
						DEBIT	CREDIT
20-- Jan.	5		J20	3 7 80		3 7 80	
	12		J21	5 9 85		9 7 65	

Problem 10-10B (Continued)

ACCOUNTS RECEIVABLE LEDGER

NAME Ray Boyd

ADDRESS 229 SE 65th Avenue, Portland, OR 97215-1451

DATE		ITEM	POST. REF.	DEBIT	CREDIT	BALANCE
20-- Jan.	1	Balance	✓			1 4 0 0 00
	1		J20		8 8 0 00	5 2 0 00
	11		J20		4 2 00	4 7 8 00

NAME Dazai Manufacturing

ADDRESS 447 6th Avenue, Flagstaff, AZ 86004-6842

DATE		ITEM	POST. REF.	DEBIT	CREDIT	BALANCE
20-- Jan.	1	Balance	✓			3 1 8 00
	25		J21		3 1 8 00	——

NAME Clint Hassell

ADDRESS 1462 N. Steves Blvd., Los Cruces, NM 88012-7791

DATE		ITEM	POST. REF.	DEBIT	CREDIT	BALANCE
20-- Jan.	1	Balance	✓			8 1 5 00
	3		J20		2 7 1 00	5 4 4 00

Problem 10-10B (Concluded)

NAME Jan Sowada

ADDRESS 5997 Blackgold Lane, Grapevine, TX 76051-2366

DATE		ITEM	POST. REF.	DEBIT	CREDIT	BALANCE
20-- Jan.	1	Balance	✓			1 4 8 1 00
	8		J20		9 1 2 00	5 6 9 00

NAME Robert Zehnle

ADDRESS 6881 Seneca Drive, San Diego, CA 92127-8671

DATE		ITEM	POST. REF.	DEBIT	CREDIT	BALANCE
20-- Jan.	1	Balance	✓			2 2 8 6 00
	15		J21		1 1 0 0 00	1 1 8 6 00
	18		J21		3 2 55	1 1 5 3 45

Problem 10-11B

1.

GENERAL JOURNAL

PAGE 7

	DATE		DESCRIPTION	POST. REF.	DEBIT	CREDIT	
1	20-- Apr.	1	Accounts Receivable/O. L. Meyers	122/✔	2 2 4 7 00		1
2			Sales	401		2 1 0 0 00	2
3			Sales Tax Payable	231		1 4 7 00	3
4			Sale No. 111				4
5							5
6		3	Accounts Receivable/A. Plaa	122/✔	1 0 7 0 00		6
7			Sales	401		1 0 0 0 00	7
8			Sales Tax Payable	231		7 0 00	8
9			Sale No. 112				9
10							10
11		6	Sales Returns and Allowances	401.1	5 0 00		11
12			Sales Tax Payable	231	3 50		12
13			Accounts Receivable/O. L. Meyers	122/✔		5 3 50	13
14			Returned merchandise—Credit Memo #42				14
15							15
16		7	Cash	101	3 4 6 6 80		16
17			Sales	401		3 2 4 0 00	17
18			Sales Tax Payable	231		2 2 6 80	18
19			Made cash sales				19
20							20
21		9	Cash	101	2 1 9 3 50		21
22			Accounts Receivable/O. L. Meyers	122/✔		2 1 9 3 50	22
23			Received cash on account				23
24							24
25		12	Accounts Receivable/M. Richfield	122/✔	1 0 4 8 60		25
26			Sales	401		9 8 0 00	26
27			Sales Tax Payable	231		6 8 60	27
28			Sale No. 113				28
29							29
30		14	Cash	101	2 3 3 2 60		30
31			Sales	401		2 1 8 0 00	31
32			Sales Tax Payable	231		1 5 2 60	32
33			Made cash sales				33
34							34

Problem 10-11B (Continued)

GENERAL JOURNAL

PAGE 8

	DATE		DESCRIPTION	POST. REF.	DEBIT	CREDIT	
1	20-- Apr.	17	Sales Returns and Allowances	401.1	4 0 00		1
2			Sales Tax Payable	231	2 80		2
3			Accounts Receivable/M. Richfield	122/✓		4 2 80	3
4			Returned merchandise—Credit Memo #43				4
5							5
6		19	Accounts Receivable/K. Munkres	122/✓	1 0 9 1 40		6
7			Sales	401		1 0 2 0 00	7
8			Sales Tax Payable	231		7 1 40	8
9			Sales No. 114				9
10							10
11		21	Cash	101	2 7 8 2 00		11
12			Sales	401		2 6 0 0 00	12
13			Sales Tax Payable	231		1 8 2 00	13
14			Made cash sales				14
15							15
16		24	Accounts Receivable/O. L. Meyers	122/✓	9 8 4 40		16
17			Sales	401		9 2 0 00	17
18			Sales Tax Payable	231		6 4 40	18
19			Sale No. 115				19
20							20
21		27	Accounts Receivable/A. Plaa	122/✓	1 4 1 2 40		21
22			Sales	401		1 3 2 0 00	22
23			Sales Tax Payable	231		9 2 40	23
24			Sale No. 116				24
25							25
26		28	Cash	101	2 9 9 6 00		26
27			Sales	401		2 8 0 0 00	27
28			Sales Tax Payable	231		1 9 6 00	28
29			Made cash sales				29
30							30
31		29	Cash	101	2 1 8 6 00		31
32			Accounts Receivable/M. Richfield	122/✓		2 1 8 6 00	32
33			Received cash on account				33
34							34

Problem 10-11B (Continued)

2.

GENERAL LEDGER

ACCOUNT   Cash

ACCOUNT NO.   101

DATE		ITEM	POST. REF.	DEBIT	CREDIT	BALANCE DEBIT	BALANCE CREDIT
20-- Apr.	1	Balance	✓			2 8 6 4 54	
	7		J7	3 4 6 6 80		6 3 3 1 34	
	9		J7	2 1 9 3 50		8 5 2 4 84	
	14		J7	2 3 3 2 60		10 8 5 7 44	
	21		J8	2 7 8 2 00		13 6 3 9 44	
	28		J8	2 9 9 6 00		16 6 3 5 44	
	29		J8	2 1 8 6 00		18 8 2 1 44	

ACCOUNT   Accounts Receivable

ACCOUNT NO.   122

DATE		ITEM	POST. REF.	DEBIT	CREDIT	BALANCE DEBIT	BALANCE CREDIT
20-- Apr.	1	Balance	✓			2 7 2 6 25	
	1		J7	2 2 4 7 00		4 9 7 3 25	
	3		J7	1 0 7 0 00		6 0 4 3 25	
	6		J7		5 3 50	5 9 8 9 75	
	9		J7		2 1 9 3 50	3 7 9 6 25	
	12		J7	1 0 4 8 60		4 8 4 4 85	
	17		J8		4 2 80	4 8 0 2 05	
	19		J8	1 0 9 1 40		5 8 9 3 45	
	24		J8	9 8 4 40		6 8 7 7 85	
	27		J8	1 4 1 2 40		8 2 9 0 25	
	29		J8		2 1 8 6 00	6 1 0 4 25	

Problem 10-11B (Continued)

ACCOUNT   Sales Tax Payable   ACCOUNT NO.   231

DATE		ITEM	POST. REF.	DEBIT	CREDIT	BALANCE DEBIT	BALANCE CREDIT
20-- Apr.	1		J7		1 4 7 00		1 4 7 00
	3		J7		7 0 00		2 1 7 00
	6		J7	3 50			2 1 3 50
	7		J7		2 2 6 80		4 4 0 30
	12		J7		6 8 60		5 0 8 90
	14		J7		1 5 2 60		6 6 1 50
	17		J8	2 80			6 5 8 70
	19		J8		7 1 40		7 3 0 10
	21		J8		1 8 2 00		9 1 2 10
	24		J8		6 4 40		9 7 6 50
	27		J8		9 2 40		1 0 6 8 90
	28		J8		1 9 6 00		1 2 6 4 90

ACCOUNT   Sales   ACCOUNT NO.   401

DATE		ITEM	POST. REF.	DEBIT	CREDIT	BALANCE DEBIT	BALANCE CREDIT
20-- Apr.	1		J7		2 1 0 0 00		2 1 0 0 00
	3		J7		1 0 0 0 00		3 1 0 0 00
	7		J7		3 2 4 0 00		6 3 4 0 00
	12		J7		9 8 0 00		7 3 2 0 00
	14		J7		2 1 8 0 00		9 5 0 0 00
	19		J8		1 0 2 0 00		10 5 2 0 00
	21		J8		2 6 0 0 00		13 1 2 0 00
	24		J8		9 2 0 00		14 0 4 0 00
	27		J8		1 3 2 0 00		15 3 6 0 00
	28		J8		2 8 0 0 00		18 1 6 0 00

ACCOUNT   Sales Returns and Allowances   ACCOUNT NO.   401.1

DATE		ITEM	POST. REF.	DEBIT	CREDIT	BALANCE DEBIT	BALANCE CREDIT
20-- Apr.	6		J7	5 0 00		5 0 00	
	17		J8	4 0 00		9 0 00	

Problem 10-11B (Concluded)

ACCOUNTS RECEIVABLE LEDGER

NAME O. L. Meyers

ADDRESS 119 Hartford Turnpike, Vernon, CT 06066-0113

DATE		ITEM	POST. REF.	DEBIT	CREDIT	BALANCE
20-- Apr.	1		J7	2 2 4 7 00		2 2 4 7 00
	6		J7		5 3 50	2 1 9 3 50
	9		J7		2 1 9 3 50	—
	24		J8	9 8 4 40		9 8 4 40

NAME Kelsay Munkres

ADDRESS 233 Cambridge Dr., Branford, CT 06405-9276

DATE		ITEM	POST. REF.	DEBIT	CREDIT	BALANCE
20-- Apr.	1	Balance	✓			4 8 2 00
	19		J8	1 0 9 1 40		1 5 7 3 40

NAME Andrew Plaa

ADDRESS 51 Bissell Ave., Old Saybrook, CT 06475-0212

DATE		ITEM	POST. REF.	DEBIT	CREDIT	BALANCE
20-- Apr.	3		J7	1 0 7 0 00		1 0 7 0 00
	27		J8	1 4 1 2 40		2 4 8 2 40

NAME Melissa Richfield

ADDRESS 1107 Silver Lane, East Hartford, CT 06108-1907

DATE		ITEM	POST. REF.	DEBIT	CREDIT	BALANCE
20-- Apr.	1	Balance	✓			2 2 4 4 25
	12		J7	1 0 4 8 60		3 2 9 2 85
	17		J8		4 2 80	3 2 5 0 05
	29		J8		2 1 8 6 00	1 0 6 4 05

Problem 10-12B

Paul Jackson					
Schedule of Accounts Receivable					
April 30, 20--					
O. L. Meyers	$	9	8	4	40
Kelsay Munkres		1	5	7	3	40
Andrew Plaa		2	4	8	2	40
Melissa Richfield		1	0	6	4	05
Total	$6	1	0	4	25

MANAGING YOUR WRITING

Last month, I paid my account in full, but you credited the payment to my spouse's account. Because of this error, you have treated my account as over the credit limit and have charged interest on the unpaid balance. Please credit my account for last month's payment and remove the interest charge. This error might have occurred because my spouse and I have the same last name and similar first names. To avoid this error in the future, please instruct your accounts receivable department to focus on our account numbers rather than our names.

ETHICS CASE: SUGGESTED SOLUTIONS

1. Yes, Robin violated her company's policy.
2. Answers will vary. Robin could have called Good Earth Foods and explained the credit policy. If this meant losing the order, she could have gone to the vice president to see if he would like to make an exception to the credit policy.
3. Answers will vary. Students should point out that new businesses do not have established credit histories.
4. Answers will vary. Possibly, the credit manager as well as the sales supervisor must approve shipments to new customers.

Mastery Problem

1.

GENERAL JOURNAL

	DATE		DESCRIPTION	POST. REF.	DEBIT	CREDIT	
1	20-- Sept.	2	Accounts Receivable/K. Shank	122/✓	1 3 2 50		1
2			Sales	401		1 2 5 00	2
3			Sales Tax Payable	231		7 50	3
4			Sale No. 101				4
5							5
6		3	Accounts Receivable/N. Truelove	122/✓	7 2 35		6
7			Sales	401		6 8 25	7
8			Sales Tax Payable	231		4 10	8
9			Sale No. 102				9
10							10
11		5	Accounts Receivable/J. Warkentin	122/✓	4 6 59		11
12			Sales	401		4 3 95	12
13			Sales Tax Payable	231		2 64	13
14			Sale No. 103				14
15							15
16		8	Cash	101	2 4 7 2 40		16
17			Sales	401		2 3 3 2 45	17
18			Sales Tax Payable	231		1 3 9 95	18
19			Made cash sales				19
20							20
21		10	Cash	101	6 6 2 50		21
22			Boarding and Grooming Revenue	402		6 2 5 00	22
23			Sales Tax Payable	231		3 7 50	23
24			Received cash for grooming				24
25							25
26		11	Sales Returns and Allowances	401.1	1 0 00		26
27			Sales Tax Payable	231	0 60		27
28			Accounts Receivable/J. Warkentin	122/✓		1 0 60	28
29			Sales allowance for defect				29
30							30
31		12	Accounts Receivable/T. Shaw	122/✓	1 2 7 2 00		31
32			Sales	401		1 2 0 0 00	32
33			Sales Tax Payable	231		7 2 00	33
34			Sale No. 104				34

Mastery Problem (Continued)

	DATE		DESCRIPTION	POST. REF.	DEBIT	CREDIT	
1	20-- Sept.	14	Cash	101	2 5 6 00		1
2			Accounts Receivable/R. Alanso	122/✓		2 5 6 00	2
3			Received cash on account				3
4							4
5		15	Sales Returns and Allowances	401.1	8 8 00		5
6			Sales Tax Payable	231	5 28		6
7			Accounts Receivable/R. Alanso	122/✓		9 3 28	7
8			Returned merchandise				8
9							9
10		15	Cash	101	2 8 1 6 26		10
11			Sales	401		2 6 5 6 85	11
12			Sales Tax Payable	231		1 5 9 41	12
13			Made cash sales				13
14							14
15		16	Cash	101	5 8 25		15
16			Accounts Receivable/N. Truelove	122/✓		5 8 25	16
17			Received cash on account				17
18							18
19		18	Cash	101	5 6 7 10		19
20			Boarding and Grooming Revenue	402		5 3 5 00	20
21			Sales Tax Payable	231		3 2 10	21
22			Received cash for grooming				22
23							23
24		19	Cash	101	6 3 25		24
25			Accounts Receivable/E. Cochran	122/✓		6 3 25	25
26			Received cash on account				26
27							27
28		20	Accounts Receivable/S. Hays	122/✓	8 8 33		28
29			Sales	401		8 3 33	29
30			Sales Tax Payable	231		5 00	30
31			Sale No. 105				31
32							32
33							33
34							34

Mastery Problem (Continued)

GENERAL JOURNAL

	DATE		DESCRIPTION	POST. REF.	DEBIT	CREDIT	
1	20-- Sept.	21	Accounts Receivable/All American Day Camp	122/✔	3 9 7 50		1
2			Sales	401		3 7 5 00	2
3			Sales Tax Payable	231		2 2 50	3
4			Sale No. 106				4
5							5
6		22	Cash	101	3 3 0 9 80		6
7			Sales	401		3 1 2 2 45	7
8			Sales Tax Payable	231		1 8 7 35	8
9			Made cash sales				9
10							10
11		23	Cash	101	5 4 5 90		11
12			Boarding and Grooming Revenue	402		5 1 5 00	12
13			Sales Tax Payable	231		3 0 90	13
14			Received cash for grooming				14
15							15
16		25	Cash	101	1 3 2 50		16
17			Accounts Receivable/K. Shank	122/✔		1 3 2 50	17
18			Received cash on account				18
19							19
20		26	Cash	101	7 2 35		20
21			Accounts Receivable/N. Truelove	122/✔		7 2 35	21
22			Received cash on account				22
23							23
24		27	Cash	101	2 7 3 25		24
25			Accounts Receivable/J. Gloy	122/✔		2 7 3 25	25
26			Received cash on account				26
27							27
28		28	Cash	101	11 0 0 0 00		28
29			Notes Payable	201		11 0 0 0 00	29
30			Borrowed cash				30
31							31
32							32
33							33
34							34

Mastery Problem (Continued)

GENERAL JOURNAL

	DATE		DESCRIPTION	POST. REF.	DEBIT	CREDIT	
1	20-- Sept.	29	Cash	101	3 0 0 5 58		1
2			Sales	401		2 8 3 5 45	2
3			Sales Tax Payable	231		1 7 0 13	3
4			Made cash sales				4
5							5
6		30	Cash	101	5 1 7 28		6
7			Boarding and Grooming Revenue	402		4 8 8 00	7
8			Sales Tax Payable	231		2 9 28	8
9			Received cash for grooming				9
10							10

2.

GENERAL LEDGER

ACCOUNT   Cash   ACCOUNT NO.   101

DATE		ITEM	POST. REF.	DEBIT	CREDIT	BALANCE	
						DEBIT	CREDIT
20-- Sept.	1	Balance	✓			23 5 0 0 25	
	8		J7	2 4 7 2 40		25 9 7 2 65	
	10		J7	6 6 2 50		26 6 3 5 15	
	14		J8	2 5 6 00		26 8 9 1 15	
	15		J8	2 8 1 6 26		29 7 0 7 41	
	16		J8	5 8 25		29 7 6 5 66	
	18		J8	5 6 7 10		30 3 3 2 76	
	19		J8	6 3 25		30 3 9 6 01	
	22		J9	3 3 0 9 80		33 7 0 5 81	
	23		J9	5 4 5 90		34 2 5 1 71	
	25		J9	1 3 2 50		34 3 8 4 21	
	26		J9	7 2 35		34 4 5 6 56	
	27		J9	2 7 3 25		34 7 2 9 81	
	28		J9	11 0 0 0 00		45 7 2 9 81	
	29		J10	3 0 0 5 58		48 7 3 5 39	
	30		J10	5 1 7 28		49 2 5 2 67	

Mastery Problem (Continued)

ACCOUNT   Accounts Receivable   ACCOUNT NO.   122

DATE		ITEM	POST. REF.	DEBIT	CREDIT	BALANCE DEBIT	BALANCE CREDIT
20-- Sept.	1	Balance	✓			8 5 0 75	
	2		J7	1 3 2 50		9 8 3 25	
	3		J7	7 2 35		1 0 5 5 60	
	5		J7	4 6 59		1 1 0 2 19	
	11		J7		1 0 60	1 0 9 1 59	
	12		J7	1 2 7 2 00		2 3 6 3 59	
	14		J8		2 5 6 00	2 1 0 7 59	
	15		J8		9 3 28	2 0 1 4 31	
	16		J8		5 8 25	1 9 5 6 06	
	19		J8		6 3 25	1 8 9 2 81	
	20		J8	8 8 33		1 9 8 1 14	
	21		J9	3 9 7 50		2 3 7 8 64	
	25		J9		1 3 2 50	2 2 4 6 14	
	26		J9		7 2 35	2 1 7 3 79	
	27		J9		2 7 3 25	1 9 0 0 54	

ACCOUNT   Notes Payable   ACCOUNT NO.   201

DATE		ITEM	POST. REF.	DEBIT	CREDIT	BALANCE DEBIT	BALANCE CREDIT
20-- Sept.	1	Balance	✓				2 5 0 0 00
	28		J9		11 0 0 0 00		13 5 0 0 00

Mastery Problem (Continued)

ACCOUNT   Sales Tax Payable   ACCOUNT NO.   231

DATE		ITEM	POST. REF.	DEBIT	CREDIT	BALANCE DEBIT	BALANCE CREDIT
20-- Sept.	1	Balance	✓				9 0 9 90
	2		J7		7 50		9 1 7 40
	3		J7		4 10		9 2 1 50
	5		J7		2 64		9 2 4 14
	8		J7		1 3 9 95		1 0 6 4 09
	10		J7		3 7 50		1 1 0 1 59
	11		J7	0 60			1 1 0 0 99
	12		J7		7 2 00		1 1 7 2 99
	15		J8	5 28			1 1 6 7 71
	15		J8		1 5 9 41		1 3 2 7 12
	18		J8		3 2 10		1 3 5 9 22
	20		J8		5 00		1 3 6 4 22
	21		J9		2 2 50		1 3 8 6 72
	22		J9		1 8 7 35		1 5 7 4 07
	23		J9		3 0 90		1 6 0 4 97
	29		J10		1 7 0 13		1 7 7 5 10
	30		J10		2 9 28		1 8 0 4 38

ACCOUNT   Sales   ACCOUNT NO.   401

DATE		ITEM	POST. REF.	DEBIT	CREDIT	BALANCE DEBIT	BALANCE CREDIT
20— Sept.	1	Balance	✓				13 0 5 0 48
	2		J7		1 2 5 00		13 1 7 5 48
	3		J7		6 8 25		13 2 4 3 73
	5		J7		4 3 95		13 2 8 7 68
	8		J7		2 3 3 2 45		15 6 2 0 13
	12		J7		1 2 0 0 00		16 8 2 0 13
	15		J8		2 6 5 6 85		19 4 7 6 98
	20		J8		8 3 33		19 5 6 0 31
	21		J9		3 7 5 00		19 9 3 5 31
	22		J9		3 1 2 2 45		23 0 5 7 76
	29		J10		2 8 3 5 45		25 8 9 3 21

Mastery Problem (Continued)

ACCOUNT   Sales Returns and Allowances   ACCOUNT NO.   401.1

DATE		ITEM	POST. REF.	DEBIT	CREDIT	BALANCE DEBIT	BALANCE CREDIT
20-- Sept.	1	Balance	✓			8 6 00	
	11		J7	1 0 00		9 6 00	
	15		J8	8 8 00		1 8 4 00	

ACCOUNT   Boarding and Grooming Revenue   ACCOUNT NO.   402

DATE		ITEM	POST. REF.	DEBIT	CREDIT	BALANCE DEBIT	BALANCE CREDIT
20-- Sept.	1	Balance	✓				2 1 1 5 00
	10		J7		6 2 5 00		2 7 4 0 00
	18		J8		5 3 5 00		3 2 7 5 00
	23		J9		5 1 5 00		3 7 9 0 00
	30		J10		4 8 8 00		4 2 7 8 00

ACCOUNTS RECEIVABLE LEDGER

NAME All American Day Camp

ADDRESS 3025 Old Mill Run, Bloomington, IN 47408-1080

DATE		ITEM	POST. REF.	DEBIT	CREDIT	BALANCE
20-- Sept.	21		J9	3 9 7 50		3 9 7 50

Mastery Problem (Continued)

NAME Rosa Alanso

ADDRESS 2541 East 2nd Street, Bloomington, IN 47401-5356

DATE		ITEM	POST. REF.	DEBIT	CREDIT	BALANCE
20-- Sept.	1	Balance	✓			4 5 6 00
	14		J8		2 5 6 00	2 0 0 00
	15		J8		9 3 28	1 0 6 72

NAME Ed Cochran

ADDRESS 2669 Windcrest Drive, Bloomington, IN 47401-5446

DATE		ITEM	POST. REF.	DEBIT	CREDIT	BALANCE
20-- Sept.	1	Balance	✓			6 3 25
	19		J8		6 3 25	—

NAME Joe Gloy

ADDRESS 1458 Parnell Avenue, Muncie, IN 47304-2682

DATE		ITEM	POST. REF.	DEBIT	CREDIT	BALANCE
20-- Sept.	1	Balance	✓			2 7 3 25
	27		J9		2 7 3 25	—

NAME Susan Hays

ADDRESS 1424 Jackson Creek Road, Nashville, IN 47448-2245

DATE		ITEM	POST. REF.	DEBIT	CREDIT	BALANCE
20-- Sept.	20		J8	8 8 33		8 8 33

Mastery Problem (Continued)

NAME Ken Shank

ADDRESS 6422 E. Bender Road, Bloomington, IN 47401-7756

DATE	ITEM	POST. REF.	DEBIT	CREDIT	BALANCE
20-- Sept. 2		J7	1 3 2 50		1 3 2 50
25		J9		1 3 2 50	—

NAME Tully Shaw

ADDRESS 3315 Longview Avenue, Bloomington, IN 47401-7223

DATE	ITEM	POST. REF.	DEBIT	CREDIT	BALANCE
20-- Sept. 12		J7	1 2 7 2 00		1 2 7 2 00

NAME Nancy Truelove

ADDRESS 2300 E. National Road, Cumberland, IN 46229-4824

DATE	ITEM	POST. REF.	DEBIT	CREDIT	BALANCE
20-- Sept. 1	Balance	✓			5 8 25
3		J7	7 2 35		1 3 0 60
16		J8		5 8 25	7 2 35
26		J9		7 2 35	—

NAME Jean Warkentin

ADDRESS 1813 Deep Well Court, Bloomington, IN 47401-5124

DATE	ITEM	POST. REF.	DEBIT	CREDIT	BALANCE
20-- Sept. 5		J7	4 6 59		4 6 59
11		J7		1 0 60	3 5 99

Mastery Problem (Concluded)

3.

Wayward Kennel and Pet Supply

Schedule of Accounts Receivable

September 30, 20--

All American Day Camp	$	3 9 7	50	
Rosa Alanso		1 0 6	72	
Susan Hays		8 8	33	
Tully Shaw		1 2 7 2	00	
Jean Warkentin		3 5	99	
Total		$1 9 0 0	54	

4.

Sales	$12,842.73
Less: Sales returns and allowances	98.00
Net sales	$12,744.73

Challenge Problem

GENERAL JOURNAL

PAGE

DATE		DESCRIPTION	POST. REF.	DEBIT	CREDIT	
20-- June	4	Accounts Receivable/T. Allen		1 5 9 0 00		1
		Sales			1 5 0 0 00	2
		Sales Tax Payable			9 0 00	3
		Made credit sale				4
						5
	7	Accounts Receivable/K. Bryant		1 9 0 8 00		6
		Sales			1 8 0 0 00	7
		Sales Tax Payable			1 0 8 00	8
		Made credit sale				9
						10
	11	Sales Returns and Allowances		3 0 0 00		11
		Sales Tax Payable		1 8 00		12
		Accounts Receivable/T. Allen			3 1 8 00	13
		Returned merchandise				14
						15
	14	Cash		1 2 6 0 00		16
		Sales Discounts		1 2 00		17
		Accounts Receivable/T. Allen			1 2 7 2 00	18
		Received cash on account				19
						20
	17	Cash		1 8 9 0 00		21
		Sales Discounts		1 8 00		22
		Accounts Receivable/K. Bryant			1 9 0 8 00	23
		Received cash on account				24
						25
						26
						27
						28
						29
						30
						31
						32
						33
						34

CHAPTER 11

ACCOUNTING FOR PURCHASES AND CASH PAYMENTS

REVIEW QUESTIONS

1. The major documents commonly used in the purchasing process are the purchase requisition, the purchase order, the receiving report, and the purchase invoice.

2. A cash discount is available if the bill is paid within the discount period. A trade discount is a reduction from the list or catalog price offered by manufacturers and wholesalers to different classes of customers.

3. The purchases account is used to record the cost of merchandise purchased. Purchases Returns and Allowances is a contra-purchases account used to record purchases returns and purchases allowances. Purchases Discounts is a contra-purchases account used to record cash discounts allowed on purchases. Freight-In is an adjunct-purchases account used to record transportation charges on merchandise purchases.

4. The cost of goods sold is the beginning merchandise inventory plus the cost of goods purchased during the period less ending merchandise inventory. The gross profit is the net sales minus the cost of goods sold.

5. To post purchases from the general journal to the general ledger:

   In the general ledger account:
   Step 1: Enter the date of the transaction in the Date column.
   Step 2: Enter the amount of the debit or credit in the Debit or Credit column.
   Step 3: Enter the new balance in the Balance columns under Debit or Credit.
   Step 4: Enter the journal page number from which each transaction is posted in the Posting Reference column.

   In the journal:
   Step 5: Enter the ledger account number in the Posting Reference column of the journal for each transaction that is posted.

6. To post purchases from the general journal to the accounts payable ledger:

   In the accounts payable ledger account:
   Step 1: Enter the date of the transaction in the Date column.
   Step 2: Enter the amount of the debit or credit in the Debit or Credit column.
   Step 3: Enter the new balance in the Balance column.
   Step 4: Enter the journal page number from which each transaction is posted in the Posting Reference column.

   In the journal:
   Step 5: Enter a slash (/) followed by a check mark (✓) in the Posting Reference column of the journal for each transaction that is posted.

7. To post purchases returns and allowances from the general journal to the general ledger and accounts payable ledger:

   The general ledger is posted using the same five steps as for purchases transactions (Figure 11-9). To post the accounts payable ledger:

In the accounts payable ledger account:

Step 1: Enter the date of the transaction in the Date column.

Step 2: Enter the amount of the debit or credit in the Debit or Credit column.

Step 3: Enter the new balance in the Balance column.

Step 4: Enter the journal page number from which each transaction is posted in the Posting Reference column.

In the journal:

Step 5: Enter a slash (/) followed by a check mark (✓) in the Posting Reference column of the journal for each transaction that is posted.

8. To post cash payments from the general journal to the general ledger, use the same five steps as for posting purchases transactions (Figure 11-9).

9. To post cash payments from the general journal to the accounts payable ledger:

In the accounts payable ledger account:

Step 1: Enter the date of the transaction in the Date column.

Step 2: Enter the amount of the debit or credit in the Debit or Credit column.

Step 3: Enter the new balance in the Balance column.

Step 4: Enter the journal page number from which each transaction is posted in the Posting Reference column.

In the journal:

Step 5: Enter a slash (/) followed by a check mark (✓) in the Posting Reference column of the journal for each transaction that is posted.

10. To find the error, use the following steps:

Step 1: Verify the total of the schedule.

Step 2: Verify the postings to the accounts payable ledger.

Step 3: Verify the postings to Accounts Payable in the general ledger.

Exercise 11-1A

1. *Purchase requisition*
2. Purchase order
3. *Receiving report*
4. *Purchase invoice*

Exercise 11-2A

1.

Gross amount	*$2,000*
Less 10% trade discount	*200*
Net amount of purchases	*$1,800*

2.

Net amount	*$1,800*
Less 2% discount	*36*
Net amount to be paid	*$1,764*

3.

GENERAL JOURNAL

PAGE

	DATE		DESCRIPTION	POST. REF.	DEBIT	CREDIT	
1	20-- May	17	**Purchases**		1 8 0 0 00		1
2			**Accounts Payable/Jacob's Distributors**			1 8 0 0 00	2
3			**Purchased merchandise**				3
4							4
5		27	**Accounts Payable/Jacob's Distributors**		1 8 0 0 00		5
6			**Cash**			1 7 6 4 00	6
7			**Purchases Discounts**			3 6 00	7
8			**Paid invoice within discount period**				8
9							9
10							10
11							11
12							12
13							13
14							14
15							15

Exercise 11-3A

1.

Cash		
	(a)	1,500
	(b)	2,975

Accounts Payable

Purchases		
(a)	1,500	
(b)	2,975	

Purchases Returns and Allowances

Purchases Discounts

Freight-In

2.

Cash		
	(c)	1,960
	(d)	1,200

Accounts Payable			
(c)	2,000	(a)	2,000
(d)	1,200	(b)	1,200

Purchases		
(a)	2,000	
(b)	1,200	

Purchases Returns and Allowances

Purchases Discounts		
	(c)	40

Freight-In

Exercise 11-3A (Concluded)

3.

	Cash	
	(c)	3,430

	Accounts Payable		
(b)	500	(a)	4,000
(c)	3,500		

	Purchases	
(a)	4,000	

	Purchases Returns and Allowances	
	(b)	500

	Purchases Discounts	
	(c)	70

	Freight-In	

4.

	Cash	
	(b)	2,600

	Accounts Payable		
(b)	2,600	(a)	2,600

	Purchases	
(a)	2,500	

	Purchases Returns and Allowances	

	Purchases Discounts	

	Freight-In	
(a)	100	

Exercise 11-4A

Sales			$113 500 00	
Less: Sales returns and allowances		$ 800 00		
Sales discounts		500 00	1 300 00	
Net sales				$112 200 00
Cost of goods sold				
Merchandise inventory, Jan. 1			$ 34 000 00	
Purchases		$76 000 00		
Less: Purchases returns and allow.	$4 000 00			
Purchases discounts	3 000 00	7 000 00		
Net purchases		$69 000 00		
Add freight-in		1 500 00		
Cost of goods purchased			70 500 00	
Goods available for sale			$104 500 00	
Less merchandise inventory, Dec. 31			30 000 00	
Cost of goods sold				74 500 00
Gross profit				$ 37 700 00

Exercise 11-5A

GENERAL JOURNAL

PAGE

	DATE		DESCRIPTION	POST. REF.	DEBIT	CREDIT	
1	20-- May	3	Purchases		6 5 0 0 00		1
2			Accounts Payable/Cintron			6 5 0 0 00	2
3			Invoice No. 321				3
4							4
5		9	Purchases		2 3 0 0 00		5
6			Accounts Payable/Mitsui			2 3 0 0 00	6
7			Invoice No. 614				7
8							8
9		18	Purchases		4 2 0 0 00		9
10			Accounts Payable/Aloha Distributors			4 2 0 0 00	10
11			Invoice No. 180				11
12							12
13		23	Purchases		6 3 0 0 00		13
14			Accounts Payable/Soto			6 3 0 0 00	14
15			Invoice No. 913				15
16							16
17							17
18							18
19							19
20							20
21							21
22							22
23							23
24							24
25							25
26							26
27							27
28							28
29							29
30							30
31							31
32							32
33							33
34							34

Exercise 11-6A

GENERAL JOURNAL

PAGE 3

	DATE		DESCRIPTION	POST. REF.	DEBIT	CREDIT	
1	20-- July	7	Accounts Payable/Starcraft Industries	202/✓	7 0 0 00		1
2			Purchases Returns and Allowances	501.1		7 0 0 00	2
3			Returned merchandise				3
4							4
5		15	Accounts Payable/XYZ, Inc.	202/✓	4 5 0 00		5
6			Purchases Returns and Allowances	501.1		4 5 0 00	6
7			Returned merchandise				7
8							8
9		27	Accounts Payable/Datamagic	202/✓	9 0 0 00		9
10			Purchases Returns and Allowances	501.1		9 0 0 00	10
11			Returned merchandise				11
12							12

GENERAL LEDGER

ACCOUNT   Accounts Payable   ACCOUNT NO.   202

DATE		ITEM	POST. REF.	DEBIT	CREDIT	BALANCE DEBIT	BALANCE CREDIT
20-- July	1	Balance	✓				10 6 5 0 00
	7		J3	7 0 0 00			9 9 5 0 00
	15		J3	4 5 0 00			9 5 0 0 00
	27		J3	9 0 0 00			8 6 0 0 00

ACCOUNT   Purchases Returns and Allowances   ACCOUNT NO.   501.1

DATE		ITEM	POST. REF.	DEBIT	CREDIT	BALANCE DEBIT	BALANCE CREDIT
20-- July	7		J3		7 0 0 00		7 0 0 00
	15		J3		4 5 0 00		1 1 5 0 00
	27		J3		9 0 0 00		2 0 5 0 00

Exercise 11-6A (Concluded)

ACCOUNTS PAYABLE LEDGER

NAME Datamagic

ADDRESS

DATE		ITEM	POST. REF.	DEBIT	CREDIT	BALANCE
20-- July	1	Balance	✓			2 6 0 0 00
	27		J3	9 0 0 00		1 7 0 0 00

NAME Starcraft Industries

ADDRESS

DATE		ITEM	POST. REF.	DEBIT	CREDIT	BALANCE
20-- July	1	Balance	✓			4 3 0 0 00
	7		J3	7 0 0 00		3 6 0 0 00

NAME XYZ, Inc.

ADDRESS

DATE		ITEM	POST. REF.	DEBIT	CREDIT	BALANCE
20-- July	1	Balance	✓			3 7 5 0 00
	15		J3	4 5 0 00		3 3 0 0 00

Exercise 11-7A

GENERAL JOURNAL

	DATE		DESCRIPTION	POST. REF.	DEBIT	CREDIT	
1	20-- Sept.	5	Accounts Payable/Clinton Corp.		6 0 0 0 00		1
2			Cash			5 8 8 0 00	2
3			Purchases Discounts			1 2 0 00	3
4			Check No. 318				4
5							5
6		12	Accounts Payable/Mitchell Company		7 0 0 0 00		6
7			Cash			6 9 3 0 00	7
8			Purchases Discounts			7 0 00	8
9			Check No. 319				9
10							10
11		19	Accounts Payable/Expert Systems		4 1 0 0 00		11
12			Cash			4 1 0 0 00	12
13			Check No. 320				13
14							14
15		27	Account Payable/Graphic Data		9 0 0 0 00		15
16			Cash			8 8 2 0 00	16
17			Purchases Discounts			1 8 0 00	17
18			Check No. 321				18
19							19
20							20
21							21

Exercise 11-8A

Ryan's Express

Schedule of Accounts Payable

October 31, 20--

Columbia Products	$ 5 3 5 0 00
Favorite Fashions	4 2 8 0 00
Rustic Legends	4 7 4 0 00
	$14 3 7 0 00

Problem 11-9A

1.

	DATE		DESCRIPTION	POST. REF.	DEBIT	CREDIT	
1	20-- Sept.	3	*Purchases*	501	2 6 5 0 00		1
2			*Accounts Payable/Smith Distributors*	202/✓		2 6 5 0 00	2
3			*Invoice No. 415*				3
4							4
5		8	*Purchases*	501	3 8 3 0 00		5
6			*Accounts Payable/Michaels Wholesaler*	202/✓		3 8 3 0 00	6
7			*Invoice No. 132*				7
8							8
9		11	*Purchases*	501	3 1 4 0 00		9
10			*Accounts Payable/J. B. Sanders & Co.*	202/✓		3 1 4 0 00	10
11			*Invoice No. 614*				11
12							12
13		18	*Purchases*	501	2 2 5 0 00		13
14			*Accounts Payable/Bateman & Jones, Inc.*	202/✓		2 2 5 0 00	14
15			*Invoice No. 329*				15
16							16
17		23	*Purchases*	501	4 1 6 0 00		17
18			*Accounts Payable/Smith Distributors*	202/✓		4 1 6 0 00	18
19			*Invoice No. 767*				19
20							20
21		27	*Purchases*	501	1 9 8 0 00		21
22			*Accounts Payable/Anderson Company*	202/✓		1 9 8 0 00	22
23			*Invoice No. 744*				23
24							24
25		30	*Purchases*	501	2 7 8 0 00		25
26			*Accounts Payable/Michaels Wholesaler*	202/✓		2 7 8 0 00	26
27			*Invoice No. 652*				27
28							28
29							29
30							30
31							31
32							32
33							33
34							34

Problem 11-9A (Continued)
2.

GENERAL LEDGER

ACCOUNT   Accounts Payable   ACCOUNT NO.   202

DATE		ITEM	POST. REF.	DEBIT	CREDIT	BALANCE DEBIT	BALANCE CREDIT
20-- Sept.	3		J16		2 6 5 0 00		2 6 5 0 00
	8		J16		3 8 3 0 00		6 4 8 0 00
	11		J16		3 1 4 0 00		9 6 2 0 00
	18		J16		2 2 5 0 00		11 8 7 0 00
	23		J16		4 1 6 0 00		16 0 3 0 00
	27		J16		1 9 8 0 00		18 0 1 0 00
	30		J16		2 7 8 0 00		20 7 9 0 00

ACCOUNT   Purchases   ACCOUNT NO.   501

DATE		ITEM	POST. REF.	DEBIT	CREDIT	BALANCE DEBIT	BALANCE CREDIT
20-- Sept.	3		J16	2 6 5 0 00		2 6 5 0 00	
	8		J16	3 8 3 0 00		6 4 8 0 00	
	11		J16	3 1 4 0 00		9 6 2 0 00	
	18		J16	2 2 5 0 00		11 8 7 0 00	
	23		J16	4 1 6 0 00		16 0 3 0 00	
	27		J16	1 9 8 0 00		18 0 1 0 00	
	30		J16	2 7 8 0 00		20 7 9 0 00	

ACCOUNTS PAYABLE LEDGER

NAME   *Anderson Company*

ADDRESS

DATE		ITEM	POST. REF.	DEBIT	CREDIT	BALANCE
20-- Sept.	27		J16		1 9 8 0 00	1 9 8 0 00

Problem 11-9A (Concluded)

NAME *Bateman & Jones, Inc.*

ADDRESS

DATE		ITEM	POST. REF.	DEBIT	CREDIT	BALANCE
20-- Sept.	18		J16		2 2 5 0 00	2 2 5 0 00

NAME *Michaels Wholesaler*

ADDRESS

DATE		ITEM	POST. REF.	DEBIT	CREDIT	BALANCE
20-- Sept.	8		J16		3 8 3 0 00	3 8 3 0 00
	30		J16		2 7 8 0 00	6 6 1 0 00

NAME *J. B. Sanders & Co.*

ADDRESS

DATE		ITEM	POST. REF.	DEBIT	CREDIT	BALANCE
20-- Sept.	11		J16		3 1 4 0 00	3 1 4 0 00

NAME *Smith Distributors*

ADDRESS

DATE		ITEM	POST. REF.	DEBIT	CREDIT	BALANCE
20-- Sept.	3		J16		2 6 5 0 00	2 6 5 0 00
	23		J16		4 1 6 0 00	6 8 1 0 00

Problem 11-10A

1.

GENERAL JOURNAL

PAGE 9

	DATE		DESCRIPTION	POST. REF.	DEBIT	CREDIT	
1	20-- May	1	Rent Expense	521	2 4 0 0 00		1
2			Cash	101		2 4 0 0 00	2
3			Check No. 426				3
4							4
5		3	Accounts Payable/Mueller's Distributors	202/✓	3 6 0 0 00		5
6			Cash	101		3 4 9 2 00	6
7			Purchases Discounts	501.2		1 0 8 00	7
8			Check No. 427				8
9							9
10		7	Accounts Payable/Van Kooning	202/✓	5 5 0 0 00		10
11			Cash	101		5 5 0 0 00	11
12			Check No. 428				12
13							13
14		12	Accounts Payable/Fantastic Toys	202/✓	5 2 0 0 00		14
15			Cash	101		5 1 4 8 00	15
16			Purchases Discounts	501.2		5 2 00	16
17			Check No. 429				17
18							18
19		15	Utilities Expense	533	1 7 2 0 00		19
20			Cash	101		1 7 2 0 00	20
21			Check No. 430				21
22							22
23		18	Purchases	501	4 8 0 0 00		23
24			Cash	101		4 8 0 0 00	24
25			Check No. 431				25
26							26
27		26	Accounts Payable/Goya Outlet	202/✓	3 8 0 0 00		27
28			Cash	101		3 7 2 4 00	28
29			Purchases Discounts	501.2		7 6 00	29
30			Check No. 432				30
31							31
32		30	Freight-In	502	1 2 0 0 00		32
33			Cash	101		1 2 0 0 00	33
34			Check No. 433				34

Problem 11-10A (Continued)

GENERAL JOURNAL

	DATE		DESCRIPTION	POST. REF.	DEBIT	CREDIT	
1	20-- May	31	Purchases	501	3 0 0 0 00		1
2			Cash	101		3 0 0 0 00	2
3			Check No. 434				3
4							4
5							5

2.

GENERAL LEDGER

ACCOUNT   Cash   ACCOUNT NO.   101

DATE		ITEM	POST. REF.	DEBIT	CREDIT	BALANCE DEBIT	BALANCE CREDIT
20-- May	1	Balance	✓			40 0 0 0 00	
	1		J9		2 4 0 0 00	37 6 0 0 00	
	3		J9		3 4 9 2 00	34 1 0 8 00	
	7		J9		5 5 0 0 00	28 6 0 8 00	
	12		J9		5 1 4 8 00	23 4 6 0 00	
	15		J9		1 7 2 0 00	21 7 4 0 00	
	18		J9		4 8 0 0 00	16 9 4 0 00	
	26		J9		3 7 2 4 00	13 2 1 6 00	
	30		J9		1 2 0 0 00	12 0 1 6 00	
	31		J10		3 0 0 0 00	9 0 1 6 00	

ACCOUNT   Accounts Payable   ACCOUNT NO.   202

DATE		ITEM	POST. REF.	DEBIT	CREDIT	BALANCE DEBIT	BALANCE CREDIT
20-- May	1	Balance	✓				20 0 0 0 00
	3		J9	3 6 0 0 00			16 4 0 0 00
	7		J9	5 5 0 0 00			10 9 0 0 00
	12		J9	5 2 0 0 00			5 7 0 0 00
	26		J9	3 8 0 0 00			1 9 0 0 00

Problem 11-10A (Continued)

ACCOUNT   Purchases   ACCOUNT NO.   501

DATE	ITEM	POST. REF.	DEBIT	CREDIT	BALANCE DEBIT	BALANCE CREDIT
20-- May 18		J9	4 8 0 0 00		4 8 0 0 00	
31		J10	3 0 0 0 00		7 8 0 0 00	

ACCOUNT   Purchases Discounts   ACCOUNT NO.   501.2

DATE	ITEM	POST. REF.	DEBIT	CREDIT	BALANCE DEBIT	BALANCE CREDIT
20-- May 3		J9		1 0 8 00		1 0 8 00
12		J9		5 2 00		1 6 0 00
26		J9		7 6 00		2 3 6 00

ACCOUNT   Freight-In   ACCOUNT NO.   502

DATE	ITEM	POST. REF.	DEBIT	CREDIT	BALANCE DEBIT	BALANCE CREDIT
20-- May 30		J9	1 2 0 0 00		1 2 0 0 00	

ACCOUNT   Rent Expense   ACCOUNT NO.   521

DATE	ITEM	POST. REF.	DEBIT	CREDIT	BALANCE DEBIT	BALANCE CREDIT
20-- May 1		J9	2 4 0 0 00		2 4 0 0 00	

ACCOUNT   Utilities Expense   ACCOUNT NO.   533

DATE	ITEM	POST. REF.	DEBIT	CREDIT	BALANCE DEBIT	BALANCE CREDIT
20-- May 15		J9	1 7 2 0 00		1 7 2 0 00	

Problem 11-10A (Concluded)

ACCOUNTS PAYABLE LEDGER

NAME Fantastic Toys

ADDRESS

DATE		ITEM	POST. REF.	DEBIT	CREDIT	BALANCE
20-- May	1	Balance	✓			5 2 0 0 00
	12		J9	5 2 0 0 00		

NAME Goya Outlet

ADDRESS

DATE		ITEM	POST. REF.	DEBIT	CREDIT	BALANCE
20-- May	1	Balance	✓			3 8 0 0 00
	26		J9	3 8 0 0 00		

NAME Mueller's Distributors

ADDRESS

DATE		ITEM	POST. REF.	DEBIT	CREDIT	BALANCE
20-- May	1	Balance	✓			3 6 0 0 00
	3		J9	3 6 0 0 00		

NAME Van Kooning

ADDRESS

DATE		ITEM	POST. REF.	DEBIT	CREDIT	BALANCE
20-- May	1	Balance	✓			7 4 0 0 00
	7		J9	5 5 0 0 00		1 9 0 0 00

Problem 11-11A

1.

GENERAL JOURNAL

PAGE 16

	DATE		DESCRIPTION	POST. REF.	DEBIT	CREDIT	
1	20-- July	1	Rent Expense	521	1 5 0 0 00		1
2			Cash	101		1 5 0 0 00	2
3			Check No. 414				3
4							4
5		1	Purchases	501	2 7 0 0 00		5
6			Accounts Payable/Tang's Toys	202/✓		2 7 0 0 00	6
7			Invoice No. 311				7
8							8
9		3	Purchases	501	3 1 0 0 00		9
10			Accounts Payable/Sillas & Company	202/✓		3 1 0 0 00	10
11			Invoice No. 812				11
12							12
13		5	Accounts Payable/Tang's Toys	202/✓	5 0 0 00		13
14			Purchases Returns and Allowances	501.1		5 0 0 00	14
15			Returned merchandise				15
16							16
17		8	Purchases	501	1 9 0 0 00		17
18			Accounts Payable/Daisy's Dolls	202/✓		1 9 0 0 00	18
19			Invoice No. 139				19
20							20
21		11	Accounts Payable/Tang's Toys	202/✓	2 2 0 0 00		21
22			Cash	101		2 1 5 6 00	22
23			Purchases Discounts	501.2		4 4 00	23
24			Check No. 415				24
25							25
26		13	Accounts Payable/Sillas & Company	202/✓	3 1 0 0 00		26
27			Cash	101		3 0 6 9 00	27
28			Purchases Discounts	501.2		3 1 00	28
29			Check No. 416				29
30							30
31		15	Accounts Payable/Daisy's Dolls	202/✓	4 0 0 00		31
32			Purchases Returns and Allowances	501.1		4 0 0 00	32
33			Returned merchandise				33
34							34

Problem 11-11A (Continued)

GENERAL JOURNAL

	DATE		DESCRIPTION	POST. REF.	DEBIT	CREDIT	
1	20-- July	18	Accounts Payable/Daisy's Dolls	202/✓	1 5 0 0 00		1
2			Cash	101		1 4 7 0 00	2
3			Purchases Discounts	501.2		3 0 00	3
4			Check No. 417				4
5							5
6		25	Purchases	501	2 4 5 0 00		6
7			Accounts Payable/Allied Business	202/✓		2 4 5 0 00	7
8			Invoice No. 489				8
9							9
10		26	Purchases	501	1 9 8 0 00		10
11			Accounts Payable/Tang's Toys	202/✓		1 9 8 0 00	11
12			Invoice No. 375				12
13							13
14		29	Purchases	501	3 4 6 0 00		14
15			Accounts Payable/Sillas & Company	202/✓		3 4 6 0 00	15
16			Invoice No. 883				16
17							17
18							18
19							19
20							20
21							21
22							22
23							23
24							24
25							25
26							26
27							27
28							28
29							29
30							30
31							31
32							32
33							33
34							34

Problem 11-11A (Continued)

2.

GENERAL LEDGER

ACCOUNT Cash   ACCOUNT NO. 101

DATE		ITEM	POST. REF.	DEBIT	CREDIT	BALANCE DEBIT	BALANCE CREDIT
20-- July	1	Balance	✓			20 0 0 0 00	
	1		J16		1 5 0 0 00	18 5 0 0 00	
	11		J16		2 1 5 6 00	16 3 4 4 00	
	13		J16		3 0 6 9 00	13 2 7 5 00	
	18		J17		1 4 7 0 00	11 8 0 5 00	

ACCOUNT Accounts Payable   ACCOUNT NO. 202

DATE		ITEM	POST. REF.	DEBIT	CREDIT	BALANCE DEBIT	BALANCE CREDIT
20-- July	1		J16		2 7 0 0 00		2 7 0 0 00
	3		J16		3 1 0 0 00		5 8 0 0 00
	5		J16	5 0 0 00			5 3 0 0 00
	8		J16		1 9 0 0 00		7 2 0 0 00
	11		J16	2 2 0 0 00			5 0 0 0 00
	13		J16	3 1 0 0 00			1 9 0 0 00
	15		J16	4 0 0 00			1 5 0 0 00
	18		J17	1 5 0 0 00			
	25		J17		2 4 5 0 00		2 4 5 0 00
	26		J17		1 9 8 0 00		4 4 3 0 00
	29		J17		3 4 6 0 00		7 8 9 0 00

Problem 11-11A (Continued)

ACCOUNT Purchases   ACCOUNT NO. 501

DATE		ITEM	POST. REF.	DEBIT	CREDIT	BALANCE	
						DEBIT	CREDIT
20-- July	1		J16	2 7 0 0 00		2 7 0 0 00	
	3		J16	3 1 0 0 00		5 8 0 0 00	
	8		J16	1 9 0 0 00		7 7 0 0 00	
	25		J17	2 4 5 0 00		10 1 5 0 00	
	26		J17	1 9 8 0 00		12 1 3 0 00	
	29		J17	3 4 6 0 00		15 5 9 0 00	

ACCOUNT Purchases Returns and Allowances   ACCOUNT NO. 501.1

DATE		ITEM	POST. REF.	DEBIT	CREDIT	BALANCE	
						DEBIT	CREDIT
20-- July	5		J16		5 0 0 00		5 0 0 00
	15		J16		4 0 0 00		9 0 0 00

ACCOUNT Purchases Discounts   ACCOUNT NO. 501.2

DATE		ITEM	POST. REF.	DEBIT	CREDIT	BALANCE	
						DEBIT	CREDIT
20-- July	11		J16		4 4 00		4 4 00
	13		J16		3 1 00		7 5 00
	18		J17		3 0 00		1 0 5 00

ACCOUNT Rent Expense   ACCOUNT NO. 521

DATE		ITEM	POST. REF.	DEBIT	CREDIT	BALANCE	
						DEBIT	CREDIT
20-- July	1		J16	1 5 0 0 00		1 5 0 0 00	

Problem 11-11A (Concluded)

ACCOUNTS PAYABLE LEDGER

NAME *Allied Business*

ADDRESS

DATE	ITEM	POST. REF.	DEBIT	CREDIT	BALANCE
20-- July 25		J17		2 4 5 0 00	2 4 5 0 00

NAME *Daisy's Dolls*

ADDRESS

DATE	ITEM	POST. REF.	DEBIT	CREDIT	BALANCE
20-- July 8		J16		1 9 0 0 00	1 9 0 0 00
15		J16	4 0 0 00		1 5 0 0 00
18		J17	1 5 0 0 00		—

NAME *Sillas & Company*

ADDRESS

DATE	ITEM	POST. REF.	DEBIT	CREDIT	BALANCE
20-- July 3		J16		3 1 0 0 00	3 1 0 0 00
13		J16	3 1 0 0 00		—
29		J17		3 4 6 0 00	3 4 6 0 00

NAME *Tang's Toys*

ADDRESS

DATE	ITEM	POST. REF.	DEBIT	CREDIT	BALANCE
20-- July 1		J16		2 7 0 0 00	2 7 0 0 00
5		J16	5 0 0 00		2 2 0 0 00
11		J16	2 2 0 0 00		—
26		J17		1 9 8 0 00	1 9 8 0 00

Problem 11-12A

Flint's Fantasy

Schedule of Accounts Payable

July 31, 20--

Allied Business	$2	4	5	0	00	
Sillas & Company	3	4	6	0	00	
Tang's Toys	1	9	8	0	00	
	$7	8	9	0	00	
Proof						
Balance of Accounts Payable, July 31	$7	8	9	0	00	

Exercise 11-1B

1. _A form used to request the purchase of merchandise or other property_ _____

2. _A written order to buy goods from a vendor_ _____

3. _A form indicating what goods have been received_ _____

4. _A bill from the vendor for goods shipped_ _____

Exercise 11-2B

1.

Gross amount	$5,000
Less 10% trade discount	500
Net amount of purchases	$4,500

2.

Net amount	$4,500
Less 3% discount	135
Net amount to be paid	$4,365

3.

GENERAL JOURNAL   PAGE ____

	DATE		DESCRIPTION	POST. REF.	DEBIT	CREDIT	
1	20-- June	12	Purchases		4 5 0 0 00		1
2			Accounts Payable/Grant's Distributors			4 5 0 0 00	2
3			Purchased merchandise				3
4							4
5		22	Accounts Payable/Grant's Distributors		4 5 0 0 00		5
6			Cash			4 3 6 5 00	6
7			Purchases Discounts			1 3 5 00	7
8			Paid invoice within discount period				8
9							9
10							10
11							11
12							12
13							13
15							15

Exercise 11-3B

1.

Cash		
	(a)	2,300
	(b)	3,600

Accounts Payable

Purchases		
(a)	2,300	
(b)	3,600	

Purchases Returns and Allowances

Purchases Discounts

Freight-In

2.

Cash		
	(c)	3,920
	(d)	2,800

Accounts Payable			
(c)	4,000	(a)	4,000
(d)	2,800	(b)	2,800

Purchases		
(a)	4,000	
(b)	2,800	

Purchases Returns and Allowances

Purchases Discounts		
	(c)	80

Freight-In

Exercise 11-3B (Concluded)

3.

Cash		
	(c)	4,900

Accounts Payable			
(b)	600	(a)	5,600
(c)	5,000		

Purchases		
(a)	5,600	

Purchases Returns and Allowances		
	(b)	600

Purchases Discounts		
	(c)	100

Freight-In

4.

Cash		
	(b)	4,000

Accounts Payable			
(b)	4,000	(a)	4,000

Purchases		
(a)	3,800	

Purchases Returns and Allowances

Purchases Discounts

Freight-In		
(a)	200	

Exercise 11-4B

Sales			$116 9 0 0 00	
Less: Sales returns and allowances		$ 1 1 0 0 00		
Sales discounts		4 0 0 00	1 5 0 0 00	
Net sales				$115 4 0 0 00
Cost of goods sold				
Merchandise inventory, Jan. 1			$ 30 0 0 0 00	
Purchases		$100 0 0 0 00		
Less: Purchases returns and allow.	$2 0 0 0 00			
Purchases discounts	2 8 0 0 00	4 8 0 0 00		
Net purchases		$ 95 2 0 0 00		
Add freight-in		1 5 0 0 00		
Cost of goods purchased			96 7 0 0 00	
Goods available for sale			$126 7 0 0 00	
Less merchandise inventory, Dec. 31			50 0 0 0 00	
Cost of goods sold				76 7 0 0 00
Gross profit				$ 38 7 0 0 00

Exercise 11-5B

GENERAL JOURNAL

PAGE

	DATE		DESCRIPTION	POST. REF.	DEBIT	CREDIT	
1	20-- Jan.	3	Purchases		6 0 0 0 00		1
2			Accounts Payable/Feng			6 0 0 0 00	2
3			Invoice No. 416				3
4							4
5		12	Purchases		9 0 0 0 00		5
6			Accounts Payable/Miranda			9 0 0 0 00	6
7			Invoice No. 624				7
8							8
9		19	Purchases		6 4 0 0 00		9
10			Accounts Payable/J. B. Barba			6 4 0 0 00	10
11			Invoice No. 190				11
12							12
13		26	Purchases		3 7 0 0 00		13
14			Accounts Payable/Ramirez			3 7 0 0 00	14
15			Invoice No. 923				15
16							16
17							17
18							18
19							19
20							20
21							21
22							22
23							23
24							24
25							25
26							26
27							27
28							28
29							29
30							30
31							31
32							32
33							33
34							34

Exercise 11-6B

GENERAL JOURNAL   PAGE 3

	DATE	DESCRIPTION	POST. REF.	DEBIT	CREDIT	
1	20-- Mar. 5	Accounts Payable/Tower Industries	202/✓	5 0 0 00		1
2		Purchases Returns and Allowances	501.1		5 0 0 00	2
3		Returned merchandise				3
4						4
5	11	Accounts Payable/A & D Arms	202/✓	6 2 5 00		5
6		Purchases Returns and Allowances	501.1		6 2 5 00	6
7		Returned merchandise				7
8						8
9	23	Accounts Payable/Mighty Mansion	202/✓	2 7 5 00		9
10		Purchases Returns and Allowances	501.1		2 7 5 00	10
11		Returned merchandise				11
12						12

GENERAL LEDGER

ACCOUNT   Accounts Payable   ACCOUNT NO. 202

DATE	ITEM	POST. REF.	DEBIT	CREDIT	BALANCE DEBIT	BALANCE CREDIT
20-- Mar. 1	Balance	✓				8 3 5 0 00
5		J3	5 0 0 00			7 8 5 0 00
11		J3	6 2 5 00			7 2 2 5 00
23		J3	2 7 5 00			6 9 5 0 00

ACCOUNT   Purchases Returns and Allowances   ACCOUNT NO. 501.1

DATE	ITEM	POST. REF.	DEBIT	CREDIT	BALANCE DEBIT	BALANCE CREDIT
20-- Mar. 5		J3		5 0 0 00		5 0 0 00
11		J3		6 2 5 00		1 1 2 5 00
23		J3		2 7 5 00		1 4 0 0 00

Exercise 11-6B (Concluded)

ACCOUNTS PAYABLE LEDGER

NAME A & D Arms

ADDRESS

DATE		ITEM	POST. REF.	DEBIT	CREDIT	BALANCE
20-- Mar.	1	Balance	✓			2 3 0 0 00
	11		J3	6 2 5 00		1 6 7 5 00

NAME Mighty Mansion

ADDRESS

DATE		ITEM	POST. REF.	DEBIT	CREDIT	BALANCE
20-- Mar.	1	Balance	✓			1 4 5 0 00
	23		J3	2 7 5 00		1 1 7 5 00

NAME Tower Industries

ADDRESS

DATE		ITEM	POST. REF.	DEBIT	CREDIT	BALANCE
20-- Mar.	1	Balance	✓			4 6 0 0 00
	5		J3	5 0 0 00		4 1 0 0 00

Exercise 11-7B

GENERAL JOURNAL

	DATE		DESCRIPTION	POST. REF.	DEBIT	CREDIT	
1	20-- Apr.	5	Accounts Payable/Standard Industries		8 0 0 0 00		1
2			Cash			7 8 4 0 00	2
3			Purchases Discounts			1 6 0 00	3
4			Check No. 429				4
5							5
6		19	Accounts Payable/Finest Company		5 0 0 0 00		6
7			Cash			4 9 5 0 00	7
8			Purchases Discounts			5 0 00	8
9			Check No. 430				9
10							10
11		21	Accounts Payable/Funny Follies		3 2 5 0 00		11
12			Cash			3 2 5 0 00	12
13			Check No. 431				13
14							14
15		29	Accounts Payable/Classic Data		7 0 0 0 00		15
16			Cash			6 8 6 0 00	16
17			Purchases Discounts			1 4 0 00	17
18			Check No. 432				18
19							19
20							20
21							21

Exercise 11-8B

Crystal's Candles

Schedule of Accounts Payable

November 30, 20--

Carl's Candle Wax	$ 3 4 8 0 00	
Handy Supplies	2 9 6 0 00	
Wishy Wicks	4 1 2 5 00	
	$10 5 6 5 00	

Problem 11-9B

1.

GENERAL JOURNAL

	DATE		DESCRIPTION	POST. REF.	DEBIT	CREDIT	
1	20-- Oct.	2	*Purchases*	*501*	1 9 5 0 00		1
2			**Accounts Payable/Boggs Distributors**	*202/✓*		1 9 5 0 00	2
3			*Invoice No. 321*				3
4							4
5		7	*Purchases*	*501*	2 9 1 5 00		5
6			**Accounts Payable/Wolfs Wholesaler**	*202/✓*		2 9 1 5 00	6
7			*Invoice No. 152*				7
8							8
9		10	*Purchases*	*501*	3 5 6 5 00		9
10			**Accounts Payable/Komuro & Co.**	*202/✓*		3 5 6 5 00	10
11			*Invoice No. 634*				11
12							12
13		16	*Purchases*	*501*	2 8 4 5 00		13
14			**Accounts Payable/Fritz & McCord, Inc.**	*202/✓*		2 8 4 5 00	14
15			*Invoice No. 349*				15
16							16
17		24	*Purchases*	*501*	3 3 7 0 00		17
18			**Accounts Payable/Boggs Distributors**	*202/✓*		3 3 7 0 00	18
19			*Invoice No. 587*				19
20							20
21		26	*Purchases*	*501*	2 2 4 0 00		21
22			**Accounts Payable/Sanderson Company**	*202/✓*		2 2 4 0 00	22
23			*Invoice No. 764*				23
24							24
25		31	*Purchases*	*501*	1 6 3 0 00		25
26			**Account Payable/Wolfs Wholesaler**	*202/✓*		1 6 3 0 00	26
27			*Invoice No. 672*				27
28							28
29							29
30							30
31							31
32							32
33							33
34							34

Problem 11-9B (Continued)

2.

GENERAL LEDGER

ACCOUNT   Accounts Payable   ACCOUNT NO.   202

DATE		ITEM	POST. REF.	DEBIT	CREDIT	BALANCE DEBIT	BALANCE CREDIT
20-- Oct.	2		J16		1 9 5 0 00		1 9 5 0 00
	7		J16		2 9 1 5 00		4 8 6 5 00
	10		J16		3 5 6 5 00		8 4 3 0 00
	16		J16		2 8 4 5 00		11 2 7 5 00
	24		J16		3 3 7 0 00		14 6 4 5 00
	26		J16		2 2 4 0 00		16 8 8 5 00
	31		J16		1 6 3 0 00		18 5 1 5 00

ACCOUNT   Purchases   ACCOUNT NO.   501

DATE		ITEM	POST. REF.	DEBIT	CREDIT	BALANCE DEBIT	BALANCE CREDIT
20-- Oct.	2		J16	1 9 5 0 00		1 9 5 0 00	
	7		J16	2 9 1 5 00		4 8 6 5 00	
	10		J16	3 5 6 5 00		8 4 3 0 00	
	16		J16	2 8 4 5 00		11 2 7 5 00	
	24		J16	3 3 7 0 00		14 6 4 5 00	
	26		J16	2 2 4 0 00		16 8 8 5 00	
	31		J16	1 6 3 0 00		18 5 1 5 00	

ACCOUNTS PAYABLE LEDGER

NAME *Boggs Distributors*

ADDRESS

DATE		ITEM	POST. REF.	DEBIT	CREDIT	BALANCE
20-- Oct.	2		J16		1 9 5 0 00	1 9 5 0 00
	24		J16		3 3 7 0 00	5 3 2 0 00

Problem 11-9B (Concluded)

NAME *Fritz & McCord, Inc.*

ADDRESS

DATE		ITEM	POST. REF.	DEBIT	CREDIT	BALANCE
20-- Oct.	16		J16		2 8 4 5 00	2 8 4 5 00

NAME *Komuro & Co.*

ADDRESS

DATE		ITEM	POST. REF.	DEBIT	CREDIT	BALANCE
20-- Oct.	10		J16		3 5 6 5 00	3 5 6 5 00

NAME *Sanderson Company*

ADDRESS

DATE		ITEM	POST. REF.	DEBIT	CREDIT	BALANCE
20-- Oct.	26		J16		2 2 4 0 00	2 2 4 0 00

NAME *Wolfs Wholesaler*

ADDRESS

DATE		ITEM	POST. REF.	DEBIT	CREDIT	BALANCE
20-- Oct.	7		J16		2 9 1 5 00	2 9 1 5 00
	31		J16		1 6 3 0 00	4 5 4 5 00

Problem 11-10B

1.

GENERAL JOURNAL

	DATE		DESCRIPTION	POST. REF.	DEBIT	CREDIT	
1	20-- May	1	Rent Expense	521	2 6 0 0 00		1
2			Cash	101		2 6 0 0 00	2
3			Check No. 326				3
4							4
5		4	Accounts Payable/Cortez Distributors	202/✓	4 2 0 0 00		5
6			Cash	101		4 0 7 4 00	6
7			Purchases Discounts	501.2		1 2 6 00	7
8			Check No. 327				8
9							9
10		7	Accounts Payable/Indra & Velga	202/✓	6 2 0 0 00		10
11			Cash	101		6 2 0 0 00	11
12			Check No. 328				12
13							13
14		11	Accounts Payable/Toy Corner	202/✓	4 6 0 0 00		14
15			Cash	101		4 5 5 4 00	15
16			Purchases Discounts	501.2		4 6 00	16
17			Check No. 329				17
18							18
19		15	Utilities Expense	533	1 5 0 0 00		19
20			Cash	101		1 5 0 0 00	20
21			Check No. 330				21
22							22
23		19	Purchases	501	3 5 0 0 00		23
24			Cash	101		3 5 0 0 00	24
25			Check No. 331				25
26							26
27		25	Accounts Payable/Troutman Outlet	202/✓	4 4 0 0 00		27
28			Cash	101		4 3 1 2 00	28
29			Purchases Discounts	501.2		8 8 00	29
30			Check No. 332				30
31							31
32		30	Freight-In	502	8 0 0 00		32
33			Cash	101		8 0 0 00	33
34			Check No. 333				34

Problem 11-10B (Continued)

GENERAL JOURNAL

	DATE	DESCRIPTION	POST. REF.	DEBIT	CREDIT	
1	20-- May 31	Purchases	501	2 3 5 0 00		1
2		Cash	101		2 3 5 0 00	2
3		Check No. 334				3
4						4
5						5

2.

GENERAL LEDGER

ACCOUNT   Cash   ACCOUNT NO.   101

DATE	ITEM	POST. REF.	DEBIT	CREDIT	BALANCE DEBIT	BALANCE CREDIT
20-- May 1	Balance	✓			40 0 0 0 00	
1		J9		2 6 0 0 00	37 4 0 0 00	
4		J9		4 0 7 4 00	33 3 2 6 00	
7		J9		6 2 0 0 00	27 1 2 6 00	
11		J9		4 5 5 4 00	22 5 7 2 00	
15		J9		1 5 0 0 00	21 0 7 2 00	
19		J9		3 5 0 0 00	17 5 7 2 00	
25		J9		4 3 1 2 00	13 2 6 0 00	
30		J9		8 0 0 00	12 4 6 0 00	
31		J10		2 3 5 0 00	10 1 1 0 00	

ACCOUNT   Accounts Payable   ACCOUNT NO.   202

DATE	ITEM	POST. REF.	DEBIT	CREDIT	BALANCE DEBIT	BALANCE CREDIT
20-- May 1	Balance	✓				20 0 0 0 00
4		J9	4 2 0 0 00			15 8 0 0 00
7		J9	6 2 0 0 00			9 6 0 0 00
11		J9	4 6 0 0 00			5 0 0 0 00
25		J9	4 4 0 0 00			6 0 0 00

Problem 11-10B (Continued)

ACCOUNT   Purchases   ACCOUNT NO.   501

DATE		ITEM	POST. REF.	DEBIT	CREDIT	BALANCE DEBIT	BALANCE CREDIT
20-- May	19		J9	3 5 0 0 00		3 5 0 0 00	
	31		J10	2 3 5 0 00		5 8 5 0 00	

ACCOUNT   Purchases Discounts   ACCOUNT NO.   501.2

DATE		ITEM	POST. REF.	DEBIT	CREDIT	BALANCE DEBIT	BALANCE CREDIT
20-- May	4		J9		1 2 6 00		1 2 6 00
	11		J9		4 6 00		1 7 2 00
	25		J9		8 8 00		2 6 0 00

ACCOUNT   Freight-In   ACCOUNT NO.   502

DATE		ITEM	POST. REF.	DEBIT	CREDIT	BALANCE DEBIT	BALANCE CREDIT
20-- May	30		J9	8 0 0 00		8 0 0 00	

ACCOUNT   Rent Expense   ACCOUNT NO.   521

DATE		ITEM	POST. REF.	DEBIT	CREDIT	BALANCE DEBIT	BALANCE CREDIT
20-- May	1		J9	2 6 0 0 00		2 6 0 0 00	

ACCOUNT   Utilities Expense   ACCOUNT NO.   533

DATE		ITEM	POST. REF.	DEBIT	CREDIT	BALANCE DEBIT	BALANCE CREDIT
20-- May	15		J9	1 5 0 0 00		1 5 0 0 00	

Problem 11-10B (Concluded)

ACCOUNTS PAYABLE LEDGER

NAME Cortez Distributors

ADDRESS

DATE		ITEM	POST. REF.	DEBIT	CREDIT	BALANCE
20-- May	1	Balance	✓			4 2 0 0 00
	4		J9	4 2 0 0 00		

NAME Indra & Velga

ADDRESS

DATE		ITEM	POST. REF.	DEBIT	CREDIT	BALANCE
20-- May	1	Balance	✓			6 8 0 0 00
	7		J9	6 2 0 0 00		6 0 0 00

NAME Toy Corner

ADDRESS

DATE		ITEM	POST. REF.	DEBIT	CREDIT	BALANCE
20-- May	1	Balance	✓			4 6 0 0 00
	11		J9	4 6 0 0 00		

NAME Troutman Outlet

ADDRESS

DATE		ITEM	POST. REF.	DEBIT	CREDIT	BALANCE
20-- May	1	Balance	✓			4 4 0 0 00
	25		J9	4 4 0 0 00		

Problem 11-11B

1.

GENERAL JOURNAL

	DATE		DESCRIPTION	POST. REF.	DEBIT	CREDIT	
1	20-- July	1	Rent Expense	521	1 4 0 0 00		1
2			Cash	101		1 4 0 0 00	2
3			Check No. 314				3
4							4
5		1	Purchases	501	2 5 0 0 00		5
6			Accounts Payable/Topper's Toys	202/✓		2 5 0 0 00	6
7			Invoice No. 211				7
8							8
9		3	Purchases	501	2 8 0 0 00		9
10			Accounts Payable/Jones & Company	202/✓		2 8 0 0 00	10
11			Invoice No. 812				11
12							12
13		5	Accounts Payable/Topper's Toys	202/✓	4 0 0 00		13
14			Purchases Returns and Allowances	501.1		4 0 0 00	14
15			Returned merchandise				15
16							16
17		8	Purchases	501	1 6 0 0 00		17
18			Accounts Payable/Downtown Merchants	202/✓		1 6 0 0 00	18
19			Invoice No. 159				19
20							20
21		11	Accounts Payable/Topper's Toys	202/✓	2 1 0 0 00		21
22			Cash	101		2 0 5 8 00	22
23			Purchases Discounts	501.2		4 2 00	23
24			Check No. 315				24
25							25
26		13	Accounts Payable/Jones & Company	202/✓	2 8 0 0 00		26
27			Cash	101		2 7 7 2 00	27
28			Purchases Discounts	501.2		2 8 00	28
29			Check No. 316				29
30							30
31		15	Accounts Payable/Downtown Merchants	202/✓	6 0 0 00		31
32			Purchases Returns and Allowances	501.1		6 0 0 00	32
33			Returned merchandise				33
34							34

Problem 11-11B (Continued)

GENERAL JOURNAL

PAGE 17

	DATE		DESCRIPTION	POST. REF.	DEBIT	CREDIT	
1	20-- July	18	Accounts Payable/Downtown Merchants	202/✓	1 0 0 0 00		1
2			Cash	101		9 8 0 00	2
3			Purchases Discounts	501.2		2 0 00	3
4			Check No. 317				4
5							5
6		25	Purchases	501	3 2 0 0 00		6
7			Accounts Payable/Columbia Products	202/✓		3 2 0 0 00	7
8			Invoice No. 468				8
9							9
10		26	Purchases	501	1 4 3 0 00		10
11			Accounts Payable/Topper's Toys	202/✓		1 4 3 0 00	11
12			Invoice No. 395				12
13							13
14		29	Purchases	501	2 9 7 0 00		14
15			Accounts Payable/Jones & Company	202/✓		2 9 7 0 00	15
16			Invoice No. 853				16
17							17
18							18
19							19
20							20
21							21
22							22
23							23
24							24
25							25
26							26
27							27
28							28
29							29
30							30
31							31
32							32
33							33
34							34

Problem 11-11B (Continued)

2.

GENERAL LEDGER

ACCOUNT Cash

ACCOUNT NO. 101

DATE		ITEM	POST. REF.	DEBIT	CREDIT	BALANCE DEBIT	BALANCE CREDIT
20-- July	1	Balance	✓			20 0 0 0 00	
	1		J16		1 4 0 0 00	18 6 0 0 00	
	11		J16		2 0 5 8 00	16 5 4 2 00	
	13		J16		2 7 7 2 00	13 7 7 0 00	
	18		J17		9 8 0 00	12 7 9 0 00	

ACCOUNT Accounts Payable

ACCOUNT NO. 202

DATE		ITEM	POST. REF.	DEBIT	CREDIT	BALANCE DEBIT	BALANCE CREDIT
20-- July	1		J16		2 5 0 0 00		2 5 0 0 00
	3		J16		2 8 0 0 00		5 3 0 0 00
	5		J16	4 0 0 00			4 9 0 0 00
	8		J16		1 6 0 0 00		6 5 0 0 00
	11		J16	2 1 0 0 00			4 4 0 0 00
	13		J16	2 8 0 0 00			1 6 0 0 00
	15		J16	6 0 0 00			1 0 0 0 00
	18		J17	1 0 0 0 00			—
	25		J17		3 2 0 0 00		3 2 0 0 00
	26		J17		1 4 3 0 00		4 6 3 0 00
	29		J17		2 9 7 0 00		7 6 0 0 00

Problem 11-11B (Continued)

ACCOUNT Purchases   ACCOUNT NO. 501

DATE		ITEM	POST. REF.	DEBIT	CREDIT	BALANCE DEBIT	BALANCE CREDIT
20-- July	1		J16	2 5 0 0 00		2 5 0 0 00	
	3		J16	2 8 0 0 00		5 3 0 0 00	
	8		J16	1 6 0 0 00		6 9 0 0 00	
	25		J17	3 2 0 0 00		10 1 0 0 00	
	26		J17	1 4 3 0 00		11 5 3 0 00	
	29		J17	2 9 7 0 00		14 5 0 0 00	

ACCOUNT Purchases Returns and Allowances   ACCOUNT NO. 501.1

DATE		ITEM	POST. REF.	DEBIT	CREDIT	BALANCE DEBIT	BALANCE CREDIT
20-- July	5		J16		4 0 0 00		4 0 0 00
	15		J16		6 0 0 00		1 0 0 0 00

ACCOUNT Purchases Discounts   ACCOUNT NO. 501.2

DATE		ITEM	POST. REF.	DEBIT	CREDIT	BALANCE DEBIT	BALANCE CREDIT
20-- July	11		J16		4 2 00		4 2 00
	13		J16		2 8 00		7 0 00
	18		J17		2 0 00		9 0 00

ACCOUNT Rent Expense   ACCOUNT NO. 521

DATE		ITEM	POST. REF.	DEBIT	CREDIT	BALANCE DEBIT	BALANCE CREDIT
20-- July	1		J16	1 4 0 0 00		1 4 0 0 00	

Problem 11-11B (Concluded)

ACCOUNTS PAYABLE LEDGER

NAME *Columbia Products*

ADDRESS

DATE		ITEM	POST. REF.	DEBIT	CREDIT	BALANCE
20-- July	25		J17		3 2 0 0 00	3 2 0 0 00

NAME *Downtown Merchants*

ADDRESS

DATE		ITEM	POST. REF.	DEBIT	CREDIT	BALANCE
20-- July	8		J16		1 6 0 0 00	1 6 0 0 00
	15		J16	6 0 0 00		1 0 0 0 00
	18		J17	1 0 0 0 00		———

NAME *Jones & Company*

ADDRESS

DATE		ITEM	POST. REF.	DEBIT	CREDIT	BALANCE
20-- July	3		J16		2 8 0 0 00	2 8 0 0 00
	13		J16	2 8 0 0 00		———
	29		J17		2 9 7 0 00	2 9 7 0 00

NAME *Topper's Toys*

ADDRESS

DATE		ITEM	POST. REF.	DEBIT	CREDIT	BALANCE
20-- July	1		J16		2 5 0 0 00	2 5 0 0 00
	5		J16	4 0 0 00		2 1 0 0 00
	11		J16	2 1 0 0 00		———
	26		J17		1 4 3 0 00	1 4 3 0 00

Problem 11-12B

Debbie's Doll House

Schedule of Accounts Payable

July 31, 20--

Columbia Products	$3	2	0	0	00
Jones & Company	2	9	7	0	00
Topper's Toys	1	4	3	0	00
	$7	6	0	0	00
Proof					
Balance of Accounts Payable, July 31	$7	6	0	0	00

MANAGING YOUR WRITING

Cash discounts of 1% or 2% seem small, but when converted to an annual rate, the discounts are substantial. For example, a $1,000 purchase with terms of 2/10, n/30, would yield a discount of only $20 if paid within the discount period. But if the invoice is not paid until the 30-day due date, the $20 lost discount is the expense the business incurs for having the use of $980 ($1,000 – $20) for only 20 days. The approximate annual interest rate is 36% (360 days/20 days × 2%). This is an expensive way to finance purchases.

The supplier invoices should be filed by due date within the discount period. This will provide a reminder to make payments within the discount period and help the business to plan for its cash needs.

ETHICS CASE: SUGGESTED SOLUTIONS

1. Although it is a good cash management practice to pay invoices on the last day of the discount period, Bob is taking more time than the seller is willing to extend him. Since the seller has contacted him, Bob is behaving in an unethical manner by his attempts to avoid paying within the discount period and still deducting the discount.
2. Answers will vary. Auto Warehouse can add on to the next invoice the discount Bob has taken or send him a separate invoice for the balance owed. Auto Warehouse can change the credit terms to net cash or refuse to extend Bob's Discount Auto Parts credit.
3. Answers will vary. Students might point out that the purpose of cash discounts is to encourage prompt payment by customers. In this case, the payment must be postmarked within 10 days of the date of the invoice.
4. Answers will vary. Advantages: attracting and retaining customers, shortening your collection of receivables time. Disadvantages: discrepancies involving cash discounts taken.

Mastery Problem

1.

GENERAL JOURNAL

	DATE		DESCRIPTION	POST. REF.	DEBIT	CREDIT	
1	20-- June	1	Purchases	501	2 1 0 0 00		1
2			Accounts Payable/Irving Publishing Company	202/✓		2 1 0 0 00	2
3			Invoice No. 101				3
4							4
5		2	Accounts Payable/Northeastern Publishing Co.	202/✓	2 0 0 0 00		5
6			Cash	101		1 9 6 0 00	6
7			Purchases Discounts	501.2		4 0 00	7
8			Check No. 300				8
9							9
10		3	Purchases	501	2 3 0 4 00		10
11			Accounts Payable/Broadway Publishing, Inc.	202/✓		2 3 0 4 00	11
12			Invoice No. 711				12
13							13
14		3	Freight-In	502	2 5 0 00		14
15			Cash	101		2 5 0 00	15
16			Check No. 301				16
17							17
18		4	Rent Expense	521	6 2 5 00		18
19			Cash	101		6 2 5 00	19
20			Check No. 302				20
21							21
22		8	Purchases	501	5 8 2 5 00		22
23			Accts. Payable/Northeastern Publishing Co.	202/✓		5 8 2 5 00	23
24			Invoice No. 268				24
25							25
26		10	Accounts Payable/Irving Publishing Company	202/✓	5 5 0 00		26
27			Purchases Returns and Allowances	501.1		5 5 0 00	27
28			Returned merchandise				28
29							29
30		13	Accounts Payable/Broadway Publishing, Inc.	202/✓	2 3 0 4 00		30
31			Cash	101		2 2 3 4 88	31
32			Purchases Discounts	501.2		6 9 12	32
33			Check No. 304				33
34							34

Mastery Problem (Continued)

GENERAL JOURNAL

	DATE		DESCRIPTION	POST. REF.	DEBIT	CREDIT	
1	20-- June	28	*Purchases*	*501*	2 3 5 0 00		1
2			*Accounts Payable/Broadway Publishing, Inc.*	*202/✓*		2 3 5 0 00	2
3			*Invoice No. 579*				3
4							4
5		28	*Purchases*	*501*	4 2 0 0 00		5
6			*Accts. Payable/Northeastern Publishing Co.*	*202/✓*		4 2 0 0 00	6
7			*Invoice No. 406*				7
8							8
9		28	*Purchases*	*501*	3 4 5 0 00		9
10			*Accounts Payable/Riley Publishing Co.*	*202/✓*		3 4 5 0 00	10
11			*Invoice No. 964*				11
12							12
13		30	*Utilities Expense*	*533*	3 2 5 00		13
14			*Cash*	*101*		3 2 5 00	14
15			*Check No. 305*				15
16							16
17		30	*M. French, Drawing*	*312*	4 5 0 0 00		17
18			*Cash*	*101*		4 5 0 0 00	18
19			*Check No. 306*				19
20							20
21		30	*Accounts Payable/Irving Publishing Company*	*202/✓*	1 5 5 0 00		21
22			*Cash*	*101*		1 5 5 0 00	22
23			*Check No. 307*				23
24							24
25		30	*Accounts Payable/Northeastern Publishing Co.*	*202/✓*	5 8 2 5 00		25
26			*Cash*	*101*		5 7 0 8 50	26
27			*Purchases Discounts*	*501.2*		1 1 6 50	27
28			*Check No. 308*				28
29							29
30		30	*Purchases*	*501*	1 3 2 8 00		30
31			*Cash*	*101*		1 3 2 8 00	31
32			*Check No. 309*				32
33							33
34							34

Mastery Problem (Continued)
2.

GENERAL LEDGER

ACCOUNT   Cash   ACCOUNT NO.   101

DATE		ITEM	POST. REF.	DEBIT	CREDIT	BALANCE DEBIT	BALANCE CREDIT
20-- June	1	Balance	✓			32 2 0 0 00	
	2		J16		1 9 6 0 00	30 2 4 0 00	
	3		J16		2 5 0 00	29 9 9 0 00	
	4		J16		6 2 5 00	29 3 6 5 00	
	13		J16		2 2 3 4 88	27 1 3 0 12	
	30		J17		3 2 5 00	26 8 0 5 12	
	30		J17		4 5 0 0 00	22 3 0 5 12	
	30		J17		1 5 5 0 00	20 7 5 5 12	
	30		J17		5 7 0 8 50	15 0 4 6 62	
	30		J17		1 3 2 8 00	13 7 1 8 62	

ACCOUNT   Accounts Payable   ACCOUNT NO.   202

DATE		ITEM	POST. REF.	DEBIT	CREDIT	BALANCE DEBIT	BALANCE CREDIT
20-- June	1	Balance	✓				2 0 0 0 00
	1		J16		2 1 0 0 00		4 1 0 0 00
	2		J16	2 0 0 0 00			2 1 0 0 00
	3		J16		2 3 0 4 00		4 4 0 4 00
	8		J16		5 8 2 5 00		10 2 2 9 00
	10		J16	5 5 0 00			9 6 7 9 00
	13		J16	2 3 0 4 00			7 3 7 5 00
	28		J17		2 3 5 0 00		9 7 2 5 00
	28		J17		4 2 0 0 00		13 9 2 5 00
	28		J17		3 4 5 0 00		17 3 7 5 00
	30		J17	1 5 5 0 00			15 8 2 5 00
	30		J17	5 8 2 5 00			10 0 0 0 00

Mastery Problem (Continued)

ACCOUNT   M. French, Drawing   ACCOUNT NO.   312

DATE		ITEM	POST. REF.	DEBIT	CREDIT	BALANCE DEBIT	BALANCE CREDIT
20-- June	1	Balance	✓			18 0 0 0 00	
	30		J17	4 5 0 0 00		22 5 0 0 00	

ACCOUNT   Purchases   ACCOUNT NO.   501

DATE		ITEM	POST. REF.	DEBIT	CREDIT	BALANCE DEBIT	BALANCE CREDIT
20-- June	1	Balance	✓			67 0 2 1 66	
	1		J16	2 1 0 0 00		69 1 2 1 66	
	3		J16	2 3 0 4 00		71 4 2 5 66	
	8		J16	5 8 2 5 00		77 2 5 0 66	
	28		J17	2 3 5 0 00		79 6 0 0 66	
	28		J17	4 2 0 0 00		83 8 0 0 66	
	28		J17	3 4 5 0 00		87 2 5 0 66	
	30		J17	1 3 2 8 00		88 5 7 8 66	

ACCOUNT   Purchases Returns and Allowances   ACCOUNT NO.   501.1

DATE		ITEM	POST. REF.	DEBIT	CREDIT	BALANCE DEBIT	BALANCE CREDIT
20-- June	1	Balance	✓				2 3 1 5 23
	10		J16		5 5 0 00		2 8 6 5 23

ACCOUNT   Purchases Discounts   ACCOUNT NO.   501.2

DATE		ITEM	POST. REF.	DEBIT	CREDIT	BALANCE DEBIT	BALANCE CREDIT
20-- June	1	Balance	✓				9 0 5 00
	2		J16		4 0 00		9 4 5 00
	13		J16		6 9 12		1 0 1 4 12
	30		J17		1 1 6 50		1 1 3 0 62

Mastery Problem (Continued)

ACCOUNT Freight-In

ACCOUNT NO. 502

DATE		ITEM	POST. REF.	DEBIT	CREDIT	BALANCE DEBIT	BALANCE CREDIT
20-- June	1	Balance	✓			5 2 2 60	
	3		J16	2 5 0 00		7 7 2 60	

ACCOUNT Rent Expense

ACCOUNT NO. 521

DATE		ITEM	POST. REF.	DEBIT	CREDIT	BALANCE DEBIT	BALANCE CREDIT
20-- June	1	Balance	✓			3 1 2 5 00	
	4		J16	6 2 5 00		3 7 5 0 00	

ACCOUNT Utilities Expense

ACCOUNT NO. 533

DATE		ITEM	POST. REF.	DEBIT	CREDIT	BALANCE DEBIT	BALANCE CREDIT
20-- June	1	Balance	✓			1 5 2 2 87	
	30		J17	3 2 5 00		1 8 4 7 87	

ACCOUNTS PAYABLE LEDGER

NAME Broadway Publishing, Inc.

ADDRESS 2300 Goodman, Cincinnati, OH 45219-2901

DATE		ITEM	POST. REF.	DEBIT	CREDIT	BALANCE
20-- June	3		J16		2 3 0 4 00	2 3 0 4 00
	13		J16	2 3 0 4 00		
	28		J17		2 3 5 0 00	2 3 5 0 00

Mastery Problem (Continued)

NAME Irving Publishing Company

ADDRESS 5200 N. Keystone Ave., Indianapolis, IN 46220-1986

DATE		ITEM	POST. REF.	DEBIT	CREDIT	BALANCE
20-- June	1		J16		2 1 0 0 00	2 1 0 0 00
	10		J16	5 5 0 00		1 5 5 0 00
	30		J17	1 5 5 0 00		

NAME Northeastern Publishing Co.

ADDRESS 874 Crescent Drive, Flint, MI 48503-7564

DATE		ITEM	POST. REF.	DEBIT	CREDIT	BALANCE
20-- June	1	Balance	✓			2 0 0 0 00
	2		J16	2 0 0 0 00		
	8		J16		5 8 2 5 00	5 8 2 5 00
	28		J17		4 2 0 0 00	10 0 2 5 00
	30		J17	5 8 2 5 00		4 2 0 0 00

NAME Riley Publishing Co.

ADDRESS 5675 Pulaski Road, Chicago, IL 60629-6705

DATE		ITEM	POST. REF.	DEBIT	CREDIT	BALANCE
20-- June	28		J17		3 4 5 0 00	3 4 5 0 00

Mastery Problem (Concluded)

3.

Books and More

Schedule of Accounts Payable

June 30, 20--

Broadway Publishing, Inc.	$ 2 3 5 0 00
Northeastern Publishing Co.	4 2 0 0 00
Riley Publishing Co.	3 4 5 0 00
	$10 0 0 0 00

4.

Cost of goods sold				
Merchandise inventory, January 1			$ 35 5 2 3 00	
Purchases		$88 5 7 8 66		
Less: Purchases returns and allowances	$2 8 6 5 23			
Purchases discounts	1 1 3 0 62	3 9 9 5 85		
Net purchases		$84 5 8 2 81		
Add freight-in		7 7 2 60		
Cost of goods purchased			85 3 5 5 41	
Goods available for sale			$120 8 7 8 41	
Less merchandise inventory, June 30			42 1 0 0 00	
Cost of goods sold			$ 78 7 7 8 41	

Challenge Problem

GENERAL JOURNAL

PAGE

	DATE		DESCRIPTION	POST. REF.	DEBIT	CREDIT	
1	20-- May	4	Purchases		2 6 1 0 00		1
2			Accounts Payable			2 6 1 0 00	2
3			Made purchases on account				3
4							4
5		8	Accounts Payable		4 6 8 00		5
6			Purchases Returns and Allowances			4 6 8 00	6
7			Returned merchandise				7
8							8
9		14	Accounts Payable		9 0 0 00		9
10			Cash			8 9 1 00	10
11			Purchases Discounts			9 00	11
12			Made payment on account				12
13							13
14	June	3	Accounts Payable		1 2 4 2 00		14
15			Cash			1 2 4 2 00	15
16			Made payment on account				16
17							17
18							18
19							19
20							20
21							21
22							22
23							23
24							24
25							25
26							26
27							27
28							28
29							29
30							30
31							31
32							32
33							33
34							34

APPENDIX: THE NET-PRICE METHOD OF RECORDING PURCHASES

REVIEW QUESTIONS

1. Under the net-price method, purchases should be recorded at the net amount, after deducting the cash discount.

2. If payment for merchandise is not made within the discount period, debits are made to Accounts Payable and Purchases Discounts Lost.

3. (a)   Purchases Discounts Lost is a temporary owner's equity account.
    (b)   Purchases Discounts Lost is reported as an expense on the income statement.

Exercise 11Apx-1A

1.

GENERAL JOURNAL

PAGE

	DATE		DESCRIPTION	POST. REF.	DEBIT	CREDIT	
1	20-- Apr.	2	Purchases		1 0 0 0 00		1
2			Accounts Payable/Alanon Valve			1 0 0 0 00	2
3			Purchased merchandise				3
4							4
5		5	Purchases		1 4 0 0 00		5
6			Accounts Payable/Leon's Garage			1 4 0 0 00	6
7			Purchased merchandise				7
8							8
9		11	Accounts Payable/Alanon Valve		1 0 0 0 00		9
10			Cash			9 8 0 00	10
11			Purchases Discounts			2 0 00	11
12			Paid invoice within discount period				12
13							13
14		25	Accounts Payable/Leon's Garage		1 4 0 0 00		14
15			Cash			1 4 0 0 00	15
16			Paid invoice				16

2.

	DATE		DESCRIPTION	POST. REF.	DEBIT	CREDIT	
1	20-- Apr.	2	Purchases		9 8 0 00		1
2			Accounts Payable/Alanon Valve			9 8 0 00	2
3			Purchased merchandise				3
4							4
5		5	Purchases		1 3 8 6 00		5
6			Accounts Payable/Leon's Garage			1 3 8 6 00	6
7			Purchased merchandise				7
8							8
9		11	Accounts Payable/Alanon Valve		9 8 0 00		9
10			Cash			9 8 0 00	10
11			Paid invoice within discount period				11
12							12
13		25	Accounts Payable/Leon's Garage		1 3 8 6 00		13
14			Purchases Discounts Lost		1 4 00		14
15			Cash			1 4 0 0 00	15
16			Paid invoice				16

Exercise 11Apx-1B

1.

GENERAL JOURNAL   PAGE

	DATE		DESCRIPTION	POST. REF.	DEBIT	CREDIT	
1	20-- May	2	Purchases		9 0 0 00		1
2			Accounts Payable/Delgado's Supply			9 0 0 00	2
3			Purchased merchandise				3
4							4
5		6	Purchases		1 2 0 0 00		5
6			Accounts Payable/Goro's Auto Care			1 2 0 0 00	6
7			Purchased merchandise				7
8							8
9		11	Accounts Payable/Delgado's Supply		9 0 0 00		9
10			Cash			8 8 2 00	10
11			Purchases Discounts			1 8 00	11
12			Paid invoice within discount period				12
13							13
14		27	Accounts Payable/Goro's Auto Care		1 2 0 0 00		14
15			Cash			1 2 0 0 00	15
16			Paid invoice				16

2.

	DATE		DESCRIPTION	POST. REF.	DEBIT	CREDIT	
1	20-- May	2	Purchases		8 8 2 00		1
2			Accounts Payable/Delgado's Supply			8 8 2 00	2
3			Purchased merchandise				3
4							4
5		6	Purchases		1 1 8 8 00		5
6			Accounts Payable/Goro's Auto Care			1 1 8 8 00	6
7			Purchased merchandise				7
8							8
9		11	Accounts Payable/Delgado's Supply		8 8 2 00		9
10			Cash			8 8 2 00	10
11			Paid invoice within discount period				11
12							12
13		27	Accounts Payable/Goro's Auto Care		1 1 8 8 00		13
14			Purchases Discounts Lost		1 2 00		14
15			Cash			1 2 0 0 00	15
16			Paid invoice				16

CHAPTER 12

SPECIAL JOURNALS

REVIEW QUESTIONS

1. The primary purpose of using special journals is to save time journalizing and posting transactions.

2. The date, sale number, customer, and dollar amounts are entered in the sales journal.

3. To post from the sales journal to the general ledger, use the following steps:

   In the sales journal:
   Step 1: Total the amount columns, verify that the total of the debit column equals the total of the credit columns, and rule the columns.

   In the general ledger account:
   Step 2: Enter the date of the transaction in the Date column.
   Step 3: Enter the amount of the debit or credit in the Debit or Credit column.
   Step 4: Enter the new balance in the Balance columns under Debit or Credit.
   Step 5: Enter the initial "S" and the journal page number in the Posting Reference column.

   In the sales journal:
   Step 6: Enter the ledger account number immediately below the column totals for each account that is posted.

4. To post from the sales journal to the accounts receivable ledger use the following steps:

   In the accounts receivable ledger account:
   Step 1: Enter the date of the transaction in the Date column.
   Step 2: Enter the amount of the debit or credit in the Debit or Credit column.
   Step 3: Enter the new balance in the Balance column.
   Step 4: Enter the initial "S" and the journal page number in the Posting Reference column.

   In the sales journal:
   Step 5: Enter a check mark (✓) in the Posting Reference column of the journal for each transaction that is posted.

5. The date, account credited (if applicable), and the dollar amounts are entered in the cash receipts journal.

6. To post from the cash receipts journal to the general ledger, use the following steps:

   To post the General Credit column, on a daily basis:

   In the general ledger account:
   Step 1: Enter the date of the transaction in the Date column.
   Step 2: Enter the amount of the debit or credit in the Debit or Credit column.
   Step 3: Enter the new balance in the Balance columns under Debit or Credit.
   Step 4: Enter the initials "CR" and the journal page number in the Posting Reference column.

   In the cash receipts journal:
   Step 5: Enter the ledger account number in the Posting Reference column for each account that is posted.

To post the other amount columns, at the end of the month, use the following steps:

In the cash receipts journal:
Step 6: Total the amount columns, verify that the total of the debit columns equals the total of the credit columns, and rule the columns.

In the general ledger account:
Step 7: Enter the date in the Date column.
Step 8: Enter the amount of the debit or credit in the Debit or Credit column.
Step 9: Enter the new balance in the Balance columns under Debit or Credit.
Step 10: Enter the initials "CR" and the journal page number in the Posting Reference column.

In the cash receipts journal:
Step 11: Enter the ledger account number immediately below the column totals for each account that is posted.
Step 12: Enter a check mark (✓) in the Posting Reference column for the cash sales and bank credit card sales, and immediately below the General Credit column.

7. To post from the cash receipts journal to the accounts receivable ledger, use the following steps:

In the accounts receivable ledger account:
Step 1: Enter the date of the transaction in the Date column.
Step 2: Enter the amount of the debit or credit in the Debit or Credit column.
Step 3: Enter the new balance in the Balance column.
Step 4: Enter the initials "CR" and the journal page number in the Posting Reference column.

In the cash receipts journal:
Step 5: Enter a check mark (✓) in the Posting Reference column of the journal for each transaction that is posted.

8. The date, invoice number, supplier (from whom purchased), and dollar amounts are entered in the purchases journal.

9. To post from the purchases journal to the general ledger, use the following steps:

In the purchases journal:
Step 1: Total and rule the amount column.

In the general ledger account:
Step 2: Enter the date in the Date column.
Step 3: Enter the amount of the debit or credit in the Debit or Credit column.
Step 4: Enter the new balance in the Balance columns under Debit or Credit.
Step 5: Enter the initial "P" and the journal page number in the Posting Reference column.

In the purchases journal:
Step 6: Enter the Purchases and Accounts Payable account numbers immediately below the column total.

10. To post from the purchases journal to the accounts payable ledger, use the following steps:

In the accounts payable ledger account:
Step 1: Enter the date of the transaction in the Date column.
Step 2: Enter the amount of the debit or credit in the Debit or Credit column.
Step 3: Enter the new balance in the Balance column.
Step 4: Enter the initial "P" and the journal page number in the Posting Reference column.

In the purchases journal:
Step 5: Enter a check mark (✓) in the Posting Reference column of the journal for each transaction that is posted.

11. The date, check number, account debited (if applicable), and dollar amounts are entered in the cash payments journal.

12. To post from the cash payments journal to the general ledger:

   To post the General Debit column, on a daily basis, use the following steps:

   In the general ledger account:
   Step 1: Enter the date of the transaction in the Date column.
   Step 2: Enter the amount of the debit or credit in the Debit or Credit column.
   Step 3: Enter the new balance in the Balance columns under Debit or Credit.
   Step 4: Enter the initials "CP" and the journal page number in the Posting Reference column.

   In the cash payments journal:
   Step 5: Enter the ledger account number in the Posting Reference column for each account that is posted.

   To post the other amount columns, at the end of the month, use the following steps:

   In the cash payments journal:
   Step 6: Total the amount columns, verify that the total of the debit columns equals the total of the credit columns, and rule the columns.

   In the general ledger account:
   Step 7: Enter the date in the Date column.
   Step 8: Enter the amount of the debit or credit in the Debit or Credit column.
   Step 9: Enter the new balance in the Balance columns under Debit or Credit.
   Step 10: Enter the initials "CP" and the journal page number in the Posting Reference column.

   In the cash payments journal:
   Step 11: Enter the ledger account number immediately below the column totals for each account that is posted.
   Step 12: Enter a check mark (✓) in the Posting Reference column for the cash purchases, and immediately below the General Debit column.

13. To post from the cash payments journal to the accounts payable ledger, use the following steps:

   In the accounts payable ledger account:
   Step 1: Enter the date of the transaction in the Date column.
   Step 2: Enter the amount of the debit or credit in the Debit or Credit column.
   Step 3: Enter the new balance in the Balance column.
   Step 4: Enter the initials "CP" and the journal page number in the Posting Reference column.

   In the cash payments journal:
   Step 5: Enter a check mark (✓) in the Posting Reference column of the journal for each transaction that is posted.

Exercise 12-1A

		Journal
a.	Sold merchandise on account.	*Sales*
b.	Purchased delivery truck on account for use in the business.	*General*
c.	Received payment from customer on account.	*Cash receipts*
d.	Purchased merchandise on account.	*Purchases*
e.	Issued check in payment of electric bill.	*Cash payments*
f.	Recorded depreciation on factory building.	*General*

Exercise 12-2A

SALES JOURNAL
PAGE

DATE		SALE NO.	TO WHOM SOLD	POST. REF.	ACCOUNTS RECEIVABLE DEBIT	SALES CREDIT	SALES TAX PAYABLE CREDIT
20-- May	1	488	J. Adams		2 1 2 0 00	2 0 0 0 00	1 2 0 00
	4	489	B. Clark		1 9 0 8 00	1 8 0 0 00	1 0 8 00
	8	490	A. Duck		1 5 9 0 00	1 5 0 0 00	9 0 00
	11	491	E. Hill		2 0 6 7 00	1 9 5 0 00	1 1 7 00

Exercise 12-3A

CASH RECEIPTS JOURNAL
PAGE

	DATE		ACCOUNT CREDITED	POST. REF.	GENERAL CREDIT	ACCOUNTS RECEIVABLE CREDIT	SALES CREDIT	SALES TAX PAYABLE CREDIT	CASH DEBIT	
1	20-- July	6	J. Adler			6 4 3 00			6 4 3 00	1
2		10					2 3 2 0 00		2 3 2 0 00	2
3		14	B. Havel			4 3 0 00			4 3 0 00	3
4		15	J. L. Borg			1 1 7 00			1 1 7 00	4
5		17					2 2 3 7 00		2 2 3 7 00	5
6										6
7										7
8										8
9										9
10										10
11										11

Exercise 12-4A

PURCHASES JOURNAL   PAGE

	DATE	INVOICE NO.	FROM WHOM PURCHASED	POST. REF.	PURCHASES DEBIT ACCTS. PAY. CREDIT	
1	20-- May 3	321	*Cintron*		6 5 0 0 00	1
2	9	614	*Mitsui*		2 3 0 0 00	2
3	18	180	*Aloha Distributors*		4 2 0 0 00	3
4	23	913	*Soto*		6 3 0 0 00	4
5						5
6						6
7						7
8						8
9						9
10						10
11						11

Exercise 12-5A

CASH PAYMENTS JOURNAL   PAGE

	DATE	CK. NO.	ACCOUNT DEBITED	POST. REF.	GENERAL DEBIT	ACCOUNTS PAYABLE DEBIT	PURCHASES DEBIT	PURCHASES DISCOUNTS CREDIT	CASH CREDIT	
1	20-- Sept. 5	318	*Clinton Corp.*			6 0 0 0 00		1 2 0 00	5 8 8 0 00	1
2	12	319	*Mitchell Co.*			7 0 0 0 00		7 0 00	6 9 3 0 00	2
3	19	320	*Expert Systems*			4 1 0 0 00			4 1 0 0 00	3
4	27	321	*Graphic Data*			9 0 0 0 00		1 8 0 00	8 8 2 0 00	4
5										5
6										6
7										7
8										8
9										9
10										10
11										11
12										12
13										13

Problem 12-6A

1.

SALES JOURNAL

DATE	SALE NO.	TO WHOM SOLD	POST. REF.	ACCOUNTS RECEIVABLE DEBIT	SALES CREDIT	SALES TAX PAYABLE CREDIT
20-- Aug. 1	213	**Jung Manufacturing Co.**	✔	1 2 7 2 00	1 2 0 0 00	7 2 00
3	214	**Hassad Co.**	✔	3 8 1 6 00	3 6 0 0 00	2 1 6 00
7	215	**Helsinki, Inc.**	✔	1 4 8 4 00	1 4 0 0 00	8 4 00
11	216	**Ardis Myler**	✔	1 3 5 6 80	1 2 8 0 00	7 6 80
18	217	**Hassad Co.**	✔	4 5 8 9 80	4 3 3 0 00	2 5 9 80
22	218	**Jung Manufacturing Co.**	✔	2 1 2 0 00	2 0 0 0 00	1 2 0 00
30	219	**Ardis Myler**	✔	1 7 0 6 60	1 6 1 0 00	9 6 60
				16 3 4 5 20	15 4 2 0 00	9 2 5 20
				(1 2 2)	(4 0 1)	(2 3 1)

Debit total:　__$16,345.20__　　*Credit total:*　　$15,420.00

　　　　　　　　　　　　　　　　　　　　　　　　925.20

　　　　　　　　　　　　　　　　　　　　　　__$16,345.20__

2.

GENERAL LEDGER

ACCOUNT　Accounts Receivable　　　　　　　　　　ACCOUNT NO.　122

DATE	ITEM	POST. REF.	DEBIT	CREDIT	BALANCE DEBIT	BALANCE CREDIT
20-- Aug. 31		S8	16 3 4 5 20		16 3 4 5 20	

ACCOUNT　Sales Tax Payable　　　　　　　　　　ACCOUNT NO.　231

DATE	ITEM	POST. REF.	DEBIT	CREDIT	BALANCE DEBIT	BALANCE CREDIT
20-- Aug. 31		S8		9 2 5 20		9 2 5 20

Problem 12-6A (Concluded)

ACCOUNT   Sales   ACCOUNT NO.   401

DATE		ITEM	POST. REF.	DEBIT	CREDIT	BALANCE DEBIT	BALANCE CREDIT
20-- Aug.	31		S8		15 4 2 0 00		15 4 2 0 00

ACCOUNTS RECEIVABLE LEDGER

NAME Hassad Co.

ADDRESS 1225 W. Temperance Street, Ellettsville, IN 47429-9976

DATE		ITEM	POST. REF.	DEBIT	CREDIT	BALANCE
20-- Aug.	3		S8	3 8 1 6 00		3 8 1 6 00
	18		S8	4 5 8 9 80		8 4 0 5 80

NAME Helsinki, Inc.

ADDRESS 125 Fishers Dr., Noblesville, IN 47870-8867

DATE		ITEM	POST. REF.	DEBIT	CREDIT	BALANCE
20-- Aug.	7		S8	1 4 8 4 00		1 4 8 4 00

NAME Jung Manufacturing Co.

ADDRESS 8825 Old State Road, Bloomington, IN 47401-8823

DATE		ITEM	POST. REF.	DEBIT	CREDIT	BALANCE
20-- Aug.	1		S8	1 2 7 2 00		1 2 7 2 00
	22		S8	2 1 2 0 00		3 3 9 2 00

NAME Ardis Myler

ADDRESS 2100 Greer Lane, Bedford, IN 47421-8876

DATE		ITEM	POST. REF.	DEBIT	CREDIT	BALANCE
20-- Aug.	11		S8	1 3 5 6 80		1 3 5 6 80
	30		S8	1 7 0 6 60		3 0 6 3 40

Problem 12-7A

1.

CASH RECEIPTS JOURNAL

	DATE		ACCOUNT CREDITED	POST. REF.	GENERAL CREDIT	ACCOUNTS RECEIVABLE CREDIT
1	20-- Dec.	1	Michael Anderson	✔		1 3 6 0 00
2		2	Ansel Manufacturing	✔		3 8 2 00
3		7		✔		
4		7		✔		
5		8	J. Gorbea	✔		8 8 0 00
6		14		✔		
7		14		✔		
8		20	Tom Wilson	✔		1 1 1 0 00
9		21		✔		
10		24	Rachel Carson	✔		2 0 0 0 00
11						5 7 3 2 00
12						(1 2 2)
13						
14						
15						
16						
17						
18						
19						
20						
21						
22						
23						
24						
25						
26						
27						
28						

Debit total:	$ 57.24	Credit total:	$ 5,732.00
	17,292.36		10,960.00
	$17,349.60		657.60
			$17,349.60

Problem 12-7A (Continued)

PAGE 10

SALES CREDIT			SALES TAX PAYABLE CREDIT		BANK CREDIT CARD EXPENSE DEBIT		CASH DEBIT		
							1 3 6 0	00	1
							3 8 2	00	2
3 1 6 0	00		1 8 9	60			3 3 4 9	60	3
1 0 0 0	00		6 0	00	3 1	80	1 0 2 8	20	4
							8 8 0	00	5
2 8 0 0	00		1 6 8	00			2 9 6 8	00	6
8 0 0	00		4 8	00	2 5	44	8 2 2	56	7
							1 1 1 0	00	8
3 2 0 0	00		1 9 2	00			3 3 9 2	00	9
							2 0 0 0	00	10
10 9 6 0	00		6 5 7	60	5 7	24	17 2 9 2	36	11
(4 0 1)			(2 3 1)		(5 1 3)		(1 0 1)		12

Problem 12-7A (Continued)

	DATE		DESCRIPTION	POST. REF.	DEBIT	CREDIT	
1	20-- Dec.	11	Sales Returns and Allowances	401.1	6 0 00		1
2			Sales Tax Payable	231	3 60		2
3			Accounts Receivable/M. Anderson	122/✓		6 3 60	3
4							4
5		21	Sales Returns and Allowances	401.1	2 2 00		5
6			Sales Tax Payable	231	1 32		6
7			Accounts Receivable/Ansel Manufacturing	122/✓		2 3 32	7
8							8
9							9
10							10
11							11
12							12
13							13
14							14
15							15
16							16
17							17
18							18
19							19
20							20
21							21
22							22
23							23
24							24
25							25
26							26
27							27
28							28
29							29
30							30
31							31
32							32
33							33
34							34

Problem 12-7A (Continued)

2.

GENERAL LEDGER

ACCOUNT Cash   ACCOUNT NO. 101

DATE		ITEM	POST. REF.	DEBIT	CREDIT	BALANCE DEBIT	BALANCE CREDIT
20-- Dec.	1	Balance	✓			9 8 6 2 00	
	31		CR10	17 2 9 2 36		27 1 5 4 36	

ACCOUNT Accounts Receivable   ACCOUNT NO. 122

DATE		ITEM	POST. REF.	DEBIT	CREDIT	BALANCE DEBIT	BALANCE CREDIT
20-- Dec.	1	Balance	✓			9 3 5 2 00	
	11		J8		6 3 60	9 2 8 8 40	
	21		J8		2 3 32	9 2 6 5 08	
	31		CR10		5 7 3 2 00	3 5 3 3 08	

ACCOUNT Sales Tax Payable   ACCOUNT NO. 231

DATE		ITEM	POST. REF.	DEBIT	CREDIT	BALANCE DEBIT	BALANCE CREDIT
20-- Dec.	11		J8	3 60		3 60	
	21		J8	1 32		4 92	
	31		CR10		6 5 7 60		6 5 2 68

ACCOUNT Sales   ACCOUNT NO. 401

DATE		ITEM	POST. REF.	DEBIT	CREDIT	BALANCE DEBIT	BALANCE CREDIT
20-- Dec.	31		CR10		10 9 6 0 00		10 9 6 0 00

Problem 12-7A (Continued)

ACCOUNT   Sales Returns and Allowances   ACCOUNT NO.   401.1

DATE		ITEM	POST. REF.	DEBIT		CREDIT		BALANCE			
								DEBIT		CREDIT	
20-- Dec.	11		J8	6 0 00				6 0 00			
	21		J8	2 2 00				8 2 00			

ACCOUNT   Bank Credit Card Expense   ACCOUNT NO.   513

DATE		ITEM	POST. REF.	DEBIT		CREDIT		BALANCE			
								DEBIT		CREDIT	
20-- Dec.	31		CR10	5 7 24				5 7 24			

ACCOUNTS RECEIVABLE LEDGER

NAME Michael Anderson

ADDRESS 233 West 11th Avenue, Detroit, MI 59500-1154

DATE		ITEM	POST. REF.	DEBIT	CREDIT	BALANCE
20-- Dec.	1	Balance	✓			2 4 8 0 00
	1		CR10		1 3 6 0 00	1 1 2 0 00
	11		J8		6 3 60	1 0 5 6 40

NAME Ansel Manufacturing

ADDRESS 284 West 88 Street, Detroit, MI 59522-1168

DATE		ITEM	POST. REF.	DEBIT	CREDIT	BALANCE
20-- Dec.	1	Balance	✓			9 8 2 00
	2		CR10		3 8 2 00	6 0 0 00
	21		J8		2 3 32	5 7 6 68

Problem 12-7A (Concluded)

NAME   J. Gorbea

ADDRESS   P.O. Box 864, Detroit, MI 59552-0864

DATE		ITEM	POST. REF.	DEBIT	CREDIT	BALANCE
20-- Dec.	1	Balance	✓			8 8 0 00
	8		CR10		8 8 0 00	

NAME   Rachel Carson

ADDRESS   11312 Fourteenth Avenue South, Detroit, MI 59221-1142

DATE		ITEM	POST. REF.	DEBIT	CREDIT	BALANCE
20-- Dec.	1	Balance	✓			3 2 0 0 00
	24		CR10		2 0 0 0 00	1 2 0 0 00

NAME   Tom Wilson

ADDRESS   100 NW Seward St., Detroit, MI 59210-1337

DATE		ITEM	POST. REF.	DEBIT	CREDIT	BALANCE
20-- Dec.	1	Balance	✓			1 8 1 0 00
	20		CR10		1 1 1 0 00	7 0 0 00

Problem 12-8A

1.

SALES JOURNAL

DATE		SALE NO.	TO WHOM SOLD	POST. REF.	ACCOUNTS RECEIVABLE DEBIT	SALES CREDIT	SALES TAX PAYABLE CREDIT
20-- Mar.	1	33C	Able & Co.	✓	1 9 4 4 00	1 8 0 0 00	1 4 4 00
	3	33D	R. J. Kalas, Inc.	✓	2 4 1 9 20	2 2 4 0 00	1 7 9 20
	11	33E	Blevins Bakery	✓	1 3 0 6 80	1 2 1 0 00	9 6 80
	18	33F	R. J. Kalas, Inc.	✓	2 8 2 9 60	2 6 2 0 00	2 0 9 60
	25	33G	Blevins Bakery	✓	2 0 6 8 20	1 9 1 5 00	1 5 3 20
	27	33H	Thompson Group	✓	2 1 7 7 28	2 0 1 6 00	1 6 1 28
					12 7 4 5 08	11 8 0 1 00	9 4 4 08
					(1 2 2)	(4 0 1)	(2 3 1)

Debit total: $12,745.08   Credit total: $11,801.00

944.08

$12,745.08

CASH RECEIPTS JOURNAL

	DATE		ACCOUNT CREDITED	POST. REF.	GENERAL CREDIT	ACCOUNTS RECEIVABLE CREDIT	SALES CREDIT	SALES TAX PAYABLE CREDIT	CASH DEBIT	
1	20-- Mar.	7		✓			3 1 6 0 00	2 5 2 80	3 4 1 2 80	1
2		10	Able & Co.	✓		1 9 1 1 60			1 9 1 1 60	2
3		13	R. J. Kalas, Inc.	✓		2 4 1 9 20			2 4 1 9 20	3
4		14		✓			4 2 0 0 00	3 3 6 00	4 5 3 6 00	4
5		20	Blevins Bakery	✓		1 2 5 9 28			1 2 5 9 28	5
6		21		✓			2 4 0 0 00	1 9 2 00	2 5 9 2 00	6
7		28		✓			3 5 0 0 00	2 8 0 00	3 7 8 0 00	7
8						5 5 9 0 08	13 2 6 0 00	1 0 6 0 80	19 9 1 0 88	8
9						(1 2 2)	(4 0 1)	(2 3 1)	(1 0 1)	9

Debit total: $19,910.88   Credit total: $ 5,590.08

13,260.00

1,060.80

$19,910.88

Problem 12-8A (Continued)

GENERAL JOURNAL

PAGE 5

	DATE		DESCRIPTION	POST. REF.	DEBIT	CREDIT	
1	20-- Mar.	5	Sales Returns and Allowances	401.1	3 0 00		1
2			Sales Tax Payable	231	2 40		2
3			Accounts Receivable/Able & Co.	122/✓		3 2 40	3
4			Credit Memo #66				4
5							5
6		16	Sales Returns and Allowances	401.1	4 4 00		6
7			Sales Tax Payable	231	3 52		7
8			Accounts Receivable/Blevins Bakery	122/✓		4 7 52	8
9			Credit Memo #67				9
10							10
11							11
12							12
13							13
14							14

2.

GENERAL LEDGER

ACCOUNT Cash   ACCOUNT NO. 101

DATE		ITEM	POST. REF.	DEBIT	CREDIT	BALANCE DEBIT	BALANCE CREDIT
20-- Mar.	1	Balance	✓			9 7 4 1 00	
	31		CR9	19 9 1 0 88		29 6 5 1 88	

ACCOUNT Accounts Receivable   ACCOUNT NO. 122

DATE		ITEM	POST. REF.	DEBIT	CREDIT	BALANCE DEBIT	BALANCE CREDIT
20-- Mar.	1	Balance	✓			1 0 5 8 25	
	5		J5		3 2 40	1 0 2 5 85	
	16		J5		4 7 52	9 7 8 33	
	31		S6	12 7 4 5 08		13 7 2 3 41	
	31		CR9		5 5 9 0 08	8 1 3 3 33	

Problem 12-8A (Continued)

ACCOUNT Sales Tax Payable   ACCOUNT NO. 231

DATE		ITEM	POST. REF.	DEBIT	CREDIT	BALANCE DEBIT	BALANCE CREDIT
20-- Mar.	5		J5	2 40		2 40	
	16		J5	3 52		5 92	
	31		S6		9 4 4 08		9 3 8 16
	31		CR9		1 0 6 0 80		1 9 9 8 96

ACCOUNT Sales   ACCOUNT NO. 401

DATE		ITEM	POST. REF.	DEBIT	CREDIT	BALANCE DEBIT	BALANCE CREDIT
20-- Mar.	31		S6		11 8 0 1 00		11 8 0 1 00
	31		CR9		13 2 6 0 00		25 0 6 1 00

ACCOUNT Sales Returns and Allowances   ACCOUNT NO. 401.1

DATE		ITEM	POST. REF.	DEBIT	CREDIT	BALANCE DEBIT	BALANCE CREDIT
20-- Mar.	5		J5	3 0 00		3 0 00	
	16		J5	4 4 00		7 4 00	

Problem 12-8A (Concluded)

ACCOUNTS RECEIVABLE LEDGER

NAME Able & Co.

ADDRESS 1424 Jackson Creek Road, Nashville, IN 47448-2245

DATE		ITEM	POST. REF.	DEBIT	CREDIT	BALANCE
20-- Mar.	1		S6	1 9 4 4 00		1 9 4 4 00
	5		J5		3 2 40	1 9 1 1 60
	10		CR9		1 9 1 1 60	——

NAME Blevins Bakery

ADDRESS 6422 E. Bender Road, Bloomington, IN 47401-7756

DATE		ITEM	POST. REF.	DEBIT	CREDIT	BALANCE
20-- Mar.	11		S6	1 3 0 6 80		1 3 0 6 80
	16		J5		4 7 52	1 2 5 9 28
	20		CR9		1 2 5 9 28	——
	25		S6	2 0 6 8 20		2 0 6 8 20

NAME R. J. Kalas, Inc.

ADDRESS 3315 Longview Avenue, Bloomington, IN 47401-7223

DATE		ITEM	POST. REF.	DEBIT	CREDIT	BALANCE
20-- Mar.	3		S6	2 4 1 9 20		2 4 1 9 20
	13		CR9		2 4 1 9 20	——
	18		S6	2 8 2 9 60		2 8 2 9 60

NAME Thompson Group

ADDRESS 2300 E. National Road, Cumberland, IN 46229-4824

DATE		ITEM	POST. REF.	DEBIT	CREDIT	BALANCE
20-- Mar.	1	Balance	✓			1 0 5 8 25
	27		S6	2 1 7 7 28		3 2 3 5 53

Problem 12-9A

1.

PURCHASES JOURNAL

PAGE 7

	DATE		INVOICE NO.	FROM WHOM PURCHASED	POST. REF.	PURCHASES DEBIT ACCTS. PAY. CREDIT	
1	20-- Sept.	3	415	Smith Distributors	✓	2 6 5 0 00	1
2		8	132	Michaels Wholesaler	✓	3 8 3 0 00	2
3		11	614	J. B. Sanders & Co.	✓	3 1 4 0 00	3
4		18	329	Bateman & Jones, Inc.	✓	2 2 5 0 00	4
5		23	867	Smith Distributors	✓	4 1 6 0 00	5
6		27	744	Anderson Company	✓	1 9 8 0 00	6
7		30	652	Michaels Wholesaler	✓	2 7 8 0 00	7
8						20 7 9 0 00	8
9						(501) (2 02)	9
10							10
11							11
12							12
13							13
14							14

2.

GENERAL LEDGER

ACCOUNT Accounts Payable

ACCOUNT NO. 202

DATE	ITEM	POST. REF.	DEBIT	CREDIT	BALANCE	
					DEBIT	CREDIT
20-- Sept. 30		P7		20 7 9 0 00		20 7 9 0 00

ACCOUNT Purchases

ACCOUNT NO. 501

DATE	ITEM	POST. REF.	DEBIT	CREDIT	BALANCE	
					DEBIT	CREDIT
20-- Sept. 30		P7	20 7 9 0 00		20 7 9 0 00	

Problem 12-9A (Concluded)

ACCOUNTS PAYABLE LEDGER

NAME   *Anderson Company*

ADDRESS

DATE		ITEM	POST. REF.	DEBIT	CREDIT	BALANCE
20-- Sept.	27		P7		1 9 8 0 00	1 9 8 0 00

NAME   *Bateman & Jones, Inc.*

ADDRESS

DATE		ITEM	POST. REF.	DEBIT	CREDIT	BALANCE
20-- Sept.	18		P7		2 2 5 0 00	2 2 5 0 00

NAME   *Michaels Wholesaler*

ADDRESS

DATE		ITEM	POST. REF.	DEBIT	CREDIT	BALANCE
20-- Sept.	8		P7		3 8 3 0 00	3 8 3 0 00
	30		P7		2 7 8 0 00	6 6 1 0 00

NAME   *J. B. Sanders & Co.*

ADDRESS

DATE		ITEM	POST. REF.	DEBIT	CREDIT	BALANCE
20-- Sept.	11		P7		3 1 4 0 00	3 1 4 0 00

NAME   *Smith Distributors*

ADDRESS

DATE		ITEM	POST. REF.	DEBIT	CREDIT	BALANCE
20-- Sept.	3		P7		2 6 5 0 00	2 6 5 0 00
	23		P7		4 1 6 0 00	6 8 1 0 00

Problem 12-10A

1.

GENERAL LEDGER

ACCOUNT   Accounts Payable   ACCOUNT NO.   202

DATE		ITEM	POST. REF.	DEBIT	CREDIT	BALANCE DEBIT	BALANCE CREDIT
20-- Jan.	31		P1		18 2 5 0 00		18 2 5 0 00

ACCOUNT   Purchases   ACCOUNT NO.   501

DATE		ITEM	POST. REF.	DEBIT	CREDIT	BALANCE DEBIT	BALANCE CREDIT
20-- Jan.	31		P1	18 2 5 0 00		18 2 5 0 00	

2.

ACCOUNTS PAYABLE LEDGER

NAME   *Helmut's Hair Supply*

ADDRESS

DATE		ITEM	POST. REF.	DEBIT	CREDIT	BALANCE
20-- Jan.	3		P1		2 4 8 0 00	2 4 8 0 00
	25		P1		1 7 6 0 00	4 2 4 0 00

NAME   *Maria's Melodies*

ADDRESS

DATE		ITEM	POST. REF.	DEBIT	CREDIT	BALANCE
20-- Jan.	18		P1		4 7 0 0 00	4 7 0 0 00

Problem 12-10A (Concluded)

NAME   *Royal Flush*

ADDRESS

DATE		ITEM	POST. REF.	DEBIT	CREDIT	BALANCE
20-- Jan.	12		P1		1 9 5 0 00	1 9 5 0 00

NAME   *Ruiz Imports*

ADDRESS

DATE		ITEM	POST. REF.	DEBIT	CREDIT	BALANCE
20-- Jan.	2		P1		3 0 0 0 00	3 0 0 0 00

NAME   *Viola's Boutique*

ADDRESS

DATE		ITEM	POST. REF.	DEBIT	CREDIT	BALANCE
20-- Jan.	7		P1		4 3 6 0 00	4 3 6 0 00

Problem 12-11A

1.

CASH PAYMENTS JOURNAL   PAGE 6

DATE	CK. NO.	ACCOUNT DEBITED	POST. REF.	GENERAL DEBIT	ACCOUNTS PAYABLE DEBIT	PURCHASES DEBIT	PURCHASES DISCOUNTS CREDIT	CASH CREDIT	
20-- May 1	426	Rent Expense	521	2 400 00				2 400 00	1
3	427	Mueller's Dist.	✓		3 600 00		108 00	3 492 00	2
7	428	Van Kooning	✓		5 500 00			5 500 00	3
12	429	Fantastic Toys	✓		5 200 00		52 00	5 148 00	4
15	430	Utilities Exp.	533	1 720 00				1 720 00	5
18	431		✓			4 800 00		4 800 00	6
26	432	Goya Outlet	✓		3 800 00		76 00	3 724 00	7
30	433	Freight-In	502	1 200 00				1 200 00	8
31	434		✓			3 000 00		3 000 00	9
				5 320 00	18 100 00	7 800 00	236 00	30 984 00	10
				(✓)	(202)	(501)	(501.2)	(101)	11

Debit total: $ 5,320   **Credit total:** $ 236
           18,100   30,984
            7,800 $31,220
          $31,220

2.

GENERAL LEDGER

ACCOUNT Cash   ACCOUNT NO. 101

DATE	ITEM	POST. REF.	DEBIT	CREDIT	BALANCE DEBIT	BALANCE CREDIT
20-- May 1	Balance	✓			40 000 00	
31		CP6		30 984 00	9 016 00	

ACCOUNT Accounts Payable   ACCOUNT NO. 202

DATE	ITEM	POST. REF.	DEBIT	CREDIT	BALANCE DEBIT	BALANCE CREDIT
20-- May 1	Balance	✓				20 000 00
31		CP6	18 100 00			1 900 00

Problem 12-11A (Continued)

ACCOUNT   Purchases   ACCOUNT NO.   501

DATE		ITEM	POST. REF.	DEBIT	CREDIT	BALANCE	
						DEBIT	CREDIT
20-- May	31		CP6	7 8 0 0 00		7 8 0 0 00	

ACCOUNT   Purchases Discounts   ACCOUNT NO.   501.2

DATE		ITEM	POST. REF.	DEBIT	CREDIT	BALANCE	
						DEBIT	CREDIT
20-- May	31		CP6		2 3 6 00		2 3 6 00

ACCOUNT   Freight-In   ACCOUNT NO.   502

DATE		ITEM	POST. REF.	DEBIT	CREDIT	BALANCE	
						DEBIT	CREDIT
20-- May	30		CP6	1 2 0 0 00		1 2 0 0 00	

ACCOUNT   Rent Expense   ACCOUNT NO.   521

DATE		ITEM	POST. REF.	DEBIT	CREDIT	BALANCE	
						DEBIT	CREDIT
20-- May	1		CP6	2 4 0 0 00		2 4 0 0 00	

ACCOUNT   Utilities Expense   ACCOUNT NO.   533

DATE		ITEM	POST. REF.	DEBIT	CREDIT	BALANCE	
						DEBIT	CREDIT
20-- May	15		CP6	1 7 2 0 00		1 7 2 0 00	

Problem 12-11A (Concluded)

ACCOUNTS PAYABLE LEDGER

NAME Fantastic Toys

ADDRESS

DATE		ITEM	POST. REF.	DEBIT	CREDIT	BALANCE
20-- May	1	Balance	✓			5 2 0 0 00
	12		CP6	5 2 0 0 00		

NAME Goya Outlet

ADDRESS

DATE		ITEM	POST. REF.	DEBIT	CREDIT	BALANCE
20-- May	1	Balance	✓			3 8 0 0 00
	26		CP6	3 8 0 0 00		

NAME Mueller's Distributors

ADDRESS

DATE		ITEM	POST. REF.	DEBIT	CREDIT	BALANCE
20-- May	1	Balance	✓			3 6 0 0 00
	3		CP6	3 6 0 0 00		

NAME Van Kooning

ADDRESS

DATE		ITEM	POST. REF.	DEBIT	CREDIT	BALANCE
20-- May	1	Balance	✓			7 4 0 0 00
	7		CP6	5 5 0 0 00		1 9 0 0 00

Problem 12-12A

1.

PURCHASES JOURNAL PAGE 7

	DATE		INVOICE NO.	FROM WHOM PURCHASED	POST. REF.	PURCHASES DEBIT ACCTS. PAY. CREDIT	
1	20-- July	1	311	Tang's Toys	✓	2 7 0 0 00	1
2		3	812	Sillas & Company	✓	3 1 0 0 00	2
3		8	139	Daisy's Dolls	✓	1 9 0 0 00	3
4		25	489	Allied Business	✓	2 4 5 0 00	4
5		26	375	Tang's Toys	✓	1 9 8 0 00	5
6		29	883	Sillas & Company	✓	3 4 6 0 00	6
7						15 5 9 0 00	7
8						(501) (2 02)	8
9							9
10							10

CASH PAYMENTS JOURNAL PAGE 9

	DATE		CK. NO.	ACCOUNT DEBITED	POST. REF.	GENERAL DEBIT	ACCOUNTS PAYABLE DEBIT	PURCHASES DEBIT	PURCHASES DISCOUNTS CREDIT	CASH CREDIT	
1	20-- July	1	414	Rent Expense	521	1 5 0 0 00				1 5 0 0 00	1
2		11	415	Tang's Toys	✓		2 2 0 0 00		4 4 00	2 1 5 6 00	2
3		13	416	Sillas & Co.	✓		3 1 0 0 00		3 1 00	3 0 6 9 00	3
4		18	417	Daisy's Dolls	✓		1 5 0 0 00		3 0 00	1 4 7 0 00	4
5		31	418	F. Flint, Drawing	312	2 0 0 0 00				2 0 0 0 00	5
6		31	419		✓			9 7 5 00		9 7 5 00	6
7						3 5 0 0 00	6 8 0 0 00	9 7 5 00	1 0 5 00	11 1 7 0 00	7
8						(✓)	(2 02)	(5 01)	(5 01 .2)	(1 01)	8
9											9
10											10
11											11
12											12

Debit total: $ 3,500   *Credit total:* $ 105

            6,800   11,170

            975                         $11,275

        $11,275

Problem 12-12A (Continued)

GENERAL JOURNAL

PAGE 3

	DATE		DESCRIPTION	POST. REF.	DEBIT	CREDIT	
1	20-- July	5	Accounts Payable/Tang's Toys	202/✓	5 0 0 00		1
2			Purchases Returns and Allowances	501.1		5 0 0 00	2
3			Returned merchandise				3
4							4
5		15	Accounts Payable/Daisy's Dolls	202/✓	4 0 0 00		5
6			Purchases Returns and Allowances	501.1		4 0 0 00	6
7			Returned merchandise				7
8							8
9							9
10							10

2.

GENERAL LEDGER

ACCOUNT Cash

ACCOUNT NO. 101

DATE		ITEM	POST. REF.	DEBIT	CREDIT	BALANCE DEBIT	BALANCE CREDIT
20-- July	1	Balance	✓			20 0 0 0 00	
	31		CP9		11 1 7 0 00	8 8 3 0 00	

ACCOUNT Accounts Payable

ACCOUNT NO. 202

DATE		ITEM	POST. REF.	DEBIT	CREDIT	BALANCE DEBIT	BALANCE CREDIT
20-- July	5		J3	5 0 0 00		5 0 0 00	
	15		J3	4 0 0 00		9 0 0 00	
	31		CP9	6 8 0 0 00		7 7 0 0 00	
	31		P7		15 5 9 0 00		7 8 9 0 00

Problem 12-12A (Continued)

ACCOUNT   F. Flint, Drawing   ACCOUNT NO.   312

DATE		ITEM	POST. REF.	DEBIT	CREDIT	BALANCE DEBIT	BALANCE CREDIT
20-- July	31		CP9	2 0 0 0 00		2 0 0 0 00	

ACCOUNT   Purchases   ACCOUNT NO.   501

DATE		ITEM	POST. REF.	DEBIT	CREDIT	BALANCE DEBIT	BALANCE CREDIT
20-- July	31		CP9	9 7 5 00		9 7 5 00	
	31		P7	15 5 9 0 00		16 5 6 5 00	

ACCOUNT   Purchases Returns and Allowances   ACCOUNT NO.   501.1

DATE		ITEM	POST. REF.	DEBIT	CREDIT	BALANCE DEBIT	BALANCE CREDIT
20-- July	5		J3		5 0 0 00		5 0 0 00
	15		J3		4 0 0 00		9 0 0 00

ACCOUNT   Purchases Discounts   ACCOUNT NO.   501.2

DATE		ITEM	POST. REF.	DEBIT	CREDIT	BALANCE DEBIT	BALANCE CREDIT
20-- July	31		CP9		1 0 5 00		1 0 5 00

ACCOUNT   Rent Expense   ACCOUNT NO.   521

DATE		ITEM	POST. REF.	DEBIT	CREDIT	BALANCE DEBIT	BALANCE CREDIT
20-- July	1		CP9	1 5 0 0 00		1 5 0 0 00	

Problem 12-12A (Concluded)

ACCOUNTS PAYABLE LEDGER

NAME *Allied Business*

ADDRESS

DATE		ITEM	POST. REF.	DEBIT	CREDIT	BALANCE
20-- July	25		P7		2 4 5 0 00	2 4 5 0 00

NAME *Daisy's Dolls*

ADDRESS

DATE		ITEM	POST. REF.	DEBIT	CREDIT	BALANCE
20-- July	8		P7		1 9 0 0 00	1 9 0 0 00
	15		J3	4 0 0 00		1 5 0 0 00
	18		CP9	1 5 0 0 00		—

NAME *Sillas & Company*

ADDRESS

DATE		ITEM	POST. REF.	DEBIT	CREDIT	BALANCE
20-- July	3		P7		3 1 0 0 00	3 1 0 0 00
	13		CP9	3 1 0 0 00		—
	29		P7		3 4 6 0 00	3 4 6 0 00

NAME *Tang's Toys*

ADDRESS

DATE		ITEM	POST. REF.	DEBIT	CREDIT	BALANCE
20-- July	1		P7		2 7 0 0 00	2 7 0 0 00
	5		J3	5 0 0 00		2 2 0 0 00
	11		CP9	2 2 0 0 00		—
	26		P7		1 9 8 0 00	1 9 8 0 00

Exercise 12-1B

		Journal
a.	Issued credit memo to customer for merchandise returned.	*General*
b.	Sold merchandise for cash.	*Cash receipts*
c.	Purchased merchandise on account.	*Purchases*
d.	Issued checks to employees in payment of wages.	*Cash payments*
e.	Purchased factory supplies on account.	*General*
f.	Sold merchandise on account.	*Sales*

Exercise 12-2B

SALES JOURNAL

PAGE

DATE	SALE NO.	TO WHOM SOLD	POST. REF.	ACCOUNTS RECEIVABLE DEBIT	SALES CREDIT	SALES TAX PAYABLE CREDIT
20-- Sept. 1	228	K. Smith		1 890 00	1 800 00	90 00
3	229	J. Arnes		3 255 00	3 100 00	155 00
5	230	M. Denison		2 940 00	2 800 00	140 00
7	231	B. Marshall		1 995 00	1 900 00	95 00

Exercise 12-3B

CASH RECEIPTS JOURNAL

PAGE

	DATE	ACCOUNT CREDITED	POST. REF.	GENERAL CREDIT	ACCOUNTS. RECEIVABLE CREDIT	SALES CREDIT	SALES TAX PAYABLE CREDIT	CASH DEBIT	
1	20-- Nov. 1	J. Haghighat			750 00			750 00	1
2	12	M. Antonoff			464 00			464 00	2
3	15					3 763 00		3 763 00	3
4	18	W. Mossein			241 00			241 00	4
5	25					2 648 00		2 648 00	5
6									6
7									7
8									8
9									9
10									10
11									11

Exercise 12-4B

PURCHASES JOURNAL
PAGE

	DATE	INVOICE NO.	FROM WHOM PURCHASED	POST. REF.	PURCHASES DEBIT ACCTS. PAY. CREDIT	
1	20-- Jan. 3	416	Feng		6 0 0 0 00	1
2	12	624	Miranda		9 0 0 0 00	2
3	19	190	J. B. Barba		6 4 0 0 00	3
4	26	923	Ramirez		3 7 0 0 00	4
5						5
6						6
7						7
8						8
9						9
10						10
11						11

Exercise 12-5B

CASH PAYMENTS JOURNAL
PAGE

	DATE	CK. NO.	ACCOUNT DEBITED	POST. REF.	GENERAL DEBIT	ACCOUNTS PAYABLE DEBIT	PURCHASES DEBIT	PURCHASES DISCOUNTS CREDIT	CASH CREDIT	
1	20-- Apr. 5	429	Standard Ind.			8 0 0 0 00		1 6 0 00	7 8 4 0 00	1
2	19	430	Finest Co.			5 0 0 0 00		5 0 00	4 9 5 0 00	2
3	21	431	Funny Follies			3 2 5 0 00			3 2 5 0 00	3
4	29	432	Classic Data			7 0 0 0 00		1 4 0 00	6 8 6 0 00	4
5										5
6										6
7										7
8										8
9										9
10										10
11										11
12										12
13										13

Problem 12-6B

1.

SALES JOURNAL

DATE		SALE NO.	TO WHOM SOLD	POST. REF.	ACCOUNTS RECEIVABLE DEBIT	SALES CREDIT	SALES TAX PAYABLE CREDIT
20-- July	1	101	Saga, Inc.	✔	1 2 6 0 00	1 2 0 0 00	6 0 00
	8	102	Vinnie Ward	✔	2 2 0 5 00	2 1 0 0 00	1 0 5 00
	15	103	Dvorak Manufacturing	✔	4 5 1 5 00	4 3 0 0 00	2 1 5 00
	21	104	Vinnie Ward	✔	1 8 9 0 00	1 8 0 0 00	9 0 00
	24	105	Zapata Co.	✔	1 6 8 0 00	1 6 0 0 00	8 0 00
	29	106	Saga, Inc.	✔	1 5 2 2 50	1 4 5 0 00	7 2 50
					13 0 7 2 50	12 4 5 0 00	6 2 2 50
					(1 2 2)	(4 0 1)	(2 3 1)

Debit total: $13,072.50   *Credit total:* $12,450.00
                                                    622.50
                                                $13,072.50

2.

GENERAL LEDGER

ACCOUNT   Accounts Receivable   ACCOUNT NO.   122

DATE		ITEM	POST. REF.	DEBIT	CREDIT	BALANCE DEBIT	BALANCE CREDIT
20-- July	31		S8	13 0 7 2 50		13 0 7 2 50	

ACCOUNT   Sales Tax Payable   ACCOUNT NO.   231

DATE		ITEM	POST. REF.	DEBIT	CREDIT	BALANCE DEBIT	BALANCE CREDIT
20-- July	31		S8		6 2 2 50		6 2 2 50

Problem 12-6B (Concluded)

ACCOUNT   Sales   ACCOUNT NO.   401

DATE		ITEM	POST. REF.	DEBIT	CREDIT	BALANCE DEBIT	BALANCE CREDIT
20-- July	31		S8		12 4 5 0 00		12 4 5 0 00

ACCOUNTS RECEIVABLE LEDGER

NAME Dvorak Manufacturing Co.

ADDRESS 2105 Williams Drive, Muncie, IN 47304-2437

DATE		ITEM	POST. REF.	DEBIT	CREDIT	BALANCE
20-- July	15		S8	4 5 1 5 00		4 5 1 5 00

NAME Saga, Inc.

ADDRESS 1453 Parnell Avenue, Indianapolis, IN 46201-6870

DATE		ITEM	POST. REF.	DEBIT	CREDIT	BALANCE
20-- July	1		S8	1 2 6 0 00		1 2 6 0 00
	29		S8	1 5 2 2 50		2 7 8 2 50

NAME Vinnie Ward

ADDRESS 308 So. Muirhead Drive, Okemos, MI 48864-5356

DATE		ITEM	POST. REF.	DEBIT	CREDIT	BALANCE
20-- July	8		S8	2 2 0 5 00		2 2 0 5 00
	21		S8	1 8 9 0 00		4 0 9 5 00

NAME Zapata Co.

ADDRESS 789 N. Stafford Dr., Bloomington, IN 47401-6201

DATE		ITEM	POST. REF.	DEBIT	CREDIT	BALANCE
20-- July	24		S8	1 6 8 0 00		1 6 8 0 00

Problem 12-7B

1.

GENERAL JOURNAL

	DATE		DESCRIPTION	POST. REF.	DEBIT	CREDIT	
1	20-- Jan.	11	Sales Returns and Allowances	401.1	4 0 00		1
2			Sales Tax Payable	231	2 00		2
3			Accounts Receivable/Ray Boyd	122/✓		4 2 00	3
4							4
5		18	Sales Returns and Allowances	401.1	3 1 00		5
6			Sales Tax Payable	231	1 55		6
7			Accounts Receivable/Robert Zehnle	122/✓		3 2 55	7
8							8
9							9
10							10
11							11
12							12
13							13
14							14
15							15
16							16
17							17
18							18
19							19
20							20
21							21
22							22
23							23
24							24
25							25
26							26
27							27
28							28
29							29
30							30
31							31
32							32
33							33
34							34

Problem 12-7B (Continued)

CASH RECEIPTS JOURNAL

	DATE		ACCOUNT CREDITED	POST. REF.	GENERAL CREDIT	ACCOUNTS RECEIVABLE CREDIT
1	20-- Jan.	1	Ray Boyd	✔		8 8 0 00
2		3	Clint Hassell	✔		2 7 1 00
3		5		✔		
4		5		✔		
5		8	Jan Sowada	✔		9 1 2 00
6		12		✔		
7		12		✔		
8		15	Robert Zehnle	✔		1 1 0 0 00
9		19		✔		
10		25	Dazai Manufacturing	✔		3 1 8 00
11						3 4 8 1 00
12						(1 2 2)
13						
14						
15						
16						
17						
18						
19						
20						
21						
22						
23						
24						
25						
26						
27						
28						

Debit total:	$15,174.85	Credit total:	$ 3,481.00
	97.65		11,230.00
	$15,272.50		561.50
			$15,272.50

Problem 12-7B (Continued)

PAGE 10

SALES CREDIT	SALES TAX PAYABLE CREDIT	BANK CREDIT CARD EXPENSE DEBIT	CASH DEBIT	
			8 80 00	1
			2 71 00	2
2 8 0 0 00	1 4 0 00		2 9 4 0 00	3
1 2 0 0 00	6 0 00	3 7 80	1 2 2 2 20	4
			9 1 2 00	5
3 1 0 0 00	1 5 5 00		3 2 5 5 00	6
1 9 0 0 00	9 5 00	5 9 85	1 9 3 5 15	7
			1 1 0 0 00	8
2 2 3 0 00	1 1 1 50		2 3 4 1 50	9
			3 1 8 00	10
11 2 3 0 00	5 6 1 50	9 7 65	15 1 7 4 85	11
(4 0 1)	(2 3 1)	(5 1 3)	(1 0 1)	12
				13
				14
				15
				16
				17
				18
				19
				20
				21
				22
				23
				24
				25
				26
				27
				28

Problem 12-7B (Continued)

2.

GENERAL LEDGER

ACCOUNT   Cash   ACCOUNT NO.   101

DATE		ITEM	POST. REF.	DEBIT	CREDIT	BALANCE	
						DEBIT	CREDIT
20-- Jan.	1	Balance	✓			2 8 9 0 75	
	31		CR10	15 1 7 4 85		18 0 6 5 60	

ACCOUNT   Accounts Receivable   ACCOUNT NO.   122

DATE		ITEM	POST. REF.	DEBIT	CREDIT	BALANCE	
						DEBIT	CREDIT
20-- Jan.	1	Balance	✓			6 3 0 0 00	
	11		J8		4 2 00	6 2 5 8 00	
	18		J8		3 2 55	6 2 2 5 45	
	31		CR10		3 4 8 1 00	2 7 4 4 45	

ACCOUNT   Sales Tax Payable   ACCOUNT NO.   231

DATE		ITEM	POST. REF.	DEBIT	CREDIT	BALANCE	
						DEBIT	CREDIT
20-- Jan.	11		J8	2 00		2 00	
	18		J8	1 55		3 55	
	31		CR10		5 6 1 50		5 5 7 95

ACCOUNT   Sales   ACCOUNT NO.   401

DATE		ITEM	POST. REF.	DEBIT	CREDIT	BALANCE	
						DEBIT	CREDIT
20-- Jan.	31		CR10		11 2 3 0 00		11 2 3 0 00

Problem 12-7B (Continued)

ACCOUNT Sales Returns and Allowances   ACCOUNT NO. 401.1

DATE		ITEM	POST. REF.	DEBIT	CREDIT	BALANCE	
						DEBIT	CREDIT
20-- Jan.	11		J8	4 0 00		4 0 00	
	18		J8	3 1 00		7 1 00	

ACCOUNT Bank Credit Card Expense   ACCOUNT NO. 513

DATE		ITEM	POST. REF.	DEBIT	CREDIT	BALANCE	
						DEBIT	CREDIT
20-- Jan.	31		CR10	9 7 65		9 7 65	

ACCOUNTS RECEIVABLE LEDGER

NAME Ray Boyd

ADDRESS 229 SE 65th Avenue, Portland, OR 97215-1451

DATE		ITEM	POST. REF.	DEBIT	CREDIT	BALANCE
20-- Jan.	1	Balance	✓			1 4 0 0 00
	1		CR10		8 8 0 00	5 2 0 00
	11		J8		4 2 00	4 7 8 00

NAME Dazai Manufacturing

ADDRESS 447 6th Avenue, Flagstaff, AZ 86004-6842

DATE		ITEM	POST. REF.	DEBIT	CREDIT	BALANCE
20-- Jan.	1	Balance	✓			3 1 8 00
	25		CR10		3 1 8 00	—

Problem 12-7B (Concluded)

NAME Clint Hassell

ADDRESS 1462 N. Steves Blvd., Los Cruces, NM 88012-7791

DATE		ITEM	POST. REF.	DEBIT	CREDIT	BALANCE
20-- Jan.	1	Balance	✓			8 1 5 00
	3		CR10		2 7 1 00	5 4 4 00

NAME Jan Sowada

ADDRESS 5997 Blackgold Lane, Grapevine, TX 76051-2366

DATE		ITEM	POST. REF.	DEBIT	CREDIT	BALANCE
20-- Jan.	1	Balance	✓			1 4 8 1 00
	8		CR10		9 1 2 00	5 6 9 00

NAME Robert Zehnle

ADDRESS 6881 Seneca Drive, San Diego, CA 92127-8671

DATE		ITEM	POST. REF.	DEBIT	CREDIT	BALANCE
20-- Jan.	1	Balance	✓			2 2 8 6 00
	15		CR10		1 1 0 0 00	1 1 8 6 00
	18		J8		3 2 55	1 1 5 3 45

Problem 12-8B

1.

SALES JOURNAL

DATE		SALE NO.	TO WHOM SOLD	POST. REF.	ACCOUNTS RECEIVABLE DEBIT	SALES CREDIT	SALES TAX PAYABLE CREDIT
20-- Apr.	1	111	O. L. Meyers	✔	2 2 4 7 00	2 1 0 0 00	1 4 7 00
	3	112	Andrew Plaa	✔	1 0 7 0 00	1 0 0 0 00	7 0 00
	12	113	Melissa Richfield	✔	1 0 4 8 60	9 8 0 00	6 8 60
	19	114	Kelsay Munkres	✔	1 0 9 1 40	1 0 2 0 00	7 1 40
	24	115	O. L. Meyers	✔	9 8 4 40	9 2 0 00	6 4 40
	27	116	Andrew Plaa	✔	1 4 1 2 40	1 3 2 0 00	9 2 40
					7 8 5 3 80	7 3 4 0 00	5 1 3 80
					(1 2 2)	(4 0 1)	(2 3 1)

Debit total: $7,853.80   Credit total: $7,340.00

                                                     513.80

                                                     $7,853.80

CASH RECEIPTS JOURNAL

	DATE		ACCOUNT CREDITED	POST. REF.	GENERAL CREDIT	ACCOUNTS. RECEIVABLE CREDIT	SALES CREDIT	SALES TAX PAYABLE CREDIT	CASH DEBIT	
1	20-- Apr.	7		✔			3 2 4 0 00	2 2 6 80	3 4 6 6 80	1
2		9	O. L. Meyers	✔		2 1 9 3 50			2 1 9 3 50	2
3		14		✔			2 1 8 0 00	1 5 2 60	2 3 3 2 60	3
4		21		✔			2 6 0 0 00	1 8 2 00	2 7 8 2 00	4
5		28		✔			2 8 0 0 00	1 9 6 00	2 9 9 6 00	5
6						2 1 9 3 50	10 8 2 0 00	7 5 7 40	13 7 7 0 90	6
7						(1 2 2)	(4 0 1)	(2 3 1)	(1 0 1)	7
8										8
9										9

Debit total: $13,770.90   Credit total: $ 2,193.50

                                                      10,820.00

                                                         757.40

                                                      $13,770.90

Problem 12-8B (Continued)

GENERAL JOURNAL

PAGE 5

	DATE		DESCRIPTION	POST. REF.	DEBIT	CREDIT	
1	20-- Apr.	6	*Sales Returns and Allowances*	*401.1*	5 0 00		1
2			*Sales Tax Payable*	*231*	3 50		2
3			Accounts Receivable/O. L. Meyers	122/✓		5 3 50	3
4							4
5		17	*Sales Returns and Allowances*	*401.1*	4 0 00		5
6			*Sales Tax Payable*	*231*	2 80		6
7			Accounts Receivable/M. Richfield	122/✓		4 2 80	7
8							8
9							9
10							10
11							11
12							12
13							13
14							14

2.

GENERAL LEDGER

ACCOUNT   Cash   ACCOUNT NO.   101

DATE		ITEM	POST. REF.	DEBIT	CREDIT	BALANCE DEBIT	BALANCE CREDIT
20-- Apr.	1	Balance	✓			2 8 6 4 54	
	30		CR9	13 7 7 0 90		16 6 3 5 44	

ACCOUNT   Accounts Receivable   ACCOUNT NO.   122

DATE		ITEM	POST. REF.	DEBIT	CREDIT	BALANCE DEBIT	BALANCE CREDIT
20-- Apr.	1	Balance	✓			2 7 2 6 25	
	6		J5		5 3 50	2 6 7 2 75	
	17		J5		4 2 80	2 6 2 9 95	
	30		S6	7 8 5 3 80		10 4 8 3 75	
	30		CR9		2 1 9 3 50	8 2 9 0 25	

Problem 12-8B (Continued)

ACCOUNT Sales Tax Payable   ACCOUNT NO. 231

DATE		ITEM	POST. REF.	DEBIT	CREDIT	BALANCE DEBIT	BALANCE CREDIT
20-- Apr.	6		J5	3 50		3 50	
	17		J5	2 80		6 30	
	30		S6		5 1 3 80		5 0 7 50
	30		CR9		7 5 7 40		1 2 6 4 90

ACCOUNT Sales   ACCOUNT NO. 401

DATE		ITEM	POST. REF.	DEBIT	CREDIT	BALANCE DEBIT	BALANCE CREDIT
20-- Apr.	30		S6		7 3 4 0 00		7 3 4 0 00
	30		CR9		10 8 2 0 00		18 1 6 0 00

ACCOUNT Sales Returns and Allowances   ACCOUNT NO. 401.1

DATE		ITEM	POST. REF.	DEBIT	CREDIT	BALANCE DEBIT	BALANCE CREDIT
20-- Apr.	6		J5	5 0 00		5 0 00	
	17		J5	4 0 00		9 0 00	

Problem 12-8B (Concluded)

ACCOUNTS RECEIVABLE LEDGER

NAME O. L. Meyers

ADDRESS 119 Hartford Turnpike, Vernon, CT 06066-0113

DATE		ITEM	POST. REF.	DEBIT	CREDIT	BALANCE
20-- Apr.	1	Balance	✓			2 1 8 6 00
	1		S6	2 2 4 7 00		4 4 3 3 00
	6		J5		5 3 50	4 3 7 9 50
	9		CR9		2 1 9 3 50	2 1 8 6 00
	24		S6	9 8 4 40		3 1 7 0 40

NAME Kelsay Munkres

ADDRESS 233 Cambridge Dr., Branford, CT 06405-9276

DATE		ITEM	POST. REF.	DEBIT	CREDIT	BALANCE
20-- Apr.	1	Balance	✓			4 8 2 00
	19		S6	1 0 9 1 40		1 5 7 3 40

NAME Andrew Plaa

ADDRESS 51 Bissell Ave., Old Saybrook, CT 06475-0212

DATE		ITEM	POST. REF.	DEBIT	CREDIT	BALANCE
20-- Apr.	3		S6	1 0 7 0 00		1 0 7 0 00
	27		S6	1 4 1 2 40		2 4 8 2 40

NAME Melissa Richfield

ADDRESS 1107 Silver Lane, East Hartford, CT 06108-1907

DATE		ITEM	POST. REF.	DEBIT	CREDIT	BALANCE
20-- Apr.	1	Balance	✓			5 8 25
	12		S6	1 0 4 8 60		1 1 0 6 85
	17		J5		4 2 80	1 0 6 4 05

Problem 12-9B

1.

PURCHASES JOURNAL   PAGE 7

	DATE		INVOICE NO.	FROM WHOM PURCHASED	POST. REF.	PURCHASES DEBIT ACCTS. PAY. CREDIT	
1	20-- Oct.	2	321	Boggs Distributors	✔	1 9 5 0 00	1
2		7	152	Wolfs Wholesaler	✔	2 9 1 5 00	2
3		10	634	Komuro & Co.	✔	3 5 6 5 00	3
4		16	349	Fritz & McCord, Inc.	✔	2 8 4 5 00	4
5		24	587	Boggs Distributors	✔	3 3 7 0 00	5
6		26	764	Sanderson Company	✔	2 2 4 0 00	6
7		31	672	Wolfs Wholesaler	✔	1 6 3 0 00	7
8						18 5 1 5 00	8
9						(501) (2 02)	9
10							10
11							11
12							12
13							13
14							14

2.

GENERAL LEDGER

ACCOUNT   Accounts Payable   ACCOUNT NO.   202

DATE	ITEM	POST. REF.	DEBIT	CREDIT	BALANCE DEBIT	CREDIT
20-- Oct. 31		P7		18 5 1 5 00		18 5 1 5 00

ACCOUNT   Purchases   ACCOUNT NO.   501

DATE	ITEM	POST. REF.	DEBIT	CREDIT	BALANCE DEBIT	CREDIT
20-- Oct. 31		P7	18 5 1 5 00		18 5 1 5 00	

Problem 12-9B (Concluded)

ACCOUNTS PAYABLE LEDGER

NAME   *Boggs Distributors*

ADDRESS

DATE		ITEM	POST. REF.	DEBIT	CREDIT	BALANCE
20-- Oct.	2		P7		1 9 5 0 00	1 9 5 0 00
	24		P7		3 3 7 0 00	5 3 2 0 00

NAME   *Fritz & McCord, Inc.*

ADDRESS

DATE		ITEM	POST. REF.	DEBIT	CREDIT	BALANCE
20-- Oct.	16		P7		2 8 4 5 00	2 8 4 5 00

NAME   *Komuro & Co.*

ADDRESS

DATE		ITEM	POST. REF.	DEBIT	CREDIT	BALANCE
20-- Oct.	10		P7		3 5 6 5 00	3 5 6 5 00

NAME   *Sanderson Company*

ADDRESS

DATE		ITEM	POST. REF.	DEBIT	CREDIT	BALANCE
20-- Oct.	26		P7		2 2 4 0 00	2 2 4 0 00

NAME   *Wolfs Wholesaler*

ADDRESS

DATE		ITEM	POST. REF.	DEBIT	CREDIT	BALANCE
20-- Oct.	7		P7		2 9 1 5 00	2 9 1 5 00
	31		P7		1 6 3 0 00	4 5 4 5 00

Problem 12-10B

1.

GENERAL LEDGER

ACCOUNT   Accounts Payable   ACCOUNT NO.   202

DATE		ITEM	POST. REF.	DEBIT	CREDIT	BALANCE	
						DEBIT	CREDIT
20-- Jan.	31		P1		22 8 4 0 00		22 8 4 0 00

ACCOUNT   Purchases   ACCOUNT NO.   501

DATE		ITEM	POST. REF.	DEBIT	CREDIT	BALANCE	
						DEBIT	CREDIT
20-- Jan.	31		P1	22 8 4 0 00		22 8 4 0 00	

2.

ACCOUNTS PAYABLE LEDGER

NAME   *Amelia & Vincente*

ADDRESS

DATE		ITEM	POST. REF.	DEBIT	CREDIT	BALANCE
20-- Jan.	5		P1		5 9 2 0 00	5 9 2 0 00
	30		P1		1 8 9 0 00	7 8 1 0 00

NAME   *Hidemi, Inc.*

ADDRESS

DATE		ITEM	POST. REF.	DEBIT	CREDIT	BALANCE
20-- Jan.	21		P1		1 3 0 0 00	1 3 0 0 00

Problem 12-10B (Concluded)

NAME *Nobuko's Nature Store*

ADDRESS

DATE		ITEM	POST. REF.	DEBIT	CREDIT	BALANCE
20-- Jan.	9		P1		2 6 8 0 00	2 6 8 0 00

NAME *Sandra's Sweets*

ADDRESS

DATE		ITEM	POST. REF.	DEBIT	CREDIT	BALANCE
20-- Jan.	3		P1		4 4 9 0 00	4 4 9 0 00

NAME *Smith and Johnson Company*

ADDRESS

DATE		ITEM	POST. REF.	DEBIT	CREDIT	BALANCE
20-- Jan.	15		P1		6 5 6 0 00	6 5 6 0 00

Problem 12-11B

1.

CASH PAYMENTS JOURNAL

PAGE 6

	DATE		CK. NO.	ACCOUNT DEBITED	POST. REF.	GENERAL DEBIT	ACCOUNTS PAYABLE DEBIT	PURCHASES DEBIT	PURCHASES DISCOUNTS CREDIT	CASH CREDIT	
1	20-- May	1	326	Rent Expense	521	2 6 0 0 00				2 6 0 0 00	1
2		4	327	Cortez Dist.	✓		4 2 0 0 00		1 26 00	4 0 7 4 00	2
3		7	328	Indra & Velga	✓		6 2 0 0 00			6 2 0 0 00	3
4		11	329	Toy Corner	✓		4 6 0 0 00		46 00	4 5 5 4 00	4
5		15	330	Utilities Exp.	533	1 5 0 0 00				1 5 0 0 00	5
6		19	331		✓			3 5 0 0 00		3 5 0 0 00	6
7		25	332	Troutman Outlet	✓		4 4 0 0 00		88 00	4 3 1 2 00	7
8		30	333	Freight-In	502	8 0 0 00				8 0 0 00	8
9		31	334		✓			2 3 5 0 00		2 3 5 0 00	9
10						4 9 0 0 00	19 4 0 0 00	5 8 5 0 00	2 60 00	29 8 9 0 00	10
11						(✓)	(2 0 2)	(5 0 1)	(5 0 1 .2)	(1 0 1)	11
12											12

Debit total:	$ 4,900	Credit total:	$ 260
	19,400		29,890
	5,850		$30,150
	$30,150		

2.

GENERAL LEDGER

ACCOUNT Cash   ACCOUNT NO. 101

DATE		ITEM	POST. REF.	DEBIT	CREDIT	BALANCE DEBIT	BALANCE CREDIT
20-- May	1	Balance	✓			40 0 0 0 00	
	31		CP6		29 8 9 0 00	10 1 1 0 00	

ACCOUNT Accounts Payable   ACCOUNT NO. 202

DATE		ITEM	POST. REF.	DEBIT	CREDIT	BALANCE DEBIT	BALANCE CREDIT
20-- May	1	Balance	✓				20 0 0 0 00
	31		CP6	19 4 0 0 00			6 0 0 00

Problem 12-11B (Continued)

ACCOUNT　Purchases　　　　　　　　　　　　　　　　ACCOUNT NO.　501

DATE	ITEM	POST. REF.	DEBIT	CREDIT	BALANCE DEBIT	BALANCE CREDIT
20-- May 31		CP6	5 8 5 0 00		5 8 5 0 00	

ACCOUNT　Purchases Discounts　　　　　　　　　　　ACCOUNT NO.　501.2

DATE	ITEM	POST. REF.	DEBIT	CREDIT	BALANCE DEBIT	BALANCE CREDIT
20-- May 31		CP6		2 6 0 00		2 6 0 00

ACCOUNT　Freight-In　　　　　　　　　　　　　　　　ACCOUNT NO.　502

DATE	ITEM	POST. REF.	DEBIT	CREDIT	BALANCE DEBIT	BALANCE CREDIT
20-- May 30		CP6	8 0 0 00		8 0 0 00	

ACCOUNT　Rent Expense　　　　　　　　　　　　　　ACCOUNT NO.　521

DATE	ITEM	POST. REF.	DEBIT	CREDIT	BALANCE DEBIT	BALANCE CREDIT
20-- May 1		CP6	2 6 0 0 00		2 6 0 0 00	

ACCOUNT　Utilities Expense　　　　　　　　　　　　ACCOUNT NO.　533

DATE	ITEM	POST. REF.	DEBIT	CREDIT	BALANCE DEBIT	BALANCE CREDIT
20-- May 15		CP6	1 5 0 0 00		1 5 0 0 00	

Problem 12-11B (Concluded)

ACCOUNTS PAYABLE LEDGER

NAME Cortez Distributors

ADDRESS

DATE		ITEM	POST. REF.	DEBIT	CREDIT	BALANCE
20-- May	1	Balance	✓			4 2 0 0 00
	4		CP6	4 2 0 0 00		————

NAME Indra & Velga

ADDRESS

DATE		ITEM	POST. REF.	DEBIT	CREDIT	BALANCE
20-- May	1	Balance	✓			6 8 0 0 00
	7		CP6	6 2 0 0 00		6 0 0 00

NAME Toy Corner

ADDRESS

DATE		ITEM	POST. REF.	DEBIT	CREDIT	BALANCE
20-- May	1	Balance	✓			4 6 0 0 00
	11		CP6	4 6 0 0 00		————

NAME Troutman Outlet

ADDRESS

DATE		ITEM	POST. REF.	DEBIT	CREDIT	BALANCE
20-- May	1	Balance	✓			4 4 0 0 00
	25		CP6	4 4 0 0 00		————

Problem 12-12B

1.

PURCHASES JOURNAL   PAGE 7

	DATE		INVOICE NO.	FROM WHOM PURCHASED	POST. REF.	PURCHASES DEBIT ACCTS. PAY. CREDIT	
1	20-- July	1	211	Topper's Toys	✔	2 5 0 0 00	1
2		3	812	Jones & Company	✔	2 8 0 0 00	2
3		8	159	Downtown Merchants	✔	1 6 0 0 00	3
4		25	468	Columbia Products	✔	3 2 0 0 00	4
5		26	395	Topper's Toys	✔	1 4 3 0 00	5
6		29	853	Jones & Company	✔	2 9 7 0 00	6
7						14 5 0 0 00	7
8						(501) (2 02)	8
9							9
10							10

CASH PAYMENTS JOURNAL   PAGE 9

	DATE		CK. NO.	ACCOUNT DEBITED	POST. REF.	GENERAL DEBIT	ACCOUNTS PAYABLE DEBIT	PURCHASES DEBIT	PURCHASES DISCOUNTS CREDIT	CASH CREDIT	
1	20-- July	1	314	Rent Expense	521	1 4 0 0 00				1 4 0 0 00	1
2		11	315	Topper's Toys	✔		2 1 0 0 00		4 2 00	2 0 5 8 00	2
3		13	316	Jones & Co.	✔		2 8 0 0 00		2 8 00	2 7 7 2 00	3
4		18	317	Downtown Mer.	✔		1 0 0 0 00		2 0 00	9 8 0 00	4
5		31	318	D. Mueller, Draw.	312	2 5 0 0 00				2 5 0 0 00	5
6		31	319		✔			1 0 5 0 00		1 0 5 0 00	6
7						3 9 0 0 00	5 9 0 0 00	1 0 5 0 00	9 0 00	10 7 6 0 00	7
8						(✔)	(2 0 2)	(5 0 1)	(5 0 1 .2)	(1 0 1)	8
9											9
10											10
11											11
12											12

Debit total: $ 3,900   **Credit total** $ 90

                              5,900   10,760

                              1,050 $10,850

                             $10,850

Problem 12-12B (Continued)

GENERAL JOURNAL

PAGE 3

	DATE		DESCRIPTION	POST. REF.	DEBIT	CREDIT	
1	20-- July	5	*Accounts Payable/Topper's Toys*	202/✓	4 0 0 00		1
2			*Purchases Returns and Allowances*	501.1		4 0 0 00	2
3			*Returned merchandise*				3
4							4
5		15	*Accounts Payable/Downtown Merchants*	202/✓	6 0 0 00		5
6			*Purchases Returns and Allowances*	501.1		6 0 0 00	6
7			*Returned merchandise*				7
8							8
9							9
10							10

2.

GENERAL LEDGER

ACCOUNT   Cash   ACCOUNT NO.   101

DATE		ITEM	POST. REF.	DEBIT	CREDIT	BALANCE DEBIT	BALANCE CREDIT
20-- July	1	Balance	✓			20 0 0 0 00	
	31		CP9		10 7 6 0 00	9 2 4 0 00	

ACCOUNT   Accounts Payable   ACCOUNT NO.   202

DATE		ITEM	POST. REF.	DEBIT	CREDIT	BALANCE DEBIT	BALANCE CREDIT
20-- July	5		J3	4 0 0 00		4 0 0 00	
	15		J3	6 0 0 00		1 0 0 0 00	
	31		CP9	5 9 0 0 00		6 9 0 0 00	
	31		P7		14 5 0 0 00		7 6 0 0 00

Problem 12-12B (Continued)

ACCOUNT   D. Mueller, Drawing   ACCOUNT NO.   312

DATE		ITEM	POST. REF.	DEBIT	CREDIT	BALANCE	
						DEBIT	CREDIT
20-- July	31		CP9	2 5 0 0 00		2 5 0 0 00	

ACCOUNT   Purchases   ACCOUNT NO.   501

DATE		ITEM	POST. REF.	DEBIT	CREDIT	BALANCE	
						DEBIT	CREDIT
20-- July	31		CP9	1 0 5 0 00		1 0 5 0 00	
	31		P7	14 5 0 0 00		15 5 5 0 00	

ACCOUNT   Purchases Returns and Allowances   ACCOUNT NO.   501.1

DATE		ITEM	POST. REF.	DEBIT	CREDIT	BALANCE	
						DEBIT	CREDIT
20-- July	5		J3		4 0 0 00		4 0 0 00
	15		J3		6 0 0 00		1 0 0 0 00

ACCOUNT   Purchases Discounts   ACCOUNT NO.   501.2

DATE		ITEM	POST. REF.	DEBIT	CREDIT	BALANCE	
						DEBIT	CREDIT
20-- July	31		CP9		9 0 00		9 0 00

ACCOUNT   Rent Expense   ACCOUNT NO.   521

DATE		ITEM	POST. REF.	DEBIT	CREDIT	BALANCE	
						DEBIT	CREDIT
20-- July	1		CP9	1 4 0 0 00		1 4 0 0 00	

Problem 12-12B (Concluded)

ACCOUNTS PAYABLE LEDGER

NAME *Columbia Products*

ADDRESS

DATE		ITEM	POST. REF.	DEBIT	CREDIT	BALANCE
20-- July	25		P7		3 2 0 0 00	3 2 0 0 00

NAME *Downtown Merchants*

ADDRESS

DATE		ITEM	POST. REF.	DEBIT	CREDIT	BALANCE
20-- July	8		P7		1 6 0 0 00	1 6 0 0 00
	15		J3	6 0 0 00		1 0 0 0 00
	18		CP9	1 0 0 0 00		——

NAME *Jones & Company*

ADDRESS

DATE		ITEM	POST. REF.	DEBIT	CREDIT	BALANCE
20-- July	3		P7		2 8 0 0 00	2 8 0 0 00
	13		CP9	2 8 0 0 00		——
	29		P7		2 9 7 0 00	2 9 7 0 00

NAME *Topper's Toys*

ADDRESS

DATE		ITEM	POST. REF.	DEBIT	CREDIT	BALANCE
20-- July	1		P7		2 5 0 0 00	2 5 0 0 00
	5		J3	4 0 0 00		2 1 0 0 00
	11		CP9	2 1 0 0 00		——
	26		P7		1 4 3 0 00	1 4 3 0 00

MANAGING YOUR WRITING

Efficiency can be increased by using special journals instead of only a general journal. Accuracy of supplier records can be increased by using an accounts payable ledger in addition to a general ledger.

The number and types of special journals to use should be decided based on the types of transactions that occur most frequently. At a minimum, sales and purchases journals should be used for this business. Use of these journals will substantially reduce the time required to enter transactions. In addition, duties can be divided so that a different person makes entries in each journal.

The accounts payable ledger would contain a separate account for each supplier. By posting these accounts daily, the amount owed to each supplier could be readily determined at any time.

ETHICS CASE

1. Yes, Sue's suggestion is unethical because she is taking credit for work that is not hers and not following her supervisor's directive to "design" special journals. It would be appropriate to use the special journals from the textbook as a guide to help prepare the ones for the company, as long as Judy was informed of the source.
2. Special journals should be designed to meet the needs of a specific company. Their design will vary depending on the nature of the business and frequency and type of transactions. If Sue and Jon use special journals that have not been customized for their company, they might not be appropriate and, consequently, might not meet their objective of saving time.
3. Answers will vary.

Mastery Problem

1.

SALES JOURNAL

PAGE 7

	DATE		SALE NO.	TO WHOM SOLD	POST. REF.	ACCOUNTS RECEIVABLE DEBIT	SALES CREDIT	SALES TAX PAYABLE CREDIT	
1	20-- Oct.	1	222	*Elizabeth Shoemaker*	✔	1050 00	1000 00	50 00	1
2		12	223	*Leigh Summers*	✔	2100 00	2000 00	100 00	2
3		27	224	*David's Decorating*	✔	3150 00	3000 00	150 00	3
4						6300 00	6000 00	300 00	4
5						(122)	(401)	(231)	5
6									6
7									7
8									8

CASH RECEIPTS JOURNAL

PAGE 10

	DATE	ACCOUNT CREDITED	POST. REF.	GENERAL CREDIT	ACCOUNTS RECEIVABLE CREDIT	SALES CREDIT	SALES TAX PAYABLE CREDIT	CASH DEBIT	
1	20-- Oct.	7	✔			3500 00	175 00	3675 00	1
2		9 *Leigh Summers*	✔		2000 00			2000 00	2
3		12 *Meg Johnson*	✔		3100 00			3100 00	3
4		24 *David's Decor.*	✔		2135 00			2135 00	4
5					7235 00	3500 00	175 00	10910 00	5
6					(122)	(401)	(231)	(101)	6
7									7
8									8
9									9
10									10
11									11
12									12
13									13

Mastery Problem (Continued)

PURCHASES JOURNAL

	DATE	INVOICE NO.	FROM WHOM PURCHASED	POST. REF.	PURCHASES DEBIT ACCTS. PAY. CREDIT	
1	20-- Oct. 2	500	*Flower Wholesalers*	✔	4 0 0 0 00	1
2	4	527	*Seidl Enterprises*	✔	7 0 0 00	2
3					4 7 0 0 00	3
4					(501) (2 02)	4
5						5
6						6
7						7
8						8
9						9
10						10
11						11

CASH PAYMENTS JOURNAL

	DATE	CK. NO.	ACCOUNT DEBITED	POST. REF.	GENERAL DEBIT	ACCOUNTS PAYABLE DEBIT	PURCHASES DEBIT	PURCHASES DISCOUNTS CREDIT	CASH CREDIT	
1	20-- Oct. 2	190	*Jill Hand*	✔		5 0 0 00		1 0 00	4 9 0 00	1
2	5	191	Telephone Exp.	525	1 5 0 00				1 5 0 00	2
3	11	192	*Flower Whole.*	✔		1 5 0 0 00			1 5 0 0 00	3
4	13	193	*Seidl Ent.*	✔		7 0 0 00		1 4 00	6 8 6 00	4
5	29	194	Wages Exp.	511	9 0 0 00				9 0 0 00	5
6					1 0 5 0 00	2 7 0 0 00		2 4 00	3 7 2 6 00	6
7					(✔)	(202)		(501.2)	(101)	7
8										8
9										9
10										10
11										11
12										12
13										13

Mastery Problem (Continued)

GENERAL JOURNAL   PAGE 5

	DATE		DESCRIPTION	POST. REF.	DEBIT	CREDIT	
1	20-- Oct.	14	Sales Returns and Allowances	401.1	3 0 0 00		1
2			Sales Tax Payable	231	1 5 00		2
3			Accounts Receivable/Meg Johnson	122/✓		3 1 5 00	3
4			Accepted returned merchandise				4
5							5
6		17	Accounts Payable/Vases Etc.	202/✓	9 0 0 00		6
7			Purchases Returns and Allowances	501.1		9 0 0 00	7
8			Returned merchandise				8
9							9
10							10
11							11
12							12

2.

GENERAL LEDGER

ACCOUNT   Cash   ACCOUNT NO. 101

DATE		ITEM	POST. REF.	DEBIT	CREDIT	BALANCE DEBIT	BALANCE CREDIT
20-- Oct.	1	Balance	✓			18 2 2 5 00	
	31		CR10	10 9 1 0 00		29 1 3 5 00	
	31		CP11		3 7 2 6 00	25 4 0 9 00	

ACCOUNT   Accounts Receivable   ACCOUNT NO. 122

DATE		ITEM	POST. REF.	DEBIT	CREDIT	BALANCE DEBIT	BALANCE CREDIT
20-- Oct.	1	Balance	✓			9 6 1 9 00	
	14		J5		3 1 5 00	9 3 0 4 00	
	31		S7	6 3 0 0 00		15 6 0 4 00	
	31		CR10		7 2 3 5 00	8 3 6 9 00	

Mastery Problem (Continued)

ACCOUNT   Accounts Payable   ACCOUNT NO.   202

DATE		ITEM	POST. REF.	DEBIT	CREDIT	BALANCE	
						DEBIT	CREDIT
20-- Oct.	1	Balance	✓				5 1 2 0 00
	17		J5	9 0 0 00			4 2 2 0 00
	31		P6		4 7 0 0 00		8 9 2 0 00
	31		CP11	2 7 0 0 00			6 2 2 0 00

ACCOUNT   Sales Tax Payable   ACCOUNT NO.   231

DATE		ITEM	POST. REF.	DEBIT	CREDIT	BALANCE	
						DEBIT	CREDIT
20-- Oct.	14		J5	1 5 00		1 5 00	
	31		S7		3 0 0 00		2 8 5 00
	31		CR10		1 7 5 00		4 6 0 00

ACCOUNT   Sales   ACCOUNT NO.   401

DATE		ITEM	POST. REF.	DEBIT	CREDIT	BALANCE	
						DEBIT	CREDIT
20-- Oct.	31		S7		6 0 0 0 00		6 0 0 0 00
	31		CR10		3 5 0 0 00		9 5 0 0 00

ACCOUNT   Sales Returns and Allowances   ACCOUNT NO.   401.1

DATE		ITEM	POST. REF.	DEBIT	CREDIT	BALANCE	
						DEBIT	CREDIT
20-- Oct.	14		J5	3 0 0 00		3 0 0 00	

Mastery Problem (Continued)

ACCOUNT Purchases   ACCOUNT NO. 501

DATE		ITEM	POST. REF.	DEBIT	CREDIT	BALANCE	
						DEBIT	CREDIT
20-- Oct.	31		P6	4 7 0 0 00		4 7 0 0 00	

ACCOUNT Purchases Returns and Allowances   ACCOUNT NO. 501.1

DATE		ITEM	POST. REF.	DEBIT	CREDIT	BALANCE	
						DEBIT	CREDIT
20-- Oct.	17		J5		9 0 0 00		9 0 0 00

ACCOUNT Purchases Discounts   ACCOUNT NO. 501.2

DATE		ITEM	POST. REF.	DEBIT	CREDIT	BALANCE	
						DEBIT	CREDIT
20-- Oct.	31		CP11		2 4 00		2 4 00

ACCOUNT Wages Expense   ACCOUNT NO. 511

DATE		ITEM	POST. REF.	DEBIT	CREDIT	BALANCE	
						DEBIT	CREDIT
20-- Oct.	29		CP11	9 0 0 00		9 0 0 00	

ACCOUNT Telephone Expense   ACCOUNT NO. 525

DATE		ITEM	POST. REF.	DEBIT	CREDIT	BALANCE	
						DEBIT	CREDIT
20-- Oct.	5		CP11	1 5 0 00		1 5 0 00	

Mastery Problem (Continued)

ACCOUNTS RECEIVABLE LEDGER

NAME David's Decorating

ADDRESS 12 Jude Lane, Hartford, CT 06117

DATE		ITEM	POST. REF.	DEBIT	CREDIT	BALANCE
20-- Oct.	1	Balance	✓			3 3 4 0 00
	24		CR10		2 1 3 5 00	1 2 0 5 00
	27		S7	3 1 5 0 00		4 3 5 5 00

NAME Meg Johnson

ADDRESS 700 Hobbes Dr., Avon, CT 06108

DATE		ITEM	POST. REF.	DEBIT	CREDIT	BALANCE
20-- Oct.	1	Balance	✓			4 0 0 0 00
	12		CR10		3 1 0 0 00	9 0 0 00
	14		J5		3 1 5 00	5 8 5 00

NAME Elizabeth Shoemaker

ADDRESS 52 Juniper Road, Hartford, CT 06118

DATE		ITEM	POST. REF.	DEBIT	CREDIT	BALANCE
20-- Oct.	1	Balance	✓			2 7 9 00
	1		S7	1 0 5 0 00		1 3 2 9 00

NAME Leigh Summers

ADDRESS 5200 Hamilton Ave., Hartford, CT 06111

DATE		ITEM	POST. REF.	DEBIT	CREDIT	BALANCE
20-- Oct.	1	Balance	✓			2 0 0 0 00
	9		CR10		2 0 0 0 00	———
	12		S7	2 1 0 0 00		2 1 0 0 00

Mastery Problem (Concluded)

ACCOUNTS PAYABLE LEDGER

NAME Flower Wholesalers

ADDRESS 43 Lucky Lane, Bristol, CT 06007

DATE		ITEM	POST. REF.	DEBIT	CREDIT	BALANCE
20-- Oct.	1	Balance	✓			1 5 0 0 00
	2		P6		4 0 0 0 00	5 5 0 0 00
	11		CP11	1 5 0 0 00		4 0 0 0 00

NAME Jill Hand

ADDRESS 1009 Drake Rd., Farmington, CT 06082

DATE		ITEM	POST. REF.	DEBIT	CREDIT	BALANCE
20-- Oct.	1	Balance	✓			5 0 0 00
	2		CP11	5 0 0 00		—

NAME Seidl Enterprises

ADDRESS 888 Anders Street, Newington, CT 06789

DATE		ITEM	POST. REF.	DEBIT	CREDIT	BALANCE
20-- Oct.	4		P6		7 0 0 00	7 0 0 00
	13		CP11	7 0 0 00		—

NAME Vases Etc.

ADDRESS 34 Harry Ave., East Hartford, CT 05234

DATE		ITEM	POST. REF.	DEBIT	CREDIT	BALANCE
20-- Oct.	1	Balance	✓			3 1 2 0 00
	17		J5	9 0 0 00		2 2 2 0 00

Challenge Problem

1.

GENERAL JOURNAL

PAGE

	DATE		DESCRIPTION	POST. REF.	DEBIT	CREDIT	
1	20-- June	1	Purchases		2 7 0 0 00		1
2			Freight-In		1 6 0 00		2
3			Accounts Payable/Acme Supply			2 8 6 0 00	3
4			Purchased merchandise on account				4
5							5
6		1	Accounts Payable/Denver Wholesalers		7 2 0 00		6
7			Cash			7 1 2 80	7
8			Purchases Discounts			7 20	8
9			Made payment on account				9
10							10
11		1	Accounts Receivable/F. Colby		2 6 3 22		11
12			Sales			2 4 6 00	12
13			State Sales Tax Payable			1 2 30	13
14			City Sales Tax Payable			4 92	14
15			Made sale on account				15
16							16
17		2	Cash		3 1 5 00		17
18			Accounts Receivable/N. Dunlop			3 1 5 00	18
19			Received cash on account				19
20							20
21		2	Cash		4 4 1 91		21
22			Sales			4 1 3 00	22
23			State Sales Tax Payable			2 0 65	23
24			City Sales Tax Payable			8 26	24
25			Made cash sale				25
26							26
27		2	Purchases		3 2 0 0 00		27
28			Freight-In		1 9 0 00		28
29			Accounts Payable/Permon Co.			3 3 9 0 00	29
30			Purchased merchandise on account				30
31							31
32							32
33							33
34							34

Challenge Problem (Continued)

GENERAL JOURNAL

PAGE

	DATE		DESCRIPTION	POST. REF.	DEBIT	CREDIT	
1	20-- June	3	Accounts Receivable/F. Ayres	.	2 2 5 77		1
2			Sales			2 1 1 00	2
3			State Sales Tax Payable			1 0 55	3
4			City Sales Tax Payable			4 22	4
5			Made sale on account	.			5
6							6
7		3	Accounts Payable/Ellis Co.		8 4 7 00		7
8			Cash			8 3 8 53	8
9			Purchases Discounts			8 47	9
10			Made payment on account				10
11							11
12		3	Cash		4 6 3 00		12
13			Accounts Receivable/F. Graves			4 6 3 00	13
14			Received cash on account				14
15							15
16		4	Accounts Payable/Penguin Warehouse		9 5 0 00		16
17			Cash			9 4 0 50	17
18			Purchases Discounts			9 50	18
19			Made payment on account				19
20							20
21		4	Accounts Receivable/K. Stanga		3 4 0 26		21
22			Sales			3 1 8 00	22
23			State Sales Tax Payable			1 5 90	23
24			City Sales Tax Payable			6 36	24
25			Made sale on account				25
26							26
27		4	Purchases		1 6 3 0 00		27
28			Freight-In		9 0 00		28
29			Accounts Payable/Mason Milling			1 7 2 0 00	29
30			Purchased merchandise on account				30
31							31
32							32
33							33
34							34

Challenge Problem (Continued)

GENERAL JOURNAL

PAGE

	DATE		DESCRIPTION	POST. REF.	DEBIT	CREDIT	
1	20-- June	4	*Cash*		3 8 1 00		1
2			*Accounts Receivable/O. Alston*			3 8 1 00	2
3			*Received cash on account*				3
4							4
5		5	*Cash*		3 4 1 33		5
6			*Sales*			3 1 9 00	6
7			*State Sales Tax Payable*			1 5 95	7
8			*City Sales Tax Payable*			6 38	8
9			*Made cash sale*				9
10							10
11		5	*Accounts Payable/Acme Supply*		9 8 0 00		11
12			*Cash*			9 7 0 20	12
13			*Purchases Discounts*			9 80	13
14			*Made payment on account*				14
15							15
16							16
17							17
18							18
19							19
20							20
21							21
22							22
23							23
24							24
25							25
26							26
27							27
28							28
29							29
30							30
31							31
32							32
33							33
34							34

Challenge Problem (Concluded)

2.

(a)

SALES JOURNAL

PAGE

DATE	SALE NO.	TO WHOM SOLD	POST. REF.	ACCOUNTS RECEIVABLE DEBIT	SALES CREDIT	STATE SALES TAX PAYABLE CREDIT	CITY SALES TAX PAYABLE CREDIT

(b)

CASH RECEIPTS JOURNAL

PAGE

DATE	ACCOUNT CREDITED	POST. REF.	GENERAL CR.	ACCOUNTS RECEIVABLE CREDIT	SALES CREDIT	STATE SALES TAX PAYABLE CREDIT	CITY SALES TAX PAYABLE CREDIT	CASH DEBIT

(c)

PURCHASES JOURNAL

PAGE

DATE	INVOICE NO.	FROM WHOM PURCHASED	POST. REF.	PURCHASES DEBIT	FREIGHT-IN DEBIT	ACCOUNTS PAYABLE CREDIT

(d)

CASH PAYMENTS JOURNAL

PAGE

DATE	CK. NO.	ACCOUNT DEBITED	POST. REF.	GENERAL DEBIT	ACCOUNTS PAYABLE DEBIT	PURCHASES DISCOUNTS CREDIT	CASH CREDIT

CHAPTER 13

ACCOUNTING FOR MERCHANDISE INVENTORY

REVIEW QUESTIONS

1. The financial statements affected by an error in ending inventory are the income statement, statement of owner's equity, and balance sheet.

2. The main difference between the periodic system and the perpetual system of accounting for inventory is that in the periodic system the balance in Merchandise Inventory is merely a record of the most recent physical inventory count, whereas in the perpetual system the balance of the inventory account represents the cost of goods on hand at all times.

3. Yes, a physical inventory is necessary under the periodic system to determine the ending inventory for the calculation of the cost of goods sold.

4. Yes, a physical inventory is necessary under the perpetual system to determine whether the amount reported in the accounts equals the actual cost of inventory on hand.

5. Teaching tip: These responses assume no material liquidation of inventory layers.
    a. LIFO
    b. FIFO
    c. FIFO
    d. LIFO
    e. FIFO
    f. LIFO

6. The two factors taken into account by the weighted-average cost method are the total cost of units available for sale and the number of units available for sale.

7. The specific identification method follows the actual physical flow of merchandise.

8. When "lower-of-cost-or-market" is used, "cost" means the dollar amount calculated by one of the four cost assignment methods. "Market" means the cost to replace the item.

9. Steps in the gross profit method are:
    1. Compute the cost of goods available for sale.
    2. Estimate cost of goods sold by deducting the normal gross profit from net sales.
    3. Estimate the ending inventory by deducting cost of goods sold from the cost of goods available for sale.

10. Steps in the retail inventory method are:
    1. Compute the cost of goods available for sale at cost and retail.
    2. Compute the ending inventory at **retail** by subtracting sales at retail from goods available for sale at retail.
    3. Compute the cost-to-retail ratio by dividing the **cost** of goods available for sale by the **retail** value of the goods available for sale.
    4. Estimate the **cost** of ending inventory by multiplying the ending inventory at retail (step 2) by the cost-to-retail ratio.
    5. Estimate cost of goods sold by:
        a. multiplying sales at retail by the cost-to-retail ratio, or
        b. subtracting the estimated cost of the ending inventory from the cost of goods available for sale.

Exercise 13-1A

	Year 1	Year 2
Ending merchandise inventory	*overstated*	*correct*
Beginning merchandise inventory	*correct*	*overstated*
Cost of goods sold	*understated*	*overstated*
Gross profit	*overstated*	*understated*
Net income	*overstated*	*understated*
Ending owner's capital	*overstated*	*correct*

Exercise 13-2A

GENERAL JOURNAL   PAGE

	DATE		DESCRIPTION	POST. REF.	DEBIT	CREDIT	
1	20-- Jan.	5	Purchases		3 7 0 0 00		1
2			Accounts Payable/Prestigious Jewelers			3 7 0 0 00	2
3							3
4		8	Freight-In		2 0 0 00		4
5			Cash			2 0 0 00	5
6							6
7		12	Accounts Receivable/Diamonds Unlimited		4 9 0 0 00		7
8			Sales			4 9 0 0 00	8
9							9
10		15	Accounts Payable/Prestigious Jewelers		6 0 0 00		10
11			Purchases Returns and Allowances			6 0 0 00	11
12							12
13		22	Sales Returns and Allowances		8 0 0 00		13
14			Accounts Receivable/Diamonds Unlimited			8 0 0 00	14
15							15
16							16
17							17
18							18
19							19
20							20
21							21
22							22
23							23

Exercise 13-3A

GENERAL JOURNAL PAGE

	DATE		DESCRIPTION	POST. REF.	DEBIT	CREDIT	
1	20-- Mar.	3	Merchandise Inventory		2 7 0 0 00		1
2			Accounts Payable/City Galleria			2 7 0 0 00	2
3							3
4		7	Merchandise Inventory		1 7 5 00		4
5			Cash			1 7 5 00	5
6							6
7		13	Accounts Receivable/Amber Specialties		3 0 0 0 00		7
8			Sales			3 0 0 0 00	8
9							9
10		13	Cost of Goods Sold		1 8 0 0 00		10
11			Merchandise Inventory			1 8 0 0 00	11
12							12
13		18	Accounts Payable/City Galleria		5 0 0 00		13
14			Merchandise Inventory			5 0 0 00	14
15							15
16		22	Sales Returns and Allowances		4 0 0 00		16
17			Accounts Receivable/Amber Specialties			4 0 0 00	17
18							18
19		22	Merchandise Inventory		2 4 0 00		19
20			Cost of Goods Sold			2 4 0 00	20
21							21
22							22
23							23

Exercise 13-4A

Cost of merchandise on the showroom floor and in the warehouse	$37,800
Goods that Chen's Chattel, as the consignor, has for sale at the location of	
the Grand Avenue Vista	4,600
Sales invoices indicate that merchandise was shipped on June 25, terms FOB	
destination, delivered at buyer's receiving dock on July 5	3,100
Ending inventory	$45,500

Exercise 13-5A

1. a. **Ending inventory under FIFO**

      10 units @ $30 = $300

   b. **Ending inventory under weighted-average**

     Average cost per unit = $970/40 = $24.25

     10 units @ $24.25 = $242.50

2. a. **FIFO lower-of-cost-or-market**

FIFO cost	*$300*
Market (10 @ $26)	*260*
Choose market	*260*

   b. **Weighted-average lower-of-cost-or-market**

Weighted-average cost	*$242.50*
Market (10 @ $26)	*260.00*
Choose weighted-average cost	*242.50*

3. (a) *Loss on Write-Down of Inventory*   *40*

       Merchandise Inventory   *40*

   (b) *No entry*

Problem 13-6A

1. FIFO Inventory Method

Date 20-1/ 20-2		Cost of Goods Sold			Cost of Ending Inventory		
		Units	Unit Price	Total	Units	Unit Price	Total
Oct. 1	Beg. inv.	300	$20.00	$ 6,000		$20.00	$ 0
Oct. 18	1st purchase	500	21.50	10,750		21.50	0
Nov. 25	2nd purchase	400	22.00	8,800		22.00	0
Jan. 12	3rd purchase	800	23.00	18,400		23.00	0
Mar. 17	4th purchase	900	23.50	21,150		23.50	0
June 2	5th purchase	500	24.00	12,000	100	24.00	2,400
Aug. 21	6th purchase		25.00	0	500	25.00	12,500
Sept. 27	7th purchase		25.75	0	400	25.75	10,300
	Total	3,400		$77,100	1,000		$25,200

Alternative calculation if given goods available for sale and CGS or EI.	Cost of goods available for sale	$102,300	Cost of goods available for sale	$102,300
	Less cost of ending inventory	(25,200)	Less cost of goods sold	(77,100)
	Cost of goods sold	$ 77,100	Cost of ending inventory	$ 25,200

2. LIFO Inventory Method

Date 20-1/ 20-2		Cost of Goods Sold			Cost of Ending Inventory		
		Units	Unit Price	Total	Units	Unit Price	Total
Oct. 1	Beg. inv.		$20.00	$ 0	300	$20.00	$ 6,000
Oct. 18	1st purchase		21.50	0	500	21.50	10,750
Nov. 25	2nd purchase	200	22.00	4,400	200	22.00	4,400
Jan. 12	3rd purchase	800	23.00	18,400		23.00	0
Mar. 17	4th purchase	900	23.50	21,150		23.50	0
June 2	5th purchase	600	24.00	14,400		24.00	0
Aug. 21	6th purchase	500	25.00	12,500		25.00	0
Sept. 27	7th purchase	400	25.75	10,300		25.75	0
	Total	3,400		$81,150	1,000		$21,150

Alternative calculation if given goods available for sale and CGS or EI.	Cost of goods available for sale	$102,300	Cost of goods available for sale	$102,300
	Less cost of ending inventory	(21,150)	Less cost of goods sold	(81,150)
	Cost of goods sold	$ 81,150	Cost of ending inventory	$ 21,150

Problem 13-6A (Concluded)

3. *Weighted-average*

Average cost per unit: $102,300 ÷ 4,400 units = $23.25

Ending inventory = 1,000 units @ $23.25 = $23,250

Cost of goods sold = 3,400 units @ $23.25 = $79,050

4. Specific Identification Method

Date 20-1/ 20-2		Cost of Goods Sold			Cost of Ending Inventory		
		Units	Unit Price	Total	Units	Unit Price	Total
Oct. 1	Beg. inv.	300	$20.00	$ 6,000		$20.00	$ 0
Oct. 18	1st purchase	400	21.50	8,600	100	21.50	2,150
Nov. 25	2nd purchase	400	22.00	8,800		22.00	0
Jan. 12	3rd purchase	500	23.00	11,500	300	23.00	6,900
Mar. 17	4th purchase	800	23.50	18,800	100	23.50	2,350
June 2	5th purchase	400	24.00	9,600	200	24.00	4,800
Aug. 21	6th purchase	400	25.00	10,000	100	25.00	2,500
Sept. 27	7th purchase	200	25.75	5,150	200	25.75	5,150
	Total	3,400		$78,450	1,000		$23,850

Alternative calculation if given goods available for sale and CGS or EI.		
Cost of goods available for sale	$102,300
Less cost of ending inventory	(23,850)
Cost of goods sold	$ 78,450

Cost of goods available for sale	$102,300
Less cost of goods sold	(78,450)
Cost of ending inventory	$ 23,850

Problem 13-7A

1.

a. FIFO Inventory Method

Date 20--		Cost of Goods Sold	Unit		Cost of Ending Inventory	Unit	
		Units	Price	Total	Units	Price	Total
Jan. 1	Beg. inv.	1,100	$ 8.00	$ 8,800		$ 8.00	$ 0
Mar. 5	1st purchase	900	9.00	8,100		9.00	0
Apr. 16	2nd purchase	400	9.50	3,800		9.50	0
June 3	3rd purchase	700	10.25	7,175		10.25	0
Aug. 18	4th purchase	600	11.00	6,600		11.00	0
Sept. 13	5th purchase	700	12.00	8,400	100	12.00	1,200
Nov. 14	6th purchase		14.00	0	400	14.00	5,600
Dec. 3	7th purchase		14.05	0	500	14.05	7,025
	Total	4,400		$42,875	1,000		$13,825

Alternative calculation if given goods available for sale and CGS or EI.	Cost of goods available for sale	$ 56,700	Cost of goods available for sale	$ 56,700
	Less cost of ending inventory	(13,825)	Less cost of goods sold	(42,875)
	Cost of goods sold	$ 42,875	Cost of ending inventory	$ 13,825

b. LIFO Inventory Method

Date 20--		Cost of Goods Sold	Unit		Cost of Ending Inventory	Unit	
		Units	Price	Total	Units	Price	Total
Jan. 1	Beg. inv.	100	$ 8.00	$ 800	1,000	$ 8.00	$8,000
Mar. 5	1st purchase	900	9.00	8,100		9.00	0
Apr. 16	2nd purchase	400	9.50	3,800		9.50	0
June 3	3rd purchase	700	10.25	7,175		10.25	0
Aug. 18	4th purchase	600	11.00	6,600		11.00	0
Sept. 13	5th purchase	800	12.00	9,600		12.00	0
Nov. 14	6th purchase	400	14.00	5,600		14.00	0
Dec. 3	7th purchase	500	14.05	7,025		14.05	0
	Total	4,400		$48,700	1,000		$8,000

Alternative calculation if given goods available for sale and CGS or EI.	Cost of goods available for sale	$56,700	Cost of goods available for sale	$56,700
	Less cost of ending inventory	(8,000)	Less cost of goods sold	(48,700)
	Cost of goods sold	$48,700	Cost of ending inventory	$ 8,000

Problem 13-7A (Concluded)

c.   **Weighted-average**

Average cost per unit: $56,700 ÷ 5,400 units = $10.50

Ending inventory = 1,000 units @ $10.50 = $10,500

Cost of goods sold = 4,400 units @ $10.50 = $46,200

2.

a.   **FIFO lower-of-cost-or-market**

FIFO cost	$13,825	
Market (1,000 @ $13)	13,000	
Choose market	13,000	

b.   **Weighted-average lower-of-cost-or-market**

Weighted-average cost	$10,500	
Market (1,000 @ $13)	13,000	
Choose weighted-average cost	10,500	

Problem 13-8A

Cost of goods available for sale:

Inventory, January 1, 20--	$100,000	
Net purchases, January 1–August 5, 20--	420,000	
Cost of goods available for sale		$520,000

Estimated cost of goods sold:

Net sales	$732,000	
Normal gross profit ($732,000 × 40%)	292,800	
Estimated cost of goods sold		439,200
Estimated inventory at August 5, 20--		$ 80,800

Problem 13-9A

1. and 2.

	Cost	Retail
Inventory, start of period, January 1, 20--	$ 32,000	$ 52,000
Net purchases during period	176,000	268,000
Goods available for sale	$208,000	$320,000
Less net sales for the period		260,000
Inventory, end of period, at retail		$ 60,000
Ratio of cost-to-retail prices of goods available for sale		
($208,000 ÷ $320,000)		65%
Inventory, end of period, at estimated cost ($60,000 × 65%)	(39,000)	
Estimated cost of goods sold ($260,000 × 65%)	$169,000	

Exercise 13-1B

	Year 1	Year 2
Ending merchandise inventory	*understated*	*correct*
Beginning merchandise inventory	*correct*	*understated*
Cost of goods sold	*overstated*	*understated*
Gross profit	*understated*	*overstated*
Net income	*understated*	*overstated*
Ending owner's capital	*understated*	*correct*

Exercise 13-2B

GENERAL JOURNAL

PAGE

	DATE		DESCRIPTION	POST. REF.	DEBIT	CREDIT	
1	20-- Jan.	5	Purchases		4 1 0 0 00		1
2			Accounts Payable/Elite Warehouse			4 1 0 0 00	2
3							3
4		8	Freight-In		3 0 0 00		4
5			Cash			3 0 0 00	5
6							6
7		12	Accounts Receivable/Memories Unlimited		5 2 0 0 00		7
8			Sales			5 2 0 0 00	8
9							9
10		15	Accounts Payable/Elite Warehouse		7 0 0 00		10
11			Purchases Returns and Allowances			7 0 0 00	11
12							12
13		22	Sales Returns and Allowances		4 0 0 00		13
14			Accounts Receivable/Memories Unlimited			4 0 0 00	14
15							15
16							16
17							17
18							18
19							19
20							20
21							21
22							22
23							23
24							24
25							25
26							26
27							27
28							28
29							29
30							30
31							31
32							32
33							33
34							34
35							35

Exercise 13-3B

GENERAL JOURNAL

PAGE

	DATE		DESCRIPTION	POST. REF.	DEBIT	CREDIT	
1	20-- Mar.	3	Merchandise Inventory		3 5 0 0 00		1
2			Accounts Payable/Corner Galleria			3 5 0 0 00	2
3							3
4		7	Merchandise Inventory		2 0 0 00		4
5			Cash			2 0 0 00	5
6							6
7		13	Accounts Receivable/Sonya Specialties		4 2 5 0 00		7
8			Sales			4 2 5 0 00	8
9							9
10		13	Cost of Goods Sold		2 5 5 0 00		10
11			Merchandise Inventory			2 5 5 0 00	11
12							12
13		18	Accounts Payable/Corner Galleria		9 0 0 00		13
14			Merchandise Inventory			9 0 0 00	14
15							15
16		22	Sales Returns and Allowances		5 0 0 00		16
17			Accounts Receivable/Sonya Specialties			5 0 0 00	17
18							18
19		22	Merchandise Inventory		3 0 0 00		19
20			Cost of Goods Sold			3 0 0 00	20
21							21
22							22
23							23

Exercise 13-4B

Cost of merchandise on the showroom floor and in the warehouse	$42,600
Goods that Steele's Storeroom, as the consignor, has for sale at the location of	
Midtown Galleria	8,300
Sales invoices indicate that merchandise was shipped on June 26, terms FOB	
destination, delivered at buyer's receiving dock on July 1	2,800
Ending inventory	$53,700

Exercise 13-5B

1. a. **Ending inventory under FIFO**

    20 units @ $40 = $800

    b. **Ending inventory under weighted-average**

    Average cost per unit = $3,068 ÷ 88 = $34.86

    20 units @ $34.86 = $697.20

2. a. **FIFO lower-of-cost-or-market**

FIFO cost	$800
Market (20 @ $39)	780
Choose market	780

    b. **Weighted-average lower-of-cost-or-market**

Weighted-average cost	$697.20
Market (20 @ $39)	780.00
Choose weighted-average cost	697.20

3. (a) Loss of Write-Down of Inventory   20

           Merchandise Inventory   20

    (b) No entry

Problem 13-6B

1. FIFO Inventory Method

Date 20-1/ 20-2		Cost of Goods Sold			Cost of Ending Inventory		
		Units	Unit Price	Total	Units	Unit Price	Total
Oct. 1	Beg. inv.	400	$15.00	$ 6,000		$15.00	$ 0
Oct. 18	1st purchase	300	16.50	4,950		16.50	0
Nov. 25	2nd purchase	600	17.00	10,200		17.00	0
Jan. 12	3rd purchase	700	17.25	12,075		17.25	0
Mar. 17	4th purchase	800	18.00	14,400		18.00	0
June 2	5th purchase	300	19.00	5,700	100	19.00	1,900
Aug. 21	6th purchase		21.00	0	300	21.00	6,300
Sept. 27	7th purchase		21.75	0	500	21.75	10,875
	Total	3,100		$53,325	900		$19,075

Alternative calculation if given goods available for sale and CGS or EI.	Cost of goods available for sale	$ 72,400	Cost of goods available for sale	$ 72,400
	Less cost of ending inventory	(19,075)	Less cost of goods sold	(53,325)
	Cost of goods sold	$ 53,325	Cost of ending inventory	$ 19,075

2. LIFO Inventory Method

Date 20-1/ 20-2		Cost of Goods Sold			Cost of Ending Inventory		
		Units	Unit Price	Total	Units	Unit Price	Total
Oct. 1	Beg. inv.		$15.00	$ 0	400	$15.00	$ 6,000
Oct. 18	1st purchase		16.50	0	300	16.50	4,950
Nov. 25	2nd purchase	400	17.00	6,800	200	17.00	3,400
Jan. 12	3rd purchase	700	17.25	12,075		17.25	0
Mar. 17	4th purchase	800	18.00	14,400		18.00	0
June 2	5th purchase	400	19.00	7,600		19.00	0
Aug. 21	6th purchase	300	21.00	6,300		21.00	0
Sept. 27	7th purchase	500	21.75	10,875		21.75	0
	Total	3,100		$58,050	900		$14,350

Alternative calculation if given goods available for sale and CGS or EI.	Cost of goods available for sale	$ 72,400	Cost of goods available for sale	$ 72,400
	Less cost of ending inventory	(14,350)	Less cost of goods sold	(58,050)
	Cost of goods sold	$ 58,050	Cost of ending inventory	$ 14,350

Problem 13-6B (Concluded)

3.　　*Weighted-average*

　　　Average cost per unit: $72,400 ÷ 4,000 units = $18.10

　　　Ending inventory = 900 units @ $18.10 = $16,290

　　　Cost of goods sold = 3,100 units @ $18.10 = $56,110

4. Specific Identification Method

Date 20-1/ 20-2		Cost of Goods Sold			Cost of Ending Inventory		
		Units	Unit Price	Total	Units	Unit Price	Total
Oct. 1	Beg. inv.	400	$15.00	$ 6,000		$15.00	$ 0
Oct. 18	1st purchase	250	16.50	4,125	50	16.50	825
Nov. 25	2nd purchase	600	17.00	10,200		17.00	0
Jan. 12	3rd purchase	400	17.25	6,900	300	17.25	5,175
Mar. 17	4th purchase	700	18.00	12,600	100	18.00	1,800
June 2	5th purchase	200	19.00	3,800	200	19.00	3,800
Aug. 21	6th purchase	250	21.00	5,250	50	21.00	1,050
Sept. 27	7th purchase	300	21.75	6,525	200	21.75	4,350
	Total	3,100		$55,400	900		$17,000
Alternative calculation if given goods available for sale and CGS or EI.		Cost of goods available for sale		$ 72,400	Cost of goods available for sale		$ 72,400
		Less cost of ending inventory		(17,000)	Less cost of goods sold		(55,400)
		Cost of goods sold		$ 55,400	Cost of ending inventory		$ 17,000

Problem 13-7B

1.

a. FIFO Inventory Method

Date 20--		Cost of Goods Sold			Cost of Ending Inventory		
		Units	Unit Price	Total	Units	Unit Price	Total
Jan. 1	Beg. inv.	800	$11.00	$ 8,800		$11.00	$ 0
Mar. 5	1st purchase	600	12.00	7,200		12.00	0
Apr. 16	2nd purchase	500	12.50	6,250		12.50	0
June 3	3rd purchase	700	14.00	9,800		14.00	0
Aug. 18	4th purchase	800	15.00	12,000		15.00	0
Sept. 13	5th purchase	700	17.00	11,900	200	17.00	3,400
Nov. 14	6th purchase		18.00	0	400	18.00	7,200
Dec. 3	7th purchase		20.30	0	500	20.30	10,150
	Total	4,100		$55,950	1,100		$20,750

Alternative calculation if given goods available for sale and CGS or EI.	Cost of goods available for sale	$ 76,700	Cost of goods available for sale	$ 76,700
	Less cost of ending inventory	(20,750)	Less cost of goods sold	(55,950)
	Cost of goods sold	$ 55,950	Cost of ending inventory	$ 20,750

b. LIFO Inventory Method

Date 20--		Cost of Goods Sold			Cost of Ending Inventory		
		Units	Unit Price	Total	Units	Unit Price	Total
Jan. 1	Beg. inv.		$11.00	$ 0	800	$11.00	$ 8,800
Mar. 5	1st purchase	300	12.00	3,600	300	12.00	3,600
Apr. 16	2nd purchase	500	12.50	6,250		12.50	0
June 3	3rd purchase	700	14.00	9,800		14.00	0
Aug. 18	4th purchase	800	15.00	12,000		15.00	0
Sept. 13	5th purchase	900	17.00	15,300		17.00	0
Nov. 14	6th purchase	400	18.00	7,200		18.00	0
Dec. 3	7th purchase	500	20.30	10,150		20.30	0
	Total	4,100		$64,300	1,100		$12,400

Alternative calculation if given goods available for sale and CGS or EI.	Cost of goods available for sale	$ 76,700	Cost of goods available for sale	$ 76,700
	Less cost of ending inventory	(12,400)	Less cost of goods sold	(64,300)
	Cost of goods sold	$ 64,300	Cost of ending inventory	$ 12,400

Problem 13-7B (Concluded)

c.   *Weighted-average*

   Average cost per unit: $76,700 ÷ 5,200 units = $14.75

   Ending inventory = 1,100 units @ $14.75 = $16,225

   Cost of goods sold = 4,100 units @ $14.75 = $60,475

2.

a.   *FIFO lower-of-cost-or-market*

FIFO cost	*$20,750*
Market (1,100 @ $16)	*17,600*
Choose market	*17,600*

b.   *Weighted-average lower-of-cost-or-market*

Weighted-average cost	*$16,225*
Market (1,100 @ $16)	*17,600*
Choose weighted-average cost	*16,225*

Problem 13-8B

Cost of goods available for sale:		
Inventory, January 1, 20--	$ 60,000	
Net purchases, January 1–July 1, 20--	380,000	
Cost of goods available for sale		$440,000

Estimated cost of goods sold:		
Net sales	$650,000	
Normal gross profit ($650,000 × 45%)	292,500	
Estimated cost of goods sold		357,500
Estimated inventory at July 1, 20--		$ 82,500

Problem 13-9B

1. and 2.

	Cost	Retail
Inventory, start of period, January 1, 20--	$ 50,000	$ 80,000
Net purchases during period	220,000	352,000
Goods available for sale	$270,000	$432,000
Less net sales for period		310,000
Inventory, end of period, at retail		$122,000
Ratio of cost-to-retail prices of goods available for sale		
($270,000 ÷ $432,000)		62.5%
Inventory, end of period, at estimated cost ($122,000 × 62.5%)	(76,250)	
Estimated cost of goods sold ($310,000 × 62.5%)	$193,750	

MANAGING YOUR WRITING

Answers will vary depending on the store visited and the patience of the manager.

Key points that the students should address include:
1. What inventory method is used? (Periodic/Perpetual; FIFO/LIFO)
2. Are the scanning devices connected directly with inventory systems?
3. Are scanners connected directly with corporate headquarters?
4. How do scanning devices affect the process of ordering inventory?

What are the advantages of the scanning devices?
1. Speed at the checkout stand.
2. Internal control:
   a. Scanning device identifies product. Without the scanner, the clerk must register the type of product (meat, produce, grocery) sold. Precision is better because the scanner identifies the specific product and there is a lower probability of error.
   b. Scanners also reduce the opportunity for theft. With regular cash registers, the clerk can enter a lower amount than marked on the package and give "discounts" to friends. The scanner will automatically enter the correct price.

ETHICS CASE: SUGGESTED SOLUTIONS

1. No. The accountant should write down the carrying amount of the computers as soon as she knows they will sell for 60–70% less.

2. Loss on Write-Down of Inventory 30,000
       Merchandise Inventory 30,000
           $1,000 × 50 × (100% − 40%) = $30,000

3. Answers will vary. Students should point out that conservatism states that when in doubt, the lower asset value and net income measure should be used. Never anticipate gains, but always anticipate and account for losses. This relates to the lower of cost or market by keeping track of decreases in value of inventory and making the appropriate entry to write the assets down to market, if necessary.

4. Answers will vary. Students might mention obsolescence, decreasing popularity, slow moving items, damage, or theft.

Mastery Problem

1.

a. FIFO Inventory Method

| Date | | Cost of Goods Sold | | | Cost of Ending Inventory | | |
| | | | Unit | | | Unit | |
20-2		Units	Price	Total	Units	Price	Total
Jan. 1	Beg. inv.	1,500	$10.00	$15,000		$10.00	$ 0
Jan. 12	1st purchase	500	11.50	5,750		11.50	0
Feb. 28	2nd purchase	600	14.50	8,700		14.50	0
June 29	3rd purchase	1,200	15.00	18,000		15.00	0
Aug. 31	4th purchase	800	16.50	13,200		16.50	0
Oct. 29	5th purchase	200	18.00	3,600	100	18.00	1,800
Nov. 30	6th purchase		18.50	0	700	18.50	12,950
Dec. 21	7th purchase		20.00	0	400	20.00	8,000
	Total	4,800		$64,250	1,200		$22,750

Alternative calculation if given goods available for sale and CGS or EI.	Cost of goods available for sale	$ 87,000	Cost of goods available for sale	$ 87,000
	Less cost of ending inventory	(22,750)	Less cost of goods sold	(64,250)
	Cost of goods sold	$ 64,250	Cost of ending inventory	$ 22,750

b. LIFO Inventory Method

| Date | | Cost of Goods Sold | | | Cost of Ending Inventory | | |
| | | | Unit | | | Unit | |
20-2		Units	Price	Total	Units	Price	Total
Jan. 1	Beg. inv.	300	$10.00	$ 3,000	1,200	$10.00	$12,000
Jan. 12	1st purchase	500	11.50	5,750		11.50	0
Feb. 28	2nd purchase	600	14.50	8,700		14.50	0
June 29	3rd purchase	1,200	15.00	18,000		15.00	0
Aug. 31	4th purchase	800	16.50	13,200		16.50	0
Oct. 29	5th purchase	300	18.00	5,400		18.00	0
Nov. 30	6th purchase	700	18.50	12,950		18.50	0
Dec. 21	7th purchase	400	20.00	8,000		20.00	0
	Total	4,800		$75,000	1,200		$12,000

Alternative calculation if given goods available for sale and CGS or EI.	Cost of goods available for sale	$ 87,000	Cost of goods available for sale	$ 87,000
	Less cost of ending inventory	(12,000)	Less cost of goods sold	(75,000)
	Cost of goods sold	$ 75,000	Cost of ending inventory	$ 12,000

Mastery Problem (Concluded)

c.   *Weighted-average method*

Average cost per unit: $87,000 ÷ 6,000 units = $14.50

Inventory, December 31, 20-2:

   1,200 units @ $14.50 = $17,400

Cost of goods sold for 20-2:

   4,800 units @ $14.50 = $69,600

2.

a.   *FIFO lower-of-cost-or-market*

FIFO cost	$22,750
Market (1,200 @ $18)	21,600
Choose market	21,600

b.   *Weighted-average lower-of-cost-or-market*

Weighted-average cost	$17,400
Market (1,200 @ $18)	21,600
Choose weighted-average cost	17,400

3.

Cost of goods available for sale:

Inventory, January 1, 20-2	$ 15,000	
Net purchases, January 1, 20-2–December 31, 20-2	72,000	
Cost of goods available for sale		$87,000

Estimated cost of goods sold:

Net sales	$100,000	
Normal gross profit ($100,000 × 35%)	35,000	
Estimated cost of goods sold		65,000
Estimated inventory at December 31, 20-2		$22,000

Challenge Problem

20-1	Units	FIFO Cost/Unit	Cost	Units	LIFO Cost/Unit	Cost
Purchase 1	100	$1.00	$ 100	100	$1.00	$ 100
Purchase 2	200	2.00	400	200	2.00	400
Purchase 3	300	3.00	900	300	3.00	900
Goods available for sale	600		$1,400	600		$1,400
Ending inventory	(200)	3.00	(600)	(100)	1.00	(100)
				(100)	2.00	(200)
Units sold/CGS	400		$ 800	400		$1,100

Details of Cost of Goods Sold 20-1	Units	FIFO Cost/Unit	Cost	Units	LIFO Cost/Unit	Cost
Purchase 1	100	$1.00	$100		$1.00	
Purchase 2	200	2.00	400	100	2.00	$ 200
Purchase 3	100	3.00	300	300	3.00	900
Total	400		$800	400		$1,100

Challenge Problem (Concluded)

20-2	Units	FIFO Cost/Unit	Cost	Units	LIFO Cost/Unit	Cost
Beginning inventory	200	$3.00	$ 600	100	$1.00	$ 100
				100	2.00	200
Purchase 4	150	4.00	600	150	4.00	600
Purchase 5	250	5.00	1,250	250	5.00	1,250
Purchase 6	350	6.00	2,100	350	6.00	2,100
Goods available for sale	950		$4,550	950		$4,250
Ending inventory	(50)	6.00	(300)	(50)	1.00	(50)
Units sold/CGS	900		$4,250	900		$4,200

Details of Cost of Goods Sold 20-2	Units	FIFO Cost/Unit	Cost	Units	LIFO Cost/Unit	Cost
Beginning inventory	200	$3.00	$ 600	50	$1.00	$ 50
				100	2.00	200
Purchase 4	150	4.00	600	150	4.00	600
Purchase 5	250	5.00	1,250	250	5.00	1,250
Purchase 6	300	6.00	1,800	350	6.00	2,100
Total	900		$4,250	900		$4,200

Note: During increasing prices, LIFO cost of goods sold is generally higher than FIFO cost of goods sold. This relationship is reversed in 20-2 because the firm "dipped" into its beginning inventory and the LIFO approach reported those lower costs ($1 and $2 units) on the income statement. The least expensive unit sold under FIFO was $3.

APPENDIX: PERPETUAL INVENTORY METHOD: LIFO AND MOVING-AVERAGE METHODS

Review Question

1. Under the periodic system, calculations are made at the end of the accounting period. Under the perpetual system, calculations are made each time inventory is purchased or sold.

Exercise 13Apx-1A

1. Perpetual LIFO

Date	Purchases Units	Purchases Cost/ Unit	Purchases Total	Cost of Goods Sold Units	Cost of Goods Sold Cost/ Unit	Cost of Goods Sold CGS	Cum. CGS	Inventory on Hand Layer	Inventory on Hand Units	Inventory on Hand Cost/ Unit	Inventory on Hand Layer Cost	Inventory on Hand Total
4/1								(1)	100	$4.30	$ 430	
(BI)								(2)	100	4.50	450	
								(3)	200	4.60	920	$1,800
4/20	400	$5.50	$2,200					(1)	100	$4.30	$ 430	
								(2)	100	4.50	450	
								(3)	200	4.60	920	
								(4)	400	5.50	2,200	$4,000
4/30				400	$5.50	$2,200		(1)	100	$4.30	$ 430	
				200	4.60	920		(2)	50	4.50	225	$ 655
				50	4.50	225	$3,345					
Cost of Goods Sold during April							$3,345					

BI: Beginning Inventory

2. Perpetual Moving-Average

Date	Purchases Units	Purchases Cost/ Unit	Purchases Total	Cost of Goods Sold Units	Cost of Goods Sold Cost/ Unit	Cost of Goods Sold CGS	Cum. CGS	Inventory on Hand and Average Cost per Unit Cost of Purchase or (Sale)	Cost of Inventory on Hand	Units on Hand	Average Cost/ Unit
4/1 (BI)									$1,800	400	$4.50
4/20	400	$5.50	$2,200					$ 2,200	4,000	800	5.00
4/30				650	$5.00	$3,250	$3,250	(3,250)	750	150	5.00
Cost of Goods Sold during April							$3,250				

BI: Beginning Inventory

Problem 13Apx-2A

1. Perpetual LIFO

Date	Purchases			Cost of Goods Sold				Inventory on Hand				
	Units	Cost/ Unit	Total	Units	Cost/ Unit	CGS	Cum. CGS	Layer	Units	Cost/ Unit	Layer Cost	Total
1/1	100	$1.00	$100					(1)	100	$1.00	$100	$ 100
1/4	400	$1.10	$440					(1)	100	$1.00	$100	
								(2)	400	1.10	440	$ 540
1/5				300	$1.10	$330	$ 330	(1)	100	$1.00	$100	
								(2)	100	1.10	110	$ 210
1/10	300	$1.30	$390					(1)	100	$1.00	$100	
								(2)	100	1.10	110	
								(3)	300	1.30	390	$ 600
1/12				200	$1.30	$260	$ 590	(1)	100	$1.00	$100	
								(2)	100	1.10	110	
								(3)	100	1.30	130	$ 340
1/15	200	$1.35	$270					(1)	100	$1.00	$100	
								(2)	100	1.10	110	
								(3)	100	1.30	130	
								(4)	200	1.35	270	$ 610
1/18	500	$1.60	$800					(1)	100	$1.00	$100	
								(2)	100	1.10	110	
								(3)	100	1.30	130	
								(4)	200	1.35	270	
								(5)	500	1.60	800	$1,410
1/22				500	$1.60	$800		(1)	100	$1.00	$100	
				200	1.35	270		(2)	100	1.10	110	$ 210
				100	1.30	130	$1,790					
1/27				100	$1.10	$110	$1,900	(1)	100	$1.00	$100	$ 100
1/31	300	$1.80	$540					(1)	100	$1.00	$100	
								(6)	300	1.80	540	$ 640
Cost of Goods Sold during January							$1,900					

Problem 13Apx-2A (Concluded)

2. Perpetual Moving-Average

Date	Purchases Units	Cost/ Unit	Total	Cost of Goods Sold Units	Cost/ Unit	CGS	Cum. CGS	Cost of Purchase or (Sale)	Cost of Inventory on Hand	Units on Hand	Average Cost/ Unit
1/1	100	$1.00	$100					$ 100.00	$ 100.00	100	$1.0000
1/4	400	1.10	440					440.00	540.00	500	1.0800
1/5				300	$1.0800	$ 324.00	$ 324.00	(324.00)	216.00	200	1.0800
1/10	300	1.30	390					390.00	606.00	500	1.2120
1/12				200	1.2120	242.40	566.40	(242.40)	363.60	300	1.2120
1/15	200	1.35	270					270.00	633.60	500	1.2672
1/18	500	1.60	800					800.00	1,433.60	1,000	1.4336
1/22				800	1.4336	1,146.88	1,713.28	(1,146.88)	286.72	200	1.4336
1/27				100	1.4336	143.36	1,856.64	(143.36)	143.36	100	1.4336
1/31	300	1.80	540					540.00	683.36	400	1.7084
Cost of Goods Sold during January							$1,856.64				

Exercise 13Apx-1B

1. Perpetual LIFO

Date	Purchases Units	Purchases Cost/ Unit	Purchases Total	COGS Units	COGS Cost/ Unit	COGS CGS	COGS Cum. CGS	Layer	Inventory Units	Inventory Cost/ Unit	Inventory Layer Cost	Inventory Total
8/1								(1)	100	$8.00	$ 800	
(BI)								(2)	150	8.10	1,215	
								(3)	250	8.30	2,075	$4,090
8/15	300	$8.50	$2,550					(1)	100	$8.00	$ 800	
								(2)	150	8.10	1,215	
								(3)	250	8.30	2,075	
								(4)	300	8.50	2,550	$6,640
8/31				300	$8.50	$2,550		(1)	100	$8.00	$ 800	
				250	8.30	2,075		(2)	50	8.10	405	$1,205
				100	8.10	810	$5,435					
Cost of Goods Sold during August							$5,435					

BI: Beginning Inventory

2. Perpetual Moving-Average

Date	Purchases Units	Purchases Cost/ Unit	Purchases Total	COGS Units	COGS Cost/ Unit	COGS CGS	COGS Cum. CGS	Cost of Purchase or (Sale)	Cost of Inventory on Hand	Units on Hand	Average Cost/ Unit
8/1 (BI)									$4,090	500	$8.18
8/15	300	$8.50	$2,550					$ 2,550	6,640	800	8.30
8/31				650	$8.30	$5,395	$5,395	(5,395)	1,245	150	8.30
Cost of Goods Sold during August							$5,395				

BI: Beginning Inventory

Problem 13Apx-2B

1. Perpetual LIFO

Date	Purchases Units	Cost/ Unit	Total	Cost of Goods Sold Units	Cost/ Unit	CGS	Cum. CGS	Layer	Inventory on Hand Units	Cost/ Unit	Layer Cost	Total
1/1	100	$2.00	$ 200					(1)	100	$2.00		$ 200
1/5	500	$2.30	$1,150					(1)	100	$2.00	$ 200	
								(2)	500	2.30	1,150	$1,350
1/7				300	$2.30	$ 690	$ 690	(1)	100	$2.00	$ 200	
								(2)	200	2.30	460	$ 660
1/12	300	$2.40	$ 720					(1)	100	$2.00	$ 200	
								(2)	200	2.30	460	
								(3)	300	2.40	720	$1,380
1/15				300	$2.40	$ 720	$1,410	(1)	100	$2.00	$ 200	
								(2)	200	2.30	460	$ 660
1/17	200	$2.50	$ 500					(1)	100	$2.00	$ 200	
								(2)	200	2.30	460	
								(4)	200	2.50	500	$1,160
1/19	500	$2.70	$1,350					(1)	100	$2.00	$ 200	
								(2)	200	2.30	460	
								(4)	200	2.50	500	
								(5)	500	2.70	1,350	$2,510
1/24				500	$2.70	$1,350		(1)	100	$2.00	$ 200	
				200	2.50	500		(2)	100	2.30	230	$ 430
				100	2.30	230	$3,490					
1/28				100	$2.30	$ 230	$3,720	(1)	100	$2.00	$ 200	$ 200
1/31	200	$2.90	$ 580					(1)	100	$2.00	$ 200	
								(6)	200	2.90	580	$ 780
Cost of Goods Sold during January							$3,720					

Problem 13Apx-2B (Concluded)

2. Perpetual Moving-Average

Date	Purchases			Cost of Goods Sold				Inventory on Hand and Average Cost per Unit			
	Units	Cost/Unit	Total	Units	Cost/Unit	CGS	Cum. CGS	Cost of Purchase or (Sale)	Cost of Inventory on Hand	Units on Hand	Average Cost/Unit
1/1	100	$2.00	$ 200					$ 200.00	$ 200.00	100	$2.0000
1/5	500	2.30	1,150					1,150.00	1,350.00	600	2.2500
1/7				300	$2.2500	$ 675.00	$ 675.00	(675.00)	675.00	300	2.2500
1/12	300	2.40	720					720.00	1,395.00	600	2.3250
1/15				300	2.3250	697.50	1,372.50	(697.50)	697.50	300	2.3250
1/17	200	2.50	500					500.00	1,197.50	500	2.3950
1/19	500	2.70	1,350					1,350.00	2,547.50	1,000	2.5475
1/24				800	2.5475	2,038.00	3,410.50	(2,038.00)	509.50	200	2.5475
1/28				100	2.5475	254.75	3,665.25	(254.75)	254.75	100	2.5475
1/31	200	2.90	580					580.00	834.75	300	2.7825
Cost of Goods Sold during January							$3,665.25				

CHAPTER 14

ADJUSTMENTS AND THE WORK SHEET FOR
A MERCHANDISING BUSINESS

REVIEW QUESTIONS

1. The balance represents the beginning inventory. This balance must be adjusted using the two-step process to reflect the ending inventory as determined by the physical inventory count.

2. The following amounts from the work sheet are used to compute cost of goods sold:
   a. Beginning merchandise inventory
   b. Purchases
   c. Purchases returns and allowances
   d. Purchases discounts
   e. Freight-in
   f. Ending merchandise inventory

3. Both are extended because the individual amounts are needed for calculation of cost of goods sold on the income statement.

4. An unearned revenue is cash received in advance. It is a liability because the company owes its customers product or service or must refund their money.

5. Three examples of unearned revenue are Unearned Ticket Revenue, Unearned Subscriptions Revenue, and Unearned Deposit Fees.

6. The five steps in preparing a work sheet are as follows:
   Step 1: Prepare the trial balance.
   Step 2: Prepare the adjustments.
   Step 3: Prepare the adjusted trial balance.
   Step 4: Extend the adjusted trial balance amounts to the Income Statement and Balance Sheet columns.
   Step 5: Total the Income Statement and Balance Sheet columns to compute the net income or net loss.

7. The difference between debits and credits for each pair of columns represents the net income or net loss.

8. The balance represents the amount of inventory that should be on hand at the end of the period. This amount may need to be adjusted based on the physical inventory.

Exercise 14-1A

Merchandise Inventory			Income Summary	
(Beg. Inv.)	47,000		(a)	47,000
		(a) 47,000	(b)	53,000
(b)	53,000			

Exercise 14-2A

Cost of goods sold:				
Merch. inv., beginning			$26 0 0 0 00	
Purchases		$71 0 0 0 00		
Less: Purch. ret. & allow.	$3 5 0 0 00			
Purchases discounts	5 5 0 0 00	9 0 0 0 00		
Net purchases		$62 0 0 0 00		
Add freight-in		2 0 0 00		
Cost of goods purchased			62 2 0 0 00	
Goods available for sale			$88 2 0 0 00	
Less merch. inv., ending			23 0 0 0 00	
Cost of goods sold				$65 2 0 0 00

Exercise 14-3A

Cash			Unearned Ticket Revenue	
(a)	45,000		(a)	45,000
			(b) 35,000	

Ticket Revenue	
(b)	35,000

This page left intentionally blank.

Exercise 14-4A

1., 2., and 3.

	ACCOUNT TITLE	TRIAL BALANCE					ADJUSTMENTS				
		DEBIT		CREDIT			DEBIT			CREDIT	
1	Merchandise Inventory	40 0 0 0 00				(b) 50 0 0 0 00			(a) 40 0 0 0 00		
12	Income Summary					(a) 40 0 0 0 00			(b) 50 0 0 0 00		
13	Purchases	90 0 0 0 00									
14	Purchases Returns and Allow.			2 0 0 0 00							
15	Purchases Discounts			3 0 0 0 00							
16	Freight-In	5 0 0 00									
17											
18											

Exercise 14-4A (Concluded)

Gift Shop

Sheet (Partial)

December 31, 20--

ADJUSTED TRIAL BALANCE		INCOME STATEMENT		BALANCE SHEET		
DEBIT	CREDIT	DEBIT	CREDIT	DEBIT	CREDIT	
50 0 0 0 00				50 0 0 0 00		1
40 0 0 0 00	50 0 0 0 00	40 0 0 0 00	50 0 0 0 00			12
90 0 0 0 00		90 0 0 0 00				13
	2 0 0 0 00		2 0 0 0 00			14
	3 0 0 0 00		3 0 0 0 00			15
5 0 0 00		5 0 0 00				16
						17
						18

4.

Cost of goods sold:			
Merch. inv., Jan. 1			$ 40 0 0 0 00
Purchases		$90 0 0 0 00	
Less: Purch. ret. & allow.	$2 0 0 0 00		
Purchases discounts	3 0 0 0 00	5 0 0 0 00	
Net purchases		$85 0 0 0 00	
Add freight-in		5 0 0 00	
Cost of goods purchased			85 5 0 0 00
Goods available for sale			$125 5 0 0 00
Less merch. inv., Dec. 31			50 0 0 0 00
Cost of goods sold			$75 5 0 0 00

Exercise 14-5A

Beginning merchandise inventory	*$55,000*
Ending merchandise inventory	*60,000*

Exercise 14-6A

GENERAL JOURNAL   PAGE

	DATE		DESCRIPTION	POST. REF.	DEBIT	CREDIT	
1			*Adjusting Entries*				1
2	20-- Dec.	31	Income Summary		45 0 0 0 00		2
3			Merchandise Inventory			45 0 0 0 00	3
4							4
5		31	Merchandise Inventory		50 0 0 0 00		5
6			Income Summary			50 0 0 0 00	6
7							7
8		31	Unearned Grooming Revenue		2 0 0 0 00		8
9			Grooming Revenue			2 0 0 0 00	9
10							10
11		31	Supplies Expense		7 0 0 0 00		11
12			Supplies			7 0 0 0 00	12
13							13
14		31	Depreciation Expense—Building		5 0 0 0 00		14
15			Accumulated Depreciation—Building			5 0 0 0 00	15
16							16
17		31	Wages Expense		1 2 0 0 00		17
18			Wages Payable			1 2 0 0 00	18
19							19
20							20
21							21
22							22
23							23
24							24
25							25
26							26
27							27

Exercise 14-7A

GENERAL JOURNAL

PAGE

	DATE		DESCRIPTION	POST. REF.	DEBIT	CREDIT	
1	20-- June	1	Merchandise Inventory		500 0 0 0 00		1
2			Accounts Payable/Brij Builder's Materials			500 0 0 0 00	2
3							3
4		3	Merchandise Inventory		400 0 0 0 00		4
5			Cash			400 0 0 0 00	5
6							6
7		5	Accounts Receivable/Champa Construction		20 0 0 0 00		7
8			Sales			20 0 0 0 00	8
9							9
10		5	Cost of Goods Sold		15 0 0 0 00		10
11			Merchandise Inventory			15 0 0 0 00	11
12							12
13							13
14							14
15							15
16							16
17							17
18							18
19							19

Exercise 14-8A

GENERAL JOURNAL

PAGE

	DATE		DESCRIPTION	POST. REF.	DEBIT	CREDIT	
			Adjusting Entry				
1	20-- Dec.	31	Inventory Short and Over		25 0 0 0 00		1
2			Merchandise Inventory			25 0 0 0 00	2
3							3
4							4
5							5
6							6
7							7
8							8
9							9
10							10
11							11

Problem 14-9A

1. and 2.

Seaside Kite

Work

For Year Ended

	ACCOUNT TITLE	TRIAL BALANCE DEBIT	TRIAL BALANCE CREDIT	ADJUSTMENTS DEBIT	ADJUSTMENTS CREDIT
1	Cash	20 0 0 0 00			
2	Accounts Receivable	14 0 0 0 00			
3	Merchandise Inventory	25 0 0 0 00		(b) 30 0 0 0 00	(a) 25 0 0 0 00
4	Supplies	8 0 0 0 00			(c) 5 3 0 0 00
5	Prepaid Insurance	5 4 0 0 00			(d) 2 5 0 0 00
6	Land	30 0 0 0 00			
7	Building	50 0 0 0 00			
8	Accumulated Depr.—Building		20 0 0 0 00		(e) 5 0 0 0 00
9	Store Equipment	35 0 0 0 00			
10	Accumulated Depr.—Store Equip.		14 0 0 0 00		(f) 3 2 0 0 00
11	Accounts Payable		9 6 0 0 00		
12	Wages Payable				(h) 9 0 0 00
13	Sales Tax Payable		5 9 0 0 00		
14	Unearned Rent Revenue		8 9 0 0 00	(g) 6 7 0 0 00	
15	Mortgage Payable		45 0 0 0 00		
16	J. Kennington, Capital		65 4 1 0 00		
17	J. Kennington, Drawing	26 0 0 0 00			
18	Income Summary			(a) 25 0 0 0 00	(b) 30 0 0 0 00
19	Sales		118 0 0 0 00		
20	Sales Returns and Allowances	1 7 0 0 00			
21	Rent Revenue				(g) 6 7 0 0 00
22	Purchases	27 0 0 0 00			
23	Purchases Returns and Allow.		1 4 0 0 00		
24	Purchases Discounts		1 8 0 0 00		
25	Freight-In	2 1 0 0 00			
26	Wages Expense	32 0 0 0 00		(h) 9 0 0 00	
27	Advertising Expense	3 6 0 0 00			
28	Supplies Expense			(c) 5 3 0 0 00	
29	Telephone Expense	1 3 5 0 00			
30	Utilities Expense	8 0 0 0 00			
31	Insurance Expense			(d) 2 5 0 0 00	
32	Depreciation Expense—Building			(e) 5 0 0 0 00	
33	Depreciation Exp.—Store Equip.			(f) 3 2 0 0 00	
34	Miscellaneous Expense	8 6 0 00			
35		290 0 1 0 00	290 0 1 0 00	78 6 0 0 00	78 6 0 0 00
36	*Net Income*				
37					
38					

Problem 14-9A (Continued)

Shop

Sheet

December 31, 20--

	ADJUSTED TRIAL BALANCE		INCOME STATEMENT		BALANCE SHEET		
	DEBIT	CREDIT	DEBIT	CREDIT	DEBIT	CREDIT	
1	20 0 0 0 00				20 0 0 0 00		
2	14 0 0 0 00				14 0 0 0 00		
3	30 0 0 0 00				30 0 0 0 00		
4	2 7 0 0 00				2 7 0 0 00		
5	2 9 0 0 00				2 9 0 0 00		
6	30 0 0 0 00				30 0 0 0 00		
7	50 0 0 0 00				50 0 0 0 00		
8		25 0 0 0 00				25 0 0 0 00	
9	35 0 0 0 00				35 0 0 0 00		
10		17 2 0 0 00				17 2 0 0 00	
11		9 6 0 0 00				9 6 0 0 00	
12		9 0 0 00				9 0 0 00	
13		5 9 0 0 00				5 9 0 0 00	
14		2 2 0 0 00				2 2 0 0 00	
15		45 0 0 0 00				45 0 0 0 00	
16		65 4 1 0 00				65 4 1 0 00	
17	26 0 0 0 00				26 0 0 0 00		
18	25 0 0 0 00	30 0 0 0 00	25 0 0 0 00	30 0 0 0 00			
19		118 0 0 0 00		118 0 0 0 00			
20	1 7 0 0 00		1 7 0 0 00				
21		6 7 0 0 00		6 7 0 0 00			
22	27 0 0 0 00		27 0 0 0 00				
23		1 4 0 0 00		1 4 0 0 00			
24		1 8 0 0 00		1 8 0 0 00			
25	2 1 0 0 00		2 1 0 0 00				
26	32 9 0 0 00		32 9 0 0 00				
27	3 6 0 0 00		3 6 0 0 00				
28	5 3 0 0 00		5 3 0 0 00				
29	1 3 5 0 00		1 3 5 0 00				
30	8 0 0 00		8 0 0 00				
31	2 5 0 0 00		2 5 0 0 00				
32	5 0 0 0 00		5 0 0 0 00				
33	3 2 0 0 00		3 2 0 0 00				
34	8 6 0 00		8 6 0 00				
35	329 1 1 0 00	329 1 1 0 00	118 5 1 0 00	157 9 0 0 00	210 6 0 0 00	171 2 1 0 00	
36			39 3 9 0 00			39 3 9 0 00	
37			157 9 0 0 00	157 9 0 0 00	210 6 0 0 00	210 6 0 0 00	
38							

Problem 14-9A (Concluded)

3.

GENERAL JOURNAL

PAGE

	DATE		DESCRIPTION	POST. REF.	DEBIT	CREDIT	
1			*Adjusting Entries*				1
2	20-- Dec.	31	Income Summary		25 0 0 0 00		2
3			Merchandise Inventory			25 0 0 0 00	3
4							4
5		31	Merchandise Inventory		30 0 0 0 00		5
6			Income Summary			30 0 0 0 00	6
7							7
8		31	Supplies Expense		5 3 0 0 00		8
9			Supplies			5 3 0 0 00	9
10							10
11		31	Insurance Expense		2 5 0 0 00		11
12			Prepaid Insurance			2 5 0 0 00	12
13							13
14		31	Depreciation Expense—Building		5 0 0 0 00		14
15			Accumulated Depreciation—Building			5 0 0 0 00	15
16							16
17		31	Depreciation Expense—Store Equipment		3 2 0 0 00		17
18			Accumulated Depreciation—Store Equipment			3 2 0 0 00	18
19							19
20		31	Unearned Rent Revenue		6 7 0 0 00		20
21			Rent Revenue			6 7 0 0 00	21
22							22
23		31	Wages Expense		9 0 0 00		23
24			Wages Payable			9 0 0 00	24
25							25
26							26
27							27
28							28
29							29
30							30
31							31
32							32
33							33
34							34

Problem 14-10A

1. and 2. (See pages 554 and 555)

3.

GENERAL JOURNAL   PAGE

	DATE		DESCRIPTION	POST. REF.	DEBIT	CREDIT	
1			*Adjusting Entries*				1
2	20-- Dec.	31	Income Summary		31 0 0 0 00		2
3			Merchandise Inventory			31 0 0 0 00	3
4							4
5		31	Merchandise Inventory		22 0 0 0 00		5
6			Income Summary			22 0 0 0 00	6
7							7
8		31	Supplies Expense		4 8 0 0 00		8
9			Supplies			4 8 0 0 00	9
10							10
11		31	Insurance Expense		2 8 5 0 00		11
12			Prepaid Insurance			2 8 5 0 00	12
13							13
14		31	Depreciation Expense—Building		4 0 0 0 00		14
15			Accumulated Depreciation—Building			4 0 0 0 00	15
16							16
17		31	Depreciation Expense—Store Equipment		3 6 0 0 00		17
18			Accumulated Depreciation—Store Equipment			3 6 0 0 00	18
19							19
20		31	Unearned Storage Revenue		3 6 5 0 00		20
21			Storage Revenue			3 6 5 0 00	21
22							22
23		31	Wages Expense		7 5 0 00		23
24			Wages Payable			7 5 0 00	24

Problem 14-10A (Continued)
1. and 2.

Cascade Bicycle

Work

For Year Ended

#	ACCOUNT TITLE	TRIAL BALANCE DEBIT	TRIAL BALANCE CREDIT	ADJUSTMENTS DEBIT	ADJUSTMENTS CREDIT
1	Cash	23 000 00			
2	Accounts Receivable	15 000 00			
3	Merchandise Inventory	31 000 00		(b) 22 000 00	(a) 31 000 00
4	Supplies	7 200 00			(c) 4 800 00
5	Prepaid Insurance	4 600 00			(d) 2 850 00
6	Land	28 000 00			
7	Building	53 000 00			
8	Accumulated Depr.—Building		17 000 00		(e) 4 000 00
9	Store Equipment	27 000 00			
10	Accumulated Depr.—Store Equip.		9 000 00		(f) 3 600 00
11	Accounts Payable		3 800 00		
12	Wages Payable				(h) 750 00
13	Sales Tax Payable		3 050 00		
14	Unearned Storage Revenue		5 600 00	(g) 3 650 00	
15	Mortgage Payable		42 000 00		
16	D. Lamond, Capital		165 760 00		
17	D. Lamond, Drawing	33 000 00			
18	Income Summary			(a) 31 000 00	(b) 22 000 00
19	Sales		51 000 00		
20	Sales Returns and Allowances	2 400 00			
21	Storage Revenue				(g) 3 650 00
22	Purchases	21 000 00			
23	Purchases Returns and Allow.		1 300 00		
24	Purchases Discounts		1 900 00		
25	Freight-In	1 800 00			
26	Wages Expense	35 000 00		(h) 750 00	
27	Advertising Expense	5 700 00			
28	Supplies Expense			(c) 4 800 00	
29	Telephone Expense	2 200 00			
30	Utilities Expense	9 600 00			
31	Insurance Expense			(d) 2 850 00	
32	Depreciation Expense—Building			(e) 4 000 00	
33	Depreciation Exp.—Store Equip.			(f) 3 600 00	
34	Miscellaneous Expense	910 00			
35		300 410 00	300 410 00	72 650 00	72 650 00
36	*Net Loss*				
37					
38					

Problem 14-10A (Concluded)

Shop

Sheet

December 31, 20--

ADJUSTED TRIAL BALANCE DEBIT	ADJUSTED TRIAL BALANCE CREDIT	INCOME STATEMENT DEBIT	INCOME STATEMENT CREDIT	BALANCE SHEET DEBIT	BALANCE SHEET CREDIT	
23 0 0 0 00				23 0 0 0 00		1
15 0 0 0 00				15 0 0 0 00		2
22 0 0 0 00				22 0 0 0 00		3
2 4 0 0 00				2 4 0 0 00		4
1 7 5 0 00				1 7 5 0 00		5
28 0 0 0 00				28 0 0 0 00		6
53 0 0 0 00				53 0 0 0 00		7
	21 0 0 0 00				21 0 0 0 00	8
27 0 0 0 00				27 0 0 0 00		9
	12 6 0 0 00				12 6 0 0 00	10
	3 8 0 0 00				3 8 0 0 00	11
	7 5 0 00				7 5 0 00	12
	3 0 5 0 00				3 0 5 0 00	13
	1 9 5 0 00				1 9 5 0 00	14
	42 0 0 0 00				42 0 0 0 00	15
	165 7 6 0 00				165 7 6 0 00	16
33 0 0 0 00				33 0 0 0 00		17
31 0 0 0 00	22 0 0 0 00	31 0 0 0 00	22 0 0 0 00			18
	51 0 0 0 00		51 0 0 0 00			19
2 4 0 0 00		2 4 0 0 00				20
	3 6 5 0 00		3 6 5 0 00			21
21 0 0 0 00		21 0 0 0 00				22
	1 3 0 0 00		1 3 0 0 00			23
	1 9 0 0 00		1 9 0 0 00			24
1 8 0 0 00		1 8 0 0 00				25
35 7 5 0 00		35 7 5 0 00				26
5 7 0 0 00		5 7 0 0 00				27
4 8 0 0 00		4 8 0 0 00				28
2 2 0 0 00		2 2 0 0 00				29
9 6 0 0 00		9 6 0 0 00				30
2 8 5 0 00		2 8 5 0 00				31
4 0 0 0 00		4 0 0 0 00				32
3 6 0 0 00		3 6 0 0 00				33
9 1 0 00		9 1 0 00				34
330 7 6 0 00	330 7 6 0 00	125 6 1 0 00	79 8 5 0 00	205 1 5 0 00	250 9 1 0 00	35
			45 7 6 0 00	45 7 6 0 00		36
		125 6 1 0 00	125 6 1 0 00	250 9 1 0 00	250 9 1 0 00	37
						38

Problem 14-11A

1.

Stark Street Computers
Work Sheet (Partial)
For Year Ended December 31, 20--

	ACCOUNT TITLE	TRIAL BALANCE DEBIT	TRIAL BALANCE CREDIT	ADJUSTMENTS DEBIT	ADJUSTMENTS CREDIT	ADJUSTED TRIAL BALANCE DEBIT	ADJUSTED TRIAL BALANCE CREDIT	
1	Cash	18 0 0 0 00				18 0 0 0 00		1
2	Accounts Receivable	11 0 0 0 00				11 0 0 0 00		2
3	Merchandise Inventory	25 0 0 0 00		(b) 35 0 0 0 00	(a) 25 0 0 0 00	35 0 0 0 00		3
4	Supplies	8 0 0 0 00			(c) 5 1 8 0 00	2 8 2 0 00		4
5	Prepaid Insurance	5 4 0 0 00			(d) 4 1 7 5 00	1 2 2 5 00		5
6	Land	27 0 0 0 00				27 0 0 0 00		6
7	Building	48 0 0 0 00				48 0 0 0 00		7
8	Accum. Depr.—Building		20 0 0 0 00		(e) 7 0 0 0 00		27 0 0 0 00	8
9	Store Equipment	33 0 0 0 00				33 0 0 0 00		9
10	Accum. Depr.—Store Equip.		8 7 0 0 00		(f) 4 1 0 0 00		12 8 0 0 00	10
11	Accounts Payable		6 4 0 0 00				6 4 0 0 00	11
12	Wages Payable				(h) 1 3 0 0 00		1 3 0 0 00	12
13	Sales Tax Payable		5 7 0 0 00				5 7 0 0 00	13
14	Unearned Repair Rev.		8 2 0 0 00	(g) 6 4 0 0 00			1 8 0 0 00	14
15	Mortgage Payable		44 0 0 0 00				44 0 0 0 00	15
16	L. Cowart, Capital		80 0 2 5 00				80 0 2 5 00	16
17	L. Cowart, Drawing	35 0 0 0 00				35 0 0 0 00		17
18	Income Summary			(a) 25 0 0 0 00	(b) 35 0 0 0 00	25 0 0 0 00	35 0 0 0 00	18
19	Sales		122 0 0 0 00				122 0 0 0 00	19
20	Sales Returns and Allow.	2 2 5 0 00				2 2 5 0 00		20
21	Repair Revenue				(g) 6 4 0 0 00		6 4 0 0 00	21
22	Purchases	29 7 5 0 00				29 7 5 0 00		22
23	Purchases Ret. and Allow.		1 8 5 0 00				1 8 5 0 00	23
24	Purchases Discounts		1 4 2 5 00				1 4 2 5 00	24
25	Freight-In	3 2 0 0 00				3 2 0 0 00		25
26	Wages Expense	37 0 0 0 00		(h) 1 3 0 0 00		38 3 0 0 00		26
27	Advertising Expense	4 1 2 5 00				4 1 2 5 00		27
28	Supplies Expense			(c) 5 1 8 0 00		5 1 8 0 00		28
29	Telephone Expense	1 6 5 0 00				1 6 5 0 00		29
30	Utilities Expense	9 1 5 0 00				9 1 5 0 00		30
31	Insurance Expense			(d) 4 1 7 5 00		4 1 7 5 00		31
32	Depr. Exp.—Building			(e) 7 0 0 0 00		7 0 0 0 00		32
33	Depr. Exp.—Store Equip.			(f) 4 1 0 0 00		4 1 0 0 00		33
34	Miscellaneous Expense	7 7 5 00				7 7 5 00		34
35		298 3 0 0 00	298 3 0 0 00	88 1 5 5 00	88 1 5 5 00	345 7 0 0 00	345 7 0 0 00	35
36								36
37								37
38								38

Problem 14-11A (Concluded)

2.

GENERAL JOURNAL

	DATE		DESCRIPTION	POST. REF.	DEBIT	CREDIT	
1			*Adjusting Entries*				1
2	20-- Dec.	31	Income Summary		25 0 0 0 00		2
3			Merchandise Inventory			25 0 0 0 00	3
4							4
5		31	Merchandise Inventory		35 0 0 0 00		5
6			Income Summary			35 0 0 0 00	6
7							7
8		31	Supplies Expense		5 1 8 0 00		8
9			Supplies			5 1 8 0 00	9
10							10
11		31	Insurance Expense		4 1 7 5 00		11
12			Prepaid Insurance			4 1 7 5 00	12
13							13
14		31	Depreciation Expense—Building		7 0 0 0 00		14
15			Accumulated Depreciation—Building			7 0 0 0 00	15
16							16
17		31	Depreciation Expense—Store Equipment		4 1 0 0 00		17
18			Accumulated Depreciation—Store Equipment			4 1 0 0 00	18
19							19
20		31	Unearned Repair Revenue		6 4 0 0 00		20
21			Repair Revenue			6 4 0 0 00	21
22							22
23		31	Wages Expense		1 3 0 0 00		23
24			Wages Payable			1 3 0 0 00	24
25							25
26							26
27							27
28							28
29							29
30							30
31							31
32							32
33							33
34							34
35							35

Problem 14-12A

1.

	ACCOUNT TITLE	TRIAL BALANCE DEBIT	TRIAL BALANCE CREDIT	ADJUSTMENTS DEBIT	ADJUSTMENTS CREDIT
1	Cash	27 0 0 0 00			
2	Accounts Receivable	13 3 0 0 00			
3	Merchandise Inventory	34 0 0 0 00		(b) 38 0 0 0 00	(a) 34 0 0 0 00
4	Supplies	5 3 0 0 00			(c) 3 8 0 0 00
5	Prepaid Insurance	6 1 0 0 00			(d) 4 3 1 5 00
6	Land	31 0 0 0 00			
7	Building	52 0 0 0 00			
8	Accumulated Depr.—Building		17 0 0 0 00		(e) 4 1 4 5 00
9	Store Equipment	39 0 0 0 00			
10	Accumulated Depr.—Store Equip.		11 9 0 0 00		(f) 2 9 7 5 00
11	Accounts Payable		6 2 5 0 00		
12	Wages Payable				(h) 8 7 5 00
13	Sales Tax Payable		6 2 0 0 00		
14	Unearned Rent Revenue		7 4 0 0 00	(g) 4 2 2 5 00	
15	Mortgage Payable		46 0 0 0 00		
16	H. Lewis, Capital		111 6 2 0 00		
17	H. Lewis, Drawing	37 0 0 0 00			
18	Income Summary			(a) 34 0 0 0 00	(b) 38 0 0 0 00
19	Sales		136 0 0 0 00		
20	Sales Returns and Allowances	3 5 0 0 00			
21	Rent Revenue				(g) 4 2 2 5 00
22	Purchases	39 0 0 0 00			
23	Purchases Returns and Allow.		2 5 3 0 00		
24	Purchases Discounts		1 9 7 5 00		
25	Freight-In	2 6 5 0 00			
26	Wages Expense	42 0 0 0 00		(h) 8 7 5 00	
27	Advertising Expense	4 1 7 5 00			
28	Supplies Expense			(c) 3 8 0 0 00	
29	Telephone Expense	1 9 8 0 00			
30	Utilities Expense	7 9 4 5 00			
31	Insurance Expense			(d) 4 3 1 5 00	
32	Depreciation Expense—Building			(e) 4 1 4 5 00	
33	Depreciation Exp.—Store Equip.			(f) 2 9 7 5 00	
34	Miscellaneous Expense	9 2 5 00			
35		346 8 7 5 00	346 8 7 5 00	92 3 3 5 00	92 3 3 5 00
36	Net Income				
37					
38					

Problem 14-12A (Continued)

Store

Sheet

December 31, 20--

	ADJUSTED TRIAL BALANCE		INCOME STATEMENT		BALANCE SHEET		
	DEBIT	CREDIT	DEBIT	CREDIT	DEBIT	CREDIT	
	27 0 0 0 00				27 0 0 0 00		1
	13 3 0 0 00				13 3 0 0 00		2
	38 0 0 0 00				38 0 0 0 00		3
	1 5 0 0 00				1 5 0 0 00		4
	1 7 8 5 00				1 7 8 5 00		5
	31 0 0 0 00				31 0 0 0 00		6
	52 0 0 0 00				52 0 0 0 00		7
		21 1 4 5 00				21 1 4 5 00	8
	39 0 0 0 00				39 0 0 0 00		9
		14 8 7 5 00				14 8 7 5 00	10
		6 2 5 0 00				6 2 5 0 00	11
		8 7 5 00				8 7 5 00	12
		6 2 0 0 00				6 2 0 0 00	13
		3 1 7 5 00				3 1 7 5 00	14
		46 0 0 0 00				46 0 0 0 00	15
		111 6 2 0 00				111 6 2 0 00	16
	37 0 0 0 00				37 0 0 0 00		17
	34 0 0 0 00	38 0 0 0 00	34 0 0 0 00	38 0 0 0 00			18
		136 0 0 0 00		136 0 0 0 00			19
	3 5 0 0 00		3 5 0 0 00				20
		4 2 2 5 00		4 2 2 5 00			21
	39 0 0 0 00		39 0 0 0 00				22
		2 5 3 0 00		2 5 3 0 00			23
		1 9 7 5 00		1 9 7 5 00			24
	2 6 5 0 00		2 6 5 0 00				25
	42 8 7 5 00		42 8 7 5 00				26
	4 1 7 5 00		4 1 7 5 00				27
	3 8 0 0 00		3 8 0 0 00				28
	1 9 8 0 00		1 9 8 0 00				29
	7 9 4 5 00		7 9 4 5 00				30
	4 3 1 5 00		4 3 1 5 00				31
	4 1 4 5 00		4 1 4 5 00				32
	2 9 7 5 00		2 9 7 5 00				33
	9 2 5 00		9 2 5 00				34
	392 8 7 0 00	392 8 7 0 00	152 2 8 5 00	182 7 3 0 00	240 5 8 5 00	210 1 4 0 00	35
			30 4 4 5 00			30 4 4 5 00	36
			182 7 3 0 00	182 7 3 0 00	240 5 8 5 00	240 5 8 5 00	37
							38

Problem 14-12A (Continued)

2.

GENERAL JOURNAL

PAGE

	DATE		DESCRIPTION	POST. REF.	DEBIT	CREDIT	
1			*Adjusting Entries*				1
2	20-- Dec.	31	Income Summary		34 0 0 0 00		2
3			Merchandise Inventory			34 0 0 0 00	3
4							4
5		31	Merchandise Inventory		38 0 0 0 00		5
6			Income Summary			38 0 0 0 00	6
7							7
8		31	Supplies Expense		3 8 0 0 00		8
9			Supplies			3 8 0 0 00	9
10							10
11		31	Insurance Expense		4 3 1 5 00		11
12			Prepaid Insurance			4 3 1 5 00	12
13							13
14		31	Depreciation Expense—Building		4 1 4 5 00		14
15			Accumulated Depreciation—Building			4 1 4 5 00	15
16							16
17		31	Depreciation Expense—Store Equipment		2 9 7 5 00		17
18			Accumulated Depreciation—Store Equipment			2 9 7 5 00	18
19							19
20		31	Unearned Rent Revenue		4 2 2 5 00		20
21			Rent Revenue			4 2 2 5 00	21
22							22
23		31	Wages Expense		8 7 5 00		23
24			Wages Payable			8 7 5 00	24
25							25
26							26
27							27
28							28
29							29
30							30
31							31
32							32
33							33
34							34

Problem 14-12A (Concluded)

3.

Cost of goods sold:										
Merch. inv., Jan. 1						$34 0 0 0 00			
Purchases			$39 0 0 0 00				
Less: Purch. ret. & allow.	$2 5 3 0 00						
Purchases discounts	1 9 7 5 00	4 5 0 5 00				
Net purchases			$34 4 9 5 00				
Add freight-in			2 6 5 0 00				
Cost of goods purchased					37 1 4 5 00			
Goods available for sale					$71 1 4 5 00			
Less merch. inv., Dec. 31					38 0 0 0 00			
Cost of goods sold							$33 1 4 5 00

Exercise 14-1B

Merchandise Inventory						Income Summary			
(Beg. Inv.)	33,000		(a)	33,000		(a)	33,000	(b)	36,000
(b)	36,000								

Exercise 14-2B

Cost of goods sold:																				
Merch. inv., beginning												$29	0	0	0	00				
Purchases							$62	0	0	0	00									
Less: Purch. ret. & allow.	$2	8	0	0	00															
Purchases discounts	3	4	0	0	00		6	2	0	0	00									
Net purchases							$55	8	0	0	00									
Add freight-in								3	0	0	00									
Cost of goods purchased												56	1	0	0	00				
Goods available for sale												$85	1	0	0	00				
Less merch. inv., ending												27	0	0	0	00				
Cost of goods sold																	$58	1	0	0	00

Exercise 14-3B

Cash				Unearned Ticket Revenue			
(a)	24,000					(a)	24,000
				(b)	19,000		

Ticket Revenue			
		(b)	19,000

This page left intentionally blank.

Exercise 14-4B

1., 2., and 3.

Nicole's

Work

For Year Ended

	ACCOUNT TITLE	TRIAL BALANCE										ADJUSTMENTS										
		DEBIT					CREDIT					DEBIT					CREDIT					
1	Merchandise Inventory	30	0	0	0	00						(b) 37	0	0	0	00	(a) 30	0	0	0	00	
12	Income Summary											(a) 30	0	0	0	00	(b) 37	0	0	0	00	
13	Purchases	85	0	0	0	00																
14	Purchases Returns and Allow.						2	2	0	0	00											
15	Purchases Discounts						2	5	0	0	00											
16	Freight-In		1	0	0	00																
17																						
18																						

Exercise 14-4B (Concluded)

Gift Shop

Sheet (Partial)

December 31, 20--

ADJUSTED TRIAL BALANCE		INCOME STATEMENT		BALANCE SHEET		
DEBIT	CREDIT	DEBIT	CREDIT	DEBIT	CREDIT	
37 0 0 0 00				37 0 0 0 00		1
30 0 0 0 00	37 0 0 0 00	30 0 0 0 00	37 0 0 0 00			12
85 0 0 0 00		85 0 0 0 00				13
	2 2 0 0 00		2 2 0 0 00			14
	2 5 0 0 00		2 5 0 0 00			15
1 0 0 00		1 0 0 00				16
						17
						18

4.

Cost of goods sold:					
Merch. inv., Jan. 1			$ 30 0 0 0 00		
Purchases		$85 0 0 0 00			
Less: Purch. ret. & allow.	$2 2 0 0 00				
Purchases discounts	2 5 0 0 00	4 7 0 0 00			
Net purchases		$80 3 0 0 00			
Add freight-in		1 0 0 00			
Cost of goods purchased			80 4 0 0 00		
Goods available for sale			$110 4 0 0 00		
Less merch. inv., Dec. 31			37 0 0 0 00		
Cost of goods sold				$73 4 0 0 00	

Exercise 14-5B

Beginning merchandise inventory	*$49,000*
Ending merchandise inventory	*45,000*

Exercise 14-6B

GENERAL JOURNAL   PAGE

	DATE		DESCRIPTION	POST. REF.	DEBIT	CREDIT	
1			**Adjusting Entries**				1
2	20-- Dec.	31	Income Summary		35 0 0 0 00		2
3			Merchandise Inventory			35 0 0 0 00	3
4							4
5		31	Merchandise Inventory		30 0 0 0 00		5
6			Income Summary			30 0 0 0 00	6
7							7
8		31	Unearned Grooming Revenue		5 5 0 0 00		8
9			Grooming Revenue			5 5 0 0 00	9
10							10
11		31	Supplies Expense		3 1 0 0 00		11
12			Supplies			3 1 0 0 00	12
13							13
14		31	Depreciation Expense—Building		6 0 0 0 00		14
15			Accumulated Depreciation—Building			6 0 0 0 00	15
16							16
17		31	Wages Expense		1 3 0 0 00		17
18			Wages Payable			1 3 0 0 00	18
19							19
20							20
21							21
22							22
23							23
24							24
25							25
26							26
27							27

Exercise 14-7B

GENERAL JOURNAL   PAGE

	DATE		DESCRIPTION	POST. REF.	DEBIT	CREDIT	
1	20-- May	1	Merchandise Inventory		200 0 0 0 00		1
2			Accounts Payable/Anju Enterprises			200 0 0 0 00	2
3							3
4		8	Merchandise Inventory		100 0 0 0 00		4
5			Cash			100 0 0 0 00	5
6							6
7		15	Accounts Receivable/Salil's Pharmacy		8 0 0 0 00		7
8			Sales			8 0 0 0 00	8
9							9
10		15	Cost of Goods Sold		5 0 0 0 00		10
11			Merchandise Inventory			5 0 0 0 00	11
12							12
13							13
14							14
15							15
16							16
17							17
18							18
19							19
20							20
21							21

Exercise 14-8B

GENERAL JOURNAL   PAGE

	DATE		DESCRIPTION	POST. REF.	DEBIT	CREDIT	
1			*Adjusting Entry*				1
2	20-- Dec.	31	Merchandise Inventory		10 0 0 0 00		2
3			Inventory Short and Over			10 0 0 0 00	3
4							4
5							5
6							6
7							7
8							8
9							9
10							10

Problem 14-9B

1. and 2.

Basket

Work

For Year Ended

	ACCOUNT TITLE	TRIAL BALANCE													ADJUSTMENTS													
		DEBIT					CREDIT								DEBIT						CREDIT					
1	Cash	25	0	0	0	00																				
2	Accounts Receivable	8	1	0	0	00																				
3	Merchandise Inventory	32	0	0	0	00							(b)	24	0	0	0	00	(a)	32	0	0	0	00
4	Supplies	7	1	0	0	00													(c)	5	0	0	0	00
5	Prepaid Insurance	3	6	0	0	00													(d)	1	0	0	0	00
6	Land	40	0	0	0	00																				
7	Building	45	0	0	0	00																				
8	Accumulated Depr.—Building						16	0	0	0	00								(e)	5	3	0	0	00
9	Store Equipment	27	0	0	0	00																				
10	Accumulated Depr.—Store Equip.						5	5	0	0	00								(f)	3	8	0	0	00
11	Accounts Payable						3	6	0	0	00															
12	Wages Payable																		(h)		7	5	0	00
13	Sales Tax Payable						6	2	0	0	00															
14	Unearned Decorating Revenue						6	3	0	0	00	(g)	4	6	5	0	00							
15	Mortgage Payable						36	0	0	0	00															
16	L. Palermo, Capital						112	0	5	0	00															
17	L. Palermo, Drawing	31	0	0	0	00																				
18	Income Summary											(a)	32	0	0	0	00	(b)	24	0	0	0	00
19	Sales						125	0	0	0	00															
20	Sales Returns and Allowances	2	6	0	0	00																				
21	Decorating Revenue																		(g)	4	6	5	0	00
22	Purchases	38	0	0	0	00																				
23	Purchases Returns and Allow.						2	2	0	0	00															
24	Purchases Discounts						1	7	0	0	00															
25	Freight-In	1	9	0	0	00																				
26	Wages Expense	38	0	0	0	00							(h)		7	5	0	00							
27	Advertising Expense	4	2	0	0	00																				
28	Supplies Expense											(c)	5	0	0	0	00							
29	Telephone Expense	1	8	7	0	00																				
30	Utilities Expense	8	4	0	0	00																				
31	Insurance Expense											(d)	1	0	0	0	00							
32	Depreciation Expense—Building											(e)	5	3	0	0	00							
33	Depreciation Exp.—Store Equip.											(f)	3	8	0	0	00							
34	Miscellaneous Expense		7	8	0	00																				
35		314	5	5	0	00	314	5	5	0	00		76	5	0	0	00		76	5	0	0	00
36	*Net Income*																									
37																										
38																										

Problem 14-9B (Continued)

Corner

Sheet

December 31, 20--

ADJUSTED TRIAL BALANCE		INCOME STATEMENT		BALANCE SHEET		
DEBIT	CREDIT	DEBIT	CREDIT	DEBIT	CREDIT	
25 0 0 0 00				25 0 0 0 00		1
8 1 0 0 00				8 1 0 0 00		2
24 0 0 0 00				24 0 0 0 00		3
2 1 0 0 00				2 1 0 0 00		4
2 6 0 0 00				2 6 0 0 00		5
40 0 0 0 00				40 0 0 0 00		6
45 0 0 0 00				45 0 0 0 00		7
	21 3 0 0 00				21 3 0 0 00	8
27 0 0 0 00				27 0 0 0 00		9
	9 3 0 0 00				9 3 0 0 00	10
	3 6 0 0 00				3 6 0 0 00	11
	7 5 0 00				7 5 0 00	12
	6 2 0 0 00				6 2 0 0 00	13
	1 6 5 0 00				1 6 5 0 00	14
	36 0 0 0 00				36 0 0 0 00	15
	112 0 5 0 00				112 0 5 0 00	16
31 0 0 0 00				31 0 0 0 00		17
32 0 0 0 00	24 0 0 0 00	32 0 0 0 00	24 0 0 0 00			18
	125 0 0 0 00		125 0 0 0 00			19
2 6 0 0 00		2 6 0 0 00				20
	4 6 5 0 00		4 6 5 0 00			21
38 0 0 0 00		38 0 0 0 00				22
	2 2 0 0 00		2 2 0 0 00			23
	1 7 0 0 00		1 7 0 0 00			24
1 9 0 0 00		1 9 0 0 00				25
38 7 5 0 00		38 7 5 0 00				26
4 2 0 0 00		4 2 0 0 00				27
5 0 0 0 00		5 0 0 0 00				28
1 8 7 0 00		1 8 7 0 00				29
8 4 0 0 00		8 4 0 0 00				30
1 0 0 0 00		1 0 0 0 00				31
5 3 0 0 00		5 3 0 0 00				32
3 8 0 0 00		3 8 0 0 00				33
7 8 0 00		7 8 0 00				34
348 4 0 0 00	348 4 0 0 00	143 6 0 0 00	157 5 5 0 00	204 8 0 0 00	190 8 5 0 00	35
		13 9 5 0 00			13 9 5 0 00	36
		157 5 5 0 00	157 5 5 0 00	204 8 0 0 00	204 8 0 0 00	37
						38

Problem 14-9B (Concluded)

3.

GENERAL JOURNAL

PAGE

	DATE		DESCRIPTION	POST. REF.	DEBIT	CREDIT	
1			*Adjusting Entries*				1
2	20-- Dec.	31	Income Summary		32 0 0 0 00		2
3			Merchandise Inventory			32 0 0 0 00	3
4							4
5		31	Merchandise Inventory		24 0 0 0 00		5
6			Income Summary			24 0 0 0 00	6
7							7
8		31	Supplies Expense		5 0 0 0 00		8
9			Supplies			5 0 0 0 00	9
10							10
11		31	Insurance Expense		1 0 0 0 00		11
12			Prepaid Insurance			1 0 0 0 00	12
13							13
14		31	Depreciation Expense—Building		5 3 0 0 00		14
15			Accumulated Depreciation—Building			5 3 0 0 00	15
16							16
17		31	Depreciation Expense—Store Equipment		3 8 0 0 00		17
18			Accumulated Depreciation—Store Equipment			3 8 0 0 00	18
19							19
20		31	Unearned Decorating Revenue		4 6 5 0 00		20
21			Decorating Revenue			4 6 5 0 00	21
22							22
23		31	Wages Expense		7 5 0 00		23
24			Wages Payable			7 5 0 00	24
25							25
26							26
27							27
28							28
29							29
30							30
31							31
32							32
33							33
34							34

Problem 14-10B

1. and 2. (See pages 572 and 573.)

3.

GENERAL JOURNAL

	DATE		DESCRIPTION	POST. REF.	DEBIT	CREDIT	
1			*Adjusting Entries*				1
2	20-- Dec.	31	Income Summary		39 0 0 0 00		2
3			Merchandise Inventory			39 0 0 0 00	3
4							4
5		31	Merchandise Inventory		26 0 0 0 00		5
6			Income Summary			26 0 0 0 00	6
7							7
8		31	Supplies Expense		3 7 0 0 00		8
9			Supplies			3 7 0 0 00	9
10							10
11		31	Insurance Expense		3 9 8 0 00		11
12			Prepaid Insurance			3 9 8 0 00	12
13							13
14		31	Depreciation Expense—Building		6 4 0 0 00		14
15			Accumulated Depreciation—Building			6 4 0 0 00	15
16							16
17		31	Depreciation Expense—Store Equipment		2 8 0 0 00		17
18			Accumulated Depreciation—Store Equipment			2 8 0 0 00	18
19							19
20		31	Unearned Rent Revenue		3 7 5 0 00		20
21			Rent Revenue			3 7 5 0 00	21
22							22
23		31	Wages Expense		1 1 0 0 00		23
24			Wages Payable			1 1 0 0 00	24
25							25
26							26
27							27
28							28
29							29
30							30
31							31
32							32
33							33
34							34

Problem 14-10B (Continued)

1. and 2.

Oregon Bike

Work

For Year Ended

	ACCOUNT TITLE	TRIAL BALANCE DEBIT	TRIAL BALANCE CREDIT	ADJUSTMENTS DEBIT	ADJUSTMENTS CREDIT
1	Cash	27 0 0 0 00			
2	Accounts Receivable	12 0 0 0 00			
3	Merchandise Inventory	39 0 0 0 00		(b) 26 0 0 0 00	(a) 39 0 0 0 00
4	Supplies	6 2 0 0 00			(c) 3 7 0 0 00
5	Prepaid Insurance	5 8 0 0 00			(d) 3 9 8 0 00
6	Land	32 0 0 0 00			
7	Building	58 0 0 0 00			
8	Accumulated Depr.—Building		27 0 0 0 00		(e) 6 4 0 0 00
9	Store Equipment	31 0 0 0 00			
10	Accumulated Depr.—Store Equip.		14 0 0 0 00		(f) 2 8 0 0 00
11	Accounts Payable		4 9 0 0 00		
12	Wages Payable				(h) 1 1 0 0 00
13	Sales Tax Payable		2 9 0 0 00		
14	Unearned Rent Revenue		6 1 0 0 00	(g) 3 7 5 0 00	
15	Mortgage Payable		49 0 0 0 00		
16	C. Moody, Capital		169 5 0 0 00		
17	C. Moody, Drawing	36 0 0 0 00			
18	Income Summary			(a) 39 0 0 0 00	(b) 26 0 0 0 00
19	Sales		58 0 0 0 00		
20	Sales Returns and Allowances	3 3 0 0 00			
21	Rent Revenue				(g) 3 7 5 0 00
22	Purchases	19 0 0 0 00			
23	Purchases Returns and Allow.		9 0 0 00		
24	Purchases Discounts		1 4 5 0 00		
25	Freight-In	8 0 0 00			
26	Wages Expense	47 0 0 0 00		(h) 1 1 0 0 00	
27	Advertising Expense	6 2 0 0 00			
28	Supplies Expense			(c) 3 7 0 0 00	
29	Telephone Expense	1 8 6 0 00			
30	Utilities Expense	8 1 0 0 00			
31	Insurance Expense			(d) 3 9 8 0 00	
32	Depreciation Expense—Building			(e) 6 4 0 0 00	
33	Depreciation Exp.—Store Equip.			(f) 2 8 0 0 00	
34	Miscellaneous Expense	4 9 0 00			
35		333 7 5 0 00	333 7 5 0 00	86 7 3 0 00	86 7 3 0 00
36	*Net Loss*				
37					
38					

Problem 14-10B (Concluded)

Company

Sheet

December 31, 20--

ADJUSTED TRIAL BALANCE DEBIT	ADJUSTED TRIAL BALANCE CREDIT	INCOME STATEMENT DEBIT	INCOME STATEMENT CREDIT	BALANCE SHEET DEBIT	BALANCE SHEET CREDIT	
27 0 0 0 00				27 0 0 0 00		1
12 0 0 0 00				12 0 0 0 00		2
26 0 0 0 00				26 0 0 0 00		3
2 5 0 0 00				2 5 0 0 00		4
1 8 2 0 00				1 8 2 0 00		5
32 0 0 0 00				32 0 0 0 00		6
58 0 0 0 00				58 0 0 0 00		7
	33 4 0 0 00				33 4 0 0 00	8
31 0 0 0 00				31 0 0 0 00		9
	16 8 0 0 00				16 8 0 0 00	10
	4 9 0 0 00				4 9 0 0 00	11
	1 1 0 0 00				1 1 0 0 00	12
	2 9 0 0 00				2 9 0 0 00	13
	2 3 5 0 00				2 3 5 0 00	14
	49 0 0 0 00				49 0 0 0 00	15
	169 5 0 0 00				169 5 0 0 00	16
36 0 0 0 00				36 0 0 0 00		17
39 0 0 0 00	26 0 0 0 00	39 0 0 0 00	26 0 0 0 00			18
	58 0 0 0 00		58 0 0 0 00			19
3 3 0 0 00		3 3 0 0 00				20
	3 7 5 0 00		3 7 5 0 00			21
19 0 0 0 00		19 0 0 0 00				22
	9 0 0 00		9 0 0 00			23
	1 4 5 0 00		1 4 5 0 00			24
8 0 0 00		8 0 0 00				25
48 1 0 0 00		48 1 0 0 00				26
6 2 0 0 00		6 2 0 0 00				27
3 7 0 0 00		3 7 0 0 00				28
1 8 6 0 00		1 8 6 0 00				29
8 1 0 0 00		8 1 0 0 00				30
3 9 8 0 00		3 9 8 0 00				31
6 4 0 0 00		6 4 0 0 00				32
2 8 0 0 00		2 8 0 0 00				33
4 9 0 00		4 9 0 00				34
370 0 5 0 00	370 0 5 0 00	143 7 3 0 00	90 1 0 0 00	226 3 2 0 00	279 9 5 0 00	35
			53 6 3 0 00	53 6 3 0 00		36
		143 7 3 0 00	143 7 3 0 00	279 9 5 0 00	279 9 5 0 00	37
						38

Problem 14-11B

1.

Burnside Auto Parts

Work Sheet (Partial)

For Year Ended December 31, 20--

	ACCOUNT TITLE	TRIAL BALANCE DEBIT	TRIAL BALANCE CREDIT	ADJUSTMENTS DEBIT	ADJUSTMENTS CREDIT	ADJUSTED TRIAL BALANCE DEBIT	ADJUSTED TRIAL BALANCE CREDIT	
1	Cash	21 0 0 0 00				21 0 0 0 00		1
2	Accounts Receivable	8 3 0 0 00				8 3 0 0 00		2
3	Merchandise Inventory	32 0 0 0 00		(b)36 0 0 0 00	(a)32 0 0 0 00	36 0 0 0 00		3
4	Supplies	6 1 5 0 00			(c)4 2 8 5 00	1 8 6 5 00		4
5	Prepaid Insurance	5 9 2 5 00			(d)4 0 9 0 00	1 8 3 5 00		5
6	Land	41 7 5 0 00				41 7 5 0 00		6
7	Building	43 0 0 0 00				43 0 0 0 00		7
8	Accum. Depr.—Building		24 0 0 0 00		(e)3 5 0 0 00		27 5 0 0 00	8
9	Store Equipment	25 4 0 0 00				25 4 0 0 00		9
10	Accum. Depr.—Store Equip.		12 4 0 0 00		(f)2 3 5 0 00		14 7 5 0 00	10
11	Accounts Payable		8 1 0 0 00				8 1 0 0 00	11
12	Wages Payable				(h)9 8 0 00		9 8 0 00	12
13	Sales Tax Payable		5 2 0 0 00				5 2 0 0 00	13
14	Unearn. Rent-A-Junk Rev.		7 9 5 0 00	(g)5 6 0 0 00			2 3 5 0 00	14
15	Mortgage Payable		26 0 0 0 00				26 0 0 0 00	15
16	B. Davis, Capital		109 1 3 0 00				109 1 3 0 00	16
17	B. Davis, Drawing	40 0 0 0 00				40 0 0 0 00		17
18	Income Summary			(a)32 0 0 0 00	(b)36 0 0 0 00	32 0 0 0 00	36 0 0 0 00	18
19	Sales		123 5 0 0 00				123 5 0 0 00	19
20	Sales Returns and Allow.	2 8 6 0 00				2 8 6 0 00		20
21	Rent-A-Junk Revenue				(g)5 6 0 0 00		5 6 0 0 00	21
22	Purchases	32 5 2 5 00				32 5 2 5 00		22
23	Purchases Ret. and Allow.		2 1 5 0 00				2 1 5 0 00	23
24	Purchases Discounts		2 4 0 0 00				2 4 0 0 00	24
25	Freight-In	3 1 7 5 00				3 1 7 5 00		25
26	Wages Expense	44 1 7 5 00		(h)9 8 0 00		45 1 5 5 00		26
27	Advertising Expense	3 2 7 5 00				3 2 7 5 00		27
28	Supplies Expense			(c)4 2 8 5 00		4 2 8 5 00		28
29	Telephone Expense	2 2 0 0 00				2 2 0 0 00		29
30	Utilities Expense	8 2 5 0 00				8 2 5 0 00		30
31	Insurance Expense			(d)4 0 9 0 00		4 0 9 0 00		31
32	Depr. Exp.—Building			(e)3 5 0 0 00		3 5 0 0 00		32
33	Depr. Exp.—Store Equip.			(f)2 3 5 0 00		2 3 5 0 00		33
34	Miscellaneous Expense	8 4 5 00				8 4 5 00		34
35		320 8 3 0 00	320 8 3 0 00	88 8 0 5 00	88 8 0 5 00	363 6 6 0 00	363 6 6 0 00	35
36								36
37								37
38								38

Problem 14-11B (Concluded)
2.

GENERAL JOURNAL

	DATE		DESCRIPTION	POST. REF.	DEBIT	CREDIT	
1			*Adjusting Entries*				1
2	20-- Dec.	31	Income Summary		32 0 0 0 00		2
3			Merchandise Inventory			32 0 0 0 00	3
4							4
5		31	Merchandise Inventory		36 0 0 0 00		5
6			Income Summary			36 0 0 0 00	6
7							7
8		31	Supplies Expense		4 2 8 5 00		8
9			Supplies			4 2 8 5 00	9
10							10
11		31	Insurance Expense		4 0 9 0 00		11
12			Prepaid Insurance			4 0 9 0 00	12
13							13
14		31	Depreciation Expense—Building		3 5 0 0 00		14
15			Accumulated Depreciation—Building			3 5 0 0 00	15
16							16
17		31	Depreciation Expense—Store Equipment		2 3 5 0 00		17
18			Accumulated Depreciation—Store Equipment			2 3 5 0 00	18
19							19
20		31	Unearned Rent-A-Junk Revenue		5 6 0 0 00		20
21			Rent-A-Junk Revenue			5 6 0 0 00	21
22							22
23		31	Wages Expense		9 8 0 00		23
24			Wages Payable			9 8 0 00	24
25							25
26							26
27							27
28							28
29							29
30							30
31							31
32							32
33							33
34							34

Problem 14-12B

1.

Diamond Music

Work

For Year Ended

#	ACCOUNT TITLE	TRIAL BALANCE DEBIT	TRIAL BALANCE CREDIT	ADJUSTMENTS DEBIT	ADJUSTMENTS CREDIT
1	Cash	31 0 0 0 00			
2	Accounts Receivable	11 9 8 0 00			
3	Merchandise Inventory	33 6 0 0 00		(b) 39 1 0 0 00	(a) 33 6 0 0 00
4	Supplies	7 1 4 0 00			(c) 5 1 7 5 00
5	Prepaid Insurance	5 9 8 5 00			(d) 4 7 5 0 00
6	Land	36 2 0 0 00			
7	Building	51 8 5 0 00			
8	Accumulated Depr.—Building		13 5 9 0 00		(e) 5 2 8 5 00
9	Store Equipment	32 6 7 5 00			
10	Accumulated Depr.—Store Equip.		10 2 9 0 00		(f) 4 4 6 5 00
11	Accounts Payable		5 8 9 5 00		
12	Wages Payable				(h) 1 2 5 0 00
13	Sales Tax Payable		6 3 7 5 00		
14	Unearned Rent Revenue		8 8 5 0 00	(g) 5 9 2 0 00	
15	Mortgage Payable		42 4 0 0 00		
16	N. Diamond, Capital		116 3 5 0 00		
17	N. Diamond, Drawing	39 5 0 0 00			
18	Income Summary			(a) 33 6 0 0 00	(b) 39 1 0 0 00
19	Sales		148 0 0 0 00		
20	Sales Returns and Allowances	2 8 0 0 00			
21	Rent Revenue				(g) 5 9 2 0 00
22	Purchases	40 7 0 0 00			
23	Purchases Returns and Allow.		2 7 7 5 00		
24	Purchases Discounts		2 3 2 5 00		
25	Freight-In	1 8 7 5 00			
26	Wages Expense	47 0 0 0 00		(h) 1 2 5 0 00	
27	Advertising Expense	4 6 9 5 00			
28	Supplies Expense			(c) 5 1 7 5 00	
29	Telephone Expense	2 2 5 0 00			
30	Utilities Expense	6 8 2 5 00			
31	Insurance Expense			(d) 4 7 5 0 00	
32	Depreciation Expense—Building			(e) 5 2 8 5 00	
33	Depreciation Exp.—Store Equip.			(f) 4 4 6 5 00	
34	Miscellaneous Expense	7 7 5 00			
35		356 8 5 0 00	356 8 5 0 00	99 5 4 5 00	99 5 4 5 00
36	Net Income				
37					
38					

Problem 14-12B (Continued)

Store

Sheet

December 31, 20--

ADJUSTED TRIAL BALANCE		INCOME STATEMENT		BALANCE SHEET		
DEBIT	CREDIT	DEBIT	CREDIT	DEBIT	CREDIT	
31 0 0 0 00				31 0 0 0 00		1
11 9 8 0 00				11 9 8 0 00		2
39 1 0 0 00				39 1 0 0 00		3
1 9 6 5 00				1 9 6 5 00		4
1 2 3 5 00				1 2 3 5 00		5
36 2 0 0 00				36 2 0 0 00		6
51 8 5 0 00				51 8 5 0 00		7
	18 8 7 5 00				18 8 7 5 00	8
32 6 7 5 00				32 6 7 5 00		9
	14 7 5 5 00				14 7 5 5 00	10
	5 8 9 5 00				5 8 9 5 00	11
	1 2 5 0 00				1 2 5 0 00	12
	6 3 7 5 00				6 3 7 5 00	13
	2 9 3 0 00				2 9 3 0 00	14
	42 4 0 0 00				42 4 0 0 00	15
	116 3 5 0 00				116 3 5 0 00	16
39 5 0 0 00				39 5 0 0 00		17
33 6 0 0 00	39 1 0 0 00	33 6 0 0 00	39 1 0 0 00			18
	148 0 0 0 00		148 0 0 0 00			19
2 8 0 0 00		2 8 0 0 00				20
	5 9 2 0 00		5 9 2 0 00			21
40 7 0 0 00		40 7 0 0 00				22
	2 7 7 5 00		2 7 7 5 00			23
	2 3 2 5 00		2 3 2 5 00			24
1 8 7 5 00		1 8 7 5 00				25
48 2 5 0 00		48 2 5 0 00				26
4 6 9 5 00		4 6 9 5 00				27
5 1 7 5 00		5 1 7 5 00				28
2 2 5 0 00		2 2 5 0 00				29
6 8 2 5 00		6 8 2 5 00				30
4 7 5 0 00		4 7 5 0 00				31
5 2 8 5 00		5 2 8 5 00				32
4 4 6 5 00		4 4 6 5 00				33
7 7 5 00		7 7 5 00				34
406 9 5 0 00	406 9 5 0 00	161 4 4 5 00	198 1 2 0 00	245 5 0 5 00	208 8 3 0 00	35
		36 6 7 5 00			36 6 7 5 00	36
		198 1 2 0 00	198 1 2 0 00	245 5 0 5 00	245 5 0 5 00	37
						38

Problem 14-12B (Continued)

2.

			GENERAL JOURNAL			PAGE	
	DATE		DESCRIPTION	POST. REF.	DEBIT	CREDIT	
1			*Adjusting Entries*				1
2	20-- Dec.	31	Income Summary		33 6 0 0 00		2
3			Merchandise Inventory			33 6 0 0 00	3
4							4
5		31	Merchandise Inventory		39 1 0 0 00		5
6			Income Summary			39 1 0 0 00	6
7							7
8		31	Supplies Expense		5 1 7 5 00		8
9			Supplies			5 1 7 5 00	9
10							10
11		31	Insurance Expense		4 7 5 0 00		11
12			Prepaid Insurance			4 7 5 0 00	12
13							13
14		31	Depreciation Expense—Building		5 2 8 5 00		14
15			Accumulated Depreciation—Building			5 2 8 5 00	15
16							16
17		31	Depreciation Expense—Store Equipment		4 4 6 5 00		17
18			Accumulated Depreciation—Store Equipment			4 4 6 5 00	18
19							19
20		31	Unearned Rent Revenue		5 9 2 0 00		20
21			Rent Revenue			5 9 2 0 00	21
22							22
23		31	Wages Expense		1 2 5 0 00		23
24			Wages Payable			1 2 5 0 00	24
25							25
26							26
27							27
28							28
29							29
30							30
31							31
32							32
33							33
34							34

Problem 14-12B (Concluded)

3.

Cost of goods sold:												
Merch. inv., Jan. 1						$33 6 0 0 00		
Purchases			$40 7 0 0 00					
Less: Purch. ret. & allow.	$2 7 7 5 00							
Purchases discounts	2 3 2 5 00	5 1 0 0 00					
Net purchases			$35 6 0 0 00					
Add freight-in			1 8 7 5 00					
Cost of goods purchased				37 4 7 5 00		
Goods available for sale				$71 0 7 5 00		
Less merch. inv., Dec. 31				39 1 0 0 00		
Cost of goods sold					$31 9 7 5 00

MANAGING YOUR WRITING

Students should make the following points:

1. It is true that your friend can compute the amount paid for inventory purchased. Now it is important to divide that amount between goods sold and not sold. Taking a physical inventory will determine the amount not sold. We assume that the remainder has been sold.

2. Under the accrual basis of accounting, expenses are recorded when incurred. Cost of goods sold is an expense. As the title suggests, it represents the cost of merchandise actually sold. The fact that the merchandise may have been paid for is not relevant. If the merchandise is still in the ending inventory, it has not been sold. Thus, the remaining inventory is an asset, not an expense. Failure to take a physical inventory would result in an overstatement of cost of goods sold.

ETHICS CASE

1. Jason should know, from past experience, that taking a physical inventory at the end of the accounting period is necessary to have the correct ending inventory amount in the accounting records.

2. If the ending inventory is understated, net income for the accounting period will be understated because the cost of goods sold will be overstated.

3. Answers will vary. Students should point out that a physical inventory is necessary to make the proper adjusting entry if the periodic inventory system is used. Even if the perpetual inventory system is used, a physical inventory will confirm the cost of ending inventory. Students might also reason that an accurate ending inventory will mean that the next period's beginning inventory is also correct.

4. Answers will vary. Possible reasons might be theft, prior period ending inventory counted incorrectly, or computer error in recording transactions affecting inventory.

This page left intentionally blank.

Mastery Problem

1.

Waikiki Surf

Work

For Year Ended

#	ACCOUNT TITLE	TRIAL BALANCE DEBIT	TRIAL BALANCE CREDIT	ADJUSTMENTS DEBIT	ADJUSTMENTS CREDIT
1	Cash	30 0 0 0 00			
2	Accounts Receivable	22 5 0 0 00			
3	Merchandise Inventory	57 0 0 0 00		(b) 45 0 0 0 00	(a) 57 0 0 0 00
4	Supplies	2 7 0 0 00			(c) 2 1 0 0 00
5	Prepaid Insurance	3 6 0 0 00			(d) 2 7 0 0 00
6	Land	15 0 0 0 00			
7	Building	135 0 0 0 00			
8	Accumulated Depr.—Building		24 0 0 0 00		(e) 6 0 0 0 00
9	Store Equipment	75 0 0 0 00			
10	Accumulated Depr.—Store Equip.		22 5 0 0 00		(f) 4 5 0 0 00
11	Notes Payable		7 5 0 0 00		
12	Accounts Payable		15 0 0 0 00		
13	Wages Payable				(g) 6 7 5 00
14	Unearned Boat Rental Revenue		33 0 0 0 00	(h) 30 0 0 0 00	
15	J. Neff, Capital		233 7 0 0 00		
16	J. Neff, Drawing	30 0 0 0 00			
17	Income Summary			(a) 57 0 0 0 00	(b) 45 0 0 0 00
18	Sales		300 7 5 0 00		
19	Sales Returns and Allowances	1 8 0 0 00			
20	Boat Rental Revenue				(h) 30 0 0 0 00
21	Purchases	157 5 0 0 00			
22	Purchases Returns and Allow.		1 2 0 0 00		
23	Purchases Discounts		1 5 0 0 00		
24	Freight-In	4 5 0 00			
25	Wages Expense	63 0 0 0 00		(g) 6 7 5 00	
26	Advertising Expense	11 2 5 0 00			
27	Supplies Expense			(c) 2 1 0 0 00	
28	Telephone Expense	5 2 5 0 00			
29	Utilities Expense	18 0 0 0 00			
30	Insurance Expense			(d) 2 7 0 0 00	
31	Depreciation Expense—Building			(e) 6 0 0 0 00	
32	Depreciation Exp.—Store Equip.			(f) 4 5 0 0 00	
33	Miscellaneous Expense	10 8 7 5 00			
34	Interest Expense	2 2 5 00			
35		639 1 5 0 00	639 1 5 0 00	147 9 7 5 00	147 9 7 5 00
36	*Net Income*				
37					
38					

Mastery Problem (Continued)

Shop

Sheet

December 31, 20--

ADJUSTED TRIAL BALANCE		INCOME STATEMENT		BALANCE SHEET		
DEBIT	CREDIT	DEBIT	CREDIT	DEBIT	CREDIT	
30 0 0 0 00				30 0 0 0 00		1
22 5 0 0 00				22 5 0 0 00		2
45 0 0 0 00				45 0 0 0 00		3
6 0 0 00				6 0 0 00		4
9 0 0 00				9 0 0 00		5
15 0 0 0 00				15 0 0 0 00		6
135 0 0 0 00				135 0 0 0 00		7
	30 0 0 0 00				30 0 0 0 00	8
75 0 0 0 00				75 0 0 0 00		9
	27 0 0 0 00				27 0 0 0 00	10
	7 5 0 0 00				7 5 0 0 00	11
	15 0 0 0 00				15 0 0 0 00	12
	6 7 5 00				6 7 5 00	13
	3 0 0 00				3 0 0 00	14
	233 7 0 0 00				233 7 0 0 00	15
30 0 0 0 00				30 0 0 0 00		16
57 0 0 0 00	45 0 0 0 00	57 0 0 0 00	45 0 0 0 00			17
	300 7 5 0 00		300 7 5 0 00			18
1 8 0 0 00		1 8 0 0 00				19
	30 0 0 0 00		30 0 0 0 00			20
157 5 0 0 00		157 5 0 0 00				21
	1 2 0 0 00		1 2 0 0 00			22
	1 5 0 0 00		1 5 0 0 00			23
4 5 0 00		4 5 0 00				24
63 6 7 5 00		63 6 7 5 00				25
11 2 5 0 00		11 2 5 0 00				26
2 1 0 0 00		2 1 0 0 00				27
5 2 5 0 00		5 2 5 0 00				28
18 0 0 0 00		18 0 0 0 00				29
2 7 0 0 00		2 7 0 0 00				30
6 0 0 0 00		6 0 0 0 00				31
4 5 0 0 00		4 5 0 0 00				32
10 8 7 5 00		10 8 7 5 00				33
2 2 5 00		2 2 5 00				34
695 3 2 5 00	695 3 2 5 00	341 3 2 5 00	378 4 5 0 00	354 0 0 0 00	316 8 7 5 00	35
		37 1 2 5 00			37 1 2 5 00	36
		378 4 5 0 00	378 4 5 0 00	354 0 0 0 00	354 0 0 0 00	37
						38

Mastery Problem (Concluded)

2.

GENERAL JOURNAL　　　　　　　　　PAGE

	DATE		DESCRIPTION	POST. REF.	DEBIT	CREDIT	
1			*Adjusting Entries*				1
2	20-- Dec.	31	Income Summary		57 0 0 0 00		2
3			Merchandise Inventory			57 0 0 0 00	3
4							4
5		31	Merchandise Inventory		45 0 0 0 00		5
6			Income Summary			45 0 0 0 00	6
7							7
8		31	Supplies Expense		2 1 0 0 00		8
9			Supplies			2 1 0 0 00	9
10							10
11		31	Insurance Expense		2 7 0 0 00		11
12			Prepaid Insurance			2 7 0 0 00	12
13							13
14		31	Depreciation Expense—Building		6 0 0 0 00		14
15			Accumulated Depreciation—Building			6 0 0 0 00	15
16							16
17		31	Depreciation Expense—Store Equipment		4 5 0 0 00		17
18			Accumulated Depreciation—Store Equipment			4 5 0 0 00	18
19							19
20		31	Wages Expense		6 7 5 00		20
21			Wages Payable			6 7 5 00	21
22							22
23		31	Unearned Boat Rental Revenue		30 0 0 0 00		23
24			Boat Rental Revenue			30 0 0 0 00	24
25							25
26							26
27							27
28							28
29							29
30							30
31							31
32							32
33							33
34							34

Challenge Problem

Cost of goods sold	$400,000
Plus increase in inventory	10,000
Net purchases in 20-1	$410,000

It appears that Block has violated its agreement and has purchased $110,000 in merchandise from other suppliers.

Alternative Solution:

Beginning inventory	(1)	$ 20,000	Given
Plus purchases	(2)	410,000	Step 2, (3) – (1)
Goods available for sale	(3)	$430,000	Step 1, (5) + (4)
Less ending inventory	(4)	30,000	Given
Cost of goods sold	(5)	$400,000	Given

The sum of the cost of goods sold and ending inventory equals the goods available for sale. If Block had $430,000 available for sale and started the period with $20,000 in inventory, it must have purchased $410,000.

APPENDIX: EXPENSE METHOD OF ACCOUNTING FOR PREPAID EXPENSES

Exercise 14Apx-1A

GENERAL JOURNAL   PAGE

	DATE		DESCRIPTION	POST. REF.	DEBIT	CREDIT	
1			*Adjusting Entry*				1
2	20-- Dec.	31	*Prepaid Advertising*		4 0 0 00		2
3			*Advertising Expense*			4 0 0 00	3
4							4
5							5
6							6
7							7
8							8
9							9
10							10
11							11
12							12

Exercise 14Apx-1B

GENERAL JOURNAL   PAGE

	DATE		DESCRIPTION	POST. REF.	DEBIT	CREDIT	
1			*Adjusting Entry*				1
2	20-- Dec.	31	*Supplies*		5 0 0 00		2
3			*Supplies Expense*			5 0 0 00	3
4							4
5							5
6							6
7							7
8							8
9							9
10							10
11							11
12							12

CHAPTER 15

FINANCIAL STATEMENTS AND YEAR-END ACCOUNTING FOR A MERCHANDISING BUSINESS

REVIEW QUESTIONS

1. The single-step form of income statement lists all revenue items and their total first, followed by all expense items and their total. The difference, which is either net income or net loss, is then calculated. The multiple-step form of income statement is commonly used for merchandising businesses. The term "multiple-step" is used because the final net income is calculated on a step-by-step basis. Gross sales is shown first, less sales returns and allowances, and sales discounts. This difference is called net sales. Cost of goods sold is next subtracted to arrive at gross profit. Operating expenses are then listed and subtracted from gross profit to compute income from operations. Finally, other revenues are added and other expenses are subtracted to arrive at net income (or net loss).

2. Two measures of the firm's ability to pay its current liabilities are the current ratio and quick ratio. The current ratio is the current assets divided by the current liabilities. The quick ratio is the quick assets divided by the current liabilities.

3. **a.** Return on owner's equity = Net income ÷ Average owner's equity
   b. Accounts receivable turnover = Net credit sales for the period ÷ Average accounts receivable
   c. Inventory turnover = Cost of goods sold for the period ÷ Average inventory

4. The work sheet contains the information needed to journalize the closing entries.

5. (1) All income statement accounts with credit balances are closed to Income Summary. (2) All income statement accounts with debit balances are closed to Income Summary. (3) The balance in Income Summary is transferred to the owner's capital account. (4) The balance in the owner's drawing account is transferred to the owner's capital account.

6. The purpose of the post-closing trial balance is to prove that the general ledger is in balance at the beginning of a new accounting period before any transactions for the new accounting period are entered.

7. Reversing entries are made to simplify the recording of transactions in the new accounting period.

8. Reversing entries are generally made on the first day of a new accounting period.

9. Except for the first year of operation, reverse all adjusting entries that increase an asset or liability account from a zero balance.

Exercise 15-1A

Revenue from sales:					
Sales			$140 0 0 0 00		
Less: Sales returns and allowances	$3 5 0 0 00				
Sales discounts	2 8 0 0 00		6 3 0 0 00		
Net sales				$133 7 0 0 00	

Exercise 15-2A

Cost of goods sold:					
Merch. inv., Jan. 1, 20--			$ 34 0 0 0 00		
Purchases		$102 0 0 0 00			
Less: Purch. ret. & allow.	$4 2 0 0 00				
Purch. discounts	2 0 4 0 00	6 2 4 0 00			
Net purchases		$ 95 7 6 0 00			
Add freight-in		8 0 0 00			
Cost of goods purchased			96 5 6 0 00		
Goods available for sale			$130 5 6 0 00		
Less mer. inv., Dec. 31, 20--			28 0 0 0 00		
Cost of goods sold				$102 5 6 0 00	

Exercise 15-3A

Rau Office Supplies
Income Statement
For Year Ended December 31, 20--

Revenue from sales:												
Sales								$148 3 0 0 00				
Less: Sales ret. & allow.					$ 1 3 8 0 00							
Sales discounts					2 1 6 6 00		3 5 4 6 00					
Net sales										$144 7 5 4 00		
Cost of goods sold:												
Merch. inv., Jan. 1, 20--								$ 26 5 0 0 00				
Purchases					$98 0 0 0 00							
Less: Purch. ret. & allow.	$2 1 8 0 00											
Purch. discounts	1 9 6 0 00			4 1 4 0 00								
Net purchases				$93 8 6 0 00								
Add freight-in				7 5 0 00								
Cost of goods purchased							94 6 1 0 00					
Goods available for sale							$121 1 1 0 00					
Less merch. inv., Dec. 31, 20--							33 2 5 0 00					
Cost of goods sold										87 8 6 0 00		
Gross profit										$ 56 8 9 4 00		
Operating expenses:												
Wages expense							$ 23 8 0 0 00					
Supplies expense							9 0 0 00					
Telephone expense							1 1 0 0 00					
Utilities expense							7 0 0 0 00					
Insurance expense							1 0 0 0 00					
Depr. exp.—equipment							3 1 0 0 00					
Miscellaneous expense							7 2 0 00					
Total operating expenses										37 6 2 0 00		
Income from operations										$ 19 2 7 4 00		
Other revenues:												
Interest revenue							$ 2 4 0 00					
Other expenses:												
Interest expense							3 8 8 0 00		(3 6 4 0 00)		
Net income										$ 15 6 3 4 00		

Exercise 15-4A

1.   Working capital:

Current Assets	$70,100
− Current Liabilities	15,100
	$55,000

2.   Current ratio:

$$\frac{\text{Current Assets}}{\text{Current Liabilities}} = \frac{\$70,100}{\$15,100} = 4.64 \text{ to } 1$$

3.   Quick ratio:

$$\frac{\text{Quick Assets}}{\text{Current Liabilities}} = \frac{\$39,700}{\$15,100} = 2.63 \text{ to } 1$$

4.   Return on owner's equity:

$$\frac{\text{Net Income}}{\text{Average Owner's Equity}} = \frac{\$27,800}{\left[\dfrac{\$88,000 + \$104,200}{2}\right]} = \frac{\$27,800}{\$96,100} = 28.9\%$$

5.   Accounts receivable turnover:

$$\frac{\text{Net Credit Sales}}{\text{Average Accounts Receivable}} = \frac{\$182,100}{\left[\dfrac{\$21,600 + \$18,900}{2}\right]} = \frac{\$182,100}{\$20,250} = 8.99$$

$$365 \div 8.99 = 40.6 \text{ days}$$

6.   Inventory turnover:

$$\frac{\text{Cost of Goods Sold}}{\text{Average Inventory}} = \frac{\$93,200}{\left[\dfrac{\$31,300 + \$28,177}{2}\right]} = \frac{\$93,200}{\$29,738.50} = 3.13$$

$$365 \div 3.13 = 116.6 \text{ days}$$

Exercise 15-5A

1.

GENERAL JOURNAL   PAGE

	DATE		DESCRIPTION	POST. REF.	DEBIT	CREDIT	
1			**Closing Entries**				1
2	20-1 Dec.	31	Sales		86 0 0 0 00		2
3			Purchases Returns and Allowances		2 8 1 3 00		3
4			Purchases Discounts		1 0 8 4 00		4
5			Income Summary			89 8 9 7 00	5
6							6
7		31	Income Summary		83 2 2 2 00		7
8			Sales Returns and Allowances			1 8 4 0 00	8
9			Purchases			54 2 0 0 00	9
10			Freight-In			8 0 0 00	10
11			Wages Expense			17 0 8 0 00	11
12			Advertising Expense			7 8 4 00	12
13			Supplies Expense			3 8 0 00	13
14			Telephone Expense			2 1 0 0 00	14
15			Utilities Expense			1 3 1 0 00	15
16			Insurance Expense			2 0 0 00	16
17			Depreciation Expense—Building			4 0 0 0 00	17
18			Miscellaneous Expense			3 8 6 00	18
19			Interest Expense			1 4 2 00	19
20							20
21		31	Income Summary		9 2 6 5 00		21
22			J. M. Gimbel, Capital			9 2 6 5 00	22
23							23
24		31	J. M. Gimbel, Capital		8 0 0 0 00		24
25			J. M. Gimbel, Drawing			8 0 0 0 00	25
26							26
27							27
28							28
29							29
30							30
31							31
32							32
33							33
34							34

Exercise 15-5A (Concluded)

2.

<table>
<tr><td colspan="2" align="center">*Gimbel's Gifts and Gadgets*</td></tr>
<tr><td colspan="2" align="center">*Post-Closing Trial Balance*</td></tr>
<tr><td colspan="2" align="center">*December 31, 20-1*</td></tr>
<tr><td>Cash</td><td>8 2 1 4 00</td><td></td></tr>
<tr><td>Accounts Receivable</td><td>6 7 2 0 00</td><td></td></tr>
<tr><td>Merchandise Inventory</td><td>16 8 0 0 00</td><td></td></tr>
<tr><td>Supplies</td><td>3 0 0 00</td><td></td></tr>
<tr><td>Prepaid Insurance</td><td>6 0 0 00</td><td></td></tr>
<tr><td>Building</td><td>80 0 0 0 00</td><td></td></tr>
<tr><td>Accum. Depr.—Building</td><td></td><td>17 6 0 0 00</td></tr>
<tr><td>Accounts Payable</td><td></td><td>5 2 8 0 00</td></tr>
<tr><td>Wages Payable</td><td></td><td>2 8 0 00</td></tr>
<tr><td>Sales Tax Payable</td><td></td><td>3 2 6 00</td></tr>
<tr><td>J. M. Gimbel, Capital</td><td></td><td>89 1 4 8 00</td></tr>
<tr><td></td><td>112 6 3 4 00</td><td>112 6 3 4 00</td></tr>
</table>

Don't forget to update the capital account before preparing the post-closing trial balance.

J. M. Gimbel, Capital

(Drawing)	8,000.00	87,883.00	
		9,265.00	(Net income)
		89,148.00	

Exercise 15-6A

	DATE		DESCRIPTION	POST. REF.	DEBIT	CREDIT	
1			*Reversing Entry*				1
2	20-2 Jan.	1	Wages Payable		2 8 0 00		2
3			Wages Expense			2 8 0 00	3
4							4
5							5

Exercise 15-7A

DATE	WITHOUT REVERSING ENTRY	WITH REVERSING ENTRY
Adjusting Entry: 12/31/-1	Wages Expense 300 Wages Payable 300	Wages Expense 300 Wages Payable 300
Closing Entry: 12/31/-1	Income Summary 21,100 Wages Expense 21,100	Income Summary 21,100 Wages Expense 21,100
Reversing Entry: 1/1/-2	No entry	Wages Payable 300 Wages Expense 300
Payment of Payroll: 1/3/-2	Wages Expense 500 Wages Payable 300 Cash 800	Wages Expense 800 Cash 800

Wages Expense

Bal.	20,800		
12/31/-1 Adj.	300	12/31/-1 Clos.	21,100
1/3/-2	500		

Wages Expense

Bal.	20,800		
12/31/-1 Adj.	300	12/31/-1 Clos.	21,100
		1/1/-2 Rev.	300
1/3/-2	800		
Bal.	500		

Wages Payable

		12/31/-1 Adj.	300
1/3/-2	300		

Wages Payable

		12/31/-1 Adj.	300
1/1/-2 Rev.	300		

Problem 15-8A

1.

Paulson's Pet Store

Income Statement

For Year Ended December 31, 20--

Revenue from sales:					
Sales				$71 5 1 0 00	
Less sales ret. & allow.				1 3 4 0 00	
Net sales					$70 1 7 0 00
Cost of goods sold:					
Merch. inv., Jan. 1, 20--				$15 0 0 0 00	
Purchases		$40 6 6 0 00			
Less: Purch. ret. & allow.	$1 0 2 0 00				
Purch. discounts	8 0 0 00	1 8 2 0 00			
Net purchases		$38 8 4 0 00			
Add freight-in		4 0 0 00			
Cost of goods purchased				39 2 4 0 00	
Goods available for sale				$54 2 4 0 00	
Less merch. inv., Dec. 31, 20--				16 5 0 0 00	
Cost of goods sold					37 7 4 0 00
Gross profit					$32 4 3 0 00
Operating expenses:					
Wages expense				$22 6 0 0 00	
Advertising expense				3 0 0 00	
Supplies expense				2 0 0 00	
Telephone expense				6 8 4 00	
Utilities expense				7 1 6 00	
Insurance expense				1 5 0 00	
Depr. exp.—equipment				4 5 0 00	
Miscellaneous expense				1 5 0 00	
Total operating expenses					25 2 5 0 00
Income from operations					$ 7 1 8 0 00
Other expenses:					
Interest expense					8 0 00
Net income					$ 7 1 0 0 00

Problem 15-8A (Continued)

2.

Paulson's Pet Store

Statement of Owner's Equity

For Year Ended December 31, 20--

B. Paulson, capital, January 1, 20--							$21	9	0	0	00
Add additional investment								2	0	0	00
Total investment							$23	9	0	0	00
Net income for the year	$7	1	0	0	00						
Less withdrawals for the year	1	2	0	0	00						
Increase in capital								5	9	0	0	00
B. Paulson, capital, December 31, 20--							$29	8	0	0	00

Problem 15-8A (Concluded)

3.

Paulson's Pet Store

Balance Sheet

December 31, 20--

Assets																			
Current assets:																			
Cash						$15	8	6	0	00									
Accounts receivable						2	3	4	0	00									
Merchandise inventory						16	5	0	0	00									
Supplies							6	0	0	00									
Prepaid insurance							4	5	0	00									
Total current assets											$35	7	5	0	00				
Property, plant, and equipment:																			
Equipment						$ 5	0	0	0	00									
Less accumulated depreciation							9	0	0	00		4	1	0	0	00			
Total assets											$39	8	5	0	00				
Liabilities																			
Current liabilities:																			
Accounts payable	$4	8	9	0	00														
Wages payable		3	0	0	00														
Sales tax payable		8	6	0	00														
Mortgage payable (current portion)		5	0	0	00														
Total current liabilities						$ 6	5	5	0	00									
Long-term liabilities:																			
Mortgage payable	$4	0	0	0	00														
Less current portion		5	0	0	00	3	5	0	0	00									
Total liabilities											$10	0	5	0	00				
Owner's Equity																			
B. Paulson, capital											29	8	0	0	00				
Total liabilities and owner's equity											$39	8	5	0	00				

Problem 15-9A

a. *Working capital:*

Current Assets	$35,750
− Current Liabilities	6,550
	$29,200

b. *Current ratio:*

$$\frac{\text{Current Assets}}{\text{Current Liabilities}} = \frac{\$35,750}{\$6,550} = 5.46 \text{ to } 1$$

c. *Quick ratio:*

$$\frac{\text{Quick Assets}}{\text{Current Liabilities}} = \frac{\$18,200}{\$6,550} = 2.78 \text{ to } 1$$

d. *Return on owner's equity:*

$$\frac{\text{Net Income}}{\text{Average Owner's Equity}} = \frac{\$7,100}{\left[\dfrac{\$21,900 + \$29,800}{2}\right]} = \frac{\$7,100}{\$25,850} = 27.5\%$$

e. *Accounts receivable turnover:*

$$\frac{\text{Net Credit Sales}}{\text{Average Accounts Receivable}} = \frac{\$70,170}{\left[\dfrac{\$3,800 + \$2,340}{2}\right]} = \frac{\$70,170}{\$3,070} = 22.86$$

$$365 \div 22.86 = 15.97 \text{ days}$$

f. *Inventory turnover:*

$$\frac{\text{Cost of Goods Sold}}{\text{Average Inventory}} = \frac{\$37,740}{\left[\dfrac{\$15,000 + \$16,500}{2}\right]} = \frac{\$37,740}{\$15,750} = 2.40$$

$$365 \div 2.40 = 152.08 \text{ days}$$

Problem 15-10A

1.

Ellis Fabric

Work

For Year Ended

	ACCOUNT TITLE	TRIAL BALANCE DEBIT	TRIAL BALANCE CREDIT	ADJUSTMENTS DEBIT	ADJUSTMENTS CREDIT
1	Cash	28 0 0 0 00			
2	Accounts Receivable	14 2 0 0 00			
3	Merchandise Inventory	33 0 0 0 00		(b) 28 9 0 0 00	(a) 33 0 0 0 00
4	Supplies	1 6 0 0 00			(c) 2 5 0 00
5	Prepaid Insurance	9 0 0 00			(d) 3 0 0 00
6	Equipment	6 6 0 0 00			
7	Accumulated Depr.—Equipment		1 0 0 0 00		(e) 5 0 0 00
8	Accounts Payable		15 6 2 0 00		
9	Wages Payable				(f) 4 8 0 00
10	Sales Tax Payable		8 5 0 00		
11	Unearned Revenue		5 0 0 0 00	(g) 4 0 0 0 00	
12	W. P. Ellis, Capital		71 2 0 0 00		
13	W. P. Ellis, Drawing	21 6 1 0 00			
14	Income Summary			(a) 33 0 0 0 00	(b) 28 9 0 0 00
15	Sales		74 5 0 0 00		(g) 4 0 0 0 00
16	Sales Returns and Allowances	1 8 5 0 00			
17	Interest Revenue		1 2 0 0 00		
18	Purchases	41 5 0 0 00			
19	Purchases Returns and Allow.		1 8 0 0 00		
20	Purchases Discounts		8 3 0 00		
21	Freight-In	6 6 0 00			
22	Wages Expense	14 8 8 0 00		(f) 4 8 0 00	
23	Advertising Expense	8 1 0 00			
24	Supplies Expense			(c) 2 5 0 00	
25	Telephone Expense	1 2 1 0 00			
26	Utilities Expense	3 2 4 0 00			
27	Insurance Expense			(d) 3 0 0 00	
28	Depreciation Expense—Equip.			(e) 5 0 0 00	
29	Miscellaneous Expense	9 2 0 00			
30	Interest Expense	1 0 2 0 00			
31		172 0 0 0 00	172 0 0 0 00	67 4 3 0 00	67 4 3 0 00
32	**Net Income**				
33					

Problem 15-10A (Continued)
Store

Sheet

December 31, 20-1

#	ADJ. TRIAL BAL. DEBIT	ADJ. TRIAL BAL. CREDIT	INCOME STMT. DEBIT	INCOME STMT. CREDIT	BALANCE SHEET DEBIT	BALANCE SHEET CREDIT
1	28 0 0 0 00				28 0 0 0 00	
2	14 2 0 0 00				14 2 0 0 00	
3	28 9 0 0 00				28 9 0 0 00	
4	1 3 5 0 00				1 3 5 0 00	
5	6 0 0 00				6 0 0 00	
6	6 6 0 0 00				6 6 0 0 00	
7		1 5 0 0 00				1 5 0 0 00
8		15 6 2 0 00				15 6 2 0 00
9		4 8 0 00				4 8 0 00
10		8 5 0 00				8 5 0 00
11		1 0 0 0 00				1 0 0 0 00
12		71 2 0 0 00				71 2 0 0 00
13	21 6 1 0 00				21 6 1 0 00	
14	33 0 0 0 00	28 9 0 0 00	33 0 0 0 00	28 9 0 0 00		
15		78 5 0 0 00		78 5 0 0 00		
16	1 8 5 0 00		1 8 5 0 00			
17		1 2 0 0 00		1 2 0 0 00		
18	41 5 0 0 00		41 5 0 0 00			
19		1 8 0 0 00		1 8 0 0 00		
20		8 3 0 00		8 3 0 00		
21	6 6 0 00		6 6 0 00			
22	15 3 6 0 00		15 3 6 0 00			
23	8 1 0 00		8 1 0 00			
24	2 5 0 00		2 5 0 00			
25	1 2 1 0 00		1 2 1 0 00			
26	3 2 4 0 00		3 2 4 0 00			
27	3 0 0 00		3 0 0 00			
28	5 0 0 00		5 0 0 00			
29	9 2 0 00		9 2 0 00			
30	1 0 2 0 00		1 0 2 0 00			
31	201 8 8 0 00	201 8 8 0 00	100 6 2 0 00	111 2 3 0 00	101 2 6 0 00	90 6 5 0 00
32			10 6 1 0 00			10 6 1 0 00
33			111 2 3 0 00	111 2 3 0 00	101 2 6 0 00	101 2 6 0 00

Problem 15-10A (Continued)

2., 3., and 5.

GENERAL JOURNAL

	DATE		DESCRIPTION	POST. REF.	DEBIT	CREDIT	
1			*Adjusting Entries*				1
2	20-1 Dec.	31	**Income Summary**		33 0 0 0 00		2
3			Merchandise Inventory			33 0 0 0 00	3
4							4
5		31	**Merchandise Inventory**		28 9 0 0 00		5
6			**Income Summary**			28 9 0 0 00	6
7							7
8		31	**Supplies Expense**		2 5 0 00		8
9			**Supplies**			2 5 0 00	9
10							10
11		31	**Insurance Expense**		3 0 0 00		11
12			**Prepaid Insurance**			3 0 0 00	12
13							13
14		31	**Depreciation Expense—Equipment**		5 0 0 00		14
15			**Accumulated Depreciation—Equipment**			5 0 0 00	15
16							16
17		31	**Wages Expense**		4 8 0 00		17
18			**Wages Payable**			4 8 0 00	18
19							19
20		31	**Unearned Revenue**		4 0 0 00		20
21			**Sales**			4 0 0 00	21
22							22
23			*Closing Entries*				23
24		31	**Sales**		78 5 0 0 00		24
25			**Interest Revenue**		1 2 0 00		25
26			**Purchases Returns and Allowances**		1 8 0 00		26
27			**Purchases Discounts**		8 3 0 00		27
28			**Income Summary**			82 3 3 0 00	28
29							29
30							30
31							31

GENERAL JOURNAL   PAGE

	DATE		DESCRIPTION	POST. REF.	DEBIT	CREDIT	
1	20-1 Dec.	31	**Income Summary**		67 6 2 0 00		1
2			**Sales Returns and Allowances**			1 8 5 0 00	2
3			**Purchases**			41 5 0 0 00	3
4			**Freight-In**			6 6 0 00	4
5			**Wages Expense**			15 3 6 0 00	5
6			**Advertising Expense**			8 1 0 00	6
7			**Supplies Expense**			2 5 0 00	7
8			**Telephone Expense**			1 2 1 0 00	8
9			**Utilities Expense**			3 2 4 0 00	9
10			**Insurance Expense**			3 0 0 00	10
11			**Depreciation Expense—Equipment**			5 0 0 00	11
12			**Miscellaneous Expense**			9 2 0 00	12
13			**Interest Expense**			1 0 2 0 00	13
14							14
15		31	**Income Summary**		10 6 1 0 00		15
16			**W. P. Ellis, Capital**			10 6 1 0 00	16
17							17
18		31	**W. P. Ellis, Capital**		21 6 1 0 00		18
19			**W. P. Ellis, Drawing**			21 6 1 0 00	19
20							20
21			**Reversing Entries**				21
22	20-2 Jan.	1	**Wages Payable**		4 8 0 00		22
23			**Wages Expense**			4 8 0 00	23
24							24
25							25
26							26
27							27
28							28
29							29
30							30
31							31
32							32
33							33
34							34

Problem 15-10A (Concluded)

4.

Ellis Fabric Store

Post-Closing Trial Balance

December 31, 20-1

ACCOUNT	DEBIT BALANCE	CREDIT BALANCE
Cash	28 0 0 0 00	
Accounts Receivable	14 2 0 0 00	
Merchandise Inventory	28 9 0 0 00	
Supplies	1 3 5 0 00	
Prepaid Insurance	6 0 0 00	
Equipment	6 6 0 0 00	
Accumulated Depreciation—Equipment		1 5 0 0 00
Accounts Payable		15 6 2 0 00
Wages Payable		4 8 0 00
Sales Tax Payable		8 5 0 00
Unearned Revenue		1 0 0 00
W. P. Ellis, Capital		60 2 0 0 00
	79 6 5 0 00	79 6 5 0 00

Exercise 15-1B

Revenue from sales:																	
Sales									$86	2	0	0	00				
Less: Sales returns and allowances	$2	2	8	0	00												
Sales discounts	1	7	2	4	00		4	0	0	4	00					
Net sales													$82	1	9	6	00

Exercise 15-2B

Cost of goods sold:																	
Merch. inv., Jan. 1, 20--									$13	8	0	0	00				
Purchases						$71	3	0	0	00							
Less: Purch. ret. & allow.	$3	1	8	8	00											
Purch. discounts	1	4	6	0	00		4	6	4	8	00					
Net purchases						$66	6	5	2	00						
Add freight-in							3	9	0	00						
Cost of goods purchased									67	0	4	2	00				
Goods available for sale									$80	8	4	2	00				
Less mer. inv., Dec. 31, 20--									21	4	0	0	00				
Cost of goods sold													$59	4	4	2	00

Exercise 15-3B

Aeito's Plumbing Supplies
Income Statement
For Year Ended December 31, 20--

Revenue from sales:						
Sales				$166 0 0 0 00		
Less: Sales ret. & allow.		$ 1 6 2 0 00				
Sales discounts		3 3 2 0 00		4 9 4 0 00		
Net sales					$161 0 6 0 00	
Cost of goods sold:						
Merch. inv., Jan. 1, 20--				$ 33 2 0 0 00		
Purchases		$111 3 0 0 00				
Less: Purch. ret. & allow.	$3 6 0 0 00					
Purch. discounts	2 2 2 6 00	5 8 2 6 00				
Net purchases		$105 4 7 4 00				
Add freight-in		6 4 0 00				
Cost of goods purchased				106 1 1 4 00		
Goods available for sale				$139 3 1 4 00		
Less merch. inv., Dec. 31, 20--				29 6 0 0 00		
Cost of goods sold					109 7 1 4 00	
Gross profit					$ 51 3 4 6 00	
Operating expenses:						
Wages expense				$ 22 0 0 0 00		
Supplies expense				6 5 0 00		
Telephone expense				1 1 0 0 00		
Utilities expense				9 0 0 0 00		
Insurance expense				1 0 0 0 00		
Depr. exp.—building				4 6 0 0 00		
Depr. exp.—equipment				2 8 0 0 00		
Miscellaneous expense				2 1 4 00		
Total operating expenses					41 3 6 4 00	
Income from operations					$ 9 9 8 2 00	
Other revenues:						
Interest revenue				$ 3 1 8 4 00		
Other expenses:						
Interest expense				1 1 2 6 00	2 0 5 8 00	
Net income					$ 12 0 4 0 00	

Exercise 15-4B

1. Working capital:

Current Assets	$37,900
− Current Liabilities	10,300
	$27,600

2. Current ratio:

$$\frac{\text{Current Assets}}{\text{Current Liabilities}} = \frac{\$37,900}{\$10,300} = 3.68 \text{ to } 1$$

3. Quick ratio:

$$\frac{\text{Quick Assets}}{\text{Current Liabilities}} = \frac{\$19,300}{\$10,300} = 1.87 \text{ to } 1$$

4. Return on owner's equity:

$$\frac{\text{Net Income}}{\text{Average Owner's Equity}} = \frac{\$25,300}{\dfrac{\$52,000 + \$66,900}{2}} = \frac{\$25,300}{\$59,450} = 42.6\%$$

5. Accounts receivable turnover:

$$\frac{\text{Net Credit Sales}}{\text{Average Accounts Receivable}} = \frac{\$121,700}{\dfrac{\$6,800 + \$8,900}{2}} = \frac{\$121,700}{\$7,850} = 15.5$$

$$365 \div 15.5 = 23.5 \text{ days}$$

6. Inventory turnover:

$$\frac{\text{Cost of Goods Sold}}{\text{Average Inventory}} = \frac{\$61,600}{\dfrac{\$19,300 + \$16,700}{2}} = \frac{\$61,600}{\$18,000} = 3.42$$

$$365 \div 3.42 = 106.7 \text{ days}$$

© 2011 Cengage Learning. All Rights Reserved. May not be scanned, copied or duplicated, or posted to a publicly accessible website, in whole or in part.

Exercise 15-5B

1.

GENERAL JOURNAL   PAGE

	DATE		DESCRIPTION	POST. REF.	DEBIT	CREDIT	
1			*Closing Entries*				1
2	20-1 Dec.	31	Sales		31 0 0 0 00		2
3			Purchases Returns and Allowances		1 8 0 0 00		3
4			Purchases Discounts		4 0 7 00		4
5			Income Summary			33 2 0 7 00	5
6							6
7		31	Income Summary		26 7 8 7 00		7
8			Sales Returns and Allowances			8 0 0 00	8
9			Purchases			22 0 0 0 00	9
10			Freight-In			2 0 0 00	10
11			Wages Expense			1 4 0 0 00	11
12			Advertising Expense			3 0 0 00	12
13			Supplies Expense			2 8 0 00	13
14			Telephone Expense			7 0 0 00	14
15			Utilities Expense			4 8 0 00	15
16			Insurance Expense			1 2 0 00	16
17			Depreciation Expense—Equipment			3 0 0 00	17
18			Miscellaneous Expense			1 1 0 00	18
19			Interest Expense			9 7 00	19
20							20
21		31	Income Summary		5 3 2 0 00		21
22			L. Marlow, Capital			5 3 2 0 00	22
23							23
24		31	L. Marlow, Capital		2 0 0 0 00		24
25			L. Marlow, Drawing			2 0 0 0 00	25
26							26
27							27
28							28
29							29
30							30
31							31
32							32
33							33
34							34

Exercise 15-5B (Concluded)

2.

Balloons and Baubbles

Post-Closing Trial Balance

December 31, 20-1

	Debit	Credit
Cash	2 8 0 0 00	
Accounts Receivable	4 2 0 0 00	
Merchandise Inventory	7 5 0 0 00	
Supplies	5 0 0 00	
Prepaid Insurance	5 0 0 00	
Equipment	3 0 0 0 00	
Accum. Depr.—Equipment		9 0 0 00
Accounts Payable		1 8 0 0 00
Wages Payable		2 0 0 00
Sales Tax Payable		8 0 00
L. Marlow, Capital		15 5 2 0 00
	18 5 0 0 00	18 5 0 0 00

Don't forget to update the capital account before preparing the post-closing trial balance.

L. Marlow, Capital

	12,200.00	
(Drawing)	2,000.00 5,320.00	(Net income)
	15,520.00	

Exercise 15-6B

GENERAL JOURNAL   PAGE

	DATE	DESCRIPTION	POST. REF.	DEBIT	CREDIT	
1		*Reversing Entry*				1
2	20-2 Jan. 1	Wages Payable		2 0 0 00		2
3		Wages Expense			2 0 0 00	3
4						4
5						5

Exercise 15-7B

DATE	WITHOUT REVERSING ENTRY		WITH REVERSING ENTRY	
Adjusting Entry: 12/31/-1	*Wages Expense* 280 *Wages Payable*	280	*Wages Expense* 280 *Wages Payable*	280
Closing Entry: 12/31/-1	*Income Summary* 20,360 *Wages Expense*	20,360	*Income Summary* 20,360 *Wages Expense*	20,360
Reversing Entry: 1/1/-2	*No entry*		*Wages Payable* 280 *Wages Expense*	280
Payment of Payroll: 1/3/-2	*Wages Expense* 560 *Wages Payable* 280 *Cash*	840	*Wages Expense* 840 *Cash*	840

Wages Expense

Bal.	**20,080**			
12/31/-1 Adj.	**280**	**12/31/-1 Clos.**	**20,360**	
1/3/-2	**560**			

Wages Expense

Bal.	**20,080**			
12/31/-1 Adj.	**280**	**12/31/-1 Clos.**	**20,360**	
		1/1/-2 Rev.	**280**	
1/3/-2	**840**			
Bal.	**560**			

Wages Payable

		12/31/-1 Adj.	**280**
1/3/-2	**280**		

Wages Payable

		12/31/-1 Adj.	**280**
1/1/-2 Rev.	**280**		

Problem 15-8B

1.

Backlund Farm Supply

Income Statement

For Year Ended December 31, 20--

Revenue from sales:																										
Sales											$141	8	0	0	00											
Less sales ret. & allow.											1	3	1	0	00											
Net sales																$140	4	9	0	00						
Cost of goods sold:																										
Merch. inv., Jan. 1, 20--											$ 42	1	6	0	00											
Purchases					$81	3	0	0	00																	
Less: Purch. ret. & allow.	$2	9	0	0	00																					
Purch. discounts	1	5	1	0	00	4	4	1	0	00																
Net purchases					$76	8	9	0	00																	
Add freight-in						6	0	0	00																	
Cost of goods purchased											77	4	9	0	00											
Goods available for sale											$119	6	5	0	00											
Less merch. inv., Dec. 31, 20--											44	3	0	0	00											
Cost of goods sold																75	3	5	0	00						
Gross profit																$ 65	1	4	0	00						
Operating expenses:																										
Wages expense											$ 41	7	2	0	00											
Advertising expense												4	0	0	00											
Supplies expense												8	6	0	00											
Telephone expense												8	0	0	00											
Utilities expense											1	3	0	0	00											
Insurance expense												7	5	0	00											
Depr. exp.—equipment												9	0	0	00											
Miscellaneous expense												2	0	0	00											
Total operating expenses																46	9	3	0	00						
Income from operations																$ 18	2	1	0	00						
Other expenses:																										
Interest expense																1	0	8	0	00						
Net income																$ 17	1	3	0	00						

Problem 15-8B (Continued)

2.

Backlund Farm Supply				
Statement of Owner's Equity				
For Year Ended December 31, 20--				
J. Backlund, capital, January 1, 20--			$50 0 0 0 00	
Add additional investment			7 0 0 0 00	
Total investment			$57 0 0 0 00	
Net income for the year	$17 1 3 0 00			
Less withdrawals for the year	6 8 0 0 00			
Increase in capital			10 3 3 0 00	
J. Backlund, capital, December 31, 20--			$67 3 3 0 00	

Problem 15-8B (Concluded)

3.

Backlund Farm Supply

Balance Sheet

December 31, 20--

Assets																			
Current assets:																			
Cash						$10	1	8	0	00									
Accounts receivable						26	4	2	0	00									
Merchandise inventory						44	3	0	0	00									
Supplies						3	5	0	0	00									
Prepaid insurance						2	2	5	0	00									
Total current assets											$ 86	6	5	0	00				
Property, plant, and equipment:																			
Equipment						$38	0	0	0	00									
Less accumulated depreciation						6	9	0	0	00	31	1	0	0	00				
Total assets											$117	7	5	0	00				
Liabilities																			
Current liabilities:																			
Accounts payable	$41	2	0	0	00														
Wages payable		4	2	0	00														
Sales tax payable		8	0	0	00														
Mortgage payable (current portion)	1	0	0	0	00														
Total current liabilities						$43	4	2	0	00									
Long-term liabilities:																			
Mortgage payable	$ 8	0	0	0	00														
Less current portion	1	0	0	0	00	7	0	0	0	00									
Total liabilities											$ 50	4	2	0	00				
Owner's Equity																			
J. Backlund, capital											67	3	3	0	00				
Total liabilities and owner's equity											$117	7	5	0	00				

Problem 15-9B

a. *Working capital:*

Current Assets	$86,650
− Current Liabilities	43,420
	$43,230

b. *Current ratio:*

$$\frac{\text{Current Assets}}{\text{Current Liabilities}} = \frac{\$86,650}{\$43,420} = 2.0 \text{ to } 1$$

c. *Quick ratio:*

$$\frac{\text{Quick Assets}}{\text{Current Liabilities}} = \frac{\$36,600}{\$43,420} = 0.84 \text{ to } 1$$

d. *Return on owner's equity:*

$$\frac{\text{Net Income}}{\text{Average Owner's Equity}} = \frac{\$17,130}{\left[\dfrac{\$50,000 + \$67,330}{2}\right]} = \frac{\$17,130}{\$58,665} = 29.2\%$$

e. *Accounts receivable turnover:*

$$\frac{\text{Net Credit Sales}}{\text{Average Accounts Receivable}} = \frac{\$140,490}{\left[\dfrac{\$38,200 + \$26,420}{2}\right]} = \frac{\$140,490}{\$32,310} = 4.35$$

$$365 \div 4.35 = 83.91 \text{ days}$$

f. *Inventory turnover:*

$$\frac{\text{Cost of Goods Sold}}{\text{Average Inventory}} = \frac{\$75,350}{\left[\dfrac{\$42,160 + \$44,300}{2}\right]} = \frac{\$75,350}{\$43,230} = 1.74$$

$$365 \div 1.74 = 209.77 \text{ days}$$

This page left intentionally blank.

Problem 15-10B
1.

Darby Kite

Work

For Year Ended

	ACCOUNT TITLE	TRIAL BALANCE DEBIT	TRIAL BALANCE CREDIT	ADJUSTMENTS DEBIT	ADJUSTMENTS CREDIT
1	Cash	11 7 0 0 00			
2	Accounts Receivable	11 2 0 0 00			
3	Merchandise Inventory	25 0 0 0 00		(b) 23 6 0 0 00	(a) 25 0 0 0 00
4	Supplies	1 2 0 0 00			(c) 1 5 0 00
5	Prepaid Insurance	8 0 0 00			(d) 2 5 0 00
6	Equipment	5 4 0 0 00			
7	Accumulated Depr.—Equipment		8 0 0 00		(e) 4 0 0 00
8	Accounts Payable		7 1 0 0 00		
9	Wages Payable				(f) 3 6 0 00
10	Sales Tax Payable		2 5 0 00		
11	Unearned Revenue		3 0 0 0 00	(g) 2 5 0 0 00	
12	M. D. Akins, Capital		50 0 0 0 00		
13	M. D. Akins, Drawing	10 5 0 0 00			
14	Income Summary			(a) 25 0 0 0 00	(b) 23 6 0 0 00
15	Sales		55 4 9 0 00		(g) 2 5 0 0 00
16	Sales Returns and Allowances	1 4 5 0 00			
17	Purchases	34 5 0 0 00			
18	Purchases Returns and Allow.		1 1 0 0 00		
19	Purchases Discounts		6 3 0 00		
20	Freight-In	3 6 0 00			
21	Wages Expense	10 8 8 0 00		(f) 3 6 0 00	
22	Advertising Expense	7 4 0 00			
23	Supplies Expense			(c) 1 5 0 00	
24	Telephone Expense	1 1 0 0 00			
25	Utilities Expense	2 3 0 0 00			
26	Insurance Expense			(d) 2 5 0 00	
27	Depreciation Expense—Equip.			(e) 4 0 0 00	
28	Miscellaneous Expense	3 2 0 00			
29	Interest Expense	9 2 0 00			
30		118 3 7 0 00	118 3 7 0 00	52 2 6 0 00	52 2 6 0 00
31	**Net Income**				
32					

Problem 15-10B (Continued)

Store _____

Sheet _____

December 31, 20-1 _____

	ADJUSTED TRIAL BALANCE		INCOME STATEMENT		BALANCE SHEET		
	DEBIT	CREDIT	DEBIT	CREDIT	DEBIT	CREDIT	
	11 7 0 0 00				11 7 0 0 00		1
	11 2 0 0 00				11 2 0 0 00		2
	23 6 0 0 00				23 6 0 0 00		3
	1 0 5 0 00				1 0 5 0 00		4
	5 5 0 00				5 5 0 00		5
	5 4 0 0 00				5 4 0 0 00		6
		1 2 0 0 00				1 2 0 0 00	7
		7 1 0 0 00				7 1 0 0 00	8
		3 6 0 00				3 6 0 00	9
		2 5 0 00				2 5 0 00	10
		5 0 0 00				5 0 0 00	11
		50 0 0 0 00				50 0 0 0 00	12
	10 5 0 0 00				10 5 0 0 00		13
	25 0 0 0 00	23 6 0 0 00	25 0 0 0 00	23 6 0 0 00			14
		57 9 9 0 00		57 9 9 0 00			15
	1 4 5 0 00		1 4 5 0 00				16
	34 5 0 0 00		34 5 0 0 00				17
		1 1 0 0 00		1 1 0 0 00			18
		6 3 0 00		6 3 0 00			19
	3 6 0 00		3 6 0 00				20
	11 2 4 0 00		11 2 4 0 00				21
	7 4 0 00		7 4 0 00				22
	1 5 0 00		1 5 0 00				23
	1 1 0 0 00		1 1 0 0 00				24
	2 3 0 0 00		2 3 0 0 00				25
	2 5 0 00		2 5 0 00				26
	4 0 0 00		4 0 0 00				27
	3 2 0 00		3 2 0 00				28
	9 2 0 00		9 2 0 00				29
	142 7 3 0 00	142 7 3 0 00	78 7 3 0 00	83 3 2 0 00	64 0 0 0 00	59 4 1 0 00	30
			4 5 9 0 00			4 5 9 0 00	31
			83 3 2 0 00	83 3 2 0 00	64 0 0 0 00	64 0 0 0 00	32

Problem 15-10B (Continued)
2., 3., and 5.

GENERAL JOURNAL

PAGE

	DATE		DESCRIPTION	POST. REF.	DEBIT	CREDIT	
1			*Adjusting Entries*				1
2	20-1 Dec.	31	Income Summary		25 0 0 0 00		2
3			Merchandise Inventory			25 0 0 0 00	3
4							4
5		31	Merchandise Inventory		23 6 0 0 00		5
6			Income Summary			23 6 0 0 00	6
7							7
8		31	Supplies Expense		1 5 0 00		8
9			Supplies			1 5 0 00	9
10							10
11		31	Insurance Expense		2 5 0 00		11
12			Prepaid Insurance			2 5 0 00	12
13							13
14		31	Depreciation Expense—Equipment		4 0 0 00		14
15			Accumulated Depreciation—Equipment			4 0 0 00	15
16							16
17		31	Wages Expense		3 6 0 00		17
18			Wages Payable			3 6 0 00	18
19							19
20		31	Unearned Revenue		2 5 0 0 00		20
21			Sales			2 5 0 0 00	21
22							22
23			*Closing Entries*				23
24		31	Sales		57 9 9 0 00		24
25			Purchases Returns and Allowances		1 1 0 0 00		25
26			Purchases Discounts		6 3 0 00		26
27			Income Summary			59 7 2 0 00	27
28							28
29							29
30							30
31							31
32							32
33							33
34							34

GENERAL JOURNAL   PAGE

	DATE		DESCRIPTION	POST. REF.	DEBIT	CREDIT	
1	20-1 Dec.	31	Income Summary		53 7 3 0 00		1
2			Sales Returns and Allowances			1 4 5 0 00	2
3			Purchases			34 5 0 0 00	3
4			Freight-In			3 6 0 00	4
5			Wages Expense			11 2 4 0 00	5
6			Advertising Expense			7 4 0 00	6
7			Supplies Expense			1 5 0 00	7
8			Telephone Expense			1 1 0 0 00	8
9			Utilities Expense			2 3 0 0 00	9
10			Insurance Expense			2 5 0 00	10
11			Depreciation Expense—Equipment			4 0 0 00	11
12			Miscellaneous Expense			3 2 0 00	12
13			Interest Expense			9 2 0 00	13
14							14
15		31	Income Summary		4 5 9 0 00		15
16			M. D. Akins, Capital			4 5 9 0 00	16
17							17
18		31	M. D. Akins, Capital		10 5 0 0 00		18
19			M. D. Akins, Drawing			10 5 0 0 00	19
20							20
21			Reversing Entries				21
22	20-2 Jan.	1	Wages Payable		3 6 0 00		22
23			Wages Expense			3 6 0 00	23
24							24
25							25
26							26
27							27
28							28
29							29
30							30
31							31
32							32
33							33
34							34

Problem 15-10B (Concluded)

4.

Darby Kite Store
Post-Closing Trial Balance
December 31, 20-1

ACCOUNT	DEBIT BALANCE	CREDIT BALANCE
Cash	11 7 0 0 00	
Accounts Receivable	11 2 0 0 00	
Merchandise Inventory	23 6 0 0 00	
Supplies	1 0 5 0 00	
Prepaid Insurance	5 5 0 00	
Equipment	5 4 0 0 00	
Accumulated Depreciation—Equipment		1 2 0 0 00
Accounts Payable		7 1 0 0 00
Wages Payable		3 6 0 00
Sales Tax Payable		2 5 0 00
Unearned Revenue		5 0 0 00
M. D. Akins, Capital		44 0 9 0 00
	53 5 0 0 00	53 5 0 0 00

MANAGING YOUR WRITING

The student's response should include a discussion of the following ratios:

a. Working capital
b. Current ratio
c. Quick ratio
d. Return on owner's equity
e. Accounts receivable turnover and average collection period
f. Inventory turnover and average days to sell inventory

ETHICS CASE

1. Brian should inform Louise that he cannot be a part of preparing financial statements he knows to be fraudulent.

2. If Brian approaches Louise with the problem, Louise might blame Martha for telling Brian that personal expenses were charged to the business. Martha knowingly made journal entries she knew would have an impact of misrepresenting Louise Michener Consulting's books.

3. Answers will vary. Students should emphasize that personal expenses are separate from business transactions. Some students might recognize that tax forms prepared from incorrect financial statements might constitute fraud.

4. Discussions will vary. The teacher can play an active role in this discussion by talking about the wide range of situations where clients unknowingly provide accountants with incorrect or incomplete information and where clients knowingly provide the accountant with incorrect or incomplete information. The conclusion should be that an accountant should not be part of any situation where he or she knows the information on the financial statements is incorrect.

Mastery Problem
1.

Dominique's Doll House

Income Statement

For Year Ended December 31, 20-3

Revenue from sales:			
Sales		$130 5 0 0 00	
Less sales returns and allowances		9 0 0 00	
Net sales			$129 6 0 0 00
Cost of goods sold:			
Merchandise inventory, Jan. 1, 20-3		$ 22 3 0 0 00	
Purchases	$72 0 0 0 00		
Less purchases discounts	7 5 0 00		
Net purchases	$71 2 5 0 00		
Add freight-in	1 2 0 0 00		
Cost of goods purchased		72 4 5 0 00	
Goods available for sale		$ 94 7 5 0 00	
Less merch. inventory, Dec. 31, 20-3		24 6 0 0 00	
Cost of goods sold			70 1 5 0 00
Gross profit			$ 59 4 5 0 00
Operating expenses:			
Wages expense		$ 42 2 0 0 00	
Rent expense		6 0 0 0 00	
Office supplies expense		6 0 0 00	
Telephone expense		1 5 0 0 00	
Utilities expense		7 6 0 0 00	
Insurance expense		4 0 0 00	
Depreciation expense—store equipment		5 0 0 0 00	
Total operating expenses			63 3 0 0 00
Income (loss) from operations			$ (3 8 5 0 00)
Other revenues:			
Rent revenue		$ 25 7 0 0 00	
Other expenses:			
Interest expense		5 0 0 00	25 2 0 0 00
Net income			$ 21 3 5 0 00

Mastery Problem (Continued)

2.

Dominique's Doll House

Statement of Owner's Equity

For Year Ended December 31, 20-3

Dominique Fouque, capital, January 1, 20-3			$75 800 00
Net income for the year	$21 350 00		
Less withdrawals for the year	21 000 00		
Increase in capital			350 00
Dominique Fouque, capital, December 31, 20-3			$76 150 00

Mastery Problem (Continued)
3.

Dominique's Doll House

Balance Sheet

December 31, 20-3

Assets			
Current assets:			
Cash	$ 5 2 0 0 00		
Accounts receivable	3 2 0 0 00		
Merchandise inventory	24 6 0 0 00		
Office supplies	2 0 0 00		
Prepaid insurance	8 0 0 00		
Total current assets		$34 0 0 0 00	
Property, plant, and equipment:			
Store equipment	$85 0 0 0 00		
Less accumulated depreciation	20 0 0 0 00	65 0 0 0 00	
Total assets		$99 0 0 0 00	
Liabilities			
Current liabilities:			
Notes payable	$ 6 0 0 0 00		
Accounts payable	5 5 0 0 00		
Wages payable	2 0 0 00		
Sales tax payable	8 5 0 00		
Unearned rent revenue	3 0 0 00		
Total current liabilities		$12 8 5 0 00	
Long-term liabilities:			
Long-term note payable		10 0 0 0 00	
Total liabilities		$22 8 5 0 00	
Owner's Equity			
Dominique Fouque, capital		76 1 5 0 00	
Total liabilities and owner's equity		$99 0 0 0 00	

Mastery Problem (Continued)

4.

a. *Current ratio:*

Current Assets	=	$34,000	=	2.65 to 1
Current Liabilities		$12,850		

b. *Quick ratio:*

Quick Assets	=	$8,400	=	0.65 to 1
Current Liabilities		$12,850		

c. *Working capital:*

Current assets	$34,000
− Current liabilities	12,850
	$21,150

d. *Return on owner's equity:*

Net Income	=	$21,350	=	$21,350	=	28.1%
Average Owner's Equity		$\dfrac{\$75,800 + \$76,150}{2}$		$75,975		

e. *Accounts receivable turnover:*

Net Credit Sales for the Year	=	$35,300	=	$35,300	=	12.39
Average Accounts Receivable		$\dfrac{\$2,500 + \$3,200}{2}$		$2,850		

Average number of days to collect an account receivable:

365 ÷ 12.39 = 29.46 days

f. *Inventory turnover:*

Cost of Goods Sold	=	$70,150	=	$70,150	=	2.99
Average Inventory		$\dfrac{\$22,300 + \$24,600}{2}$		$23,450		

Average number of days to sell inventory:

365 ÷ 2.99 = 122.07 days

Mastery Problem (Continued)

5.

GENERAL JOURNAL

	DATE		DESCRIPTION	POST. REF.	DEBIT	CREDIT	
1	20-3 Dec.		*Adjusting Entries*				1
2	*a.*	31	Income Summary		22 3 0 0 00		2
3			Merchandise Inventory			22 3 0 0 00	3
4							4
5	*b.*	31	Merchandise Inventory		24 6 0 0 00		5
6			Income Summary			24 6 0 0 00	6
7							7
8	*c.*	31	Office Supplies Expense		6 0 0 00		8
9			Office Supplies			6 0 0 00	9
10							10
11	*d.*	31	Insurance Expense		4 0 0 00		11
12			Prepaid Insurance			4 0 0 00	12
13							13
14	*e.*	31	Depreciation Expense—Store Equipment		5 0 0 0 00		14
15			Accumulated Depreciation—Store Equipment			5 0 0 0 00	15
16							16
17	*f.*	31	Unearned Rent Revenue		7 0 0 00		17
18			Rent Revenue			7 0 0 00	18
19							19
20	*g.*	31	Wages Expense		2 0 0 00		20
21			Wages Payable			2 0 0 00	21
22							22

Should the adjustment be reversed?

a.	**Never reverse adjustments for merchandise inventory.**
b.	**Never reverse adjustments for merchandise inventory.**
c.	**No. No asset or liability with a zero balance has been increased.**
d.	**No. No asset or liability with a zero balance has been increased.**
e.	**Never reverse adjustments for depreciation.**
f.	**No. No asset or liability with a zero balance has been increased.**
g.	**Yes. A liability with a zero balance has been increased.**

Mastery Problem (Concluded)
6. and 7.

GENERAL JOURNAL　　　　　　　　　　　　PAGE 4

	DATE		DESCRIPTION	POST. REF.	DEBIT	CREDIT	
1			*Closing Entries*				1
2	20-3 Dec.	31	Sales		130 500 00		2
3			Rent Revenue		25 700 00		3
4			Purchases Discounts		750 00		4
5			Income Summary			156 950 00	5
6							6
7		31	Income Summary		137 900 00		7
8			Sales Returns and Allowances			900 00	8
9			Purchases			72 000 00	9
10			Freight-In			1 200 00	10
11			Wages Expense			42 200 00	11
12			Rent Expense			6 000 00	12
13			Office Supplies Expense			600 00	13
14			Telephone Expense			1 500 00	14
15			Utilities Expense			7 600 00	15
16			Insurance Expense			400 00	16
17			Depreciation Expense—Store Equipment			5 000 00	17
18			Interest Expense			500 00	18
19							19
20		31	Income Summary		21 350 00		20
21			Dominique Fouque, Capital			21 350 00	21
22							22
23		31	Dominique Fouque, Capital		21 000 00		23
24			Dominique Fouque, Drawing			21 000 00	24
25							25
26			*Reversing Entry*				26
27	20-4 Jan.	1	Wages Payable		200 00		27
28			Wages Expense			200 00	28
29							29
30							30
31							31
32							32
33							33
34							34
35							35

Challenge Problem

To compute the average number of days to convert inventory to cash, the average days to sell inventory and the average collection period for accounts receivable must be computed.

Average Inventory = $\dfrac{\text{Beginning Inventory + Ending Inventory}}{2}$ = $\dfrac{\$100 + \$300}{2}$ = $200

Inventory Turnover = $\dfrac{\text{Cost of Goods Sold for the Period}}{\text{Average Inventory}}$ = $\dfrac{\$5,000}{\$200}$ = 25

Average days to sell inventory = 365 days ÷ 25 = 14.6 days

Average Accounts Receivable = $\dfrac{\text{Beginning Balance + Ending Balance}}{2}$ = $\dfrac{\$500 + \$700}{2}$ = $600

Accounts Receivable Turnover = $\dfrac{\text{Net Credit Sales for the Period}}{\text{Average Accounts Receivable}}$ = $\dfrac{\$7,200}{\$600}$ = 12

Average collection period = 365 days ÷ 12 = 30.4 days

Average days to sell inventory	*14.6 days*
Average days to collect receivables	*30.4 days*
Average days to convert inventory to cash	*45.0 days*

Comprehensive Problem 2—General Journal Based, Part 1
Requirements 2. and 3.

GENERAL JOURNAL

PAGE 3

	DATE		DESCRIPTION	POST. REF.	DEBIT	CREDIT	
1	20-1 Dec.	16	Cash	101	1 9 6 0 00		1
2			Accounts Receivable/Lucy Greene	122		1 9 6 0 00	2
3			Received cash on account				3
4							4
5		16	Accounts Receivable/Kim Fields	122	1 6 8 00		5
6			Sales	401		1 6 0 00	6
7			Sales Tax Payable	231		8 00	7
8			Sale No. 640				8
9							9
10		17	Accounts Payable/Evans Essentials	202	1 5 0 00		10
11			Purchases Returns and Allowances	501.1		1 5 0 00	11
12			Returned goods purchased				12
13							13
14		18	Accounts Payable/Evans Essentials	202	1 1 0 0 00		14
15			Cash	101		1 1 0 0 00	15
16			Check No. 813				16
17							17
18		19	Accounts Receivable/Lucy Greene	122	6 5 1 00		18
19			Sales	401		6 2 0 00	19
20			Sales Tax Payable	231		3 1 00	20
21			Sale No. 641				21
22							22
23		22	Cash	101	1 5 6 0 00		23
24			Accounts Receivable/John Dempsey	122		1 5 6 0 00	24
25			Received cash on account				25
26							26
27		23	Supplies	141	1 2 0 00		27
28			Cash	101		1 2 0 00	28
29			Check No. 814				29
30							30
31		24	Purchases	501	1 2 0 0 00		31
32			Accounts Payable/West Wholesalers	202		1 2 0 0 00	32
33			Invoice No. 465				33
34							34
35		26	Purchases	501	8 0 0 00		35
36			Accounts Payable/Nathen Co.	202		8 0 0 00	36
37			Invoice No. 817				37
38							38
39		27	Utilities Expense	533	6 3 0 00		39
40			Cash	101		6 3 0 00	40
41			Check No. 815				41

Comprehensive Problem 2—General Journal Based, Part 1 (Requirements 2. and 3. Continued)

GENERAL JOURNAL

PAGE 4

	DATE		DESCRIPTION	POST. REF.	DEBIT	CREDIT	
1	20-1 Dec.	27	Accounts Receivable/John Dempsey	122	2 1 2 1 00		1
2			Sales	401		2 0 2 0 00	2
3			Sales Tax Payable	231		1 0 1 00	3
4			Sale No. 642				4
5							5
6		29	Cash	101	2 4 7 3 00		6
7			Accounts Receivable/Martha Boyle	122		2 4 7 3 00	7
8			Received cash on account				8
9							9
10		29	Wages Expense	511	1 1 0 0 00		10
11			Cash	101		1 1 0 0 00	11
12			Check No. 816				12
13							13
14		30	Purchases	501	2 0 0 00		14
15			Cash	101		2 0 0 00	15
16			Check No. 817				16
17							17

Requirements 1., 2., 3., 6., 7., and 9.

GENERAL LEDGER

ACCOUNT Cash

ACCOUNT NO. 101

DATE		ITEM	POST. REF.	DEBIT	CREDIT	BALANCE DEBIT	BALANCE CREDIT
20-1 Dec.	16	Balance	✓			9 7 0 5 00	
	16		J3	1 9 6 0 00		11 6 6 5 00	
	18		J3		1 1 0 0 00	10 5 6 5 00	
	22		J3	1 5 6 0 00		12 1 2 5 00	
	23		J3		1 2 0 00	12 0 0 5 00	
	27		J3		6 3 0 00	11 3 7 5 00	
	29		J4	2 4 7 3 00		13 8 4 8 00	
	29		J4		1 1 0 0 00	12 7 4 8 00	
	30		J4		2 0 0 00	12 5 4 8 00	

Comprehensive Problem 2—General Journal Based, Part 1 (Requirements 1., 2., 3., 6., 7., and 9. Continued)

ACCOUNT Accounts Receivable   ACCOUNT NO. 122

DATE		ITEM	POST. REF.	DEBIT	CREDIT	BALANCE DEBIT	BALANCE CREDIT
20-1 Dec.	16	Balance	✓			10 2 5 6 00	
	16		J3		1 9 6 0 00	8 2 9 6 00	
	16		J3	1 6 8 00		8 4 6 4 00	
	19		J3	6 5 1 00		9 1 1 5 00	
	22		J3		1 5 6 0 00	7 5 5 5 00	
	27		J4	2 1 2 1 00		9 6 7 6 00	
	29		J4		2 4 7 3 00	7 2 0 3 00	

ACCOUNT Merchandise Inventory   ACCOUNT NO. 131

DATE		ITEM	POST. REF.	DEBIT	CREDIT	BALANCE DEBIT	BALANCE CREDIT
20-1 Dec.	16	Balance	✓			21 8 0 0 00	
	31	Adjusting	J5		21 8 0 0 00	—	—
	31	Adjusting	J5	19 7 0 0 00		19 7 0 0 00	

ACCOUNT Supplies   ACCOUNT NO. 141

DATE		ITEM	POST. REF.	DEBIT	CREDIT	BALANCE DEBIT	BALANCE CREDIT
20-1 Dec.	16	Balance	✓			1 0 3 5 00	
	23		J3	1 2 0 00		1 1 5 5 00	
	31	Adjusting	J5		6 3 0 00	5 2 5 00	

ACCOUNT Prepaid Insurance   ACCOUNT NO. 145

DATE		ITEM	POST. REF.	DEBIT	CREDIT	BALANCE DEBIT	BALANCE CREDIT
20-1 Dec.	16	Balance	✓			1 3 8 0 00	
	31	Adjusting	J5		3 8 0 00	1 0 0 0 00	

Comprehensive Problem 2—General Journal Based, Part 1 (Requirements 1., 2., 3., 6., 7., and 9. Continued)

ACCOUNT   Land   ACCOUNT NO.   161

DATE		ITEM	POST. REF.	DEBIT	CREDIT	BALANCE DEBIT	BALANCE CREDIT
20-1 Dec.	16	Balance	✓			8 7 0 0 00	

ACCOUNT   Building   ACCOUNT NO.   171

DATE		ITEM	POST. REF.	DEBIT	CREDIT	BALANCE DEBIT	BALANCE CREDIT
20-1 Dec.	16	Balance	✓			52 0 0 0 00	

ACCOUNT   Accumulated Depreciation—Building   ACCOUNT NO.   171.1

DATE		ITEM	POST. REF.	DEBIT	CREDIT	BALANCE DEBIT	BALANCE CREDIT
20-1 Dec.	16	Balance	✓				9 2 0 0 00
	31	*Adjusting*	*J5*		8 0 0 00		10 0 0 0 00

ACCOUNT   Store Equipment   ACCOUNT NO.   181

DATE		ITEM	POST. REF.	DEBIT	CREDIT	BALANCE DEBIT	BALANCE CREDIT
20-1 Dec.	16	Balance	✓			28 7 5 0 00	

Comprehensive Problem 2—General Journal Based, Part 1
(Requirements 1., 2., 3., 6., 7., and 9. Continued)

ACCOUNT Accumulated Depreciation—Store Equipment   ACCOUNT NO. 181.1

DATE		ITEM	POST. REF.	DEBIT	CREDIT	BALANCE DEBIT	BALANCE CREDIT
20-1 Dec.	16	Balance	✓				9 3 0 0 00
	31	Adjusting	J5		4 5 0 00		9 7 5 0 00

ACCOUNT Accounts Payable   ACCOUNT NO. 202

DATE		ITEM	POST. REF.	DEBIT	CREDIT	BALANCE DEBIT	BALANCE CREDIT
20-1 Dec.	16	Balance	✓				3 6 0 0 00
	17		J3	1 5 0 00			3 4 5 0 00
	18		J3	1 1 0 0 00			2 3 5 0 00
	24		J3		1 2 0 0 00		3 5 5 0 00
	26		J3		8 0 0 00		4 3 5 0 00

ACCOUNT Wages Payable   ACCOUNT NO. 219

DATE		ITEM	POST. REF.	DEBIT	CREDIT	BALANCE DEBIT	BALANCE CREDIT
20-1 Dec.	31	Adjusting	J5		3 3 0 00		3 3 0 00
20-2 Jan.	1	Reversing	J6	3 3 0 00			

Comprehensive Problem 2—General Journal Based, Part 1
(Requirements 1., 2., 3., 6., 7., and 9. Continued)

ACCOUNT   Sales Tax Payable   ACCOUNT NO.   231

DATE		ITEM	POST. REF.	DEBIT	CREDIT	BALANCE DEBIT	BALANCE CREDIT
20-1 Dec.	16	Balance	✓				1 3 7 8 00
	16		J3		8 00		1 3 8 6 00
	19		J3		3 1 00		1 4 1 7 00
	27		J4	1 0 1 00			1 5 1 8 00

ACCOUNT   Mortgage Payable   ACCOUNT NO.   251

DATE		ITEM	POST. REF.	DEBIT	CREDIT	BALANCE DEBIT	BALANCE CREDIT
20-1 Dec.	16	Balance	✓				12 5 2 5 00

ACCOUNT   Tom Jones, Capital   ACCOUNT NO.   311

DATE		ITEM	POST. REF.	DEBIT	CREDIT	BALANCE DEBIT	BALANCE CREDIT
20-1 Dec.	16	Balance	✓				90 0 0 0 00
	31	Closing	J6		10 4 5 3 00		100 4 5 3 00
	31	Closing	J6	8 5 0 0 00			91 9 5 3 00

ACCOUNT   Tom Jones, Drawing   ACCOUNT NO.   312

DATE		ITEM	POST. REF.	DEBIT	CREDIT	BALANCE DEBIT	BALANCE CREDIT
20-1 Dec.	16	Balance	✓			8 5 0 0 00	
	31	Closing	J6		8 5 0 0 00		

Comprehensive Problem 2—General Journal Based, Part 1 (Requirements 1., 2., 3., 6., 7., and 9. Continued)

ACCOUNT Income Summary   ACCOUNT NO. 313

DATE		ITEM	POST. REF.	DEBIT	CREDIT	BALANCE DEBIT	BALANCE CREDIT
20-1 Dec.	31	Adjusting	J5	21 8 0 0 00		21 8 0 0 00	
	31	Adjusting	J5		19 7 0 0 00	2 1 0 0 00	
	31	Closing	J6		129 0 0 8 00		126 9 0 8 00
	31	Closing	J6	116 4 5 5 00			10 4 5 3 00
	31	Closing	J6	10 4 5 3 00			

ACCOUNT Sales   ACCOUNT NO. 401

DATE		ITEM	POST. REF.	DEBIT	CREDIT	BALANCE DEBIT	BALANCE CREDIT
20-1 Dec.	16	Balance	✓				124 9 0 0 00
	16		J3		1 6 0 00		125 0 6 0 00
	19		J3		6 2 0 00		125 6 8 0 00
	27		J4		2 0 2 0 00		127 7 0 0 00
	31	Closing	J6	127 7 0 0 00			

ACCOUNT Sales Returns and Allowances   ACCOUNT NO. 401.1

DATE		ITEM	POST. REF.	DEBIT	CREDIT	BALANCE DEBIT	BALANCE CREDIT
20-1 Dec.	16	Balance	✓			1 4 3 0 00	
	31	Closing	J6		1 4 3 0 00		

Comprehensive Problem 2—General Journal Based, Part 1 (Requirements 1., 2., 3., 6., 7., and 9. Continued)

ACCOUNT Purchases   ACCOUNT NO. 501

DATE		ITEM	POST. REF.	DEBIT	CREDIT	BALANCE DEBIT	BALANCE CREDIT
20-1 Dec.	16	Balance	✓			64 4 0 0 00	
	24		J3	1 2 0 0 00		65 6 0 0 00	
	26		J3	8 0 0 00		66 4 0 0 00	
	30		J4	2 0 0 00		66 6 0 0 00	
	31	Closing	J6		66 6 0 0 00		

ACCOUNT Purchases Returns and Allowances   ACCOUNT NO. 501.1

DATE		ITEM	POST. REF.	DEBIT	CREDIT	BALANCE DEBIT	BALANCE CREDIT
20-1 Dec.	16	Balance	✓				4 6 0 00
	17		J3		1 5 0 00		6 1 0 00
	31	Closing	J6	6 1 0 00			

ACCOUNT Purchases Discounts   ACCOUNT NO. 501.2

DATE		ITEM	POST. REF.	DEBIT	CREDIT	BALANCE DEBIT	BALANCE CREDIT
20-1 Dec.	16	Balance	✓				6 9 8 00
	31	Closing	J6	6 9 8 00			

ACCOUNT Freight-In   ACCOUNT NO. 502

DATE		ITEM	POST. REF.	DEBIT	CREDIT	BALANCE DEBIT	BALANCE CREDIT
20-1 Dec.	16	Balance	✓			1 7 5 00	
	31	Closing	J6		1 7 5 00		

Comprehensive Problem 2—General Journal Based, Part 1
(Requirements 1., 2., 3., 6., 7., and 9. Continued)

ACCOUNT   Wages Expense   ACCOUNT NO.   511

DATE		ITEM	POST. REF.	DEBIT	CREDIT	BALANCE DEBIT	BALANCE CREDIT
20-1 Dec.	16	Balance	✓			26 1 0 0 00	
	29		J4	1 1 0 0 00		27 2 0 0 00	
	31	Adjusting	J5	3 3 0 00		27 5 3 0 00	
	31	Closing	J6		27 5 3 0 00		
20-2 Jan.	1	Reversing	J6		3 3 0 00		3 3 0 00

ACCOUNT   Advertising Expense   ACCOUNT NO.   512

DATE		ITEM	POST. REF.	DEBIT	CREDIT	BALANCE DEBIT	BALANCE CREDIT
20-1 Dec.	16	Balance	✓			4 7 0 0 00	
	31	Closing	J6		4 7 0 0 00		

ACCOUNT   Supplies Expense   ACCOUNT NO.   524

DATE		ITEM	POST. REF.	DEBIT	CREDIT	BALANCE DEBIT	BALANCE CREDIT
20-1 Dec.	31	Adjusting	J5	6 3 0 00		6 3 0 00	
	31	Closing	J6		6 3 0 00		

ACCOUNT   Telephone Expense   ACCOUNT NO.   525

DATE		ITEM	POST. REF.	DEBIT	CREDIT	BALANCE DEBIT	BALANCE CREDIT
20-1 Dec.	16	Balance	✓			2 1 8 0 00	
	31	Closing	J6		2 1 8 0 00		

Comprehensive Problem 2—General Journal Based, Part 1
(Requirements 1., 2., 3., 6., 7., and 9. Continued)

ACCOUNT Utilities Expense   ACCOUNT NO. 533

DATE		ITEM	POST. REF.	DEBIT	CREDIT	BALANCE DEBIT	BALANCE CREDIT
20-1 Dec.	16	Balance	✓			6 9 0 0 00	
	27		J4	6 3 0 00		7 5 3 0 00	
	31	Closing	J6		7 5 3 0 00		

ACCOUNT Insurance Expense   ACCOUNT NO. 535

DATE		ITEM	POST. REF.	DEBIT	CREDIT	BALANCE DEBIT	BALANCE CREDIT
20-1 Dec.	31	Adjusting	J5	3 8 0 00		3 8 0 00	
	31	Closing	J6		3 8 0 00		

ACCOUNT Depreciation Expense—Building   ACCOUNT NO. 540

DATE		ITEM	POST. REF.	DEBIT	CREDIT	BALANCE DEBIT	BALANCE CREDIT
20-1 Dec.	31	Adjusting	J5	8 0 0 00		8 0 0 00	
	31	Closing	J6		8 0 0 00		

ACCOUNT Depreciation Expense—Store Equipment   ACCOUNT NO. 541

DATE		ITEM	POST. REF.	DEBIT	CREDIT	BALANCE DEBIT	BALANCE CREDIT
20-1 Dec.	31	Adjusting	J5	4 5 0 00		4 5 0 00	
	31	Closing	J6		4 5 0 00		

Comprehensive Problem 2—General Journal Based, Part 1 (Requirements 1., 2., 3., 6., 7., and 9. Continued)

ACCOUNT Miscellaneous Expense   ACCOUNT NO. 549

DATE		ITEM	POST. REF.	DEBIT	CREDIT	BALANCE DEBIT	BALANCE CREDIT
20-1 Dec.	16	Balance	✓			2 7 0 0 00	
	31	Closing	J6		2 7 0 0 00		

ACCOUNT Interest Expense   ACCOUNT NO. 551

DATE		ITEM	POST. REF.	DEBIT	CREDIT	BALANCE DEBIT	BALANCE CREDIT
20-1 Dec.	16	Balance	✓			1 3 5 0 00	
	31	Closing	J6		1 3 5 0 00		

ACCOUNTS RECEIVABLE LEDGER

NAME Martha Boyle
ADDRESS 12 Jude Lane, Hartford, CT 06117

DATE		ITEM	POST. REF.	DEBIT	CREDIT	BALANCE
20-1 Dec.	16	Balance	✓			3 7 9 6 00
	29		J4		2 4 7 3 00	1 3 2 3 00

NAME Anne Clark
ADDRESS 52 Juniper Road, Hartford, CT 06118

DATE		ITEM	POST. REF.	DEBIT	CREDIT	BALANCE
20-1 Dec.	16	Balance	✓			2 1 0 0 00

**Comprehensive Problem 2—General Journal Based, Part 1
(Requirements 1., 2., 3., 6., 7., and 9. Continued)**

NAME John Dempsey

ADDRESS 700 Hobbes Dr., Avon, CT 06108

DATE		ITEM	POST. REF.	DEBIT	CREDIT	BALANCE
20-1 Dec.	16	Balance	✓			1 5 6 0 00
	22		J3		1 5 6 0 00	
	27		J4	2 1 2 1 00		2 1 2 1 00

NAME Kim Fields

ADDRESS 5200 Hamilton Ave., Hartford, CT 06117

DATE		ITEM	POST. REF.	DEBIT	CREDIT	BALANCE
20-1 Dec.	16	Balance	✓			
	16		J3	1 6 8 00		1 6 8 00

NAME Lucy Greene

ADDRESS 236 Bally Lane, Simsbury, CT 06123

DATE		ITEM	POST. REF.	DEBIT	CREDIT	BALANCE
20-1 Dec.	16	Balance	✓			2 8 0 0 00
	16		J3		1 9 6 0 00	8 4 0 00
	19		J3	6 5 1 00		1 4 9 1 00

Comprehensive Problem 2—General Journal Based, Part 1 (Requirements 1., 2., 3., 6., 7., and 9. Concluded)

ACCOUNTS PAYABLE LEDGER

NAME Evans Essentials

ADDRESS 34 Harry Ave., East Hartford, CT 05234

DATE		ITEM	POST. REF.	DEBIT	CREDIT	BALANCE
20-1 Dec.	16	Balance	✓			3 6 0 0 00
	17		J3	1 5 0 00		3 4 5 0 00
	18		J3	1 1 0 0 00		2 3 5 0 00

NAME Nathen Co.

ADDRESS 1009 Drake Rd., Farmington, CT 06082

DATE		ITEM	POST. REF.	DEBIT	CREDIT	BALANCE
20-1 Dec.	16	Balance	✓			— — —
	26		J3		8 0 0 00	8 0 0 00

NAME Owen Enterprises

ADDRESS 43 Lucky Lane, Bristol, CT 06007

DATE		ITEM	POST. REF.	DEBIT	CREDIT	BALANCE
20-1 Dec.	16	Balance	✓			— — —

NAME West Wholesalers

ADDRESS 888 Anders Street, Newington, CT 06789

DATE		ITEM	POST. REF.	DEBIT	CREDIT	BALANCE
20-1 Dec.	16	Balance	✓			— — —
	24		J3		1 2 0 0 00	1 2 0 0 00

Comprehensive Problem 2—General Journal Based, Part 1

Requirement 4.

TJ's Specialty Shop
Schedule of Accounts Receivable
December 31, 20-1

Martha Boyle	$1 323 00
Anne Clark	2 100 00
John Dempsey	2 121 00
Kim Fields	168 00
Lucy Greene	1 491 00
	$7 203 00

TJ's Specialty Shop
Schedule of Accounts Payable
December 31, 20-1

Evans Essentials	$2 350 00
Nathen Co.	800 00
West Wholesalers	1 200 00
	$4 350 00

This page left intentionally blank.

Comprehensive Problem 2—General Journal Based, Part 1

Requirement 5.

TJ's Specialty
Work
For Year Ended

	TRIAL BALANCE DEBIT	TRIAL BALANCE CREDIT	ADJUSTMENTS DEBIT	ADJUSTMENTS CREDIT
1 Cash	12 5 4 8 00			
2 Accounts Receivable	7 2 0 3 00			
3 Merchandise Inventory	21 8 0 0 00		(b) 19 7 0 0 00	(a) 21 8 0 0 00
4 Supplies	1 1 5 5 00			(c) 6 3 0 00
5 Prepaid Insurance	1 3 8 0 00			(d) 3 8 0 00
6 Land	8 7 0 0 00			
7 Building	52 0 0 0 00			
8 Accum. Depr.—Building		9 2 0 0 00		(e) 8 0 0 00
9 Store Equipment	28 7 5 0 00			
10 Accum. Depr.—Store Equip.		9 3 0 0 00		(f) 4 5 0 00
11 Accounts Payable		4 3 5 0 00		
12 Wages Payable				(g) 3 3 0 00
13 Sales Tax Payable		1 5 1 8 00		
14 Mortgage Payable		12 5 2 5 00		
15 Tom Jones, Capital		90 0 0 0 00		
16 Tom Jones, Drawing	8 5 0 0 00			
17 Income Summary			(a) 21 8 0 0 00	(b) 19 7 0 0 00
18 Sales		127 7 0 0 00		
19 Sales Returns & Allowances	1 4 3 0 00			
20 Purchases	66 6 0 0 00			
21 Purchases Returns & Allow.		6 1 0 00		
22 Purchases Discounts		6 9 8 00		
23 Freight-In	1 7 5 00			
24 Wages Expense	27 2 0 0 00		(g) 3 3 0 00	
25 Advertising Expense	4 7 0 0 00			
26 Supplies Expense			(c) 6 3 0 00	
27 Telephone Expense	2 1 8 0 00			
28 Utilities Expense	7 5 3 0 00			
29 Insurance Expense			(d) 3 8 0 00	
30 Depr. Exp.—Building			(e) 8 0 0 00	
31 Depr. Exp.—Store Equip.			(f) 4 5 0 00	
32 Miscellaneous Expense	2 7 0 0 00			
33 Interest Expense	1 3 5 0 00			
34	255 9 0 1 00	255 9 0 1 00	44 0 9 0 00	44 0 9 0 00
35 Net Income				
36				

Comprehensive Problem 2—General Journal Based, Part 1 (Requirement 5. Continued)

Shop

Sheet

December 31, 20-1

	ADJUSTED TRIAL BALANCE DEBIT	ADJUSTED TRIAL BALANCE CREDIT	INCOME STATEMENT DEBIT	INCOME STATEMENT CREDIT	BALANCE SHEET DEBIT	BALANCE SHEET CREDIT	
	12 5 4 8 00				12 5 4 8 00		1
	7 2 0 3 00				7 2 0 3 00		2
	19 7 0 0 00				19 7 0 0 00		3
	5 2 5 00				5 2 5 00		4
	1 0 0 0 00				1 0 0 0 00		5
	8 7 0 0 00				8 7 0 0 00		6
	52 0 0 0 00				52 0 0 0 00		7
		10 0 0 0 00				10 0 0 0 00	8
	28 7 5 0 00				28 7 5 0 00		9
		9 7 5 0 00				9 7 5 0 00	10
		4 3 5 0 00				4 3 5 0 00	11
		3 3 0 00				3 3 0 00	12
		1 5 1 8 00				1 5 1 8 00	13
		12 5 2 5 00				12 5 2 5 00	14
		90 0 0 0 00				90 0 0 0 00	15
	8 5 0 0 00				8 5 0 0 00		16
	21 8 0 0 00	19 7 0 0 00	21 8 0 0 00	19 7 0 0 00			17
		127 7 0 0 00		127 7 0 0 00			18
	1 4 3 0 00		1 4 3 0 00				19
	66 6 0 0 00		66 6 0 0 00				20
		6 1 0 00		6 1 0 00			21
		6 9 8 00		6 9 8 00			22
	1 7 5 00		1 7 5 00				23
	27 5 3 0 00		27 5 3 0 00				24
	4 7 0 0 00		4 7 0 0 00				25
	6 3 0 00		6 3 0 00				26
	2 1 8 0 00		2 1 8 0 00				27
	7 5 3 0 00		7 5 3 0 00				28
	3 8 0 00		3 8 0 00				29
	8 0 0 00		8 0 0 00				30
	4 5 0 00		4 5 0 00				31
	2 7 0 0 00		2 7 0 0 00				32
	1 3 5 0 00		1 3 5 0 00				33
	277 1 8 1 00	277 1 8 1 00	138 2 5 5 00	148 7 0 8 00	138 9 2 6 00	128 4 7 3 00	34
			10 4 5 3 00			10 4 5 3 00	35
			148 7 0 8 00	148 7 0 8 00	138 9 2 6 00	138 9 2 6 00	36

Comprehensive Problem 2—General Journal Based, Part 1 (Requirement 5. Continued)

TJ's Specialty Shop
Income Statement
For Year Ended December 31, 20-1

Revenue from sales:					
Sales			$127 7 0 0 00		
Less sales ret. & allow.			1 4 3 0 00		
Net sales				$126 2 7 0 00	
Cost of goods sold:					
Merch. inv., Jan. 1			$ 21 8 0 0 00		
Purchases		$66 6 0 0 00			
Less: Purch. ret. & allow.	$ 6 1 0 00				
Purch. discounts	6 9 8 00	1 3 0 8 00			
Net purchases		$65 2 9 2 00			
Add freight-in		1 7 5 00			
Cost of goods purch.			65 4 6 7 00		
Goods avail. for sale			$ 87 2 6 7 00		
Less merch. inv., Dec. 31.			19 7 0 0 00		
Cost of goods sold				67 5 6 7 00	
Gross profit				$ 58 7 0 3 00	
Operating expenses:					
Wages expense			$ 27 5 3 0 00		
Advertising expense			4 7 0 0 00		
Supplies expense			6 3 0 00		
Telephone expense			2 1 8 0 00		
Utilities expense			7 5 3 0 00		
Insurance expense			3 8 0 00		
Depr. exp.—building			8 0 0 00		
Depr. exp.—store equip.			4 5 0 00		
Miscellaneous expense			2 7 0 0 00		
Total operating exp.				46 9 0 0 00	
Income from operations				$ 11 8 0 3 00	
Other expenses:					
Interest expense				1 3 5 0 00	
Net income				$ 10 4 5 3 00	

Comprehensive Problem 2—General Journal Based, Part 1 (Requirement 5. Continued)

TJ's Specialty Shop				
Statement of Owner's Equity				
For Year Ended December 31, 20-1				
Tom Jones, capital, January 1, 20-1				$90 0 0 0 00
Net income for year	$10 4 5 3 00			
Less withdrawals for year	8 5 0 0 00			
Increase in capital				1 9 5 3 00
Tom Jones, capital, December 31, 20-1				$91 9 5 3 00

Comprehensive Problem 2—General Journal Based, Part 1
(Requirement 5. Concluded)

TJ's Specialty Shop

Balance Sheet

December 31, 20-1

Assets				
Current assets:				
Cash		$12,548.00		
Accounts receivable		7,203.00		
Merchandise inventory		19,700.00		
Supplies		525.00		
Prepaid insurance		1,000.00		
Total current assets			$40,976.00	
Property, plant, and equipment:				
Land		$8,700.00		
Building	$52,000.00			
Less accumulated depreciation	10,000.00	42,000.00		
Store equipment	$28,750.00			
Less accumulated depreciation	9,750.00	19,000.00		
Total property, plant, and equipment			69,700.00	
Total assets			$110,676.00	
Liabilities				
Current liabilities:				
Accounts payable	$4,350.00			
Wages payable	330.00			
Sales tax payable	1,518.00			
Mortgage payable (current portion)	600.00			
Total current liabilities		$6,798.00		
Long-term liabilities:				
Mortgage payable	$12,525.00			
Less current portion	600.00	11,925.00		
Total liabilities			$18,723.00	
Owner's Equity				
Tom Jones, capital			91,953.00	
Total liabilities and owner's equity			$110,676.00	

Comprehensive Problem 2—General Journal Based, Part 1
Requirement 6.

GENERAL JOURNAL

PAGE 5

	DATE		DESCRIPTION	POST. REF.	DEBIT	CREDIT	
1			*Adjusting Entries*				1
2	20-1 Dec.	31	Income Summary	313	21 800 00		2
3			Merchandise Inventory	131		21 800 00	3
4							4
5		31	Merchandise Inventory	131	19 700 00		5
6			Income Summary	313		19 700 00	6
7							7
8		31	Supplies Expense	524	630 00		8
9			Supplies	141		630 00	9
10							10
11		31	Insurance Expense	535	380 00		11
12			Prepaid Insurance	145		380 00	12
13							13
14		31	Depreciation Expense—Building	540	800 00		14
15			Accumulated Depreciation—Building	171.1		800 00	15
16							16
17		31	Depreciation Expense—Store Equipment	541	450 00		17
18			Accumulated Depreciation—Store Equipment	181.1		450 00	18
19							19
20		31	Wages Expense	511	330 00		20
21			Wages Payable	219		330 00	21
22							22
23							23
24							24
25							25
26							26
27							27
28							28
29							29
30							30
31							31
32							32
33							33
34							34

Comprehensive Problem 2—General Journal Based, Part 1
Requirements 7. and 9.

GENERAL JOURNAL   PAGE 6

	DATE		DESCRIPTION	POST. REF.	DEBIT	CREDIT	
1			*Closing Entries*				1
2	20-1 Dec.	31	Sales	401	127 7 0 0 00		2
3			Purchases Returns and Allowances	501.1	6 1 0 00		3
4			Purchases Discounts	501.2	6 9 8 00		4
5			Income Summary	313		129 0 0 8 00	5
6							6
7		31	Income Summary	313	116 4 5 5 00		7
8			Sales Returns and Allowances	401.1		1 4 3 0 00	8
9			Purchases	501		66 6 0 0 00	9
10			Freight-In	502		1 7 5 00	10
11			Wages Expense	511		27 5 3 0 00	11
12			Advertising Expense	512		4 7 0 0 00	12
13			Supplies Expense	524		6 3 0 00	13
14			Telephone Expense	525		2 1 8 0 00	14
15			Utilities Expense	533		7 5 3 0 00	15
16			Insurance Expense	535		3 8 0 00	16
17			Depreciation Expense—Building	540		8 0 0 00	17
18			Depreciation Expense—Store Equipment	541		4 5 0 00	18
19			Miscellaneous Expense	549		2 7 0 0 00	19
20			Interest Expense	551		1 3 5 0 00	20
21							21
22		31	Income Summary	313	10 4 5 3 00		22
23			Tom Jones, Capital	311		10 4 5 3 00	23
24							24
25		31	Tom Jones, Capital	311	8 5 0 0 00		25
26			Tom Jones, Drawing	312		8 5 0 0 00	26
27							27
28			*Reversing Entries*				28
29	20-2 Jan.	1	Wages Payable	219	3 3 0 00		29
30			Wages Expense	511		3 3 0 00	30
31							31
32							32
33							33
34							34

Comprehensive Problem 2—General Journal Based, Part 1

Requirement 8.

TJ's Specialty Shop

Post-Closing Trial Balance

December 31, 20-1

ACCOUNT	DEBIT BALANCE	CREDIT BALANCE
Cash	12 548 00	
Accounts Receivable	7 203 00	
Merchandise Inventory	19 700 00	
Supplies	525 00	
Prepaid Insurance	1 000 00	
Land	8 700 00	
Building	52 000 00	
Accumulated Depreciation—Building		10 000 00
Store Equipment	28 750 00	
Accumulated Depreciation—Store Equipment		9 750 00
Accounts Payable		4 350 00
Wages Payable		330 00
Sales Tax Payable		1 518 00
Mortgage Payable		12 525 00
Tom Jones, Capital		91 953 00
	130 426 00	130 426 00

Comprehensive Problem 2—General Journal Based, Part 2

Requirements 2. and 3.

GENERAL JOURNAL

PAGE 1

	DATE		DESCRIPTION	POST. REF.	DEBIT	CREDIT	
1	20-2 Jan.	1	Accounts Receivable/Anne Clark	122	3 1 5 0 00		1
2			Sales	401		3 0 0 0 00	2
3			Sales Tax Payable	231		1 5 0 00	3
4			Sale No. 643				4
5							5
6		2	Accounts Payable/Nathen Co.	202	8 0 0 00		6
7			Cash	101		7 8 4 00	7
8			Purchases Discounts	501.2		1 6 00	8
9			Check No. 818				9
10							10
11		3	Purchases	501	1 5 0 0 00		11
12			Accounts Payable/West Wholesalers	202		1 5 0 0 00	12
13			Invoice No. 678				13
14							14
15		4	Purchases	501	2 0 0 0 00		15
16			Accounts Payable/Owen Enterprises	202		2 0 0 0 00	16
17			Invoice No. 767				17
18							18
19		4	Telephone Expense	525	1 8 0 00		19
20			Cash	101		1 8 0 00	20
21			Check No. 819				21
22							22
23		8	Cash	101	3 7 8 0 00		23
24			Sales	401		3 6 0 0 00	24
25			Sales Tax Payable	231		1 8 0 00	25
26			Made cash sale				26
27							27
28		9	Cash	101	1 4 9 1 00		28
29			Accounts Receivable/Lucy Greene	122		1 4 9 1 00	29
30			Received cash on account				30
31							31
32		10	Accounts Payable/West Wholesalers	202	1 2 0 0 00		32
33			Cash	101		1 2 0 0 00	33
34			Check No. 820				34
35							35
36		12	Accounts Receivable/Martha Boyle	122	1 0 5 0 00		36
37			Sales	401		1 0 0 0 00	37
38			Sales Tax Payable	231		5 0 00	38
39			Sale No. 644				39

Comprehensive Problem 2—General Journal Based, Part 2 (Requirements 2. and 3. Concluded)

GENERAL JOURNAL

PAGE 2

	DATE		DESCRIPTION	POST. REF.	DEBIT	CREDIT	
1	20-2 Jan.	12	Cash	101	2 1 0 0 00		1
2			Accounts Receivable/Anne Clark	122		2 1 0 0 00	2
3			Received cash on account				3
4							4
5		12	Wages Expense	511	1 1 0 0 00		5
6			Cash	101		1 1 0 0 00	6
7			Check No. 821				7
8							8
9		13	Accounts Payable/Owen Enterprises	202	2 0 0 0 00		9
10			Cash	101		1 9 6 0 00	10
11			Purchases Discounts	501.2		4 0 00	11
12			Check No. 822				12
13							13
14		13	Sales Returns and Allowances	401.1	8 0 0 00		14
15			Sales Tax Payable	231	4 0 00		15
16			Accounts Receivable/Martha Boyle	122		8 4 0 00	16
17			Accepted return of goods sold				17
18							18
19		17	Accounts Payable/Evans Essentials	202	3 0 0 00		19
20			Purchases Returns and Allowances	501.1		3 0 0 00	20
21			Returned goods purchased				21
22							22
23		22	Cash	101	2 1 2 1 00		23
24			Accounts Receivable/John Dempsey	122		2 1 2 1 00	24
25			Received cash on account				25
26							26
27		26	Wages Expense	511	1 1 0 0 00		27
28			Cash	101		1 1 0 0 00	28
29			Check No. 823				29
30							30
31		27	Utilities Expense	533	6 3 0 00		31
32			Cash	101		6 3 0 00	32
33			Check No. 824				33
34							34
35		27	Accounts Receivable/John Dempsey	122	2 1 0 0 00		35
36			Sales	401		2 0 0 0 00	36
37			Sales Tax Payable	231		1 0 0 00	37
38			Sale No. 645				38
39							39

Comprehensive Problem 2—General Journal Based, Part 2

Requirements 1., 2., 3., 6., and 7.

GENERAL LEDGER

ACCOUNT Cash   ACCOUNT NO. 101

DATE		ITEM	POST. REF.	DEBIT	CREDIT	BALANCE DEBIT	BALANCE CREDIT
20-2 Jan.	1	Balance	✓			12 5 4 8 00	
	2		J1		7 8 4 00	11 7 6 4 00	
	4		J1		1 8 0 00	11 5 8 4 00	
	8		J1	3 7 8 0 00		15 3 6 4 00	
	9		J1	1 4 9 1 00		16 8 5 5 00	
	10		J1		1 2 0 0 00	15 6 5 5 00	
	12		J2	2 1 0 0 00		17 7 5 5 00	
	12		J2		1 1 0 0 00	16 6 5 5 00	
	13		J2		1 9 6 0 00	14 6 9 5 00	
	22		J2	2 1 2 1 00		16 8 1 6 00	
	26		J2		1 1 0 0 00	15 7 1 6 00	
	27		J2		6 3 0 00	15 0 8 6 00	

ACCOUNT Accounts Receivable   ACCOUNT NO. 122

DATE		ITEM	POST. REF.	DEBIT	CREDIT	BALANCE DEBIT	BALANCE CREDIT
20-2 Jan.	1	Balance	✓			7 2 0 3 00	
	1		J1	3 1 5 0 00		10 3 5 3 00	
	9		J1		1 4 9 1 00	8 8 6 2 00	
	12		J1	1 0 5 0 00		9 9 1 2 00	
	12		J2		2 1 0 0 00	7 8 1 2 00	
	13		J2		8 4 0 00	6 9 7 2 00	
	22		J2		2 1 2 1 00	4 8 5 1 00	
	27		J2	2 1 0 0 00		6 9 5 1 00	

Comprehensive Problem 2—General Journal Based, Part 2
(Requirements 1., 2., 3., 6., and 7. Continued)

ACCOUNT Merchandise Inventory   ACCOUNT NO. 131

DATE		ITEM	POST. REF.	DEBIT	CREDIT	BALANCE	
						DEBIT	CREDIT
20-2 Jan.	1	Balance	✓			19 7 0 0 00	
	31	*Adjusting*	*J3*		19 7 0 0 00		
	31	*Adjusting*	*J3*	19 0 0 0 00		19 0 0 0 00	

ACCOUNT Supplies   ACCOUNT NO. 141

DATE		ITEM	POST. REF.	DEBIT	CREDIT	BALANCE	
						DEBIT	CREDIT
20-2 Jan.	1	Balance	✓			5 2 5 00	
	31	*Adjusting*	*J3*		4 1 0 00	1 1 5 00	

ACCOUNT Prepaid Insurance   ACCOUNT NO. 145

DATE		ITEM	POST. REF.	DEBIT	CREDIT	BALANCE	
						DEBIT	CREDIT
20-2 Jan.	1	Balance	✓			1 0 0 0 00	
	31	*Adjusting*	*J3*		3 2 00	9 6 8 00	

ACCOUNT Land   ACCOUNT NO. 161

DATE		ITEM	POST. REF.	DEBIT	CREDIT	BALANCE	
						DEBIT	CREDIT
20-2 Jan.	1	Balance	✓			8 7 0 0 00	

Comprehensive Problem 2—General Journal Based, Part 2
(Requirements 1., 2., 3., 6., and 7. Continued)

ACCOUNT Building   ACCOUNT NO. 171

DATE		ITEM	POST. REF.	DEBIT	CREDIT	BALANCE DEBIT	BALANCE CREDIT
20-2 Jan.	1	Balance	✓			52 0 0 0 00	

ACCOUNT Accumulated Depreciation—Building   ACCOUNT NO. 171.1

DATE		ITEM	POST. REF.	DEBIT	CREDIT	BALANCE DEBIT	BALANCE CREDIT
20-2 Jan.	1	Balance	✓				10 0 0 0 00
	31	Adjusting	J3		6 7 00		10 0 6 7 00

ACCOUNT Store Equipment   ACCOUNT NO. 181

DATE		ITEM	POST. REF.	DEBIT	CREDIT	BALANCE DEBIT	BALANCE CREDIT
20-2 Jan.	1	Balance	✓			28 7 5 0 00	

Comprehensive Problem 2—General Journal Based, Part 2 (Requirements 1., 2., 3., 6., and 7. Continued)

ACCOUNT Accumulated Depreciation—Store Equipment   ACCOUNT NO. 181.1

DATE		ITEM	POST. REF.	DEBIT	CREDIT	BALANCE DEBIT	BALANCE CREDIT
20-2 Jan.	1	Balance	✓				9 7 5 0 00
	31	Adjusting	J3		3 8 00		9 7 8 8 00

ACCOUNT Accounts Payable   ACCOUNT NO. 202

DATE		ITEM	POST. REF.	DEBIT	CREDIT	BALANCE DEBIT	BALANCE CREDIT
20-2 Jan.	1	Balance	✓				4 3 5 0 00
	2		J1	8 0 0 00			3 5 5 0 00
	3		J1		1 5 0 0 00		5 0 5 0 00
	4		J1		2 0 0 0 00		7 0 5 0 00
	10		J1	1 2 0 0 00			5 8 5 0 00
	13		J2	2 0 0 0 00			3 8 5 0 00
	17		J2	3 0 0 00			3 5 5 0 00

ACCOUNT Wages Payable   ACCOUNT NO. 219

DATE		ITEM	POST. REF.	DEBIT	CREDIT	BALANCE DEBIT	BALANCE CREDIT
20-2 Jan.	31	Adjusting	J3		3 3 0 00		3 3 0 00

Comprehensive Problem 2—General Journal Based, Part 2
(Requirements 1., 2., 3., 6., and 7. Continued)

ACCOUNT Sales Tax Payable   ACCOUNT NO. 231

DATE		ITEM	POST. REF.	DEBIT	CREDIT	BALANCE DEBIT	BALANCE CREDIT
20-2 Jan.	1	Balance	✓				1 5 1 8 00
	1		J1		1 5 0 00		1 6 6 8 00
	8		J1		1 8 0 00		1 8 4 8 00
	12		J1		5 0 00		1 8 9 8 00
	13		J2	4 0 00			1 8 5 8 00
	27		J2		1 0 0 00		1 9 5 8 00

ACCOUNT Mortgage Payable   ACCOUNT NO. 251

DATE		ITEM	POST. REF.	DEBIT	CREDIT	BALANCE DEBIT	BALANCE CREDIT
20-2 Jan.	1	Balance	✓				12 5 2 5 00

ACCOUNT Tom Jones, Capital   ACCOUNT NO. 311

DATE		ITEM	POST. REF.	DEBIT	CREDIT	BALANCE DEBIT	BALANCE CREDIT
20-2 Jan.	1	Balance	✓				91 9 5 3 00
	31	Closing	J4		1 3 9 9 00		93 3 5 2 00

ACCOUNT Tom Jones, Drawing   ACCOUNT NO. 312

DATE		ITEM	POST. REF.	DEBIT	CREDIT	BALANCE DEBIT	BALANCE CREDIT

Comprehensive Problem 2—General Journal Based, Part 2
(Requirements 1., 2., 3., 6., and 7. Continued)

ACCOUNT Income Summary   ACCOUNT NO. 313

DATE		ITEM	POST. REF.	DEBIT	CREDIT	BALANCE DEBIT	BALANCE CREDIT
20-2 Jan.	31	Adjusting	J3	19 7 0 0 00		19 7 0 0 00	
	31	Adjusting	J3		19 0 0 0 00	7 0 0 00	
	31	Closing	J4		9 9 5 6 00		9 2 5 6 00
	31	Closing	J4	7 8 5 7 00			1 3 9 9 00
	31	Closing	J4	1 3 9 9 00			

ACCOUNT Sales   ACCOUNT NO. 401

DATE		ITEM	POST. REF.	DEBIT	CREDIT	BALANCE DEBIT	BALANCE CREDIT
20-2 Jan.	1		J1		3 0 0 0 00		3 0 0 0 00
	8		J1		3 6 0 0 00		6 6 0 0 00
	12		J1		1 0 0 0 00		7 6 0 0 00
	27		J2		2 0 0 0 00		9 6 0 0 00
	31	Closing	J4	9 6 0 0 00			

ACCOUNT Sales Returns and Allowances   ACCOUNT NO. 401.1

DATE		ITEM	POST. REF.	DEBIT	CREDIT	BALANCE DEBIT	BALANCE CREDIT
20-2 Jan.	13		J2	8 0 0 00		8 0 0 00	
	31	Closing	J4		8 0 0 00		

ACCOUNT Purchases   ACCOUNT NO. 501

DATE		ITEM	POST. REF.	DEBIT	CREDIT	BALANCE DEBIT	BALANCE CREDIT
20-2 Jan.	3		J1	1 5 0 0 00		1 5 0 0 00	
	4		J1	2 0 0 0 00		3 5 0 0 00	
	31	Closing	J4		3 5 0 0 00		

Comprehensive Problem 2—General Journal Based, Part 2
(Requirements 1., 2., 3., 6., and 7. Continued)

ACCOUNT Purchases Returns and Allowances   ACCOUNT NO. 501.1

DATE		ITEM	POST. REF.	DEBIT	CREDIT	BALANCE DEBIT	BALANCE CREDIT
20-2 Jan.	17		J2		3 0 0 00		3 0 0 00
	31	Closing	J4	3 0 0 00			

ACCOUNT Purchases Discounts   ACCOUNT NO. 501.2

DATE		ITEM	POST. REF.	DEBIT	CREDIT	BALANCE DEBIT	BALANCE CREDIT
20-2 Jan.	2		J1		1 6 00		1 6 00
	13		J2		4 0 00		5 6 00
	31	Closing	J4	5 6 00			

ACCOUNT Freight-In   ACCOUNT NO. 502

DATE	ITEM	POST. REF.	DEBIT	CREDIT	BALANCE DEBIT	BALANCE CREDIT

Comprehensive Problem 2—General Journal Based, Part 2
(Requirements 1., 2., 3., 6., and 7. Continued)

ACCOUNT Wages Expense   ACCOUNT NO. 511

DATE		ITEM	POST. REF.	DEBIT	CREDIT	BALANCE DEBIT	BALANCE CREDIT
20-2 Jan.	1	Balance	✓				3 3 0 00
	12		J2	1 1 0 0 00		7 7 0 00	
	26		J2	1 1 0 0 00		1 8 7 0 00	
	31	Adjusting	J3	3 3 0 00		2 2 0 0 00	
	31	Closing	J4		2 2 0 0 00	—	—

ACCOUNT Advertising Expense   ACCOUNT NO. 512

DATE	ITEM	POST. REF.	DEBIT	CREDIT	BALANCE DEBIT	BALANCE CREDIT

ACCOUNT Supplies Expense   ACCOUNT NO. 524

DATE		ITEM	POST. REF.	DEBIT	CREDIT	BALANCE DEBIT	BALANCE CREDIT
20-2 Jan.	31	Adjusting	J3	4 1 0 00		4 1 0 00	
	31	Closing	J4		4 1 0 00	—	—

ACCOUNT Telephone Expense   ACCOUNT NO. 525

DATE		ITEM	POST. REF.	DEBIT	CREDIT	BALANCE DEBIT	BALANCE CREDIT
20-2 Jan.	4		J1	1 8 0 00		1 8 0 00	
	31	Closing	J4		1 8 0 00	—	—

Comprehensive Problem 2—General Journal Based, Part 2 (Requirements 1., 2., 3., 6., and 7. Continued)

ACCOUNT   Utilities Expense   ACCOUNT NO.   533

DATE		ITEM	POST. REF.	DEBIT	CREDIT	BALANCE DEBIT	BALANCE CREDIT
20-2 Jan.	27		J2	6 3 0 00		6 3 0 00	
	31	Closing	J4		6 3 0 00	—	—

ACCOUNT   Insurance Expense   ACCOUNT NO.   535

DATE		ITEM	POST. REF.	DEBIT	CREDIT	BALANCE DEBIT	BALANCE CREDIT
20-2 Jan.	31	Adjusting	J3	3 2 00		3 2 00	
	31	Closing	J4		3 2 00	—	—

ACCOUNT   Depreciation Expense—Building   ACCOUNT NO.   540

DATE		ITEM	POST. REF.	DEBIT	CREDIT	BALANCE DEBIT	BALANCE CREDIT
20-2 Jan.	31	Adjusting	J3	6 7 00		6 7 00	
	31	Closing	J4		6 7 00	—	—

ACCOUNT   Depreciation Expense—Store Equipment   ACCOUNT NO.   541

DATE		ITEM	POST. REF.	DEBIT	CREDIT	BALANCE DEBIT	BALANCE CREDIT
20-2 Jan.	31	Adjusting	J3	3 8 00		3 8 00	
	31	Closing	J4		3 8 00	—	—

Comprehensive Problem 2—General Journal Based, Part 2 (Requirements 1., 2., 3., 6., and 7. Continued)

ACCOUNT Miscellaneous Expense   ACCOUNT NO. 549

DATE	ITEM	POST. REF.	DEBIT	CREDIT	BALANCE DEBIT	BALANCE CREDIT

ACCOUNT Interest Expense   ACCOUNT NO. 551

DATE	ITEM	POST. REF.	DEBIT	CREDIT	BALANCE DEBIT	BALANCE CREDIT

ACCOUNTS RECEIVABLE LEDGER

NAME Martha Boyle
ADDRESS 12 Jude Lane, Hartford, CT 06117

DATE	ITEM	POST. REF.	DEBIT	CREDIT	BALANCE
20-2 Jan. 1	Balance	✓			1 3 2 3 00
12		J1	1 0 5 0 00		2 3 7 3 00
13		J2		8 4 0 00	1 5 3 3 00

NAME Anne Clark
ADDRESS 52 Juniper Road, Hartford, CT 06118

DATE	ITEM	POST. REF.	DEBIT	CREDIT	BALANCE
20-2 Jan. 1	Balance	✓			2 1 0 0 00
1		J1	3 1 5 0 00		5 2 5 0 00
12		J2		2 1 0 0 00	3 1 5 0 00

Comprehensive Problem 2—General Journal Based, Part 2
(Requirements 1., 2., 3., 6., and 7. Continued)

NAME John Dempsey

ADDRESS 700 Hobbes Dr., Avon, CT 06108

DATE		ITEM	POST. REF.	DEBIT	CREDIT	BALANCE
20-2 Jan.	1	Balance	✓			2 1 2 1 00
	22		J2		2 1 2 1 00	
	27		J2	2 1 0 0 00		2 1 0 0 00

NAME Kim Fields

ADDRESS 5200 Hamilton Ave., Hartford, CT 06117

DATE		ITEM	POST. REF.	DEBIT	CREDIT	BALANCE
20-2 Jan.	1	Balance	✓			1 6 8 00

NAME Lucy Greene

ADDRESS 236 Bally Lane, Simsbury, CT 06123

DATE		ITEM	POST. REF.	DEBIT	CREDIT	BALANCE
20-2 Jan.	1	Balance	✓			1 4 9 1 00
	9		J1		1 4 9 1 00	

Comprehensive Problem 2—General Journal Based, Part 2 (Requirements 1., 2., 3., 6., and 7. Concluded)

ACCOUNTS PAYABLE LEDGER

NAME Evans Essentials

ADDRESS 34 Harry Ave., East Hartford, CT 05234

DATE		ITEM	POST. REF.	DEBIT	CREDIT	BALANCE
20-2 Jan.	1	Balance	✓			2 3 5 0 00
	17		J2	3 0 0 00		2 0 5 0 00

NAME Nathen Co.

ADDRESS 1009 Drake Rd., Farmington, CT 06082

DATE		ITEM	POST. REF.	DEBIT	CREDIT	BALANCE
20-2 Jan.	1	Balance	✓			8 0 0 00
	2		J1	8 0 0 00		— — —

NAME Owen Enterprises

ADDRESS 43 Lucky Lane, Bristol, CT 06007

DATE		ITEM	POST. REF.	DEBIT	CREDIT	BALANCE
20-2 Jan.	4		J1		2 0 0 0 00	2 0 0 0 00
	13		J2	2 0 0 0 00		— — —

NAME West Wholesalers

ADDRESS 888 Anders Street, Newington, CT 06789

DATE		ITEM	POST. REF.	DEBIT	CREDIT	BALANCE
20-2 Jan.	1	Balance	✓			1 2 0 0 00
	3		J1		1 5 0 0 00	2 7 0 0 00
	10		J1	1 2 0 0 00		1 5 0 0 00

Comprehensive Problem 2—General Journal Based, Part 2

Requirement 4.

TJ's Specialty Shop

Schedule of Accounts Receivable

January 31, 20-2

Martha Boyle	$1 5 3 3 00
Anne Clark	3 1 5 0 00
John Dempsey	2 1 0 0 00
Kim Fields	1 6 8 00
	$6 9 5 1 00

TJ's Specialty Shop

Schedule of Accounts Payable

January 31, 20-2

Evans Essentials	$2 0 5 0 00
West Wholesalers	1 5 0 0 00
	$3 5 5 0 00

This page left intentionally blank.

Comprehensive Problem 2—General Journal Based, Part 2

Requirement 5.

TJ's Specialty
Work
For Month Ended

		TRIAL BALANCE		ADJUSTMENTS	
		DEBIT	CREDIT	DEBIT	CREDIT
1	Cash	15 086 00			
2	Accounts Receivable	6 951 00			
3	Merchandise Inventory	19 700 00		(b) 19 000 00	(a) 19 700 00
4	Supplies	525 00			(c) 410 00
5	Prepaid Insurance	1 000 00			(d) 32 00
6	Land	8 700 00			
7	Building	52 000 00			
8	Accum. Depr.—Building		10 000 00		(e) 67 00
9	Store Equipment	28 750 00			
10	Accum. Depr.—Store Equip.		9 750 00		(f) 38 00
11	Accounts Payable		3 550 00		
12	Wages Payable				(g) 330 00
13	Sales Tax Payable		1 958 00		
14	Mortgage Payable		12 525 00		
15	Tom Jones, Capital		91 953 00		
16	Tom Jones, Drawing				
17	Income Summary			(a) 19 700 00	(b) 19 000 00
18	Sales		9 600 00		
19	Sales Returns & Allowances	800 00			
20	Purchases	3 500 00			
21	Purchases Returns & Allow.		300 00		
22	Purchases Discounts		56 00		
23	Freight-In				
24	Wages Expense	1 870 00		(g) 330 00	
25	Advertising Expense				
26	Supplies Expense			(c) 410 00	
27	Telephone Expense	180 00			
28	Utilities Expense	630 00			
29	Insurance Expense			(d) 32 00	
30	Depr. Exp.—Building			(e) 67 00	
31	Depr. Exp.—Store Equip.			(f) 38 00	
32	Miscellaneous Expense				
33	Interest Expense				
34		139 692 00	139 692 00	39 577 00	39 577 00
35	Net Income				
36					

Comprehensive Problem 2—General Journal Based, Part 2
(Requirement 5. Continued)
Shop

Sheet

January 31, 20-2

| ADJUSTED TRIAL BALANCE | | INCOME STATEMENT | | BALANCE SHEET | | |
DEBIT	CREDIT	DEBIT	CREDIT	DEBIT	CREDIT	
15 0 8 6 00				15 0 8 6 00		1
6 9 5 1 00				6 9 5 1 00		2
19 0 0 0 00				19 0 0 0 00		3
1 1 5 00				1 1 5 00		4
9 6 8 00				9 6 8 00		5
8 7 0 0 00				8 7 0 0 00		6
52 0 0 0 00				52 0 0 0 00		7
	10 0 6 7 00				10 0 6 7 00	8
28 7 5 0 00				28 7 5 0 00		9
	9 7 8 8 00				9 7 8 8 00	10
	3 5 5 0 00				3 5 5 0 00	11
	3 3 0 00				3 3 0 00	12
	1 9 5 8 00				1 9 5 8 00	13
	12 5 2 5 00				12 5 2 5 00	14
	91 9 5 3 00				91 9 5 3 00	15
						16
19 7 0 0 00	19 0 0 0 00	19 7 0 0 00	19 0 0 0 00			17
	9 6 0 0 00		9 6 0 0 00			18
8 0 0 00		8 0 0 00				19
3 5 0 0 00		3 5 0 0 00				20
	3 0 0 00		3 0 0 00			21
	5 6 00		5 6 00			22
						23
2 2 0 0 00		2 2 0 0 00				24
						25
4 1 0 00		4 1 0 00				26
1 8 0 00		1 8 0 00				27
6 3 0 00		6 3 0 00				28
3 2 00		3 2 00				29
6 7 00		6 7 00				30
3 8 00		3 8 00				31
						32
						33
159 1 2 7 00	159 1 2 7 00	27 5 5 7 00	28 9 5 6 00	131 5 7 0 00	130 1 7 1 00	34
		1 3 9 9 00			1 3 9 9 00	35
		28 9 5 6 00	28 9 5 6 00	131 5 7 0 00	131 5 7 0 00	36

Comprehensive Problem 2—General Journal Based, Part 2
(Requirement 5. Continued)

TJ's Specialty Shop

Income Statement

For Month Ended January 31, 20-2

Revenue from sales:				
Sales			$ 9 6 0 0 00	
Less sales ret. & allow.			8 0 0 00	
Net sales				$8 8 0 0 00
Cost of goods sold:				
Merch. inv., Jan 1			$19 7 0 0 00	
Purchases		$3 5 0 0 00		
Less: Purch. ret. & allow.	$ 3 0 0 00			
Purch. discounts	5 6 00	3 5 6 00		
Cost of goods purch.			3 1 4 4 00	
Goods avail. for sale			$22 8 4 4 00	
Less merch. inv., Jan. 31			19 0 0 0 00	
Cost of goods sold				3 8 4 4 00
Gross profit				$4 9 5 6 00
Operating expenses:				
Wages expense			$ 2 2 0 0 00	
Supplies expense			4 1 0 00	
Telephone expense			1 8 0 00	
Utilities expense			6 3 0 00	
Insurance expense			3 2 00	
Depr. exp.—building			6 7 00	
Depr. exp.—store equip.			3 8 00	
Total operating exp.				3 5 5 7 00
Net income				$1 3 9 9 00

Comprehensive Problem 2—General Journal Based, Part 2 (Requirement 5. Continued)

TJ's Specialty Shop
Statement of Owner's Equity
For Month Ended January 31, 20-2

Tom Jones, capital, January 1, 20-2			$91 9 5 3 00
Net income for month			1 3 9 9 00
Tom Jones, capital, January 31, 20-2			$93 3 5 2 00

Comprehensive Problem 2—General Journal Based, Part 2 (Requirement 5. Concluded)

TJ's Specialty Shop

Balance Sheet

January 31, 20-2

Assets				
Current assets:				
Cash		$15 086 00		
Accounts receivable		6 951 00		
Merchandise inventory		19 000 00		
Supplies		1 15 00		
Prepaid insurance		9 68 00		
Total current assets			$ 42 120 00	
Property, plant, and equipment:				
Land		$ 8 700 00		
Building	$52 000 00			
Less accumulated depreciation	10 067 00	41 933 00		
Store equipment	$28 750 00			
Less accumulated depreciation	9 788 00	18 962 00		
Total property, plant, and equipment			69 595 00	
Total assets			$111 715 00	
Liabilities				
Current liabilities:				
Accounts payable	$ 3 550 00			
Wages payable	3 30 00			
Sales tax payable	1 958 00			
Mortgage payable (current portion)	6 00 00			
Total current liabilities		$ 6 438 00		
Long-term liabilities:				
Mortgage payable	$12 525 00			
Less current portion	6 00 00	11 925 00		
Total liabilities			$ 18 363 00	
Owner's Equity				
Tom Jones, capital			93 352 00	
Total liabilities and owner's equity			$111 715 00	

Comprehensive Problem 2—General Journal Based, Part 2

Requirement 6.

GENERAL JOURNAL

PAGE 3

	DATE		DESCRIPTION	POST. REF.	DEBIT	CREDIT	
1			*Adjusting Entries*				1
2	20-2 Jan.	31	Income Summary	313	19 7 0 0 00		2
3			Merchandise Inventory	131		19 7 0 0 00	3
4							4
5		31	Merchandise Inventory	131	19 0 0 0 00		5
6			Income Summary	313		19 0 0 0 00	6
7							7
8		31	Supplies Expense	524	4 1 0 00		8
9			Supplies	141		4 1 0 00	9
10							10
11		31	Insurance Expense	535	3 2 00		11
12			Prepaid Insurance	145		3 2 00	12
13							13
14		31	Depreciation Expense—Building	540	6 7 00		14
15			Accumulated Depreciation—Building	171.1		6 7 00	15
16							16
17		31	Depreciation Expense—Store Equipment	541	3 8 00		17
18			Accumulated Depreciation—Store Equipment	181.1		3 8 00	18
19							19
20		31	Wages Expense	511	3 3 0 00		20
21			Wages Payable	219		3 3 0 00	21
22							22
23							23
24							24
25							25
26							26
27							27
28							28
29							29
30							30
31							31
32							32
33							33
34							34

Comprehensive Problem 2—General Journal Based, Part 2

Requirement 7.

GENERAL JOURNAL

PAGE 4

	DATE		DESCRIPTION	POST. REF.	DEBIT	CREDIT	
1			*Closing Entries*				1
2	20-2 Jan.	31	Sales	401	9 6 0 0 00		2
3			Purchases Returns and Allowances	501.1	3 0 0 00		3
4			Purchases Discounts	501.2	5 6 00		4
5			Income Summary	313		9 9 5 6 00	5
6							6
7		31	Income Summary	313	7 8 5 7 00		7
8			Sales Returns and Allowances	401.1		8 0 0 00	8
9			Purchases	501		3 5 0 0 00	9
10			Wages Expense	511		2 2 0 0 00	10
11			Supplies Expense	524		4 1 0 00	11
12			Telephone Expense	525		1 8 0 00	12
13			Utilities Expense	533		6 3 0 00	13
14			Insurance Expense	535		3 2 00	14
15			Depreciation Expense—Building	540		6 7 00	15
16			Depreciation Expense—Store Equipment	541		3 8 00	16
17							17
18		31	Income Summary	313	1 3 9 9 00		18
19			Tom Jones, Capital	311		1 3 9 9 00	19
20							20
21							21
22							22
23							23
24							24
25							25
26							26
27							27
28							28
29							29
30							30
31							31
32							32
33							33
34							34

Comprehensive Problem 2—General Journal Based, Part 2

Requirement 8.

TJ's Specialty Shop
Post-Closing Trial Balance
January 31, 20-2

ACCOUNT	DEBIT BALANCE	CREDIT BALANCE
Cash	15 086 00	
Accounts Receivable	6 951 00	
Merchandise Inventory	19 000 00	
Supplies	1 115 00	
Prepaid Insurance	968 00	
Land	8 700 00	
Building	52 000 00	
Accumulated Depreciation—Building		10 067 00
Store Equipment	28 750 00	
Accumulated Depreciation—Store Equipment		9 788 00
Accounts Payable		3 550 00
Wages Payable		330 00
Sales Tax Payable		1 958 00
Mortgage Payable		12 525 00
Tom Jones, Capital		93 352 00
	131 570 00	131 570 00

Comprehensive Problem 2—Special Journals Based, Part 1

Requirements 2. and 3.

SALES JOURNAL

PAGE 6

DATE		SALE NO.	TO WHOM SOLD	POST. REF.	ACCOUNTS RECEIVABLE DEBIT	SALES CREDIT	SALES TAX PAYABLE CREDIT
20-1 Dec.	1-15		Cumulative Amount	✓	4 2 6 3 00	4 0 6 0 00	2 0 3 00
	16	640	Kim Fields	✓	1 6 8 00	1 6 0 00	8 00
	19	641	Lucy Greene	✓	6 5 1 00	6 2 0 00	3 1 00
	27	642	John Dempsey	✓	2 1 2 1 00	2 0 2 0 00	1 0 1 00
					7 2 0 3 00	6 8 6 0 00	3 4 3 00
					(1 2 2)	(4 0 1)	(2 3 1)

Proof:

Debit total:	$7,203.00	Credit total:	$6,860.00
			343.00
			$7,203.00

CASH RECEIPTS JOURNAL

PAGE 9

	DATE		ACCOUNT CREDITED	POST. REF.	GENERAL CREDIT	ACCOUNTS RECEIVABLE CREDIT	SALES CREDIT	SALES TAX PAYABLE CREDIT	CASH DEBIT	
1	20-1 Dec.	1-15	Cumulative Amount	✓		1 8 3 0 00	4 8 4 0 00	2 4 2 00	6 9 1 2 00	1
2		16	L. Greene	✓		1 9 6 0 00			1 9 6 0 00	2
3		22	J. Dempsey	✓		1 5 6 0 00			1 5 6 0 00	3
4		29	M. Boyle	✓		2 4 7 3 00			2 4 7 3 00	4
5						7 8 2 3 00	4 8 4 0 00	2 4 2 00	12 9 0 5 00	5
6						(1 2 2)	(4 0 1)	(2 3 1)	(1 0 1)	6
7										7

Proof:

Debit total:	$12,905.00	Credit total:	$ 7,823.00
			4,840.00
			242.00
			$12,905.00

Comprehensive Problem 2—Special Journals Based, Part 1 (Requirements 2. and 3. Continued)

PURCHASES JOURNAL

PAGE 5

	DATE	INVOICE NO.	FROM WHOM PURCHASED	POST. REF.	PURCHASES DEBIT ACCTS. PAY. CREDIT	
1	20-1 Dec. 1-15		Cumulative Amount	✓	3 9 0 0 00	1
2	24	465	West Wholesalers	✓	1 2 0 0 00	2
3	26	817	Nathen Co.	✓	8 0 0 00	3
4					5 9 0 0 00	4
5					(501) (2 02)	5
6						6

CASH PAYMENTS JOURNAL

PAGE 10

	DATE	CK. NO.	ACCOUNT DEBITED	POST. REF.	GENERAL DEBIT	ACCOUNTS PAYABLE DEBIT	PURCHASES DEBIT	PURCHASES DISCOUNTS CREDIT	CASH CREDIT	
1	20-1 Dec. 1-15		Cumulative Amount	✓	1 6 8 0 00	7 1 5 0 00		1 2 3 00	8 7 0 7 00	1
2	18	813	Evans Essentials	✓		1 1 0 0 00			1 1 0 0 00	2
3	23	814	Supplies	141	1 2 0 00				1 2 0 00	3
4	27	815	Utilities Exp.	533	6 3 0 00				6 3 0 00	4
5	29	816	Wages Exp.	511	1 1 0 0 00				1 1 0 0 00	5
6	30	817		✓			2 0 0 00		2 0 0 00	6
7					3 5 3 0 00	8 2 5 0 00	2 0 0 00	1 2 3 00	11 8 5 7 00	7
8					(✓)	(202)	(501)	(501 .2)	(101)	8
9										9
10										10
11										11
12										12
13										13
14										14
15										15

Proof:

Debit total:	$ 3,530.00	Credit total:	$ 123.00
	8,250.00		11,857.00
	200.00		$11,980.00
	$11,980.00		

Comprehensive Problem 2—Special Journals Based, Part 1 (Requirements 2. and 3. Concluded)

GENERAL JOURNAL

PAGE 3

	DATE		DESCRIPTION	POST. REF.	DEBIT	CREDIT	
1	20-1 Dec.	17	Accounts Payable/Evans Essentials	202/✓	1 5 0 00		1
2			Purchases Returns and Allowances	501.1		1 5 0 00	2
3			Returned goods purchased				3
4							4
5							5
6							6
7							7
8							8
9							9
10							10
11							11
12							12

Requirements 1., 2., 3., 6., 7., and 9.

GENERAL LEDGER

ACCOUNT Cash   ACCOUNT NO. 101

DATE		ITEM	POST. REF.	DEBIT	CREDIT	BALANCE DEBIT	BALANCE CREDIT
20-1 Dec.	16	Balance	✓			11 5 0 0 00	
	31		CR9	12 9 0 5 00		24 4 0 5 00	
	31		CP10		11 8 5 7 00	12 5 4 8 00	

ACCOUNT Accounts Receivable   ACCOUNT NO. 122

DATE		ITEM	POST. REF.	DEBIT	CREDIT	BALANCE DEBIT	BALANCE CREDIT
20-1 Dec.	16	Balance	✓			7 8 2 3 00	
	31		S6	7 2 0 3 00		15 0 2 6 00	
	31		CR9		7 8 2 3 00	7 2 0 3 00	

Comprehensive Problem 2—Special Journals Based, Part 1
(Requirements 1., 2., 3., 6., 7., and 9. Continued)

ACCOUNT   Merchandise Inventory   ACCOUNT NO.   131

DATE		ITEM	POST. REF.	DEBIT	CREDIT	BALANCE DEBIT	BALANCE CREDIT
20-1 Dec.	16	Balance	✓			21 8 0 0 00	
	31	Adjusting	J5		21 8 0 0 00		
	31	Adjusting	J5	19 7 0 0 00		19 7 0 0 00	

ACCOUNT   Supplies   ACCOUNT NO.   141

DATE		ITEM	POST. REF.	DEBIT	CREDIT	BALANCE DEBIT	BALANCE CREDIT
20-1 Dec.	16	Balance	✓			1 0 3 5 00	
	23		CP10	1 2 0 00		1 1 5 5 00	
	31	Adjusting	J5		6 3 0 00	5 2 5 00	

ACCOUNT   Prepaid Insurance   ACCOUNT NO.   145

DATE		ITEM	POST. REF.	DEBIT	CREDIT	BALANCE DEBIT	BALANCE CREDIT
20-1 Dec.	16	Balance	✓			1 3 8 0 00	
	31	Adjusting	J5		3 8 0 00	1 0 0 0 00	

ACCOUNT   Land   ACCOUNT NO.   161

DATE		ITEM	POST. REF.	DEBIT	CREDIT	BALANCE DEBIT	BALANCE CREDIT
20-1 Dec.	16	Balance	✓			8 7 0 0 00	

Comprehensive Problem 2—Special Journals Based, Part 1
(Requirements 1., 2., 3., 6., 7., and 9. Continued)

ACCOUNT Building   ACCOUNT NO. 171

DATE		ITEM	POST. REF.	DEBIT	CREDIT	BALANCE DEBIT	BALANCE CREDIT
20-1 Dec.	16	Balance	✓			52 0 0 0 00	

ACCOUNT Accumulated Depreciation—Building   ACCOUNT NO. 171.1

DATE		ITEM	POST. REF.	DEBIT	CREDIT	BALANCE DEBIT	BALANCE CREDIT
20-1 Dec.	16	Balance	✓				9 2 0 0 00
	31	*Adjusting*	J5		8 0 0 00		10 0 0 0 00

ACCOUNT Store Equipment   ACCOUNT NO. 181

DATE		ITEM	POST. REF.	DEBIT	CREDIT	BALANCE DEBIT	BALANCE CREDIT
20-1 Dec.	16	Balance	✓			28 7 5 0 00	

ACCOUNT Accumulated Depreciation—Store Equipment   ACCOUNT NO. 181.1

DATE		ITEM	POST. REF.	DEBIT	CREDIT	BALANCE DEBIT	BALANCE CREDIT
20-1 Dec.	16	Balance	✓				9 3 0 0 00
	31	*Adjusting*	J5		4 5 0 00		9 7 5 0 00

Comprehensive Problem 2—Special Journals Based, Part 1
(Requirements 1., 2., 3., 6., 7., and 9. Continued)

ACCOUNT Accounts Payable

ACCOUNT NO. 202

DATE		ITEM	POST. REF.	DEBIT	CREDIT	BALANCE DEBIT	BALANCE CREDIT
20-1 Dec.	16	Balance	✓				6 8 5 0 00
	17		J3	1 5 0 00			6 7 0 0 00
	31		P5		5 9 0 0 00		12 6 0 0 00
	31		CP10	8 2 5 0 00			4 3 5 0 00

ACCOUNT Wages Payable

ACCOUNT NO. 219

DATE		ITEM	POST. REF.	DEBIT	CREDIT	BALANCE DEBIT	BALANCE CREDIT
20-1 Dec.	31	*Adjusting*	J5		3 3 0 00		3 3 0 00
20-2 Jan.	1	*Reversing*	J6	3 3 0 00			

ACCOUNT Sales Tax Payable

ACCOUNT NO. 231

DATE		ITEM	POST. REF.	DEBIT	CREDIT	BALANCE DEBIT	BALANCE CREDIT
20-1 Dec.	16	Balance	✓				9 3 3 00
	31		S6		3 4 3 00		1 2 7 6 00
	31		CR9		2 4 2 00		1 5 1 8 00

ACCOUNT Mortgage Payable

ACCOUNT NO. 251

DATE		ITEM	POST. REF.	DEBIT	CREDIT	BALANCE DEBIT	BALANCE CREDIT
20-1 Dec.	16	Balance	✓				12 5 2 5 00

Comprehensive Problem 2—Special Journals Based, Part 1 (Requirements 1., 2., 3., 6., 7., and 9. Continued)

ACCOUNT Tom Jones, Capital   ACCOUNT NO. 311

DATE		ITEM	POST. REF.	DEBIT	CREDIT	BALANCE DEBIT	BALANCE CREDIT
20-1 Dec.	16	Balance	✓				90 0 0 0 00
	31	Closing	J6		10 4 5 3 00		100 4 5 3 00
	31	Closing	J6	8 5 0 0 00			91 9 5 3 00

ACCOUNT Tom Jones, Drawing   ACCOUNT NO. 312

DATE		ITEM	POST. REF.	DEBIT	CREDIT	BALANCE DEBIT	BALANCE CREDIT
20-1 Dec.	16	Balance	✓			8 5 0 0 00	
	31	Closing	J6		8 5 0 0 00	—	—

ACCOUNT Income Summary   ACCOUNT NO. 313

DATE		ITEM	POST. REF.	DEBIT	CREDIT	BALANCE DEBIT	BALANCE CREDIT
20-1 Dec.	31	Adjusting	J5	21 8 0 0 00		21 8 0 0 00	
	31	Adjusting	J5		19 7 0 0 00	2 1 0 0 00	
	31	Closing	J6		129 0 0 8 00		126 9 0 8 00
	31	Closing	J6	116 4 5 5 00			10 4 5 3 00
	31	Closing	J6	10 4 5 3 00		—	—

ACCOUNT Sales   ACCOUNT NO. 401

DATE		ITEM	POST. REF.	DEBIT	CREDIT	BALANCE DEBIT	BALANCE CREDIT
20-1 Dec.	16	Balance	✓				116 0 0 0 00
	31		S6		6 8 6 0 00		122 8 6 0 00
	31		CR9		4 8 4 0 00		127 7 0 0 00
	31	Closing	J6	127 7 0 0 00		—	—

Comprehensive Problem 2—Special Journals Based, Part 1 (Requirements 1., 2., 3., 6., 7., and 9. Continued)

ACCOUNT   Sales Returns and Allowances   ACCOUNT NO.   401.1

DATE		ITEM	POST. REF.	DEBIT	CREDIT	BALANCE DEBIT	BALANCE CREDIT
20-1 Dec.	16	Balance	✓			1 4 3 0 00	
	31	Closing	J6		1 4 3 0 00		

ACCOUNT   Purchases   ACCOUNT NO.   501

DATE		ITEM	POST. REF.	DEBIT	CREDIT	BALANCE DEBIT	BALANCE CREDIT
20-1 Dec.	16	Balance	✓			60 5 0 0 00	
	31		P5	5 9 0 0 00		66 4 0 0 00	
	31		CP10	2 0 0 00		66 6 0 0 00	
	31	Closing	J6		66 6 0 0 00		

ACCOUNT   Purchases Returns and Allowances   ACCOUNT NO.   501.1

DATE		ITEM	POST. REF.	DEBIT	CREDIT	BALANCE DEBIT	BALANCE CREDIT
20-1 Dec.	16	Balance	✓				4 6 0 00
	17		J3		1 5 0 00		6 1 0 00
	31	Closing	J6	6 1 0 00			

ACCOUNT   Purchases Discounts   ACCOUNT NO.   501.2

DATE		ITEM	POST. REF.	DEBIT	CREDIT	BALANCE DEBIT	BALANCE CREDIT
20-1 Dec.	16	Balance	✓				5 7 5 00
	31		CP10		1 2 3 00		6 9 8 00
	31	Closing	J6	6 9 8 00			

Comprehensive Problem 2—Special Journals Based, Part 1 (Requirements 1., 2., 3., 6., 7., and 9. Continued)

ACCOUNT   Freight-In   ACCOUNT NO.   502

DATE		ITEM	POST. REF.	DEBIT	CREDIT	BALANCE DEBIT	BALANCE CREDIT
20-1 Dec.	16	Balance	✓			1 7 5 00	
	31	Closing	J6		1 7 5 00		

ACCOUNT   Wages Expense   ACCOUNT NO.   511

DATE		ITEM	POST. REF.	DEBIT	CREDIT	BALANCE DEBIT	BALANCE CREDIT
20-1 Dec.	16	Balance	✓			26 1 0 0 00	
	29		CP10	1 1 0 0 00		27 2 0 0 00	
	31	Adjusting	J5	3 3 0 00		27 5 3 0 00	
	31	Closing	J6		27 5 3 0 00		
20-2 Jan.	1	Reversing	J6		3 3 0 00		3 3 0 00

ACCOUNT   Advertising Expense   ACCOUNT NO.   512

DATE		ITEM	POST. REF.	DEBIT	CREDIT	BALANCE DEBIT	BALANCE CREDIT
20-1 Dec.	16	Balance	✓			4 7 0 0 00	
	31	Closing	J6		4 7 0 0 00		

ACCOUNT   Supplies Expense   ACCOUNT NO.   524

DATE		ITEM	POST. REF.	DEBIT	CREDIT	BALANCE DEBIT	BALANCE CREDIT
20-1 Dec	31	Adjusting	J5	6 3 0 00		6 3 0 00	
	31	Closing	J6		6 3 0 00		

Comprehensive Problem 2—Special Journals Based, Part 1 (Requirements 1, 2., 3., 6., 7., and 9. Continued)

ACCOUNT   Telephone Expense   ACCOUNT NO.   525

DATE		ITEM	POST. REF.	DEBIT	CREDIT	BALANCE DEBIT	BALANCE CREDIT
20-1 Dec.	16	Balance	✓			2 1 8 0 00	
	31	Closing	J6		2 1 8 0 00		

ACCOUNT   Utilities Expense   ACCOUNT NO.   533

DATE		ITEM	POST. REF.	DEBIT	CREDIT	BALANCE DEBIT	BALANCE CREDIT
20-1 Dec.	16	Balance	✓			6 9 0 0 00	
	27		CP10	6 3 0 00		7 5 3 0 00	
	31	Closing	J6		7 5 3 0 00		

ACCOUNT   Insurance Expense   ACCOUNT NO.   535

DATE		ITEM	POST. REF.	DEBIT	CREDIT	BALANCE DEBIT	BALANCE CREDIT
20-1 Dec.	31	Adjusting	J5	3 8 0 00		3 8 0 00	
	31	Closing	J6		3 8 0 00		

ACCOUNT   Depreciation Expense—Building   ACCOUNT NO.   540

DATE		ITEM	POST. REF.	DEBIT	CREDIT	BALANCE DEBIT	BALANCE CREDIT
20-1 Dec.	31	Adjusting	J5	8 0 0 00		8 0 0 00	
	31	Closing	J6		8 0 0 00		

Comprehensive Problem 2—Special Journals Based, Part 1
(Requirements 1., 2., 3., 6., 7., and 9. Continued)

ACCOUNT Depreciation Expense—Store Equipment   ACCOUNT NO. 541

DATE		ITEM	POST. REF.	DEBIT	CREDIT	BALANCE DEBIT	BALANCE CREDIT
20-1 Dec.	31	Adjusting	J5	4 5 0 00		4 5 0 00	
	31	Closing	J6		4 5 0 00		

ACCOUNT Miscellaneous Expense   ACCOUNT NO. 549

DATE		ITEM	POST. REF.	DEBIT	CREDIT	BALANCE DEBIT	BALANCE CREDIT
20-1 Dec.	16	Balance	✓			2 7 0 0 00	
	31	Closing	J6		2 7 0 0 00		

ACCOUNT Interest Expense   ACCOUNT NO. 551

DATE		ITEM	POST. REF.	DEBIT	CREDIT	BALANCE DEBIT	BALANCE CREDIT
20-1 Dec.	16	Balance	✓			1 3 5 0 00	
	31	Closing	J6		1 3 5 0 00		

ACCOUNTS RECEIVABLE LEDGER

NAME Martha Boyle

ADDRESS 12 Jude Lane, Hartford, CT 06117

DATE		ITEM	POST. REF.	DEBIT	CREDIT	BALANCE
20-1 Dec.	16	Balance	✓			3 7 9 6 00
	29		CR9		2 4 7 3 00	1 3 2 3 00

**Comprehensive Problem 2—Special Journals Based, Part 1
(Requirements 1., 2., 3., 6., 7., and 9. Continued)**

NAME Anne Clark

ADDRESS 52 Juniper Road, Hartford, CT 06118

DATE		ITEM	POST. REF.	DEBIT	CREDIT	BALANCE
20-1 Dec.	16	Balance	✓			2 1 0 0 00

NAME John Dempsey

ADDRESS 700 Hobbes Dr., Avon, CT 06108

DATE		ITEM	POST. REF.	DEBIT	CREDIT	BALANCE
20-1 Dec.	16	Balance	✓			1 5 6 0 00
	22		CR9		1 5 6 0 00	
	27		S6	2 1 2 1 00		2 1 2 1 00

NAME Kim Fields

ADDRESS 5200 Hamilton Ave., Hartford, CT 06117

DATE		ITEM	POST. REF.	DEBIT	CREDIT	BALANCE
20-1 Dec.	16	Balance	✓			
	16		S6	1 6 8 00		1 6 8 00

NAME Lucy Greene

ADDRESS 236 Bally Lane, Simsbury, CT 06123

DATE		ITEM	POST. REF.	DEBIT	CREDIT	BALANCE
20-1 Dec.	16	Balance	✓			2 8 0 0 00
	16		CR9		1 9 6 0 00	8 4 0 00
	19		S6	6 5 1 00		1 4 9 1 00

Comprehensive Problem 2—Special Journals Based, Part 1
(Requirements 1., 2., 3., 6., 7., and 9. Continued)

ACCOUNTS PAYABLE LEDGER

NAME Evans Essentials

ADDRESS 34 Harry Ave., East Hartford, CT 05234

DATE		ITEM	POST. REF.	DEBIT	CREDIT	BALANCE
20-1 Dec.	16	Balance	✓			3 6 0 0 00
	17		J3	1 5 0 00		3 4 5 0 00
	18		CP10	1 1 0 0 00		2 3 5 0 00

NAME Nathen Co.

ADDRESS 1009 Drake Rd., Farmington, CT 06082

DATE		ITEM	POST. REF.	DEBIT	CREDIT	BALANCE
20-1 Dec.	16	Balance	✓			
	26		P5		8 0 0 00	8 0 0 00

Comprehensive Problem 2—Special Journals Based, Part 1
(Requirements 1., 2., 3., 6., 7., and 9. Concluded)

NAME   Owen Enterprises

ADDRESS   43 Lucky Lane, Bristol, CT 06007

DATE		ITEM	POST. REF.	DEBIT	CREDIT	BALANCE
20-1 Dec.	16	Balance	✓			

NAME   West Wholesalers

ADDRESS   888 Anders Street, Newington, CT 06789

DATE		ITEM	POST. REF.	DEBIT	CREDIT	BALANCE
20-1 Dec.	16	Balance	✓			
	24		P5		1 2 0 0 00	1 2 0 0 00

Comprehensive Problem 2—Special Journals Based, Part 1

Requirement 4.

TJ's Specialty Shop
Schedule of Accounts Receivable
December 31, 20-1

Martha Boyle	$1 3 2 3 00
Anne Clark	2 1 0 0 00
John Dempsey	2 1 2 1 00
Kim Fields	1 6 8 00
Lucy Greene	1 4 9 1 00
	$7 2 0 3 00

TJ's Specialty Shop
Schedule of Accounts Payable
December 31, 20-1

Evans Essentials	$2 3 5 0 00
Nathen Co.	8 0 0 00
West Wholesalers	1 2 0 0 00
	$4 3 5 0 00

Comprehensive Problem 2—Special Journals Based, Part 1

Requirement 5.

TJ's Specialty
Work
For Year Ended

	TRIAL BALANCE DEBIT	TRIAL BALANCE CREDIT	ADJUSTMENTS DEBIT	ADJUSTMENTS CREDIT
1 Cash	12 5 4 8 00			
2 Accounts Receivable	7 2 0 3 00			
3 Merchandise Inventory	21 8 0 0 00		(b) 19 7 0 0 00	(a) 21 8 0 0 00
4 Supplies	1 1 5 5 00			(c) 6 3 0 00
5 Prepaid Insurance	1 3 8 0 00			(d) 3 8 0 00
6 Land	8 7 0 0 00			
7 Building	52 0 0 0 00			
8 Accum. Depr.—Building		9 2 0 0 00		(e) 8 0 0 00
9 Store Equipment	28 7 5 0 00			
10 Accum. Depr.—Store Equip.		9 3 0 0 00		(f) 4 5 0 00
11 Accounts Payable		4 3 5 0 00		
12 Wages Payable				(g) 3 3 0 00
13 Sales Tax Payable		1 5 1 8 00		
14 Mortgage Payable		12 5 2 5 00		
15 Tom Jones, Capital		90 0 0 0 00		
16 Tom Jones, Drawing	8 5 0 0 00			
17 Income Summary			(a) 21 8 0 0 00	(b) 19 7 0 0 00
18 Sales		127 7 0 0 00		
19 Sales Returns & Allowances	1 4 3 0 00			
20 Purchases	66 6 0 0 00			
21 Purchases Returns & Allow.		6 1 0 00		
22 Purchases Discounts		6 9 8 00		
23 Freight-In	1 7 5 00			
24 Wages Expense	27 2 0 0 00		(g) 3 3 0 00	
25 Advertising Expense	4 7 0 0 00			
26 Supplies Expense			(c) 6 3 0 00	
27 Telephone Expense	2 1 8 0 00			
28 Utilities Expense	7 5 3 0 00			
29 Insurance Expense			(d) 3 8 0 00	
30 Depr. Exp.—Building			(e) 8 0 0 00	
31 Depr. Exp.—Store Equip.			(f) 4 5 0 00	
32 Miscellaneous Expense	2 7 0 0 00			
33 Interest Expense	1 3 5 0 00			
34	255 9 0 1 00	255 9 0 1 00	44 0 9 0 00	44 0 9 0 00
35 Net Income				
36				

Comprehensive Problem 2—Special Journals Based, Part 1 (Requirement 5. Continued)

Shop

Sheet

December 31, 20-1

	ADJUSTED TRIAL BALANCE		INCOME STATEMENT		BALANCE SHEET		
	DEBIT	CREDIT	DEBIT	CREDIT	DEBIT	CREDIT	
1	12 5 4 8 00				12 5 4 8 00		1
2	7 2 0 3 00				7 2 0 3 00		2
3	19 7 0 0 00				19 7 0 0 00		3
4	5 2 5 00				5 2 5 00		4
5	1 0 0 0 00				1 0 0 0 00		5
6	8 7 0 0 00				8 7 0 0 00		6
7	52 0 0 0 00				52 0 0 0 00		7
8		10 0 0 0 00				10 0 0 0 00	8
9	28 7 5 0 00				28 7 5 0 00		9
10		9 7 5 0 00				9 7 5 0 00	10
11		4 3 5 0 00				4 3 5 0 00	11
12		3 3 0 00				3 3 0 00	12
13		1 5 1 8 00				1 5 1 8 00	13
14		12 5 2 5 00				12 5 2 5 00	14
15		90 0 0 0 00				90 0 0 0 00	15
16	8 5 0 0 00				8 5 0 0 00		16
17	21 8 0 0 00	19 7 0 0 00	21 8 0 0 00	19 7 0 0 00			17
18		127 7 0 0 00		127 7 0 0 00			18
19	1 4 3 0 00		1 4 3 0 00				19
20	66 6 0 0 00		66 6 0 0 00				20
21		6 1 0 00		6 1 0 00			21
22		6 9 8 00		6 9 8 00			22
23	1 7 5 00		1 7 5 00				23
24	27 5 3 0 00		27 5 3 0 00				24
25	4 7 0 0 00		4 7 0 0 00				25
26	6 3 0 00		6 3 0 00				26
27	2 1 8 0 00		2 1 8 0 00				27
28	7 5 3 0 00		7 5 3 0 00				28
29	3 8 0 00		3 8 0 00				29
30	8 0 0 00		8 0 0 00				30
31	4 5 0 00		4 5 0 00				31
32	2 7 0 0 00		2 7 0 0 00				32
33	1 3 5 0 00		1 3 5 0 00				33
34	277 1 8 1 00	277 1 8 1 00	138 2 5 5 00	148 7 0 8 00	138 9 2 6 00	128 4 7 3 00	34
35			10 4 5 3 00			10 4 5 3 00	35
36			148 7 0 8 00	148 7 0 8 00	138 9 2 6 00	138 9 2 6 00	36

Comprehensive Problem 2—Special Journals Based, Part 1 (Requirement 5. Continued)

TJ's Specialty Shop

Income Statement

For Year Ended December 31, 20-1

Revenue from sales:					
Sales				$127 700 00	
Less sales ret. & allow.				1 430 00	
Net sales					$126 270 00
Cost of goods sold:					
Merch. inv., Jan. 1				$ 21 800 00	
Purchases			$66 600 00		
Less: Purch. ret. & allow.	$ 610 00				
Purch. discounts	698 00	1 308 00			
Net purchases			$65 292 00		
Add freight-in			175 00		
Cost of goods purch.				65 467 00	
Goods avail. for sale				$ 87 267 00	
Less merch. inv., Dec. 31				19 700 00	
Cost of goods sold					67 567 00
Gross profit					$ 58 703 00
Operating expenses:					
Wages expense				$ 27 530 00	
Advertising expense				4 700 00	
Supplies expense				630 00	
Telephone expense				2 180 00	
Utilities expense				7 530 00	
Insurance expense				380 00	
Depr. exp.—building				800 00	
Depr. exp.—store equip.				450 00	
Miscellaneous expense				2 700 00	
Total operating exp.					46 900 00
Income from operations					$ 11 803 00
Other expenses:					
Interest expense					1 350 00
Net income					$ 10 453 00

Comprehensive Problem 2—Special Journals Based, Part 1 (Requirement 5. Continued)

TJ's Specialty Shop

Statement of Owner's Equity

For Year Ended December 31, 20-1

Tom Jones, capital, January 1, 20-1			$90 0 0 0 00
Net income for year	$10 4 5 3 00		
Less withdrawals for year	8 5 0 0 00		
Increase in capital			1 9 5 3 00
Tom Jones, capital, December 31, 20-1			$91 9 5 3 00

Comprehensive Problem 2—Special Journals Based, Part 1 (Requirement 5. Concluded)

TJ's Specialty Shop
Balance Sheet
December 31, 20-1

Assets									
Current assets:									
Cash					$12 5 4 8 00				
Accounts receivable					7 2 0 3 00				
Merchandise inventory					19 7 0 0 00				
Supplies					5 2 5 00				
Prepaid insurance					1 0 0 0 00				
Total current assets							$ 40 9 7 6 00		
Property, plant, and equipment:									
Land					$ 8 7 0 0 00				
Building	$52 0 0 0 00								
Less accumulated depreciation	10 0 0 0 00				42 0 0 0 00				
Store equipment	$28 7 5 0 00								
Less accumulated depreciation	9 7 5 0 00				19 0 0 0 00				
Total property, plant, and equipment							69 7 0 0 00		
Total assets							$110 6 7 6 00		
Liabilities									
Current liabilities:									
Accounts payable	$ 4 3 5 0 00								
Wages payable	3 3 0 00								
Sales tax payable	1 5 1 8 00								
Mortgage payable (current portion)	6 0 0 00								
Total current liabilities					$ 6 7 9 8 00				
Long-term liabilities:									
Mortgage payable	$12 5 2 5 00								
Less current portion	6 0 0 00				11 9 2 5 00				
Total liabilities							$ 18 7 2 3 00		
Owner's Equity									
Tom Jones, capital							91 9 5 3 00		
Total liabilities and owner's equity							$110 6 7 6 00		

Comprehensive Problem 2—Special Journals Based, Part 1

Requirement 6.

GENERAL JOURNAL

PAGE 5

	DATE		DESCRIPTION	POST. REF.	DEBIT	CREDIT	
1			*Adjusting Entries*				1
2	20-1 Dec.	31	Income Summary	313	21 8 0 0 00		2
3			Merchandise Inventory	131		21 8 0 0 00	3
4							4
5		31	Merchandise Inventory	131	19 7 0 0 00		5
6			Income Summary	313		19 7 0 0 00	6
7							7
8		31	Supplies Expense	524	6 3 0 00		8
9			Supplies	141		6 3 0 00	9
10							10
11		31	Insurance Expense	535	3 8 0 00		11
12			Prepaid Insurance	145		3 8 0 00	12
13							13
14		31	Depreciation Expense—Building	540	8 0 0 00		14
15			Accumulated Depreciation—Building	171.1		8 0 0 00	15
16							16
17		31	Depreciation Expense—Store Equipment	541	4 5 0 00		17
18			Accumulated Depreciation—Store Equipment	181.1		4 5 0 00	18
19							19
20		31	Wages Expense	511	3 3 0 00		20
21			Wages Payable	219		3 3 0 00	21
22							22
23							23
24							24
25							25
26							26
27							27
28							28
29							29
30							30
31							31
32							32
33							33
34							34

Comprehensive Problem 2—Special Journals Based, Part 1

Requirements 7. and 9.

GENERAL JOURNAL   PAGE 6

DATE		DESCRIPTION	POST. REF.	DEBIT	CREDIT	
		Closing Entries				1
20-1 Dec.	31	Sales	401	127 700 00		2
		Purchases Returns and Allowances	501.1	610 00		3
		Purchases Discounts	501.2	698 00		4
		Income Summary	313		129 008 00	5
						6
	31	Income Summary	313	116 455 00		7
		Sales Returns and Allowances	401.1		1 430 00	8
		Purchases	501		66 600 00	9
		Freight-In	502		175 00	10
		Wages Expense	511		27 530 00	11
		Advertising Expense	512		4 700 00	12
		Supplies Expense	524		630 00	13
		Telephone Expense	525		2 180 00	14
		Utilities Expense	533		7 530 00	15
		Insurance Expense	535		380 00	16
		Depreciation Expense—Building	540		800 00	17
		Depreciation Expense—Store Equipment	541		450 00	18
		Miscellaneous Expense	549		2 700 00	19
		Interest Expense	551		1 350 00	20
						21
	31	Income Summary	313	10 453 00		22
		Tom Jones, Capital	311		10 453 00	23
						24
	31	Tom Jones, Capital	311	8 500 00		25
		Tom Jones, Drawing	312		8 500 00	26
						27
		Reversing Entries				28
20-2 Jan.	1	Wages Payable	219	330 00		29
		Wages Expense	511		330 00	30
						31
						32
						33
						34

Comprehensive Problem 2—Special Journals Based, Part 1

Requirement 8.

TJ's Specialty Shop
Post-Closing Trial Balance
December 31, 20-1

ACCOUNT	DEBIT BALANCE	CREDIT BALANCE
Cash	12 5 4 8 00	
Accounts Receivable	7 2 0 3 00	
Merchandise Inventory	19 7 0 0 00	
Supplies	5 2 5 00	
Prepaid Insurance	1 0 0 0 00	
Land	8 7 0 0 00	
Building	52 0 0 0 00	
Accumulated Depreciation—Building		10 0 0 0 00
Store Equipment	28 7 5 0 00	
Accumulated Depreciation—Store Equipment		9 7 5 0 00
Accounts Payable		4 3 5 0 00
Wages Payable		3 3 0 00
Sales Tax Payable		1 5 1 8 00
Mortgage Payable		12 5 2 5 00
Tom Jones, Capital		91 9 5 3 00
	130 4 2 6 00	130 4 2 6 00

Comprehensive Problem 2—Special Journals Based, Part 2
Requirements 2. and 3.

SALES JOURNAL   PAGE 7

DATE		SALE NO.	TO WHOM SOLD	POST. REF.	ACCOUNTS RECEIVABLE DEBIT	SALES CREDIT	SALES TAX PAYABLE CREDIT
20-2 Jan.	1	643	Anne Clarke	✓	3 1 5 0 00	3 0 0 0 00	1 5 0 00
	12	644	Martha Boyle	✓	1 0 5 0 00	1 0 0 0 00	5 0 00
	27	645	John Dempsey	✓	2 1 0 0 00	2 0 0 0 00	1 0 0 00
					6 3 0 0 00	6 0 0 0 00	3 0 0 00
					(1 2 2)	(4 0 1)	(2 3 1)

Proof:

Debit total:	$6,300.00	Credit total:	$6,000.00
			300.00
			$6,300.00

CASH RECEIPTS JOURNAL   PAGE 10

	DATE		ACCOUNT CREDITED	POST. REF.	GENERAL CREDIT	ACCOUNTS RECEIVABLE CREDIT	SALES CREDIT	SALES TAX PAYABLE CREDIT	CASH DEBIT	
1	20-2 Jan.	8		✓			3 6 0 0 00	1 8 0 00	3 7 8 0 00	1
2		9	Lucy Greene	✓		1 4 9 1 00			1 4 9 1 00	2
3		12	Anne Clark	✓		2 1 0 0 00			2 1 0 0 00	3
4		22	John Dempsey	✓		2 1 2 1 00			2 1 2 1 00	4
5						5 7 1 2 00	3 6 0 0 00	1 8 0 00	9 4 9 2 00	5
6						(1 2 2)	(4 0 1)	(2 3 1)	(1 0 1)	6
7										7
8										8
9										9

Proof:

Debit total:	$9,492.00	Credit total:	$5,712.00
			3,600.00
			180.00
			$9,492.00

Comprehensive Problem 2—Special Journals Based, Part 2 (Requirements 2. and 3. Continued)

PURCHASES JOURNAL

PAGE 6

	DATE		INVOICE NO.	FROM WHOM PURCHASED	POST. REF.	PURCHASES DEBIT ACCTS. PAY. CREDIT	
1	20-2 Jan.	3	678	West Wholesalers	✓	1500 00	1
2		4	767	Owen Enterprises	✓	2000 00	2
3						3500 00	3
4						(501) (202)	4
5							5
6							6
7							7
8							8
9							9

CASH PAYMENTS JOURNAL

PAGE 11

	DATE		CK. NO.	ACCOUNT DEBITED	POST. REF.	GENERAL DEBIT	ACCOUNTS PAYABLE DEBIT	PURCHASES DEBIT	PURCHASES DISCOUNTS CREDIT	CASH CREDIT	
1	20-2 Jan.	2	818	Nathen Co.	✓		800 00		16 00	784 00	1
2		4	819	Telephone Exp.	525	180 00				180 00	2
3		10	820	West Wholesalers	✓		1200 00			1200 00	3
4		12	821	Wages Expense	511	1100 00				1100 00	4
5		13	822	Owen Enterprises	✓		2000 00		40 00	1960 00	5
6		26	823	Wages Expense	511	1100 00				1100 00	6
7		27	824	Utilities Expense	533	630 00				630 00	7
8						3010 00	4000 00		56 00	6954 00	8
9						(✓)	(202)		(501 .2)	(101)	9
10											10
11											11
12											12
13											13

Proof:

Debit Total:	$3,010.00	Credit Total:	$ 56.00
	4,000.00		6,954.00
	$7,010.00		$7,010.00

Comprehensive Problem 2—Special Journals Based, Part 2
(Requirements 2. and 3. Concluded)

GENERAL JOURNAL   PAGE 1

	DATE	DESCRIPTION	POST. REF.	DEBIT	CREDIT	
1	20-2 Jan. 13	**Sales Returns and Allowances**	401.1	8 0 0 00		1
2		**Sales Tax Payable**	231	4 0 00		2
3		*Accounts Receivable/Martha Boyle*	122/✓		8 4 0 00	3
4		*Accepted return of goods sold*				4
5						5
6	17	**Accounts Payable/Evans Essentials**	202/✓	3 0 0 00		6
7		*Purchases Returns and Allowances*	501.1		3 0 0 00	7
8		*Returned goods purchased*				8
9						9
10						10
11						11
12						12

Requirements 1., 2., 3., 6., and 7.
GENERAL LEDGER

ACCOUNT Cash   ACCOUNT NO. 101

DATE	ITEM	POST. REF.	DEBIT	CREDIT	BALANCE DEBIT	BALANCE CREDIT
20-2 Jan. 1	Balance	✓			12 5 4 8 00	
31		CR10	9 4 9 2 00		22 0 4 0 00	
31		CP11		6 9 5 4 00	15 0 8 6 00	

ACCOUNT Accounts Receivable   ACCOUNT NO. 122

DATE	ITEM	POST. REF.	DEBIT	CREDIT	BALANCE DEBIT	BALANCE CREDIT
20-2 Jan. 1	Balance	✓			7 2 0 3 00	
13		J1		8 4 0 00	6 3 6 3 00	
31		S7	6 3 0 0 00		12 6 6 3 00	
31		CR10		5 7 1 2 00	6 9 5 1 00	

Comprehensive Problem 2—Special Journals Based, Part 2
(Requirements 1., 2., 3., 6., and 7. Continued)

ACCOUNT   Merchandise Inventory   ACCOUNT NO.   131

DATE		ITEM	POST. REF.	DEBIT	CREDIT	BALANCE DEBIT	BALANCE CREDIT
20-2 Jan.	1	Balance	✓			19 7 0 0 00	
	31	Adjusting	J2		19 7 0 0 00		
	31	Adjusting	J2	19 0 0 0 00		19 0 0 0 00	

ACCOUNT   Supplies   ACCOUNT NO.   141

DATE		ITEM	POST. REF.	DEBIT	CREDIT	BALANCE DEBIT	BALANCE CREDIT
20-2 Jan.	1	Balance	✓			5 2 5 00	
	31	Adjusting	J2		4 1 0 00	1 1 5 00	

ACCOUNT   Prepaid Insurance   ACCOUNT NO.   145

DATE		ITEM	POST. REF.	DEBIT	CREDIT	BALANCE DEBIT	BALANCE CREDIT
20-2 Jan.	1	Balance	✓			1 0 0 0 00	
	31	Adjusting	J2		3 2 00	9 6 8 00	

ACCOUNT   Land   ACCOUNT NO.   161

DATE		ITEM	POST. REF.	DEBIT	CREDIT	BALANCE DEBIT	BALANCE CREDIT
20-2 Jan.	1	Balance	✓			8 7 0 0 00	

Comprehensive Problem 2—Special Journals Based, Part 2 (Requirements 1., 2., 3., 6., and 7. Continued)

ACCOUNT Building   ACCOUNT NO. 171

DATE		ITEM	POST. REF.	DEBIT	CREDIT	BALANCE DEBIT	BALANCE CREDIT
20-2 Jan.	1	Balance	✓			52 0 0 0 00	

ACCOUNT Accumulated Depreciation—Building   ACCOUNT NO. 171.1

DATE		ITEM	POST. REF.	DEBIT	CREDIT	BALANCE DEBIT	BALANCE CREDIT
20-2 Jan.	1	Balance	✓				10 0 0 0 00
	31	*Adjusting*	J2		6 7 00		*10 0 6 7 00*

ACCOUNT Store Equipment   ACCOUNT NO. 181

DATE		ITEM	POST. REF.	DEBIT	CREDIT	BALANCE DEBIT	BALANCE CREDIT
20-2 Jan.	1	Balance	✓			28 7 5 0 00	

ACCOUNT Accumulated Depreciation—Store Equipment   ACCOUNT NO. 181.1

DATE		ITEM	POST. REF.	DEBIT	CREDIT	BALANCE DEBIT	BALANCE CREDIT
20-2 Jan.	1	Balance	✓				9 7 5 0 00
	31	*Adjusting*	J2		3 8 00		*9 7 8 8 00*

Comprehensive Problem 2—Special Journals Based, Part 2
(Requirements 1., 2., 3., 6., and 7. Continued)

ACCOUNT   Accounts Payable   ACCOUNT NO.   202

DATE		ITEM	POST. REF.	DEBIT	CREDIT	BALANCE DEBIT	BALANCE CREDIT
20-2 Jan.	1	Balance	✓				4 3 5 0 00
	17		J1	3 0 0 00			4 0 5 0 00
	31		P6		3 5 0 0 00		7 5 5 0 00
	31		CP11	4 0 0 0 00			3 5 5 0 00

ACCOUNT   Wages Payable   ACCOUNT NO.   219

DATE		ITEM	POST. REF.	DEBIT	CREDIT	BALANCE DEBIT	BALANCE CREDIT
20-2 Jan.	31	*Adjusting*	J2		3 3 0 00		3 3 0 00

ACCOUNT   Sales Tax Payable   ACCOUNT NO.   231

DATE		ITEM	POST. REF.	DEBIT	CREDIT	BALANCE DEBIT	BALANCE CREDIT
20-2 Jan.	1	Balance	✓				1 5 1 8 00
	13		J1	4 0 00			1 4 7 8 00
	31		S7		3 0 0 00		1 7 7 8 00
	31		CR10		1 8 0 00		1 9 5 8 00

ACCOUNT   Mortgage Payable   ACCOUNT NO.   251

DATE		ITEM	POST. REF.	DEBIT	CREDIT	BALANCE DEBIT	BALANCE CREDIT
20-2 Jan.	1	Balance	✓				12 5 2 5 00

Comprehensive Problem 2—Special Journals Based, Part 2 (Requirements 1., 2., 3., 6., and 7. Continued)

ACCOUNT Tom Jones, Capital   ACCOUNT NO. 311

DATE		ITEM	POST. REF.	DEBIT	CREDIT	BALANCE DEBIT	BALANCE CREDIT
20-2 Jan.	1	Balance	✓				91 9 5 3 00
	31	Closing	J3		1 3 9 9 00		93 3 5 2 00

ACCOUNT Tom Jones, Drawing   ACCOUNT NO. 312

DATE		ITEM	POST. REF.	DEBIT	CREDIT	BALANCE DEBIT	BALANCE CREDIT

ACCOUNT Income Summary   ACCOUNT NO. 313

DATE		ITEM	POST. REF.	DEBIT	CREDIT	BALANCE DEBIT	BALANCE CREDIT
20-2 Jan.	31	Adjusting	J2	19 7 0 0 00		19 7 0 0 00	
	31	Adjusting	J2		19 0 0 0 00	7 0 0 00	
	31	Closing	J3		9 9 5 6 00		9 2 5 6 00
	31	Closing	J3	7 8 5 7 00			1 3 9 9 00
	31	Closing	J3	1 3 9 9 00			

ACCOUNT Sales   ACCOUNT NO. 401

DATE		ITEM	POST. REF.	DEBIT	CREDIT	BALANCE DEBIT	BALANCE CREDIT
20-2 Jan.	31		S7		6 0 0 0 00		6 0 0 0 00
	31		CR10		3 6 0 0 00		9 6 0 0 00
	31	Closing	J3	9 6 0 0 00			

Comprehensive Problem 2—Special Journals Based, Part 2 (Requirements 1., 2., 3., 6., and 7. Continued)

ACCOUNT   Sales Returns and Allowances   ACCOUNT NO.   401.1

DATE		ITEM	POST. REF.	DEBIT	CREDIT	BALANCE DEBIT	BALANCE CREDIT
20-2 Jan.	13		J1	8 0 0 00		8 0 0 00	
	31	Closing	J3		8 0 0 00		

ACCOUNT   Purchases   ACCOUNT NO.   501

DATE		ITEM	POST. REF.	DEBIT	CREDIT	BALANCE DEBIT	BALANCE CREDIT
20-2 Jan.	31		P6	3 5 0 0 00		3 5 0 0 00	
	31	Closing	J3		3 5 0 0 00		

ACCOUNT   Purchases Returns and Allowances   ACCOUNT NO.   501.1

DATE		ITEM	POST. REF.	DEBIT	CREDIT	BALANCE DEBIT	BALANCE CREDIT
20-2 Jan.	17		J1		3 0 0 00		3 0 0 00
	31	Closing	J3	3 0 0 00			

ACCOUNT   Purchases Discounts   ACCOUNT NO.   501.2

DATE		ITEM	POST. REF.	DEBIT	CREDIT	BALANCE DEBIT	BALANCE CREDIT
20-2 Jan.	31		CP11		5 6 00		5 6 00
	31	Closing	J3	5 6 00			

Comprehensive Problem 2—Special Journals Based, Part 2 (Requirements 1., 2., 3., 6., and 7. Continued)

ACCOUNT   Freight-In   ACCOUNT NO.   502

DATE	ITEM	POST. REF.	DEBIT	CREDIT	BALANCE DEBIT	BALANCE CREDIT

ACCOUNT   Wages Expense   ACCOUNT NO.   511

DATE		ITEM	POST. REF.	DEBIT	CREDIT	BALANCE DEBIT	BALANCE CREDIT
20-2 Jan.	1	Balance	✓				3 3 0 00
	12		CP11	1 1 0 0 00		7 7 0 00	
	26		CP11	1 1 0 0 00		1 8 7 0 00	
	31	Adjusting	J2	3 3 0 00		2 2 0 0 00	
	31	Closing	J3		2 2 0 0 00	—	—

ACCOUNT   Advertising Expense   ACCOUNT NO.   512

DATE	ITEM	POST. REF.	DEBIT	CREDIT	BALANCE DEBIT	BALANCE CREDIT

ACCOUNT   Supplies Expense   ACCOUNT NO.   524

DATE		ITEM	POST. REF.	DEBIT	CREDIT	BALANCE DEBIT	BALANCE CREDIT
20-2 Jan.	31	Adjusting	J2	4 1 0 00		4 1 0 00	
	31	Closing	J3		4 1 0 00	—	—

Comprehensive Problem 2—Special Journals Based, Part 2
(Requirements 1., 2., 3., 6., and 7. Continued)

ACCOUNT   Telephone Expense   ACCOUNT NO.   525

DATE		ITEM	POST. REF.	DEBIT	CREDIT	BALANCE DEBIT	BALANCE CREDIT
20-2 Jan.	4		CP11	1 8 0 00		1 8 0 00	
	31	Closing	J3		1 8 0 00		

ACCOUNT   Utilities Expense   ACCOUNT NO.   533

DATE		ITEM	POST. REF.	DEBIT	CREDIT	BALANCE DEBIT	BALANCE CREDIT
20-2 Jan.	27		CP11	6 3 0 00		6 3 0 00	
	31	Closing	J3		6 3 0 00		

ACCOUNT   Insurance Expense   ACCOUNT NO.   535

DATE		ITEM	POST. REF.	DEBIT	CREDIT	BALANCE DEBIT	BALANCE CREDIT
20-2 Jan.	31	Adjusting	J2	3 2 00		3 2 00	
	31	Closing	J3		3 2 00		

ACCOUNT   Depreciation Expense—Building   ACCOUNT NO.   540

DATE		ITEM	POST. REF.	DEBIT	CREDIT	BALANCE DEBIT	BALANCE CREDIT
20-2 Jan.	31	Adjusting	J2	6 7 00		6 7 00	
	31	Closing	J3		6 7 00		

ACCOUNT   Depreciation Expense—Store Equipment   ACCOUNT NO.   541

DATE		ITEM	POST. REF.	DEBIT	CREDIT	BALANCE DEBIT	BALANCE CREDIT
20-2 Jan.	31	Adjusting	J2	3 8 00		3 8 00	
	31	Closing	J3		3 8 00		

Comprehensive Problem 2—Special Journals Based, Part 2
(Requirements 1., 2., 3., 6., and 7. Continued)

ACCOUNT Miscellaneous Expense   ACCOUNT NO. 549

DATE	ITEM	POST. REF.	DEBIT	CREDIT	BALANCE DEBIT	BALANCE CREDIT

ACCOUNT Interest Expense   ACCOUNT NO. 551

DATE	ITEM	POST. REF.	DEBIT	CREDIT	BALANCE DEBIT	BALANCE CREDIT

ACCOUNTS RECEIVABLE LEDGER

NAME Martha Boyle

ADDRESS 12 Jude Lane, Hartford, CT 06117

DATE		ITEM	POST. REF.	DEBIT	CREDIT	BALANCE
20-2 Jan.	1	Balance	✓			1 3 2 3 00
	12		S7	1 0 5 0 00		2 3 7 3 00
	13		J1		8 4 0 00	1 5 3 3 00

NAME Anne Clark

ADDRESS 52 Juniper Road, Hartford, CT 06118

DATE		ITEM	POST. REF.	DEBIT	CREDIT	BALANCE
20-2 Jan.	1	Balance	✓			2 1 0 0 00
	1		S7	3 1 5 0 00		5 2 5 0 00
	12		CR10		2 1 0 0 00	3 1 5 0 00

Comprehensive Problem 2—Special Journals Based, Part 2
(Requirements 1., 2., 3., 6., and 7. Continued)

NAME John Dempsey

ADDRESS 700 Hobbes Dr., Avon, CT 06108

DATE		ITEM	POST. REF.	DEBIT	CREDIT	BALANCE
20-2 Jan.	1	Balance	✓			2 1 2 1 00
	22		CR10		2 1 2 1 00	
	27		S7	2 1 0 0 00		2 1 0 0 00

NAME Kim Fields

ADDRESS 5200 Hamilton Ave., Hartford, CT 06117

DATE		ITEM	POST. REF.	DEBIT	CREDIT	BALANCE
20-2 Jan.	1	Balance	✓			1 6 8 00

NAME Lucy Greene

ADDRESS 236 Bally Lane, Simsbury, CT 06123

DATE		ITEM	POST. REF.	DEBIT	CREDIT	BALANCE
20-2 Jan.	1	Balance	✓			1 4 9 1 00
	9		CR10		1 4 9 1 00	

**Comprehensive Problem 2—Special Journals Based, Part 2
(Requirements 1., 2., 3., 6., and 7. Concluded)**

ACCOUNTS PAYABLE LEDGER

NAME Evans Essentials

ADDRESS 34 Harry Ave., East Hartford, CT 05234

DATE		ITEM	POST. REF.	DEBIT	CREDIT	BALANCE
20-2 Jan.	1	Balance	✓			2 3 5 0 00
	17		J1	3 0 0 00		2 0 5 0 00

NAME Nathen Co.

ADDRESS 1009 Drake Rd., Farmington, CT 06082

DATE		ITEM	POST. REF.	DEBIT	CREDIT	BALANCE
20-2 Jan.	1	Balance	✓			8 0 0 00
	2		CP11	8 0 0 00		—

NAME Owen Enterprises

ADDRESS 43 Lucky Lane, Bristol, CT 06007

DATE		ITEM	POST. REF.	DEBIT	CREDIT	BALANCE
20-2 Jan.	4		P6		2 0 0 00	2 0 0 00
	13		CP11	2 0 0 00		—

NAME West Wholesalers

ADDRESS 888 Anders Street, Newington, CT 06789

DATE		ITEM	POST. REF.	DEBIT	CREDIT	BALANCE
20-2 Jan.	1	Balance	✓			1 2 0 0 00
	3		P6		1 5 0 0 00	2 7 0 0 00
	10		CP11	1 2 0 0 00		1 5 0 0 00

Comprehensive Problem 2—Special Journals Based, Part 2

Requirement 4.

TJ's Specialty Shop
Schedule of Accounts Receivable
January 31, 20-2

Martha Boyle	$1 533 00
Anne Clark	3 150 00
John Dempsey	2 100 00
Kim Fields	168 00
	$6 951 00

TJ's Specialty Shop
Schedule of Accounts Payable
January 31, 20-2

Evans Essentials	$2 050 00
West Wholesalers	1 500 00
	$3 550 00

Comprehensive Problem 2—Special Journals Based, Part 2

Requirement 5.

TJ's Specialty

Work

For Month Ended

	TRIAL BALANCE DEBIT	TRIAL BALANCE CREDIT	ADJUSTMENTS DEBIT	ADJUSTMENTS CREDIT
1 Cash	15 0 8 6 00			
2 Accounts Receivable	6 9 5 1 00			
3 Merchandise Inventory	19 7 0 0 00		(b) 19 0 0 0 00	(a) 19 7 0 0 00
4 Supplies	5 2 5 00			(c) 4 1 0 00
5 Prepaid Insurance	1 0 0 0 00			(d) 3 2 00
6 Land	8 7 0 0 00			
7 Building	52 0 0 0 00			
8 Accum. Depr.—Building		10 0 0 0 00		(e) 6 7 00
9 Store Equipment	28 7 5 0 00			
10 Accum. Depr.—Store Equip.		9 7 5 0 00		(f) 3 8 00
11 Accounts Payable		3 5 5 0 00		
12 Wages Payable				(g) 3 3 0 00
13 Sales Tax Payable		1 9 5 8 00		
14 Mortgage Payable		12 5 2 5 00		
15 Tom Jones, Capital		91 9 5 3 00		
16 Tom Jones, Drawing				
17 Income Summary			(a) 19 7 0 0 00	(b) 19 0 0 0 00
18 Sales		9 6 0 0 00		
19 Sales Returns & Allowances	8 0 0 00			
20 Purchases	3 5 0 0 00			
21 Purchases Returns & Allow.		3 0 0 00		
22 Purchases Discounts		5 6 00		
23 Freight-In				
24 Wages Expense	1 8 7 0 00		(g) 3 3 0 00	
25 Advertising Expense				
26 Supplies Expense			(c) 4 1 0 00	
27 Telephone Expense	1 8 0 00			
28 Utilities Expense	6 3 0 00			
29 Insurance Expense			(d) 3 2 00	
30 Depr. Exp.—Building			(e) 6 7 00	
31 Depr. Exp.—Store Equip.			(f) 3 8 00	
32 Miscellaneous Expense				
33 Interest Expense				
34	139 6 9 2 00	139 6 9 2 00	39 5 7 7 00	39 5 7 7 00
35 Net Income				
36				

COMPREHENSIVE PROBLEM

Comprehensive Problem 2—Special Journals Based, Part 2
(Requirement 5. Continued)

Shop

Sheet

January 31, 20-2

ADJUSTED TRIAL BALANCE		INCOME STATEMENT		BALANCE SHEET		
DEBIT	CREDIT	DEBIT	CREDIT	DEBIT	CREDIT	
15 086 00				15 086 00		1
6 951 00				6 951 00		2
19 000 00				19 000 00		3
115 00				115 00		4
968 00				968 00		5
8 700 00				8 700 00		6
52 000 00				52 000 00		7
	10 067 00				10 067 00	8
28 750 00				28 750 00		9
	9 788 00				9 788 00	10
	3 550 00				3 550 00	11
	330 00				330 00	12
	1 958 00				1 958 00	13
	12 525 00				12 525 00	14
	91 953 00				91 953 00	15
						16
19 700 00	19 000 00	19 700 00	19 000 00			17
	9 600 00		9 600 00			18
800 00		800 00				19
3 500 00		3 500 00				20
	300 00		300 00			21
	56 00		56 00			22
						23
2 200 00		2 200 00				24
						25
410 00		410 00				26
180 00		180 00				27
630 00		630 00				28
32 00		32 00				29
67 00		67 00				30
38 00		38 00				31
						32
						33
159 127 00	159 127 00	27 557 00	28 956 00	131 570 00	130 171 00	34
		1 399 00			1 399 00	35
		28 956 00	28 956 00	131 570 00	131 570 00	36

Comprehensive Problem 2—Special Journals Based, Part 2
(Requirement 5. Continued)

TJ's Specialty Shop
Income Statement
For Month Ended January 31, 20-2

Revenue from sales:					
Sales			$ 9 6 0 0 00		
Less sales ret. & allow.			8 0 0 00		
Net sales				$8 8 0 0 00	
Cost of goods sold:					
Merch. inv., Jan. 1			$19 7 0 0 00		
Purchases		$3 5 0 0 00			
Less: Purch. ret. & allow.	$ 3 0 0 00				
Purch. discounts	5 6 00	3 5 6 00			
Cost of goods purchased			3 1 4 4 00		
Goods avail. for sale			$22 8 4 4 00		
Less merch. inv., Jan. 31			19 0 0 0 00		
Cost of goods sold				3 8 4 4 00	
Gross profit				$4 9 5 6 00	
Operating expenses:					
Wages expense			$ 2 2 0 0 00		
Supplies expense			4 1 0 00		
Telephone expense			1 8 0 00		
Utilities expense			6 3 0 00		
Insurance expense			3 2 00		
Depr. exp.—building			6 7 00		
Depr. exp.—store equip.			3 8 00		
Total operating exp.				3 5 5 7 00	
Net income				$1 3 9 9 00	

Comprehensive Problem 2—Special Journals Based, Part 2 (Requirement 5. Continued)

TJ's Specialty Shop

Statement of Owner's Equity

For Month Ended January 31, 20-2

Tom Jones, capital, January 1, 20-2							$91	9	5	3	00
Net income for month								1	3	9	9	00
Tom Jones, capital, January 31, 20-2							$93	3	5	2	00

Comprehensive Problem 2—Special Journals Based, Part 2
(Requirement 5. Concluded)

TJ's Specialty Shop
Balance Sheet
January 31, 20-2

Assets																
Current assets:																
Cash						$15	0	8	6	00						
Accounts receivable						6	9	5	1	00						
Merchandise inventory						19	0	0	0	00						
Supplies						1	1	5	00							
Prepaid insurance						9	6	8	00							
Total current assets											$ 42	1	2	0	00	
Property, plant, and equipment:																
Land						$ 8	7	0	0	00						
Building	$52	0	0	0	00											
Less accumulated depreciation	10	0	6	7	00	41	9	3	3	00						
Store equipment	$28	7	5	0	00											
Less accumulated depreciation	9	7	8	8	00	18	9	6	2	00						
Total property, plant, and equipment											69	5	9	5	00	
Total assets											$111	7	1	5	00	
Liabilities																
Current liabilities:																
Accounts payable	$ 3	5	5	0	00											
Wages payable		3	3	0	00											
Sales tax payable	1	9	5	8	00											
Mortgage payable (current portion)		6	0	0	00											
Total current liabilities						$ 6	4	3	8	00						
Long-term liabilities:																
Mortgage payable	$12	5	2	5	00											
Less current portion		6	0	0	00	11	9	2	5	00						
Total liabilities											$ 18	3	6	3	00	
Owner's Equity																
Tom Jones, capital											93	3	5	2	00	
Total liabilities and owner's equity											$111	7	1	5	00	

Comprehensive Problem 2—Special Journals Based, Part 2
Requirement 6.

GENERAL JOURNAL

PAGE 2

	DATE		DESCRIPTION	POST. REF.	DEBIT	CREDIT	
1			*Adjusting Entries*				1
2	20-2 Jan.	31	Income Summary	313	19 7 0 0 00		2
3			Merchandise Inventory	131		19 7 0 0 00	3
4							4
5		31	Merchandise Inventory	131	19 0 0 0 00		5
6			Income Summary	313		19 0 0 0 00	6
7							7
8		31	Supplies Expense	524	4 1 0 00		8
9			Supplies	141		4 1 0 00	9
10							10
11		31	Insurance Expense	535	3 2 00		11
12			Prepaid Insurance	145		3 2 00	12
13							13
14		31	Depreciation Expense—Building	540	6 7 00		14
15			Accumulated Depreciation—Building	171.1		6 7 00	15
16							16
17		31	Depreciation Expense—Store Equipment	541	3 8 00		17
18			Accumulated Depreciation—Store Equipment	181.1		3 8 00	18
19							19
20		31	Wages Expense	511	3 3 0 00		20
21			Wages Payable	219		3 3 0 00	21
22							22
23							23
24							24
25							25
26							26
27							27
28							28
29							29
30							30
31							31
32							32
33							33
34							34

Comprehensive Problem 2—Special Journals Based, Part 2

Requirement 7.

GENERAL JOURNAL

PAGE 3

	DATE		DESCRIPTION	POST. REF.	DEBIT	CREDIT	
1			*Closing Entries*				1
2	20-2 Jan.	31	Sales	401	9 6 0 0 00		2
3			Purchases Returns and Allowances	501.1	3 0 0 00		3
4			Purchases Discounts	501.2	5 6 00		4
5			Income Summary	313		9 9 5 6 00	5
6							6
7		31	Income Summary	313	7 8 5 7 00		7
8			Sales Returns and Allowances	401.1		8 0 0 00	8
9			Purchases	501		3 5 0 0 00	9
10			Wages Expense	511		2 2 0 0 00	10
11			Supplies Expense	524		4 1 0 00	11
12			Telephone Expense	525		1 8 0 00	12
13			Utilities Expense	533		6 3 0 00	13
14			Insurance Expense	535		3 2 00	14
15			Depreciation Expense—Building	540		6 7 00	15
16			Depreciation Expense—Store Equipment	541		3 8 00	16
17							17
18		31	Income Summary	313	1 3 9 9 00		18
19			Tom Jones, Capital	311		1 3 9 9 00	19
20							20
21							21
22							22
23							23
24							24
25							25
26							26
27							27
28							28
29							29
30							30
31							31
32							32
33							33
34							34

Comprehensive Problem 2—Special Journals Based, Part 2

Requirement 8.

TJ's Specialty Shop

Post-Closing Trial Balance

January 31, 20-2

ACCOUNT	DEBIT BALANCE	CREDIT BALANCE
Cash	15 086 00	
Accounts Receivable	6 951 00	
Merchandise Inventory	19 000 00	
Supplies	115 00	
Prepaid Insurance	968 00	
Land	8 700 00	
Building	52 000 00	
Accumulated Depreciation—Building		10 067 00
Store Equipment	28 750 00	
Accumulated Depreciation—Store Equipment		9 788 00
Accounts Payable		3 550 00
Wages Payable		330 00
Sales Tax Payable		1 958 00
Mortgage Payable		12 525 00
Tom Jones, Capital		93 352 00
	131 570 00	131 570 00

MODULE

ACCOUNTING FOR A PROFESSIONAL SERVICE BUSINESS: THE COMBINATION JOURNAL

REVIEW QUESTIONS

1. Under the accrual basis of accounting, revenues are recorded when earned. Revenues are considered earned when a service is provided or a product sold regardless of whether cash has been received. Under the modified cash basis, revenues are recorded when cash is received.

2. Under the accrual basis of accounting, wages expense is recorded when incurred. Expenses are considered incurred when a service is received, regardless of when cash is paid. Under the modified cash basis, wages expense is recognized when employees are paid.

3. The purpose of an appointment record is to schedule appointments and to maintain a record of the services rendered, fees charged, and payments received.

4. The purpose of the patient ledger is to show the amount owed by each client or patient for services performed. The information is copied from the appointment record to the patient ledger. A copy of the patient ledger may also be used for billing purposes.

5. The purpose of a special column in a combination journal is to save time and space in entering and posting transactions to frequently used accounts.

6. The purpose of the General columns in the combination journal is to record transactions for those accounts that are infrequently used.

7. The combination journal saves time and space in entering transactions in which the same account is frequently used. For example, if a business has 30 transactions in one month that increase cash and 40 transactions that decrease cash, the cash account title would be entered 70 times in a two-column general journal. Using a combination journal, the total of the Cash Debit column is posted as one amount to the debit side of the cash account, and the total of the Cash Credit column is posted as one amount to the credit side of the cash account. Thus, instead of 70 postings, Cash receives only two: one debit and one credit.

8. The Description column is used for the following:
   a. To enter the account titles for the General Debit and General Credit columns.
   b. To identify specific creditors when assets are purchased on account using the modified cash basis. Using the accrual basis, this column would also be used to identify specific customers receiving services on account.
   c. To identify specific creditors when payments are made on account.
   d. To identify adjusting and closing entries.
   e. To identify amounts forwarded.

9. The purpose of proving the totals is to compare the sum of the Debit columns with the sum of the Credit columns to verify that they are equal to guard against errors.

10. In the combination journal, the account number of the general ledger account to which the amount has been posted is placed in the Posting Reference column. In the general ledger, "CJ" and the page number are entered in each account's Posting Reference column.

Exercise M-1A

	DATE		CASH DEBIT	CASH CREDIT	DESCRIPTION	POST. REF.	
1	20-- Jan.	1	10 0 0 0 00		Jean Akins, Capital		1
2		2		5 0 0 00	Rent Expense		2
3		3			Office Equipment		3
4					Accounts Payable—Business Machines, Inc.		4
5		5	7 5 0 00			—	5
6		8		6 5 00	Telephone Expense		6
7		10		1 5 00	Miscellaneous Expense		7
8		11			Office Supplies		8
9					Accounts Payable—Leo's Office Supplies		9
10		15		1 5 0 00	Prepaid Insurance		10
11		18		5 0 0 00		—	11
12		21	3 5 0 00			—	12
13		25		8 5 00	Utilities Expense		13
14		27		1 0 0 00	Jean Akins, Drawing		14
15		29		5 0 0 00		—	15
16							16
17							17
18							18
19							19
20							20
21							21
22							22
23							23
24							24
25							25
26							26
27							27
28							28
29							29
30							30
31							31
32							32
33							33
34							34

Exercise M-1A (Concluded)

PAGE 1

	GENERAL				CONSULTING FEES CREDIT		WAGES EXPENSE DEBIT		
	DEBIT		CREDIT					
1			10 0 0 0 00						1
2	5 0 0 00								2
3	1 5 0 0 00								3
4			1 5 0 0 00						4
5					7 5 0 00				5
6	6 5 00								6
7	1 5 00								7
8	3 0 0 00								8
9			3 0 0 00						9
10	1 5 0 00								10
11							5 0 0 00		11
12					3 5 0 00				12
13	8 5 00								13
14	1 0 0 00								14
15							5 0 0 00		15
16									16
17									17
18									18
19									19
20									20
21									21
22									22
23									23
24									24
25									25
26									26
27									27
28									28
29									29
30									30
31									31
32									32
33									33
34									34

Exercise M-2A

COMBINATION JOURNAL

	DATE		CASH DEBIT	CASH CREDIT	DESCRIPTION	POST. REF.	
1	20-- Oct.	1	15 000 00		Bill Rackes, Capital		1
2		2		300 00	Rent Expense		2
3		3			Bicycle Parts		3
4					Accounts Payable—Tracker's Bicycle Parts		4
5		5			Office Supplies		5
6					Accounts Payable—Downtown Office Supplies		6
7		8		38 00	Telephone Expense		7
8		9	140 00			—	8
9		11		15 00	Miscellaneous Expense		9
10		12		100 00	Accounts Payable—Tracker's Bicycle Parts		10
11		14		300 00		—	11
12		15	350 00			—	12
13		16		48 00	Utilities Expense		13
14		19	250 00			—	14
15		23		50 00	Bill Rackes, Drawing		15
16		25		50 00	Accounts Payable—Downtown Office Supplies		16
17		29		300 00		—	17
18			15 740 00	1 201 00			18
19							19
20							20
21							21
22							22
23							23
24							24
25							25
26							26
27							27
28							28

Proving the Combination Journal:

Debit columns:		Credit columns:	
Cash	$15,740	Cash	$ 1,201
General	2,851	General	17,250
Wages Expense	600	Repair Fees	740
	$19,191		$19,191

Exercise M-2A (Concluded)

PAGE 1

	GENERAL		REPAIR FEES	WAGES EXPENSE	
	DEBIT	CREDIT	CREDIT	DEBIT	
1		15 0 0 0 00			1
2	3 0 0 00				2
3	2 0 0 0 00				3
4		2 0 0 0 00			4
5	2 5 0 00				5
6		2 5 0 00			6
7	3 8 00				7
8			1 4 0 00		8
9	1 5 00				9
10	1 0 0 00				10
11				3 0 0 00	11
12			3 5 0 00		12
13	4 8 00				13
14			2 5 0 00		14
15	5 0 00				15
16	5 0 00				16
17				3 0 0 00	17
18	2 8 5 1 00	17 2 5 0 00	7 4 0 00	6 0 0 00	18
19					19
20					20
21					21
22					22
23					23
24					24
25					25
26					26
27					27
28					28

Problem M-3A

1. and 4.

COMBINATION JOURNAL

	DATE		CASH DEBIT	CASH CREDIT	DESCRIPTION	POST. REF.	
1	20-- Jan.	1	10 0 0 0 00		Angela McWharton, Capital	311	1
2		1		5 0 0 00	Rent Expense	521	2
3		2			Office Supplies	142	3
4					Accounts Payable—Crestline Office Supplies	202	4
5		4			Office Equipment	181	5
6					Accounts Payable—Office Technology, Inc.	202	6
7		6	5 8 0 00			—	7
8		7		4 2 00	Telephone Expense	525	8
9		8		3 8 00	Electricity Expense	533	9
10		10	3 6 0 00			—	10
11		12		5 0 00	Accounts Payable—Crestline Office Supplies	202	11
12		13	10 9 4 0 00	6 3 0 00 / 1 5 0 00		—	12
13		15		3 6 0 00		—	13
14		17	4 2 0 00			—	14
15		18		1 0 0 00	Angela McWharton, Drawing	312	15
16		20		2 6 00	Advertising Expense	512	16
17		22		3 5 00		—	17
18		24		2 8 00	Miscellaneous Expense	549	18
19		25	3 2 0 00			—	19
20		27		1 5 0 00	Accounts Payable—Office Technology, Inc.	202	20
21		29		3 6 0 00		—	21
22		30	1 8 0 00			—	22
23			11 8 6 0 00	1 8 3 9 00			23
24			(1 0 1)	(1 0 1)			24
25							25
26							26
27							27
28							28
29							29
30							30
31							31
32							32
33							33
34							34

Problem M-3A (Continued)

PAGE 1

	GENERAL		NURSING CARE	WAGES EXPENSE	TRANS. EXPENSE	
	DEBIT	CREDIT	FEES CREDIT	DEBIT	DEBIT	
1		10 0 0 0 00				1
2	5 0 0 00					2
3	3 0 0 00					3
4		3 0 0 00				4
5	1 5 0 0 00					5
6		1 5 0 0 00				6
7			5 8 0 00			7
8	4 2 00					8
9	3 8 00					9
10			3 6 0 00			10
11	5 0 00					11
12					1 5 0 00	12
13				3 6 0 00		13
14			4 2 0 00			14
15	1 0 0 00					15
16	2 6 00					16
17					3 5 00	17
18	2 8 00					18
19			3 2 0 00			19
20	1 5 0 00					20
21				3 6 0 00		21
22			1 8 0 00			22
23	2 7 3 4 00	11 8 0 0 00	1 8 6 0 00	7 2 0 00	1 8 5 00	23
24	(✔)	(✔)	(4 0 1)	(5 1 1)	(5 2 6)	24
25						25
26						26
27						27
28						28
29						29
30						30
31						31
32						32
33						33
34						34

Problem M-3A (Continued)

2. Cash balance, January 12:

Beginning balance	$ 0
Cash debits	10,940
Less: Cash credits	630
Balance	$10,310

3. Proving the Combination Journal:

Debit columns:		Credit columns:	
Cash	$11,860	Cash	$ 1,839
General	2,734	General	11,800
Wages Expense	720	Nursing Care Fees	1,860
Trans. Expense	185		
	$15,499		$15,499

5.

Angela McWharton Nursing Services
Trial Balance
January 31, 20--

ACCOUNT	ACCT. NO.	DEBIT BALANCE	CREDIT BALANCE
Cash	101	10 0 2 1 00	
Office Supplies	142	3 0 0 00	
Office Equipment	181	1 5 0 0 00	
Accounts Payable	202		1 6 0 0 00
Angela McWharton, Capital	311		10 0 0 0 00
Angela McWharton, Drawing	312	1 0 0 00	
Nursing Care Fees	401		1 8 6 0 00
Wages Expense	511	7 2 0 00	
Advertising Expense	512	2 6 00	
Rent Expense	521	5 0 0 00	
Telephone Expense	525	4 2 00	
Transportation Expense	526	1 8 5 00	
Electricity Expense	533	3 8 00	
Miscellaneous Expense	549	2 8 00	
		13 4 6 0 00	13 4 6 0 00

Problem M-3A (Continued)

4.

PARTIAL GENERAL LEDGER

ACCOUNT Cash   ACCOUNT NO. 101

DATE		ITEM	POST. REF.	DEBIT	CREDIT	BALANCE DEBIT	BALANCE CREDIT
20-- Jan.	31		CJ1	11 8 6 0 00		11 8 6 0 00	
	31		CJ1		1 8 3 9 00	10 0 2 1 00	

ACCOUNT Office Supplies   ACCOUNT NO. 142

DATE		ITEM	POST. REF.	DEBIT	CREDIT	BALANCE DEBIT	BALANCE CREDIT
20-- Jan.	2		CJ1	3 0 0 00		3 0 0 00	

ACCOUNT Office Equipment   ACCOUNT NO. 181

DATE		ITEM	POST. REF.	DEBIT	CREDIT	BALANCE DEBIT	BALANCE CREDIT
20-- Jan.	4		CJ1	1 5 0 0 00		1 5 0 0 00	

ACCOUNT Accounts Payable   ACCOUNT NO. 202

DATE		ITEM	POST. REF.	DEBIT	CREDIT	BALANCE DEBIT	BALANCE CREDIT
20-- Jan.	2		CJ1		3 0 0 00		3 0 0 00
	4		CJ1		1 5 0 0 00		1 8 0 0 00
	12		CJ1	5 0 00			1 7 5 0 00
	27		CJ1	1 5 0 00			1 6 0 0 00

Problem M-3A (Continued)

ACCOUNT Angela McWharton, Capital   ACCOUNT NO. 311

DATE	ITEM	POST. REF.	DEBIT	CREDIT	BALANCE DEBIT	BALANCE CREDIT
20-- Jan. 1		CJ1		10 0 0 0 00		10 0 0 0 00

ACCOUNT Angela McWharton, Drawing   ACCOUNT NO. 312

DATE	ITEM	POST. REF.	DEBIT	CREDIT	BALANCE DEBIT	BALANCE CREDIT
20-- Jan. 18		CJ1	1 0 0 00		1 0 0 00	

ACCOUNT Income Summary   ACCOUNT NO. 313

DATE	ITEM	POST. REF.	DEBIT	CREDIT	BALANCE DEBIT	BALANCE CREDIT

ACCOUNT Nursing Care Fees   ACCOUNT NO. 401

DATE	ITEM	POST. REF.	DEBIT	CREDIT	BALANCE DEBIT	BALANCE CREDIT
20-- Jan. 31		CJ1		1 8 6 0 00		1 8 6 0 00

ACCOUNT Wages Expense   ACCOUNT NO. 511

DATE	ITEM	POST. REF.	DEBIT	CREDIT	BALANCE DEBIT	BALANCE CREDIT
20-- Jan. 31		CJ1	7 2 0 00		7 2 0 00	

Problem M-3A (Continued)

ACCOUNT   Advertising Expense   ACCOUNT NO.   512

DATE	ITEM	POST. REF.	DEBIT	CREDIT	BALANCE	
					DEBIT	CREDIT
20-- Jan. 20		CJ1	2 6 00		2 6 00	

ACCOUNT   Rent Expense   ACCOUNT NO.   521

DATE	ITEM	POST. REF.	DEBIT	CREDIT	BALANCE	
					DEBIT	CREDIT
20-- Jan. 1		CJ1	5 0 0 00		5 0 0 00	

ACCOUNT   Telephone Expense   ACCOUNT NO.   525

DATE	ITEM	POST. REF.	DEBIT	CREDIT	BALANCE	
					DEBIT	CREDIT
20-- Jan. 7		CJ1	4 2 00		4 2 00	

ACCOUNT   Transportation Expense   ACCOUNT NO.   526

DATE	ITEM	POST. REF.	DEBIT	CREDIT	BALANCE	
					DEBIT	CREDIT
20-- Jan. 31		CJ1	1 8 5 00		1 8 5 00	

ACCOUNT   Electricity Expense   ACCOUNT NO.   533

DATE	ITEM	POST. REF.	DEBIT	CREDIT	BALANCE	
					DEBIT	CREDIT
20-- Jan. 8		CJ1	3 8 00		3 8 00	

Problem M-3A (Concluded)

ACCOUNT   Miscellaneous Expense   ACCOUNT NO.   549

DATE		ITEM	POST. REF.	DEBIT				CREDIT				BALANCE							
												DEBIT				CREDIT			
20-- Jan.	24		CJ1		2	8	00						2	8	00				

This page left intentionally blank.

Problem M-4A

1. and 4.

COMBINATION JOURNAL

	DATE	CASH DEBIT	CASH CREDIT	DESCRIPTION	POST. REF.
1	Nov. 1		300 00	Rent Expense	521
2	2			Tailoring Supplies	141
3				Accounts Payable—Sew Easy Supplies	202
4	3			Tailoring Equipment	188
5				Accounts Payable—Seam's Sewing Machines	202
6	5	400 00			—
7	8		13 00		—
8	9		28 00	Telephone Expense	525
9	10		21 00	Electricity Expense	533
10	12	200 00			—
11	15	600 00	362 00 / 400 00		—
12	16		100 00	Accounts Payable—Sew Easy Supplies	202
13	17		12 00	Miscellaneous Expense	549
14	19	450 00			—
15	21		500 00	Prepaid Insurance	145
16	23	300 00			—
17	24		13 00		—
18	26		12 00	Miscellaneous Expense	549
19	29	600 00			—
20		1950 00	1399 00		
21		(101)	(101)		
22					
23					
24					
25					
26					
27					
28					
29					
30					
31					
32					
33					
34					

Problem M-4A (Continued)

	GENERAL		TAILORING FEES CREDIT	WAGES EXPENSE DEBIT	ADVERTISING EXPENSE DEBIT	
	DEBIT	CREDIT				
1	3 0 0 00					1
2	1 5 0 00					2
3		1 5 0 00				3
4	3 0 0 0 00					4
5		3 0 0 0 00				5
6			4 0 0 00			6
7					1 3 00	7
8	2 8 00					8
9	2 1 00					9
10			2 0 0 00			10
11				4 0 0 00		11
12	1 0 0 00					12
13	1 2 00					13
14			4 5 0 00			14
15	5 0 0 00					15
16			3 0 0 00			16
17					1 3 00	17
18	1 2 00					18
19			6 0 0 00			19
20	4 1 2 3 00	3 1 5 0 00	1 9 5 0 00	4 0 0 00	2 6 00	20
21	(✔)	(✔)	(4 0 1)	(5 1 1)	(5 1 2)	21
22						22
23						23
24						24
25						25
26						26
27						27
28						28
29						29
30						30
31						31
32						32
33						33
34						34

Problem M-4A (Continued)

2. Cash balance, November 12:

Beginning balance	*$5,711*
Cash debits	*600*
	$6,311
Less: Cash credits	*362*
Balance	*$5,949*

3. Proving the Combination Journal:

Debit columns:		*Credit columns:*	
Cash	*$1,950*	*Cash*	*$1,399*
General	*4,123*	*General*	*3,150*
Wages Expense	*400*	*Tailoring Fees*	*1,950*
Advertising Expense	*26*		
	$6,499		*$6,499*

4., 6., and 8.

GENERAL LEDGER

ACCOUNT   Cash   ACCOUNT NO.   101

DATE		ITEM	POST. REF.	DEBIT	CREDIT	BALANCE DEBIT	BALANCE CREDIT
20-- Nov.	1	*Balance*	✔			5 7 1 1 00	
	30		CJ5	1 9 5 0 00		7 6 6 1 00	
	30		CJ5		1 3 9 9 00	6 2 6 2 00	

ACCOUNT   Tailoring Supplies   ACCOUNT NO.   141

DATE		ITEM	POST. REF.	DEBIT	CREDIT	BALANCE DEBIT	BALANCE CREDIT
20-- Nov.	1	*Balance*	✔			1 0 0 0 00	
	2		CJ5	1 5 0 00		1 1 5 0 00	
	30	*Adjusting*	CJ6		7 0 0 00	4 5 0 00	

Problem M-4A (Continued)

ACCOUNT   Office Supplies   ACCOUNT NO.   142

DATE		ITEM	POST. REF.	DEBIT	CREDIT	BALANCE	
						DEBIT	CREDIT
20-- Nov.	1	Balance	✔			4 8 5 00	
	30	Adjusting	CJ6		2 0 0 00	2 8 5 00	

ACCOUNT   Prepaid Insurance   ACCOUNT NO.   145

DATE		ITEM	POST. REF.	DEBIT	CREDIT	BALANCE	
						DEBIT	CREDIT
20-- Nov.	1	Balance	✔			1 0 0 00	
	21		CJ5	5 0 0 00		6 0 0 00	
	30	Adjusting	CJ6		1 5 0 00	4 5 0 00	

ACCOUNT   Tailoring Equipment   ACCOUNT NO.   188

DATE		ITEM	POST. REF.	DEBIT	CREDIT	BALANCE	
						DEBIT	CREDIT
20-- Nov.	1	Balance	✔			3 8 0 0 00	
	3		CJ5	3 0 0 0 00		6 8 0 0 00	

ACCOUNT   Accumulated Depreciation—Tailoring Equipment   ACCOUNT NO.   188.1

DATE		ITEM	POST. REF.	DEBIT	CREDIT	BALANCE	
						DEBIT	CREDIT
20-- Nov.	30	Adjusting	CJ6		3 0 0 00		3 0 0 00

Problem M-4A (Continued)

ACCOUNT Accounts Payable   ACCOUNT NO. 202

DATE		ITEM	POST. REF.	DEBIT	CREDIT	BALANCE DEBIT	BALANCE CREDIT
20-- Nov.	1	Balance	✓				4 1 2 5 00
	2		CJ5		1 5 0 00		4 2 7 5 00
	3		CJ5		3 0 0 0 00		7 2 7 5 00
	16		CJ5	1 0 0 00			7 1 7 5 00

ACCOUNT Sue Reyton, Capital   ACCOUNT NO. 311

DATE		ITEM	POST. REF.	DEBIT	CREDIT	BALANCE DEBIT	BALANCE CREDIT
20-- Nov.	1	Balance	✓				5 4 3 0 00
	30	Closing	CJ6		1 8 4 2 00		7 2 7 2 00
	30	Closing	CJ6	5 0 0 00			6 7 7 2 00

ACCOUNT Sue Reyton, Drawing   ACCOUNT NO. 312

DATE		ITEM	POST. REF.	DEBIT	CREDIT	BALANCE DEBIT	BALANCE CREDIT
20-- Nov.	1	Balance	✓			5 0 0 00	
	30	Closing	CJ6		5 0 0 00	—	—

ACCOUNT Income Summary   ACCOUNT NO. 313

DATE		ITEM	POST. REF.	DEBIT	CREDIT	BALANCE DEBIT	BALANCE CREDIT
20-- Nov.	30	Closing	CJ6		5 5 5 0 00		5 5 5 0 00
	30	Closing	CJ6	3 7 0 8 00			1 8 4 2 00
	30	Closing	CJ6	1 8 4 2 00		—	—

Problem M-4A (Continued)

ACCOUNT   Tailoring Fees   ACCOUNT NO.   401

DATE		ITEM	POST. REF.	DEBIT	CREDIT	BALANCE DEBIT	BALANCE CREDIT
20-- Nov.	1	Balance	✔				3 6 0 0 00
	30		CJ5		1 9 5 0 00		5 5 5 0 00
	30	Closing	CJ6	5 5 5 0 00		——	——

ACCOUNT   Wages Expense   ACCOUNT NO.   511

DATE		ITEM	POST. REF.	DEBIT	CREDIT	BALANCE DEBIT	BALANCE CREDIT
20-- Nov.	1	Balance	✔			8 0 0 00	
	30		CJ5	4 0 0 00		1 2 0 0 00	
	30	Closing	CJ6		1 2 0 0 00	——	——

ACCOUNT   Advertising Expense   ACCOUNT NO.   512

DATE		ITEM	POST. REF.	DEBIT	CREDIT	BALANCE DEBIT	BALANCE CREDIT
20-- Nov.	1	Balance	✔			3 3 00	
	30		CJ5	2 6 00		5 9 00	
	30	Closing	CJ6		5 9 00	——	——

ACCOUNT   Rent Expense   ACCOUNT NO.   521

DATE		ITEM	POST. REF.	DEBIT	CREDIT	BALANCE DEBIT	BALANCE CREDIT
20-- Nov.	1	Balance	✔			6 0 0 00	
	1		CJ5	3 0 0 00		9 0 0 00	
	30	Closing	CJ6		9 0 0 00	——	——

Problem M-4A (Continued)

ACCOUNT Office Supplies Expense   ACCOUNT NO. 523

DATE		ITEM	POST. REF.	DEBIT	CREDIT	BALANCE DEBIT	BALANCE CREDIT
20-- Nov.	30	Adjusting	CJ6	2 0 0 00		2 0 0 00	
	30	Closing	CJ6		2 0 0 00		

ACCOUNT Tailoring Supplies Expense   ACCOUNT NO. 524

DATE		ITEM	POST. REF.	DEBIT	CREDIT	BALANCE DEBIT	BALANCE CREDIT
20-- Nov.	30	Adjusting	CJ6	7 0 0 00		7 0 0 00	
	30	Closing	CJ6		7 0 0 00		

ACCOUNT Telephone Expense   ACCOUNT NO. 525

DATE		ITEM	POST. REF.	DEBIT	CREDIT	BALANCE DEBIT	BALANCE CREDIT
20-- Nov.	1	Balance	✔			6 0 00	
	9		CJ5	2 8 00		8 8 00	
	30	Closing	CJ6		8 8 00		

ACCOUNT Electricity Expense   ACCOUNT NO. 533

DATE		ITEM	POST. REF.	DEBIT	CREDIT	BALANCE DEBIT	BALANCE CREDIT
20-- Nov.	1	Balance	✔			4 4 00	
	10		CJ5	2 1 00		6 5 00	
	30	Closing	CJ6		6 5 00		

Problem M-4A (Continued)

ACCOUNT Insurance Expense   ACCOUNT NO. 535

DATE		ITEM	POST. REF.	DEBIT	CREDIT	BALANCE	
						DEBIT	CREDIT
20-- Nov.	30	Adjusting	CJ6	1 5 0 00		1 5 0 00	
	30	Closing	CJ6		1 5 0 00		

ACCOUNT Depreciation Expense—Tailoring Equipment   ACCOUNT NO. 542

DATE		ITEM	POST. REF.	DEBIT	CREDIT	BALANCE	
						DEBIT	CREDIT
20-- Nov.	30	Adjusting	CJ6	3 0 0 00		3 0 0 00	
	30	Closing	CJ6		3 0 0 00		

ACCOUNT Miscellaneous Expense   ACCOUNT NO. 549

DATE		ITEM	POST. REF.	DEBIT	CREDIT	BALANCE	
						DEBIT	CREDIT
20-- Nov.	1	Balance	✔			2 2 00	
	17		CJ5	1 2 00		3 4 00	
	26		CJ5	1 2 00		4 6 00	
	30	Closing	CJ6		4 6 00		

Problem M-4A (Continued)

5.

Sue Reyton

Work

For Three Months

		TRIAL BALANCE						ADJUSTMENTS							
ACCOUNT TITLE		DEBIT				CREDIT				DEBIT				CREDIT		
1	Cash	6	2	6	2	00										
2	Tailoring Supplies	1	1	5	0	00							(a)	7	0	0	00
3	Office Supplies		4	8	5	00							(b)	2	0	0	00
4	Prepaid Insurance		6	0	0	00							(c)	1	5	0	00
5	Tailoring Equipment	6	8	0	0	00										
6	Accum. Depr.—Tailoring Equip.												(d)	3	0	0	00
7	Accounts Payable					7	1	7	5	00						
8	Sue Reyton, Capital					5	4	3	0	00						
9	Sue Reyton, Drawing		5	0	0	00										
10	Tailoring Fees					5	5	5	0	00						
11	Wages Expense	1	2	0	0	00										
12	Advertising Expense		5	9	00											
13	Rent Expense		9	0	0	00										
14	Office Supplies Expense									(b)	2	0	0	00			
15	Tailoring Supplies Expense									(a)	7	0	0	00			
16	Telephone Expense		8	8	00											
17	Electricity Expense		6	5	00											
18	Insurance Expense									(c)	1	5	0	00			
19	Depr. Exp.—Tailoring Equip.									(d)	3	0	0	00			
20	Miscellaneous Expense		4	6	00											
21		18	1	5	5	00	18	1	5	5	00	1	3	5	0	00	1	3	5	0	00
22	Net Income															
23																
24																
25																
26																
27																
28																
29																
30																
31																
32																

Problem M-4A (Continued)

Tailors

Sheet

Ended November 30, 20--

ADJUSTED TRIAL BALANCE		INCOME STATEMENT		BALANCE SHEET		
DEBIT	CREDIT	DEBIT	CREDIT	DEBIT	CREDIT	
6 2 6 2 00				6 2 6 2 00		1
4 5 0 00				4 5 0 00		2
2 8 5 00				2 8 5 00		3
4 5 0 00				4 5 0 00		4
6 8 0 0 00				6 8 0 0 00		5
	3 0 0 00				3 0 0 00	6
	7 1 7 5 00				7 1 7 5 00	7
	5 4 3 0 00				5 4 3 0 00	8
5 0 0 00				5 0 0 00		9
	5 5 5 0 00		5 5 5 0 00			10
1 2 0 0 00		1 2 0 0 00				11
5 9 00		5 9 00				12
9 0 0 00		9 0 0 00				13
2 0 0 00		2 0 0 00				14
7 0 0 00		7 0 0 00				15
8 8 00		8 8 00				16
6 5 00		6 5 00				17
1 5 0 00		1 5 0 00				18
3 0 0 00		3 0 0 00				19
4 6 00		4 6 00				20
18 4 5 5 00	18 4 5 5 00	3 7 0 8 00	5 5 5 0 00	14 7 4 7 00	12 9 0 5 00	21
		1 8 4 2 00			1 8 4 2 00	22
		5 5 5 0 00	5 5 5 0 00	14 7 4 7 00	14 7 4 7 00	23
						24
						25
						26
						27
						28
						29
						30
						31
						32

Problem M-4A (Continued)

7.

Sue Reyton Tailors

Income Statement

For Three Months Ended November 30, 20--

Revenue:				
Tailoring fees			$5 5 5 0 00	
Expenses:				
Wages expense	$1 2 0 0 00			
Advertising expense	5 9 00			
Rent expense	9 0 0 00			
Office supplies expense	2 0 0 00			
Tailoring supplies expense	7 0 0 00			
Telephone expense	8 8 00			
Electricity expense	6 5 00			
Insurance expense	1 5 0 00			
Depreciation expense—tailoring equipment	3 0 0 00			
Miscellaneous expense	4 6 00			
Total expenses			3 7 0 8 00	
Net income			$1 8 4 2 00	

Problem M-4A (Continued)

Sue Reyton Tailors
Statement of Owner's Equity
For Three Months Ended November 30, 20--

Sue Reyton, capital, September 1, 20--		$
Investment from September through November		5 4 3 0 00
Total investment		$5 4 3 0 00
Net income for September through November	$1 8 4 2 00	
Less withdrawals for September through November	5 0 0 00	
Increase in capital		1 3 4 2 00
Sue Reyton, capital, November 30, 20--		$6 7 7 2 00

Sue Reyton Tailors
Balance Sheet
November 30, 20--

Assets		
Current assets:		
Cash	$6 2 6 2 00	
Tailoring supplies	4 5 0 00	
Office supplies	2 8 5 00	
Prepaid insurance	4 5 0 00	
Total current assets		$ 7 4 4 7 00
Property, plant, and equipment:		
Tailoring equipment	$6 8 0 0 00	
Less accumulated depreciation	3 0 0 00	6 5 0 0 00
Total assets		$13 9 4 7 00
Liabilities		
Current liabilities:		
Accounts payable		$ 7 1 7 5 00
Owner's Equity		
Sue Reyton, capital		6 7 7 2 00
Total liabilities and owner's equity		$13 9 4 7 00

Problem M-4A (Continued)
6. and 8.

COMBINATION JOURNAL

	DATE		CASH						DESCRIPTION	POST. REF.	
			DEBIT			CREDIT					
1									**Adjusting Entries**		1
2	20-- Nov.	30							Tailoring Supplies Expense	524	2
3									Tailoring Supplies	141	3
4		30							Office Supplies Expense	523	4
5									Office Supplies	142	5
6		30							Insurance Expense	535	6
7									Prepaid Insurance	145	7
8		30							Depreciation Expense—Tailoring Equipment	542	8
9									Accumulated Depreciation—Tailoring Equipment	188.1	9
10									**Closing Entries**		10
11		30							Tailoring Fees	401	11
12									Income Summary	313	12
13		30							Income Summary	313	13
14									Wages Expense	511	14
15									Advertising Expense	512	15
16									Rent Expense	521	16
17									Office Supplies Expense	523	17
18									Tailoring Supplies Expense	524	18
19									Telephone Expense	525	19
20									Electricity Expense	533	20
21									Insurance Expense	535	21
22									Depreciation Expense—Tailoring Equipment	542	22
23									Miscellaneous Expense	549	23
24		30							Income Summary	313	24
25									Sue Reyton, Capital	311	25
26		30							Sue Reyton, Capital	311	26
27									Sue Reyton, Drawing	312	27
28											28
29											29
30											30
31											31
32											32
33											33
34											34

Problem M-4A (Concluded)

PAGE 6

	GENERAL		TAILORING FEES CREDIT	WAGES EXPENSE DEBIT	ADVERTISING EXPENSE DEBIT	
	DEBIT	CREDIT				
1						1
2	7 0 0 00					2
3		7 0 0 00				3
4	2 0 0 00					4
5		2 0 0 00				5
6	1 5 0 00					6
7		1 5 0 00				7
8	3 0 0 00					8
9		3 0 0 00				9
10						10
11	5 5 5 0 00					11
12		5 5 5 0 00				12
13	3 7 0 8 00					13
14		1 2 0 0 00				14
15		5 9 00				15
16		9 0 0 00				16
17		2 0 0 00				17
18		7 0 0 00				18
19		8 8 00				19
20		6 5 00				20
21		1 5 0 00				21
22		3 0 0 00				22
23		4 6 00				23
24	1 8 4 2 00					24
25		1 8 4 2 00				25
26	5 0 0 00					26
27		5 0 0 00				27
28	12 9 5 0 00	12 9 5 0 00				28
29						29
30						30
31						31
32						32
33						33
34						34

Exercise M-1B

COMBINATION JOURNAL

	DATE		CASH DEBIT	CASH CREDIT	DESCRIPTION	POST. REF.	
1	20-- Mar.	1	7 5 0 0 00		Bill Miller, Capital		1
2		3		5 0 0 00	Rent Expense		2
3		5			Office Equipment		3
4					Accounts Payable—Desk Top Office Equipment		4
5		6	4 0 0 00			—	5
6		8		4 8 00	Telephone Expense		6
7		10		2 5 00	Miscellaneous Expense		7
8		11		2 0 0 00	Office Supplies		8
9		14	5 2 0 00			—	9
10		16		2 0 0 00	Prepaid Insurance		10
11		18		4 0 0 00		—	11
12		21	3 8 0 00			—	12
13		22		1 0 0 00	Accounts Payable—Desk Top Office Equipment		13
14		24		5 6 00	Utilities Expense		14
15		27		2 0 0 00	Bill Miller, Drawing		15
16		29		4 0 0 00		—	16
17		30	6 0 0 00			—	17
18							18
19							19
20							20
21							21
22							22
23							23
24							24
25							25
26							26
27							27
28							28
29							29
30							30
31							31
32							32
33							33
34							34

Exercise M-1B (Concluded)

PAGE 1

	GENERAL				BOOKKEEPING		WAGES EXPENSE	
	DEBIT		CREDIT		FEES CREDIT		DEBIT	
1			7 5 0 0 00					1
2	5 0 0 00							2
3	8 0 0 00							3
4			8 0 0 00					4
5					4 0 0 00			5
6	4 8 00							6
7	2 5 00							7
8	2 0 0 00							8
9					5 2 0 00			9
10	2 0 0 00							10
11							4 0 0 00	11
12					3 8 0 00			12
13	1 0 0 00							13
14	5 6 00							14
15	2 0 0 00							15
16							4 0 0 00	16
17					6 0 0 00			17
18								18
19								19
20								20
21								21
22								22
23								23
24								24
25								25
26								26
27								27
28								28
29								29
30								30
31								31
32								32
33								33
34								34

Exercise M-2B

	DATE		CASH DEBIT		CASH CREDIT		DESCRIPTION	POST. REF.	
1	20-- Jan.	1	10 0 0 0 00				Amy Anjelo, Capital		1
2		2			4 0 0 00		Rent Expense		2
3		3					Delivery Cart		3
4							Accounts Payable—Walt's Wheels		4
5		5			2 5 0 00		Office Supplies		5
6		6			5 1 00		Telephone Expense		6
7		8	4 2 8 00					—	7
8		11			3 7 00		Utilities Expense		8
9		12			4 8 0 00			—	9
10		13			2 9 00		Miscellaneous Expense		10
11		15	3 8 2 00					—	11
12		18			9 0 00		Accounts Payable—Walt's Wheels		12
13		21			2 5 0 00		Amy Anjelo, Drawing		13
14		24			1 8 0 00		Prepaid Insurance		14
15		26	2 9 2 00					—	15
16		29			4 8 0 00			—	16
17			11 1 0 2 00		2 2 4 7 00				17
18									18
19									19
20									20
21									21
22									22
23									23
24									24
25									25
26									26
27									27
28									28

Proving the Combination Journal:

Debit columns:		Credit columns:	
Cash	$11,102	Cash	$ 2,247
General	2,287	General	11,000
Wages Expense	960	Delivery Fees	1,102
	$14,349		$14,349

Exercise M-2B (Concluded)

PAGE 1

	GENERAL		DELIVERY FEES	WAGES EXPENSE	
	DEBIT	CREDIT	CREDIT	DEBIT	
1		10 0 0 0 00			1
2	4 0 0 00				2
3	1 0 0 0 00				3
4		1 0 0 0 00			4
5	2 5 0 00				5
6	5 1 00				6
7			4 2 8 00		7
8	3 7 00				8
9				4 8 0 00	9
10	2 9 00				10
11			3 8 2 00		11
12	9 0 00				12
13	2 5 0 00				13
14	1 8 0 00				14
15			2 9 2 00		15
16				4 8 0 00	16
17	2 2 8 7 00	11 0 0 0 00	1 1 0 2 00	9 6 0 00	17
18					18
19					19
20					20
21					21
22					22
23					23
24					24
25					25
26					26
27					27
28					28

Problem M-3B

1. and 4.

COMBINATION JOURNAL

	DATE		CASH DEBIT	CASH CREDIT	DESCRIPTION	POST. REF.	
1	20-- July	1	5000 00		J. B. Hoyt, Capital	311	1
2		2		250 00	Rent Expense	521	2
3		3		150 00	Office Supplies	142	3
4		4			Skiing Equipment	183	4
5					Accounts Payable—Water Fun, Inc.	202	5
6		6		36 00	Telephone Expense	525	6
7		7	200 00			—	7
8		10		28 00	Electricity Expense	533	8
9		12		250 00		—	9
10		14	300 00			—	10
11		16	5500 00	714 00 / 60 00	Transportation Expense	526	11
12		17	250 00			—	12
13		20		20 00		—	13
14		21		100 00	Accounts Payable—Water Fun, Inc.	202	14
15		24	310 00			—	15
16		26		18 00	Miscellaneous Expense	549	16
17		28		250 00		—	17
18		30	230 00			—	18
19		31		20 00		—	19
20			6290 00	1182 00			20
21			(101)	(101)			21

Problem M-3B (Continued)

PAGE 1

	GENERAL		TRAINING FEES	WAGES EXPENSE	REPAIR EXPENSE	
	DEBIT	CREDIT	CREDIT	DEBIT	DEBIT	
1		5 0 0 0 00				1
2	2 5 0 00					2
3	1 5 0 00					3
4	2 0 0 0 00					4
5		2 0 0 0 00				5
6		3 6 00				6
7			2 0 0 00			7
8		2 8 00				8
9				2 5 0 00		9
10			3 0 0 00			10
11		6 0 00				11
12			2 5 0 00			12
13					2 0 00	13
14	1 0 0 00					14
15			3 1 0 00			15
16		1 8 00				16
17				2 5 0 00		17
18			2 3 0 00			18
19					2 0 00	19
20	2 6 4 2 00	7 0 0 0 00	1 2 9 0 00	5 0 0 00	4 0 00	20
21	(✔)	(✔)	(4 0 1)	(5 1 1)	(5 3 7)	21
22						22
23						23
24						24
25						25
26						26
27						27
28						28
29						29
30						30
31						31
32						32
33						33
34						34

Problem M-3B (Continued)

2. Cash balance, July 14:

Beginning balance	$ 0
Cash debits	5,500
Less: Cash credits	714
Balance	$4,786

3. Proving the Combination Journal:

Debit columns:		Credit columns:	
Cash	$6,290	Cash	$1,182
General	2,642	General	7,000
Wages Expense	500	Training Fees	1,290
Repair Expense	40		
	$9,472		$9,472

5.

Water Walking by Hoyt

Trial Balance

July 31, 20--

ACCOUNT	ACCT. NO.	DEBIT BALANCE	CREDIT BALANCE
Cash	101	5 1 0 8 00	
Office Supplies	142	1 5 0 00	
Skiing Equipment	183	2 0 0 0 00	
Accounts Payable	202		1 9 0 0 00
J. B. Hoyt, Capital	311		5 0 0 0 00
Training Fees	401		1 2 9 0 00
Wages Expense	511	5 0 0 00	
Rent Expense	521	2 5 0 00	
Telephone Expense	525	3 6 00	
Transportation Expense	526	6 0 00	
Electricity Expense	533	2 8 00	
Repair Expense	537	4 0 00	
Miscellaneous Expense	549	1 8 00	
		8 1 9 0 00	8 1 9 0 00

Problem M-3B (Continued)

4.

GENERAL LEDGER

ACCOUNT   Cash   ACCOUNT NO.   101

DATE		ITEM	POST. REF.	DEBIT	CREDIT	BALANCE	
						DEBIT	CREDIT
20-- July	31		CJ1	6 2 9 0 00		6 2 9 0 00	
	31		CJ1		1 1 8 2 00	5 1 0 8 00	

ACCOUNT   Office Supplies   ACCOUNT NO.   142

DATE		ITEM	POST. REF.	DEBIT	CREDIT	BALANCE	
						DEBIT	CREDIT
20-- July	3		CJ1	1 5 0 00		1 5 0 00	

ACCOUNT   Skiing Equipment   ACCOUNT NO.   183

DATE		ITEM	POST. REF.	DEBIT	CREDIT	BALANCE	
						DEBIT	CREDIT
20-- July	4		CJ1	2 0 0 0 00		2 0 0 0 00	

ACCOUNT   Accounts Payable   ACCOUNT NO.   202

DATE		ITEM	POST. REF.	DEBIT	CREDIT	BALANCE	
						DEBIT	CREDIT
20-- July	4		CJ1		2 0 0 0 00		2 0 0 0 00
	21		CJ1	1 0 0 00			1 9 0 0 00

Problem M-3B (Continued)

ACCOUNT J. B. Hoyt, Capital   ACCOUNT NO. 311

DATE		ITEM	POST. REF.	DEBIT	CREDIT	BALANCE DEBIT	BALANCE CREDIT
20-- July	1		CJ1		5 0 0 0 00		5 0 0 0 00

ACCOUNT J. B. Hoyt, Drawing   ACCOUNT NO. 312

DATE	ITEM	POST. REF.	DEBIT	CREDIT	BALANCE DEBIT	BALANCE CREDIT

ACCOUNT Income Summary   ACCOUNT NO. 313

DATE	ITEM	POST. REF.	DEBIT	CREDIT	BALANCE DEBIT	BALANCE CREDIT

ACCOUNT Training Fees   ACCOUNT NO. 401

DATE		ITEM	POST. REF.	DEBIT	CREDIT	BALANCE DEBIT	BALANCE CREDIT
20-- July	31		CJ1		1 2 9 0 00		1 2 9 0 00

ACCOUNT Wages Expense   ACCOUNT NO. 511

DATE		ITEM	POST. REF.	DEBIT	CREDIT	BALANCE DEBIT	BALANCE CREDIT
20-- July	31		CJ1	5 0 0 00		5 0 0 00	

Problem M-3B (Continued)

ACCOUNT   Rent Expense   ACCOUNT NO.   521

DATE	ITEM	POST. REF.	DEBIT	CREDIT	BALANCE DEBIT	BALANCE CREDIT
20-- July 2		CJ1	2 5 0 00		2 5 0 00	

ACCOUNT   Telephone Expense   ACCOUNT NO.   525

DATE	ITEM	POST. REF.	DEBIT	CREDIT	BALANCE DEBIT	BALANCE CREDIT
20-- July 6		CJ1	3 6 00		3 6 00	

ACCOUNT   Transportation Expense   ACCOUNT NO.   526

DATE	ITEM	POST. REF.	DEBIT	CREDIT	BALANCE DEBIT	BALANCE CREDIT
20-- July 16		CJ1	6 0 00		6 0 00	

ACCOUNT   Electricity Expense   ACCOUNT NO.   533

DATE	ITEM	POST. REF.	DEBIT	CREDIT	BALANCE DEBIT	BALANCE CREDIT
20-- July 10		CJ1	2 8 00		2 8 00	

ACCOUNT   Repair Expense   ACCOUNT NO.   537

DATE	ITEM	POST. REF.	DEBIT	CREDIT	BALANCE DEBIT	BALANCE CREDIT
20-- July 31		CJ1	4 0 00		4 0 00	

Problem M-3B (Concluded)

ACCOUNT Miscellaneous Expense

ACCOUNT NO. 549

DATE		ITEM	POST. REF.	DEBIT			CREDIT			BALANCE					
										DEBIT			CREDIT		
20-- July	26		CJ1	1	8	00				1	8	00			

This page left intentionally blank.

Problem M-4B
1. and 4.

COMBINATION JOURNAL

	DATE	CASH DEBIT	CASH CREDIT	DESCRIPTION	POST. REF.	
1	20-- June 1		200 00	Rent Expense	521	1
2	2		230 00	Office Supplies	142	2
3	3			Lawn Care Equipment	189	3
4				Accounts Payable—Earth Care, Inc.	202	4
5	5		31 00	Telephone Expense	525	5
6	6	640 00			—	6
7	8		31 00	Electricity Expense	533	7
8	10		300 00		—	8
9	11	580 00			—	9
10	12		200 00	Prepaid Insurance	145	10
11	14	¹²²⁰ 00	⁹⁹² 100 00	Accounts Payable—Earth Care, Inc.	202	11
12	15		40 00	Gas and Oil Expense	538	12
13	19		25 00		—	13
14	21	310 00			—	14
15	24		100 00	Molly Claussen, Drawing	312	15
16	26		20 00		—	16
17	28	480 00			—	17
18	29		300 00		—	18
19		2010 00	1577 00			19
20		(101)	(101)			20
21						21
22						22
23						23
24						24
25						25
26						26
27						27
28						28
29						29
30						30
31						31
32						32
33						33
34						34

Problem M-4B (Continued)

PAGE 5

	GENERAL DEBIT	GENERAL CREDIT	LAWN CARE FEES CREDIT	REPAIR EXPENSE DEBIT	WAGES EXPENSE DEBIT	
1	200 00					1
2	230 00					2
3	1000 00					3
4		1000 00				4
5	31 00					5
6			640 00			6
7	31 00					7
8					300 00	8
9			580 00			9
10	200 00					10
11	100 00					11
12	40 00					12
13				25 00		13
14			310 00			14
15	100 00					15
16				20 00		16
17			480 00			17
18					300 00	18
19	1932 00	1000 00	2010 00	45 00	600 00	19
20	(✓)	(✓)	(401)	(537)	(511)	20
21						21
22						22
23						23
24						24
25						25
26						26
27						27
28						28
29						29
30						30
31						31
32						32
33						33
34						34

Problem M-4B (Continued)

2. Cash balance, June 12:

Beginning balance	$4,604
Cash debits	1,220
	$5,824
Less: Cash credits	992
Balance	$4,832

3. Proving the Combination Journal:

Debit columns:		*Credit columns:*	
Cash	$2,010	Cash	$1,577
General	1,932	General	1,000
Repair Expense	45	Lawn Care Fees	2,010
Wages Expense	600		
	$4,587		$4,587

4., 6., and 8.

GENERAL LEDGER

ACCOUNT   Cash   ACCOUNT NO.   101

DATE		ITEM	POST. REF.	DEBIT	CREDIT	BALANCE DEBIT	BALANCE CREDIT
20-- June	1	Balance	✔			4 6 0 4 00	
	30		CJ5	2 0 1 0 00		6 6 1 4 00	
	30		CJ5		1 5 7 7 00	5 0 3 7 00	

ACCOUNT   Lawn Care Supplies   ACCOUNT NO.   141

DATE		ITEM	POST. REF.	DEBIT	CREDIT	BALANCE DEBIT	BALANCE CREDIT
20-- June	1	Balance	✔			5 8 8 00	
	30	Adjusting	CJ6		2 8 8 00	3 0 0 00	

Problem M-4B (Continued)

ACCOUNT Office Supplies   ACCOUNT NO. 142

DATE		ITEM	POST. REF.	DEBIT	CREDIT	BALANCE	
						DEBIT	CREDIT
20-- June	1	Balance	✔			2 4 3 00	
	2		CJ5	2 3 0 00		4 7 3 00	
	30	Adjusting	CJ6		2 0 0 00	2 7 3 00	

ACCOUNT Prepaid Insurance   ACCOUNT NO. 145

DATE		ITEM	POST. REF.	DEBIT	CREDIT	BALANCE	
						DEBIT	CREDIT
20-- June	1	Balance	✔			1 5 0 00	
	12		CJ5	2 0 0 00		3 5 0 00	
	30	Adjusting	CJ6		1 0 0 00	2 5 0 00	

ACCOUNT Lawn Care Equipment   ACCOUNT NO. 189

DATE		ITEM	POST. REF.	DEBIT	CREDIT	BALANCE	
						DEBIT	CREDIT
20-- June	1	Balance	✔			2 4 0 8 00	
	3		CJ5	1 0 0 0 00		3 4 0 8 00	

ACCOUNT Accumulated Depreciation—Lawn Care Equipment   ACCOUNT NO. 189.1

DATE		ITEM	POST. REF.	DEBIT	CREDIT	BALANCE	
						DEBIT	CREDIT
20-- June	30	Adjusting	CJ6		2 6 0 00		2 6 0 00

Problem M-4B (Continued)

ACCOUNT Accounts Payable   ACCOUNT NO. 202

DATE		ITEM	POST. REF.	DEBIT	CREDIT	BALANCE DEBIT	BALANCE CREDIT
20-- June	1	Balance	✓				1 0 8 0 00
	3		CJ5		1 0 0 0 00		2 0 8 0 00
	14		CJ5	1 0 0 00			1 9 8 0 00

ACCOUNT Molly Claussen, Capital   ACCOUNT NO. 311

DATE		ITEM	POST. REF.	DEBIT	CREDIT	BALANCE DEBIT	BALANCE CREDIT
20-- June	1	Balance	✓				5 0 0 0 00
	30	Closing	CJ6		2 9 2 8 00		7 9 2 8 00
	30	Closing	CJ6	9 0 0 00			7 0 2 8 00

ACCOUNT Molly Claussen, Drawing   ACCOUNT NO. 312

DATE		ITEM	POST. REF.	DEBIT	CREDIT	BALANCE DEBIT	BALANCE CREDIT
20-- June	1	Balance	✓			8 0 0 00	
	24		CJ5	1 0 0 00		9 0 0 00	
	30	Closing	CJ6		9 0 0 00	—	—

ACCOUNT Income Summary   ACCOUNT NO. 313

DATE		ITEM	POST. REF.	DEBIT	CREDIT	BALANCE DEBIT	BALANCE CREDIT
20-- June	30	Closing	CJ6		6 0 4 3 00		6 0 4 3 00
	30	Closing	CJ6	3 1 1 5 00			2 9 2 8 00
	30	Closing	CJ6	2 9 2 8 00		—	—

Problem M-4B (Continued)

ACCOUNT   Lawn Care Fees   ACCOUNT NO.   401

DATE		ITEM	POST. REF.	DEBIT	CREDIT	BALANCE DEBIT	BALANCE CREDIT
20-- June	1	Balance	✓				4 0 3 3 00
	30		CJ5		2 0 1 0 00		6 0 4 3 00
	30	Closing	CJ6	6 0 4 3 00		——	——

ACCOUNT   Wages Expense   ACCOUNT NO.   511

DATE		ITEM	POST. REF.	DEBIT	CREDIT	BALANCE DEBIT	BALANCE CREDIT
20-- June	1	Balance	✓			6 0 0 00	
	30		CJ5	6 0 0 00		1 2 0 0 00	
	30	Closing	CJ6		1 2 0 0 00	——	——

ACCOUNT   Rent Expense   ACCOUNT NO.   521

DATE		ITEM	POST. REF.	DEBIT	CREDIT	BALANCE DEBIT	BALANCE CREDIT
20-- June	1	Balance	✓			4 0 0 00	
	1		CJ5	2 0 0 00		6 0 0 00	
	30	Closing	CJ6		6 0 0 00	——	——

ACCOUNT   Office Supplies Expense   ACCOUNT NO.   523

DATE		ITEM	POST. REF.	DEBIT	CREDIT	BALANCE DEBIT	BALANCE CREDIT
20-- June	30	Adjusting	CJ6	2 0 0 00		2 0 0 00	
	30	Closing	CJ6		2 0 0 00	——	——

Problem M-4B (Continued)

ACCOUNT   Lawn Care Supplies Expense   ACCOUNT NO.   524

DATE		ITEM	POST. REF.	DEBIT	CREDIT	BALANCE	
						DEBIT	CREDIT
20-- June	30	Adjusting	CJ6	2 8 8 00		2 8 8 00	
	30	Closing	CJ6		2 8 8 00		

ACCOUNT   Telephone Expense   ACCOUNT NO.   525

DATE		ITEM	POST. REF.	DEBIT	CREDIT	BALANCE	
						DEBIT	CREDIT
20-- June	1	Balance	✔			8 8 00	
	5		CJ5	3 1 00		1 1 9 00	
	30	Closing	CJ6		1 1 9 00		

ACCOUNT   Electricity Expense   ACCOUNT NO.   533

DATE		ITEM	POST. REF.	DEBIT	CREDIT	BALANCE	
						DEBIT	CREDIT
20-- June	1	Balance	✔			6 2 00	
	8		CJ5	3 1 00		9 3 00	
	30	Closing	CJ6		9 3 00		

ACCOUNT   Insurance Expense   ACCOUNT NO.   535

DATE		ITEM	POST. REF.	DEBIT	CREDIT	BALANCE	
						DEBIT	CREDIT
20-- June	30	Adjusting	CJ6	1 0 0 00		1 0 0 00	
	30	Closing	CJ6		1 0 0 00		

Problem M-4B (Continued)

ACCOUNT Repair Expense   ACCOUNT NO. 537

DATE		ITEM	POST. REF.	DEBIT	CREDIT	BALANCE DEBIT	BALANCE CREDIT
20-- June	1	Balance	✓			5 0 00	
	30		CJ5	4 5 00		9 5 00	
	30	Closing	CJ6		9 5 00		

ACCOUNT Gas and Oil Expense   ACCOUNT NO. 538

DATE		ITEM	POST. REF.	DEBIT	CREDIT	BALANCE DEBIT	BALANCE CREDIT
20-- June	1	Balance	✓			1 2 0 00	
	15		CJ5	4 0 00		1 6 0 00	
	30	Closing	CJ6		1 6 0 00		

ACCOUNT Depreciation Expense—Lawn Care Equipment   ACCOUNT NO. 542

DATE		ITEM	POST. REF.	DEBIT	CREDIT	BALANCE DEBIT	BALANCE CREDIT
20-- June	30	Adjusting	CJ6	2 6 0 00		2 6 0 00	
	30	Closing	CJ6		2 6 0 00		

Problem M-4B (Continued)

5.

	ACCOUNT TITLE	TRIAL BALANCE						ADJUSTMENTS						
		DEBIT				CREDIT		DEBIT				CREDIT		
1	Cash	5	0	3	7	00								
2	Lawn Care Supplies		5	8	8	00					(b)	2	8	8	00
3	Office Supplies		4	7	3	00					(a)	2	0	0	00
4	Prepaid Insurance		3	5	0	00					(c)	1	0	0	00
5	Lawn Care Equipment	3	4	0	8	00								
6	Accum. Depr.—Lawn Care Eq.										(d)	2	6	0	00
7	Accounts Payable						1	9	8	0	00			
8	Molly Claussen, Capital						5	0	0	0	00			
9	Molly Claussen, Drawing		9	0	0	00								
10	Lawn Care Fees						6	0	4	3	00			
11	Wages Expense	1	2	0	0	00								
12	Rent Expense		6	0	0	00								
13	Office Supplies Expense								(a)	2	0	0	00		
14	Lawn Care Supplies Expense								(b)	2	8	8	00		
15	Telephone Expense		1	1	9	00								
16	Electricity Expense			9	3	00								
17	Insurance Expense								(c)	1	0	0	00		
18	Repair Expense			9	5	00								
19	Gas and Oil Expense		1	6	0	00								
20	Depr. Exp.—Lawn Care Equip.								(d)	2	6	0	00		
21		13	0	2	3	00	13	0	2	3	00		8	4	8	00		8	4	8	00
22	Net Income													
23														
24														
25														
26														
27														
28														
29														
30														
31														
32														

Problem M-4B (Continued)

Green Thumb

Sheet

Ended June 30, 20--

ADJUSTED TRIAL BALANCE		INCOME STATEMENT		BALANCE SHEET		
DEBIT	CREDIT	DEBIT	CREDIT	DEBIT	CREDIT	
5 0 3 7 00				5 0 3 7 00		1
3 0 0 00				3 0 0 00		2
2 7 3 00				2 7 3 00		3
2 5 0 00				2 5 0 00		4
3 4 0 8 00				3 4 0 8 00		5
	2 6 0 00				2 6 0 00	6
	1 9 8 0 00				1 9 8 0 00	7
	5 0 0 0 00				5 0 0 0 00	8
9 0 0 00				9 0 0 00		9
	6 0 4 3 00		6 0 4 3 00			10
1 2 0 0 00		1 2 0 0 00				11
6 0 0 00		6 0 0 00				12
2 0 0 00		2 0 0 00				13
2 8 8 00		2 8 8 00				14
1 1 9 00		1 1 9 00				15
9 3 00		9 3 00				16
1 0 0 00		1 0 0 00				17
9 5 00		9 5 00				18
1 6 0 00		1 6 0 00				19
2 6 0 00		2 6 0 00				20
13 2 8 3 00	13 2 8 3 00	3 1 1 5 00	6 0 4 3 00	10 1 6 8 00	7 2 4 0 00	21
		2 9 2 8 00			2 9 2 8 00	22
		6 0 4 3 00	6 0 4 3 00	10 1 6 8 00	10 1 6 8 00	23
						24
						25
						26
						27
						28
						29
						30
						31
						32

Problem M-4B (Continued)

7.

Molly Claussen's Green Thumb
Income Statement
For Three Months Ended June 30, 20--

Revenue:			
Lawn care fees			$6 043 00
Expenses:			
Wages expense	$1 200 00		
Rent expense	600 00		
Office supplies expense	200 00		
Lawn care supplies expense	288 00		
Telephone expense	119 00		
Electricity expense	93 00		
Insurance expense	100 00		
Repair expense	95 00		
Gas and oil expense	160 00		
Depreciation expense—lawn care equipment	260 00		
Total expenses			3 115 00
Net income			$2 928 00

Problem M-4B (Continued)

Molly Claussen's Green Thumb

Statement of Owner's Equity

For Three Months Ended June 30, 20--

Molly Claussen, capital, April 1, 20--			$
Investment from April through June			5 0 0 0 00
Total investment			$5 0 0 0 00
Net income for April through June	$2 9 2 8 00		
Less withdrawals for April through June	9 0 0 00		
Increase in capital			2 0 2 8 00
Molly Claussen, capital, June 30, 20--			$7 0 2 8 00

Molly Claussen's Green Thumb

Balance Sheet

June 30, 20--

Assets			
Current assets:			
Cash	$5 0 3 7 00		
Lawn care supplies	3 0 0 00		
Office supplies	2 7 3 00		
Prepaid insurance	2 5 0 00		
Total current assets			$5 8 6 0 00
Property, plant, and equipment:			
Lawn care equipment	$3 4 0 8 00		
Less accumulated depreciation	2 6 0 00		3 1 4 8 00
Total assets			$9 0 0 8 00
Liabilities			
Current liabilities:			
Accounts payable			$1 9 8 0 00
Owner's Equity			
Molly Claussen, capital			7 0 2 8 00
Total liabilities and owner's equity			$9 0 0 8 00

Problem M-4B (Continued)
6. and 8.

COMBINATION JOURNAL

	DATE		CASH			DESCRIPTION	POST. REF.	
			DEBIT	CREDIT				
1						*Adjusting Entries*		1
2	20-- June	30				Office Supplies Expense	523	2
3						Office Supplies	142	3
4		30				Lawn Care Supplies Expense	524	4
5						Lawn Care Supplies	141	5
6		30				Insurance Expense	535	6
7						Prepaid Insurance	145	7
8		30				Depreciation Expense—Lawn Care Equipment	542	8
9						Accumulated Depreciation—Lawn Care Equipment	189.1	9
10						*Closing Entries*		10
11		30				Lawn Care Fees	401	11
12						Income Summary	313	12
13		30				Income Summary	313	13
14						Wages Expense	511	14
15						Rent Expense	521	15
16						Office Supplies Expense	523	16
17						Lawn Care Supplies Expense	524	17
18						Telephone Expense	525	18
19						Electricity Expense	533	19
20						Insurance Expense	535	20
21						Repair Expense	537	21
22						Gas and Oil Expense	538	22
23						Depreciation Expense—Lawn Care Equipment	542	23
24		30				Income Summary	313	24
25						Molly Claussen, Capital	311	25
26		30				Molly Claussen, Capital	311	26
27						Molly Claussen, Drawing	312	27
28								28
29								29
30								30
31								31
32								32
33								33
34								34

Problem M-4B (Concluded)

	GENERAL		LAWN CARE	REPAIR EXPENSE	WAGES EXPENSE	
	DEBIT	CREDIT	FEES CREDIT	DEBIT	DEBIT	
1						1
2	2 0 0 00					2
3		2 0 0 00				3
4	2 8 8 00					4
5		2 8 8 00				5
6	1 0 0 00					6
7		1 0 0 00				7
8	2 6 0 00					8
9		2 6 0 00				9
10						10
11	6 0 4 3 00					11
12		6 0 4 3 00				12
13	3 1 1 5 00					13
14		1 2 0 0 00				14
15		6 0 0 00				15
16		2 0 0 00				16
17		2 8 8 00				17
18		1 1 9 00				18
19		9 3 00				19
20		1 0 0 00				20
21		9 5 00				21
22		1 6 0 00				22
23		2 6 0 00				23
24	2 9 2 8 00					24
25		2 9 2 8 00				25
26	9 0 0 00					26
27		9 0 0 00				27
28	13 8 3 4 00	13 8 3 4 00				28
29	(✔)	(✔)				29
30						30
31						31
32						32
33						33
34						34

MANAGING YOUR WRITING

The memos should define each method and offer advice on the method to use with specific types of businesses.

Definitions for each method:

Under the **accrual basis of accounting**, revenues are recorded when earned. Revenues are considered earned when a service is provided or a product sold, regardless of whether cash has been received. The accrual basis also assumes that expenses are recorded when incurred. Expenses are considered incurred when a service is received or an asset consumed, regardless of when cash is paid.

The modified cash and accrual bases of accounting are the same except for three types of events. The **modified cash basis** differs from the accrual basis of accounting in the following ways.

1. Expenses for services received are not recorded until paid. Thus, accounts payable is not used under the modified cash basis for services received.

2. Accrued expenses are not recognized. Examples of accrued expenses include wages that were earned by the employees, but not yet paid, and interest expense that has been incurred, but not yet paid. Thus, no end-of-period adjusting entries are made for these types of events.

3. Revenues from services performed on account are not recorded until cash is received. Thus, no accounts receivable are entered in the accounting system.

Most Appropriate Type of Business for Each Method:

The accrual basis is the best method of measuring income for the vast majority of businesses. Revenues are recorded when earned. If cash is not received, receivables are established. If expenses are not paid in cash, payables are set up. Finally, assets are recognized and expensed as consumed or as their useful lives expire. This method provides reasonable measures of income, even when the business has long-term assets, receivables, and payables.

Many small professional service businesses use the modified cash basis of accounting. A few examples include law, dentistry, medicine, optometry, architecture, engineering, and accounting. Since adjustments are made for long-term assets and prepaid items, some of the accrual basis advantages are retained. However, the modified cash basis does not account for receivables for services rendered, payables for services received, or accrued expenses. Thus, measures of net income may be distorted if the business has large amounts of receivables and payables.

ETHICS CASE

1. Although Nancy's explanation makes sense (the transaction will make her financial statements look better), this decision is unethical. She is overstating her cash and revenue.
2. The transaction can be entered in either of the following ways:
   a. If the $10,000 is a loan from her father, Cash should be debited and Loans Payable should be credited.
   b. If the $10,000 is a gift from her father that Nancy wants to invest in her company, Cash should be debited and Nancy Bowles, Capital should be credited. In either case, revenue is not affected.
   Since this is a cash transaction, it doesn't matter if the modified cash or accrual basis of accounting is used.
3. Answers may vary. Nancy could be denied a loan by the bank based on their discovery of fraudulent financial statements. Sarah might turn her in or quit and find another job. Nancy could get the loan and not be able to pay it back.
4. Answers will vary.

Mastery Problem

1. The combination journal can be found on pages M-56 and M-57.

2. Proving the Combination Journal:

Debit columns:		Credit columns:	
Cash	$163,900	Cash	$ 44,405
General	112,705	General	187,000
Wages Expense	2,000	Registration Fees	73,900
Food Supplies	26,700		
	$305,305		$305,305

Mastery Problem (Continued)
1.

	DATE		CASH DEBIT	CASH CREDIT	DESCRIPTION	POST. REF.	
1	20-- June	1	90 0 0 0 00		John McRoe, Capital	311	1
2		1		9 0 0 0 00	Exercise Equipment	186	2
3		2	15 0 0 0 00			—	3
4		2		2 5 0 0 00	Rent Expense	521	4
5		2			Tennis Facilities	184	5
6					Accounts Payable—Rogers Construction	202	6
7		3			Accounts Payable—Au Naturel Foods	202	7
8		5			Office Supplies	142	8
9					Accounts Payable—Gordon Office Supplies	202	9
10		7	16 2 0 0 00			—	10
11		10			Accounts Payable—Au Naturel Foods	202	11
12		10		5 0 0 00		—	12
13		14	13 5 0 0 00			—	13
14		16			Accounts Payable—Au Naturel Foods	202	14
15		17		5 0 0 00		—	15
16		18		8 5 00	Postage Expense	536	16
17		21	15 2 0 0 00			—	17
18		24			Accounts Payable—Au Naturel Foods	202	18
19		24		5 0 0 00		—	19
20		28	14 0 0 0 00			—	20
21		30			Accounts Payable—Au Naturel Foods	202	21
22		30		5 0 0 00		—	22
23		30		28 7 0 0 00	Accounts Payable—Au Naturel Foods	202	23
24		30		5 0 0 00	Utilities Expense	533	24
25		30		1 2 0 00	Telephone Expense	525	25
26		30		1 5 0 0 00	John McRoe, Drawing	312	26
27			163 9 0 0 00	44 4 0 5 00			27
28			(1 0 1)	(1 0 1)			28
29							29
30							30
31							31
32							32
33							33
34							34

Mastery Problem (Continued)

PAGE 1

	GENERAL DEBIT	GENERAL CREDIT	REGISTRATION FEES CREDIT	WAGES EXPENSE DEBIT	FOOD SUPPLIES DEBIT	
1		90 0 0 0 00				1
2	9 0 0 0 00					2
3			15 0 0 0 00			3
4	2 5 0 0 00					4
5	70 0 0 0 00					5
6		70 0 0 0 00				6
7		5 0 0 0 00			5 0 0 0 00	7
8	3 0 0 00					8
9		3 0 0 00				9
10			16 2 0 0 00			10
11		6 2 0 0 00			6 2 0 0 00	11
12				5 0 0 00		12
13			13 5 0 0 00			13
14		4 0 0 0 00			4 0 0 0 00	14
15				5 0 0 00		15
16	8 5 00					16
17			15 2 0 0 00			17
18		5 5 0 0 00			5 5 0 0 00	18
19				5 0 0 00		19
20			14 0 0 0 00			20
21		6 0 0 0 00			6 0 0 0 00	21
22				5 0 0 00		22
23	28 7 0 0 00					23
24	5 0 0 00					24
25	1 2 0 00					25
26	1 5 0 0 00					26
27	112 7 0 5 00	187 0 0 0 00	73 9 0 0 00	2 0 0 0 00	26 7 0 0 00	27
28	(✓)	(✓)	(4 0 1)	(5 1 1)	(1 4 4)	28
29						29
30						30
31						31
32						32
33						33
34						34

Mastery Problem (Continued)

3.

GENERAL LEDGER

ACCOUNT Cash   ACCOUNT NO. 101

DATE	ITEM	POST. REF.	DEBIT	CREDIT	BALANCE DEBIT	BALANCE CREDIT
20-- June 30		CJ1	163 9 0 0 00		163 9 0 0 00	
30		CJ1		44 4 0 5 00	119 4 9 5 00	

ACCOUNT Office Supplies   ACCOUNT NO. 142

DATE	ITEM	POST. REF.	DEBIT	CREDIT	BALANCE DEBIT	BALANCE CREDIT
20-- June 5		CJ1	3 0 0 00		3 0 0 00	

ACCOUNT Food Supplies   ACCOUNT NO. 144

DATE	ITEM	POST. REF.	DEBIT	CREDIT	BALANCE DEBIT	BALANCE CREDIT
20-- June 30		CJ1	26 7 0 0 00		26 7 0 0 00	

ACCOUNT Tennis Facilities   ACCOUNT NO. 184

DATE	ITEM	POST. REF.	DEBIT	CREDIT	BALANCE DEBIT	BALANCE CREDIT
20-- June 2		CJ1	70 0 0 0 00		70 0 0 0 00	

Mastery Problem (Continued)

ACCOUNT Accumulated Depreciation—Tennis Facilities   ACCOUNT NO. 184.1

DATE	ITEM	POST. REF.	DEBIT	CREDIT	BALANCE DEBIT	BALANCE CREDIT

ACCOUNT Exercise Equipment   ACCOUNT NO. 186

DATE		ITEM	POST. REF.	DEBIT	CREDIT	BALANCE DEBIT	BALANCE CREDIT
20-- June	1		CJ1	9 0 0 0 00		9 0 0 0 00	

ACCOUNT Accumulated Depreciation—Exercise Equipment   ACCOUNT NO. 186.1

DATE	ITEM	POST. REF.	DEBIT	CREDIT	BALANCE DEBIT	BALANCE CREDIT

ACCOUNT Accounts Payable   ACCOUNT NO. 202

DATE		ITEM	POST. REF.	DEBIT	CREDIT	BALANCE DEBIT	BALANCE CREDIT
20-- June	2		CJ1		70 0 0 0 00		70 0 0 0 00
	3		CJ1		5 0 0 0 00		75 0 0 0 00
	5		CJ1		3 0 0 00		75 3 0 0 00
	10		CJ1		6 2 0 0 00		81 5 0 0 00
	16		CJ1		4 0 0 0 00		85 5 0 0 00
	24		CJ1		5 5 0 0 00		91 0 0 0 00
	30		CJ1		6 0 0 0 00		97 0 0 0 00
	30		CJ1	28 7 0 0 00			68 3 0 0 00

Mastery Problem (Continued)

ACCOUNT   John McRoe, Capital   ACCOUNT NO.   311

DATE	ITEM	POST. REF.	DEBIT	CREDIT	BALANCE DEBIT	BALANCE CREDIT
20-- June 1		CJ1		90 0 0 0 00		90 0 0 0 00

ACCOUNT   John McRoe, Drawing   ACCOUNT NO.   312

DATE	ITEM	POST. REF.	DEBIT	CREDIT	BALANCE DEBIT	BALANCE CREDIT
20-- June 30		CJ1	1 5 0 0 00		1 5 0 0 00	

ACCOUNT   Income Summary   ACCOUNT NO.   313

DATE	ITEM	POST. REF.	DEBIT	CREDIT	BALANCE DEBIT	BALANCE CREDIT

ACCOUNT   Registration Fees   ACCOUNT NO.   401

DATE	ITEM	POST. REF.	DEBIT	CREDIT	BALANCE DEBIT	BALANCE CREDIT
20-- June 30		CJ1		73 9 0 0 00		73 9 0 0 00

ACCOUNT   Wages Expense   ACCOUNT NO.   511

DATE	ITEM	POST. REF.	DEBIT	CREDIT	BALANCE DEBIT	BALANCE CREDIT
20-- June 30		CJ1	2 0 0 0 00		2 0 0 0 00	

Mastery Problem (Continued)

ACCOUNT Rent Expense   ACCOUNT NO. 521

DATE		ITEM	POST. REF.	DEBIT	CREDIT	BALANCE	
						DEBIT	CREDIT
20-- June	2		CJ1	2 5 0 0 00		2 5 0 0 00	

ACCOUNT Office Supplies Expense   ACCOUNT NO. 523

DATE		ITEM	POST. REF.	DEBIT	CREDIT	BALANCE	
						DEBIT	CREDIT

ACCOUNT Food Supplies Expense   ACCOUNT NO. 524

DATE		ITEM	POST. REF.	DEBIT	CREDIT	BALANCE	
						DEBIT	CREDIT

ACCOUNT Telephone Expense   ACCOUNT NO. 525

DATE		ITEM	POST. REF.	DEBIT	CREDIT	BALANCE	
						DEBIT	CREDIT
20-- June	30		CJ1	1 2 0 00		1 2 0 00	

ACCOUNT Utilities Expense   ACCOUNT NO. 533

DATE		ITEM	POST. REF.	DEBIT	CREDIT	BALANCE	
						DEBIT	CREDIT
20-- June	30		CJ1	5 0 0 00		5 0 0 00	

Mastery Problem (Continued)

ACCOUNT   Insurance Expense   ACCOUNT NO. 535

DATE	ITEM	POST. REF.	DEBIT	CREDIT	BALANCE DEBIT	BALANCE CREDIT

ACCOUNT   Postage Expense   ACCOUNT NO. 536

DATE		ITEM	POST. REF.	DEBIT	CREDIT	BALANCE DEBIT	BALANCE CREDIT
20-- June	18		CJ1	8 5 00		8 5 00	

ACCOUNT   Depreciation Expense—Tennis Facilities   ACCOUNT NO. 541

DATE	ITEM	POST. REF.	DEBIT	CREDIT	BALANCE DEBIT	BALANCE CREDIT

ACCOUNT   Depreciation Expense—Exercise Equipment   ACCOUNT NO. 542

DATE	ITEM	POST. REF.	DEBIT	CREDIT	BALANCE DEBIT	BALANCE CREDIT

Mastery Problem (Concluded)

4.

McRoe Tennis Resort

Trial Balance

June 30, 20--

ACCOUNT	ACCT. NO.	DEBIT BALANCE	CREDIT BALANCE
Cash	101	119 495 00	
Office Supplies	142	3 00 00	
Food Supplies	144	26 700 00	
Tennis Facilities	184	70 000 00	
Exercise Equipment	186	9 000 00	
Accounts Payable	202		68 300 00
John McRoe, Capital	311		90 000 00
John McRoe, Drawing	312	1 500 00	
Registration Fees	401		73 900 00
Wages Expense	511	2 000 00	
Rent Expense	521	2 500 00	
Telephone Expense	525	1 20 00	
Utilities Expense	533	5 00 00	
Postage Expense	536	85 00	
		232 200 00	232 200 00

Challenge Problem

	Resler Financial Consulting
	Income Statements
	For Month Ended June 20--

	Modified Cash Basis		Accrual Basis	
Revenue		$10,000		$10,500
Expenses:				
Supplies expense	$ 900		$ 900	
Wages expense	2,000		2,200	
Computer expense				
Depr. exp.—computer	100		100	
Total expenses		3,000		3,200
Net income		$ 7,000		$ 7,300

Explanation:

Modified Cash Basis
Revenues are recorded on a cash basis. No payables are recorded for services received. Therefore, Wages Expense is recorded on the cash basis. Prepaid and long-term assets are recorded. Therefore, Supplies Expense and Depreciation Expense on the computer are recognized on the accrual basis as shown below.

Beginning inventory of supplies	$ 500
Plus purchases of supplies	1,000
Supplies available	$1,500
Ending inventory of supplies	(600)
Cost of supplies used	$ 900

Challenge Problem (Continued)

Supplies			
Bal.	500		
Purchases (1)	1,000	(plug)	900
End. inv.	600		

Accounts Payable		
	(1)	1,000

Supplies Expense		
(plug)	900	

Depreciation: $2,400/24 months = $100 per month

Accrual Basis
All revenues and expenses are recorded on the accrual basis:

Revenues:

Cash received	$10,000
Less revenues earned in May, but paid in June	(1,500)
Plus revenues earned in June to be paid in July	2,000
Revenue recorded in June	$10,500

Cash			
Bal.	?		
Cash rec'd in			
June (1)	10,000		
End. bal.	?		

Accounts Receivable			
Bal.	1,500	(1)	10,000
(2) plug	10,500		
End. bal.	2,000		

Consulting Fees		
	(2)	10,500

Or, another way of thinking about entries to the T accounts:

Cash			
Bal.	?		
(1)	10,000		
End. bal.	?		

Accounts Receivable		
Bal.	1,500	
(2) plug	500	
End. bal.	2,000	

Consulting Fees		
	(1)	10,000
	(2)	500
	End. bal.	10,500

Wages expense:

Cash paid in June	$2,000
Less wages earned in May, but paid in June	(300)
Plus wages earned in June, but paid in July	500
	$2,200

Challenge Problem (Concluded)

Cash			
Bal.	?		
		(1)	2,000
End. bal.	?		

Wages Payable			
			300
		(2) plug	200
		End. bal.	500

Wages Expense			
(1)	2,000		
(2) plug	200		
End. bal.	2,200		

Or, another way of thinking about entries to the T accounts:

Cash			
Bal.	?		
		(1)	2,000
End. bal.	?		

Wages Payable			
			300
		(1) (plug)	200
		End. bal.	500

Wages Expense			
(1)	2,200		

NOTES

NOTES

NOTES

NOTES

NOTES

NOTES